W9-AYG-660

Generic Goals and Practices as Presented in the Continuous Representation

GG 1   Achieve Specific Goals

     GP 1.1   Perform Base Practices

GG 2   Institutionalize a Managed Process

     GP 2.1   Establish an Organizational Policy

     GP 2.2   Plan the Process

     GP 2.3   Provide Resources

     GP 2.4   Assign Responsibility

     GP 2.5   Train People

     GP 2.6   Manage Configurations

     GP 2.7   Identify and Involve Relevant Stakeholders

     GP 2.8   Monitor and Control the Process

     GP 2.9   Objectively Evaluate Adherence

     GP 2.10 Review Status with Higher Level Management

GG 3   Institutionalize a Defined Process

     GP 3.1   Establish a Defined Process

     GP 3.2   Collect Improvement Information

GG 4   Institutionalize a Quantitatively Managed Process

     GP 4.1   Establish Quantitative Objectives for the Process

     GP 4.2   Stabilize Subprocess Performance

GG 5   Institutionalize an Optimizing Process

     GP 5.1   Ensure Continuous Process Improvement

     GP 5.2   Correct Root Causes of Problems

Bodies of Knowledge Covered in this Book

Software Engineering

Systems Engineering

Integrated Product and Process Development

Supplier Sourcing

CMMI®

CMMI®

Guidelines for Process Integration and Product Improvement

Mary Beth Chrissis
Mike Konrad
Sandy Shrum

✦✦Addison-Wesley

Boston • San Francisco • New York • Toronto • Montreal
London • Munich • Paris • Madrid
Capetown • Sydney • Tokyo • Singapore • Mexico City

Carnegie Mellon
Software Engineering Institute

The SEI Series in Software Engineering

Many of the designations used by manufacturers and sellers to distinguish their products are claimed as trademarks. Where those designations appear in this book, and Addison-Wesley was aware of a trademark claim, the designations have been printed with initial capital letters or in all capitals.

CMM, CMMI, Capability Maturity Model, Capability Maturity Modeling, Carnegie Mellon, CERT, and CERT Coordination Center are registered in the U.S. Patent and Trademark Office by Carnegie Mellon University.

ATAM; Architecture Tradeoff Analysis Method; CMM Integration; CURE; IDEAL; Interim Profile; OCTAVE; Operationally Critical Threat, Asset, and Vulnerability Evaluation; Personal Software Process; PSP; SCAMPI; SCAMPI Lead Assessor; SCE; Team Software Process; and TSP are service marks of Carnegie Mellon University.

Special permission to reproduce portions from *CMMI^SM for Systems Engineering/ Software Engineering/ Integrated Product and Process Development/Supplier Sourcing, Version 1.1, Staged Representation* and *CMMI^SM for Systems Engineering/ Software Engineering/Integrated Product and Process Development/Supplier Sourcing, Version 1.1, Continuous Representation* © 2002, by Carnegie Mellon University, is granted by the Software Engineering Institute.

The publisher offers discounts on this book when ordered in quantity for bulk purchases and special sales. For more information, please contact:

U.S. Corporate and Government Sales
(800) 382-3419
corpsales@pearsontechgroup.com

For sales outside of the U.S., please contact:
International Sales
(317) 581-3793
international@pearsontechgroup.com

Visit Addison-Wesley on the Web: *www.awprofessional.com*

Library of Congress Cataloging-in-Publication Data

Chrissis, Mary Beth.
  CMMI®: guidelines for process integration and product improvement /
For: Chrissis, Mary Beth/ Konrad, Mike/ Shrum, Sandy
      p.   cm.
Includes bibliographical references and index.
  ISBN 0-321-15496-7
  1. Capability maturity model (Computer software)   I. Konrad, Mike.
II. Shrum, Sandy.   III. Title.
  QA76.758 .C518 2003
  005.1'068'5—dc21   2002152784

Text printed on recycled and acid-free paper.

ISBN 0321154967

8 9 10111213 CRW 07 06 05

8th Printing   June 2005

CONTENTS

PREFACE

CMMI® (Capability Maturity Model® Integration) consists of best practices that address the development and maintenance of products and services covering the product life cycle from conception through delivery and maintenance.

A product can be an airplane, a digital camera, a video game component, an automated teller machine, a missile guidance system, or a software package available from a commercial retailer. It can also be a service such as delivering a training class, technical support for a software product, long-distance telephone service, data-processing services, and online banking.

CMMI integrates bodies of knowledge that are essential when developing products, but that have been addressed separately in the past, such as software engineering, systems engineering, and acquisition. By integrating these bodies of knowledge, CMMI provides a comprehensive solution for development and maintenance of products and services.

Purpose of This Book

This book is an extension of the CMMI Framework,[1] which generated the full set of CMMI models released by the Software Engineering Institute (SEI) in January 2002. To use a CMMI model released by the SEI, you must choose from among the multiple models available based on your improvement needs. Therefore, to use the CMMI models published by the SEI, you need to know the content of each model and the area that you want to improve.

Unfortunately for many users, selecting a model from the SEI Web site appears difficult because they must make the up-front decision about which bodies of knowledge they want to address in their organizations and the approach they want to take to their process improvement efforts.

---

1. The CMMI Framework is the basic structure that organizes CMMI components and combines them into CMMI models.

To facilitate CMMI use, this book provides a single source for all CMMI model information—a functional equivalent of the CMMI Framework. You do not have to select a particular model to get started—all of your choices are compiled here into one book. The book describes what is common across all CMMI models as well as what is different. It describes the basic concepts and the ways processes evolve as your organization improves. It will help you to understand the content of each CMMI model and to decide how CMMI can best address your needs.

Audience

The audience for this book includes anyone interested in process improvement—whether you are familiar with the concept of Capability Maturity Models or whether you are seeking information to get started on your improvement efforts. It is intended for people who want an appraisal[2] to see where they are, those who already know what they want to improve, and those who are just getting started and want to develop a general understanding of CMMI. This book is a must-have for process appraisal teams; members of process improvement groups; product development managers; product developers and maintainers, including software and systems engineers; and project management, computer science, and engineering educators.

Organization of This Book

This book maintains the integrity of the CMMI v1.1 models available on the SEI's Web site and serves as a guide for improvement of organizational processes. It is organized into three main parts:

Part One—About CMMI
Part Two—The Process Areas
Part Three—The Appendices and Glossary

In writing this book, we enhanced and supplemented the original SEI materials. These improvements appear in Part One. Given the nature of the material in Part Two, we made only minor changes and added markings to identify and classify the content. In the glossary in Part Three, we've compiled a practical resource for understanding the "language" of CMMI.

---

2. An appraisal is an examination of one or more processes by a trained team of professionals using a reference model (e.g., CMMI) as the basis for determining strengths and weaknesses.

Part One, "About CMMI," consists of seven chapters:

- Chapter 1, "Introduction," offers a broad view of CMMI. It introduces you to the concepts of process improvement and describes the benefits of CMMI, the history of models used for process improvement, and different process improvement approaches.
- Chapter 2, "Process Area Components," describes all of the components of the CMMI process areas.
- Chapter 3, "Process Institutionalization," describes the model components that ensure that the implementation of processes is effective, repeatable, and lasting.
- Chapter 4, "Relationships among Process Areas," provides insight into the meaning and interactions of the major CMMI components.
- Chapter 5, "Tying It All Together," assembles the model components and process infrastructure into the representations and explains the concepts of maturity level and capability level.
- Chapter 6, "Using CMMI Models," describes paths to adoption and use of CMMI for process improvement and benchmarking.
- Chapter 7, "A CMMI Case Study: United Space Alliance, LLC," describes the real-life experiences of an organization as it prepared to adopt CMMI. This chapter may help you plan your own organization's adoption of CMMI.

Part Two, "The Process Areas," contains 25 sections, one for each of the CMMI process areas.[3] To facilitate your referring to them, these chapters are organized alphabetically by process area acronym. Each chapter contains descriptions of goals, best practices, and examples.

Part Three, "The Appendices and Glossary," consists of four information resources:

- Appendix A, "References," contains references you can use to locate documented sources of information such as reports, process-improvement models, industry standards, and books that are related to CMMI.
- Appendix B, "Acronyms," defines the acronyms used in CMMI.
- Appendix C, "CMMI Project Participants," contains a list of people and their organizations who participated in the CMMI project. That project developed the models on which this book is based.
- The "Glossary" defines the terms used in CMMI.

---

3. A "process area" is a cluster of related best practices in an area that, when implemented collectively, satisfy a set of goals considered important for making significant improvement in that area. We will cover this concept in detail in chapter 2.

How to Use This Book

Whether you are new to process improvement, new to CMMI, or already familiar with CMMI, this book can help you understand why CMMI is the best model to use for improving your product life-cycle processes.

Readers New to Process Improvement

If you are new to process improvement or new to the CMM® concept, we suggest that you read chapter 1, "Introduction," and the case study in chapter 7 first. Chapter 1 will give you an overview of process improvement and explain what CMMI is all about. Chapter 7 will help you to see how CMMI can be used by an organization. When you read chapter 7 the first time, don't be concerned about understanding all the terminology or details. Just read it to get an overall feel for what's going on in the case study. Then, go back and read chapters 1 through 7. When you read chapter 7 again, after reading the balance of Part One, you will understand the details much better.

Next, skim Part Two to get a feel for the scope of the best practices contained in CMMI. Pay closest attention to the statement of purpose at the beginning of each section.

In Part Three, look through the references in Appendix A and select additional sources you think would be beneficial to read before moving forward with using CMMI. Read through the acronyms and glossary to become familiar with the language of CMMI. Then, go back and read the details of Part Two.

Readers Experienced with Process Improvement

If you are new to CMMI but have experience with other process-improvement models, such as the Software CMM or the Systems Engineering CM (i.e., EIA 731), you will immediately recognize many similarities.

We recommend that you read Part One to understand how CMMI is different from other process-improvement models, but you may want to read some of the sections more quickly than others. Read Part Two with an eye open for best practices you recognize from the models you have already tried. Identifying familiar material gives you a feel for what is new and what has been carried over from the model you already know.

Next, review the glossary to understand how some terminology may differ from that used in the process-improvement model you know. Many concepts will be repeated, but they may be called something different.

Readers Familiar with CMMI

If you have reviewed or used one of the CMMI models available on the SEI Web site, you will quickly recognize the CMMI concepts discussed and the best practices presented. The differences between this book and the SEI-released models are mainly found in Part One, "About CMMI."

Although the continuous and staged representations of the models' best practices are presented together in Part Two, no changes were made that affect the meaning or applicability of these best practices. In Part One, we added information about the benefits of process improvement and historical information about process-improvement models for readers new to process improvement or to the CMM® concept. We explained the vast similarities of the two representations reflected in the models and included detailed discussions of both capability levels and maturity levels and their importance in CMMI. To understand how the two representations have been formatted for Part Two, see the descriptions and illustrations of typographical conventions (Figures 2.2, 2.3, and 2.4) in chapter 2.

We also expanded the discussion of generic model components into a chapter that you will find more informative than what is found in the SEI-released models (see chapter 3). A chapter containing a case study of CMMI (chapter 7) was added to describe the real-life experience of an organization preparing to adopt CMMI.

In Part Three, "The Appendices and Glossary," we combined all terms and their definitions into the glossary, so that you can find definitions more quickly and easily. Terms are no longer addressed in a separate chapter in Part One.

As you read Part One, we recommend that you pay closest attention to chapter 3, "Process Institutionalization," and chapter 7, "CMMI Case Study: United Space Alliance, LLC." Review the format used in Part Two. This format helps you differentiate between the two representations.

Additional Information and Reader Feedback

You can find additional information from various other sources about CMMI, such as the background and history of the CMMI models, as well as the benefits of using CMMI models. Many of these sources are listed in Appendix A and are also documented on the CMMI Web site—*http://www.sei.cmu.edu/cmmi/.*

Suggestions for improving CMMI are welcomed by the SEI. For information on how to provide feedback, see the CMMI Web site at *http://www.sei. cmu.edu/cmmi/models/change-requests.html.* If you have questions about CMMI, send an e-mail to cmmi-comments@sei.cmu.edu.

ACKNOWLEDGMENTS

It would not have been possible to write this book without the work of numerous people and organizations. This book builds on the CMMI Framework developed by the CMMI project, which involved numerous people from different organizations throughout the world. These organizations were using a CMM or multiple CMMs and were interested in the benefits of developing an integrated framework to aid in enterprise-wide process improvement.

Organizations from industry, government, and the Software Engineering Institute (SEI) joined together to develop CMMI. The organizations donated the time of one or more of their people to participate in the CMMI project. Many of those who contributed to CMMI are listed in Appendix C. In particular, we appreciate the leadership and support Jack Ferguson and Mike Phillips provided throughout the CMMI project.

There are a few people we feel need special recognition because of the support they provided during the writing of this book. First of all, we'd like to thank Bill Peterson for encouraging us to write it, his continued support while we were writing the book, and his detailed review comments that helped us to improve it.

We also would like to thank our significant others, Chuck, Patti, and Mark, for supporting our families and us while we were spending the many long hours that were necessary to write this book. We'd also like to thank our children Adam, Pamela, Kevin, Paul, Katie, Alison, David, Walter, and "Abby." There were many times they would rather have had us doing something with them when we just had to be in our offices working. You have our heartfelt thanks for your patience, support, and understanding.

We would also like to thank NASA, United Space Alliance (USA), and especially Julie Bernard who coordinated the writing of the case study for this book. Thanks also to the following people at USA for conducting the case study and providing information about it to us:

- Tom Peterson, Jim Orr, Mary Burgess, Earl Lee—senior management sponsors who provided the enthusiastic support and resources to pursue this activity
- Julie Bernard, Rich DeBernardo, Johnnie Henderson, Steve Kinstle, Allen Prescott—case study team members who learned about CMMI and diligently assessed the projects

Numerous others at USA provided supporting data to the activity for making the case study possible.

We owe our gratitude to the reviewers of this book: Yoshi Akiyama, Julia Allen, Aaron Clouse, Jay Douglass, Jon Gross, Mark Paulk, Mary Lynn Penn, Bill Peterson, Mike Phillips, Karen Richter, Gary Wolf, and others. Their in-depth and insightful comments were invaluable in helping us create a book that conveys our ideas clearly and concisely. A special thanks goes to Addison-Wesley Publishing Partner Peter Gordon for his continued assistance and support and to Joan Flaherty, Ruth Maassen, and Marilyn Rash for their help with the design and final production of this book.

Last, we'd like to especially thank Roger Bate and Mark Paulk, our friends and colleagues, who were there throughout the process with advice, opinions, and knowledge.

During the writing of this book and the publication of CMMI v1.1, we lost a special friend and coworker, Carolyn Tady. Her smile and kindness will be remembered always.

PART ONE

About CMMI

CHAPTER 1

INTRODUCTION

More now than ever, companies today want to deliver products better, faster, and cheaper. At the same time, in the high-technology environment of the twenty-first century, nearly all organizations have found themselves building more and more complex products. Today, a single company usually does not develop all the components that compose a product. More commonly, some components are built in-house and some are acquired; then all the components are integrated into the final product. Organizations must be able to manage and control this complex product development and maintenance.

Many organizations have also found themselves in the software business. Organizations that were not typically software companies—such as financial institutions, car manufacturers, airplane manufacturers, and insurance companies—find that much of their business relies on software. Software is often what differentiates them from their competitors. The problems these organizations address today involve both software and systems engineering. More and more, these disciplines are becoming a critical part of their business. In essence, these organizations are product developers that need a way to manage an integrated approach to their software and systems engineering as part of reaching their business objectives.

In the current marketplace, there are maturity models, standards, methodologies, and guidelines that can help an organization improve the way it does business. However, most available improvement approaches focus on a specific part of the business and do not take a systemic approach to the problems that most organizations are facing. For example, there are many maturity models available such as the Software Engineering Institute's (SEI's) Capability Maturity Model® for Software (SW-CMM®), which focuses on improving software, and the Electronic Industries Alliance's (EIA's) Systems Engineering Capability Model (SECM), which focuses on systems engineering. By focusing on improving one area of a business, these models have unfortunately perpetuated the stovepipes and barriers that exist in organizations.

Capability Maturity Model® Integration (CMMI®) provides an opportunity to avoid or eliminate these stovepipes and barriers through integrated models that transcend disciplines. CMMI consists of best practices that address product development and maintenance. It addresses practices that cover the product's life cycle from conception through delivery and maintenance. There is an emphasis on both systems engineering and software engineering and the integration necessary to build and maintain the total product.

About Capability Maturity Models

The SEI has found several dimensions that an organization can focus on to improve its business. Figure 1.1 illustrates the three critical dimensions that organizations typically focus on: people, procedures and methods, and tools and equipment.

But what holds everything together? It is the processes used in your organization. Processes allow you to align the way you do business. They allow you to address scalability and provide a way to incorporate knowledge of how to do things better. Processes allow you to leverage your resources and to examine business trends.

This is not to say that people and technology are not important. We are living in a world where technology is changing by an order of magnitude every ten years. Similarly, people typically work for many companies throughout their careers. We live in a dynamic world. A focus on process provides the infrastruc-

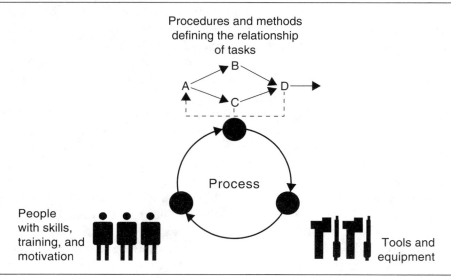

FIGURE 1.1
The Three Critical Dimensions

ture necessary to deal with an ever-changing world and to maximize personnel and technology to be more competitive.

Manufacturing has long recognized the importance of process effectiveness and efficiency. Today, many organizations in manufacturing and service industries recognize the importance of quality processes. Process helps an organization's workforce meet business objectives by helping them work smarter, not harder, and with improved consistency. Effective processes also provide a vehicle for introducing and using new technology in a way that best meets the business objectives of the organization.

In the 1930s, Walter Shewhart began work in process improvement with his principles of statistical quality control [Shewhart 31]. These principles were refined by W. Edwards Deming [Deming 86] and Joseph Juran [Juran 88]. Watts Humphrey, Ron Radice, and others extended these principles even further and began applying them to software in their work at IBM and the SEI. Humphrey's book *Managing the Software Process* [Humphrey 89] provides a description of the basic principles and concepts on which many of the capability maturity models are based.

The SEI has taken the process-management premise, "the quality of a system or product is highly influenced by the quality of the process used to develop and maintain it," and defined capability maturity models that embody this premise. The belief in this premise is worldwide in quality movements, as evidenced by the International Organization for Standardization/ International Electrotechnical Commission (ISO/IEC) body of standards.

Capability maturity models (CMMs) focus on improving processes in an organization. They contain the essential elements of effective processes for one or more disciplines and describe an evolutionary improvement path from ad hoc, immature processes to disciplined, mature processes with improved quality and effectiveness.

Mark Paulk and others at the Software Engineering Institute created the first capability maturity model designed for software organizations and published it in a book, *The Capability Maturity Model: Guidelines for Improving the Software Process* [SEI 95].

The SEI's book took the principles introduced almost a century ago and applied them to this never-ending cycle of process improvement. The value of this process improvement approach has been confirmed over time. Organizations have experienced increased productivity and quality, improved cycle time, and more accurate and predictable schedules and budgets [Herbsleb 97].

Evolution of CMMI

Since 1991, CMMs have been developed for a myriad of disciplines. Some of the most notable include models for systems engineering, software engineering, software acquisition, workforce management and development, and integrated product and process development.

Although these models have proved useful to many organizations, the use of multiple models has been problematic. Many organizations would like to focus their improvement efforts across the disciplines in their organizations. However, the differences among these discipline-specific models, including their architecture, content, and approach, have limited these organizations' ability to focus their improvements successfully. Further, applying multiple models that are not integrated within and across an organization is costly in terms of training, appraisals, and improvement activities.

The CMM Integration^SM project was formed to sort out the problem of using multiple CMMs. The CMMI Product Team's mission was to combine three source models:

1. The Capability Maturity Model for Software (SW-CMM) v2.0 draft C
2. The Systems Engineering Capability Model[1] (SECM)
3. The Integrated Product Development Capability Maturity Model (IPD-CMM) v 0.98

The combination of these models into a single improvement framework was intended for use by organizations in their pursuit of enterprise-wide process improvement.

These three source models were selected because of their widespread adoption in the software and systems engineering communities and because of their different approaches to improving processes in an organization.

Using information from these popular and well-regarded models as source material, the CMMI Product Team created a cohesive set of integrated models that can be adopted by those currently using the source models, as well as by those new to the CMM concept. Hence, CMMI is a result of the evolution of the SW-CMM, the SECM, and the IPD-CMM.

Developing a set of integrated models involved more than simply adding existing model materials together. Using processes that promote consensus, the CMMI Product Team built a framework that accommodates multiple disciplines and is flexible enough to support the different approaches of the source models.

CMMI is the designated successor of the three source models. The SEI has released a policy to sunset the Software CMM; the revisions and improvements made during development of the Software CMM version 2.0 draft C are captured in CMMI with further improvements incorporated that were

---

1. The Systems Engineering Capability Model is also known as Electronic Industries Alliance 731 (EIA 731) [EIA 98].

discovered since 1997. The same can be said for the SECM and the IPD-CMM. These models are expected to be succeeded by CMMI.

The CMMI Framework was also designed to support the future integration of other disciplines. Furthermore, CMMI was developed to be consistent and compatible with the ISO/IEC 15504 Technical Report for Software Process Assessment [ISO 98].

CMMI has gone through an extensive review process. CMMI version 0.2 was publicly reviewed and used in pilot activities. Following release of that version, improvement was guided by change requests from public reviewers, piloting organizations, and focus groups.

The CMMI Product Team evaluated more than 3,000 change requests to create CMMI version 1.0. Shortly thereafter, version 1.02 was released, which incorporated several minor improvements. As with any release, opportunities for improvement remained.

Version 1.1 incorporated improvements guided by feedback from early use, more than 1,500 change requests submitted as part of the public review, and hundreds of comments as part of the change control process. No major changes to CMMI version 1.1 are expected before 2004.

Coverage of the Bodies of Knowledge

The intent of CMMI is to provide a CMM that covers product and service development and maintenance but also provides an extensible framework so that new bodies of knowledge can be added. Currently, four bodies of knowledge are available to you when planning process improvement using CMMI:

- Systems engineering
- Software engineering
- Integrated product and process development
- Supplier sourcing

This text refers to these bodies of knowledge as "disciplines." In other words, when we refer to selecting a "discipline," it can be one of the bodies of knowledge listed above. Other bodies of knowledge may be integrated into the CMMI Framework in the future; however, none are planned at this time.

Systems Engineering

Systems engineering covers the development of total systems, which may or may not include software. Systems engineers focus on transforming customers' needs, expectations, and constraints into products and supporting these products throughout their life.

Software Engineering

Software engineering covers the development of software systems. Software engineers focus on applying systematic, disciplined, and quantifiable approaches to the development, operation, and maintenance of software.

Integrated Product and Process Development

Integrated product and process development (IPPD) is a systematic approach that achieves a timely collaboration of relevant stakeholders throughout the life of the product to satisfy customers' needs, expectations, and requirements. The processes to support an IPPD approach are integrated with the other processes in the organization.

If a project or organization chooses IPPD, it performs the IPPD best practices concurrently with other best practices used to produce products (e.g., those related to systems engineering). That is, if an organization or project wishes to use IPPD, it must select one or more disciplines in addition to IPPD.

Supplier Sourcing

As work efforts become more complex, project managers may use suppliers to perform functions or add modifications to products that are specifically needed by the project. When those activities are critical, the project benefits from enhanced source analysis and from monitoring supplier activities before product delivery. Under these circumstances, the supplier sourcing discipline covers the acquisition of products from suppliers

Similar to IPPD best practices, supplier sourcing best practices must be selected in conjunction with best practices used to produce products.

Selecting Disciplines

Disciplines are addressed in this book by the process areas associated with them and by model components called discipline amplifications.

A process area is a cluster of related best practices in an area that, when implemented collectively, satisfies a set of goals considered important for making significant improvement in that area.

A discipline amplification is a model component that contains information relevant to a particular discipline. In Part Two, you will find paragraphs labeled "For Software Engineering." These paragraphs are discipline amplifications for software engineers. This information applies only if you are improving your software engineering processes. The same is true for the other disciplines.

Because this book contains all of the disciplines currently available in CMMI, you must selectively apply the process areas found in this book to achieve your objectives.

Process Areas for Systems Engineering

If you are improving your systems engineering processes, you should select from the following process areas. The discipline amplifications for systems engineering receive special emphasis.

- Causal Analysis and Resolution
- Configuration Management
- Decision Analysis and Resolution
- Integrated Project Management (the first two specific goals)
- Measurement and Analysis
- Organizational Innovation and Deployment
- Organizational Process Definition
- Organizational Process Focus
- Organizational Process Performance
- Organizational Training
- Product Integration
- Project Monitoring and Control
- Project Planning
- Process and Product Quality Assurance
- Quantitative Project Management
- Requirements Development
- Requirements Management
- Risk Management
- Supplier Agreement Management
- Technical Solution
- Validation
- Verification

Process Areas for Software Engineering

If you are improving your software engineering processes, you will choose from the process areas that are the same as those listed for systems engineering. The only differences are that the discipline amplifications for software engineering receive special emphasis.

Process Areas for Integrated Product and Process Development

If you are improving your integrated product and process development processes, you will choose from the process areas that are the same as those listed for systems engineering with two additional process areas and additional best practices in the Integrated Project Management process area. The discipline amplifications for IPPD receive special emphasis.

The additional process areas are as follows:

- Integrated Teaming
- Organizational Environment for Integration

Process Areas for Supplier Sourcing

If you are improving your source selection processes, you will choose from the process areas that are the same as those listed for systems engineering with one additional process area. The discipline amplifications for supplier sourcing receive special emphasis

The additional process area is as follows:

- Integrated Supplier Management

Multiple Disciplines

If you are improving multiple disciplines, choose from the process areas listed under all of the relevant disciplines and pay attention to all of the discipline amplifications for those disciplines.

A Conclusion

The only distinction between CMMI models for systems engineering and software engineering is the type of discipline amplifications included. This similarity of material was an intentional decision made during the development of CMMI. CMMI focuses on product development, improving both your systems engineering and software engineering functions with an integrated approach.

Resolving Different Approaches of CMMs

The definition of a capability maturity model allows the community to develop models having different approaches. As long a model contains the essential elements of effective processes for one or more disciplines and describes an evolutionary improvement path from ad hoc, immature processes to disciplined, mature processes with improved quality and effectiveness, it is considered a CMM.

All of the source models for CMMI are considered capability maturity models; however, each has a different approach. Review and examination of each source model led to the discovery of two types of approaches to presenting capability maturity models. These types of approaches have been given the label "representations" in the process improvement community. A representation reflects the organization, use, and presentation of components in a model.

All capability maturity models have process areas that are defined by levels.[2] An example of a process area is Project Planning. There are two types of CMMI model representations: staged and continuous.

The staged representation is the approach used in the Software CMM. It is an approach that uses predefined sets of process areas to define an improvement path for an organization. This improvement path is described by a model component called a maturity level. A maturity level is a well-defined evolutionary plateau toward achieving improved organizational processes.

The continuous representation is the approach used in the SECM and the IPD-CMM. This approach allows an organization to select a specific process area and improve relative to it. The continuous representation uses capability levels to characterize improvement relative to an individual process area.

CMMI supports both representations because of the familiarity that people had with the source models and the concern that if one representation were selected over the other, part of the community would not adopt CMMI. Although this adds complexity to CMMI, it also provides an easier transition to CMMI for people familiar with one representation or the other.

Choosing a Representation

If you are new to process improvement and are not familiar with either the staged or continuous representation, you cannot go wrong if you choose one representation or the other. There are many valid reasons to select either representation.

If you have been using a CMM and you are familiar with a particular representation, we suggest that you continue to use that representation because it will make the transition to CMMI easier. Once you have become completely comfortable with CMMI, you might then decide to use the other representation.

---

2. Two of the source models use other terms for the concept of a process area. The Software CMM uses the term *key process areas*; the SECM uses the term *focus areas*.

Because each representation has advantages over the other, some organizations use both representations to address particular needs at various times in their improvement programs. We provide the advantages and disadvantages of each representation to help you decide which representation is best for your organization.

Continuous Representation

The continuous representation offers a flexible approach to process improvement. An organization may choose to improve the performance of a single process-related trouble spot, or it can work on several areas that are closely aligned to the organization's business objectives. The continuous representation also allows an organization to improve different processes at different rates. There are some limitations on an organization's choices because of the dependencies among some process areas.

Capability levels are used to measure the improvement path through each process area from an unperformed process to an optimizing process. For example, an organization may wish to strive for reaching capability level 2 in one process area and capability level 4 in another. As the organization's process reaches a capability level, it sets its sights on the next capability level for that same process area or decides to widen its scope and create the same level of capability across a larger number of process areas.

If you know the processes that need improvement in your organization and you understand the dependencies among the process areas described in CMMI, the continuous representation would be a good choice for your organization.

Staged Representation

The staged representation offers a systematic, structured way to approach process improvement one step at a time. Achieving each stage ensures that an adequate improvement has been laid as a foundation for the next stage.

Process areas are organized by maturity levels that take much of the guesswork out of process improvement. The staged representation prescribes the order for implementing each process area according to maturity levels, which define the improvement path for an organization from the initial level to the optimizing level. Achieving each maturity level ensures that an adequate improvement foundation has been laid for the next maturity level and allows for lasting, incremental improvement.

If you do not know where to start and which processes to choose to improve, the staged representation is a good choice for you. It gives you a specific set of processes to improve that have been determined through more than a decade of research and experience in the software community.

Comparison of the Continuous and Staged Representations

Table 1.1 compares the advantages of each representation and may assist you with determining which representation is right for your organization.

Factors in Your Decision

Three categories of factors that may influence your decision when selecting a representation are business, culture, and legacy.

Business Factors

An organization with mature knowledge of its own business objectives is likely to have a strong mapping of its processes to its business objectives. Such an organization may find the continuous representation useful to appraise its

TABLE 1.1   Comparative Advantages of Continuous and Staged Representations

Continuous Representation	Staged Representation
Grants explicit freedom to select the order of improvement that best meets the organization's business objectives and mitigates the organization's areas of risk	Enables organizations to have a predefined and proved improvement path
Enables increased visibility of the capability achieved in each individual process area	Focuses on a set of processes that provide an organization with a specific capability that is characterized by each maturity level
Provides a capability-level rating that is used primarily for improvement in an organization and is rarely communicated externally	Provides a maturity-level rating that is often used in internal management communication, statements external to the organization, and during acquisitions as a means to qualify bidders
Allows improvements of different processes to be performed at different rates	Summarizes process-improvement results in a simple form—a single maturity-level number
Reflects a newer approach that does not yet have the data to demonstrate its ties to return on investment	Builds on a relatively long history of use that includes case studies and data that demonstrate proved return on investment
Provides an easy migration from the SECM to the CMMI	Provides an easy migration from the Software CMM to CMMI
Affords an easy comparison of process improvement to ISO/IEC 15504 because the organization of process areas is derived from 15504	Allows comparison to 15504, but the organization of process areas does not correspond to the organization used in ISO/IEC 15504

processes and in determining how well the organization's processes support and meet its business objectives.

If an organization with a product lines focus decides to improve processes across the entire organization, it might be served best by the staged representation. The staged representation will help an organization select the critical processes to focus on for improvement.

The same organization may opt to improve processes by product line. In that case, it might select the continuous representation—and a different appraised rating of capability might be achieved for each product line. Both approaches are valid. The most important consideration is which business objectives you would like your process improvement program to support and how these business objectives align with the two representations.

Cultural Factors

Cultural factors to consider when selecting a representation have to do with an organization's ability to deploy a process improvement program. For instance, an organization might select the continuous representation if the corporate culture is process based and experienced in process improvement or has a specific process that needs to be improved quickly. An organization that has little experience in process improvement may choose the staged representation, which provides additional guidance on the order in which changes should occur.

Legacy

If an organization has experience with a staged representation, it may be wise to continue with the staged representation of CMMI, especially if it has invested resources and deployed processes across the organization that are associated with a staged representation. The same is true for the continuous representation.

Both staged and continuous representations were included in CMMI so that the communities that have used them successfully could continue in a manner that is comfortable and familiar as well as successful.

Why Not Both Representations?

Whether used for process improvement or appraisals, both representations are designed to offer essentially equivalent results. More than eighty percent of the CMMI model's content is common to both representations. Therefore, an organization need not select one representation over another.

In fact, an organization may find utility in both representations. It is rare that an organization will implement either representation exactly as prescribed. Organizations that are successful in process improvement often define an improvement plan that focuses on the unique needs of that organization and therefore use the principles of both the staged and continuous representations.

For example, organizations that select the staged representation and are at maturity level 1 often implement the maturity level 2 process areas but also the Organizational Process Focus process area, which is included at maturity level 3. Another example is an organization that chooses the continuous representation for guiding its internal process improvement effort and then chooses the staged representation to conduct an appraisal.

Choosing Your Approach to Process Improvement

Now that you know the differences between the two representations, you should be able to decide on the approach that best fits your organization. To use CMMI as intended, you select two things: a set of disciplines and a representation. Unlike the CMMI models on the SEI Web site, this book contains both representations and all of the current disciplines that compose the CMMI Framework. This "complete picture" of the CMMI Framework in Part Two enables you to use exactly what you need as you learn about it. It also allows you to quickly use other information if you decide to change the representation or disciplines that you are using.

In Part Two, markings in the margins indicate when model components are "Staged Only" (apply only when using the staged representation) or "Continuous Only" (apply only when using the continuous representation).

To use one representation or the other in this book, locate the text in Part Two that is shaded and has margin notes. The model components that are unmarked apply when using either representation. (See pages 30 through 32 for a description of other typographical conventions used in this book.)

To demonstrate how to use this book, let's look at two different scenarios. The first scenario is an organization that wants to improve its product development processes using a continuous approach. The second scenario is a software development company that uses IPPD, has been using the Software CMM, and now wants to use CMMI. This company has recently been rated at maturity level 3 according to the Software CMM version 1.1.

Scenario 1

In this scenario, you are using a continuous approach and therefore you select the processes that are important to your business objectives. Since there are twenty-five process areas to choose from, this is usually too many to focus on when starting out. You may need to narrow your focus. For example, you may find that your competitor is always getting its product released before yours. You may then choose to focus on improving your engineering and project management processes.

Building on this decision, you select these engineering process areas as a starting point: Product Integration, Requirements Development, Requirements Management, Technical Solution, Validation, and Verification. You also select Project Planning and Project Monitoring and Control.

You may at this point decide that eight process areas are still too many to focus on initially and you decide that the requirements process is really where the problems are. Consequently, you select the Requirements Development and Requirements Management process areas to begin your improvement efforts.

Next you decide how much improvement is needed in the requirements area. Do you have any processes in place already? If you don't, your process-improvement objectives may be to get to capability level 1.

Do you have your requirements development and management processes in place for each project but they are not repeatable processes? For example, policies, training, and tools are not implemented to support the processes. If your requirement processes are in place but there is no supporting infrastructure, then your process-improvement objectives may be to get to capability level 2.

Do you have all your requirements development and management processes in place but each project performs these processes differently? For example, your requirements elicitation process is not performed consistently across the organization. If this is the case, then your process-improvement objectives may be to get to capability level 3.

Do you consistently perform your requirements development and management processes but do not have an objective way to measure and improve these processes? If this is the case, then your process-improvement objectives may be to get to capability level 4.

Do you want to ensure that you are selecting the right processes to improve based on quantitative objectives to maximize your business? If yes, then your process-improvement objectives may be to get to capability level 5 for selected processes. In the description of each process area, remember to look for discipline amplications introduced by the phrases, "For Systems Engineering" and "For Software Engineering." Use all information that has no specific markings and the material that has the markings "Continuous Only" in the margins.

As you can see from this scenario, you need to understand what processes need improvement and also how much you want to improve each process. This is the fundamental principle behind the continuous representation.

Scenario 2

In the second scenario, you are a software development company using IPPD, using the Software CMM, and wanting to use CMMI. You select the process areas at maturity levels 2 and 3 for both the software and IPPD disciplines.

This selection includes the following seven process areas at maturity level 2: Requirements Management, Project Planning, Project Monitoring and Control, Supplier Agreement Management, Measurement and Analysis, Process and Product Quality Assurance, and Configuration Management. It also includes the following thirteen process areas at maturity level 3: Requirements Development, Technical Solution, Product Integration, Verification, Validation, Organizational Process Focus, Organizational Process Definition, Organizational Training, Integrated Project Management (all the specific goals), Risk Management, Integrated Teaming, Decision Analysis and Resolution, and Organizational Environment for Integration.

Since you have already been rated at maturity level 3 for the Software CMM, look at the CMMI process areas that were not in the Software CMM. These process areas include Measurement and Analysis, Requirements Development, Technical Solution, Product Integration, Verification, Validation, Risk Management, Integrated Teaming, Decision Analysis and Resolution, and Organizational Environment for Integration. Determine if you have these processes in your organization even though they were not described in the Software CMM. If there are processes in place that correspond to these process areas and for the other process areas that were in the Software CMM, perform a gap analysis against the goals and practices to make sure that you addressed the intent of each of the CMMI process areas.

Remember, in each process area you select, to look for the discipline amplications introduced by the phrases "For Software Engineering" and "For Integrated Product and Process Development." Use all information that has no specific markings and the material that has the markings "Staged Only" in the margins.

This has been an initial look at the two representations. A more detailed description is provided in chapter 5.

The Advantages of CMMI

Since many organizations have been using the Software CMM or the SECM, it is important to see how CMMI is the next generation of process improvement—a clear step forward and upward. There are unmistakable benefits to making the transition to CMMI products or to beginning process improvement using CMMI products instead of others.

CMMI provides more detailed coverage of the product life cycle than other process-improvement products used alone. For example, the engineering emphasis of CMMI has exceeded that found in the Software CMM. The process management emphasis of CMMI has exceeded that found in the SECM.

CMMI products incorporate many lessons that were learned during the development, maintenance, and use of the source models from which they were developed. Therefore, CMMI products have addressed some of the problems found in both the Software CMM and the SECM, for example.

Organizations that achieved maturity levels 4 or 5 using the Software CMM provided information to the SEI on their successes and difficulties. This information was used to develop more robust, high-level best practices in CMMI. Therefore, CMMI products better address the needs of organizations at higher maturity levels.

CMMI provides an opportunity to eliminate the stovepipes and barriers that typically exist in different parts of an organization and that typically are not addressed by other process-improvement models. The combination of useful information on engineering a product and proved practices for managing processes results in a set of well-integrated models that will facilitate project management and improve the development process—and the resulting products.

CMMI, which integrates software engineering and systems engineering into product engineering, is a valuable tool for many organizations. CMMI promotes collaboration between systems engineering and software engineering, thereby shifting the focus to the end product and its associated processes. Further, CMMI enables model and appraisal training to be simpler and more effective.

CMMI is valuable to organizations that produce software-only solutions. The systems engineering functions, not typically addressed in detail in other software-only models, are valuable to those producing software-only solutions. The handling of requirements, for example, is discussed in much more detail than in the Software CMM. Although not previously addressed in CMMs for software-only organizations, these practices use familiar terminology and model architecture and help to manage and prevent difficulties related to software requirements—a concept that is not new to many software organizations.

CMMI allows users to select the model representation (or both representations) that best suits their business objectives. The flexibility built into every CMMI model supports both staged and continuous approaches to process improvement with common terminology, architecture, and appraisal methods.

Although the initial focus of CMMI was on product and service engineering, CMMI was designed for other disciplines as well, thereby supporting enterprise-wide process improvement.

Like any other CMM, CMMI requires you to use professional judgment to interpret the information in Part Two. Although process areas describe behavior that should be exhibited in any organization, all practices must be interpreted using an in-depth knowledge of CMMI, the organization, the business environment, and the circumstances involved.

CHAPTER 2

PROCESS AREA COMPONENTS

This chapter describes the components that comprise each process area. Process areas are the primary vehicle for presenting information in Part Two. If you are unfamiliar with Part Two, you may want to skim a couple of sections to get a general feel for the layout before reading this chapter.

Required, Expected, and Informative Components

Process area components are grouped into three categories—required, expected, and informative—that reflect how to interpret them.

Required Components

Required components describe what an organization must achieve to satisfy a process area. This achievement must be visibly implemented in an organization's processes. The required components in CMMI are the specific and generic goals. Goal satisfaction is used in appraisals as the basis for deciding if a process area has been achieved and satisfied.

Expected Components

Expected components describe what an organization will typically implement to achieve a required component. Expected components guide those who implement improvements or perform appraisals. Expected components include the specific and generic practices.

Before goals can be considered satisfied, either the practices as described or acceptable alternatives to them are present in the planned and implemented processes of the organization.

Informative Components

Informative components provide details that help organizations get started in thinking about how to approach the required and expected components.

Subpractices, typical work products, discipline amplifications, generic practice elaborations, goal and practice titles, goal and practice notes, and references are all informative model components.

The CMMI glossary of terms is not a required, expected, or informative element of CMMI models. The terms in the glossary should be interpreted in the context of the model component in which they appear.

Components Associated with Part Two

The model components associated with Part Two can be summarized to illustrate their relationships, as in Figure 2.1.

The following sections provide detailed descriptions of the process area components.

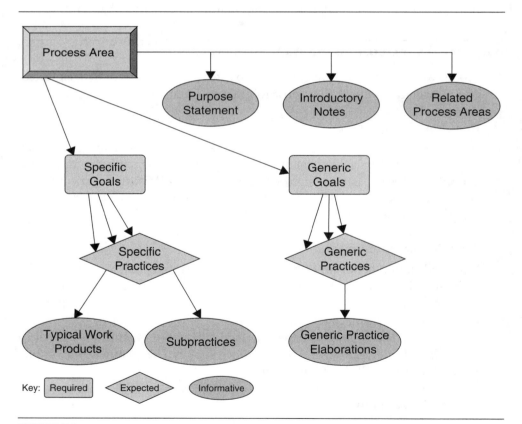

FIGURE 2.1
CMMI Model Components

Process Areas

A process area is a cluster of related practices in an area that, when implemented collectively, satisfies a set of goals considered important for making significant improvement in that area.

There are twenty-five process areas, presented in alphabetical order by acronym:

- Causal Analysis and Resolution (CAR)
- Configuration Management (CM)
- Decision Analysis and Resolution (DAR)
- Integrated Project Management (IPM)
- Integrated Supplier Management (ISM)
- Integrated Teaming (IT)
- Measurement and Analysis (MA)
- Organizational Environment for Integration (OEI)
- Organizational Innovation and Deployment (OID)
- Organizational Process Definition (OPD)
- Organizational Process Focus (OPF)
- Organizational Process Performance (OPP)
- Organizational Training (OT)
- Product Integration (PI)
- Project Monitoring and Control (PMC)
- Project Planning (PP)
- Process and Product Quality Assurance (PPQA)
- Quantitative Project Management (QPM)
- Requirements Development (RD)
- Requirements Management (REQM)
- Risk Management (RSKM)
- Supplier Agreement Management (SAM)
- Technical Solution (TS)
- Validation (VAL)
- Verification (VER)

Purpose Statements

The purpose statement describes the purpose of the process area and is an informative component.

For example, the purpose statement of the Requirements Development process area is "The purpose of Requirements Development is to produce and analyze customer, product, and product-component requirements."

Introductory Notes

The introductory notes section of the process area describes the major concepts covered in the process area and is an informative component.

An example from the introductory notes of the Project Planning process area is "Planning begins with requirements that define the product and project."

Related Process Areas

The related process areas section lists references to related process areas and reflects the high-level relationships among the process areas. The related process area section is an informative component.

An example of a reference found in the related process areas section of the Project Planning process area is "Refer to the Risk Management process area for more information about identifying and managing risks."

Specific Goals

A specific goal describes the unique characteristics that must be present to satisfy the process area. A specific goal is a required model component and is used in appraisals to help determine whether a process area is satisfied.

For example, a specific goal from the Configuration Management process area is "Integrity of baselines is established and maintained."

Only the statement of the specific goal is a required model component. The title of a specific goal (preceded by the goal number) and any notes associated with the goal are considered informative model components.

Generic Goals

Generic goals appear near the end of a process area and are called "generic" because the same goal statement appears in multiple process areas. A generic goal describes the characteristics that must be present to institutionalize the processes that implement a process area. A generic goal is a required model component and is used in appraisals to determine whether a process area is satisfied. (See chapter 3 for a more detailed description of generic goals.)

An example of a generic goal is "The process is institutionalized as a defined process."

Only the statement of the generic goal is a required model component. The title of a generic goal (preceded by the goal number) and any notes associated with the goal are considered informative model components.

Practice-to-Goal Relationship Tables

The practice-to-goal relationship table illustrates the relationships among the practices that are expected components and the goals that are required components. These relationships are critical during an appraisal to help determine when a goal is satisfied. This table contains a summary of all the goals and practices. The practice-to-goal relationship table is an informative component.

Specific Practices

A specific practice is the description of an activity that is considered important in achieving the associated specific goal. The specific practices describe the activities expected to result in achievement of the specific goals of a process area. A specific practice is an expected model component.

For example, a specific practice from the Integrated Supplier Management process area is "Identify and analyze potential sources of products that may be used to satisfy the project's requirements."

Only the statement of the specific practice is an expected model component. The title of a specific practice (preceded by the practice number) and any notes associated with the specific practice are considered informative model components.

Typical Work Products

The typical work products section lists sample outputs from a specific practice. These examples are called "typical work products" because there are often other work products that are just as effective but are not listed. A typical work product is an informative model component.

For example, a typical work product for the specific practice "Establish and maintain verification procedures and criteria for the selected work products" in the Verification process area is "verification criteria."

Subpractices

A subpractice is a detailed description that provides guidance for interpreting and implementing a specific practice. Subpractices may be worded as if prescriptive, but are actually an informative component meant only to provide ideas that may be useful for process improvement.

For example, a subpractice for the specific practice "Take corrective action on identified issues" in the Project Monitoring and Control process area is "Determine and document the appropriate actions needed to address the identified issues."

Generic Practices

Generic practices appear near the end of a process area and are called "generic" because the same practice appears in multiple process areas. A generic practice is the description of an activity that is considered important in achieving the associated generic goal. A generic practice is an expected model component. (See chapter 3 for a more detailed description of generic practices.)

For example, a generic practice for the generic goal "The process is institutionalized as a managed process" is "Provide adequate resources for performing the process, developing the work products, and providing the services of the process."

Only the statement of the generic practice is an expected model component. The title of a generic practice (preceded by the practice number) and any notes associated with the practice are considered informative model components.

To reduce the repetitiveness of this information and to conserve the number of pages required to present this information, only the generic practice title, statement, and elaborations appear in Part Two, "Process Areas." (See chapter 3, pages 39 through 54, for a complete description of the generic practices.)

Generic Practice Elaborations

A generic practice elaboration appears after a generic practice in a process area to provide guidance on how the generic practice should be applied uniquely to the process area. A generic practice elaboration is an informative model component.

For example, a generic practice elaboration after the generic practice "Establish and maintain an organizational policy for planning and performing the verification process" in the Verification process area is "This policy establishes organizational expectations for establishing and maintaining verification methods, procedures, criteria, verification environment, performing peer reviews, and verifying selected work products."

Supporting Informative Components

There are many places where further information is needed to describe a concept. This informative material is provided in the form of the following components:

- Notes
- Examples
- Discipline amplifications
- References

Notes

A note is text that can accompany nearly any other model component. It may provide detail, background, or rationale. A note is an informative model component.

For example, a note that accompanies the specific practice "Implement the selected action proposals that were developed in causal analysis" in the

Causal Analysis and Resolution process area is "Only changes that prove to be of value should be considered for broad implementation."

Examples

An example is a component comprising text and often a list of items, usually in a box, that can accompany nearly any other component and provides one or more examples to clarify a concept or described activity. An example is an informative model component.

The following is an example that accompanies the specific practice "Establish and maintain procedures and criteria for validation" in the Validation process area.

Examples of sources for validation criteria include the following:
- Product and product-component requirements
- Standards
- Customer acceptance criteria
- Environmental performance
- Thresholds of performance deviation

Discipline Amplifications

A discipline amplification is a specialized piece of information that is relevant to a particular discipline. Each discipline amplification is labeled with a heading that indicates which discipline it applies to. For example, a discipline amplification for software engineering is labeled "For Software Engineering." A discipline amplification is an informative model component.

For example, a discipline amplification that accompanies the specific practice "Establish and maintain procedures and criteria for integration of the product components" in the Product Integration process area is "*For Supplier Sourcing*: Pertinent parts of the schedule and criteria for assembly should be shared with suppliers of work products to reduce the occurrence of delays and component failure."

References

A reference is a pointer to additional or more detailed information in related process areas and can accompany nearly any other model component. A reference is an informative model component.

For example, a reference that accompanies the specific practice "Determine the type of acquisition for each product or product component to be acquired" in the Supplier Agreement Management process area is "Refer to the Technical Solution process area for more information about identifying the products and product components to be acquired."

Numbering Scheme

Specific and generic goals are numbered sequentially. Each specific goal begins with the prefix SG (e.g., SG 1). Each generic goal begins with the prefix GG (e.g., GG 2).

Each specific practice begins with the prefix SP, followed by a number in the form $x.y$-z (e.g., SP 1.1-1). The x is the same number as the goal the specific practice maps to. The y is the sequence number of the specific practice under the specific goal. The z is the capability level of the specific practice.[1]

An example of specific practice numbering is in the Project Planning process area. The first specific practice is numbered SP 1.1-1 and the second is SP 1.2-1.

Each generic practice begins with the prefix GP, followed by a number in the form $x.y$ (e.g., GP 1.1).

The x corresponds to the number of the generic goal. The y is the sequence number of the generic practice under the generic goal. For example, the first generic practice associated with GG 2 is numbered GP 2.1.

Now that you are familiar with the purpose of each of the process area components, the following typographical conventions section explains how to identify them in Part Two.

Typographical Conventions

The typographical conventions used in this book were designed to enable you to select what you need and use it effectively. We present model components in formats that allow you to find them quickly on the page.

Figures 2.2 through 2.4 are sample pages from Part Two of this book; they show the different process area components, labeled so that you can identify them. Notice that components differ typographically so that you can easily identify each one.

Representation-Specific Content

In Part Two, you will notice that some components of the process areas are shaded and labeled "Staged Only," "Continuous Only," or "Continuous/ Maturity Levels 3–5." Sometimes these labels are abbreviated, if the amount of space available makes it necessary.

Components that are not marked apply to both representations. Components marked "Staged Only" apply only if you are using the staged representation. Components marked "Continuous Only" apply only if you are using the continuous representation. (See Figure 2.4 for an example.)

---

1. A detailed discussion of capability levels can be found in chapter 5.

Components marked "Continuous/Maturity Levels 3–5" apply if you are using the continuous representation OR if you are using the staged representation and are pursuing maturity levels 3, 4, or 5. However, these components DO NOT apply if you are pursuing a maturity level 2 rating using the staged representation.

Discipline-Specific Content

A subset of the Integrated Project Management process area is only used when you have included integrated product and process development in your process-improvement program. The "IPPD Only" marking (similar to the other markings for representations) enables you to easily identify these components.

*Process
Area*

PPQA

PROCESS AND PRODUCT QUALITY ASSURANCE
A Support Process Area at Maturity Level 2

*Maturity
Level*

Purpose

The purpose of Process and Product Quality Assurance (PPQA) is to provide staff and management with objective insight into processes and associated work products.

Introductory Notes

The Process and Product Quality Assurance process area involves the following:

- Objectively evaluating performed processes, work products, and services against the applicable process descriptions, standards, and procedures
- Identifying and documenting noncompliance issues
- Providing feedback to project staff and managers on the results of quality assurance activities
- Ensuring that noncompliance issues are addressed

The Process and Product Quality Assurance process area supports the delivery of high-quality products and services by providing the project staff and managers at all levels with appropriate visibility into, and feedback on, processes and associated work products throughout the life of the project.

The practices in the Process and Product Quality Assurance process area ensure that planned processes are implemented, while the practices in the Verification process area ensure that the specified requirements are satisfied. These two process areas may on occasion address the same work product but from different perspectives. Projects should take care to minimize duplication of effort.

Objectivity in process and product quality assurance evaluations is critical to the success of the project. (See the definition of "objectively evaluate" in the glossary.) Objectivity is achieved by both independence and the use of

429

FIGURE 2.2
Sample Page from Process and Product Quality Assurance

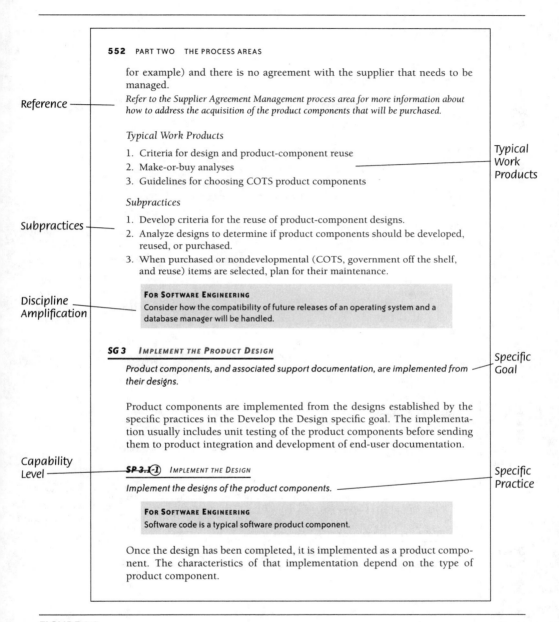

552   PART TWO   THE PROCESS AREAS

for example) and there is no agreement with the supplier that needs to be managed.

Refer to the Supplier Agreement Management process area for more information about how to address the acquisition of the product components that will be purchased.

Reference

Typical Work Products

1. Criteria for design and product-component reuse
2. Make-or-buy analyses
3. Guidelines for choosing COTS product components

Typical Work Products

Subpractices

1. Develop criteria for the reuse of product-component designs.
2. Analyze designs to determine if product components should be developed, reused, or purchased.
3. When purchased or nondevelopmental (COTS, government off the shelf, and reuse) items are selected, plan for their maintenance.

Subpractices

> **FOR SOFTWARE ENGINEERING**
> Consider how the compatibility of future releases of an operating system and a database manager will be handled.

Discipline Amplification

SG 3   *IMPLEMENT THE PRODUCT DESIGN*

Product components, and associated support documentation, are implemented from their designs.

Specific Goal

Product components are implemented from the designs established by the specific practices in the Develop the Design specific goal. The implementation usually includes unit testing of the product components before sending them to product integration and development of end-user documentation.

SP 3.1-1   *IMPLEMENT THE DESIGN*

Implement the designs of the product components.

Capability Level

Specific Practice

> **FOR SOFTWARE ENGINEERING**
> Software code is a typical software product component.

Once the design has been completed, it is implemented as a product component. The characteristics of that implementation depend on the type of product component.

FIGURE 2.3
Sample Page from Technical Solution

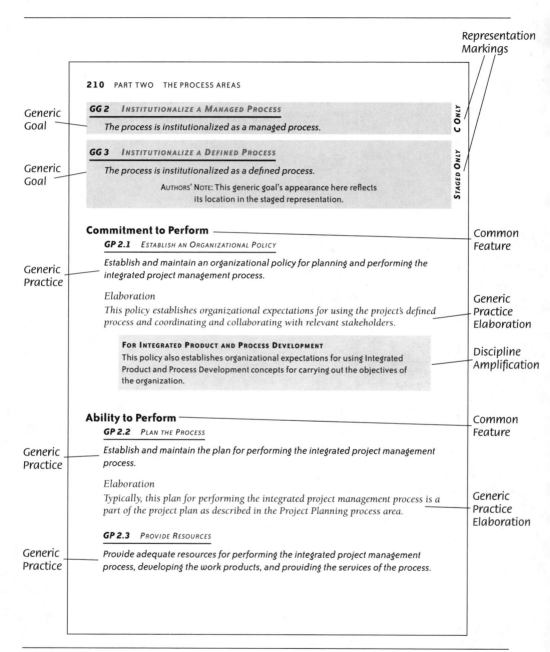

Representation
Markings

210   PART TWO   THE PROCESS AREAS

Generic
Goal

GG 2   *INSTITUTIONALIZE A MANAGED PROCESS*

The process is institutionalized as a managed process.

Generic
Goal

GG 3   *INSTITUTIONALIZE A DEFINED PROCESS*

The process is institutionalized as a defined process.

AUTHORS' NOTE: This generic goal's appearance here reflects
its location in the staged representation.

Commitment to Perform

Common
Feature

GP 2.1   *ESTABLISH AN ORGANIZATIONAL POLICY*

Generic
Practice

Establish and maintain an organizational policy for planning and performing the
integrated project management process.

Elaboration
This policy establishes organizational expectations for using the project's defined
process and coordinating and collaborating with relevant stakeholders.

Generic
Practice
Elaboration

FOR INTEGRATED PRODUCT AND PROCESS DEVELOPMENT
This policy also establishes organizational expectations for using Integrated
Product and Process Development concepts for carrying out the objectives of
the organization.

Discipline
Amplification

Ability to Perform

Common
Feature

GP 2.2   *PLAN THE PROCESS*

Generic
Practice

Establish and maintain the plan for performing the integrated project management
process.

Elaboration
Typically, this plan for performing the integrated project management process is a
part of the project plan as described in the Project Planning process area.

Generic
Practice
Elaboration

GP 2.3   *PROVIDE RESOURCES*

Generic
Practice

Provide adequate resources for performing the integrated project management
process, developing the work products, and providing the services of the process.

C ONLY

STAGED ONLY

FIGURE 2.4
Sample Page from Integrated Project Management

CHAPTER 3

PROCESS INSTITUTIONALIZATION

Overview

This chapter describes process institutionalization and presents, in detail, all the generic goals and generic practices—model components that directly address process institutionalization.

In Part Two, generic goals and generic practices appear at the end of each process area. Generic practice elaborations may appear after generic practices to show how these practices should uniquely be applied to the process area.

The entire text of the generic goals and generic practices is not repeated in the process areas (i.e., subpractices, notes, examples, and references are omitted). Instead, only the generic goal and generic practice titles and statements appear. As you address each process area, refer to this chapter for the details of all generic practices.

Process Institutionalization

"Institutionalization" is an important concept in process improvement. When mentioned in the generic goal and generic practice descriptions, institutionalization implies that the process is ingrained in the way the work is performed and there is commitment and consistency to performing the process.

An institutionalized process is more likely to be retained during times of stress. When the requirements and objectives for the process change, however, the implementation of the process may also need to change to ensure that it remains effective. The generic practices describe activities that address these aspects of institutionalization.

The degree of institutionalization is captured in the generic goals and expressed in the names of the processes associated with each goal as indicated in Table 3.1.

TABLE 3.1   Generic Goals and Process Names

Generic Goal	Progression of Processes
GG 1	Performed process
GG 2	Managed process
GG 3	Defined process
GG 4	Quantitatively managed process
GG 5	Optimizing process

The progression of process institutionalization is described in the following descriptions of each process.

Performed Process

A performed process is a process that accomplishes the work necessary to produce work products. The specific goals of the process area are satisfied.

Managed Process

A managed process is a performed process that is planned and executed in accordance with policy; employs skilled people who have adequate resources to produce controlled outputs; involves relevant stakeholders; is monitored, controlled, and reviewed; and is evaluated for adherence to its process description. The process may be instantiated by a project, group, or organizational function. Management of the process is concerned with the institutionalization of the process area and the achievement of other specific objectives established for the process, such as cost, schedule, and quality objectives. The control provided by a managed process helps ensure that the established process is retained during times of stress.

The requirements and objectives for the process are established. The status of the work products and delivery of the services are visible to management at defined points (e.g., at major milestones and completion of major tasks). Commitments are established among those performing the work and the relevant stakeholders and are revised as necessary. Work products are reviewed with relevant stakeholders and are controlled. The work products and services satisfy their specified requirements.

A critical distinction between a performed process and a managed process is the extent to which the process is managed. A managed process is planned (the plan may be part of a more encompassing plan) and the performance of the process is managed against the plan. Corrective actions are taken when the actual results and performance deviate significantly from the plan. A managed process achieves the objectives of the plan and is institutionalized for consistent performance.

Defined Process

A defined process is a managed process that is tailored from the organization's set of standard processes according to the organization's tailoring guidelines; has a maintained process description; and contributes work products, measures, and other process improvement information to the organizational process assets.

The organizational process assets are artifacts that relate to describing, implementing, and improving processes. These artifacts are assets because they are developed or acquired to meet the business objectives of the organization, and they represent investments by the organization that are expected to provide current and future business value.

The organization's set of standard processes, which are the basis of the defined process, are established and improved over time. Standard processes describe the fundamental process elements that are expected in the defined processes. Standard processes also describe the relationships (e.g., the ordering and the interfaces) among these process elements. The organization-level infrastructure to support current and future use of the organization's set of standard processes is established and improved over time. (See the definition of "standard process" in the glossary.)

A project's defined process provides a basis for planning, performing, and improving the project's tasks and activities. A project may have more than one defined process (e.g., one for developing the product and another for testing the product).

A defined process clearly states the following:

- Purpose
- Inputs
- Entry criteria
- Activities
- Roles
- Measures
- Verification steps
- Outputs
- Exit criteria

A critical distinction between a managed process and a defined process is the scope of application of the process descriptions, standards, and procedures. For a managed process, the process descriptions, standards, and procedures are applicable to a particular project, group, or organizational function. As a result, the managed processes of two projects in one organization may be different.

Another critical distinction is that a defined process is described in more detail and performed more rigorously than a managed process. This means that improvement information is easier to understand, analyze, and use. Finally, management of the defined process is based on the additional insight provided by an understanding of the interrelationships of the process activities and detailed measures of the process, its work products, and its services.

Quantitatively Managed Process

A quantitatively managed process is a defined process that is controlled using statistical and other quantitative techniques. The product quality, service quality, and process performance attributes are measurable and controlled throughout the project.

Quantitative objectives are established based on the capability of the organization's set of standard processes; the organization's business objectives; and the needs of the customer, end users, organization, and process implementers, subject to available resources. The people performing the process are directly involved in quantitatively managing the process.

Quantitative management is performed on the overall set of processes that produces a product or provides a service. The subprocesses that are significant contributors to overall process performance are statistically managed. For these selected subprocesses, detailed measures of process performance are collected and statistically analyzed. Special causes of process variation are identified and, where appropriate, the source of the special cause is addressed to prevent its recurrence.

The quality and process performance measures are incorporated into the organization's measurement repository to support future fact-based decision making.

Activities for quantitatively managing the performance of a process include the following:

- Identifying the subprocesses that are to be brought under statistical management
- Identifying and measuring product and process attributes that are important contributors to quality and process performance
- Identifying and addressing special causes of subprocess variations (based on the selected product and process attributes and subprocesses selected for statistical management)
- Managing each of the selected subprocesses, with the objective of bringing their performance within natural bounds (i.e., making the subprocess performance statistically stable and predictable based on the selected product and process attributes)
- Predicting the ability of the process to satisfy established quantitative quality and process-performance objectives

- Taking appropriate corrective actions when it is determined that the established quantitative quality and process-performance objectives will not be satisfied

These corrective actions include changing the objectives or ensuring that relevant stakeholders have a quantitative understanding of, and have agreed to, the performance shortfall.

A critical distinction between a defined process and a quantitatively managed process is the predictability of the process performance. The term "quantitatively managed" implies using appropriate statistical and other quantitative techniques to manage the performance of one or more critical subprocesses so that the performance of the process can be predicted. A defined process provides only qualitative predictability.

Optimizing Process

An optimizing process is a quantitatively managed process that is changed and adapted to meet relevant current and projected business objectives. An optimizing process focuses on continually improving process performance through both incremental and innovative technological improvements. Process improvements that address common causes of process variation, root causes of defects and other problems, and those that would measurably improve the organization's processes are identified, evaluated, and deployed as appropriate. These improvements are selected based on a quantitative understanding of their expected contribution to achieving the organization's process-improvement objectives versus the cost and impact to the organization. The process performance of the organization's processes is continually improved.

Selected incremental and innovative technological process improvements are systematically managed and deployed into the organization. The effects of the deployed process improvements are measured and evaluated against the quantitative process-improvement objectives.

In a process that is optimized, common causes of process variation are addressed by changing the process in a way that will shift the mean or decrease variation when the process is restabilized. These changes are intended to improve process performance and achieve the organization's established process-improvement objectives.

A critical distinction between a quantitatively managed process and an optimizing process is that the optimizing process is continuously improved by addressing common causes of process variation. A quantitatively managed process is concerned with addressing special causes of process variation and providing statistical predictability of the results. Although the process may produce predictable results, the results may be insufficient to achieve the organization's process-improvement objectives.

Relationships among Processes

The generic goals evolve so that each goal provides a foundation for the next. Therefore the following conclusions can be made:

- A managed process is a performed process.
- A defined process is a managed process.
- A quantitatively managed process is a defined process.
- An optimizing process is a quantitatively managed process.

Thus, applied sequentially and in order, the generic goals describe a process that is increasingly institutionalized, from a performed process to an optimizing process.

Achieving GG 1 for a process area is equivalent to saying you achieve the specific goals of the process area.

Achieving GG 2 for a process area is equivalent to saying you manage the performance of processes associated with the process area. There is a policy that indicates you will perform it. There is a plan for performing it. There are resources provided, responsibilities assigned, training on how to perform it, selected work products from performing the process are controlled, and so on. In other words, the process is planned and monitored just like any project or support activity.

Achieving GG 3 for a process area assumes that an organizational standard process exists that can be tailored to result in the process you will use. Tailoring *might* result in making no changes to the standard process. In other words, the process used and the standard process may be identical. Using the standard process "as is" is tailoring because the choice is made that no further modification is required.

Each process area describes multiple activities, some of which are repeatedly performed. You may need to tailor the way one of these activities is performed to account for new capabilities or circumstances. For example, you may have a standard for developing or obtaining organizational training that does not consider Web-based training. When preparing to develop or obtain a Web-based course, you may need to tailor that standard process to account for the particular challenges and benefits of Web-based training.

Achieving GG 4 or GG 5 for a process area is conceptually feasible but may not be economical except, perhaps, in situations where the product domain has become stable for an extended period of time or in situations in which the process area or domain is a critical business driver.

Generic Goals and Generic Practices

This section describes all of the generic goals and generic practices, as well as their associated subpractices, notes, examples, and references. The generic goals are organized in numerical order, GG 1 through GG 5. The generic practices are also organized in numerical order under the generic goal they support.

As mentioned earlier in this chapter, the subpractices, notes, examples, and references are not repeated in Part Two; the details of each generic goal and generic practice are found only here.

GG 1   ACHIEVE SPECIFIC GOALS

The process supports and enables achievement of the specific goals of the process area by transforming identifiable input work products to produce identifiable output work products.

GP 1.1   PERFORM BASE PRACTICES

Perform the base practices of the process area to develop work products and provide services to achieve the specific goals of the process area.

The purpose of this generic practice is to produce the work products and deliver the services that are expected by performing the process. These practices may be done informally, without following a documented process description or plan. The rigor with which these practices are performed depends on the individuals managing and performing the work and may vary considerably.

GG 2   INSTITUTIONALIZE A MANAGED PROCESS

The process is institutionalized as a managed process.

GP 2.1   ESTABLISH AN ORGANIZATIONAL POLICY

Establish and maintain an organizational policy for planning and performing the process.

The purpose of this generic practice is to define the organizational expectations for the process and make these expectations visible to those in the organization who are affected. In general, senior management is responsible for establishing and communicating guiding principles, direction, and expectations for the organization.

Not all direction from senior management will bear the label "policy." The existence of appropriate organizational direction is the expectation of this generic practice, regardless of what it is called or how it is imparted.

GP 2.2   *PLAN THE PROCESS*

Establish and maintain the plan for performing the process.

The purpose of this generic practice is to determine what is needed to perform the process and to achieve the established objectives, to prepare a plan for performing the process, to prepare a process description, and to get agreement on the plan from relevant stakeholders.

Requirements for the process's specified work products and for performing the work may be derived from other requirements. In the case of a project's processes, they may come from that project's requirements-management process; in the case of an organization's process, they may come from organizational sources.

The objectives for the process may be derived from other plans (e.g., the project plans). Included are objectives for the specific situation, including quality, cost, and schedule objectives. For example, an objective might be to reduce the cost of performing a process for this implementation over the previous implementation.

Although a generic practice, by definition, applies to all process areas, the practical implications of applying a generic practice vary for each process area. Consider two examples that illustrate these differences as they relate to planning the process.

First, the planning described by this generic practice as applied to the Project Monitoring and Control process area may be carried out in full by the processes associated with the Project Planning process area. In such a situation, the generic practice imposes no additional expectations for planning. Second, the planning described by this generic practice as applied to the Project Planning process area typically would not be addressed by the processes associated with other process areas. Therefore, the generic practice sets an expectation that the project planning process itself be planned. It is important to be aware of the extent to which this generic practice may either reinforce expectations set elsewhere in CMMI or set new expectations that should be addressed.

Establishing a plan includes documenting the plan and providing a process description. Maintaining the plan includes changing it, as necessary, in response to either corrective actions or to changes in requirements and objectives for the process.

The plan for performing the process typically includes the following:

- Process description
- Standards for the work products and services of the process
- Requirements for the work products and services of the process
- Specific objectives for the performance of the process (e.g., quality, time scale, cycle time, and resource usage)
- Dependencies among the activities, work products, and services of the process
- Resources (including funding, people, and tools) needed to perform the process
- Assignment of responsibility and authority
- Training needed for performing and supporting the process
- Work products to be placed under configuration management and the level of configuration management for each work product
- Measurement requirements to provide insight into the performance of the process, its work products, and its services
- Involvement of identified stakeholders
- Activities for monitoring and controlling the process
- Objective evaluation activities of the process
- Management review activities for the process and the work products

Subpractices

1. Obtain management sponsorship for performing the process.
2. Define and document the process description.

   The process description, which includes relevant standards and procedures, may be included as part of the plan for performing the process or may be included in the plan by reference.
3. Define and document the plan for performing the process.

   This plan may be a stand-alone document, embedded in a more comprehensive document, or distributed across multiple documents. In the case of the plan being distributed across multiple documents, ensure that a coherent picture of who does what is preserved. Documents may be hardcopy or softcopy.
4. Review the plan with relevant stakeholders and get their agreement.

   This includes reviewing that the planned process satisfies the applicable policies, plans, requirements, and standards to provide assurance to relevant stakeholders.
5. Revise the plan as necessary.

GP 2.3 PROVIDE RESOURCES

Provide adequate resources for performing the process, developing the work products, and providing the services of the process.

The purpose of this generic practice is to ensure that the resources necessary to perform the process as defined by the plan are available when they are needed. Resources include adequate funding, appropriate physical facilities, skilled people, and appropriate tools.

The interpretation of the term *adequate* depends on many factors and can change over time. Inadequate resources may be addressed by increasing resources or by removing requirements, constraints, and commitments.

GP 2.4 ASSIGN RESPONSIBILITY

Assign responsibility and authority for performing the process, developing the work products, and providing the services of the process.

The purpose of this generic practice is to ensure that there is accountability for performing the process and achieving the specified results throughout the life of the process. The people assigned must have the appropriate authority to perform the assigned responsibilities.

Responsibility can be assigned using detailed job descriptions or in living documents, such as the plan for performing the process. Dynamic assignment of responsibility is another legitimate way to perform this generic practice, as long as the assignment and acceptance of responsibility are ensured throughout the life of the process.

Subpractices

1. Assign overall responsibility and authority for performing the process.
2. Assign responsibility for performing the specific tasks of the process.
3. Confirm that the people assigned to the responsibilities and authorities understand and accept them.

GP 2.5 TRAIN PEOPLE

Train the people performing or supporting the process as needed.

The purpose of this generic practice is to ensure that the people have the necessary skills and expertise to perform or support the process.

Appropriate training is provided to the people who will be performing the work. Overview training is provided to orient people who interact with those performing the work.

Examples of methods for providing training include self-study; self-directed training; self-paced, programmed instruction; formalized on-the-job training; mentoring; and formal and classroom training.

Training supports the successful performance of the process by establishing a common understanding of the process and by imparting the skills and knowledge needed to perform the process.

GP 2.6 MANAGE CONFIGURATIONS

Place designated work products of the process under appropriate levels of configuration management.

The purpose of this generic practice is to establish and maintain the integrity of the designated work products of the process (or their descriptions) throughout their useful life.

Refer to the Configuration Management process area for more information on placing work products under configuration management.

The designated work products are specifically identified in the plan for performing the process, along with a specification of the level of configuration management.

Different levels of configuration management are appropriate for different work products and for different points in time. For some work products, it may be sufficient to maintain version control (i.e., the version of the work product in use at a given time, past or present, is known and changes are incorporated in a controlled manner). Version control is usually under the sole control of the work product owner (which may be an individual, a group, or a team).

Sometimes, it may be critical that work products be placed under formal or "baseline" configuration management. This type of configuration management includes defining and establishing baselines at predetermined points. These baselines are formally reviewed and agreed on, and serve as the basis for further development of the designated work products.

Additional levels of configuration management between version control and formal configuration management are possible. An identified work product may be under various levels of configuration management at different points in time.

GP 2.7 IDENTIFY AND INVOLVE RELEVANT STAKEHOLDERS

Identify and involve the relevant stakeholders as planned.

The purpose of this generic practice is to establish and maintain the expected involvement of stakeholders during the execution of the process.

Involve relevant stakeholders as described in an appropriate plan for stakeholder involvement. Involve them appropriately in activities such as the following:

- Planning
- Decisions
- Commitments
- Communications
- Coordination
- Reviews
- Appraisals
- Requirements definitions
- Resolution of problems/issues

Refer to the Project Planning process area for information on the project planning for stakeholder involvement.

The objective of planning the stakeholder involvement is to ensure that interactions necessary to the process are accomplished, while not allowing excessive numbers of affected groups and individuals to impede process execution.

Subpractices

1. Identify stakeholders relevant to this process and decide what type of involvement should be practiced.

    Relevant stakeholders are identified among the suppliers of inputs to, the users of outputs from, and the performers of the activities within the process. Once the relevant stakeholders are identified, the appropriate level of their involvement in process activities is planned.

2. Share these identifications with project planners or other planners as appropriate.

3. Involve relevant stakeholders as planned.

GP 2.8   MONITOR AND CONTROL THE PROCESS

Monitor and control the process against the plan for performing the process and take appropriate corrective action.

The purpose of this generic practice is to perform the direct day-to-day monitoring and controlling of the process. Appropriate visibility into the process is maintained so that appropriate corrective action can be taken when necessary. Monitoring and controlling the process involves measuring appropriate attributes of the process or work products produced by the process.

Refer to the Project Monitoring and Control process area for more information about monitoring and controlling the project and taking corrective action.

Refer to the Measurement and Analysis process area for more information about measurement.

Subpractices

1. Measure actual performance against the plan for performing the process.

    The measures are of the process, its work products, and its services.
2. Review accomplishments and results of the process against the plan for performing the process.
3. Review activities, status, and results of the process with the immediate level of management responsible for the process and identify issues. The reviews are intended to provide the immediate level of management with appropriate visibility into the process. The reviews can be both periodic and event driven.
4. Identify and evaluate the effects of significant deviations from the plan for performing the process.
5. Identify problems in the plan for performing the process and in the execution of the process.
6. Take corrective action when requirements and objectives are not being satisfied, when issues are identified, or when progress differs significantly from the plan for performing the process.

    There are inherent risks that should be considered before any corrective action is taken.

     Corrective action may include the following:
    - Taking remedial action to repair defective work products or services
    - Changing the plan for performing the process
    - Adjusting resources, including people, tools, and other resources
    - Negotiating changes to the established commitments
    - Securing change to the requirements and objectives that have to be satisfied
    - Terminating the effort
7. Track corrective action to closure.

GP 2.9   OBJECTIVELY EVALUATE ADHERENCE

Objectively evaluate adherence of the process against its process description, standards, and procedures, and address noncompliance.

The purpose of this generic practice is to provide credible assurance that the process is implemented as planned and adheres to its process description, standards, and procedures. (See the definition of *objectively evaluate* in the glossary.)

People not directly responsible for managing or performing the activities of the process typically evaluate adherence. In many cases, adherence is evaluated by people within the organization, but external to the process or project, or by people external to the organization. As a result, credible assurance of adherence can be provided even during times when the process is under stress (e.g., when the effort is behind schedule or over budget).

Refer to the Process and Product Quality Assurance process area for more information about objectively evaluating adherence.

GP 2.10 REVIEW STATUS WITH HIGHER LEVEL MANAGEMENT

Review the activities, status, and results of the process with higher level management and resolve issues.

The purpose of this generic practice is to provide higher level management with the appropriate visibility into the process.

Higher level management includes those levels of management in the organization above the immediate level of management responsible for the process. In particular, higher level management includes senior management. These reviews are for managers who provide the policy and overall guidance for the process, not for those who perform the direct day-to-day monitoring and controlling of the process.

Different managers have different needs for information about the process. These reviews help ensure that informed decisions on the planning and performing of the process can be made. Therefore, these reviews are expected to be both periodic and event driven.

GG 3 INSTITUTIONALIZE A DEFINED PROCESS

The process is institutionalized as a defined process.

GP 3.1 ESTABLISH A DEFINED PROCESS

Establish and maintain the description of a defined process.

The purpose of this generic practice is to establish and maintain a description of the process that is tailored from the organization's set of standard processes to address the needs of a specific instantiation. The organization should have standard processes that cover the process area, as well as have guidelines for tailoring these standard processes to meet the needs of a project or organizational function. With a defined process, variability in how the processes are performed across the organization is reduced and process assets, data, and learning can be effectively shared.

Refer to the Organizational Process Definition process area for more information about the organization's set of standard processes and tailoring guidelines.

The descriptions of the defined processes provide the basis for planning, performing, and managing the activities, work products, and services associated with the process.

Subpractices

1. Select from the organization's set of standard processes those processes that cover the process area and best meet the needs of the project or organizational function.
2. Establish the defined process by tailoring the selected processes according to the organization's tailoring guidelines.
3. Ensure that the organization's process objectives are appropriately addressed in the defined process.
4. Document the defined process and the records of the tailoring.
5. Revise the description of the defined process as necessary.

GP 3.2   COLLECT IMPROVEMENT INFORMATION

Collect work products, measures, measurement results, and improvement information derived from planning and performing the process to support the future use and improvement of the organization's processes and process assets.

The purpose of this generic practice is to collect information and artifacts derived from planning and performing the process. This generic practice is performed so that the information and artifacts can be included in the organizational process assets and made available to those who are (or who will be) planning and performing the same or similar processes. The information and artifacts are stored in the organization's measurement repository and the organization's process asset library.

> Examples of relevant information include the effort expended for the various activities, defects injected or removed in a particular activity, and lessons learned.

Refer to the Organizational Process Definition process area for more information about the organization's measurement repository and process asset library and for more information about the work products, measures, and improvement information that are incorporated into these organizational process assets.

Subpractices

1. Store process and product measures in the organization's measurement repository.

    The process and product measures are primarily those that are defined in the common set of measures for the organization's set of standard processes.
2. Submit documentation for inclusion in the organization's process asset library.
3. Document lessons learned from the process for inclusion in the organization's process asset library.
4. Propose improvements to the organizational process assets.

GG 4 INSTITUTIONALIZE A QUANTITATIVELY MANAGED PROCESS

The process is institutionalized as a quantitatively managed process.

GP 4.1 ESTABLISH QUANTITATIVE OBJECTIVES FOR THE PROCESS

Establish and maintain quantitative objectives for the process that address quality and process performance based on customer needs and business objectives.

The purpose of this generic practice is to determine and obtain agreement from relevant stakeholders about specific quantitative objectives for the process. These quantitative objectives can be expressed in terms of product quality, service quality, and process performance.

Refer to the Quantitative Project Management process area for information on how quantitative objectives are set for subprocesses of the project's defined process.

The quantitative objectives may be specific to the process or they may be defined for a broader scope (e.g., for a set of processes). In the latter case, these quantitative objectives may be allocated to some of the included processes.

These quantitative objectives are criteria used to judge whether the products, services, and process performance will satisfy the customers, end users, organization management, and process implementers. These quantitative objectives go beyond the traditional end-product objectives. They also cover intermediate objectives that are used to manage the achievement of the objectives over time. They reflect, in part, the demonstrated performance of the organization's set of standard processes. These quantitative objectives should be set to values that are likely to be achieved when the processes involved are stable and within their natural bounds.

Subpractices

1. Establish the quantitative objectives that pertain to the process.
2. Allocate the quantitative objectives to the process or its subprocesses.

GP 4.2 STABILIZE SUBPROCESS PERFORMANCE

Stabilize the performance of one or more subprocesses to determine the ability of the process to achieve the established quantitative quality and process-performance objectives.

The purpose of this generic practice is to stabilize the performance of one or more subprocesses of the defined process that are critical contributors to the overall performance using appropriate statistical and other quantitative techniques. Stabilizing selected subprocesses supports predicting the ability of the process to achieve the established quantitative quality and process-performance objectives.

A stable subprocess shows no significant indication of special causes of process variation. Stable subprocesses are predictable within the limits established by the natural bounds of the subprocess. Variations in the stable subprocess are due to a constant system of chance causes, and the magnitude of the variations can be small or large.

Predicting the ability of the process to achieve the established quantitative objectives requires a quantitative understanding of the contributions of the subprocesses that are critical to achieving these objectives and establishing and managing against interim quantitative objectives over time.

Selected process and product measures are incorporated into the organization's measurement repository to support process performance analysis and future fact-based decision making.

Subpractices

1. Statistically manage the performance of one or more subprocesses that are critical contributors to the overall performance of the process.
2. Predict the ability of the process to achieve its established quantitative objectives considering the performance of the statistically managed subprocesses.
3. Incorporate selected process performance measurements into the organization's process performance baselines.

GG 5   INSTITUTIONALIZE AN OPTIMIZING PROCESS

The process is institutionalized as an optimizing process.

GP 5.1   ENSURE CONTINUOUS PROCESS IMPROVEMENT

Ensure continuous improvement of the process in fulfilling the relevant business objectives of the organization.

The purpose of this generic practice is to select and systematically deploy process and technology improvements that contribute to meeting established quality and process-performance objectives.

Optimizing processes that are agile and innovative depends on the participation of an empowered workforce aligned with the business values and objectives of the organization. The organization's ability to rapidly respond to changes and opportunities is enhanced by finding ways to accelerate and share learning. Improvement of the processes is inherently part of everybody's role, resulting in a cycle of continual improvement.

Subpractices

1. Establish and maintain quantitative process-improvement objectives that support the organization's business objectives.

   The quantitative process-improvement objectives may be specific to the individual process or they may be defined for a broader scope (i.e., for a set of processes), with the individual processes contributing to achieving these objectives. Objectives that are specific to the individual process are typically allocated from quantitative objectives established for a broader scope.

   These process-improvement objectives are primarily derived from the organization's business objectives and from a detailed understanding of process capability. These objectives are the criteria used to judge whether the process performance is quantitatively improving the organization's ability to meet its business objectives. These process-improvement objectives are often set to values beyond the current process performance, and both incremental and innovative technological improvements may be needed to achieve these objectives. These objectives may also be revised frequently to continue to drive the improvement of the process (i.e., when an objective is achieved, it may be set to a new value that is again beyond the new process performance).

   These process-improvement objectives may be the same as, or a refinement of, the objectives established in the Establish Quantitative Objectives for the Process generic practice, as long as they can serve as both drivers and criteria for successful process improvement.

2. Identify process improvements that would result in measurable improvements to process performance.

   Process improvements include both incremental changes and innovative technological improvements. The innovative technological improvements are typically pursued as efforts that are separately planned, performed, and managed. Piloting is often performed. These efforts often address specific areas of the processes that are determined by analyzing process performance and identifying specific opportunities for significant measurable improvement.

3. Define strategies and manage deployment of selected process improvements based on the quantified expected benefits, the estimated costs and impacts, and the measured change to process performance.

   The costs and benefits of these improvements are estimated quantitatively, and the actual costs and benefits are measured. Benefits are primarily considered relative to the organization's quantitative process-improvement objectives. Improvements are made to both the organization's set of standard processes and the defined processes.

   Managing deployment of the process improvements includes piloting of changes and implementing adjustments where appropriate, addressing potential and real barriers to deployment, minimizing disruption to ongoing efforts, and managing risks.

GP 5.2   CORRECT ROOT CAUSES OF PROBLEMS

Identify and correct the root causes of defects and other problems in the process.

The purpose of this generic practice is to analyze defects and other problems that were encountered, to correct the root causes of these types of defects and problems, and to prevent these defects and problems from occurring in the future.

Refer to the Causal Analysis and Resolution process area for more information on identifying and correcting root causes of selected defects. Even though the Causal Analysis and Resolution process area has a project context, it can be applied to processes in other contexts as well.

Applying Generic Practices

This section helps you to develop a better understanding of the generic practices and provides information for interpreting and applying the generic practices in your organization.

Generic practices are components that are common to all process areas. Think of generic practices as reminders. They serve the purpose of reminding you to do things right, and are expected model components.

For example, when you are achieving the specific goals of the Project Planning process area, you are establishing and maintaining a plan that defines project activities. One of the generic practices that applies to the Project Planning process area is "Establish and maintain the plan for performing the project planning process" (GP 2.2). When applied to this process area, this generic practice ensures that you planned the activities for creating the plan for the project.

When you are satisfying the specific goals of the Organizational Training process area, you are developing the skills and knowledge of people in your project and organization so that they can perform their roles effectively and efficiently. When applying the same generic practice (GP 2.2) to the Organizational Training process area, this generic practice ensures that you planned the activities for developing the skills and knowledge of people in the organization.

Process Areas That Support Generic Practices

While generic goals and generic practices are the model components that directly address the institutionalization of a process across the organization, many process areas likewise address institutionalization by supporting the implementation of the generic practices. Knowing these relationships will help you effectively implement the generic practices.

Such process areas contain one or more specific practices that when implemented

1. may also fully implement a generic practice.
2. generate a work product that is used in the implementation of a generic practice.

An example is the Configuration Management process area and GP 2.6, "Place designated work products of the process under appropriate levels of configuration management." To implement the generic practice for one or more process areas, you might choose to implement the Configuration Management process area, all or in part, to implement the generic practice.

Another example is the Organizational Process Definition process area and GP 3.1, "Establish and maintain the description of a defined process." To implement this generic practice for one or more process areas, you should first implement the Organizational Process Definition process area, all or in part, to establish the organizational process assets that are needed to implement the generic practice.

Table 3.2 identifies which process areas support the implementation of which generic practices, and briefly summarizes their relationships. These relationships are important to remember during appraisals because observations can be duplicated between the generic practices and their related process areas.

Given the dependencies that generic practices have on these process areas, and given the more "holistic" view that many of these process areas provide, these process areas are often implemented early, in whole or in part, before or concurrent with implementing the associated generic practices.

There are also a few situations where the result of applying a generic practice to a particular process area would seem to make a whole process area redundant, but, in fact, it does not. It may be natural to think that applying GP 3.1, *Establish a Defined Process,* to the Project Planning and Project Monitoring and Control process areas gives the same effect as the first specific goal of Integrated Project Management, "The project is conducted using a defined process that is tailored from the organization's set of standard processes."

Although it is true that there is some overlap, the application of the generic practice to these two process areas provides defined processes covering project planning and project monitoring and control activities. These defined processes do not necessarily cover support activities (such as configuration management), other project-management processes (such as Supplier Agreement Management), or the engineering processes. In contrast, the project's defined process, provided by the Integrated Project Management process area, covers all fundamental project management, engineering, and support processes.

TABLE 3.2   Generic Practice and Process Area Relationships

Generic Practice	*Roles of Process Areas in Implementation of the Generic Practice*
GP 2.2 Plan the Process	*Project Planning:* The project planning process can implement GP 2.2 in full for all project-related process areas (except for Project Planning itself).
GP 2.5 Train People	*Organizational Training and Project Planning:* The organizational training process supports the implementation of GP 2.5 as applied to all process areas by making the training that addresses strategic or organization-wide training needs available to those who will perform or support the process. In addition, the part of the project planning process that implements Project Planning SP 2.5-1, "Plan for knowledge and skills needed to perform the project," together with the organizational training process, supports the implementation of GP 2.5 in full for all project-related process areas.
GP 2.6 Manage Configurations	*Configuration Management:* The configuration management process can implement GP 2.6 in full for all project-related process areas as well as some of the organizational process areas.
GP 2.7 Identify and Involve Relevant Stakeholders	*Project Planning:* The part of the project planning process that implements Project Planning SP 2.6-1, "Plan the involvement of identified stakeholders," can implement the stakeholder identification part (first two subpractices) of GP 2.7 in full for all project-related process areas.
GP 2.8 Monitor and Control the Process	*Project Monitoring and Control and Measurement and Analysis:* The project monitoring and control process can implement GP 2.8 in full for all project-related process areas. For all processes, not just project-related processes, the Measurement and Analysis process area provides general guidance about measuring, analyzing, and recording information that can be used in establishing measures for monitoring actual performance of the process.
GP 2.9 Objectively Evaluate Adherence	*Process and Product Quality Assurance:* The process and product quality assurance process can implement GP 2.9 in full for all process areas (except perhaps for Process and Product Quality Assurance itself).
GP 3.1 Establish a Defined Process	*Integrated Project Management and Organizational Process Definition:* The part of the integrated project-management process that implements Integrated Project Management SP 1.1-1, "Establish and maintain the project's defined process," can implement GP 3.1 in full for all project-related process areas. For all processes, not just project-related processes, the organizational process definition process establishes the organizational process assets needed to implement GP 3.1.

continued

TABLE 3.2   Generic Practice and Process Area Relationships   *continued*

Generic Practice	Roles of Process Areas in Implementation of the Generic Practice
GP 3.2 Collect Improvement Information	*Integrated Project Management, Organizational Process Focus, and Organizational Process Definition:* The part of the integrated project-management process that implements Integrated Project Management SP 1.5-1, "Contribute work products, measures, and documented experiences to the organizational process assets," can implement GP 3.2 in full for all project-related process areas.
	Also, the part of the organizational process focus process that implements Organizational Process Focus SP 2.4-1, "Incorporate process-related work products, measures, and improvement information derived from planning and performing the process into the organizational process assets," can implement GP 3.2 in part or full for all process areas.
	For all processes, the organizational process definition process establishes the organizational process assets needed to implement GP 3.2.
GP 4.1 Establish Quantitative Objectives for the Process	*Quantitative Project Management and Organizational Process Performance:* The part of the quantitative project-management process that implements Quantitative Project Management SP 1.1-1, "Establish and maintain the project's quality and process-performance objectives," supports the implementation of GP 4.1 for all project-related process areas by providing objectives from which the objectives for each particular process can be derived. If these objectives become addressed as part of implementing subpractices 5 and 8 of Quantitative Project Management SP 1.1-1, then the quantitative project-management process implements GP 4.1 in full.
	Similarly, the part of the organizational process performance process that implements Organizational Process Performance SP 1.3-1, "Establish and maintain quantitative objectives for quality and process performance for the organization," supports the implementation of GP 4.1 for all process areas.
GP 4.2 Stabilize Subprocess Performance	*Quantitative Project Management and Organizational Process Performance:* The part of the quantitative project-management process that implements Quantitative Project Management SG 2, "Statistically Manage Subprocess Performance," can implement GP 4.2 in full for all project-related process areas to which a statistically managed subprocess can be mapped.
	For all processes, not just project-related processes, the organizational process performance process establishes organizational process assets that may be needed to implement GP 4.2.
GP 5.1 Ensure Continuous Process Improvement	*Organizational Innovation and Deployment:* The organizational innovation and deployment process can implement GP 5.1 in full for all process areas providing that quality and process-performance objectives for the organization have been defined. (The latter would be the case, say, if the Organizational Process Performance process area has been implemented.)
GP 5.2 Correct Root Causes of Problems	*Causal Analysis and Resolution:* The causal analysis and resolution process can implement GP 5.2 in full for all project-related process areas.

CHAPTER 4

RELATIONSHIPS AMONG PROCESS AREAS

In this chapter, we describe interactions among process areas to help you see the organization's view of process improvement and also which process areas build on the implementation of other process areas. Relationships among process areas are presented in two dimensions.

The first dimension is the interactions of individual process areas that show how information and artifacts flow from one process area to another. Shown by the multiple figures and descriptions in this chapter, these interactions help you see a larger view of process improvement.

The second dimension is the interactions of groups of process areas. Shown by the classification of some process areas as *Fundamental* and others as *Progressive*, these classifications illustrate that the Fundamental process areas should be implemented before the Progressive process areas to ensure that the prerequisites are met to successfully implement the Progressive process areas.

Successful process-improvement initiatives must be driven by the business objectives of the organization. For example, a common business objective is to reduce the time it takes to get a product to market. The process-improvement objective derived from that might be to improve the project-management processes to ensure on-time delivery; those improvements rely on best practices in the Project Planning and Project Monitoring and Control process areas.

Four Categories of CMMI Process Areas

Process areas can be grouped into four categories:

- Process Management
- Project Management
- Engineering
- Support

Although we are grouping process areas this way to discuss their interactions, process areas often interact and have an effect on one another regardless of their defined group. For example, the Decision Analysis and Resolution process area provides specific practices to address formal evaluation that are used in the Technical Solution process area for selecting a technical solution from alternative solutions. Technical Solution is an Engineering process area and Decision Analysis and Resolution is a Support process area.

Being aware of the interactions that exist among CMMI process areas and which process areas are Fundamental and Progressive will help you apply CMMI in a useful and productive way. The following sections mainly describe the interactions of process areas within the categories and only briefly describe the interactions among process areas in other categories. Interactions among process areas that belong to different categories are described in the process areas in Part Two by references. Refer to chapter 2, page 27, for more information about references.

Process Management

Process Management process areas contain the cross-project activities related to defining, planning, deploying, implementing, monitoring, controlling, appraising, measuring, and improving processes.

The Process Management process areas of CMMI are as follows:

- Organizational Process Focus
- Organizational Process Definition
- Organizational Training
- Organizational Process Performance
- Organizational Innovation and Deployment

Fundamental Process Management Process Areas

The Fundamental Process Management process areas provide the organization with a capability to document and share best practices, organizational process assets, and learning across the organization.

Figure 4.1 provides a bird's-eye view of the interactions among the Fundamental Process Management process areas and with other process area categories. As illustrated in Figure 4.1, the Organizational Process Focus process area helps the organization plan and implement organizational process improvement based on an understanding of the current strengths and weaknesses of the organization's processes and process assets.

Candidate improvements to the organization's processes are obtained through various means. These include process-improvement proposals,

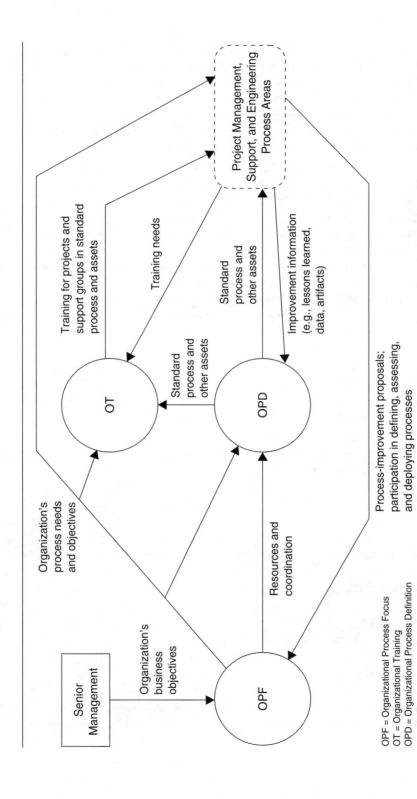

OPF = Organizational Process Focus
OT = Organizational Training
OPD = Organizational Process Definition

FIGURE 4.1
Fundamental Process Management Process Areas

measurement of the processes, lessons learned in implementing the processes, and results of process appraisal and product-evaluation activities.

The Organizational Process Definition process area establishes and maintains the organization's set of standard processes and other assets based on the process needs and objectives of the organization. These other assets include descriptions of life-cycle models, process tailoring guidelines, and process-related documentation and data. Projects tailor the organization's set of standard processes to create their defined processes. The other assets support tailoring as well as implementation of the defined processes. Experiences and work products from performing these defined processes, including measurement data, process descriptions, process artifacts, and lessons learned, are incorporated as appropriate into the organization's set of standard processes and other assets.

The Organizational Training process area identifies the strategic training needs of the organization as well as the tactical training needs that are common across projects and support groups. In particular, training is developed or obtained to develop the skills required to perform the organization's set of standard processes. The main components of training include a managed training-development program, documented plans, personnel with appropriate knowledge, and mechanisms for measuring the effectiveness of the training program.

Progressive Process Management Process Areas

The Progressive Process Management process areas provide the organization with an improved capability to achieve its quantitative objectives for quality and process performance.

Figure 4.2 provides a bird's-eye view of the interactions among the Progressive Process Management process areas and with other process area categories. Each of the Progressive Process Management process areas depends on the ability to develop and deploy processes and supporting assets. The Fundamental Process Management process areas provide this ability.

As illustrated in Figure 4.2, the Organizational Process Performance process area derives quantitative objectives for quality and process performance from the organization's business objectives. The organization provides projects and support groups with common measures, process performance baselines, and process-performance models. These additional organizational assets support quantitative project management and statistical management of critical subprocesses for both projects and support groups. The organization analyzes the process performance data collected from these defined processes to develop a quantitative understanding of product quality, service quality, and process performance of the organization's set of standard processes.

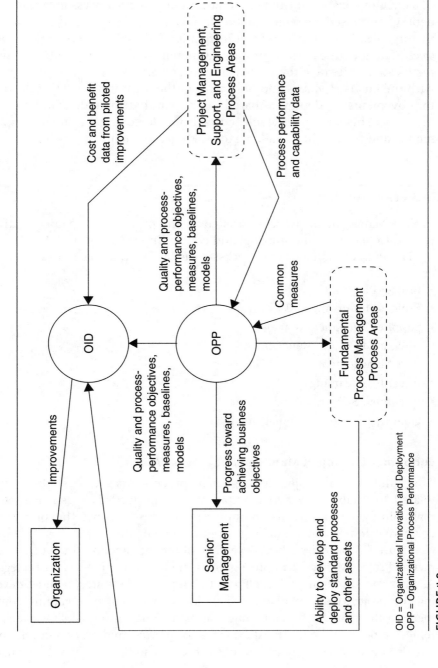

FIGURE 4.2
Progressive Process Management Process Areas

OID = Organizational Innovation and Deployment
OPP = Organizational Process Performance

The Organizational Innovation and Deployment process area selects and deploys proposed incremental and innovative improvements that improve the organization's ability to meet its quality and process-performance objectives. The identification of promising incremental and innovative improvements should involve the participation of an empowered workforce aligned with the business values and objectives of the organization. The selection of improvements to deploy is based on a quantitative understanding of the likely benefits and predictable costs from deploying candidate improvements, and the funding available for such deployment.

Project Management

Project Management process areas cover the project-management activities related to planning, monitoring, and controlling the project.

The Project Management process areas of CMMI are as follows:

- Project Planning
- Project Monitoring and Control
- Supplier Agreement Management
- Integrated Project Management[1]
- Risk Management
- Integrated Teaming
- Integrated Supplier Management
- Quantitative Project Management

Fundamental Project Management Process Areas

The Fundamental Project Management process areas address the activities related to establishing and maintaining the project plan, establishing and maintaining commitments, monitoring progress against the plan, taking corrective action, and managing supplier agreements.

Figure 4.3 provides a bird's-eye view of the interactions among the Fundamental Project Management process areas and with other process area categories. As illustrated in Figure 4.3, the Project Planning process area includes developing the project plan, involving stakeholders appropriately, obtaining commitment to the plan, and maintaining the plan. When using IPPD, stakeholders represent not just the technical expertise for product and process development, but also the business implications of the product and process development.

---

1. In CMMI, Integrated Project Management (IPM) has two goals that apply only when using CMMI for the IPPD discipline. Keep this in mind when viewing the interactions with Integrated Teaming.

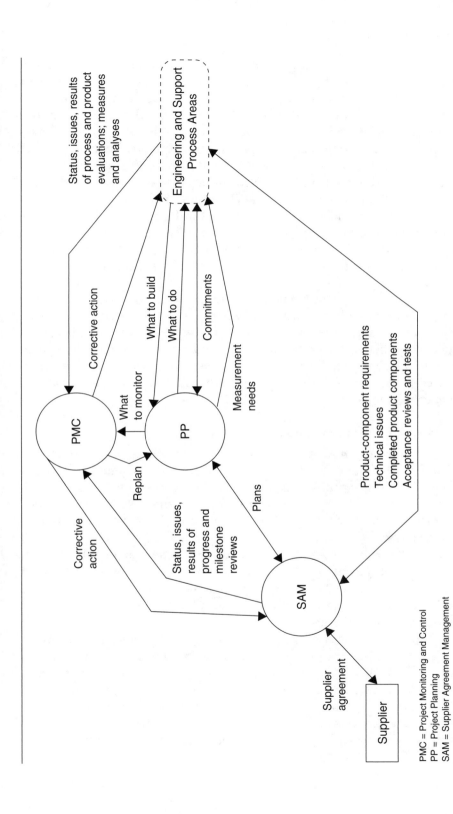

FIGURE 4.3
Fundamental Project Management Process Areas

PMC = Project Monitoring and Control
PP = Project Planning
SAM = Supplier Agreement Management

61

Planning begins with requirements that define the product and project ("What to build" in Figure 4.3). The project plan covers the various project management and engineering activities that will be performed by the project. The project will review other plans that affect the project from various relevant stakeholders and establish commitments with those relevant stakeholders for their contributions to the project. For example, these plans cover configuration management, verification, and measurement and analysis.

The Project Monitoring and Control process area includes monitoring activities and taking corrective action. The project plan specifies the appropriate level of project monitoring, the frequency of progress reviews, and the measures used to monitor progress. Progress is determined primarily by comparing project status to the plan. When actual status deviates significantly from the expected values, corrective actions are taken as appropriate. These actions may include replanning.

The Supplier Agreement Management process area addresses the need of the project to acquire those portions of work that are produced by suppliers. Once a product component is identified and the supplier that will produce it is selected, a supplier agreement is established and maintained that will be used to manage the supplier. The supplier's progress and performance are monitored. Acceptance reviews and tests are conducted on the supplier-produced product component.

Progressive Project Management Process Areas

The Progressive Project Management process areas address activities such as establishing a defined process that is tailored from the organization's set of standard processes, coordinating and collaborating with relevant stakeholders (including suppliers), managing risk, forming and sustaining integrated teams for the conduct of projects, and quantitatively managing the project's defined process.

Figure 4.4 provides a bird's-eye view of the interactions among the Progressive Project Management process areas and with other process area categories. Each Progressive Project Management process area depends on the ability to plan, monitor, and control the project. The Fundamental Project Management process areas provide this ability.

The Integrated Project Management process area establishes and maintains the project's defined process that is tailored from the organization's set of standard processes. The project is managed using the project's defined process. The project uses and contributes to the organization's process assets.

The management of the project ensures that the relevant stakeholders associated with the project coordinate their efforts in a timely manner. It does this by providing for the management of stakeholder involvement; the identification,

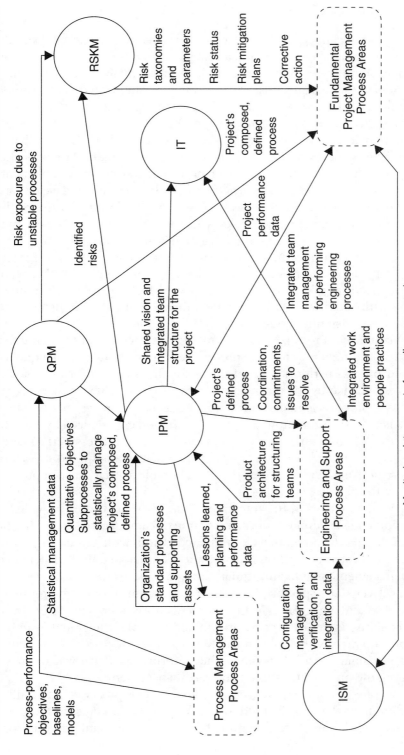

FIGURE 4.4
Progressive Project Management Process Areas

IPM = Integrated Project Management
ISM = Integrated Supplier Management
IT = Integrated Teaming

QPM = Quantitative Project Management
RSKM = Risk Management

negotiation, and tracking of critical dependencies; and the resolution of coordination issues within the project with relevant stakeholders.

The Integrated Project Management process area contains additional information that creates the shared vision of the project. This shared vision should align both horizontally and vertically with both the organization's and the integrated team's shared visions, created in the Organizational Environment for Integration and Integrated Teaming process areas, respectively. These shared visions collectively support the coordination and collaboration among stakeholders. Finally, the Integrated Project Management process area implements an integrated team structure to perform the work of the project in developing a product. This team structure is typically based on the decomposition of the product itself, much like a work breakdown structure (WBS). This activity is accomplished in conjunction with the Integrated Teaming process area.

Although risk identification and monitoring are covered in the Project Planning and Project Monitoring and Control process areas, the Risk Management process area takes a continuing, forward-looking approach to managing risks with activities that include identification of risk parameters, risk assessments, and risk mitigation.

The Quantitative Project Management process area applies quantitative and statistical techniques to manage process performance and product quality. Quality and process-performance objectives for the project are based on the objectives established by the organization. The project's defined process comprises, in part, process elements and subprocesses whose process performance can be predicted. At a minimum, the process variation experienced by subprocesses critical to achieving the project's quality and process-performance objectives is understood. Corrective action is taken when special causes of process variation are identified. (See the definition of "special cause of process variation" in the glossary.)

The specific practices in the Integrated Teaming process area provide for the formation and sustainment of each integrated team. Part of sustaining the team is developing the integrated team's shared vision, which must align with the project's and the organization's shared visions developed in the Integrated Project Management and Organizational Environment for Integration process areas, respectively. The specific practices in the Organizational Environment for Integration and Integrated Teaming process areas then set the environment for enabling integrated teamwork. In addition, the Integrated Teaming process area interacts with other Project Management processes by supplying team commitments, work plans, and other information that form the basis for managing the project and supporting risk management.

The Integrated Supplier Management process area proactively identifies sources of products that may be used to satisfy project requirements and monitors selected supplier work products and processes while maintaining a cooperative project-supplier relationship. The specific practices of the Integrated Supplier Management process area cover selecting possible sources of products, evaluating those sources to select suppliers, monitoring selected supplier processes and work products, and revising the supplier agreement or relationship as appropriate.

The Integrated Supplier Management process area works closely with the Supplier Agreement Management process area during the supplier selection process. Integrated Supplier Management also shares monitoring information with the Engineering and Support process areas in the form of technical solution, product integration, and validation data as well as process and product quality assurance and configuration management data.

Engineering

Engineering process areas cover the development and maintenance activities that are shared across engineering disciplines. The Engineering process areas were written using general engineering terminology so that any technical discipline involved in the product development process (e.g., software engineering, mechanical engineering) can use them for process improvement.

The Engineering process areas also integrate software engineering and systems engineering processes into a single product development process, supporting a product-oriented process improvement strategy. Such a strategy targets essential business objectives rather than specific technical disciplines. This approach to processes effectively avoids the tendency toward an organizational "stovepipe" mentality.

The Engineering process areas apply to the development of any product or service in the engineering development domain (e.g., software products, hardware products, services, or processes).

The technical foundation for IPPD is grounded in a robust systems engineering approach that encompasses development in the context of the phases of the product's life. The Engineering process areas provide this technical foundation. The implementation of IPPD is further addressed through amplifications to specific practices in the Engineering process areas that emphasize concurrent development and focus on all phases of the product's life.

The Engineering process areas of CMMI are as follows:

- Requirements Development
- Requirements Management
- Technical Solution
- Product Integration
- Verification
- Validation

Figure 4.5 provides a bird's-eye view of the interactions among the six Engineering process areas.

The Requirements Development process area identifies customer needs and translates these needs into product requirements. The set of product requirements is analyzed to produce a high-level conceptual solution. This set of requirements is then allocated to establish an initial set of product-component requirements. Other requirements that help define the product are derived and allocated to product components. This set of product and product-component requirements clearly describes the product's performance, design features, verification requirements, and so forth in terms the developer understands and uses.

The Requirements Development process area supplies requirements to the Technical Solution process area, where the requirements are converted into the product architecture, product-component design, and the product component itself (e.g., coding, fabrication). Requirements are also supplied to the Product Integration process area, where product components are combined and interfaces are verified to ensure that they meet the interface requirements supplied by Requirements Development.

The Requirements Management process area maintains the requirements. It describes activities for obtaining and controlling requirement changes and ensuring that other relevant plans and data are kept current. It provides traceability of requirements from customer to product to product component.

Requirements Management ensures that changes to requirements are reflected in project plans, activities, and work products. This cycle of changes may affect all the other Engineering process areas; thus requirements management is a dynamic and often recursive sequence of events. The Requirements Management process area is fundamental to a controlled and disciplined engineering design process.

The Technical Solution process area develops technical data packages for product components that will be used by the Product Integration or Supplier Agreement Management process areas. Alternative solutions are examined with the intent of selecting the optimum design based on established criteria. These criteria may be significantly different across products, depending on product type, operational environment, performance requirements, support requirements, and cost or delivery schedules. The task of selecting the final solution makes use of the specific practices in the Decision Analysis and Resolution process area.

The Technical Solution process area relies on the specific practices in the Verification process area to perform design verification and peer reviews during design and prior to final build.

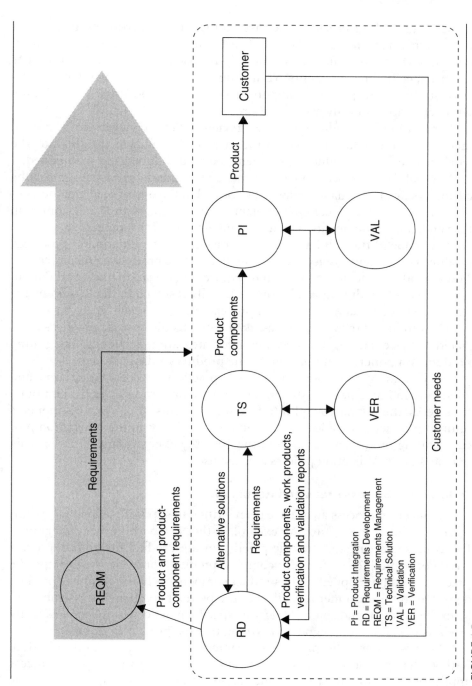

Requirements

REQM

Product and product-
component requirements

Alternative solutions

RD

Requirements

Requirements

TS

Product
components

PI

Product

Customer

Product components, work products,
verification and validation reports

VER

VAL

Customer needs

PI = Product Integration
RD = Requirements Development
REQM = Requirements Management
TS = Technical Solution
VAL = Validation
VER = Verification

FIGURE 4.5
Engineering Process Areas

The Verification process area ensures that selected work products meet the specified requirements. The Verification process area selects work products and verification methods that will be used to verify work products against specified requirements. Verification is generally an incremental process, starting with product-component verification and usually concluding with verification of fully assembled products.

Verification also addresses peer reviews. Peer reviews are a proved method for removing defects early and provide valuable insight into the work products and product components being developed and maintained.

The Validation process area incrementally validates products against the customer's needs. Validation may be performed in the operational environment or a simulated operational environment. Coordination with the customer on the validation requirements is an important element of this process area.

The scope of the Validation process area includes validation of products, product components, selected intermediate work products, and processes. These validated elements may often require reverification and revalidation. Issues discovered during validation are usually resolved in the Requirements Development or Technical Solution process areas.

The Product Integration process area contains the specific practices associated with generating the best possible integration sequence, integrating product components, and delivering the product to the customer.

Product Integration uses the specific practices of both Verification and Validation in implementing the product integration process. Verification practices verify the interfaces and interface requirements of product components prior to product integration. This is an essential event in the integration process. During product integration in the operational environment, the specific practices of the Validation process area are used.

Engineering Process Areas and Recursion

All Engineering process areas have been written to support recursion throughout the product architecture. An example is the "Establish Product Integration Procedures and Criteria" specific practice in the Product Integration process area. For a product with many complex product components, this specific practice would be applied to the product components of the complete product delivered to the customer as well as to the product components assembled to form the product, and so on. Thus, this specific practice is applied to as many levels as necessary to integrate everything that the product comprises.

There is no specific practice that forces recursive process application. Rather, the specific practices are written in a fashion that expects process application throughout the product architecture. When implementing the specific practices of an Engineering process area, you must interpret them according to the needs of your product. You may be more comfortable viewing this approach as providing a sufficiently generic set of expectations that can be applied at any level of product detail rather than as enabling recursive behavior of a process. Either description of this approach is appropriate.

There are a number of advantages gained by this approach. For example, the Engineering process areas can be applied to a product that has several layers of product components and can ensure that the specific practices will address each layer. Thus, different segments of a very large project can be appraised using the same model.

Support

Support process areas cover the activities that support product development and maintenance. The Support process areas address processes that are used in the context of performing other processes. In general, the Support process areas address processes that are targeted toward the project, and may address processes that apply more generally to the organization. For example, Process and Product Quality Assurance can be used with all the process areas to provide an objective evaluation of the processes and work products described in all of the process areas.

The Support process areas of CMMI are as follows:

- Configuration Management
- Process and Product Quality Assurance
- Measurement and Analysis
- Organizational Environment for Integration
- Decision Analysis and Resolution
- Causal Analysis and Resolution

Fundamental Support Process Areas

The Fundamental Support process areas address fundamental support functions that are used by all process areas. Although all Support process areas rely on the other process areas for input, the Fundamental Support process areas provide support functions that also help implement several generic practices.

Figure 4.6 provides a bird's-eye view of the interactions among the Fundamental Support process areas and with all other process areas.

The Measurement and Analysis process area supports all process areas by providing specific practices that guide projects and organizations in aligning measurement needs and objectives with a measurement approach that will provide objective results. These results can be used in making informed decisions and taking appropriate corrective actions.

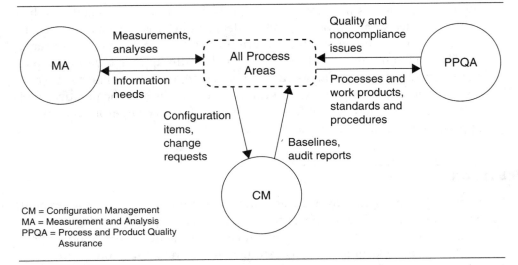

FIGURE 4.6
Fundamental Support Process Areas

The Process and Product Quality Assurance process area supports all process areas by providing specific practices for objectively evaluating performed processes, work products, and services against the applicable process descriptions, standards, and procedures and ensuring that any issues arising from these reviews are addressed. Process and Product Quality Assurance supports the delivery of high-quality products and services by providing the project staff and all levels of managers with appropriate visibility into, and feedback on, the processes and associated work products throughout the life of the project.

The Configuration Management process area supports all process areas by establishing and maintaining the integrity of work products using configuration identification, configuration control, configuration status accounting, and configuration audits. The work products placed under configuration management include the products that are delivered to the customer, designated internal work products, acquired products, tools, and other items that are used in creating and describing these work products. Examples of work products that may be placed under configuration management include plans, process descriptions, requirements, design data, drawings, product specifications, code, compilers, product data files, and product technical publications.

Progressive Support Process Areas

The Progressive Support process areas provide the projects and organization with an improved support capability. Each of these process areas relies on specific inputs or practices from other process areas.

Figure 4.7 provides a bird's-eye view of the interactions among the Progressive Support process areas and with all other process areas.

Using the Causal Analysis and Resolution process area, project members identify causes of selected defects and other problems and take action to prevent them from occurring in the future. While the project's defined processes are the principal targets for identifying the cause of the defect, the process improvement proposals they create target the organization's set of standard processes, which will prevent recurrence of the defect across the organization.

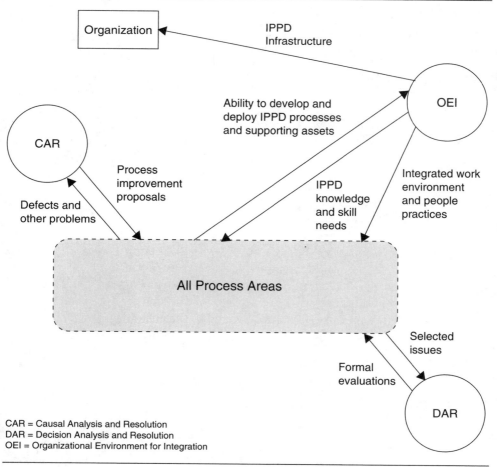

CAR = Causal Analysis and Resolution
DAR = Decision Analysis and Resolution
OEI = Organizational Environment for Integration

FIGURE 4.7
Progressive Support Process Areas

The Decision Analysis and Resolution process area supports all the process areas by determining which issues should be subjected to a formal evaluation process and then applying a formal evaluation process to them.

The Organizational Environment for Integration process area establishes the approach and environment for the implementation of IPPD. The environment is established by obtaining, adapting, or developing processes that facilitate effective integrated team behavior as well as stakeholder communication and collaboration, creating the organization's shared vision, and managing people to promote integrative behavior. Specific practices in the Organizational Environment for Integration process area promote both team and individual excellence while enabling and rewarding integration across all business and technical functions in the execution of the projects.

CHAPTER 5

TYING IT ALL TOGETHER

Now that you have been introduced to the components of CMMI® models, you need to understand how they all fit together to meet your process improvement needs. This chapter introduces the concept of levels and shows how the process areas are organized and used in the two representations. To do this, we need to revisit the representations discussion that began in chapter 1.

Understanding Levels

Levels are used in CMMI to describe the evolutionary path recommended for an organization that wants to improve the processes it uses to develop and maintain its products and services. CMMI supports two improvement paths. The first path enables organizations to incrementally improve processes corresponding to an individual process area (or process areas) selected by the organization. The second path enables organizations to improve a set of related processes by incrementally addressing successive sets of process areas.

These two improvement paths are associated with two types of levels that correspond to the two representations discussed in chapter 1. For the continuous representation, we use the term *capability level*. For the staged representation, we use the term *maturity level*.

Regardless of which representation you select, the concept of levels is the same. Levels characterize improvement from an ill-defined state to a state that uses quantitative information to determine and manage improvements that are needed to meet an organization's business objectives. This improvement path is similar to the one described for generic goals in chapter 3.

To reach a particular level, an organization must satisfy all of the appropriate goals of the process area or set of process areas that are targeted for improvement, regardless of whether it is a capability or maturity level.

Both representations provide ways to implement process improvement to achieve business objectives. Both representations provide the same essential content and use the same model components.

Structures of the Continuous and Staged Representations

The structures of the continuous and staged representations are illustrated in Figure 5.1. Some differences jump out at you immediately when you look at the structure of both representations. The staged representation has maturity levels and common features, whereas the continuous representation does not.

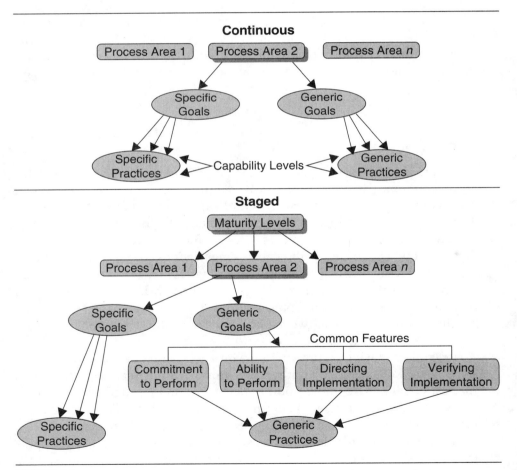

FIGURE 5.1
Structure of the Continuous and Staged Representations

What may strike you as you compare these two representations is their similarity. Both representations have many of the same components (e.g., process areas, specific goals, and specific practices). Furthermore, these components have the same general hierarchy and a similar configuration.

What is not readily apparent from the high-level view of Figure 5.1 is that the continuous representation focuses on *process area capability* as measured by capability levels and that the staged representation focuses on *organizational maturity* as measured by maturity levels. These dimensions (the capability/maturity dimensions) of CMMI are used for benchmarking and appraisal activities, as well as guiding an organization's improvement efforts.

- *Capability* levels, which belong to a continuous representation, apply to an organization's process improvement achievement in individual process areas. These levels are a means for incrementally improving the processes corresponding to a given process area. There are six capability levels, numbered 0 through 5.
- *Maturity* levels, which belong to a staged representation, apply to an organization's process improvement achievement across multiple process areas. These levels are a means of predicting the general outcomes of the next project undertaken. There are five maturity levels, numbered 1 through 5.

Table 5.1 compares the six capability levels to the five maturity levels. Notice that the names of four of the levels are the same in both representations. The difference is that there is no maturity level 0 for the staged representation and at level 1, the capability level is Performed whereas the maturity level is Initial. Therefore, the starting point is different for the two representations.

The continuous representation is concerned with selecting both a particular process area to improve and the granularity of improvement within that

TABLE 5.1   Comparison of Capability and Maturity Levels

Level	*Continuous Representation* Capability Levels	*Staged Representation* Maturity Levels
Level 0	Incomplete	N/A
Level 1	Performed	Initial
Level 2	Managed	Managed
Level 3	Defined	Defined
Level 4	Quantitatively Managed	Quantitatively Managed
Level 5	Optimizing	Optimizing

process area (i.e., you are improving not only "what you do" but also "how you do it). In this context, whether the specific goals are performed or incomplete is important. Therefore, the name "Incomplete" is given to the continuous representation starting point.

Because the staged representation is concerned with the overall maturity of a set of processes, whether individual processes are performed or incomplete is of little consequence. Therefore, the name "Initial" is given to the staged representation starting point.

Both capability levels and maturity levels provide a way to measure how well organizations can and do improve their processes. However, the approach to process improvement is different.

Understanding Capability Levels

All CMMI models with a continuous representation reflect capability levels in their design and content. A capability level consists of related specific and generic practices for a process area that can improve the organization's processes associated with that process area. As you satisfy the specific and generic goals of a process area at a particular capability level, you reap the benefits of process improvement.

The six capability levels, designated by the numbers 0 through 5, are:

0. Incomplete
1. Performed
2. Managed
3. Defined
4. Quantitatively Managed
5. Optimizing

The fact that capability levels 2 through 5 use the same terms as generic goals 2 through 5 was intentional because the concepts of generic goals and capability levels are highly related. Generic goals represent the process institutionalization of best practices in an organization. Capability levels represent the process improvement attained in an organization. Since institutionalization and process improvement attainment are interdependent, the same characterization applies to both concepts. To get a complete understanding of capability levels 1 through 5, refer to chapter 3. A short description of each capability level follows.

Capability Level 0: Incomplete

An "incomplete process" is a process that is either not performed or partially performed. One or more of the specific goals of the process area are not satisfied and no generic goals exist for this level since there is no reason to institutionalize a partially performed process.

Capability Level 1: Performed

A capability level 1 process is characterized as a "performed process." A performed process is a process that satisfies the specific goals of the process area. It supports and enables the work needed to produce work products.

Capability Level 2: Managed

A capability level 2 process is characterized as a "managed process." A managed process is a performed (capability level 1) process that has the basic infrastructure in place to support the process. It is planned and executed in accordance with policy; employs skilled people who have adequate resources to produce controlled outputs; involves relevant stakeholders; is monitored, controlled, and reviewed; and is evaluated for adherence to its process description.

Capability Level 3: Defined

A capability level 3 process is characterized as a "defined process." A defined process is a managed (capability level 2) process that is tailored from the organization's set of standard processes according to the organization's tailoring guidelines, and contributes work products, measures, and other process-improvement information to the organizational process assets.

Capability Level 4: Quantitatively Managed

A capability level 4 process is characterized as a "quantitatively managed process." A quantitatively managed process is a defined (capability level 3) process that is controlled using statistical and other quantitative techniques. Quantitative objectives for quality and process performance are established and used as criteria in managing the process. Quality and process performance is understood in statistical terms and is managed throughout the life of the process.

Capability Level 5: Optimizing

A capability level 5 process is characterized as an "optimizing process." An optimizing process is a quantitatively managed (capability level 4) process that is improved based on an understanding of the common causes of variation inherent in the process. The focus of an optimizing process is on continually improving the range of process performance through both incremental and innovative improvements.

Remember that capability levels 2 through 5 use the same terms as generic goals 2 through 5, and a detailed description of these terms appears in chapter 3.

Advancing through Capability Levels

The capability levels of process areas are achieved through the application of generic practices or suitable alternatives.

Reaching capability level 1 for a process area is equivalent to saying you have achieved the specific goals of the process area.

Reaching capability level 2 for a process area is equivalent to saying that there is a policy that indicates you will perform the process. There is a plan for performing it, resources provided, responsibilities assigned, training to perform it, selected work products from performing the process are controlled, and so on. In other words, a capability level 2 process can be planned and monitored just like any project or support activity.

Reaching capability level 3 for a process area assumes that an organizational standard process or processes exist associated with that process area that can be tailored to the needs of the projects. The processes in the organization are now more consistently defined and applied because they are based on organizational standard processes.

Reaching capability level 4 for a process area assumes that this process area is a key business driver that the organization wants to manage using quantitative and statistical techniques. This analysis gives the organization more visibility into the performance of selected subprocesses that will make it more competitive in the marketplace.

Reaching capability level 5 for a process area assumes that you have stabilized the selected subprocesses and that you want to reduce the common causes of variation within that process. Remember that variation is a natural occurrence in any process, so although it is conceptually feasible to improve all processes, it would not be economical to improve all processes to level 5. Again, you would concentrate on those processes that would help you to meet your business objectives.

Understanding Maturity Levels

All CMMI models with a staged representation reflect maturity levels in their design and content. A maturity level consists of related specific and generic practices for a predefined set of process areas that improve the organization's overall performance. The maturity level of an organization provides a way to predict an organization's performance in a given discipline or set of disciplines. Experience has shown that organizations do their best when they focus their process improvement efforts on a manageable number of process areas at a time and that those areas require increasing sophistication as the organization improves.

A maturity level is a defined evolutionary plateau for organizational process improvement. Each maturity level stabilizes an important part of the organization's processes, preparing it to move to the next maturity level. The maturity levels are measured by the achievement of the specific and generic goals associated with each predefined set of process areas.

There are five maturity levels, each a layer in the foundation for ongoing process improvement, designated by the numbers 1 through 5:

1. Initial
2. Managed
3. Defined
4. Quantitatively Managed
5. Optimizing

Remember that maturity levels 2 through 5 use the same terms as capability levels 2 through 5. This was intentional because the concepts of maturity levels and capability levels are complementary. Maturity levels are used to characterize organizational improvement relative to a set of process areas, and capability levels characterize organizational improvement relative to an individual process area.

Maturity Level 1: Initial

At maturity level 1, processes are usually ad hoc and chaotic. The organization usually does not provide a stable environment to support the processes. Success in these organizations depends on the competence and heroics of the people in the organization and not on the use of proved processes. In spite of this chaos, maturity level 1 organizations often produce products and services that work; however, they frequently exceed their budgets and do not meet their schedules.

Maturity level 1 organizations are characterized by a tendency to over-commit, abandonment of processes in a time of crisis, and an inability to repeat their successes.

Maturity Level 2: Managed

At maturity level 2, the projects of the organization have ensured that requirements are managed and that processes are planned, performed, measured, and controlled. The process discipline reflected by maturity level 2 helps to ensure that existing practices are retained during times of stress. When these practices are in place, projects are performed and managed according to their documented plans.

At maturity level 2, the status of the work products and the delivery of services are visible to management at defined points (e.g., at major milestones and at the completion of major tasks). Commitments are established among relevant stakeholders and are revised as needed. Work products are appropriately controlled. The work products and services satisfy their specified process descriptions, standards, and procedures.

Maturity Level 3: Defined

At maturity level 3, processes are well characterized and understood, and are described in standards, procedures, tools, and methods. The organization's set of standard processes, which is the basis for maturity level 3, is established and improved over time. These standard processes are used to establish consistency across the organization. Projects establish their defined processes by tailoring the organization's set of standard processes according to tailoring guidelines. (See the glossary, for a definition of "organization's set of standard processes.")

A critical distinction between maturity levels 2 and 3 is the scope of standards, process descriptions, and procedures. At maturity level 2, the standards, process descriptions, and procedures may be quite different in each specific instance of the process (e.g., on a particular project). At maturity level 3, the standards, process descriptions, and procedures for a project are tailored from the organization's set of standard processes to suit a particular project or organizational unit and therefore are more consistent except for the differences allowed by the tailoring guidelines.

Another critical distinction is that at maturity level 3, processes are typically described more rigorously than at maturity level 2. A defined process clearly states the purpose, inputs, entry criteria, activities, roles, measures, verification steps, outputs, and exit criteria. At maturity level 3, processes are managed more proactively using an understanding of the interrelationships of the process activities and detailed measures of the process, its work products, and its services.

Remember that at maturity level 3, the organization must revisit the maturity level 2 process areas. The generic practices in maturity level 3 that were not present at maturity level 2 are applied to achieve maturity level 3.

Maturity Level 4: Quantitatively Managed

At maturity level 4, the organization and projects establish quantitative objectives for quality and process performance and use them as criteria in managing processes. Quantitative objectives are based on the needs of the customer, end users, organization, and process implementers. Quality and process performance is understood in statistical terms and is managed throughout the life of the processes.

For selected subprocesses, detailed measures of process performance are collected and statistically analyzed. Quality and process performance measures are incorporated into the organization's measurement repository to support fact-based decision making. Special causes of process variation are identified and, where appropriate, the sources of special causes are corrected to prevent future occurrences. (See the definition of "special cause of process variation" in the glossary.)

A critical distinction between maturity levels 3 and 4 is the predictability of process performance. At maturity level 4, the performance of processes is controlled using statistical and other quantitative techniques, and is quantitatively predictable. At maturity level 3, processes are typically only qualitatively predictable.

Maturity Level 5: Optimizing

At maturity level 5, an organization continually improves its processes based on a quantitative understanding of the common causes of variation inherent in processes. See the definition of "common cause of process variation" in the glossary.

Maturity level 5 focuses on continually improving process performance through incremental and innovative process and technological improvements. Quantitative process-improvement objectives for the organization are established, continually revised to reflect changing business objectives, and used as criteria in managing process improvement. The effects of deployed process improvements are measured and evaluated against the quantitative process-improvement objectives. Both the defined processes and the organization's set of standard processes are targets of measurable improvement activities.

A critical distinction between maturity levels 4 and 5 is the type of process variation addressed. At maturity level 4, the organization is concerned with addressing special causes of process variation and providing statistical predictability of the results. Although processes may produce predictable results, the results may be insufficient to achieve the established objectives. At maturity level 5, the organization is concerned with addressing common causes of process variation and changing the process (to shift the mean of the process performance or reduce the inherent process variation experienced) to improve process performance and to achieve the established quantitative process-improvement objectives.

Advancing through Maturity Levels

Organizations can achieve progressive improvements in their organizational maturity by achieving control first at the project level and continuing to the most advanced level, organization-wide continuous process improvement, using both quantitative and qualitative data to make decisions.

Since improved organizational maturity is associated with improvement in the range of expected results that can be achieved by an organization, it is one means of predicting the general outcomes of the organization's next project. For instance, at maturity level 2, the organization has been elevated from ad hoc to disciplined by establishing sound project management. As your organization achieves the generic and specific goals for the set of process areas in a maturity level, you are increasing your organizational maturity and reaping the benefits of process improvement. Because each maturity level forms a necessary foundation for the next level, trying to skip maturity levels is usually counterproductive.

At the same time, you must recognize that process improvement efforts should focus on the needs of the organization in the context of its business environment and that process areas at higher maturity levels may address the current needs of an organization or project. For example, organizations seeking to move from maturity level 1 to maturity level 2 are frequently encouraged to establish a process group, which is addressed by the Organizational Process Focus process area that resides at maturity level 3. Although a process group is not a necessary characteristic of a maturity level 2 organization, it can be a useful part of the organization's approach to achieving maturity level 2.

This situation is sometimes characterized as "establishing a maturity level 1 process group to bootstrap the maturity level 1 organization to maturity level 2." Maturity level 1 process improvement activities may depend primarily on the insight and competence of the process group staff until an infrastructure to support more disciplined and widespread improvement is in place.

Organizations can institute specific process improvements at any time they choose, even before they are prepared to advance to the maturity level at which the specific practice is recommended. In such situations, however, organizations should understand that the stability of these improvements is at a greater risk because the foundation for their successful institutionalization has not been completed. Processes without the proper foundation may fail at the very point they are needed most—under stress.

A defined process that is characteristic of a maturity level 3 organization can be placed at great risk if maturity level 2 management practices are deficient. For example, management may commit to a poorly planned schedule or fail to control changes to baselined requirements. Similarly, many organizations prematurely collect the detailed data characteristic of maturity level 4, only to find the data uninterpretable because of inconsistency in processes and measurement definitions.

Another example of using processes associated with higher maturity level process areas is in the building of products. Certainly, we would expect maturity level 1 organizations to perform requirements analysis, design, integration, and verification. These activities are not described until maturity level 3, however, where they are described as the coherent, well-integrated engineering processes that complement a maturing project management capability, put in place so that the engineering improvements are not lost by an ad hoc management process.

Process Areas

Process areas are present in both representations; however, they are viewed differently in the two representations. Figure 5.2 compares views of how process areas are used in the continuous representation (at the top) and the staged representation (at the bottom).

The continuous representation enables the organization to choose the focus of its process improvement efforts by choosing those process areas, or sets of interrelated process areas, that best benefit the organization and its business objectives. Although there are some limits on what an organization can choose because of the dependencies among process areas, the organization has considerable freedom in its selection.

The process areas in the continuous representation are organized in four categories: Process Management, Project Management, Engineering, and Support. These categories emphasize the relationships that exist among the process areas and are discussed in chapter 4.

Once you select the process areas, you must also select how much you would like to improve the processes associated with those process areas (i.e., select the appropriate capability level). Capability levels and generic goals and practices support the improvement of processes in individual process areas. For example, an organization may wish to strive to reach capability level 2 in one process area and capability level 4 in another. As the organization reaches a capability level, it sets its sights on the next capability level for one of these same process areas or decides to widen its view and address a larger number of process areas.

This selection is typically described through a target profile. A target profile defines all of the process areas to be addressed and the targeted capability level for each. This profile then governs which goals and practices the organization will address in its process-improvement efforts.

Most organizations will, at minimum, target capability level 1, which requires that all specific goals of the process area be achieved. However, organizations that target capability levels higher than 1 will concentrate on the institutionalization of the selected processes in the organization by targeting the generic goals and practices.

Conversely, you will see that the staged representation encourages you to always look at process areas in the context of the maturity level to which they belong. The process areas are organized by maturity levels to reinforce

Continuous
Target Profile

Process Areas	Capability Levels Chosen for Target Profile				
	CL1	CL2	CL3	CL4	CL5
PA1					

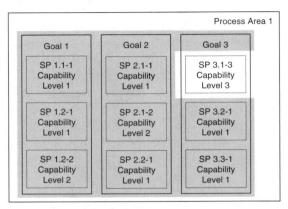

= Process area and capability levels chosen for process improvement

Staged
Specific Goals and Practices

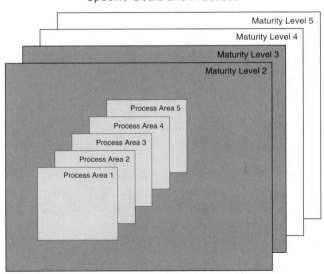

= Groups of process areas chosen for process improvement to achieve maturity level 3

FIGURE 5.2
Process areas in Continuous and Staged Representations

this concept. When you use a process area, you use the entire process area: all goals and all practices.

The staged representation provides a predetermined path of improvement from maturity level 1 to maturity level 5 that involves achieving the goals of the process areas at each maturity level. The staged representation groups process areas by maturity level, indicating which process areas to implement to achieve each maturity level. For example, at maturity level 2, there is a set of process areas that an organization would use to guide its process improvement until it could achieve all the goals of all these process areas. Once maturity level 2 is achieved this way, the organization focuses its efforts on maturity level 3 process areas, and so on. The generic goals that apply to each process area are also predetermined. Generic goal 2 applies to maturity level 2 and generic goal 3 applies to maturity levels 3 through 5.

Table 5.2 provides a list of all process areas and their associated categories and maturity levels. To explain how the components of the process areas are presented in each representation, we must discuss how the representations address specific practices.

Specific Practices

Specific practices are expected model components that are considered important guidance for achieving specific goals. Most specific practices are exactly the same in both representations. The exceptions are a few practices that are viewed differently when using one or the other model representation.

In the staged representation, all specific practices are viewed equally. Capability levels of specific practices are not recognized (they appear in the numbering of the specific practice but this information is considered irrelevant in the staged representation); therefore, base and advanced practices are not recognized concepts.

Base and Advanced Practices

In the continuous representation, each specific practice is assigned a capability level. Practices with a capability level of one are called *base practices*. Those with capability levels greater than one are called *advanced practices*.

For example, within the Requirements Management process area, "Develop an understanding with the requirements providers on the meaning of the requirements" is a capability level 1 (base) specific practice, whereas "Obtain commitment to the requirements from the project participants" is a capability level 2 (advanced) specific practice.

TABLE 5.2   Process Areas and Their Associated Categories and Maturity Levels

Process Area	Category	Maturity Level
Causal Analysis and Resolution	Support	5
Configuration Management	Support	2
Decision Analysis and Resolution	Support	3
Integrated Project Management	Project Management	3
Integrated Supplier Management	Project Management	3
Integrated Teaming	Project Management	3
Measurement and Analysis	Support	2
Organizational Environment for Integration	Support	3
Organizational Innovation and Deployment	Process Management	5
Organizational Process Definition	Process Management	3
Organizational Process Focus	Process Management	3
Organizational Process Performance	Process Management	4
Organizational Training	Process Management	3
Product Integration	Engineering	3
Project Monitoring and Control	Project Management	2
Project Planning	Project Management	2
Process and Product Quality Assurance	Support	2
Quantitative Project Management	Project Management	4
Requirements Development	Engineering	3
Requirements Management	Engineering	2
Risk Management	Project Management	3
Supplier Agreement Management	Project Management	2
Technical Solution	Engineering	3
Validation	Engineering	3
Verification	Engineering	3

There are two types of advanced practices. The first type is an advanced practice that does not build on a base practice. When this happens, the advanced practice is included in the staged representation.

The second type of advanced practice is an advanced practice that builds on a base practice. When this happens, the advanced practice is included in the staged representation as a specific practice, but the base practice is not included because the concept is very similar and is already captured in the advanced practice.[1]

An example of this is in the Requirements Development process area, SP1.1-1, Collect Stakeholder Needs, and SP1.1-2, Elicit Needs. SP 1.1-1 states: "Identify and collect stakeholder needs, expectations, constraints, and interfaces for all phases of the product life cycle." SP 1.1-2 states: "Elicit stakeholder needs, expectations, constraints, and interfaces for all phases of the product life cycle." As you can see, the only difference in the specific practices is that SP1.1-1 uses "collect" (which is more passive) and SP1.1-2 uses "elicit" (which is much more proactive).

Because of the second type of advanced practice, there is not always a one-to-one relationship between the specific practices in the continuous and the staged representations.

In Part Two, you will see both continuous and staged views of the specific practices. The base practices that are not included in the staged representation (those that are built on by an advanced practice) are displayed in the same process area, but are marked "Continuous Only."

The specific practice-numbering scheme identifies these two types of advanced practices. Specific practices are numbered so that you can identify to which specific goal the practice is mapped, its sequence number, and its capability level. For example, in Requirements Management, the first specific practice of the first specific goal is numbered 1.1-1 and the second is 1.2-2. The numbering indicates that there is an advanced practice, SP 1.2-2.

The number also indicates that this is the first type of advanced practice that does not build on the preceding base practice. In the case of the second type of advanced practice, the sequence number is the same for both specific practices; for example, in Requirements Development the first specific practice of the first specific goal is numbered 1.1-1 and the second is numbered 1.1-2.

Figure 5.3 illustrates these different views. In the continuous representation, advanced practices appear with the base practices as expected model components. If an organization chooses to pursue capability level 3 in a process area, it will use all of the base practices as well as the capability level 2 and level 3 advanced practices when trying to achieve the goals of the process area.

---

1. This happens four times in CMMI, twice in the Requirements Development process area and twice in the Technical Solution process area.

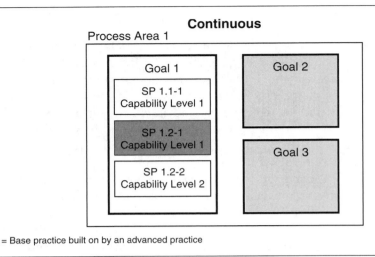

= Base practice built on by an advanced practice

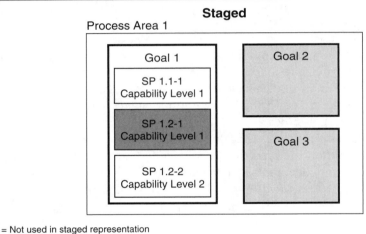

= Not used in staged representation

FIGURE 5.3
How Advanced Practices Are Handled in Each Representation

Generic Goals and Practices

Generic goals are required model components that apply to all process areas. Figure 5.4 illustrates the generic goals and practices. All of the generic goals and practices are used in the continuous representation. The capability level you are targeting for your improvement effort will determine which generic goals and practices you will apply to the process area you've selected.

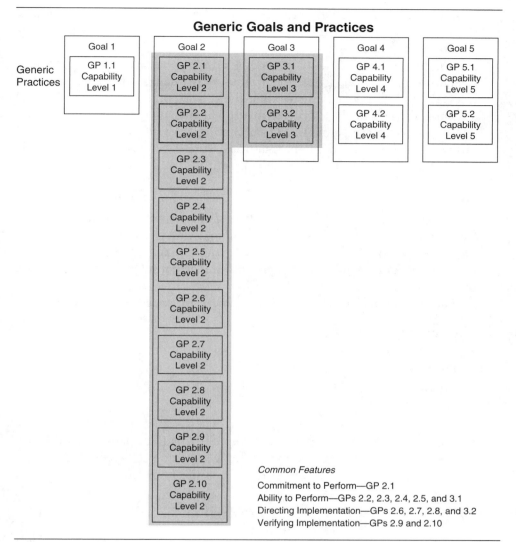

FIGURE 5.4
Generic Practices Mapped to Common Features

In the staged representation, only generic goals 2 and 3 are used, as illustrated by the goals and practices highlighted in gray in Figure 5.4. When you try to reach maturity level 2, you use the process areas at maturity level 2 as well as generic goal 2 and the generic practices at level 2.

Notice that generic goals 4 and 5 are not used. This is because not all processes will be "raised" above a defined process. Only select processes and subprocesses will be quantitatively managed and optimized and these processes are addressed by the process areas at maturity levels 4 and 5 in the staged representation.

When you reach maturity levels 3, 4, and 5, you use the process areas at the appropriate maturity levels as well as all of those at the lower maturity levels. In addition, generic goal 3 and the generic practices at levels 2 and 3 are applied to all of these process areas. This means that even though you have already achieved a maturity level 2 rating, to achieve a maturity level 3 rating you must return to the maturity level 2 process areas and apply generic goal 3 and the level 3 generic practices.

Common Features

A concept unique to the staged representation is common features. Common features are model components that are not rated in any way. They are groupings that provide a way to present the generic practices. Figure 5.4 shows how the generic practices are organized under common features within a process area.

Four common features organize the generic practices of each process area:

- Ability to Perform
- Commitment to Perform
- Directing Implementation
- Verifying Implementation

Ability to Perform groups the generic practices related to ensuring that the process is ready for execution (e.g., there is a plan for performing the process, there are adequate resources for performing it, responsibilities are assigned, and those who perform it have the knowledge and skills they need).

Commitment to Perform groups the generic practices related to creating policies and securing sponsorship.

Directing Implementation groups the generic practices related to managing the performance of the process (e.g., monitoring actual performance of the process against the plan, managing the integrity of its work products, and involving relevant stakeholders).

Verifying Implementation groups the generic practices related to review by higher level management and objective evaluation of conformance to process descriptions, procedures, and standards.

The difference between the way generic goals and practices are applied in the continuous and staged representations brings us back to the question of equivalence. How can these two representations be functionally equivalent if they do not apply the same generic goals and practices? We will answer this question in the section called "Equivalent Staging," but first let's summarize and compare the concepts by representation.

Representation Comparison

Because CMMI supports two representations, many concepts are discussed in this chapter from capability and maturity levels, to the ordering of process areas, to base and advanced practices. Table 5.3 summarizes the differences between the two representations. However, remember that the two representations bear many similarities, which were discussed in previous chapters. Representations are merely two views into the same CMMI best practices.

TABLE 5.3   Comparing Continuous and Staged Representations

Continuous Representation	*Staged Representation*
Process areas are organized by process area categories.	Process areas are organized by maturity level.
Improvement is measured using capability levels. Capability levels • measure maturity of a particular process across an organization. • range from 0 through 5.	Improvement is measured using maturity levels. Maturity levels • measure maturity of a set of processes across an organization. • range from 1 through 5.
There are two types of specific practices: base and advanced. All specific practices appear in the continuous representation.	There is only one type of specific practice. The concepts of base and advanced practices is not used. All specific practices appear in the staged representation except when a related base-advanced pair of practices appears in the continuous representation, in which case only the advanced practice appears in the staged representation.
Capability levels are used to organize the generic practices.	Common features are used to organize generic practices.
All generic practices are included in each process area.	Only the level 2 and level 3 generic practices are included.
Equivalent staging allows determination of a maturity level from an organization's achievement profile.	There is no need for an equivalence mechanism back to the continuous representation because each organization can choose what to improve and how much to improve it using the staged representation.

Equivalent Staging

Equivalent staging is a way to compare results from using the continuous representation to those of the staged representation. In essence, if improvement relative to selected process areas is measured using capability levels in the continuous representation, how would you compare that to maturity levels? Is this possible?

Up to this point, we have not discussed process appraisals in much detail. The SCAMPI[SM] method is used for appraising organizations using CMMI and one result of an appraisal is a rating. If the continuous representation is used for an appraisal, the rating is a capability level profile. If the staged representation is used for an appraisal, the rating is a maturity level (e.g., maturity level 3).

A capability level profile is a list of process areas and the corresponding capability level achieved for each. This profile enables an organization to track its capability level by process area. The profile is an *achievement profile* when it represents the organization's actual progress for each process area. Alternatively, the profile is a *target profile* when it represents the organization's planned process-improvement objectives. Figure 5.5 illustrates both a target profile and achievement profile. The gray portion of each bar represents what has been achieved. The unshaded portion represents what remains to be accomplished to meet the target profile.

An achievement profile, when compared with a target profile, enables an organization to plan and track its progress for each selected process area. Maintaining capability level profiles is advisable when using a continuous representation.

Target staging is a sequence of target profiles that describes the path of process improvement to be followed by the organization. When building target profiles, the organization should pay attention to the dependencies between generic practices and process areas. If a generic practice depends on a certain process area, either to carry out the generic practice or to provide a prerequisite product, the generic practice may be much less effective when the process area is not implemented.[2]

Although there are many reasons to use the continuous representation, the ratings provided by capability level profiles are limited in their ability to provide organizations with a way to generally compare themselves with other organizations. Capability level profiles could be used if each organization selected the same process areas; however, maturity levels have been

---

2. See chapter 3 for a detailed discussion of the relationships between the generic practices and process areas.

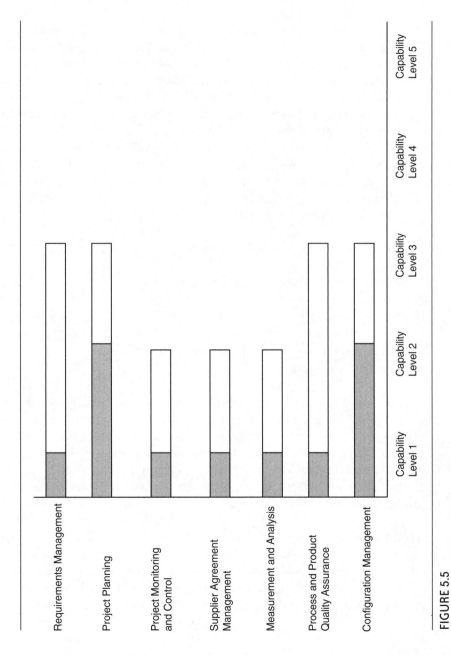

FIGURE 5.5
An Example of an Achievement Profile and a Target Profile

used to compare organizations for years and already provide predefined sets of process areas.

Because of this situation, equivalent staging was created. Equivalent staging enables an organization that used the continuous representation for an appraisal to convert the capability level profile to a maturity level rating.

The most effective way to depict equivalent staging is to provide a sequence of target profiles, each of which is equivalent to a maturity level rating of the staged representation. The result is a target staging that is equivalent to the maturity levels of the staged representation.

Figure 5.6 shows a summary of the target profiles that must be achieved when using the continuous representation to be equivalent to maturity levels 2 through 5. Each shaded area in the capability level columns represents a target profile that is equivalent to a maturity level in the staged representation.

The following rules summarize equivalent staging:

- To achieve maturity level 2, all process areas assigned to maturity level 2 must achieve capability level 2 or higher.
- To achieve maturity level 3, all process areas assigned to maturity levels 2 and 3 must achieve capability level 3 or higher.
- To achieve maturity level 4, all process areas assigned to maturity levels 2, 3, and 4 must achieve capability level 3 or higher.
- To achieve maturity level 5, all process areas must achieve capability level 3 or higher.

These rules and Figure 5.6 are complete; however, you may ask why target profiles 4 and 5 do not extend into the CL4 and CL5 columns. The reason is that the maturity level 4 process areas describe a selection of the subprocesses to be stabilized based on, in part, the quality and process-performance objectives of the organization and projects. Not every process area will be addressed in the selection and CMMI does not presume in advance which process areas might be addressed in the selection.

So, the achievement of capability level 4 for process areas cannot be predetermined because the choices depend on the selections made by the organization in its implementation of the maturity level 4 process areas. Thus, Figure 5.6 does not show target profile 4 extending into the CL4 column, although some process areas will have achieved capability level 4. The situation for maturity level 5 and target profile 5 is similar.

The existence of equivalent staging should not discourage users of the continuous representation from establishing target profiles that extend above capability level 3. Such a target profile would be determined in part by the selections made by the organization to meet its business objectives.

Name	Abbr	ML	CL1	CL2	CL3	CL4	CL5
Requirements Management	REQM	2					
Project Planning	PP	2					
Project Monitoring and Control	PMC	2					
Supplier Agreement Management	SAM	2	Target Profile 2				
Measurement and Analysis	MA	2					
Process and Product Quality Assurance	PPQA	2					
Configuration Management	CM	2					
Requirements Development	RD	3					
Technical Solution	TS	3					
Product Integration	PI	3					
Verification	VER	3					
Validation	VAL	3					
Organizational Process Focus	OPF	3					
Organizational Process Definition	OPD	3		Target Profile 3			
Organizational Training	OT	3					
Integrated Project Management	IPM	3					
Risk Management	RSKM	3					
Integrated Teaming	IT	3					
Integrated Supplier Management	ISM	3					
Decision Analysis and Resolution	DAR	3					
Organizational Environment for Integration	OEI	3					
Organizational Process Performance	OPP	4		Target Profile 4			
Quantitative Project Management	QPM	4					
Organizational Innovation and Deployment	OID	5		Target Profile 5			
Causal Analysis and Resolution	CAR	5					

Key: Name = the full name of the process area.
  Abbr = the acronym that corresponds to the Name.
  ML = the maturity level assignment of the process area in the staged representation.
  CL1,CL2 CL3, CL4, and CL5 are capability levels in the continuous representation.

FIGURE 5.6
Target Profiles and Equivalent Staging

CHAPTER 6

USING CMMI MODELS

The complexity of today's products demands that an integrated view of systems and software engineering be used. CMMI reduces the cost of process improvement efforts across an enterprise that depends on multiple disciplines to produce products or services. To accomplish this, CMMI provides common terminology, common components, common appraisal methods, and common training materials, regardless of the disciplines involved. This chapter describes how organizations can use CMMI models for both process improvement and benchmarking

Interpreting CMMI Models

CMMI describes the best practices of organizations. These best practices can be used by organizations to improve their processes for developing, acquiring, and maintaining products and services. While a new enterprise might wish to establish its processes using these best practices, they are more commonly of interest to organizations that are seeking to improve their existing processes.

Such organizations must use professional judgment to interpret CMMI practices. Although process areas depict behavior that should be exhibited in any organization, practices must be interpreted using an in-depth knowledge of CMMI, the discipline(s), the organization, the business environment, and the specific circumstances involved.

As you begin using a CMMI model for improving processes, you should map your processes to CMMI process areas. This mapping enables you to track your organization's level of conformance to the CMMI model you are using and to easily identify opportunities for improvement.

To interpret practices, it is important to consider the overall context in which they will be used and to determine how well the practices satisfy the goals of a process area in that context. CMMI models do not imply which processes are right for an organization or project. Instead, CMMI establishes minimal criteria necessary to plan and implement processes selected by the organization for improvement based on business objectives.

CMMI practices purposely use nonspecific phrases such as "relevant stakeholders," "as appropriate," and "as necessary" to accommodate the needs of different organizations or projects. Specific needs may also differ at various points during a project's life.

Appraisals and Benchmarking

Many organizations find value in benchmarking their progress (e.g., ascertaining maturity level "scores," a capability level profile) in process improvement for both internal purposes and with external customers and suppliers. The organization sets its priorities based on its business and process-improvement objectives, as well as its collection of business and technical processes.

Process appraisals focus on identifying improvement opportunities and understanding the organization's position relative to the selected model or standard. Appraisal teams use CMMI to guide their identification and prioritization of findings. These findings, with guidance provided by CMMI practices, are used (by a process group, for example) to plan improvements for the organization.

For organizations that wish to appraise multiple disciplines, CMMI's integrated approach permits some economy of scale in model and appraisal training. One appraisal method can provide separate or combined results for multiple disciplines.

The appraisal principles for the CMMI Product Suite[1] remain the same as those used in appraisals for other process-improvement models. Those principles are:

- Senior management sponsorship
- A focus on the organization's business objectives
- Confidentiality for interviewees
- Use of a documented appraisal method
- Use of a process reference model (e.g., a CMMI model) as a base
- A collaborative team approach
- A focus on actions for process improvement

The CMMI Product Suite provides a rigorous appraisal method for benchmarking that implements these appraisal principles. It is called the *Standard CMMI Appraisal Method for Process Improvement* (SCAMPI[SM]).

---

1. See the glossary for the definition of *CMMI Product Suite*.

For benchmarking against other organizations, appraisals must ensure consistent ratings. The achievement of a specific maturity level or the satisfaction of a process area must mean the same thing for different appraised organizations. Rules for ensuring this consistency are provided in the *SCAMPI Method Definition Document.*

Details on this method are available on the Software Engineering Institute Web site at the following URL: *http://www.sei.cmu.edu/cmmi/appraisals/appraisals.html.*

Appraisal Requirements for CMMI

Other CMMI-based appraisal methods may be more appropriate for a given set of sponsor needs, including self-assessments, initial appraisals, quicklook or mini-appraisals, incremental appraisals, and external appraisals.

To assist in identifying or developing appraisal methods that will be compatible with CMMI, the CMMI Product Suite provides a document called the *Appraisal Requirements for CMMI* (ARC). The ARC provides requirements for multiple types of appraisal methods with guidelines for determining the suitability of a particular appraisal method. Suitability addresses the accuracy and repeatability of appraisal results [SEI 0la].

The ARC document was designed to help improve consistency across multiple disciplines and appraisal methods, and to help appraisal method developers, sponsors, and users understand the tradeoffs associated with various methods. More information and a matrix detailing ARC requirements are available on the Software Engineering Institute's Web site at *http://www.sei.cmu.edu/cmmi/appraisals/appraisals.html.*

ISO/IEC 15504 Compatibility and Conformance

The International Organization for Standardization and International Electrotechnical Commission (ISO/IEC) Technical Report 15504 is an emerging standard for software process assessment [ISO 98].

The 1998 Technical Report version of ISO/IEC 15504 identifies two aspects of conformance: model compatibility and appraisal conformance.

For an appraisal model (e.g., Bootstrap, CMMI-SE/SW) to be in conformance with ISO/IEC 15504 (i.e., to be an ISO/IEC 15504–compatible model), it must have a "demonstration of compatibility" document to show how the model compatibility requirements of ISO/IEC 15504-2 have been addressed. These requirements are constructed to provide reasonable assurance that the model content will be reasonably broad but detailed enough to work properly with the associated documented appraisal method.

There are also ISO/IEC 15504 requirements that pertain to the actual conduct (planning as well as performance) of an appraisal. If the conduct of an appraisal is such that the requirements in ISO/IEC 15504-3 are satisfied, then the appraisal is said to be ISO/IEC 15504 conformant. One of these requirements is that an ISO/IEC 15504-compatible appraisal model be used.

The CMMI models and SCAMPI were written to support the conduct of appraisals that conform to the 1998 version of Technical Report 15504. Sponsors interested in performing an ISO/IEC 15504-conformant CMMI appraisal must provide necessary information including a demonstration of compatibility to support their needs.

Adopting CMMI

Two types of organizations are likely to adopt CMMI: those who have already used process-improvement models and those that are new to process improvement. Many organizations have been using the SW-CMM® or the SECM, so these organizations are specifically addressed.

Organizations with Experience

Organizations that have used the SW-CMM or the SECM will have an easier time adopting CMMI than organizations that haven't because these two older models share many similarities with CMMI. Also, a significant portion of the practices found in each model also appears in CMMI.

As demonstrated in chapter 7, organizations, such as United Space Alliance, that have experience with an older model can adopt CMMI in a way that preserves their existing investment in process improvement, while at the same time leveraging what they have already learned to more rapidly benefit from the additional best practices provided by CMMI. They can readily identify differences between CMMI and the model they know, thus identifying process-improvement opportunities and gaps.

Of course, this strategy can be used by any organization using any process-improvement model. Compare your current efforts and achievements to CMMI. Most likely, you'll find that you are already implementing many of the best practices in CMMI and you'll see the value in the best practices you have yet to implement.

The Capability Maturity Model for Software

CMMI incorporates the version 2.0 draft C improvements to the Capability Maturity Model for Software [SEI 97b], or SW-CMM version 1.1, as well as other improvement information gained from research at the SEI. Compared to the SW-CMM, CMMI has significantly improved coverage of the engineering, risk management, and measurement and analysis processes.

The Software CMM practices at maturity levels 4 and 5 have been improved based on experience gained since the publication of the SW-CMM version 2.0 draft C. These practices have been further refined based on studies conducted by the SEI that analyzed the implementation of maturity level 4 and 5 practices by leading organizations.

Organizations that have achieved maturity level 4 or 5 may wish to make the transition more quickly to take advantage of the additional organizational coverage described in the CMMI models. Organizations that have begun significant efforts toward a maturity-level 2, 3, or 4 rating must carefully determine the best timing for the transition to CMMI. A possible approach to easing into CMMI is to augment current plans with selected process areas that would be of greatest business value.

For example, a company with several months remaining before a maturity level 4 appraisal might want to charter small teams to investigate Risk Management and Measurement and Analysis, and add them to the appraisal scope to begin the transition without affecting current efforts. This improvement approach allows members of the organization to have a "first look" at new process areas and to gain insight and experience that will be useful as CMMI adoption continues. This approach also allows the organization to sample CMMI to see how they like it.

Electronic Industries Alliance's Systems Engineering Capability Model

CMMI incorporates many of the practices from the Electronic Industries Alliance's (EIA's) Systems Engineering Capability Model, or SECM [EIA 98]. In fact, CMMI Engineering process areas are built mainly from SECM practices. CMMI's organization is different from that of the SECM. There are no themes and some practices appear in different process areas.

The most noticeable difference between CMMI and the SECM is that CMMI provides a great abundance of informative material. This additional material provides detailed implementation guidance that the SECM did not provide.

Organizations that have achieved high capability levels using the SECM may wish to make the transition to CMMI quickly to take advantage of the additional informative material and organizational coverage described in CMMI models. Organizations that have begun significant effort toward achieving a target profile that contains lower capability levels must carefully determine the best timing for the transition to CMMI. A possible approach to easing into CMMI adoption is to augment current plans with selected process areas that would be of the greatest business value.

For example, a company with several months remaining before an appraisal might want to charter small teams to investigate process areas related to the target profile currently used and to identify gaps and opportunities from the differences found between the two models. This improvement approach allows members of the organization to have a "first look" at new process areas and to gain insight and experience that will be useful as CMMI adoption continues. This approach also allows the organization to sample CMMI to see how they like it.

Organizations New to Process Improvement

Organizations without process improvement experience can, in general, approach the adoption of CMMI as they would approach the adoption of any process-improvement model. The advantage to beginning their improvement efforts using CMMI is that expansion of the process improvement program to include multiple disciplines, groups, and organizations is easier and more straightforward than with any other process-improvement model.

Once your organization has decided to adopt CMMI, planning can begin with an improvement approach such as the IDEAL[SM] (Initiating, Diagnosing, Establishing, Acting, Learning) model [SEI 2]. For more information about the IDEAL model, see the Software Engineering Institute Web site at the following URL: *http://www.sei.cmu.edu/ideal/ideal.html.*

Research has shown that the most powerful initial step to process improvement is to build strong organizational sponsorship before investing in process appraisals. Given sufficient senior management sponsorship, establishing a specific, technically competent process group that represents relevant stakeholders to guide process-improvement efforts has proved to be an effective approach.

For an organization with a mission to develop software-intensive systems, the process group might include systems engineers and software engineers from projects across the organization, and other selected members based on the business needs driving improvement. For example, a systems administrator may focus on information-technology support, whereas a marketing representative may focus on integrating customers' needs. Both members could make powerful additions to the process group.

CMMI Model Training

Whether your organization is new to process improvement or is already familiar with process-improvement models, training is a key element in the ability of organizations to adopt CMMI. An initial set of courses is provided by the SEI and its transition partners, but your organization may wish to supplement these courses with internal instruction. This approach allows your organization to focus on the areas that provide the greatest business value.

The SEI and its transition partners offer the Introduction to CMMI course, which provides a basic overview of the CMMI models. The SEI also offers the Intermediate Concepts of CMMI course to those who plan to become more deeply involved in CMMI adoption or appraisal—for example, those who will guide improvement as part of a process group, those who will lead SCAMPI appraisals, and those who will teach the Introduction to

CMMI course. Current information about CMMI training is available on the Software Engineering Institute Web site at the following URL: *http://www. sei.cmu.edu/cmmi/training/training.html.*

Model Tailoring

Tailoring[2] a CMMI model is a process whereby only a subset of a model is used to suit the needs of a specific domain of application. Model tailoring should be done cautiously and an organization should be aware that it can result in significant gaps in efforts to improve or appraise an organization's or a project's capabilities.

Tailoring of a CMMI model can be viewed from two perspectives:

- Model tailoring for process improvement
- Model tailoring for benchmarking

Many organizations will use a CMMI model for benchmarking as well as process improvement. Such tailoring is constrained by the intersection of criteria outlined in the next two sections.

Tailoring Constraints for Process Improvement

For internal process improvement, it is appropriate to restrict or expand the scope of an organization's or project's improvement effort (including appraisals). The tailoring may address individual disciplines, process areas, maturity levels, and/or capability levels. The tailoring of a model should focus on identifying the process areas and practices that support an organization's business needs and objectives.

Care must be taken when considering whether to exclude portions of a CMMI model. Given a CMMI model's focus on the essential characteristics of an effective process, the majority of the process areas and practices in a model should be addressed.

Organizations and projects implementing less than a full set of process areas, goals, or practices can still achieve significant value from a CMMI model. However, because of the interrelationship of model components, exclusion of process areas, goals, or practices may diminish the benefits. The wholesale exclusion of fundamental process areas or specific practices defeats the purpose of process improvement.

---

2. The tailoring discussed in this section does not address adaptation of an organization's set of standard processes for use on a specific project. Such tailoring is driven by tailoring guidelines defined in this book's glossary.

Goals cannot be excluded from the process areas included in the scope of a process improvement effort. Goals reflect the minimum requirements for satisfying a process area. Goals work together to support a process area and may not be individually designated as "not applicable."

Tailoring a model also affects comparability of process improvement efforts undertaken by different projects. If one project excludes parts of a model and the other excludes other parts of the same model, the degree of comparability of results is reduced.

Tailoring Constraints for Benchmarking

Using CMMI for benchmarking allows an organization to compare its appraisal results to other organizations. Comparison to competitors is aided by state-of-the-practice reports. Appraisal results can also be used to compare a group of organizations such as potential suppliers. Tailoring a CMMI model used for such benchmarking is extremely dependent on how closely each organization follows the complete collection of process areas, goals, and practices.

Realistically, benchmarking is possible only when the results of an appraisal can be expressed as a maturity level. Until such time that achievement profiles (results of the continuous representation) are publicly shared, the value of benchmarking is found in the maturity level rating. A maturity level rating can be achieved directly using the staged representation. Such a rating can also be achieved using the continuous representation by the extra step of employing equivalent staging to convert the achievement profile to a maturity level.

The maturity level ratings resulting from the use of models in multiple appraisals is useful only to the extent that there is consistency of use among the organizations being compared. Consequently, model tailoring for benchmarking is significantly constrained, especially where maturity levels resulting from appraisals are disseminated publicly.

The scope of the organization chosen for an appraisal affects the usefulness of benchmarking. If one organization chooses to appraise only the software engineering function while another chooses to appraise both software and systems engineering functions, comparing the two would not be fair or accurate even if they implemented all of the same CMMI process areas, goals, and practices.

Planning Tailoring for Benchmarking

There are some issues to consider well in advance of planning to have an appraisal conducted. The way you construct your process improvement program will affect how easily you can achieve a rating that is meaningful to your organization.

Process Areas' Appraisal Scope

Process areas cannot be excluded except to omit process areas that are outside of the scope of an appraisal. For example, an organization using a staged representation can exclude process areas at maturity levels 4 and 5 when the organization is focused on achieving maturity level 3.

An organization using a continuous representation can exclude process areas outside the scope of the target profile; however, benchmarking opportunities using the continuous representation are possible only through the use of equivalent staging, so careful analysis should be used before deciding to exclude a process area.

Not Applicable

Process areas can be excluded when they are determined to be not applicable to the organization being appraised. This means that goals and practices of the process area are inherently outside of the organization's scope of work. For example, if an organization does not use suppliers for products or services critical to its product development efforts, it can exclude Supplier Agreement Management from its appraisal.

Under these circumstances, a maturity level rating could still be determined; however, that maturity level rating must also state which process areas were considered not applicable.

Not Rated

A process area is designated "not rated" if it is outside the appraisal scope or if insufficient data is available to satisfy the data-coverage criteria. A maturity level cannot be determined if process areas at that maturity level (or below) are not rated. In other words, "not rated" process areas are interpreted as not achieved and act against the achievement of a maturity level.

Goals

Specific goals and generic goals cannot be excluded from process areas included in the scope of an appraisal effort. Goals reflect the minimum requirements for satisfying a process area. If a process area is applicable, each of its specific goals is applicable as well as the generic goals within the scope of the appraisal.

Practices

Specific practices and generic practices are typical activities necessary to implement and institutionalize the goals of the process area. Therefore, appropriate alternative practices can be substituted for specific practices and generic practices if the alternatives are effective in implementing and institutionalizing the goals.

Informative Components

All other model components (subpractices, typical work products, examples, amplifications, elaborations, and references) are informative and can be excluded at will.

Appraisal Considerations

Choices that affect a CMMI-based appraisal include the following:

- Establishing the appraisal scope, including the organizational entity to be appraised, the CMMI process areas to be investigated, and the maturity level or capability level(s) to be appraised
- Selecting the appraisal method
- Selecting the appraisal team members
- Selecting appraisal participants from the appraisal entities to be interviewed
- Establishing appraisal outputs (e.g., ratings, instantiation-specific findings)
- Establishing appraisal constraints (e.g., time spent on site)

The *SCAMPI Method Definition Document* allows the selection of predefined options for use in an appraisal. These appraisal options are designed to help organizations align CMMI with their business needs and objectives.

Documentation of CMMI appraisal plans and results must always include a description of the appraisal options, model scope, and organizational scope selected. This documentation confirms whether an appraisal meets the requirements for benchmarking.

CHAPTER 7

CMMI CASE STUDY
UNITED SPACE ALLIANCE, LLC

United Space Alliance (USA) is a limited liability company owned equally by The Boeing Company and Lockheed Martin Corporation. USA was formed as a result of the consolidation of National Aeronautics and Space Administration (NASA) contracts for the Space Shuttle program. USA is chartered for space operations: operating and maintaining space systems (hardware/software) after they have been put into use. The USA principal markets are those space operation tasks identified within human space-flight operations. The core competencies of USA include space hardware processing, launch and recovery, on-orbit operations, and space systems training. USA is currently performing work on the NASA Space Shuttle and International Space Station programs, with a staff of more than 10,000 employees.

Background

USA enjoys a strong heritage in software process improvement, including being the first SW-CMM Level 5 project. In 1989, the Flight Software project earned the highest rating, maturity level 5. The Flight Software project was described in *The Capability Maturity Model: Guidelines for Improving the Software Process* [SEI 95]. United Space Alliance embraces the SW-CMM and uses it as the basis for corporate-wide software process-improvement planning. USA has not previously used the Systems Engineering Capability Model *(EIA 731)* [EIA 98].

Note: This case study was written in 2001 when United Space Alliance was in the early stages of investigation and adoption of CMMI. As you would expect, they have continued their process improvement efforts, so this case study reflects only their early decisions, issues, and activities. We hope this will help you with the opportunities and challenges that you may face with adopting CMMI.

USA Mission and Vision

The United Space Alliance vision is to be the world leader in space operations on Earth, in orbit, and beyond. The USA mission is to provide safe, high-quality, best-value space operations services to government and commercial customers. To achieve the vision and mission, the company established six key goals.

- Provide for safe operations for all aspects of our business.
- Achieve excellent customer satisfaction and program performance.
- Improve, grow, and diversify our business.
- Be the company of choice for our employees.
- Contribute positively to the enrichment of our communities.
- Provide excellent financial returns to our stakeholders.

Deploying Company Goals

One of the concepts in CMMI is to explicitly link activities and business objectives. USA supports this concept through the Vision Support Plan, which defines the company's shared vision. To align all goals in the organization to achieve the corporate vision, this initiative links company goals and individual department and employee goals. Further, this initiative ensures that all employees understand how their work helps the company reach its shared vision.

Each year, executive managers establish goals to support the organization's vision and mission. Process owners establish the company-level goals for their disciplines. The owner of each company goal must define the goal, collect requirements, and track comments for that goal.

Managers then use these higher level goals to develop supporting goals and initiatives for their areas. The Vision Support Plan goal-deployment process requires a standard metric for measuring the progress of each goal/objective/initiative and each related year-end metric target. This same process of refining higher level goals to supporting goals continues until each employee's goals are defined.

Each owner of a goal/objective/initiative must monitor the status of progress using stoplight colors (red, yellow, and green).

> *Green:* Performance met the target or is projected to meet the target.
> *Yellow:* Performance is projected to miss the target, but a corrective action plan is in place.
> *Red:* Performance did not meet the target or is projected to not meet the target.

If the status is yellow or red, a plan of action must be available for review and attention is given to the goal/objective/initiative.

In addition to entering information into the Vision Support Plan Web-based system, managers display information on bulletin boards known as Vision Support Plan wall boards. Each department maintains a Vision Support Plan wall board that displays its progress toward its goals and stimulates discussion of related work. Progress toward USA goals is reviewed periodically by management at all levels of the company. Once a quarter, the senior management team formally reviews progress by reviewing the wall boards with all members of the department.

Process Ownership

To achieve corporate goals, USA initiated a number of process-improvement activities that are organized around designated process owners. These process owners are the focus of technical process excellence and employee development. Process owners are identified for Software, Engineering, Quality Assurance, Process and Manufacturing, Logistics, and Program Management disciplines and report to the chief executive officer of USA.

Under the United Space Alliance Process Owners Charter, each process owner must accomplish the following:

- Develop and maintain technical processes that support core competencies.
- Develop and maintain core technical processes and tools.
- Ensure that technical processes are implemented consistently according to policy.
- Look for cross-program synergy and horizontal integration opportunities, including identifying and developing best internal practices for company-wide application.
- Assure availability and efficient use of technical resources.
- Support new business development.
- Infuse technology throughout the company for tools within his or her area.

Under the leadership of the Software process owner, USA is currently in the midst of rolling out a SW-CMM–based set of standard process assets as a part of the software process improvement initiative. At some point, CMMI practices that are different from the SW-CMM will be folded into these assets.

USA will continue to use the SW-CMM as a basis for improvement since a significant investment has already been made. That is, current plans are not being sidetracked or drastically revised to change course and start immediate widespread adoption of CMMI. Transition to CMMI will be a gradual move of the entire software process from SW-CMM to CMMI within the next four years.

Since most of the Software Engineering Process Group (SEPG) representatives attended the training course, "Introduction to CMMI," they are familiar with CMMI and the differences between the SW-CMM and CMMI. The SEPG is able to easily incorporate the aspects of CMMI that are compatible with SW-CMM. For example, the standard software process may require review of activities with higher level management (CMMI oriented) instead of dictating review of activities with project management and senior management (SW-CMM oriented).

The USA Engineering Process Owner is currently evaluating the more immediate use of CMMI for process definition. Presumably this approach will allow CMMI to become a binding agent to unite the work of software and engineering process owners when the two separate improvement initiatives converge. The process owners currently coordinate activities at regular face-to-face meetings. CMMI, however, has not yet been adopted as the company standard to span multiple company-wide processes.

Since the case study was conducted, the Logistics process owner has begun applying a CMMI model during process definition activities. This area is related to neither systems nor software and was not a target area for which CMMI was anticipated to be applied.

Because of the tight relationship between NASA and USA, NASA policy strongly influences USA policy and process direction. The USA decisions to adopt SW-CMM and subsequently CMMI are influenced heavily by NASA decisions. Policies are pending at NASA that will more broadly apply CMMI across the agency.

CMMI Case Study Activity

In 2001, USA began investigating the use of CMMI within the company. To determine the feasibility of using CMMI, USA piloted CMMI in part of the company through an informal assessment of specific projects following SEI's IDEAL guidelines for instituting process improvement. The IDEAL model is an organizational improvement model that serves as a road map for initiating, planning, and implementing improvement actions [SEI 2]. During the CMMI case study, the initiating and diagnosing phases of the IDEAL model were launched.

The Initiating Phase

The first critical step to adopting CMMI is the involvement of management. Among the first to be involved was USA senior management, including the USA Software Process owner and the Flight Software Program Element Associate Program Manager. In addition, the NASA Technical Management Representative was involved in discussions and decisions regarding this effort.

Involving these key players enabled USA to establish goals and expectations, determine the scope of the effort, communicate plans, establish sponsorship, and obtain commitment of resources. To ensure the success of the CMMI case study, it was managed as a project. Schedules were established and planning was conducted to obtain commitments, resources, tools, personnel, and training.

A detailed project plan was created. Such a plan is important for successful execution of such projects, and is especially critical for early identification of risks. Internal meetings were held to select projects, to identify and assign project members to tasks, and to determine the appropriate scope of support required for the case study. Relevant stakeholders participated in the development and review of the plan.

The goals of the case study were established in the planning stages:

- Provide awareness of CMMI throughout USA.
- Determine the extent of compliance with CMMI in a high-maturity software environment.

Project Selection

During the planning stages, USA invited a variety of projects to participate in the CMMI case study. To gain the most benefit from applying CMMI, the use of a systems-level project was preferred. However, existing work commitments precluded their involvement during the case study time period.

Two projects were selected. Members of both software project teams were familiar and comfortable with process discussions, models, and assessments. This allowed for a quick startup of the case study. The CMMI case study participants were from the Flight Software Program Element:

- Primary Avionics Software System (PASS)
- Cockpit Avionics Upgrade (CAU)

The legacy PASS project was selected because the core processes in place for this case study were the same as the core processes in place at the time of the SW-CMM case study. Participation of this project provided continuity in case studies from the SW-CMM book to this book and is an example of a high-maturity project implementing CMMI practices.

The CAU project was selected because it is a new project in its process definition phase and can easily implement CMMI practices. This project also has customer and USA management visibility and therefore must have sound processes in place.

Primary Avionics Software System Project Background

The Space Shuttle's flight software is responsible for the guidance, naviga-
tion, and flight control functions performed during all phases of shuttle
flight. Flight software consists of more than 400,000 lines of code that run
on the shuttle's onboard computers. USA also develops and maintains more
than one million lines of application tools code that supports configuration
management, software builds, test, simulation, automatic verification, and
software reconfiguration.

The USA software development efforts include requirements analysis, design, development, testing, certification, and maintenance of the avionics software for the data processing system of the Space Shuttle Orbiter. Responsibilities
include development of the flight, test, and support software; integration of
software furnished by NASA; and design, analysis, and test support to NASA.

The unique requirements for flight software, such as redundancy management, fail-safe operations, complex timing, and synchronization, had to be developed to produce human-rated, error-free flight software for shuttle space flight.

Cockpit Avionics Upgrade Project Background

The Cockpit Avionics Upgrade (CAU) project is a major hardware and software development project responsible for the design, development, verification, and delivery of hardware and software for four orbiters, an initial lay-in
of spares, and ground avionics facilities. With the goal of first flight in 2006,
the CAU project aims to enhance the cockpit to include many state-of-the-
art features available in other avionics systems.

The CAU represents a third generation of avionics for the orbiters and
builds on the Multifunction Electronic Display System, or "glass cockpit,"
already installed onboard *Atlantis* and *Columbia*. CAU Command and Display Processors will replace the Multifunction Electronic Display System
integrated display processors. With these new devices, a much greater variety of displays and more data filtering and analysis will be possible.

The CAU project includes two significantly new software applications. The
first of these applications will continuously determine which launch abort
option is most attractive based on the current state of the vehicle. The second
new application will reduce crew workload by providing more sophisticated
vehicle health monitoring functions and by limiting the number of alarms that
sound for nonemergencies.

CMMI Model Selection and Scope

USA selected the CMMI Systems Engineering/Software Engineering version
1.02 model with a staged representation for the case study (version 1.1 was

not yet available). This model version exhibited adequate shelf life and its use would result in only minor modifications during CMMI version 1.1 development. The use of version 1.02 would not generally negate the results of the case study.

The CMMI model selected most accurately reflected the core businesses within the company: software engineering. There was no need to review the draft IPPD or acquisition practices since these were not considered a part of the typical business profile of a USA project. USA selected the staged representation of the model because the case study participants were familiar with previous staged models (i.e., SW-CMM) and because the case study did not intend to isolate a subset of process areas for intense scrutiny (as the continuous representation would facilitate).

Since the CMMI model contains nearly 500 practices and the amount of time to conduct the case study was limited, only a subset of the CMMI practices was evaluated for each project. The case study's purpose was to sample the examination of process areas (PAs) suitable to selected projects in a planned and meaningful way to determine how well CMMI could be implemented at USA. As such, not all PAs at all maturity levels were investigated in total for each project. However, between the two projects, all of the practices were examined, but not all practices were examined for each project.

Different criteria were used for the two flight software projects to determine which CMMI practices to apply. Since the PASS project conducted SW-CMM self-assessments in 1996 and 1999 with results that mapped evidence to key practices, there was no perceived need to revisit the SW-CMM key practices at maturity levels 2 and 3, which are unchanged between SW-CMM and CMMI. The CMMI scope for PASS was based on significant differences from SW-CMM 1.1 to CMMI and high-maturity practices. In addition, all CMMI maturity level 4 and 5 PAs were examined.

The CMMI scope for the CAU project was based on its life-cycle progress (i.e., process areas and practices that can be reasonably applied to CAU at its current life-cycle stage). With the CAU project early in its life cycle, limited defined processes were operating. It was not feasible to assess CAU planned processes not yet established or operating.

Figure 7.1 identifies the process areas examined for each project. Each project considered all practices for the process areas examined. For example, all SPs and GPs for the Requirements Management PA were examined for CAU and all SPs and GPs for the Measurement and Analysis PA were examined for PASS.

The case study does not represent a comprehensive Standard CMMI Appraisal Method for Process Improvement (SCAMPI) appraisal of all PAs for all maturity levels for representative organizational projects. USA anticipates that future efforts will more broadly cover the PAs and practices across the company.

PA/Project	REQM	PP	PMC	SAM	MA	PPQA	CM	RD	TS	PI	VER	VAL	OPF	OPD	OT	IPM	RSKM	DAR	OPP	QPM	OID	CAR
PASS					X			X	X	X	X	X	X	X	X		X	X	X	X	X	X
CAU	X	X	X	X		X	X	X								X	X	X				

FIGURE 7.1
CMMI Process Areas Examined by Project

CMMI Training

USA planned for CMMI training to ensure that the team in the case study had the requisite knowledge and a foundational understanding of the model to support evaluation of processes against the model. To obtain these skills, students attended the course "Introduction to CMMI." The team leader for the case study attended the "CMMI Intermediate" course for an advanced understanding of the model.

The majority of the students were familiar with the SW-CMM. Participants other than those involved in the case study were also included in training. This approach introduced the idea to others that future deployment of CMMI at the corporate level across company-wide processes may occur. As a result of this approach, the Logistics group has since adopted CMMI.

Most of the case study participants (e.g., managers and practitioners interviewed or solicited for project information) did not attend CMMI training. The case study team translated project practices to eliminate the need for other case study participants to learn about CMMI model content.

CMMI Supplemental Resources

USA also used a number of other publicly available CMMI resources to prepare for the case study and to help with CMMI familiarization, training, and transition:

- "Advice for Change Agents" [SEI 3]
- *CMMI Distilled: A Practical Introduction to Integrated Process Improvement* [Ahern 01]
- "CMMI Frequently Asked Questions" [SEI 4]
- "CMMI Risk Management Requirements" [Hefner 01]
- *The 2001 High Maturity Workshop* Technical Report [SEI 01c]
- Mapping of SW-CMM 1.1 to CMMI SE/SW 1.0 [STSC 1]
- *The Measurement and Analysis Process Area in CMMI 2002* [SEI 02g]
- "Transitioning Your Organization from SW CMM Version1.1 to CMMI-SW Version 1.0" [SEI 1]

To enable standardization across projects, the team chose to use a spreadsheet template for recording data. This template was based on Microsoft's Excel program, contained the CMMI practices, and was organized by PA. The Excel files linked to the model to enable easy access when team members needed to review more details about a practice.

The Diagnosing Phase

The case study team was divided into two mini-teams, each with responsibility for one of the projects. Each team gathered the information from the projects using a variety of means, including informal interviews, facilitated questionnaires, document review, and e-mail. This approach was chosen as the least intrusive to the participating projects.

Collecting Information

The team members compared project processes to PAs using their knowledge of the processes and collected information (e.g., documented policies, plans, procedures, and other project documentation).

PA examination was conducted using required and expected CMMI components (i.e., goals and practices). The informative material, while helpful to understand the specific and generic practices, was not explicitly reviewed for compliance as a part of this activity.

The case study team identified where the processes met or did not meet practices. A process was determined to meet the practices of the model if it was sufficiently institutionalized (i.e., is followed consistently, yields repeatable results, is used throughout the project, is known and understood by constituents, and is documented). Team members' experience with SW-CMM and assessments aided in making objective rulings about alignment of the project practices with the model.

For purposes of the organizational-based PAs and practices at maturity levels 3 through 5, the team interpreted "organization" to mean United Space Alliance because it is the level at which organizational activity is performed.

The team relied on its understanding of the model during the course of the case study and interpreted practices using the "Introduction to CMMI" course materials. The team did not rely on SEI staff, consultants, or other model experts for model interpretation issues or for further model amplification or elaboration.

Recording Observations

Using results from the review, the team members wrote observations for each specific and generic practice. They recorded whether the process met (strength) or did not meet (weakness) the intent of the practices. Team members identified no alternative practices or practices that were considered not applicable.

Team members recorded at least one observation (strength or weakness) for every specific and generic practice in the examined scope to describe what the project did to satisfy or not satisfy the practice. The team also implemented the "partial credit" technique. Team members wrote separate observations for each practice to note strengths and weaknesses associated with the practice in the event some, but not all, of a given practice was being done. There were more than 650 observations written for the practices examined.

The team documented a mapping of project processes to the model that facilitated a gap analysis between the processes and the model. This analysis resulted in recommendations for changes to processes. Teams reviewed the observations while developing the results.

CMMI Model Results

The following section demonstrates how USA processes relate to CMMI process areas. Remember that organization's processes and CMMI PAs do not always map one to one and that is, of course, the case with USA. The discussion is organized from the model perspective. So, you will see the name of one or more process areas followed by a discussion of related USA processes. The discussion contains highlights, not a complete description, of what USA does.

Specific USA projects or products are mentioned only when relevant. The majority of the discussion does not mention this information. However, the process areas considered for each of the projects are illustrated in Figure 7.1.

Engineering Process Areas

Requirements Management and Requirements Development

The CAU project patterns its requirements-generation and evaluation process after the robust PASS requirements evaluation process. This accelerates the deployment of practices related to Requirements Development and Requirements Management process areas.

USA and NASA work closely together for requirements elicitation, development, and management. For the CAU project, the Space Shuttle Cockpit Council is composed of USA representatives and shuttle astronauts who identify the desired features to be included in the CAU system, particularly in the area of shuttle cockpit displays. The customer provides USA with data dictionary documents to ensure that a clear understanding of the requirement is communicated.

USA then transforms the Cockpit Council products into detailed software requirements. The highest-level requirements document is the System Specification Document. The lowest level of software requirements is documented in the Software Requirements Specification. Use cases are created to analyze and validate both the System Specification Document and lower-level specifications.

The project uses a tool to track the traceability from the Software Requirements Specification to the System Specification Document. This tool will also be used during code, design, and test to document traceability to the requirements. USA tracks metrics for requirements-generation schedules, issues, readiness status, and quality. For the PASS project, similar forums are used, such as technical mode teams to formulate requirements concepts.

Scenario reviews of preliminary requirements concepts are conducted prior to formal requirements inspections. The purpose of the scenario review is to present community-identified scenarios to increase the team's understanding of intended functionality and usage and to develop other scenarios that might have been overlooked by the technical community. The review is designed to stimulate thought about scenarios to provoke "what-if" analysis. The scenario review is also designed to help increase the understanding of the requirements and to reduce the number of scenario-related discrepancies in requirements and design/code. The review includes scenarios from the following perspectives:

- *User*—Overview of impacts on operational scenarios and user interface
- *Performance*—Overview of intended vehicle-performance impacts and algorithmic accuracy requirements
- *Software/System Integration*—New interfaces and interactions
- *Off-nominal*—System response to failures and how it might be used for secondary purposes
- *Known discrepancies and maintenance traps*—Explanations of known maintenance traps associated with software areas being updated
- *A list of applicable user notes*—Insight into potential traps and possibly a chance to get rid of some nuisance user notes

The case study team identified a gap of a deficient requirements-generation process/procedure. While the evaluation, inspection, approval, and change-management aspects of requirements are covered in depth, there are limited guidelines for the actual writing of the requirements. This area has an existing process improvement action plan that is focusing on the requirements-writing guidelines and deployment of a corresponding course.

All requirements must go through formal requirements inspection. To ensure their commitment to the requirements, project participants attend the requirements inspections. Requirements inspections identify issues and errors with the documented requirements. After sections of the requirements are formally inspected and issues resolved, the requirements sections are submitted to control boards for approval.

In summary, projects' processes are in place to elicit customer requirements, translate those requirements into product requirements, obtain commitments to requirements, analyze and verify requirements, and maintain and control those requirements.

Technical Solution

Operational concepts, alternative solutions, and architectures are developed, and make/buy/reuse decisions are performed in the early phases of a program and typically require minimal adjustment during maintenance.

The PASS project has been in existence for more than 20 years and operates in a predominantly maintenance mode. The project performs design maintenance activities for each proposed software change. However, specific goals 1 and 2 of the Technical Solution process area are geared toward new projects in their early stages and do not seem well suited to the PASS long-term maintenance project.

For the CAU project, the decision regarding acquiring two parts of the software through a subcontract agreement was the only item described in the Technical Solution process area that was applicable at the time of the case study. Many of the practices called for by the Technical Solution process area will be more beneficial to the CAU project during its design phase.

For make/buy decisions, white papers are developed and reviewed to scope the software development effort. A make/buy decision panel is formed in accordance with the USA make/buy process.

One noted deficiency of the design process was that documented rationale was weak (i.e., not comprehensive or consistently applied) for design decisions. However, projects develop designs, code, and end-use documentation using defined standards, guidelines, and processes.

Product Integration

Detailed procedures are used for integrating software components as part of the project's build process. The build function is a highly tooled process that is controlled by the overall configuration management system and is managed through project schedules by the project Baseline Control Board.

The planning performed for each software release includes an integration strategy that specifies the software functions to be implemented for each build, the ordering, and the component dependencies. Tools support the detailed interface documentation.

The development load modules and the build release testing ensure the integrity of the initially compiled units. The detailed product specifications and delivery procedures support the packaging and delivery of the final software assembly.

Verification and Validation

The objective of software system verification is to perform an independent test, analysis, and evaluation of the software to ensure full conformity to specification and satisfaction of operational needs. Within the PASS verification/validation process, four levels of testing are performed: subsystem testing

(Level 3), detailed/functional testing (Level 6), performance testing (Level 7), and reconfiguration testing (Level 8). USA uses the term *verification* for all four levels of testing; however, Level 7 and Level 8 verification activities represent validation as that term is used in the Validation process area. The testing cycle for the PASS project is illustrated in Figure 7.2.

Detailed/functional testing verifies that the software system meets all specified requirements. The testing is organized by functional area along the lines of the software requirements. In addition to dynamic testing, complementary static analyses may be performed. Examples of static analyses are multipass analysis and standards compliance audits. Level 6 verification focuses on verifying the letter of the requirements.

For each software system, verification plans define the planned testing, scenarios, and test environments. Detailed plans are established and maintained for the verification and validation of selected work products. For Level 6 Verification, the verification test procedures describe each detailed functional test to be performed. They are based on the requirements but also consider software design decisions and test facility capabilities. Each verification test procedure is reviewed prior to final testing.

Performance testing, on the other hand, is directed at how the software system as a whole performs in nominal, off-nominal, and stressed situations. Performance testing is organized primarily by flight phases and attempts to duplicate as closely as possible actual trajectory and environmental conditions. Level 7 testing concentrates on demonstrating that the software produces the functional intent of the requirements and meets the desired performance constraints. Level 7 tests are performed by simulating user operational scenarios.

For Level 7, Verification pretesting, analysis, and planning activities culminate with the documentation of the verification approach in the performance test plan. The performance test plan includes overall testing objectives and the set of individual performance verification test specifications. The performance test plan defines test requirements based on requirements and interface control documents. It provides a functional, narrative description of testing to be conducted. Included in the performance test plan are (a) identification of requirements against which each computer program end item will be tested, (b) methods employed in testing the requirements, and (c) selected success criteria.

Level 8 testing consists of a standard set of verification test cases that are executed against the software after it has been reconfigured to support the specific mission objectives. This testing is performed according to predefined schedule templates for each flight.

Additional validation is performed after the software release. During this testing phase for the PASS project, the software is integrated as an element of

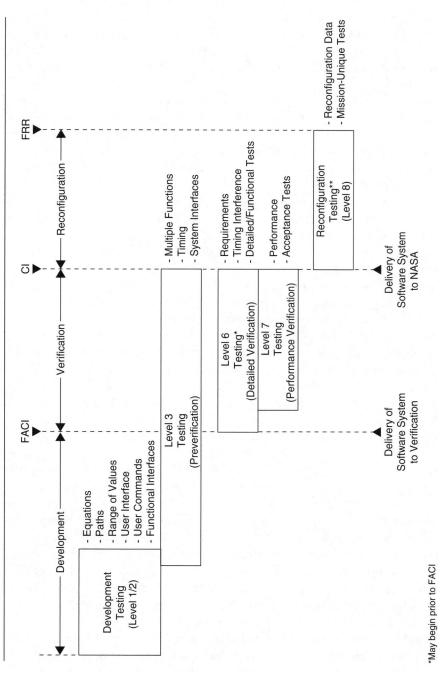

FIGURE 7.2
PASS Software Testing

*May begin prior to FACI
**May involve Level 6 and 7 testing for post-CI CR/DR implementations

121

the overall avionics system. Testing and integration are performed in the Shuttle Avionics Integration Laboratory. This laboratory contains avionics hardware and software systems as well as environmental and vehicle models, forming a closed-loop system. The purpose of this validation testing is to ensure that all subsystems interface correctly and that the system functions properly when integrated.

Quality control of testing is a key element of the verification process. Measures taken to ensure quality include the use of checklists, audits, and test coverage analysis of both requirements and code. Furthermore, reported software anomalies not found by verification testing are analyzed and reviewed with management in an effort to identify and correct deficiencies of the verification process.

In addition to the testing, rigorous formal inspections are performed for most project work products. Formal inspections are conducted on identified work products (e.g., requirements, design, code, development test scenarios) and issues are identified that must be addressed before the inspection can be closed.

Preparation for inspections includes developing a schedule for conducting reviews (inspection prescheduling) and defining required lead time for preparation. Inspection moderators verify adequate preparation of inspectors at the start of each inspection. Criteria are defined and followed for entry and exit requirements, re-review thresholds, issue closure, required participants, and responsibilities of each role.

The inspection technique has proved to be the bread and butter of processes; as the associate program manager likes to say, "PASS depends heavily on this technique throughout the project life cycle for defect identification." The CAU project has similarly planned to adopt formal inspections for its work products and is currently applying them to requirements products. Because of the importance placed on this verification method, the project requires every participant to take a mandatory computer-based training course on the inspection process.

For each software system, formal verification begins with the completion of software development marked by the First Article Configuration Inspection milestone. Tests are executed and analyzed in accordance with the approved performance test plan, verification test procedure, and project standards and procedures. In addition, desk analysis of noncode change items, including documentation-only items, tool inputs, and review of program notes, is performed in accordance with procedures.

Software errors identified by testing are analyzed, formally documented as discrepancy reports, and tracked in the configuration management system. Regression testing is scheduled, as required, to reverify software areas affected by program correction.

Results of verification testing are reflected in verification test reports. All test results are reviewed and approved prior to the software delivery milestone at configuration inspection.

The appropriate technical community and NASA participate in the development of the test plans and the review of the test results.

Many tools, such as the simulator/models, test analysis and reporting tools, and test status and tracking tools, are used to support the verification processes.

As with the other engineering process areas, the outputs of the processes (work products) are declared as quality records, placed under configuration management, and handled according to detailed NASA records retention requirements.

Since the USA policy was formulated using the SW-CMM as its process-improvement model, the policy is currently deficient in fully addressing the engineering process areas. Also, the corresponding company assets, such as the standard software process, do not yet fully address these areas. For example, there is no company-level, documented, standard integration process; this will be one of the areas to address.

Project Management Process Areas

Project Planning

The CAU project was strategically populated with experienced personnel from the PASS project to allow rapid transfer of experience in the Project Planning process area. This permitted the champions who were placed into CAU to contribute their intense process culture, experience base, and history to this start-up project.

Projects develop software estimates based on experience with similar functions. Initial estimates are developed from the top down with historical costing factors applied. A bottom-up costing activity is then used for tuning. For the CAU project, following the generation of estimates, three independent assessments are used for a sanity check using industry tools. Independent estimates are generated by the customer, consultants, and an independent subcontractor.

The basic inputs to the estimates are source lines of code, projected error rates, and level of testing required. A basis of estimate is developed for each estimate. The basis for the estimate includes product size (e.g., lines of code, number of test cases) and the computations using that data to generate an estimate.

Project budgets are based on the estimates. These are developed against an Integrated Master Schedule, which takes into account task size, complexity, and dependencies.

Assessment of the growth in the work scope based on requirements creep is conducted on a schedule that has been accepted by the customer. Source lines of code estimates are used to determine the impact of requirements creep. This data is used to renegotiate the scope of the work. Requirements growth beyond a negotiated threshold will result in a customer-directed scrub of the requirements.

The staffing plan is developed based on the agreed-on product content, schedule, and budget. Equipment and system resources to support all project activities are estimated and funding is allocated. Actual plans for obtaining this equipment are documented in the Information Technology Plan. Task charge numbers are opened for each activity, decomposed from the work breakdown structure, with funding loaded using the earned-value system. Allocation of facilities for housing the staff and performing testing and integration are included in the plan. Funding is allocated for these facilities and they are now in place.

Three levels of schedule plans are covered by the project Integrated Management Schedule. Plans are also in place for verification and validation, integration, facilities, and software via the Software Development Management Plan (SDMP). The SDMP covers planning for the processes to be used in developing the software. Subordinate plans are a direct fallout of the plans documented in the Project Management Plan and SDMP. Subordinate plans are developed to be consistent with those upper-level documents.

Data management plans include the use of the project's intranet Web page—the Integrated Collaborative Environment, which includes such project data as presentations, trade studies, product team agendas and minutes, and requirements documents.

A training plan is developed that identifies the skills required by the project team. For the CAU project, skills are required in three areas: the legacy system that the project interfaces with, the commercial off-the-shelf (COTS) real-time operating system, and the language and tools to be used.

Relevant stakeholders participate in planning through the various product teams, as defined in the Project Management Plan. Participation of relevant stakeholders is also defined in the process documents for each phase of the development cycle (e.g., requirements generation and evaluation, development process, and detailed test process). Relevant stakeholders participate through attendance at both formal and informal reviews and inspections.

Project Monitoring and Control

Performance progress is monitored through two specific tools. First, the earned-value system provides timely insight into the completion of project milestones. Milestones are of sufficient detail to allow close review of project progress.

Following customer acceptance, the project's budget is loaded into an earned-value schedule that is used to manage the execution of the project. Parameters developed during planning (specifically, effort to accomplish specific deliverables and milestones) are entered and are tracked closely for variances. Training is provided in the use of the earned-value system with guidance on the rules for resource-loaded schedules.

The program-level schedules include milestones at which project accomplishments are to be reviewed. For example, reviews occur at the System Design Review, the System Requirements Review, the Preliminary Design Review, and the Critical Design Review, among others.

Until the project begins to develop code, actual measures cannot be generated against the planning size parameters. Instead, size is reestimated based on iterative deliveries of requirements from the customer to determine the delta to original estimates so that scope can be renegotiated with the customer.

The second tool consists of a set of performance metrics that have been established to provide project management with more information to assess progress and address problem areas. Actual staffing is tracked against the staffing plan. Staffing and training are guided by the training plan to ensure that the necessary skills are available to the project. The Information Technology Plan is executed and closely tracked for variances.

Deliverable data is specifically identified in the decision packages. These documents are assigned control numbers and are maintained in a project library tracked by project librarians. For the CAU project, this library is managed at the program level, not the software project level.

The various product teams carry out monitoring of project commitments. Product team leads are responsible for ensuring that stakeholder attendance and participation is appropriate at each product team meeting.

Issues that require special corrective action normally result in development of unique plans with special schedules for issue resolution. Issues are identified, responsibility for the issue is assigned, and a schedule for resolution is developed. Impacts to project schedules are communicated to the appropriate product team or to the project manager so that appropriate action can be taken. For the CAU project, this is now being done for issues concerning the System Software, Software Requirements Specification.

Integrated Project Management

CAU project processes are patterned after the PASS processes and are tailored to meet the specific requirements of the project. (The PASS processes and historical data have influenced the USA organizational process and database that is being developed. See the section on Organizational Process Definition, pages 131–132.) The project processes and the integration of these processes are described in the Project Management Plan. The Software Development Management Plan further defines the software processes and how they are integrated. The integration of these processes is implemented through the Integrated Management Plan. An important aspect of the plans is the use of integrated product teams to ensure that the integration of project activities includes all relevant stakeholders.

Historical data from the PASS project is used in project estimating and planning. The estimates developed from this data are tested against industry models.

Also, the project uses the lessons learned by other projects, particularly PASS. As the project itself progresses, it will, in turn, contribute lessons learned to other projects that might benefit from its experiences.

Dependencies are documented in the Integrated Master Schedule. Responsibility to manage and track these dependencies is accomplished by the individual product teams. The Development Product Team addresses significant project dependency issues. Coordination issues are addressed through the individual product teams, with significant issues communicated to the Development Product Team. The Development Product Team calls meetings with relevant stakeholders to coordinate resolution of issues.

Integrated product teams are the focal point for managing project activities. A series of product teams (e.g., Flight Software Product Team, Hardware Product Team, Operations Product Team, and Project Product Team) are used to involve relevant stakeholders in planning and in technical decision making. All the product teams regularly monitor progress with overall status reviewed at the product team level. Product teams meet on a weekly basis to perform integrated planning/decision making.

Supplier Agreement Management

The CAU project forms a source selection team that will use criteria in accordance with the source selection process. The supplier is required to describe its management approach, technical approach, past performance on similar programs, and pricing. Detailed evaluation criteria are applied to the bids received. A scale is used to evaluate each criterion. The contract is awarded to the supplier with the highest score. Risks are identified and mitigation plans established for the contracting and performance phases. The selection process, evaluation criteria, rationale for candidate selection, and risk information are reviewed at multiple management levels.

The selected subcontractor provides a rough order of magnitude cost based on USA's initial estimate. The subcontractor revises the estimate by applying an appropriate estimation method (e.g., IBM's Function Point Analysis) to the revised Software Requirements Specification. USA performs a parallel effort.

The subcontractor typically participates in the project's requirements processes to obtain an understanding of and make a commitment to the software requirements. The subcontractor-developed software design, code, test plans, and results will be inspected in accordance with USA's practices. The subcontractor will support (not perform) USA's integration, and detailed verification testing efforts. For the CAU project, formal acceptance testing of the subcontractor-developed software will be done at least one year prior to the first flight with the software installed. The subcontractor will remain in a supporting role through the completion of the first shuttle flight with the software. USA will then assume control of the software.

The project works with USA's Contracting Office and Purchasing. They follow the processes documented in the company policies, functional procedures, and company acquisition procedures to establish supplier agreements and procure well-defined products.

USA employees receive computer-based training to learn the concepts and process for effective subcontract management. This includes compliance with government regulations, acquisition strategies, source selection, and management of subcontractors' performance.

Because there is no specific USA commercial off-the-shelf policy, this is handled as a make/buy decision. Nonstandard COTS products incorporated as a significant part of the developed software are evaluated against a documented set of criteria in a trade study. A decision package agreement reviewed by NASA lists the COTS products to be acquired. An internal Information Technology Plan specifies the timing of the COTS acquisitions.

Risk Management

Risk management is an integral part of USA program management. USA emphasizes that risk is goal-based. If you have a goal, you have the potential to miss that goal. USA integrates risk management into its day-to-day decision making by employing a collective set of activities for identifying, assessing, handling, monitoring, and communicating risk information (Figure 7.3).

Proactive risk management is designed to uncover potential issues before they can disrupt normal operations. USA targets two areas for proactive risk management:

- Change as a major source for introducing new risks into a system or process —a risk assessment will be performed whenever changes to the baseline are proposed.
- Communication and monthly reviews of significant risks as proactive measures—the presentation of risk information from one program element may help identify collateral risks in other areas.

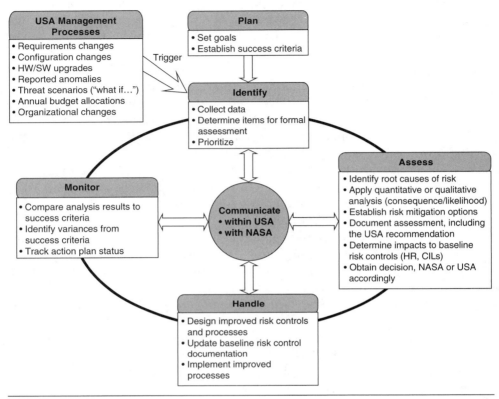

FIGURE 7.3
USA Risk Management Process

The USA Risk Assessment Scorecard (Figure 7.4) is the primary tool for prioritizing risks against goals. It contains predefined descriptions for consequence and likelihood on an increasing scale from 1 to 5. The consequence descriptions are grouped in risk measures that represent risks to contract goals so that risks from different functional program elements can be expressed in the same "scorecard" language. The likelihood descriptions are scaled according to the expectation of occurrence for the undesirable event.

The risk score is computed by multiplying highest consequence by the likelihood. Risks are ranked to make the best use of resources and to prioritize the handling actions. The risk matrix has three regions: low (green) or scores 1–6, medium (yellow) or scores 7–14, and high (red) or scores 15–25. Colors correspond to the USA stoplight status reporting method.

A green risk is one of either relatively low likelihood or low consequence or both, and does not normally require action. A yellow risk can occur when a risk has a high consequence, but a low likelihood; or a high likelihood, but

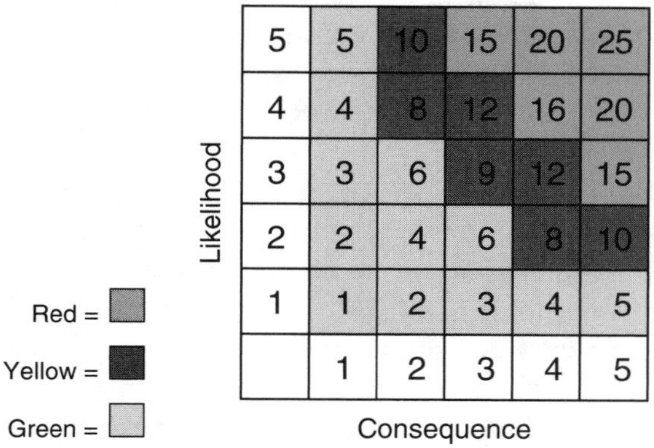

Likelihood					
5	5	10	15	20	25
4	4	8	12	16	20
3	3	6	9	12	15
2	2	4	6	8	10
1	1	2	3	4	5
	1	2	3	4	5

Red = ▢
Yellow = ▦
Green = ▢

Consequence

FIGURE 7.4
USA Risk Assessment Scorecard

a low consequence; or a medium score on both. For yellow risks, action and notification to appropriate management is recommended. A red risk is one that is of both high likelihood and undesirable consequence. Red risks require action and notification.

When a risk assessment is performed, multiple options for handling the risk are usually presented. Actions can fall into three categories: accept, mitigate, or prevent.

Risks are "accepted" when the action is totally outside of USA's control or the risk is low priority. Management is aware that the risk condition exists, but no further action will be taken. Risks are "mitigated" when control measures have been put in place to reduce the consequence if the event were to occur. Risks are "prevented" when some form of action has been taken to reduce the likelihood of an undesirable event.

A well-defined USA company risk management process is in place to identify, assess, and address program risks. It includes mechanisms to ensure communication of the risk to appropriate management and objective criteria defining when actions are required. Significant risks on the project are reviewed with top USA management and also reviewed with the NASA customer at regularly scheduled integrated product team meetings.

Quantitative Project Management

The primary quality objective set for process performance is the product error rate threshold (errors/KSLOC) defined in the contract. NASA and USA set the project process-performance objectives jointly through contract negotiations. The current threshold was set based on historical process performance. The processes examined for process performance data include the development,

development test, design/code inspection, and verification test processes. Data from these processes are used to determine process performance.

Emphasis is placed on inspection results/performance and inserted errors or defect density. The design/code inspection process is statistically analyzed using statistical process control techniques to determine how current process performance compares to historical performance and to identify any special causes of variation (signals) in the current execution of the process. When special causes of variations are noted, they are investigated to determine if action is required.

The measurements are monitored throughout product development to determine if the actual results support achievement of the established objectives. Management is involved in reviewing the process performance through internal quality review meetings. The process owners are involved, as needed, to make changes to the process based on feedback from the statistical process control analysis (e.g., data collection changes, refresher training).

For most USA software projects, there are no defined subprocesses that are statistically managed and monitored for process capability. The USA standard software process has not yet been institutionalized in a way that it can collect historical process stability and capability data. Additionally, no USA measurement repository, in which to store such data, has been established yet.

Process Management Process Areas

Many of the Process Management Process Area practices apply to organization-level, not project-level, activities. The organization represents the USA Company. Because two software projects were the primary focus of the CMMI case study, the way to address the organizational practices posed a problem. To solve this dilemma, the team looked at the organizational practices for the USA software organization (i.e., the software process across USA).

Organizational Process Focus and Organizational Process Definition

The USA software policy establishes the means for coordinating software process development and improvement activities across projects. These activities include development and maintenance of the USA standard software process, collection and review of information related to the use of the USA standard software process, assessment of strengths and weaknesses of the software process against a process standard, and planned and coordinated development and improvement activities for the software process across USA.

The USA standard software process defines the minimum requirements for satisfying the USA software policy. Standard processes for nonsoftware areas (e.g., Engineering, Program Management) are being developed. The USA Software Process Asset Library is in its early stages with a small number of process assets in existence. A more robust and populated process asset library is planned. The existing USA online documentation systems also provide mechanisms for process asset storage and retrieval.

To implement improvement for the USA software process, the USA process owner outlined a plan to achieve the improvement. As part of this plan's development and implementation, each USA program element assessed its software development processes against the USA standard software process, identifying strengths, weaknesses, and process gaps that formed the basis of the program elements' action plans for attaining compliance with requirements of the USA standard software process.

Each USA process owner organized an infrastructure that supports the implementation of her or his improvement plan. The USA software process owner established a common process improvement network to effect major improvements in software product quality in the most cost-effective manner. Figure 7.5 displays the functional organization and roles involved in the improvement effort.

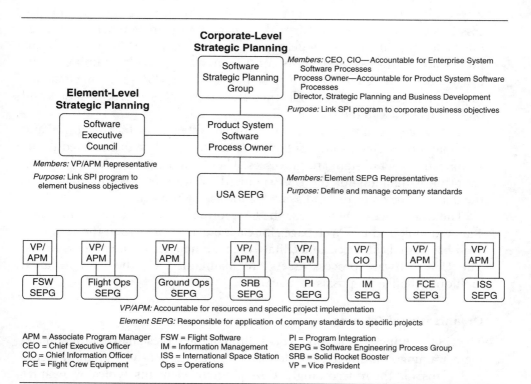

FIGURE 7.5
Software Process Improvement Infrastructure

The USA SEPG is responsible for developing and deploying the USA software process assets. The management oversight committees include the Software Strategic Planning Group and Software Executive Council (SEC). The Software Strategic Planning Group is responsible for linking the software process improvement program to corporate business objectives. The Software Strategic Planning Group is composed of the Chief Executive Officer, Chief Information Officer, Director of Strategic Business Planning and Development, and the USA Software Process Owner. The SEC is responsible for linking the software process improvement program to the program elements' business objectives. The SEC is composed of executive representatives from each USA program element.

The USA SEPG coordinates the software process improvement activities through its representatives to company element SEPGs and communicates changes through this infrastructure. The USA SEPG meets with groups from each program element, as needed, to deploy planned improvements. In addition, the USA Software Process Owners meet with peer executive managers of business areas to communicate strategic direction.

The USA SEPG used lessons learned from its initial development and review cycle of the USA software process assets to improve its subsequent process asset releases (e.g., required documentation of recommended change information, refined process definition standards). The SEPG also controls the release of process assets to its constituency and provides training on the use of assets through its SEPG representatives to the USA program elements. Representatives derive lessons learned from the deployed process assets and provide feedback to the USA SEPG.

The existing company-wide standardized systems in which technical and financial measurements are contained do not yet provide data related to the organization's set of standard processes. There is a plan to deploy a common set of measurements for the USA standard software process. At such time, the data will be collected and available for use by projects.

The USA Process Owners use the USA intranet as a means of establishing standard look-and-feel Web pages for each business process in the company. Web-based tools are used to facilitate the maintenance of the process assets. The USA software process assets are maintained via the USA intranet, including change proposals to assets.

Organizational Training

The USA training organization works through the representative program element training coordinators to identify the organization-wide training needs and plans for them accordingly. USA program elements typically organize their unique training needs specific to their application domains; however, the USA-wide training organization also coordinates the program element training in some instances. A training process owner is assigned for USA at the corporate level with corresponding staff in the training department.

USA is developing career tracks for roles within the company processes to identify key required skills that represent strategic needs of the company. The career tracks are intended to define requirements for progression along identified career paths in the USA disciplines. In addition, there is an extensive leadership development program that is available for USA employees across the company.

Some mandatory computer-based training (CBT) courses include embedded tests to determine the effectiveness of the individual training. In addition, some certification programs that require completion of staged requirements (e.g., through testing) are used in conjunction with USA training to assess effectiveness. Most USA training courses use a standard satisfaction survey to evaluate individual classes. Vendor-provided training for purchased courseware is evaluated to determine if the supplier should be used for future course offerings.

Records of completed employee training are maintained in the company's training records management system. There are limited records of staff that have been waived from specific training.

The USA intranet and online course registration processes are in place to facilitate the deployment of training. Numerous CBT courses are available as well as a large catalog of courses. The training group provides the necessary support to administer the training program. CBT development software and experts are available to prepare internally developed online courses. The training organization is equipped to help with instructional design and course content design/development. The training academy facility includes allocated rooms with permanently housed workstations and equipment to conduct regular classes.

Organizational Process Performance

Because the USA standard software process is in early stages of deployment, the activities of the Organizational Process Performance process area are premature and therefore no observations were recorded.

Organizational Innovation and Deployment

As part of their responsibility, the corporate process owners, continuous improvement team, and associate program managers identify innovative process and technology improvements. There are some documented plans for deploying process and technology improvements for USA processes. The USA Continuous Improvement Plan identifies activities that will result in measurable change, including quality and process performance.

The USA intranet (and planned process asset library to be used by all USA process owners) will provide a base on which to build changes; however, there are limited tools in place to model changes to processes or technologies in support of innovative and technological advancements.

Support Process Areas

Configuration Management

The items that require configuration management have been identified. The items currently under configuration management for the CAU project include the System Specification Document, numerous software requirements specifications, and interface requirements definition documents. Test facilities, including labs, will have configuration management policies. Test cases will also be under configuration management.

The Documentum™ tool is used for managing most of the documentation associated with the project. This tool is also used across USA for management of many documents. The USA standard document templates contain change notices in the front of documents.

The planning activity to support the software system builds is under way. The project is currently documenting the procedures to be followed with the open-standard concurrent versions system. There will be eight incremental system builds with the final system being used for formal testing.

Change instruments will be used to investigate and track changes to the configuration items. The first time items are delivered, the change request is linked to the initial submittal. Documentum, the concurrent versions system, and the build system will all provide version control and provide for the recovery of each version. The source code will contain identifiers that indicate when a specific line was modified.

The Version Description Document will contain the documented base release configuration. Software Quality Assurance will perform configuration audits.

Process and Product Quality Assurance

Quality engineers from Safety Quality and Mission Assurance independently audit the development of software requirements and will continue to audit the software products. It is USA policy to deliver Human Space Flight products and services safely, on time, and error-free. The USA Safety Quality and Mission Assurance organization provides independent oversight to ensure the associated technical processes are implemented in accordance with this policy. Routine performance data, in the form of Safety Quality and Mission Assurance integrated metrics, will be collected and analyzed to measure the effectiveness of these processes.

The programmers, testers, and requirements analysts audit the technical quality of the flight software products (e.g., software requirement specifications, design, code, test results) by participating in inspections during each phase of the development process. All issues from inspections and testing are recorded. Issues are written and tracked until closure. Currently, requirements inspection issues are recorded and maintained. This practice will be carried forward to design, code, and test as these project phases are reached.

Measurement and Analysis

Within the Flight Software Program Element, the associate program manager expects support to the USA Vision Support Plan Program as well as expects measurements to be rolled out at the lowest levels of the process. The associate program manager directs the processes to collect and present their measurements annually at the internal quality review meeting.

Some objectives for measurement are stated in the project documentation (e.g., use to track the quality and timeliness of products, focus analysis to identify trends that ensure steady progress against goals or suggest areas of concern, provide a basis of communication within the USA Flight software program element concerning the evaluation of technical issues and accomplishments, analyze schedule adherence, identify areas where improvements or corrections are required).

The metrics-related documents provide high-level information that indicates the sources of metrics data and the collection approach. The process documents define the base measure collection.

The list of derived measures is contained in the Metrics Product Development Plan, which USA and NASA have approved. Measure definitions are contained in the quarterly quality report, which is a contract deliverable. The PASS measurement reports include some analysis summary conclusions. Some of the reports are previewed prior to broader dissemination. There is some documentation that represents administrative procedures for analyzing the measurement data and communicating the results.

The base measurement data is collected from multiple sources (e.g., development environment database, configuration management database, SLOC reports) and derived measures are computed based on established Excel file links/computations. Derived measurements are kept in Excel/Word/PowerPoint files stored on the local area network.

Data integrity, accuracy, completeness, and currency checks are typically performed for each Flight Software build and quarterly when discrepancy report data is reconciled during generation of the quarterly quality report. Some data integrity checks are built in to the "process enactment" system at the source of the data recording. Discrepancies noted in collected base measures are reported to the appropriate data source (e.g., control board, process owner).

The appropriate measurement data analysis methods and tools have been established for the project data (e.g., error predictions, reliability models, trend analysis). The analysis results (reports) are stored on the local area network or the USA intranet for contract deliverables. A long-standing process of not using measurement data inappropriately for performance evaluations has been established. The project culture supports the open collection and reporting of measurements across the board.

Measurement reports (e.g., monthly key project metrics, quarterly quality reports, milestone error predictions) are distributed to managers and key staff who have a vested interest in the report's content.

Measurement collection, analysis, and use to support managerial decision making are ingrained in all development processes. Measurement activities are also a means for identifying areas for process improvement.

Decision Analysis and Resolution

The formal evaluation process has been applied for two key aspects of the project: subcontractor source selection and trade studies. The subcontractor source selection is described in the Supplier Agreement Management PA.

Decisions were made early in the project life cycle to use prototyping as USA and NASA met to discuss the best way to determine possible software solutions. Where choices were to be made between commercial products (or build vs. buy decisions), company and customer expectations dictated the use of trade studies.

Trade studies were selected as the method of choice for three different areas where decisions were needed. These areas were (1) operating system selection, (2) implementation language selection, and (3) display tool selection. Prototyping was also used to evaluate implementation techniques.

A trade study methodology was documented, evaluation criteria were defined and weighted, and alternative solutions were identified and documented, along with the trade study results in the reports.

Risk Management is another area where a formal evaluation process is used. Medium- and high-risk areas are also subject to formal evaluation as identified by the company risk mitigation policy.

The USA decision package process is another form of structured decision making that is used across the company. USA requirements dictate when a decision package is needed. Developing a decision package requires identification and consideration of alternative solutions. The decision package documents the results of the evaluation and recommendation of a specific solution.

Causal Analysis and Resolution

Discrepancy reports are subject to causal analysis. Additional problems selected for causal analysis are based on the significance decided by management or control boards. Analysts record the root cause of the problem and any proposed solutions in the discrepancy report analysis to prevent recurrence of the problem. Additional analysts with knowledge in the same technical area review the root cause analysis information. These reviewers also have input on why the problem was missed and may suggest ways to prevent missing the problem in the future.

For identified deficiencies in the process, the process teams determine which of the proposed actions will be implemented. Depending on the seriousness of the problem, they may be directed to implement some action proposals by customer, management, Discrepancy Report Board, or other control boards.

Discrepancy report causal analysis information is recorded and maintained on the discrepancy report quality analysis form. However, sometimes detailed supplemental presentations contain causal analysis data. This information is not controlled in the same manner as the discrepancy report analyses. It is usually maintained but not easily available. Causal analysis data from other activities is similarly maintained but is not readily available.

There is no systematic method in place to evaluate the effect of (individual) changes on process performance.

USA formed a company-wide team to support corporate standardization of root cause analysis. The team defined a standard process and selected a corresponding tool (REASON®) to support the tracking of root causes across the company for defined incidents.

Lessons Learned

Several points could have been addressed better during the CMMI case study:

1. As a result of interviewing the newer (software) project, the team discovered how much more meaningful some of the PAs (e.g., Requirements Development, Project Planning, Project Monitoring and Control, Integrated Project Management, and Risk Management) would have been had they been evaluated at the program element level, which joins the software and systems engineering efforts.

2. The use of defined criteria worked well for selecting the PAs that would be examined for each project. This allowed sampling of PAs to get a sense of the model without performing a comprehensive or exhaustive formal assessment.
   However, in retrospect, the selection of PAs fell short in a few places.
   - Process and Product Quality Assurance
   - Integrated Project Management for IPPD
   - Integrated Teaming
   - Organizational Environment for Integration

3. The newer project (CAU) planned to review Process and Product Quality Assurance but could not because attempts to fill the Software Quality Assurance role had not been successful at that time.

4. The team decided early on to use the systems engineering/software version of CMMI without the three IPPD-related PAs. It was initially understood that the IPPD PAs and practices would not be applicable to USA projects based on preliminary feedback. Later interviews with the newer project uncovered that much of the structure in place relies on the use of product development teams, and that a network of product development teams exists. The IPPD practices would have been applicable even though the project did not relate to the use of the IPPD term. The team should have probed a little deeper here during planning to more fully understand the applicability of the IPPD practices.

5. The case study mini-teams used any techniques they were comfortable using to elicit information from projects for writing observations. Some of the mini-teams elected to use the SEI questionnaires to solicit data and information on current project practices from participants. In some cases, the team amplified the questions with more explanatory text, making for long surveys. A lengthy survey and busy project participants did not make a good combination; only one respondent chose to complete the instrument. There was minimal return on investment for the effort expended to augment the existing instrument.

The informal techniques of conducting meetings, interviews, and distributing e-mail worked well. This placed the burden on the team member and not the project to collect, format, and report results rather than to depend on the project member to record all of the information on an instrument.

Interpretation Issues

In general, the team could apply CMMI practices with a comfortable understanding of the intent. The team encountered a few interpretation issues in trying to understand and apply the model. A few times the information contained in the practices caused a bit of confusion or struggle in interpretation. Some of the examples involved the application of generic practices to certain PAs.

One example of an interpretation issue was the application of generic practice (GP) 2.2 in some of the PAs. GP 2.2 states "Establish and maintain the requirements and objectives, and plan for performing the process." The model elaborates the meaning of GP 2.2 with, "In some CMMI PAs, there are specific practices that also talk about developing strategies or plans. This generic practice addresses overall planning for the entire PA, whereas the specific practices address a topic for more detailed or focused planning."

In applying GP 2.2 to the Risk Management PA, it was difficult to distinguish the overall plan for risk management and the strategy for risk management. Elaboration of the PA indicates that the risk management strategy addresses risk sources, categories, parameters, and management control and reporting requirements; whereas the plan for risk management addresses high-level planning for all the risk management activities.

In the Risk Management PA, GP 2.1 discusses documenting policy for the risk management process, specific practice 1.3 discusses documenting risk strategy (typically) in a project risk management plan and specific practice 3.1 discusses documenting risk mitigation plans for (important) risks.

In a documentation hierarchy, it would be expected that project risk documentation would flow in an increasing level of detail from a risk management policy to a risk management strategy (plan) to risk management mitigation plan(s).

It was not clear where the GP 2.2 documentation of requirements, objectives, and plans for risk management would fall in these three document layers. Would it be a higher level than policy, or is policy equivalent to a requirement and objective? Would it fall below policy and above strategy?

USA does not believe in performing activities or creating artifacts for the sake of CMMI satisfaction, but rather in applying the practices in a sensible manner that suits the business. If the CMMI practice is a reasonable practice that would help the business and support achievement of goals, then the practice would be adopted. In this example, the USA documentation exists for the policy, strategy, and risk mitigation plans. However, it was unclear if GP 2.2 would require something more or different.

Note: In CMMI v1.1, additional informative material has been added to clarify, where needed, how the plans described in GP 2.2 relate to the plans described in the specific practices. The Risk Management PA is one example of where this confusion has been addressed.

In addition to GP 2.2, the application of GP 2.8 was awkward at times for some of the PAs. Generic practice 2.8 states "Monitor and control the process against the plan and take appropriate corrective action." In applying GP 2.8 to the Project Monitoring and Control PA, it was difficult to determine what type of monitoring and controlling would be performed for the monitoring and controlling process. This seemed similar to some of the "unnatural" or forced measurement of processes that are not naturally conducive to meaningful measurement, just as some of the "contrived" measurements were awkward in the SW-CMM for measuring the status of activities that may not normally be measured or useful.

Next Steps

Now that USA has experienced the flavor of CMMI, the company is better educated and equipped to move forward with broader deployment when the decision is made to transition from the CMM to CMMI at USA. The case study results include a number of identified weaknesses in the projects examined.

The first next step is to communicate the results. The team will provide the projects with more detailed feedback on the results of the case study, including the identified weaknesses. The two projects will then be able to prepare action plans and to address the significant weaknesses.

The case study team will also more broadly communicate the case study results within USA beyond just the two projects. A starting point will be to review the results with the USA SEPG. In this forum, the group can discuss some of the known organizational weaknesses that apply to the USA software process as well as the activities that should be undertaken at the company level for organizational practices in the future. For example, the case study identified areas in the corporate software policy that need to be upgraded to address the "new" PAs in CMMI.

The second next step is to expand the use of CMMI. Adoption of CMMI will require that a strategy be developed for corporate-wide adoption and will require coordination of USA process owners regarding how CMMI will apply to their separate processes and how it will apply to overlapping or common USA processes.

PART TWO

The Process Areas

CAUSAL ANALYSIS AND RESOLUTION
A Support Process Area at Maturity Level 5

Purpose

The purpose of Causal Analysis and Resolution (CAR) is to identify causes of defects and other problems and take action to prevent them from occurring in the future.

Introductory Notes

The Causal Analysis and Resolution process area involves the following:

- Identifying and analyzing causes of defects and other problems
- Taking specific actions to remove the causes and prevent the occurrence of those types of defects and problems in the future

Causal analysis and resolution improves quality and productivity by preventing the introduction of defects into a product. Reliance on detecting defects after they have been introduced is not cost effective. It is more effective to prevent defects from being introduced by integrating causal analysis and resolution activities into each phase of the project.

Since defects and problems may have been previously encountered on other projects or in earlier phases or tasks of the current project, causal analysis and resolution activities are a mechanism for communicating lessons learned among projects.

The types of defects and other problems encountered are analyzed to identify any trends. Based on an understanding of the defined process and how it is implemented, the root causes of the defects and the future implications of the defects are determined.

Causal analysis may also be performed on problems unrelated to defects. For example, causal analysis may be used to improve quality attributes such as cycle time. Improvement proposals, simulations, dynamic systems models, engineering analyses, new business directives, or other items may initiate such analysis.

Sometimes it may be impractical to perform causal analysis on all defects. In these cases, tradeoffs are made between estimated investments and estimated returns in quality, productivity, and cycle time, and defect targets are selected.

A measurement process should already be in place. The defined measures can be used, though in some instances new measures may be needed to analyze the effects of the process change.

Refer to the Measurement and Analysis process area for more information about establishing objectives for measurement and analysis, specifying the measures and analyses to be performed, obtaining and analyzing measures, and reporting results.

Causal Analysis and Resolution activities provide a mechanism for projects to evaluate their processes at the local level and look for improvements that can be implemented.

When improvements are judged to be effective, the information is extended to the organizational level.

Refer to the Organizational Innovation and Deployment process area for more information about improving organizational level processes through proposed improvements and action proposals.

The informative material in this process area is written with the assumption that the specific practices are applied to a quantitatively managed process. The specific practices of this process area may be applicable, but with reduced value, if the assumption is not met.

See the definitions of "stable process" and "common cause of process variation" in the glossary.

Related Process Areas

Refer to the Quantitative Project Management process area for more information about the analysis of process performance and the creation of process capability measures for selected project processes.

Refer to the Organizational Innovation and Deployment process area for more information about the selection and deployment of improvements to organizational processes and technologies.

Refer to the Measurement and Analysis process area for more information about establishing objectives for measurement and analysis, specifying the measures and analyses to be performed, obtaining and analyzing measures, and reporting results.

Practice-to-Goal Relationship Table

Continuous Representation	*Staged Representation*

SG 1 Determine Causes of Defects
    SP 1.1-1 Select Defect Data for Analysis
    SP 1.2-1 Analyze Causes

SG 2 Address Causes of Defects
    SP 2.1-1 Implement the Action
            Proposals
    SP 2.2-1 Evaluate the Effect of Changes
    SP 2.3-1 Record Data

GG 1 Achieve Specific Goals
    GP 1.1 Perform Base Practices

GG 2 Institutionalize a Managed Process
    GP 2.1 Establish an Organizational
           Policy
    GP 2.2 Plan the Process
    GP 2.3 Provide Resources
    GP 2.4 Assign Responsibility
    GP 2.5 Train People
    GP 2.6 Manage Configurations
    GP 2.7 Identify and Involve Relevant
           Stakeholders
    GP 2.8 Monitor and Control the Process
    GP 2.9 Objectively Evaluate Adherence
   GP 2.10 Review Status with Higher Level
           Management

GG 3 Institutionalize a Defined Process
    GP 3.1 Establish a Defined Process
    GP 3.2 Collect Improvement
           Information

GG 4 Institutionalize a Quantitatively
Managed Process
    GP 4.1 Establish Quantitative Objectives
           for the Process
    GP 4.2 Stabilize Subprocess
           Performance

GG 5 Institutionalize an Optimizing Process
    GP 5.1 Ensure Continuous Process
           Improvement
    GP 5.2 Correct Root Causes of Problems

SG 1 Determine Causes of Defects
    SP 1.1-1 Select Defect Data for Analysis
    SP 1.2-1 Analyze Causes

SG 2 Address Causes of Defects
    SP 2.1-1 Implement the Action
            Proposals
    SP 2.2-1 Evaluate the Effect of Changes
    SP 2.3-1 Record Data

GG 3 Institutionalize a Defined Process
    GP 2.1 Establish an Organizational
           Policy
    GP 2.2 Plan the Process
    GP 2.3 Provide Resources
    GP 2.4 Assign Responsibility
    GP 2.5 Train People
    GP 2.6 Manage Configurations
    GP 2.7 Identify and Involve Relevant
           Stakeholders
    GP 2.8 Monitor and Control the Process
    GP 2.9 Objectively Evaluate Adherence
   GP 2.10 Review Status with Higher Level
           Management

    GP 3.1 Establish a Defined Process
    GP 3.2 Collect Improvement
           Information

Specific Practices by Goal

SG 1 DETERMINE CAUSES OF DEFECTS

Root causes of defects and other problems are systematically determined.

A root cause is a source of a defect such that if it is removed, the defect is decreased or removed.

SP 1.1-1 SELECT DEFECT DATA FOR ANALYSIS

Select the defects and other problems for analysis.

Typical Work Products

1. Defect and problem data selected for further analysis

Subpractices

1. Gather relevant defect data.

> Examples of relevant defect data may include the following:
> • Project-management problem reports requiring corrective action
> • Defects reported by the customer
> • Defects reported by end user
> • Defects found in peer reviews
> • Defects found in testing
> • Process capability problems

> *Refer to the Verification process area for more information about work product verification.*
>
> *Refer to the Quantitative Project Management process area for more information about statistical management.*

2. Determine which defects and other problems will be analyzed further.

   When determining which defects to analyze further, consider the impact of the defects, the frequency of occurrence, the similarity between defects, the cost of analysis, the time and resources needed, the safety considerations, etc.

> Examples of methods for selecting defects and other problems include the following:
> • Pareto analysis
> • Histograms
> • Process capability analysis

SP 1.2-1 ANALYZE CAUSES

Perform causal analysis of selected defects and other problems and propose actions to address them.

The purpose of this analysis is to develop solutions to the identified problems by analyzing the relevant data and producing action proposals for implementation.

Typical Work Products

1. Action proposal

Subpractices

1. Conduct causal analysis with the people who are responsible for performing the task.

   Causal analysis is performed with those people who have an understanding of the selected defect or problem under study, typically in meetings. The people who have the best understanding of the selected defect are typically those responsible for performing the task.

   > Examples of when to perform causal analysis include the following:
   > - When a stable process does not meet its specified quality and process-performance objectives
   > - During the task, if and when problems warrant additional meetings
   > - When a work product exhibits an unexpected deviation from its requirements

   Refer to the Quantitative Project Management process area for more information about achieving the project's quality and process-performance objectives.

2. Analyze selected defects and other problems to determine their root causes.

   Depending on the type and number of defects, it may make sense to first group the defects before identifying their root causes.

   > Examples of methods to determine root causes include the following:
   > - Cause-and-effect (fishbone) diagrams
   > - Check sheets

3. Group the selected defects and other problems based on their root causes.

   > Examples of cause groups, or categories, include the following:
   > - Inadequate training
   > - Breakdown of communications
   > - Not accounting for all details of the task
   > - Making mistakes in manual procedures (e.g., typing)
   > - Process deficiency

4. Propose and document actions that need to be taken to prevent the future occurrence of similar defects or other problems.

> Examples of proposed actions include changes to the following:
> - The process in question
> - Training
> - Tools
> - Methods
> - Communications
> - Work products

> Examples of specific actions include the following:
> - Providing training in common problems and techniques for preventing them
> - Changing a process so that error-prone steps do not occur
> - Automating all or part of a process
> - Reordering process activities
> - Adding process steps to prevent defects, such as task kickoff meetings to review common defects and actions to prevent them

An action proposal usually documents the following:
- Originator of the action proposal
- Description of the problem
- Description of the defect cause
- Defect cause category
- Phase when the problem was introduced
- Phase when the defect was identified
- Description of the action proposal
- Action proposal category

SG 2   ADDRESS CAUSES OF DEFECTS

Root causes of defects and other problems are systematically addressed to prevent their future occurrence.

Projects operating according to a well-defined process will systematically analyze the operation where problems still occur and implement process changes to eliminate root causes of selected problems.

SP 2.1-1   IMPLEMENT THE ACTION PROPOSALS

Implement the selected action proposals that were developed in causal analysis.

Action proposals describe the tasks necessary to remove the root causes of the analyzed defects or problems and avoid their reoccurrence.

Only changes that prove to be of value should be considered for broad implementation.

Typical Work Products

1. Action proposals selected for implementation
2. Improvement proposals

Subpractices

1. Analyze the action proposals and determine their priorities.

   Criteria for prioritizing action proposals include the following:
   - Implications of not addressing the defects
   - Cost to implement process improvements to prevent the defects
   - Expected impact on quality
2. Select the action proposals that will be implemented.
3. Create action items for implementing the action proposals.

   > Examples of information provided in an action item include the following:
   > - Person responsible for implementing it
   > - Description of the areas affected by it
   > - People who are to be kept informed of its status
   > - Next date that status will be reviewed
   > - Rationale for key decisions
   > - Description of implementation actions
   > - Time and cost for identifying the defect and correcting it
   > - Estimated cost of not fixing the problem

   To implement the action proposals, the following tasks must be done:
   - Make assignments
   - Coordinate the persons doing the work
   - Review the results
   - Track the action items to closure

   Experiments may be conducted for particularly complex changes.

   > Examples of experiments include the following:
   > - Using a temporarily modified process
   > - Using a new tool

   Action items may be assigned to members of the causal analysis team, members of the project team, or other members of the organization.
4. Identify and remove similar defects that may exist in other processes and work products.
5. Identify and document improvement proposals for the organization's set of standard processes.

Refer to the Organizational Innovation and Deployment process area for more information about the selection and deployment of improvement proposals for the organization's set of standard processes.

SP 2.2-1 EVALUATE THE EFFECT OF CHANGES

Evaluate the effect of changes on process performance.

Refer to the Quantitative Project Management process area for more information about analyzing process performance and creating process capability measures for selected processes.

Once the changed process is deployed across the project, the effect of the changes must be checked to gather evidence that the process change has corrected the problem and improved performance.

Typical Work Products

1. Measures of performance and performance change

Subpractices

1. Measure the change in the performance of the project's defined process as appropriate.

    This subpractice determines whether the selected change has positively influenced the process performance and by how much.

    > An example of a change in the performance of the project's defined design process would be the change in the defect density of the design documentation, as statistically measured through peer reviews before and after the improvement has been made. On a statistical process control chart, this would be represented by a change in the mean.

2. Measure the capability of the project's defined process as appropriate.

    This subpractice determines whether the selected change has positively influenced the ability of the process to meet its quality and process-performance objectives, as determined by relevant stakeholders.

    > An example of a change in the capability of the project's defined design process would be a change in the ability of the process to stay within its process-specification boundaries. This can be statistically measured by calculating the range of the defect density of design documentation, as collected in peer reviews before and after the improvement has been made. On a statistical process control chart, this would be represented by lowered control limits.

SP 2.3-1 RECORD DATA

Record causal analysis and resolution data for use across the project and organization.

Data are recorded so that other projects and organizations can make appropriate process changes and achieve similar results.

Record the following:

- Data on defects and other problems that were analyzed
- Rationale for decisions
- Action proposals from causal analysis meetings
- Action items resulting from action proposals
- Cost of the analysis and resolution activities
- Measures of changes to the performance of the defined process resulting from resolutions

Typical Work Products

1. Causal analysis and resolution records

Generic Practices by Goal

GG 1 ACHIEVE SPECIFIC GOALS

The process supports and enables achievement of the specific goals of the process area by transforming identifiable input work products to produce identifiable output work products.

GP 1.1 PERFORM BASE PRACTICES

Perform the base practices of the causal analysis and resolution process to develop work products and provide services to achieve the specific goals of the process area.

GG 2 INSTITUTIONALIZE A MANAGED PROCESS

The process is institutionalized as a managed process.

GG 3 INSTITUTIONALIZE A DEFINED PROCESS

The process is institutionalized as a defined process.

> AUTHORS' NOTE: This generic goal's appearance here reflects its location in the staged representation.

CONTINUOUS ONLY

STAGED ONLY

Commitment to Perform

GP 2.1   ESTABLISH AN ORGANIZATIONAL POLICY

Establish and maintain an organizational policy for planning and performing the causal analysis and resolution process.

Elaboration

This policy establishes organizational expectations for identifying and systematically addressing root causes of defects and other problems.

Ability to Perform

GP 2.2   PLAN THE PROCESS

Establish and maintain the plan for performing the causal analysis and resolution process.

Elaboration

This plan for performing the causal analysis and resolution process may be included in (or referenced by) the project plan, which is described in the Project Planning process area. This plan differs from the action proposals and associated action items described in several specific practices in this process area. The plan called for in this generic practice would address the project's overall causal analysis and resolution process (perhaps tailored from a standard process maintained by the organization). In contrast, the process action proposals and associated action items address the activities needed to remove a specific root cause under study.

GP 2.3   PROVIDE RESOURCES

Provide adequate resources for performing the causal analysis and resolution process, developing the work products, and providing the services of the process.

Elaboration

Examples of resources provided include the following tools:
- Database systems
- Process modeling tools
- Statistical analysis packages
- Tools, methods, and analysis techniques (e.g., Ishikawa or fishbone diagram, Pareto analysis, histograms, process capability studies, control charts)

GP 2.4   ASSIGN RESPONSIBILITY

Assign responsibility and authority for performing the process, developing the work products, and providing the services of the causal analysis and resolution process.

GP 2.5 TRAIN PEOPLE

Train the people performing or supporting the causal analysis and resolution process as needed.

Elaboration

> Examples of training topics include the following:
> * Quality management methods (e.g., root cause analysis)

Directing Implementation

GP 2.6 MANAGE CONFIGURATIONS

Place designated work products of the causal analysis and resolution process under appropriate levels of configuration management.

Elaboration

> Examples of work products placed under configuration management include the following:
> * Action proposals
> * Action proposals selected for implementation
> * Causal analysis and resolution records

GP 2.7 IDENTIFY AND INVOLVE RELEVANT STAKEHOLDERS

Identify and involve the relevant stakeholders of the causal analysis and resolution process as planned.

Elaboration

> Examples of activities for stakeholder involvement include the following:
> * Conducting causal analysis
> * Assessing the action proposals

GP 2.8 MONITOR AND CONTROL THE PROCESS

Monitor and control the causal analysis and resolution process against the plan for performing the process and take appropriate corrective action.

Elaboration

> Examples of measures used in monitoring and controlling include the following:
> * Number of root causes removed
> * Change in quality or process performance per instance of the causal analysis and resolution process

Verifying Implementation

GP 2.9 *Objectively Evaluate Adherence*

Objectively evaluate adherence of the causal analysis and resolution process against its process description, standards, and procedures, and address noncompliance.

Elaboration

> Examples of activities reviewed include the following:
> - Determining causes of defects
> - Addressing causes of defects

> Examples of work products reviewed include the following:
> - Action proposals selected for implementation
> - Causal analysis and resolution records

GP 2.10 *Review Status with Higher Level Management*

Review the activities, status, and results of the causal analysis and resolution process with higher level management and resolve issues.

GG 3 *Institutionalize a Defined Process*

The process is institutionalized as a defined process.

> Authors' Note: This generic goal's appearance here reflects its location in the continuous representation.

C Only

Ability to Perform

GP 3.1 *Establish a Defined Process*

Establish and maintain the description of a defined causal analysis and resolution process.

Directing Implementation

GP 3.2 *Collect Improvement Information*

Collect work products, measures, measurement results, and improvement information derived from planning and performing the causal analysis and resolution process to support the future use and improvement of the organization's processes and process assets.

GG 4   *INSTITUTIONALIZE A QUANTITATIVELY MANAGED PROCESS*

The process is institutionalized as a quantitatively managed process.

GP 4.1   *ESTABLISH QUANTITATIVE OBJECTIVES FOR THE PROCESS*

Establish and maintain quantitative objectives for the causal analysis and resolution process that address quality and process performance based on customer needs and business objectives.

GP 4.2   *STABILIZE SUBPROCESS PERFORMANCE*

Stabilize the performance of one or more subprocesses to determine the ability of the causal analysis and resolution process to achieve the established quantitative quality and process-performance objectives.

GG 5   *INSTITUTIONALIZE AN OPTIMIZING PROCESS*

The process is institutionalized as an optimizing process.

GP 5.1   *ENSURE CONTINUOUS PROCESS IMPROVEMENT*

Ensure continuous improvement of the causal analysis and resolution process in fulfilling the relevant business objectives of the organization.

GP 5.2   *CORRECT ROOT CAUSES OF PROBLEMS*

Identify and correct the root causes of defects and other problems in the causal analysis and resolution process.

CONFIGURATION MANAGEMENT
A Support Process Area at Maturity Level 2

Purpose

The purpose of Configuration Management (CM) is to establish and maintain the integrity of work products using configuration identification, configuration control, configuration status accounting, and configuration audits.

Introductory Notes

The Configuration Management process area involves the following:

- Identifying the configuration of selected work products that compose the baselines at given points in time
- Controlling changes to configuration items
- Building or providing specifications to build work products from the configuration management system
- Maintaining the integrity of baselines
- Providing accurate status and current configuration data to developers, end users, and customers

The work products placed under configuration management include the products that are delivered to the customer, designated internal work products, acquired products, tools, and other items that are used in creating and describing these work products. (See the definition of "configuration management" in the glossary.)

> **FOR SUPPLIER SOURCING**
> Acquired products may need to be placed under configuration management by both the supplier and the project. Provisions for conducting configuration management should be established in supplier agreements. Methods to ensure that the data is complete and consistent should be established and maintained.

Examples of work products that may be placed under configuration management include the following:

- Plans
- Process descriptions
- Requirements
- Design data
- Drawings
- Product specifications
- Code
- Compilers
- Product data files
- Product technical publications

Configuration management of work products may be performed at several levels of granularity. Configuration items can be decomposed into configuration components and configuration units. Only the term "configuration item" is used in this process area. Therefore, in these practices, "configuration item" may be interpreted as "configuration component" or "configuration unit" as appropriate. (See the definition of "configuration item" in the glossary.)

Baselines provide a stable basis for continuing evolution of configuration items.

An example of a baseline is an approved description of a product that includes internally consistent versions of requirements, requirement traceability matrices, design, discipline-specific items, and end-user documentation.

Baselines are added to the configuration management system as they are developed. Changes to baselines and the release of work products built from the configuration management system are systematically controlled and monitored via the configuration control, change management, and configuration auditing functions of configuration management.

This process area applies not only to configuration management on projects, but also to configuration management on organization work products such as standards, procedures, and reuse libraries.

Configuration management is focused on the rigorous control of the managerial and technical aspects of work products, including the delivered system.

This process area covers the practices for performing the configuration management function and is applicable to all work products that are placed under configuration management.

Practice-to-Goal Relationship Table

Continuous Representation	*Staged Representation*
SG 1 Establish Baselines	SG 1 Establish Baselines
SP 1.1-1 Identify Configuration Items	SP 1.1-1 Identify Configuration Items
SP 1.2-1 Establish a Configuration Management System	SP 1.2-1 Establish a Configuration Management System
SP 1.3-1 Create or Release Baselines	SP 1.3-1 Create or Release Baselines
SG 2 Track and Control Changes	SG 2 Track and Control Changes
SP 2.1-1 Track Change Requests	SP 2.1-1 Track Change Requests
SP 2.2-1 Control Configuration Items	SP 2.2-1 Control Configuration Items
SG 3 Establish Integrity	SG 3 Establish Integrity
SP 3.1-1 Establish Configuration Management Records	SP 3.1-1 Establish Configuration Management Records
SP 3.2-1 Perform Configuration Audits	SP 3.2-1 Perform Configuration Audits
GG 1 Achieve Specific Goals	
GP 1.1 Perform Base Practices	
GG 2 Institutionalize a Managed Process	GG 2 Institutionalize a Managed Process
GP 2.1 Establish an Organizational Policy	GP 2.1 Establish an Organizational Policy
GP 2.2 Plan the Process	GP 2.2 Plan the Process
GP 2.3 Provide Resources	GP 2.3 Provide Resources
GP 2.4 Assign Responsibility	GP 2.4 Assign Responsibility
GP 2.5 Train People	GP 2.5 Train People
GP 2.6 Manage Configurations	GP 2.6 Manage Configurations
GP 2.7 Identify and Involve Relevant Stakeholders	GP 2.7 Identify and Involve Relevant Stakeholders
GP 2.8 Monitor and Control the Process	GP 2.8 Monitor and Control the Process
GP 2.9 Objectively Evaluate Adherence	GP 2.9 Objectively Evaluate Adherence
GP 2.10 Review Status with Higher Level Management	GP 2.10 Review Status with Higher Level Management
GG 3 Institutionalize a Defined Process	GG 3 Institutionalize a Defined Process
GP 3.1 Establish a Defined Process	GP 3.1 Establish a Defined Process
GP 3.2 Collect Improvement Information	GP 3.2 Collect Improvement Information
GG 4 Institutionalize a Quantitatively Managed Process	
GP 4.1 Establish Quantitative Objectives for the Process	
GP 4.2 Stabilize Subprocess Performance	
GG 5 Institutionalize an Optimizing Process	
GP 5.1 Ensure Continuous Process Improvement	
GP 5.2 Correct Root Causes of Problems	

CM

C/ML 3–5

Related Process Areas

Refer to the Project Planning process area for information on developing plans and work breakdown structures, which may be useful for determining configuration items.

Refer to the Causal Analysis and Resolution process area for more information about both the method to use for analyzing the impact of change requests and the method to use when evaluating changes.

Refer to the Project Monitoring and Control process area for more information about performance analyses and corrective actions.

Specific Practices by Goal

SG 1   ESTABLISH BASELINES

Baselines of identified work products are established.

Specific practices to establish baselines are covered by this specific goal. The specific practices under the Track and Control Changes specific goal serve to maintain the baselines. The specific practices of the Establish Integrity specific goal document and audit the integrity of the baselines.

SP 1.1-1   IDENTIFY CONFIGURATION ITEMS

Identify the configuration items, components, and related work products that will be placed under configuration management.

Configuration identification is the selection, creation, and specification of the following:

- Products that are delivered to the customer
- Designated internal work products
- Acquired products
- Tools
- Other items that are used in creating and describing these work products

Items under configuration management will include specifications and interface documents that define the requirements for the product. Other documents, such as test results, may also be included, depending on their criticality to defining the product.

A "configuration item" is an entity designated for configuration management, which may consist of multiple related work products that form a baseline. This logical grouping provides ease of identification and controlled access.

The selection of work products for configuration management should be based on criteria established during planning.

> **FOR SYSTEMS ENGINEERING**
> In a system that includes both hardware and software, where software represents a small part of the system, all of the software may be designated as a single configuration item. In other cases, the software may be decomposed into multiple configuration items.

Configuration items can be decomposed into configuration components and configuration units. Only the term "configuration item" is used in this process area. In these practices, "configuration item" may be interpreted as "configuration component" or "configuration unit" as appropriate. For example, configuration items in the area of requirements management could vary from each individual requirement to a set of requirements.

Typical Work Products

1. Identified configuration items

Subpractices

1. Select the configuration items and the work products that compose them based on documented criteria.

> Example criteria for selecting configuration items at the appropriate work product level include the following:
> - Work products that may be used by two or more groups
> - Work products that are expected to change over time either because of errors or change of requirements
> - Work products that are dependent on each other in that a change in one mandates a change in the others
> - Work products that are critical for the project

> Examples of work products that may be part of a configuration item include the following:
> - Process descriptions
> - Requirements
> - Design
> - Test plans and procedures
> - Test results
> - Interface descriptions

> **FOR SOFTWARE ENGINEERING**
>
> Examples of software work products that may be part of a configuration item include the following:
>
> • Code/module
> • Tools (e.g., compilers)

2. Assign unique identifiers to configuration items.
3. Specify the important characteristics of each configuration item.

> Example characteristics of configuration items include author, document or file type, and programming language for software code files.

4. Specify when each configuration item is placed under configuration management.

> Example criteria for determining when to place work products under configuration management include the following:
>
> • Stage of the project life cycle
> • When the work product is ready for test
> • Degree of control desired on the work product
> • Cost and schedule limitations
> • Customer requirements

5. Identify the owner responsible for each configuration item.

SP 1.2-1   ESTABLISH A CONFIGURATION MANAGEMENT SYSTEM

Establish and maintain a configuration management and change management system for controlling work products.

A configuration management system includes the storage media, the procedures, and the tools for accessing the configuration system.

A change management system includes the storage media, the procedures, and tools for recording and accessing change requests.

Typical Work Products

1. Configuration management system with controlled work products
2. Configuration management system access control procedures
3. Change request database

Subpractices

1. Establish a mechanism to manage multiple control levels of configuration management.

> Examples of situations leading to multiple levels of control include the following:
> - Differences in the levels of control needed at different times in the project life cycle (e.g., tighter control as product matures)
> - Differences in the levels of control needed for different types of systems (e.g., software-only systems versus systems that include hardware and software)
> - Differences in the levels of control needed to satisfy privacy and security requirements for the configuration items

2. Store and retrieve configuration items in configuration management system.

> Examples of configuration management systems include the following:
> - Dynamic (or developer's) systems contain components currently being created or revised. They are in the developer's workspace and are controlled by the developer. Configuration items in a dynamic system are under version control.
> - Master (or controlled) systems contain current baselines and changes to them. Configuration items in a master system are under full configuration management as described in this process area.
> - Static systems contain archives of various baselines released for use. Static systems are under full configuration management as described in this process area.

3. Share and transfer configuration items between control levels within the configuration management system.
4. Store and recover archived versions of configuration items.
5. Store, update, and retrieve configuration management records.
6. Create configuration management reports from the configuration management system.
7. Preserve the contents of the configuration management system.

> Examples of preservation functions of the configuration management system include the following:
> - Backups and restoration of configuration management files
> - Archiving of configuration management files
> - Recovery from configuration management errors

8. Revise the configuration management structure as necessary.

SP 1.3-1   CREATE OR RELEASE BASELINES

Create or release baselines for internal use and for delivery to the customer.

A baseline is a set of specifications or work products that has been formally reviewed and agreed on, that thereafter serves as the basis for further development, and that can be changed only through change control procedures. A baseline represents the assignment of an identifier to a configuration item and its associated entities.

> **FOR SYSTEMS ENGINEERING**
> Release of a baseline involves approving a set of configuration data for the agreed-on set of configuration items from the configuration management system and releasing the baseline for further development. Multiple baselines may be used to define an evolving product during its development cycle. One common set includes the system-level requirements, system-element-level design requirements, and the product definition at the end of development/beginning of production. These are referred to as the "functional baseline," "allocated baseline," and "product baseline."

> **FOR SOFTWARE ENGINEERING**
> A set of requirements, design, source code files and the associated executable code, build files, and user documentation (associated entities) that have been assigned a unique identifier can be considered to be a baseline. Release of a baseline constitutes retrieval of source code files (configuration items) from the configuration management system and generating the executable files. A baseline that is delivered to a customer is typically called a "release" whereas a baseline for an internal use is typically called a "build."

Typical Work Products

1. Baselines
2. Description of baselines

Subpractices

1. Obtain authorization from the configuration control board (CCB) before creating or releasing baselines of configuration items.
2. Create or release baselines only from configuration items in the configuration management system.

> **FOR SYSTEMS ENGINEERING**
> Ensure that the configuration items are built to the correct drawing.

3. Document the set of configuration items that are contained in a baseline.
4. Make the current set of baselines readily available.

SG 2 TRACK AND CONTROL CHANGES

Changes to the work products under configuration management are tracked and controlled.

The specific practices under this specific goal serve to maintain the baselines after they are established by the specific practices under the Establish Baselines specific goal.

SP 2.1-1 TRACK CHANGE REQUESTS

Track change requests for the configuration items.

Change requests address not only new or changed requirements, but also failures and defects in the work products.

Change requests are analyzed to determine the impact that the change will have on the work product, related work products, and schedule and cost.

Typical Work Products

1. Change requests

Subpractices

1. Initiate and record change requests in the change request database.
2. Analyze the impact of changes and fixes proposed in the change requests.

    Changes are evaluated through activities that ensure that they are consistent with all technical and project requirements.

    Changes are evaluated for their impact beyond immediate project or contract requirements. Changes to an item used in multiple products can resolve an immediate issue while causing a problem in other applications.

3. Review change requests that will be addressed in the next baseline with those who will be affected by the changes and get their agreement.

    Conduct the change request review with appropriate participants. Record the disposition of each change request and the rationale for the decision, including success criteria, a brief action plan if appropriate, and needs met or unmet by the change. Perform the actions required in the disposition, and report the results to relevant stakeholders.

4. Track the status of change requests to closure.

    Change requests brought into the system need to be handled in an efficient and timely manner. Once a change request has been processed, it is critical to close the request with the appropriate approved action as soon as it is practical. Actions left open result in larger than necessary status lists, which in turn result in added costs and confusion.

SP 2.2-1 CONTROL CONFIGURATION ITEMS

Control changes to the configuration items.

Control is maintained over the configuration of the work product baseline. This control includes tracking the configuration of each of the configuration items, approving a new configuration if necessary, and updating the baseline.

Typical Work Products

1. Revision history of configuration items
2. Archives of the baselines

Subpractices

1. Control changes to configuration items throughout the life of the product.
2. Obtain appropriate authorization before changed configuration items are entered into the configuration management system.

> For example, authorization may come from the CCB, the project manager, or the customer.

3. Check in and check out configuration items from the configuration management system for incorporation of changes in a manner that maintains the correctness and integrity of the configuration items.

> Examples of check-in and check-out steps include the following:
> - Confirming that the revisions are authorized
> - Updating the configuration items
> - Archiving the replaced baseline and retrieving the new baseline

4. Perform reviews to ensure that changes have not caused unintended effects on the baselines (e.g., ensure that the changes have not compromised the safety and/or security of the system).
5. Record changes to configuration items and the reasons for the changes as appropriate.

    If a proposed change to the work product is accepted, a schedule is identified for incorporating the change into the work product and other affected areas.

    Configuration control mechanisms can be tailored to categories of changes. For example, the approval considerations could be less stringent for component changes that do not affect other components.

    Changed configuration items are released after review and approval of configuration changes. Changes are not official until they are released.

SG 3 ESTABLISH INTEGRITY

Integrity of baselines is established and maintained.

The integrity of the baselines, established by processes associated with the Establish Baselines specific goal, and maintained by processes associated with the Track and Control Changes specific goal, is provided by the specific practices under this specific goal.

SP 3.1-1 ESTABLISH CONFIGURATION MANAGEMENT RECORDS

Establish and maintain records describing configuration items.

Typical Work Products

1. Revision history of configuration items
2. Change log
3. Copy of the change requests
4. Status of configuration items
5. Differences between baselines

Subpractices

1. Record configuration management actions in sufficient detail so the content and status of each configuration item is known and previous versions can be recovered.

2. Ensure that relevant stakeholders have access to and knowledge of the configuration status of the configuration items.

> Examples of activities for communicating configuration status include the following:
> - Providing access permissions to authorized end users
> - Making baseline copies readily available to authorized end users

3. Specify the latest version of the baselines.
4. Identify the version of configuration items that constitute a particular baseline.
5. Describe the differences between successive baselines.
6. Revise the status and history (i.e., changes and other actions) of each configuration item as necessary.

SP 3.2-1 PERFORM CONFIGURATION AUDITS

Perform configuration audits to maintain integrity of the configuration baselines.

Audit configuration management activities and processes to confirm that the resulting baselines and documentation are accurate, and record the audit results as appropriate.

Typical Work Products

1. Configuration audit results
2. Action items

Subpractices

1. Assess the integrity of the baselines.
2. Confirm that the configuration records correctly identify the configuration of the configuration items.
3. Review the structure and integrity of the items in the configuration management system.
4. Confirm the completeness and correctness of the items in the configuration management system.

   Completeness and correctness of the content is based on the requirements as stated in the plan and the disposition of approved change requests.
5. Confirm compliance with applicable configuration management standards and procedures.
6. Track action items from the audit to closure.

Generic Practices by Goal

GG 1 ACHIEVE SPECIFIC GOALS

The process supports and enables achievement of the specific goals of the process area by transforming identifiable input work products to produce identifiable output work products.

GP 1.1 PERFORM BASE PRACTICES

Perform the base practices of the configuration management process to develop work products and provide services to achieve the specific goals of the process area.

CONTINUOUS ONLY

GG 2 INSTITUTIONALIZE A MANAGED PROCESS

The process is institutionalized as a managed process.

Commitment to Perform

GP 2.1 ESTABLISH AN ORGANIZATIONAL POLICY

Establish and maintain an organizational policy for planning and performing the configuration management process.

Elaboration

This policy establishes organizational expectations for establishing and maintaining baselines, tracking and controlling changes to the work products (under configuration management), and establishing and maintaining integrity of the baselines.

Ability to Perform

GP 2.2 PLAN THE PROCESS

Establish and maintain the plan for performing the configuration management process.

Elaboration

This plan for performing the configuration management process can be included in (or referenced by) the project plan, which is described in the Project Planning process area.

GP 2.3 PROVIDE RESOURCES

Provide adequate resources for performing the configuration management process, developing the work products, and providing the services of the process.

Elaboration

Examples of resources provided include the following tools:
- Configuration management tools
- Data management tools
- Archiving and reproduction tools
- Database programs

GP 2.4 ASSIGN RESPONSIBILITY

Assign responsibility and authority for performing the process, developing the work products, and providing the services of the configuration management process.

GP 2.5   *TRAIN PEOPLE*

Train the people performing or supporting the configuration management process as needed.

Elaboration

Examples of training topics include the following:
- Roles, responsibilities, and authority of the configuration management staff
- Configuration management standards, procedures, and methods
- Configuration library system

Directing Implementation

GP 2.6   *MANAGE CONFIGURATIONS*

Place designated work products of the configuration management process under appropriate levels of configuration management.

Elaboration

Examples of work products placed under configuration management include the following:
- Access lists
- Change status reports
- Change request database
- CCB meeting minutes
- Archived baselines

GP 2.7   *IDENTIFY AND INVOLVE RELEVANT STAKEHOLDERS*

Identify and involve the relevant stakeholders of the configuration management process as planned.

Elaboration

Examples of activities for stakeholder involvement include the following:
- Establishing baselines
- Reviewing configuration management system reports and resolving issues
- Assessing the impact of changes for the configuration items
- Performing configuration audits
- Reviewing the results of configuration management audits

GP 2.8 Monitor and Control the Process

Monitor and control the configuration management process against the plan for performing the process and take appropriate corrective action.

Elaboration

Examples of measures used in monitoring and controlling include the following:
- Number of changes to configuration items
- Number of configuration audits conducted

Verifying Implementation

GP 2.9 Objectively Evaluate Adherence

Objectively evaluate adherence of the configuration management process against its process description, standards, and procedures, and address noncompliance.

Elaboration

Examples of activities reviewed include the following:
- Establishing baselines
- Tracking and controlling changes
- Establishing and maintaining integrity of baselines

Examples of work products reviewed include the following:
- Archives of the baselines
- Change request database

GP 2.10 Review Status with Higher Level Management

Review the activities, status, and results of the configuration management process with higher level management and resolve issues.

AUTHORS' NOTE: GG3 and its practices do not apply for a maturity level 2 rating, but do apply for a maturity level 3 rating and above.

GG 3 Institutionalize a Defined Process

The process is institutionalized as a defined process.

Ability to Perform

GP 3.1 Establish a Defined Process

Establish and maintain the description of a defined configuration management process.

Directing Implementation

GP 3.2   COLLECT IMPROVEMENT INFORMATION

Collect work products, measures, measurement results, and improvement information derived from planning and performing the configuration management process to support the future use and improvement of the organization's processes and process assets.

GG 4   INSTITUTIONALIZE A QUANTITATIVELY MANAGED PROCESS

The process is institutionalized as a quantitatively managed process.

GP 4.1   ESTABLISH QUANTITATIVE OBJECTIVES FOR THE PROCESS

Establish and maintain quantitative objectives for the configuration management process that address quality and process performance based on customer needs and business objectives.

GP 4.2   STABILIZE SUBPROCESS PERFORMANCE

Stabilize the performance of one or more subprocesses to determine the ability of the configuration management process to achieve the established quantitative quality and process-performance objectives.

GG 5   INSTITUTIONALIZE AN OPTIMIZING PROCESS

The process is institutionalized as an optimizing process.

GP 5.1   ENSURE CONTINUOUS PROCESS IMPROVEMENT

Ensure continuous improvement of the configuration management process in fulfilling the relevant business objectives of the organization.

GP 5.2   CORRECT ROOT CAUSES OF PROBLEMS

Identify and correct the root causes of defects and other problems in the configuration management process.

C/ML 3–5

CONTINUOUS ONLY

DECISION ANALYSIS AND RESOLUTION
A Support Process Area at Maturity Level 3

Purpose

The purpose of Decision Analysis and Resolution (DAR) is to analyze possible decisions using a formal evaluation process that evaluates identified alternatives against established criteria.

Introductory Notes

The Decision Analysis and Resolution process area involves establishing guidelines to determine which issues should be subjected to a formal evaluation process and then applying formal evaluation processes to these issues.

A formal evaluation process is a structured approach to evaluating alternative solutions against established criteria to determine a recommended solution to address an issue. A formal evaluation process involves the following actions:

- Establishing the criteria for evaluating alternatives
- Identifying alternative solutions
- Selecting methods for evaluating alternatives
- Evaluating the alternative solutions using the established criteria and methods
- Selecting recommended solutions from the alternatives based on the evaluation criteria

Rather than using the phrase "alternative solutions to address issues" each time it is needed, we will use one of two shorter phrases: "alternative solutions" or "alternatives."

A formal evaluation process reduces the subjective nature of the decision and has a higher probability of selecting a solution that meets the multiple demands of the relevant stakeholders.

While the primary application of this process area is for selected technical concerns, formal evaluation processes can also be applied to many nontechnical issues, particularly when a project is being planned. Issues that have multiple alternative solutions and evaluation criteria lend themselves to a formal evaluation process.

> Trade studies of equipment or software are typical examples of formal evaluation processes.

During planning, specific issues requiring a formal evaluation process are identified. Typical issues include selection among architectural or design alternatives, use of reusable or commercial off-the-shelf (COTS) components, supplier selection, engineering support environments or associated tools, test environments, and logistics and production. A formal evaluation process can also be used to address a make-or-buy decision, the development of manufacturing processes, the selection of distribution locations, and other decisions.

Guidelines are created for deciding when to use formal evaluation processes to address unplanned issues. Guidelines often suggest using formal evaluation processes when issues are associated with medium to high risks or when issues affect the ability to achieve project objectives.

Formal evaluation processes can vary in formality, type of criteria, and methods employed. Less formal decisions can be analyzed in a few hours, use only a few criteria (e.g., effectiveness and cost to implement), and result in a one- or two-page report. More formal decisions may require separate plans, months of effort, meetings to develop and approve criteria, simulations, prototypes, piloting, and extensive documentation.

Both numeric and non-numeric criteria can be used in a formal evaluation process. Numeric criteria use weights to reflect the relative importance of the criteria. Non-numeric criteria use a more subjective ranking scale (e.g., high, medium, low). More formal decisions may require a full trade study.

A formal evaluation process identifies and evaluates alternative solutions. The eventual selection of a solution may involve iterative activities of identification and evaluation. Portions of identified alternatives may be combined, emerging technologies may change alternatives, and the business situation of vendors may change during the evaluation period.

A recommended alternative is accompanied by documentation of the selected methods, criteria, alternatives, and rationale for the recommendation. The documentation is distributed to the relevant stakeholders; it provides a record of the formal evaluation process and rationale that is useful to other projects that encounter a similar issue.

Practice-to-Goal Relationship Table

Continuous Representation	*Staged Representation*

SG 1 Evaluate Alternatives

    SP 1.1-1 Establish Guidelines for Decision Analysis

    SP 1.2-1 Establish Evaluation Criteria

    SP 1.3-1 Identify Alternative Solutions

    SP 1.4-1 Select Evaluation Methods

    SP 1.5-1 Evaluate Alternatives

    SP 1.6-1 Select Solutions

GG 1 Achieve Specific Goals

    GP 1.1 Perform Base Practices

GG 2 Institutionalize a Managed Process

    GP 2.1 Establish an Organizational Policy

    GP 2.2 Plan the Process

    GP 2.3 Provide Resources

    GP 2.4 Assign Responsibility

    GP 2.5 Train People

    GP 2.6 Manage Configurations

    GP 2.7 Identify and Involve Relevant Stakeholders

    GP 2.8 Monitor and Control the Process

    GP 2.9 Objectively Evaluate Adherence

    GP 2.10 Review Status with Higher Level Management

GG 3 Institutionalize a Defined Process

    GP 3.1 Establish a Defined Process

    GP 3.2 Collect Improvement Information

GG 4 Institutionalize a Quantitatively Managed Process

    GP 4.1 Establish Quantitative Objectives for the Process

    GP 4.2 Stabilize Subprocess Performance

GG 5 Institutionalize an Optimizing Process

    GP 5.1 Ensure Continuous Process Improvement

    GP 5.2 Correct Root Causes of Problems

Staged Representation

SG 1 Evaluate Alternatives

    SP 1.1-1 Establish Guidelines for Decision Analysis

    SP 1.2-1 Establish Evaluation Criteria

    SP 1.3-1 Identify Alternative Solutions

    SP 1.4-1 Select Evaluation Methods

    SP 1.5-1 Evaluate Alternatives

    SP 1.6-1 Select Solutions

GG 3 Institutionalize a Defined Process

    GP 2.1 Establish an Organizational Policy

    GP 2.2 Plan the Process

    GP 2.3 Provide Resources

    GP 2.4 Assign Responsibility

    GP 2.5 Train People

    GP 2.6 Manage Configurations

    GP 2.7 Identify and Involve Relevant Stakeholders

    GP 2.8 Monitor and Control the Process

    GP 2.9 Objectively Evaluate Adherence

    GP 2.10 Review Status with Higher Level Management

    GP 3.1 Establish a Defined Process

    GP 3.2 Collect Improvement Information

DAR

Related Process Areas

Refer to the Project Planning process area for more information about general planning for projects.

Refer to the Integrated Project Management process area for more information about establishing the project's defined process. The project's defined process includes a formal evaluation process for each selected issue and incorporates the use of guidelines for applying a formal evaluation process to unforeseen issues.

Refer to the Risk Management process area for more information about identifying and mitigating risks. A formal evaluation process is often used to address issues with identified medium or high risks. Selected solutions typically affect risk mitigation plans.

Specific Practices by Goal

SG 1   EVALUATE ALTERNATIVES

Decisions are based on an evaluation of alternatives using established criteria.

Issues requiring a formal evaluation process may be identified during any phase of a product or project life cycle. The objective should be to identify issues as early as possible to maximize the time available to resolve them.

SP 1.1-1   ESTABLISH GUIDELINES FOR DECISION ANALYSIS

Establish and maintain guidelines to determine which issues are subject to a formal evaluation process.

Not every decision is significant enough to require a formal evaluation process. The choice between the trivial and the truly important will be unclear without explicit guidance. Whether a decision is significant or not is dependent on the project and circumstances, and is determined by the established guidelines.

Typical guidelines for determining when to require a formal evaluation process include the following:

- When a decision is directly related to topics assessed as being of medium or high risk
- When a decision is related to changing work products under configuration management
- When a decision would cause schedule delays over a certain percentage or specific amount of time
- When a decision affects the ability to achieve project objectives

- When the costs of the formal evaluation process are reasonable when compared to the decision's impact

Refer to the Risk Management process area for more information about determining which issues are medium or high risk.

DAR

Examples of when to use a formal evaluation process include the following:

- On material procurement when 20 percent of the material parts constitute 80 percent of the total material costs
- On design-implementation decisions when technical performance failure may cause a catastrophic failure (e.g., safety of flight item)
- On decisions with the potential to significantly reduce design risk, engineering changes, cycle time, and production costs (e.g., to use lithography models to assess form and fit capability before releasing engineering drawings and production builds)

Typical Work Products

1. Guidelines for when to apply a formal evaluation process

Subpractices

1. Establish guidelines.
2. Incorporate the use of the guidelines into the defined process where appropriate.

    Refer to the Integrated Project Management process area for more information about establishing the project's defined process.

SP 1.2-1   ESTABLISH EVALUATION CRITERIA

Establish and maintain the criteria for evaluating alternatives, and the relative ranking of these criteria.

The evaluation criteria provide the basis for evaluating alternative solutions. The criteria are ranked so that the highest ranked criteria exert the most influence on the evaluation.

This process area is referenced by many other process areas in the model, and there are many contexts in which a formal evaluation process can be used. Therefore, in some situations you may find that criteria have already been defined as part of another process. This specific practice does not suggest that a second development of criteria be conducted.

Document the evaluation criteria to minimize the possibility that decisions will be second-guessed, or that the reason for making the decision will be forgotten. Decisions based on criteria that are explicitly defined and established remove barriers to stakeholder buy-in.

Typical Work Products

1. Documented evaluation criteria
2. Rankings of criteria importance

Subpractices

1. Define the criteria for evaluating alternative solutions.

   Criteria should be traceable to requirements, scenarios, business case assumptions, business objectives, or other documented sources. Types of criteria to consider include the following:
   - Technology limitations
   - Environmental impact
   - Risks
   - Total ownership and life-cycle costs

2. Define the range and scale for ranking the evaluation criteria.

   Scales of relative importance for evaluation criteria can be established with non-numeric values or with formulas that relate the evaluation parameter to a numerical weight.

3. Rank the criteria.

   The criteria are ranked according to the defined range and scale to reflect the needs, objectives, and priorities of the relevant stakeholders.

4. Assess the criteria and their relative importance.

5. Evolve the evaluation criteria to improve their validity.

6. Document the rationale for the selection and rejection of evaluation criteria.

   Documentation of selection criteria and rationale may be needed to justify solutions or for future reference and use.

SP 1.3-1 *IDENTIFY ALTERNATIVE SOLUTIONS*

Identify alternative solutions to address issues.

A wider range of alternatives can surface by soliciting as many stakeholders as practical for input. Input from stakeholders with diverse skills and backgrounds can help teams identify and address assumptions, constraints, and biases. Brainstorming sessions may stimulate innovative alternatives through rapid interaction and feedback. Sufficient candidate solutions may not be furnished for analysis. As the analysis proceeds, other alternatives should be added to the list of potential candidate solutions. The generation and consideration of multiple alternatives early in a decision analysis and resolution process increases the likelihood that an acceptable decision will be made, and that consequences of the decision will be understood.

Typical Work Products

1. Identified alternatives

Subpractices

1. Perform a literature search.

   A literature search can uncover what others have done both inside and outside the organization. It may provide a deeper understanding of the problem, alternatives to consider, barriers to implementation, existing trade studies, and lessons learned from similar decisions.

2. Identify alternatives for consideration in addition to those that may be provided with the issue.

   Evaluation criteria are an effective starting point for identifying alternatives. The evaluation criteria identify the priorities of the relevant stakeholders and the importance of technical challenges.

   Combining key attributes of existing alternatives can generate additional and sometimes stronger alternatives.

   Solicit alternatives from relevant stakeholders. Brainstorming sessions, interviews, and working groups can be used effectively to uncover alternatives.

3. Document the proposed alternatives.

SP 1.4-1   SELECT EVALUATION METHODS

Select the evaluation methods.

Methods for evaluating alternative solutions against established criteria can range from simulations to the use of probabilistic models and decision theory. These methods need to be carefully selected. The level of detail of a method should be commensurate with cost, schedule, performance, and risk impacts.

While many problems may need only one evaluation method, some problems may require multiple methods. For instance, simulations may augment a trade study to determine which design alternative best meets a given criterion.

Typical Work Products

1. Selected evaluation methods

Subpractices

1. Select the methods based on the purpose for analyzing a decision and on the availability of the information used to support the method.

   > For example, the methods used for evaluating a technical solution when requirements are weakly defined may be different from the methods used when the requirements are well defined.

Typical evaluation methods include the following:

- Simulations
- Engineering studies
- Manufacturing studies
- Cost studies
- Business opportunity studies
- Surveys
- Extrapolations based on field experience and prototypes
- User review and comment
- Testing

2. Select evaluation methods based on their ability to focus on the issues at hand without being overly influenced by side issues.

   Results of simulations can be skewed by random activities in the solution that are not directly related to the issues at hand.

3. Determine the measures needed to support the evaluation method.

   Consider the impact on cost, schedule, performance, and risks.

SP 1.5-1   EVALUATE ALTERNATIVES

Evaluate alternative solutions using the established criteria and methods.

Evaluating alternative solutions involves analysis, discussion, and review. Iterative cycles of analysis are sometimes necessary. Supporting analyses, experimentation, prototyping, or simulations may be needed to substantiate scoring and conclusions.

Often, the relative importance of criteria is imprecise and the total effect on a solution is not apparent until after the analysis is performed. In cases where the resulting scores differ by relatively small amounts, the best selection among alternative solutions may not be clearcut. Challenges to criteria and assumptions should be encouraged.

Typical Work Products

1. Evaluation results

Subpractices

1. Evaluate the proposed alternative solutions using the established evaluation criteria and selected methods.

2. Evaluate the assumptions related to the evaluation criteria and the evidence that supports the assumptions.

3. Evaluate whether uncertainty in the values for alternative solutions affects the evaluation and address as appropriate.

   For instance, if the score can vary between two values, is the difference significant enough to make a difference in the final solution set? Does the variation in score represent a high risk? To address these concerns, simulations may be run, further studies may be performed, or evaluation criteria may be modified, among other things.

4. Perform simulations, modeling, prototypes, and pilots as necessary to exercise the evaluation criteria, methods, and alternative solutions.

   Untested criteria, their relative importance, and supporting data or functions may cause the validity of solutions to be questioned. Criteria and their relative priorities and scales can be tested with trial runs against a set of alternatives. These trial runs of a select set of criteria allow for the evaluation of the cumulative impact of the criteria on a solution. If the trials reveal problems, different criteria or alternatives might be considered to avoid biases.

5. Consider new alternative solutions, criteria, or methods if the proposed alternatives do not test well; repeat the evaluations until alternatives do test well.

6. Document the results of the evaluation.

   Document the rationale for the addition of new alternatives or methods and changes to criteria, as well as the results of interim evaluations.

SP 1.6-1 SELECT SOLUTIONS

Select solutions from the alternatives based on the evaluation criteria.

Selecting solutions involves weighing the results from the evaluation of alternatives. Risks associated with implementation of the solutions must be assessed.

Typical Work Products

1. Recommended solutions to address significant issues

Subpractices

1. Assess the risks associated with implementing the recommended solution.

   Refer to the Risk Management process area for more information about identifying and managing risks.

   Decisions must often be made with incomplete information. There can be substantial risk associated with the decision because of having incomplete information.

   When decisions must be made according to a specific schedule, time and resources may not be available for gathering complete information. Consequently, risky decisions made with incomplete information may require re-analysis later. Identified risks should be monitored.

2. Document the results and rationale for the recommended solution.

   It is important to record both why a solution is selected and why another solution was rejected.

Generic Practices by Goal

GG 1 ACHIEVE SPECIFIC GOALS

The process supports and enables achievement of the specific goals of the process area by transforming identifiable input work products to produce identifiable output work products.

GP 1.1 PERFORM BASE PRACTICES

Perform the base practices of the decision analysis and resolution process to develop work products and provide services to achieve the specific goals of the process area.

GG 2 INSTITUTIONALIZE A MANAGED PROCESS

The process is institutionalized as a managed process.

GG 3 INSTITUTIONALIZE A DEFINED PROCESS

The process is institutionalized as a defined process.

> AUTHORS' NOTE: This generic goal's appearance here reflects its location in the staged representation.

(margin: CONTINUOUS ONLY)

(margin: STAGED ONLY)

Commitment to Perform

GP 2.1 ESTABLISH AN ORGANIZATIONAL POLICY

Establish and maintain an organizational policy for planning and performing the decision analysis and resolution process.

Elaboration

This policy establishes organizational expectations for selectively analyzing possible decisions using a formal evaluation process that evaluates identified alternatives against established criteria. The policy should also provide guidance on which decisions require a formal evaluation process.

Ability to Perform

GP 2.2 PLAN THE PROCESS

Establish and maintain the plan for performing the decision analysis and resolution process.

Elaboration

Typically, this plan for performing the decision analysis and resolution process is included in (or is referenced by) the project plan, which is described in the Project Planning process area.

GP 2.3   PROVIDE RESOURCES

Provide adequate resources for performing the decision analysis and resolution process, developing the work products, and providing the services of the process.

Elaboration

Examples of resources provided include the following tools:
- Simulators and modeling tools
- Prototyping tools
- Tools for conducting surveys

GP 2.4   ASSIGN RESPONSIBILITY

Assign responsibility and authority for performing the process, developing the work products, and providing the services of the decision analysis and resolution process.

GP 2.5   TRAIN PEOPLE

Train the people performing or supporting the decision analysis and resolution process as needed.

Elaboration

Examples of training topics include the following:
- Formal decision analysis
- Methods for evaluating alternative solutions against criteria

Directing Implementation

GP 2.6   MANAGE CONFIGURATIONS

Place designated work products of the decision analysis and resolution process under appropriate levels of configuration management.

Elaboration

Examples of work products placed under configuration management include the following:
- Guidelines for when to apply a formal evaluation process
- Evaluation reports containing recommended solutions

GP 2.7   IDENTIFY AND INVOLVE RELEVANT STAKEHOLDERS

Identify and involve the relevant stakeholders of the decision analysis and resolution process as planned.

Elaboration

> Examples of activities for stakeholder involvement include the following:
> - Establishing guidelines for which issues are subject to a formal evaluation process
> - Establishing evaluation criteria
> - Identifying and evaluating alternatives
> - Selecting evaluation methods
> - Selecting solutions

GP 2.8   MONITOR AND CONTROL THE PROCESS

Monitor and control the decision analysis and resolution process against the plan for performing the process and take appropriate corrective action.

Elaboration

> Examples of measures used in monitoring and controlling include the following:
> - Cost-to-benefit ratio of using formal evaluation processes

Verifying Implementation

GP 2.9   OBJECTIVELY EVALUATE ADHERENCE

Objectively evaluate adherence of the decision analysis and resolution process against its process description, standards, and procedures, and address noncompliance.

Elaboration

> Examples of activities reviewed include the following:
> - Evaluating alternatives using established criteria and methods

> Examples of work products reviewed include the following:
> - Guidelines for when to apply a formal evaluation process
> - Evaluation reports containing recommended solutions

GP 2.10   REVIEW STATUS WITH HIGHER LEVEL MANAGEMENT

Review the activities, status, and results of the decision analysis and resolution process with higher level management and resolve issues.

GG 3   INSTITUTIONALIZE A DEFINED PROCESS

The process is institutionalized as a defined process.

> AUTHORS' NOTE: This generic goal's appearance here reflects its location in the continuous representation.

C ONLY

Ability to Perform

GP 3.1   ESTABLISH A DEFINED PROCESS

Establish and maintain the description of a defined decision analysis and resolution process.

Directing Implementation

GP 3.2   COLLECT IMPROVEMENT INFORMATION

Collect work products, measures, measurement results, and improvement information derived from planning and performing the decision analysis and resolution process to support the future use and improvement of the organization's processes and process assets.

GG 4   INSTITUTIONALIZE A QUANTITATIVELY MANAGED PROCESS

The process is institutionalized as a quantitatively managed process.

GP 4.1   ESTABLISH QUANTITATIVE OBJECTIVES FOR THE PROCESS

Establish and maintain quantitative objectives for the decision analysis and resolution process that address quality and process performance based on customer needs and business objectives.

GP 4.2   STABILIZE SUBPROCESS PERFORMANCE

Stabilize the performance of one or more subprocesses to determine the ability of the decision analysis and resolution process to achieve the established quantitative quality and process-performance objectives.

GG 5   INSTITUTIONALIZE AN OPTIMIZING PROCESS

The process is institutionalized as an optimizing process.

GP 5.1   ENSURE CONTINUOUS PROCESS IMPROVEMENT

Ensure continuous improvement of the decision analysis and resolution process in fulfilling the relevant business objectives of the organization.

GP 5.2   CORRECT ROOT CAUSES OF PROBLEMS

Identify and correct the root causes of defects and other problems in the decision analysis and resolution process.

INTEGRATED PROJECT MANAGEMENT
A Project Management Process Area at Maturity Level 3

Purpose

The purpose of Integrated Project Management (IPM) is to establish and manage the project and the involvement of the relevant stakeholders according to an integrated and defined process that is tailored from the organization's set of standard processes.

For Integrated Product and Process Development, Integrated Project Management also covers the establishment of a shared vision for the project and a team structure for integrated teams that will carry out the objectives of the project.

Introductory Notes

Integrated Project Management involves the following:

- Establishing the project's defined process by tailoring the organization's set of standard processes
- Managing the project using the project's defined process
- Using and contributing to the organizational process assets
- Enabling relevant stakeholders' concerns to be identified, considered, and, when appropriate, addressed during the development of the product
- Ensuring that the relevant stakeholders perform their tasks in a coordinated and timely manner (1) to address product and product-component requirements, plans, objectives, issues, and risks; (2) to fulfill their commitments; and (3) to identify, track, and resolve issues

> **FOR INTEGRATED PRODUCT AND PROCESS DEVELOPMENT**
> Integrated Project Management also involves the following:
> - Establishing a shared vision by and for the project
> - Establishing a structure of integrated teams that are tasked to accomplish the objectives of the project

> **FOR SUPPLIER SOURCING**
>
> Integrated Project Management also involves the following:
>
> - Including suppliers as relevant stakeholders
> - Coordinating the activities of critical suppliers with project activities

The integrated and defined process that is tailored from the organization's set of standard processes is called the project's defined process.

Managing the project's effort, cost, schedule, staffing, risks, and other factors is tied to the tasks of the project's defined process. The implementation and management of the project's defined process are typically described in the project plan. Certain activities may be covered in other plans that affect the project, such as the quality assurance plan, risk management strategy, and the configuration management plan.

Since the defined process for each project is tailored from the organization's set of standard processes, variability among projects is typically reduced and projects can more easily share process assets, data, and lessons learned.

This process area also addresses the coordination of all activities associated with the project including the following:

- Technical activities such as requirements development, design, and verification
- Support activities such as configuration management, documentation, marketing, and training

The working interfaces and interactions among relevant stakeholders internal and external to the project are planned and managed to ensure the quality and integrity of the entire product. Relevant stakeholders participate, as appropriate, in defining the project's defined process and the project plan. Reviews and exchanges are regularly conducted with the relevant stakeholders and coordination issues receive appropriate attention. Reviews and exchanges are regularly conducted with the relevant stakeholders to ensure that coordination issues receive appropriate attention and everyone involved with the project is appropriately aware of the status, plans, and activities. (See the definition of "relevant stakeholder" in the glossary.) In defining the project's defined process, formal interfaces are created as necessary to ensure that appropriate coordination and collaboration occurs.

This process area applies in any organizational structure, including projects that are structured as line organizations, matrix organizations, or integrated teams. The terminology should be appropriately interpreted for the organizational structure in place.

Practice-to-Goal Relationship Table

Continuous Representation	Staged Representation

SG 1 Use the Project's Defined Process
- SP 1.1-1 Establish the Project's Defined Process
- SP 1.2-1 Use Organizational Process Assets for Planning Project Activities
- SP 1.3-1 Integrate Plans
- SP 1.4-1 Manage the Project Using the Integrated Plans
- SP 1.5-1 Contribute to the Organizational Process Assets

SG 2 Coordinate and Collaborate with Relevant Stakeholders
- SP 2.1-1 Manage Stakeholder Involvement
- SP 2.2-1 Manage Dependencies
- SP 2.3-1 Resolve Coordination Issues

SG 3 Use the Project's Shared Vision for IPPD
- SP 3.1-1 Define Project's Shared Vision Context
- SP 3.2-1 Establish the Project's Shared Vision

SG 4 Organize Integrated Teams for IPPD
- SP 4.1-1 Determine Integrated Team Structure for the Project
- SP 4.2-1 Develop a Preliminary Distribution of Requirements to Integrated Teams
- SP 4.3-1 Establish Integrated Teams

GG 1 Achieve Specific Goals
- GP 1.1 Perform Base Practices

GG 2 Institutionalize a Managed Process
- GP 2.1 Establish an Organizational Policy
- GP 2.2 Plan the Process
- GP 2.3 Provide Resources
- GP 2.4 Assign Responsibility
- GP 2.5 Train People
- GP 2.6 Manage Configurations
- GP 2.7 Identify and Involve Relevant Stakeholders
- GP 2.8 Monitor and Control the Process
- GP 2.9 Objectively Evaluate Adherence
- GP 2.10 Review Status with Higher Level Management

GG 3 Institutionalize a Defined Process
- GP 3.1 Establish a Defined Process
- GP 3.2 Collect Improvement Information

GG 4 Institutionalize a Quantitatively Managed Process
- GP 4.1 Establish Quantitative Objectives for the Process
- GP 4.2 Stabilize Subprocess Performance

GG 5 Institutionalize an Optimizing Process
- GP 5.1 Ensure Continuous Process Improvement
- GP 5.2 Correct Root Causes of Problems

SG 1 Use the Project's Defined Process
- SP 1.1-1 Establish the Project's Defined Process
- SP 1.2-1 Use Organizational Process Assets for Planning Project Activities
- SP 1.3-1 Integrate Plans
- SP 1.4-1 Manage the Project Using the Integrated Plans
- SP 1.5-1 Contribute to the Organizational Process Assets

SG 2 Coordinate and Collaborate with Relevant Stakeholders
- SP 2.1-1 Manage Stakeholder Involvement
- SP 2.2-1 Manage Dependencies
- SP 2.3-1 Resolve Coordination Issues

SG 3 Use the Project's Shared Vision for IPPD
- SP 3.1-1 Define Project's Shared Vision Context
- SP 3.2-1 Establish the Project's Shared Vision

SG 4 Organize Integrated Teams for IPPD
- SP 4.1-1 Determine Integrated Team Structure for the Project
- SP 4.2-1 Develop a Preliminary Distribution of Requirements to Integrated Teams
- SP 4.3-1 Establish Integrated Teams

GG 3 Institutionalize a Defined Process
- GP 2.1 Establish an Organizational Policy
- GP 2.2 Plan the Process
- GP 2.3 Provide Resources
- GP 2.4 Assign Responsibility
- GP 2.5 Train People
- GP 2.6 Manage Configurations
- GP 2.7 Identify and Involve Relevant Stakeholders
- GP 2.8 Monitor and Control the Process
- GP 2.9 Objectively Evaluate Adherence
- GP 2.10 Review Status with Higher Level Management

- GP 3.1 Establish a Defined Process
- GP 3.2 Collect Improvement Information

IPM

If you are using the continuous representation, the first specific goal in this process area may be redundant when applying the capability level 3 generic practices to project-related process areas. However, the specific practices, subpractices, and notes will provide many details that will assist you with this application.

C Only

Related Process Areas

Refer to the Project Planning process area for more information about planning the project.

Refer to the Project Monitoring and Control process area for more information about monitoring and controlling the project.

Refer to the Project Planning process area for more information about identifying relevant stakeholders and their appropriate involvement in the project.

Refer to the Verification process area for more information about peer reviews.

Refer to the Organizational Process Definition process area for more information about organizational process assets.

Refer to the Measurement and Analysis process area for more information about defining a process for measuring and analyzing processes.

Refer to the Integrated Teaming process area for more information about how teams are established and maintained.

Refer to the Organizational Environment for Integration process area for more information about the work environment, the creation of the organization's shared vision, and managing people for integration.

IPPD Only

Specific Practices by Goal

SG 1 USE THE PROJECT'S DEFINED PROCESS

The project is conducted using a defined process that is tailored from the organization's set of standard processes.

The project's defined process must include those processes from the organization's set of standard processes that address all processes necessary to develop and maintain the product. The product-related life-cycle processes, such as the manufacturing and support processes, are developed concurrently with the product.

SP 1.1-1 ESTABLISH THE PROJECT'S DEFINED PROCESS

Establish and maintain the project's defined process.

Refer to the Organizational Process Definition process area for more information about the organizational process assets.

Refer to the Organizational Process Focus process area for more information about organizational process needs and objectives.

The project's defined process consists of defined processes that form an integrated, coherent life cycle for the project.

The project's defined process covers all of the processes needed by the project, including those processes that are addressed by the process areas at maturity level 2.

S ONLY

IPM

FOR INTEGRATED PRODUCT AND PROCESS DEVELOPMENT
The project's defined process includes all life-cycle processes including the IPPD processes that will be applied by the project (tailored from the organization's IPPD processes). Processes to select the team structure, allocate limited personnel resources, implement cross-integrated team communication, and conduct issue-resolution processes are part of the project's defined process.

The project's defined process should satisfy the project's contractual and operational needs, opportunities, and constraints. It is designed to provide a best fit for the project's needs. A project's defined process is based on the following factors:

- Customer requirements
- Product and product-component requirements
- Commitments
- Organizational process needs and objectives
- Operational environment
- Business environment

Typical Work Products

1. The project's defined process

Subpractices

1. Select a life-cycle model from those available from the organizational process assets.
2. Select the standard processes from the organization's set of standard processes that best fit the needs of the project.
3. Tailor the organization's set of standard processes and other organizational process assets according to the tailoring guidelines to produce the project's defined process.

    Sometimes the available life-cycle models and standard processes are inadequate to meet a specific project's needs. Sometimes the project will be unable to produce required work products or measures. In such circumstances, the project will need to seek approval to deviate from what is required by the organization. Waivers are provided for this purpose.

4. Use other artifacts from the organization's process asset library as appropriate.

   Other artifacts may include the following:
   - Lessons-learned documents
   - Templates
   - Example documents
   - Estimating models

5. Document the project's defined process.

   The project's defined process covers all the engineering, management, and support activities for the project and its interfaces to relevant stakeholders.

   Examples of project activities include the following:
   - Project planning
   - Project monitoring and controlling
   - Requirements development
   - Requirements management
   - Design and implementation
   - Verification and validation
   - Product integration
   - Supplier agreement management
   - Configuration management
   - Quality assurance
   ---

6. Conduct peer reviews of the project's defined process.

   Refer to the Verification process area for more information about conducting peer reviews.

7. Revise the project's defined process as necessary.

SP 1.2-1 USE ORGANIZATIONAL PROCESS ASSETS FOR PLANNING PROJECT ACTIVITIES

Use the organizational process assets and measurement repository for estimating and planning the project's activities.

Refer to the Organizational Process Definition process area for more information about organizational process assets and the organization's measurement repository.

Typical Work Products

1. Project estimates
2. Project plans

Subpractices

1. Base the activities for estimating and planning on the tasks and work products of the project's defined process.

An understanding of the relationships among the various tasks and work products of the project's defined process, and of the roles to be performed by the relevant stakeholders, is a basis for developing a realistic plan.

2. Use the organization's measurement repository in estimating the project's planning parameters.

    This estimate typically includes the following:

    - Using appropriate historical data from this project or similar projects
    - Accounting for and recording similarities and differences between the current project and those projects whose historical data will be used
    - Independently validating the historical data
    - Recording the reasoning, assumptions, and rationale used to select the historical data

---

Examples of parameters that are considered for similarities and differences include the following:

- Work product and task attributes
- Application domain
- Design approach
- Operational environment
- Experience of the people

Examples of data contained in the organization's measurement repository include the following:

- Size of work products or other work product attributes
- Effort
- Cost
- Schedule
- Staffing
- Defects

SP 1.3-1 INTEGRATE PLANS

Integrate the project plan and the other plans that affect the project to describe the project's defined process.

Refer to the Project Planning process area for more information about establishing and maintaining a project plan.

Refer to the Organizational Process Definition process area for more information about organizational process assets and, in particular, the organization's measurement repository.

Refer to the Measurement and Analysis process area for more information about defining measures and measurement activities and using analytic techniques.

Refer to the Risk Management process area for more information about identifying and analyzing risks.

Refer to the Organizational Process Focus process area for more information about organizational process needs and objectives.

This specific practice extends the specific practices for establishing and maintaining a project plan to address additional planning activities such as incorporating the project's defined process, coordinating with relevant stakeholders, using organizational process assets, incorporating plans for peer reviews, and establishing objective entry and exit criteria for tasks.

The development of the project plan should account for current and projected needs, objectives, and requirements of the organization, customer, and end users, as appropriate.

FOR INTEGRATED PRODUCT AND PROCESS DEVELOPMENT
The plans of the integrated teams are included in this integration. Developing a complete project plan and the project's defined process may require an iterative effort if a complex, multi-layered, integrated team structure is being deployed.

FOR SUPPLIER SOURCING
The plans for integrated supplier management are included in this integration of plans. Plans for integrated supplier management must be coordinated with other related plans.

Typical Work Products

1. Integrated plans

Subpractices

1. Integrate other plans that affect the project with the project plan.
   Other plans that affect the project may include the following:
   - Quality assurance plans
   - Configuration management plans
   - Risk management strategy
   - Documentation plans
2. Incorporate into the project plan the definitions of measures and measurement activities for managing the project.

   Examples of measures that would be incorporated include the following:
   - Organization's common set of measures
   - Additional project-specific measures

3. Identify and analyze product and project interface risks.

> Examples of product and project interface risks include the following:
> - Incomplete interface descriptions
> - Unavailability of tools or test equipment
> - Availability of COTS components
> - Inadequate or ineffective team interfaces

4. Schedule the tasks in a sequence that accounts for critical development factors and project risks.

> Examples of factors considered in scheduling include the following:
> - Size and complexity of the tasks
> - Integration and test issues
> - Needs of the customer and end users
> - Availability of critical resources
> - Availability of key personnel

5. Incorporate the plans for performing peer reviews on the work products of the project's defined process.

   Refer to the Verification process area for more information about peer reviews.

6. Incorporate the training needed to perform the project's defined process in the project's training plans.

   This task typically involves negotiating with the organizational training group the support they will provide.

7. Establish objective entry and exit criteria to authorize the initiation and completion of the tasks described in the work breakdown structure (WBS).

   Refer to the Project Planning process area for more information about the WBS.

8. Ensure that the project plan is appropriately compatible with the plans of relevant stakeholders.

   Typically the plan and changes to the plan will be reviewed for compatibility.

> **FOR SUPPLIER SOURCING**
> Ensure that the plans for the integrated supplier management process are compatible with related plans.

9. Identify how conflicts will be resolved that arise among relevant stakeholders.

SP 1.4-1   *MANAGE THE PROJECT USING THE INTEGRATED PLANS*

Manage the project using the project plan, the other plans that affect the project, and the project's defined process.

Refer to the Organizational Process Definition process area for more information about the organizational process assets.

Refer to the Organizational Process Focus process area for more information about organizational process needs and objectives and coordinating process improvement activities with the rest of the organization.

Refer to the Risk Management process area for more information about managing risks.

Refer to the Project Monitoring and Control process area for more information about monitoring and controlling the project.

Typical Work Products

1. Work products created by performing the project's defined process
2. Collected measures ("actuals") and progress records or reports
3. Revised requirements, plans, and commitments
4. Integrated plans

Subpractices

1. Implement the project's defined process using the organization's process asset library.

    This task typically includes the following:

    - Incorporating artifacts from the organization's process asset library into the project as appropriate
    - Using lessons learned from the organization's process asset library to manage the project

2. Monitor and control the project's activities and work products using the project's defined process, project plan, and other plans that affect the project.

    This task typically includes the following:

    - Using the defined entry and exit criteria to authorize the initiation and determine the completion of the tasks
    - Monitoring the activities that could significantly affect the actual values of the project's planning parameters
    - Tracking the project's planning parameters using measurable thresholds that will trigger investigation and appropriate actions
    - Monitoring product and project interface risks
    - Managing external and internal commitments based on the plans for the tasks and work products of implementing the project's defined process

    An understanding of the relationships among the various tasks and work products of the project's defined process, and of the roles to be performed by the relevant stakeholders, along with well-defined control mechanisms (e.g., peer reviews) achieves better visibility into the project's performance and better control of the project.

3. Obtain and analyze the selected measures to manage the project and support the organization's needs.

    Refer to the Measurement and Analysis process area for more information about defining a process for obtaining and analyzing measures.

4. Periodically review the adequacy of the environment to meet the project's needs and to support coordination.

> **Examples of actions that might be taken include the following:**
> - Adding new tools
> - Acquiring additional networks, equipment, training, and support

5. Periodically review and align the project's performance with the current and anticipated needs, objectives, and requirements of the organization, customer, and end users, as appropriate.

   This review includes alignment with the organizational process needs and objectives.

> **Examples of actions that achieve alignment include the following:**
> - Accelerating the schedule, with appropriate adjustments to other planning parameters and the project risks
> - Changing the requirements in response to a change in market opportunities or customer and end-user needs
> - Terminating the project

SP 1.5-1   CONTRIBUTE TO THE ORGANIZATIONAL PROCESS ASSETS

Contribute work products, measures, and documented experiences to the organizational process assets.

Refer to the Organizational Process Focus process area for more information about process improvement proposals.

Refer to the Organizational Process Definition process area for more information about the organizational process assets, the organization's measurement repository, and the organization's process asset library.

This specific practice addresses collecting information from processes in the project's defined process.

Typical Work Products

1. Proposed improvements to the organizational process assets
2. Actual process and product measures collected from the project
3. Documentation (e.g., exemplary process descriptions, plans, training modules, checklists, and lessons learned)

Subpractices

1. Propose improvements to the organizational process assets.
2. Store process and product measures in the organization's measurement repository.

Refer to the Project Planning process area for more information about recording planning and replanning data.

Refer to the Project Monitoring and Control process area for more information about recording measures.

This typically includes the following:

- Planning data
- Replanning data
- Measures

Examples of data recorded by the project include the following:
- Task descriptions
- Assumptions
- Estimates
- Revised estimates
- Definitions of recorded data and measures
- Measures
- Context information that relates the measures to the activities performed and work products produced
- Associated information needed to reconstruct the estimates, assess their reasonableness, and derive estimates for new work

---

3. Submit documentation for possible inclusion in the organization's process asset library.

Examples of documentation include the following:
- Exemplary process descriptions
- Training modules
- Exemplary plans
- Checklists

---

4. Document lessons learned from the project for inclusion in the organization's process asset library.

SG 2   COORDINATE AND COLLABORATE WITH RELEVANT STAKEHOLDERS

Coordination and collaboration of the project with relevant stakeholders is conducted.

SP 2.1-1   MANAGE STAKEHOLDER INVOLVEMENT

Manage the involvement of the relevant stakeholders in the project.

Refer to the Project Planning process area for more information about identifying stakeholders and their appropriate involvement and about establishing and maintaining commitments.

Typical Work Products

1. Agendas and schedules for collaborative activities
2. Documented issues (e.g., issues with customer requirements, product and product-component requirements, product architecture, and product design)
3. Recommendations for resolving relevant stakeholder issues

Subpractices

1. Coordinate with the relevant stakeholders who should participate in the project's activities.

   The relevant stakeholders should already be identified in the project plan.

2. Ensure that work products that are produced to satisfy commitments meet the requirements of the recipient projects.

   Refer to the Verification process area for more information about determining acceptability of work products.

   This task typically includes the following:
   - Reviewing, demonstrating, or testing, as appropriate, each work product produced by relevant stakeholders
   - Reviewing, demonstrating, or testing, as appropriate, each work product produced by the project for other projects with representatives of the projects receiving the work product
   - Resolving issues related to the acceptance of the work products

3. Develop recommendations and coordinate the actions to resolve misunderstandings and problems with the product and product-component requirements, product and product-component architecture, and product and product-component design.

SP 2.2-1 MANAGE DEPENDENCIES

Participate with relevant stakeholders to identify, negotiate, and track critical dependencies.

Refer to the Project Planning process area for more information about identifying stakeholders and their appropriate involvement and about establishing and maintaining commitments.

Typical Work Products

1. Defects, issues, and action items resulting from reviews with relevant stakeholders
2. Critical dependencies
3. Commitments to address critical dependencies
4. Status of critical dependencies

Subpractices

1. Conduct reviews with relevant stakeholders.
2. Identify each critical dependency.
3. Establish need dates and plan dates for each critical dependency based on the project schedule.
4. Review and get agreement on the commitments to address each critical dependency with the people responsible for providing the work product and the people receiving the work product.
5. Document the critical dependencies and commitments.

    Documentation of commitments typically includes the following:
    - Describing the commitment
    - Identifying who made the commitment
    - Identifying who is responsible for satisfying the commitment
    - Specifying when the commitment will be satisfied
    - Specifying the criteria for determining if the commitment has been satisfied

6. Track the critical dependencies and commitments and take corrective action as appropriate.

    Refer to the Project Monitoring and Control process area for more information about tracking commitments.

    Tracking the critical dependencies typically includes the following:
    - Evaluating the effects of late and early completion for impacts on future activities and milestones
    - Resolving actual and potential problems with the responsible people whenever possible
    - Escalating to the appropriate managers the actual and potential problems not resolvable with the responsible people

SP 2.3-1 RESOLVE COORDINATION ISSUES

Resolve issues with relevant stakeholders.

Examples of coordination issues include the following:
- Late critical dependencies and commitments
- Product and product-component requirements and design defects
- Product-level problems
- Unavailability of critical resources or personnel

Typical Work Products

1. Relevant stakeholder coordination issues
2. Status of relevant stakeholder coordination issues

Subpractices

1. Identify and document issues.
2. Communicate issues to the relevant stakeholders.
3. Resolve issues with the relevant stakeholders.
4. Escalate to the appropriate managers those issues not resolvable with the relevant stakeholders.
5. Track the issues to closure.
6. Communicate with the relevant stakeholders on the status and resolution of the issues.

The following two specific goals, Use the Project's Shared Vision for IPPD and Organize Integrated Teams for IPPD, are only required for IPPD.

SG 3 USE THE PROJECT'S SHARED VISION FOR IPPD

The project is conducted using the project's shared vision.

The purpose of creating a shared vision is to achieve a unity of purpose. Creating a shared vision requires that all people in the project have an opportunity to speak and be heard about what really matters to them. The project's shared vision captures the project's guiding principles, including mission, objectives, expected behavior, and values. The project's guiding principles should be consistent with those of the organization. The implementation of the project's shared vision in work can become part of the project's process for doing that work. As a result, it is subject to the same requirements for measurement, review, and corrective action as other processes.

The value of a shared vision is that people understand and can adopt its principles to guide their actions and decisions. Shared visions tend to focus on an end state while leaving room for personal and team innovation, creativity, and enthusiasm. The activities of the individuals, teams, and project are aligned with the shared vision (i.e., the activities contribute to the achievement of the objectives expressed in the shared vision).

SP 3.1-1 DEFINE PROJECT'S SHARED-VISION CONTEXT

Identify expectations, constraints, interfaces, and operational conditions applicable to the project's shared vision.

Refer to the Organizational Environment for Integration process area for more information about the organization's shared vision.

A project does not operate in isolation. Understanding organizational expectations and constraints allows for alignment of the project's direction, activities, and shared vision with the organization's and helps create a common purpose within which project activities can be coordinated. To enable this, it is critical to understand (1) the interfaces between the project and stakeholders external to the project, (2) the objectives and expectations of all relevant stakeholders (internal and external), and (3) conditions within which the project must operate. Gaining awareness in these three areas ensures that the project's direction and activities are consistent with the broader objectives of the organization.

The project's shared-vision context has both an external and internal aspect. The external aspect has to do with the overlying vision and objectives as well as interfaces outside of the project. The internal aspect is about aligning project members' personal aspirations and objectives with the project's vision and purpose.

Typical Work Products

1. Organizational expectations and constraints that apply to the project
2. Summary of project members' personal aspirations for the project
3. External interfaces that the project is required to observe
4. Operational conditions that affect the project's activities
5. Project's shared-vision context

Subpractices

1. Identify expectations, constraints, interfaces, and operational conditions about the organization and the project that affect the project's shared vision.
2. Elicit project members' perspectives and aspirations for the project.
3. Create a description of the project's shared-vision context.

SP 3.2-1 *ESTABLISH THE PROJECT'S SHARED VISION*

Establish and maintain a shared vision for the project.

A shared vision is created by the project and for the project, in alignment with the organization's shared vision.

Refer to the Organizational Environment for Integration process area for more information about the organization's shared vision.

When creating a shared vision, consider:

- external stakeholder expectations and requirements
- the aspirations and expectations of the leader and project members

- the project's objectives
- the conditions and outcomes the project will create
- interfaces the project needs to maintain
- the visions created by the organization and interfacing groups
- the constraints imposed by outside authorities (e.g., environmental regulations)
- project operation while working to achieve its objectives (both principles and behaviors)

When creating a shared vision, all people in the project should be invited to participate. Although there may be a draft proposal, the larger population must have an opportunity to speak and be heard about what really matters to them. The shared vision is articulated in terms of both the core ideology (values, principles, and behaviors) and the desired future to which each member of the project can commit.

An effective communications strategy is key to implementing and focusing the shared vision throughout the project. Promulgation of the shared vision is a public declaration of the commitment of the project to their shared vision and provides the opportunity for others to examine, understand, and align their activities in a common direction. The shared vision should be communicated, and agreement and commitment of the relevant stakeholders should be obtained.

Effective communications are also especially important when incorporating new project members. New members of the project often need more or special attention to ensure that they understand the shared vision, have a stake in it, and are prepared to follow it in doing their work.

Typical Work Products

1. Meeting minutes for team-building exercises
2. Shared vision and objective statements
3. Statement of values and principles
4. Communications strategy
5. Handbook for new members of the project
6. Presentations to relevant stakeholders
7. Published principles, shared vision statement, mission statement, and objectives (e.g., posters, wallet cards)

Subpractices

1. Hold meetings or workshops to create the project's shared vision.
2. Articulate the project's shared vision in terms of purpose or mission, vision, values, and objectives.

3. Reach consensus on the project's shared vision.

4. Establish a strategy to communicate the project's shared vision both externally and internally.

5. Make presentations suitable for the various audiences that need to be informed about the project's shared vision.

6. Check that project and individual activities and tasks are aligned with the project's shared vision.

SG 4   ORGANIZE INTEGRATED TEAMS FOR IPPD

The integrated teams needed to execute the project are identified, defined, structured, and tasked.

The purpose of this specific goal and its specific practices is to create an integrated team structure that will efficiently meet the project's requirements and produce a quality product. The integrated team structure partitions responsibilities, requirements, and resources to teams so that the right expertise and abilities are available to produce the assigned products. The integrated teams are organized to facilitate communications among teams and to honor interfaces between product components.

Organizing integrated teams to realize IPPD requires care and deliberation. As the project evolves, integrated team structures are reevaluated for continued applicability. For example, once the product-component requirements are established, it may be appropriate to replace a leader having expertise in design with one having more expertise in manufacturing or in verification.

The teams in the structure must be appropriately integrated with each other. The interface between two integrated teams should be specified when one team has responsibility for a work product that has an interface requirement referring to a work product of the other team. An interface between teams should be specified when one team produces a work product that will be used by another. An interface should exist when two teams share responsibility for a general requirement of the product. Each of these types of interfaces between integrated teams may require a different type of collaboration as appropriate.

IPPD ONLY

SP 4.1-1   DETERMINE INTEGRATED TEAM STRUCTURE FOR THE PROJECT

Determine the integrated team structure that will best meet the project objectives and constraints.

Product requirements, cost, schedule, risk, resource projections, business processes, the project's defined process, and organizational guidelines are evaluated to establish the basis for defining integrated teams and their responsibilities, authorities, and interrelationships.

The simplest integrated team structure from an IPPD perspective evolves when the WBS is a work-product-oriented hierarchy, and resources are available to staff a team with the expertise needed to adequately address the entire life of the product for each work product in that hierarchy. More complex structuring occurs when the WBS is not product oriented, product risks are not uniform, and resources are constrained.

Structuring integrated teams is dependent on:

- Product risk and complexity
- Location and types of risks
- Integration risks, including product-component interfaces and inter-team communication
- Resources, including availability of appropriately skilled people
- Limitations on team size for effective collaboration
- Need for team membership of stakeholders external to the project
- Business processes
- Organizational structure

The integrated team structure can include the whole project as an integrated team. In this case, the project team would need to satisfy the requirements of the Integrated Teaming process area (e.g., it would need a shared vision [created in the Use the Project's Shared Vision for IPPD specific goal of this process area], a charter, clearly defined responsibilities, operating principles, and collaborative interfaces with other teams outside of the project).

If a project team has too many members for effective collaboration, the project team should be divided into subteams of appropriate size.

Typical Work Products

1. Assessments of the product and product architectures, including risk and complexity
2. Integrated team structures based on the WBS and adaptations
3. Alternative concepts for integrated team structures that include responsibilities, scope, and interfaces
4. Selected integrated team structure

Subpractices

1. Determine the risks in the products and product suite.

   Refer to the Risk Management process area for more information about practices associated with risk determination.

2. Determine likely resource requirements and availability.

   Refer to the Project Planning process area for more information about resource assignments.

   Constraints on the available assets impact which teams are formed and how the teams are structured.

3. Establish work-product-based responsibilities.

   Each team in the team structure should be responsible for specific tasks and work products. The team structure should tie to the WBS used by the project.

4. Consider organizational process assets for opportunities, constraints, and other factors that might influence integrated team structure.

   Organizational process assets can provide guidance to assist the project in structuring and implementing integrated teams. Such assets may include:

   - Team formation and structures
   - Team authority guidelines
   - Implementation techniques for IPPD
   - Guidelines for managing risks in IPPD
   - Guidelines for establishing lines of communication and authority
   - Team leader selection criteria
   - Team responsibility guidelines

5. Develop an understanding of the organization's shared vision, the project's shared vision, and the organization's standard processes and organizational process assets applicable to teams and team structures.

   The shared visions for the organization and project are examined. These visions help the planners focus on attributes critical to the organization and the project. Organizational processes provide information to streamline the planning process. These may be particularly useful when establishing reporting mechanisms for integrated teams and when integrated team structures are constructed in hybrid situations, such as project teams consisting of both functional and product teams.

6. Identify alternative integrated team structures.

   Alternative integrated team structures are frequently developed for collaborative evaluation prior to selection of the structure to be employed. Much like any other set of design alternatives, extreme cases should be included to test the adequacy of the solution set. Innovative concepts in integrated team structure that promote integration as well as efficiency can be overlooked if planning is limited to devising a single team structure.

7. Evaluate alternatives and select an integrated team structure.

   Refer to the Decision Analysis and Resolution process area for more information about a formal evaluation process for selecting the team structure.

   The integrated team structure that meets the objectives, subject to the constraints of time, money, and people, is collaboratively evaluated and selected from the alternative integrated team structures. From the perspective of team-structure maintenance, this activity would include assessments of the teams already deployed and candidate alternative structures.

SP 4.2-1 DEVELOP A PRELIMINARY DISTRIBUTION OF REQUIREMENTS TO INTEGRATED TEAMS

Develop a preliminary distribution of requirements, responsibilities, authorities, tasks, and interfaces to teams in the selected integrated team structure.

This preliminary distribution of requirements to integrated teams is done before any teams are formed to verify that the selected team structure is workable and covers all the necessary requirements, responsibilities, authorities, tasks, and interfaces. If this check is not satisfied, it is necessary to repeat the selection of team structure to meet this check. This preliminary distribution is a useful compendium of information that the integrated teams must know to effectively carry out their tasks in an integrated way.

Typical Work Products

1. Preliminary distribution of integrated team authorities and responsibilities
2. Preliminary distribution of the work product requirements, technical interfaces, and business (e.g., cost accounting, project management) interfaces each integrated team will be responsible for satisfying

Subpractices

1. Assemble requirements and interfaces for integrated teams.

   Assemble the tasks and work products, and the associated requirements and interfaces. Assign these to the appropriate integrated teams.

2. Check that the preliminary distribution of requirements and interfaces covers all specified product requirements and other requirements.

   In the event that complete coverage of requirements is not achieved, corrective action should be taken to redistribute requirements or to alter the integrated team structure.

3. Define responsibilities and authorities for integrated teams.

   Business, management, and other nontechnical responsibilities and authorities for the integrated team are necessary elements to proper team function. Integrated team responsibilities and authorities are normally developed by the project and are consistent with established organization practices. Such factors include:

   - Authority of teams to pick their own leader
   - Authority of teams to implement subteams (e.g., a product team forming an integration subteam)
   - Reporting chains

IPM

IPPD ONLY

- Reporting requirements (cost, schedule, and performance status)
- Progress reporting measures and methods

4. Designate the sponsor for each integrated team.

An integrated team sponsor is a manager (individual or team) who is responsible for establishing an integrated team, monitoring its activities and progress, and taking corrective action when needed. A manager may sponsor one or many teams.

SP 4.3-1 ESTABLISH INTEGRATED TEAMS

Establish and maintain teams in the integrated team structure.

The teams within the selected and satisfactory integrated team structure are established. This process encompasses the choosing of team leaders and the assignment of planned responsibilities and requirements for each team. It also involves providing the resources required to accomplish the tasks assigned to the team.

The integrated team structure is a dynamic entity that must be able to adjust to changes in people, requirements, and the nature of tasks, and to tackle many difficulties. The integrated team structure should be continuously monitored to detect malfunctions, mismanaged interfaces, and mismatches of the work to the staff. Corrective action should be taken when performance does not meet expectations.

Typical Work Products

1. A list of project integrated teams
2. List of team leaders
3. Responsibilities and authorities for each integrated team
4. Requirements allocated to each integrated team
5. Measures for evaluating the performance of integrated teams
6. Quality assurance reports
7. Periodic status reports
8. New integrated team structures

Subpractices

1. Choose integrated team leaders.

Integrated team leaders are selected who can achieve the expectations of the product in the context of organizational limitations (project priority and the needs of other projects). Integrated teams need a great deal of autonomy to faithfully implement IPPD. That autonomy is at risk if project or organizational leadership does not have confidence in the leader. The extent of organizational and project direction in selecting the leader is often a function of product risk and complexity. It can also be related to an organization's need to "grow" new leaders.

2. Allocate responsibilities and requirements to each integrated team.

The planned responsibilities and requirements are issued to the integrated team. These items are discussed with the team to encourage collaborative buy-in. Some adjustments may be made at this time.

3. Allocate resources to each integrated team.

The people and other resources are allocated to each integrated team. These items are discussed with the team to ensure that the resources are adequate and that the people are adequate to carry out the tasks and are compatible with other members of the team.

4. Create each integrated team.

Refer to the Integrated Teaming process area for more information about forming and sustaining each of the integrated teams in the team structure.

For each integrated team in the selected structure, create a team that has a shared vision, charter, and operating principles as described in the Integrated Teaming process area. Creating the integrated team is a collaborative effort of the team sponsor and the members of the team. Other relevant stakeholders may be involved in accordance with the plan for stakeholder involvement. The teams that interface with the target team should be involved to ensure that the specified interfaces are honored.

5. Integrated team composition and structures are periodically evaluated and modified to best reflect project needs.

Changes in team structure could include:

- Retiring a team for a period of time (e.g., while long duration manufacturing or verifications are done)
- Disbanding a team when it is no longer cost effective in serving the project
- Combining teams to achieve operating efficiencies
- Adding teams as new product components are identified for development

6. When a change of team leader or a significant change of membership of the team occurs, review the integrated team composition and its place in the integrated team structure.

A change of this kind may significantly affect the ability of the team to accomplish its objectives. A review of the match between the new composition and the current responsibilities should be made. If the match is not satisfactory, the team composition should be changed or the team's responsibility should be modified. One complication of changed responsibility is that other teams may have to adjust and add tasks to cover the change. This fact may cause a domino effect in the team structure. Such a change should be undertaken carefully.

7. When a change in team responsibility occurs, review the team composition and its tasking.

> These changes often occur as the project moves from one phase to the next. For example, less design expertise on teams may be needed when detailed design is completed and fabrication and integration of product components begins.

8. Manage the overall performance of the teams.

Generic Practices by Goal

GG 1   ACHIEVE SPECIFIC GOALS

The process supports and enables achievement of the specific goals of the process area by transforming identifiable input work products to produce identifiable output work products.

GP 1.1   PERFORM BASE PRACTICES

Perform the base practices of the integrated project management process to develop work products and provide services to achieve the specific goals of the process area.

GG 2   INSTITUTIONALIZE A MANAGED PROCESS

The process is institutionalized as a managed process.

GG 3   INSTITUTIONALIZE A DEFINED PROCESS

The process is institutionalized as a defined process.

> AUTHORS' NOTE: This generic goal's appearance here reflects its location in the staged representation.

Commitment to Perform

GP 2.1   ESTABLISH AN ORGANIZATIONAL POLICY

Establish and maintain an organizational policy for planning and performing the integrated project management process.

Elaboration

This policy establishes organizational expectations for using the project's defined process and coordinating and collaborating with relevant stakeholders.

> **FOR INTEGRATED PRODUCT AND PROCESS DEVELOPMENT**
> This policy also establishes organizational expectations for using Integrated Product and Process Development concepts for carrying out the objectives of the organization.

Ability to Perform

GP 2.2   PLAN THE PROCESS

Establish and maintain the plan for performing the integrated project management process.

Elaboration

Typically, this plan for performing the integrated project management process is a part of the project plan as described in the Project Planning process area.

GP 2.3   PROVIDE RESOURCES

Provide adequate resources for performing the integrated project management process, developing the work products, and providing the services of the process.

Elaboration

Examples of resources provided include the following tools:
- Problem-tracking and trouble-reporting packages
- Groupware
- Video conferencing
- Integrated decision database
- Integrated product support environments

GP 2.4   ASSIGN RESPONSIBILITY

Assign responsibility and authority for performing the process, developing the work products, and providing the services of the integrated project management process.

GP 2.5   TRAIN PEOPLE

Train the people performing or supporting the integrated project management process as needed.

Elaboration

Examples of training topics include the following:
- Tailoring the organization's set of standard processes to meet the needs of the project
- Procedures for managing the project based on the project's defined process
- Using the organization's measurement repository
- Using the organizational process assets
- Integrated management
- Intergroup coordination
- Group problem solving

FOR INTEGRATED PRODUCT AND PROCESS DEVELOPMENT

Examples of training topics also include the following:

- Building the project's shared vision
- Team building

Directing Implementation

GP 2.6   MANAGE CONFIGURATIONS

Place designated work products of the integrated project management process under appropriate levels of configuration management.

Elaboration

Examples of work products placed under configuration management include the following:

- The project's defined process
- Project plans
- Other plans that affect the project
- Integrated plans
- Actual process and product measures collected from the project

FOR INTEGRATED PRODUCT AND PROCESS DEVELOPMENT

Examples of work products placed under configuration management also include the following:

- Integrated team structure

GP 2.7   IDENTIFY AND INVOLVE RELEVANT STAKEHOLDERS

Identify and involve the relevant stakeholders of the integrated project management process as planned.

Elaboration

This generic practice is different from managing stakeholder involvement for the project, which is covered by specific practices within this process area.

Examples of activities for stakeholder involvement include:

- Resolving issues about the tailoring of the organizational process assets
- Resolving issues among the project plan and the other plans that affect the project
- Reviewing project performance to align with current and projected needs, objectives, and requirements

FOR INTEGRATED PRODUCT AND PROCESS DEVELOPMENT
Examples of activities for stakeholder involvement also include:
- Creating the project's shared vision
- Defining the integrated team structure for the project

GP 2.8   *MONITOR AND CONTROL THE PROCESS*

Monitor and control the integrated project management process against the plan for performing the process and take appropriate corrective action.

Elaboration

> Examples of measures used in monitoring and controlling include the following:
> - Number of changes to the project's defined process
> - Schedule and effort to tailor the organization's set of standard processes
> - Interface coordination issue trends (i.e., number identified and number closed)

FOR INTEGRATED PRODUCT AND PROCESS DEVELOPMENT
Examples of measures used in monitoring and controlling also include the following:
- Project's shared vision usage and effectiveness
- Integrated team-structure usage and effectiveness
- Select indicators of shared vision effectiveness that show (1) that there is unity of purpose within the project; (2) that project members are working together and meeting the project's objectives; (3) that behaviors and principles have been established and are being used while team members work to achieve objectives; and (4) that the shared vision of the project aligns with the existing visions of the organization and other projects, particularly those with which close interaction is expected

Verifying Implementation

GP 2.9   *OBJECTIVELY EVALUATE ADHERENCE*

Objectively evaluate adherence of the integrated project management process against its process description, standards, and procedures, and address non-compliance.

Elaboration

> Examples of activities reviewed include the following:
> - Establishing, maintaining, and using the project's defined process
> - Coordinating and collaborating with relevant stakeholders

FOR INTEGRATED PRODUCT AND PROCESS DEVELOPMENT

Examples of activities reviewed also include the following:

- Using the project's shared vision

Examples of work products reviewed include the following:

- Project's defined process
- Project plans
- Other plans that affect the project

FOR INTEGRATED PRODUCT AND PROCESS DEVELOPMENT

Examples of work products reviewed also include the following:

- Integrated plans
- Shared vision statements

GP 2.10 *REVIEW STATUS WITH HIGHER LEVEL MANAGEMENT*

Review the activities, status, and results of the integrated project management process with higher level management and resolve issues.

GG 3 *INSTITUTIONALIZE A DEFINED PROCESS*

The process is institutionalized as a defined process.

> AUTHORS' NOTE: This generic goal's appearance here reflects its location in the continuous representation.

C ONLY

Ability to Perform

GP 3.1 *ESTABLISH A DEFINED PROCESS*

Establish and maintain the description of a defined integrated project management process.

Elaboration

This generic practice is different from the Establish the Project's Defined Process specific practice in this process area. This generic practice establishes and maintains a defined integrated project management process. The Establish the Project's Defined Process specific practice defines the project's defined process, which includes all processes that affect the project.

Directing Implementation

GP 3.2 COLLECT IMPROVEMENT INFORMATION

Collect work products, measures, measurement results, and improvement information derived from planning and performing the integrated project management process to support the future use and improvement of the organization's processes and process assets.

Elaboration

This generic practice is different from the Contribute to the Organizational Process Assets specific practice in this process area. This generic practice collects improvement information about the integrated project management processes. The Contribute to the Organizational Process Assets specific practice collects information from processes in the project's defined process.

GG 4 INSTITUTIONALIZE A QUANTITATIVELY MANAGED PROCESS

The process is institutionalized as a quantitatively managed process.

GP 4.1 ESTABLISH QUANTITATIVE OBJECTIVES FOR THE PROCESS

Establish and maintain quantitative objectives for the integrated project management process that address quality and process performance based on customer needs and business objectives.

GP 4.2 STABILIZE SUBPROCESS PERFORMANCE

Stabilize the performance of one or more subprocesses to determine the ability of the integrated project management process to achieve the established quantitative quality and process-performance objectives.

GG 5 INSTITUTIONALIZE AN OPTIMIZING PROCESS

The process is institutionalized as an optimizing process.

GP 5.1 ENSURE CONTINUOUS PROCESS IMPROVEMENT

Ensure continuous improvement of the integrated project management process in fulfilling the relevant business objectives of the organization.

GP 5.2 CORRECT ROOT CAUSES OF PROBLEMS

Identify and correct the root causes of defects and other problems in the integrated project management process.

INTEGRATED SUPPLIER MANAGEMENT
A Project Management Process Area at Maturity Level 3

Purpose

The purpose of Integrated Supplier Management (ISM) is to proactively identify sources of products that may be used to satisfy the project's requirements and to manage selected suppliers while maintaining a cooperative project-supplier relationship.

Introductory Notes

Integrated Supplier Management involves monitoring the new products available on the market, evaluating sources of products that might help satisfy project requirements, and using this information to select suppliers. Integrated Supplier Management also involves maintaining a cooperative project-supplier relationship, monitoring selected supplier processes, evaluating selected work products, and making appropriate adjustments in the supplier relationship and agreement.

Integrated Supplier Management involves the following activities:

- Identifying, analyzing, and selecting potential sources of products
- Evaluating and determining the sources to be used for acquiring products
- Monitoring and analyzing selected supplier processes
- Evaluating selected supplier work products
- Revising the supplier agreement or relationship as appropriate

The Integrated Supplier Management process area builds on the concepts established in the Supplier Agreement Management process area by adding practices that emphasize a cooperative relationship with suppliers. Integrated Supplier Management is designed for situations in which projects use suppliers to perform functions that are critical to the success of the project. Analyzing sources and monitoring selected supplier processes and work products before delivery of the product to the project are two such functions described in this process area.

The practices in Supplier Agreement Management, such as Select Suppliers, Establish Supplier Agreements, and Execute the Supplier Agreement, are critically tied to Integrated Supplier Management. Appropriate references are provided in both process areas to emphasize these relationships.

Integrated Supplier Management emphasizes relationships with suppliers that are collaborative and coordinated. Projects evaluate the supplier's performance and the quality of the work products for compliance with the requirements in the supplier agreement. Integrated Supplier Management is not required for projects using off-the-shelf items that are generally available and that are not modified in any way; there, the use of Supplier Agreement Management is sufficient.

The term "source" refers to a potential supplier or suppliers before selection. (See the definitions of "supplier" and "product" in the glossary.)

The supplier agreement establishes the mechanism to allow the project to oversee supplier processes and work products and to evaluate any products being acquired. It also provides the vehicle for mutual understanding between the project and the supplier.

The specific practices of this process area can be implemented either within each project, by a separate group in the organization that supports multiple projects (e.g., contract management), or some combination of the two.

Related Process Areas

Refer to the Supplier Agreement Management process area for more information about establishing and maintaining agreements with suppliers.

Refer to the Project Planning process area for more information about planning and managing the involvement of stakeholders.

Refer to the Integrated Project Management process area for more information about establishing and maintaining the project's defined process and about implementing and managing integrated teams.

Refer to the Risk Management process area for more information about managing risks.

Refer to the Requirements Management process area for more information about managing requirements.

Refer to the Requirements Development process area for more information about developing product and product-component requirements.

Refer to the Technical Solution process area for more information about the products and product components to be acquired.

Practice-to-Goal Relationship Table

Continuous Representation	*Staged Representation*
SG 1 Analyze and Select Sources of Products	SG 1 Analyze and Select Sources of Products
SP 1.1-1 Analyze Potential Sources of Products	SP 1.1-1 Analyze Potential Sources of Products
SP 1.2-1 Evaluate and Determine Sources of Products	SP 1.2-1 Evaluate and Determine Sources of Products
SG 2 Coordinate Work with Suppliers	SG 2 Coordinate Work with Suppliers
SP 2.1-1 Monitor Selected Supplier Processes	SP 2.1-1 Monitor Selected Supplier Processes
SP 2.2-1 Evaluate Selected Supplier Work Products	SP 2.2-1 Evaluate Selected Supplier Work Products
SP 2.3-1 Revise the Supplier Agreement or Relationship	SP 2.3-1 Revise the Supplier Agreement or Relationship
GG 1 Achieve Specific Goals	
GP 1.1 Perform Base Practices	
GG 2 Institutionalize a Managed Process	GG 3 Institutionalize a Defined Process
GP 2.1 Establish an Organizational Policy	GP 2.1 Establish an Organizational Policy
GP 2.2 Plan the Process	GP 2.2 Plan the Process
GP 2.3 Provide Resources	GP 2.3 Provide Resources
GP 2.4 Assign Responsibility	GP 2.4 Assign Responsibility
GP 2.5 Train People	GP 2.5 Train People
GP 2.6 Manage Configurations	GP 2.6 Manage Configurations
GP 2.7 Identify and Involve Relevant Stakeholders	GP 2.7 Identify and Involve Relevant Stakeholders
GP 2.8 Monitor and Control the Process	GP 2.8 Monitor and Control the Process
GP 2.9 Objectively Evaluate Adherence	GP 2.9 Objectively Evaluate Adherence
GP 2.10 Review Status with Higher Level Management	GP 2.10 Review Status with Higher Level Management
GG 3 Institutionalize a Defined Process	
GP 3.1 Establish a Defined Process	GP 3.1 Establish a Defined Process
GP 3.2 Collect Improvement Information	GP 3.2 Collect Improvement Information
GG 4 Institutionalize a Quantitatively Managed Process	
GP 4.1 Establish Quantitative Objectives for the Process	
GP 4.2 Stabilize Subprocess Performance	
GG 5 Institutionalize an Optimizing Process	
GP 5.1 Ensure Continuous Process Improvement	
GP 5.2 Correct Root Causes of Problems	

Specific Practices by Goal

SG 1 ANALYZE AND SELECT SOURCES OF PRODUCTS

Potential sources of products that best fit the needs of the project are identified, analyzed, and selected.

The specific practices associated with this specific goal enhance the approach to selecting suppliers described in the Supplier Agreement Management process area by proactively identifying potential sources of products that satisfy the project's requirements and by using this information when selecting suppliers.

The specific practices associated with this specific goal augment those that help achieve the Establish Supplier Agreements specific goal of the Supplier Agreement Management process area and contribute to making the supplier selection decisions described in that process area.

SP 1.1-1 ANALYZE POTENTIAL SOURCES OF PRODUCTS

Identify and analyze potential sources of products that may be used to satisfy the project's requirements.

Identifying sources of products that might be used to satisfy the project's requirements involves monitoring the market to identify potential sources of such products. The products available in the market continually change, as does the information about the capabilities of products and their suppliers. Thus, new information that may be essential to deciding which potential sources are most effective continually becomes available. Monitoring the market to identify potential sources involves proactively searching for such information and incorporating it into ongoing and future decisions.

Typical Work Products

1. List of potential sources of products that might be acquired
2. Market studies
3. Trade studies
4. Information about potential sources such as past performance, post-delivery support, corporate viability, and risks

Subpractices

1. Conduct market research to identify potential sources of candidate products to be acquired, including candidates from suppliers of custom-made products and vendors of COTS products.

> *Refer to the Organizational Innovation and Deployment process area for examples of sources of process and technology improvements and how to pilot and evaluate such improvements.*

2. Evaluate potential sources against established criteria by performing trade studies, as appropriate.

   The purpose of evaluating sources is to achieve a better understanding of the relative merits of alternative sources in terms of their potential to satisfy project requirements.

3. Identify risks associated with the potential sources.

SP 1.2-1 *EVALUATE AND DETERMINE SOURCES OF PRODUCTS*

Use a formal evaluation process to determine which sources of custom-made and off-the-shelf products to use.

Factors that may affect the evaluation include the following:
- Core competencies
- Functions the products will provide and how these functions relate to customer needs
- Availability of on-site support such as responses to queries and problem reports
- Availability of maintenance support after delivery
- Availability of project resources and skills
- Ability to commit to critical delivery and integration dates
- Skills and capabilities
- Licenses, warranties, responsibilities, and limitations associated with the products
- Results of cost-to-benefit ratio analyses, as appropriate

Refer to the Decision Analysis and Resolution process area for more information about formal evaluation approaches that can be used to select suppliers.

Typical Work Products

1. Analysis and evaluation reports
2. Revised list of product sources

Subpractices

1. Determine the feasibility of acquiring custom-made or off-the-shelf products.
2. Determine product life-cycle costs of custom-made or off-the-shelf products.
3. Use the results of these analyses to select a supplier.

   Refer to the Select Suppliers specific practice of the Supplier Agreement Management process area for more information about selecting suppliers.

SG 2 COORDINATE WORK WITH SUPPLIERS

Work is coordinated with suppliers to ensure the supplier agreement is executed appropriately.

The relationship that exists among the project, supplier, customer, and end user requires special emphasis.

Achieving project success increasingly demands closely aligned, if not integrated, processes across organizational boundaries. The specific practices associated with this specific goal augment those that help achieve the Satisfy Supplier Agreements specific goal of the Supplier Agreement Management process area.

SP 2.1-1 MONITOR SELECTED SUPPLIER PROCESSES

Monitor and analyze selected processes used by the supplier.

In situations where there must be tight alignment between some of the processes implemented by the supplier and those of the project, monitoring these processes will help prevent interface problems.

The processes selected for monitoring should include engineering, project management (including contracting), and support processes critical to successful project performance.

Monitoring, if not performed with adequate care, can at one extreme be invasive and burdensome, or at the other extreme be uninformative and ineffective. There should be sufficient monitoring to detect issues, as early as possible, that may affect the supplier's ability to satisfy the requirements of the supplier agreement.

Analyzing selected processes involves taking the data obtained from monitoring selected supplier processes and analyzing it to determine whether there are serious issues.

Typical Work Products

1. List of processes selected for monitoring
2. Activity reports
3. Performance reports
4. Performance curves
5. Discrepancy reports

Subpractices

1. Identify the supplier processes that are critical to the success of the project.
2. Monitor the selected supplier's processes for compliance with requirements of the agreement.

3. Analyze the results of monitoring the selected processes to detect issues as early as possible that may affect the supplier's ability to satisfy the requirements of the agreement.

> Trend analysis can rely on internal and external data.
>
> *Refer to the Verification process area for more information about recording the results of verification and analyses.*
>
> *Refer to the Project Monitoring and Control process area for more information about taking corrective action.*

SP 2.2-1 EVALUATE SELECTED SUPPLIER WORK PRODUCTS

For custom-made products, evaluate selected supplier work products.

The scope of this specific practice is limited to suppliers providing the project with custom-made products. The intent of this specific practice is to evaluate selected work products produced by the supplier to help detect issues as early as possible that may affect the supplier's ability to satisfy the requirements of the agreement. The work products selected for evaluation should include critical products, product components, and work products that provide insight into quality issues as early as possible.

Typical Work Products

1. List of work products selected for monitoring
2. Activity reports
3. Discrepancy reports

Subpractices

1. Identify those work products that are critical to the success of the project and that should be evaluated to help detect issues as early as possible that may affect the supplier's ability to satisfy the requirements of the agreement.

> Examples of work products that may be critical to the success of the project include:
> - Requirements
> - Architecture
> - Documentation

2. Evaluate the selected work products.

> Work products are evaluated to ensure the following:
> - Derived requirements are traceable to higher level requirements.
> - The architecture is feasible and will satisfy future product growth and reuse needs.
> - Documentation that will be used to operate and to support the product is adequate.

- Work products are consistent with one another.
- Products and product components (e.g., custom-made, off-the-shelf, and customer-supplied products) can be integrated.

3. Determine and document actions needed to address deficiencies identified in the evaluations.

Refer to the Project Monitoring and Control process area for more information about taking corrective action.

SP 2.3-1   REVISE THE SUPPLIER AGREEMENT OR RELATIONSHIP

Revise the supplier agreement or relationship, as appropriate, to reflect changes in conditions.

There are a number of conditions that occur throughout the life of the supplier agreement that warrant changing this agreement or changing the project's relationship with the supplier. These conditions include changes in the business environment of the project or supplier; availability of new products in the market that can better satisfy the needs of the project; and deficiencies in supplier performance, project performance, or work product performance.

When the level of risk associated with satisfying the supplier agreement increases significantly, the project may make changes to the supplier agreement or to the relationship with the supplier. When the supplier's level of risk is low, the project should be careful not to impede the execution of the supplier's processes. This situation may also warrant making changes to the supplier agreement to minimize intervention.

Refer to the Establish Supplier Agreements specific practice of the Supplier Agreement Management process area for more information about establishing and maintaining formal agreements with the supplier.

Typical Work Products

1. Revisions to the supplier agreement
2. Revisions to the project's and supplier's processes and work products

Subpractices

1. Review the supplier agreement to ensure it accurately reflects the project's relationship with the supplier and current market conditions.
2. Revise the project's defined process or work products as necessary to reflect changes in the project-supplier relationship.

    Refer to the Integrated Project Management process area for more information about establishing and maintaining the project's defined process.

3. Ensure that the supplier's processes or work products are revised as necessary to reflect changes in the project-supplier relationship.

4. Coordinate changes to the supplier agreement with the supplier to ensure that changes in the project-supplier relationship are understood by both the project and the supplier.

    Make any adjustments that affect requirements in the supplier agreement through official channels.

5. Adapt the supplier agreement or relationship to better match the supplier's performance based on the results of risk evaluations.

6. Communicate to project members and other relevant stakeholders all changes to the supplier agreement and to the project-supplier relationship.

Generic Practices by Goal

GG 1 ACHIEVE SPECIFIC GOALS

The process supports and enables achievement of the specific goals of the process area by transforming identifiable input work products to produce identifiable output work products.

GP 1.1 PERFORM BASE PRACTICES

Perform the base practices of the integrated supplier management process to develop work products and provide services to achieve the specific goals of the process area.

GG 2 INSTITUTIONALIZE A MANAGED PROCESS

The process is institutionalized as a managed process.

GG 3 INSTITUTIONALIZE A DEFINED PROCESS

The process is institutionalized as a defined process.

> AUTHORS' NOTE: This generic goal's appearance here reflects its location in the staged representation.

Sidebar: CONTINUOUS ONLY / STAGED ONLY

Commitment to Perform

GP 2.1 ESTABLISH AN ORGANIZATIONAL POLICY

Establish and maintain an organizational policy for planning and performing the integrated supplier management process.

Elaboration

This policy establishes organizational expectations for identifying, analyzing, and selecting suppliers and for monitoring supplier processes, work products, and performance.

This policy also establishes organizational expectations for analyzing and managing risks relevant to potential sources and the project-supplier relationship.

Ability to Perform

GP 2.2 PLAN THE PROCESS

Establish and maintain the plan for performing the integrated supplier management process.

Elaboration

Typically, this plan for performing the integrated supplier management process is a part of the project plan as described in the Project Planning process area.

GP 2.3 PROVIDE RESOURCES

Provide adequate resources for performing the integrated supplier management process, developing the work products, and providing the services of the process.

Elaboration

Special expertise may be required including the following:
- *Ability to evaluate potential sources and select suppliers*
- *Knowledge of supplier management, including appraising a supplier's planning documents, processes, work products, and services*
- *Knowledge of risk management*
- *Knowledge of the domain of the product being acquired*
- *Knowledge of current engineering processes, work products, verification methods, technology, costing methodologies, and tools*

GP 2.4 ASSIGN RESPONSIBILITY

Assign responsibility and authority for performing the process, developing the work products, and providing the services of the integrated supplier management process.

GP 2.5 TRAIN PEOPLE

Train the people performing or supporting the integrated supplier management process as needed.

Elaboration

Examples of training topics include the following:
- Identifying potential sources for candidate products to be acquired
- Acquisition feasibility and product life-cycle costs analysis
- Evaluating supplier work products
- Monitoring supplier processes

Directing Implementation

GP 2.6 MANAGE CONFIGURATIONS

Place designated work products of the integrated supplier management process under appropriate levels of configuration management.

Elaboration

Examples of work products placed under configuration management include the following:

- Results of the acquisition feasibility and product life-cycle costs analysis
- Supplier agreements
- Discrepancy reports

GP 2.7 IDENTIFY AND INVOLVE RELEVANT STAKEHOLDERS

Identify and involve the relevant stakeholders of the integrated supplier management process as planned.

Elaboration

Examples of activities for stakeholder involvement include:

- Resolving issues about the improvements to supplier agreements
- Resolving issues about the meaning of the requirements to be fulfilled by the supplied products
- Resolving issues about the reporting of performance data and the handling of discrepancies

GP 2.8 MONITOR AND CONTROL THE PROCESS

Monitor and control the integrated supplier management process against the plan for performing the process and take appropriate corrective action.

Elaboration

Examples of measures used in monitoring and controlling include the following:

- Effort expended to manage the evaluation of sources and selection of suppliers
- Number of changes to the requirements in the supplier agreement
- Number of documented commitments between the project and the supplier
- Interface coordination issue trends (i.e., number identified and number closed)
- Quality measures of the supplied products

Verifying Implementation

GP 2.9 *OBJECTIVELY EVALUATE ADHERENCE*

Objectively evaluate adherence of the integrated supplier management process against its process description, standards, and procedures, and address noncompliance.

Elaboration

Examples of activities reviewed include the following:
- Managing the evaluation of sources and selection of suppliers according to the project's defined process
- Collecting data and providing appropriate data to the organization's measurement repository
- Using the organization's measurement repository to support management activities
- Ensuring that appropriate project subgroups participate in technical activities
- Identifying, negotiating, and tracking critical dependencies and commitments among the functions involved with the integrated supplier management process
- Handling agreement-coordination issues

GP 2.10 *REVIEW STATUS WITH HIGHER LEVEL MANAGEMENT*

Review the activities, status, and results of the integrated supplier management process with higher level management and resolve issues.

GG 3 *INSTITUTIONALIZE A DEFINED PROCESS*

The process is institutionalized as a defined process.

AUTHORS' NOTE: This generic goal's appearance here reflects its location in the continuous representation.

C ONLY

Ability to Perform

GP 3.1 *ESTABLISH A DEFINED PROCESS*

Establish and maintain the description of a defined integrated supplier management process.

Directing Implementation

GP 3.2 *COLLECT IMPROVEMENT INFORMATION*

Collect work products, measures, measurement results, and improvement information derived from planning and performing the integrated supplier management process to support the future use and improvement of the organization's processes and process assets.

GG 4 INSTITUTIONALIZE A QUANTITATIVELY MANAGED PROCESS

The process is institutionalized as a quantitatively managed process.

GP 4.1 ESTABLISH QUANTITATIVE OBJECTIVES FOR THE PROCESS

Establish and maintain quantitative objectives for the integrated supplier management process that address quality and process performance based on customer needs and business objectives.

GP 4.2 STABILIZE SUBPROCESS PERFORMANCE

Stabilize the performance of one or more subprocesses to determine the ability of the integrated supplier management process to achieve the established quantitative quality and process-performance objectives.

GG 5 INSTITUTIONALIZE AN OPTIMIZING PROCESS

The process is institutionalized as an optimizing process.

GP 5.1 ENSURE CONTINUOUS PROCESS IMPROVEMENT

Ensure continuous improvement of the integrated supplier management process in fulfilling the relevant business objectives of the organization.

GP 5.2 CORRECT ROOT CAUSES OF PROBLEMS

Identify and correct the root causes of defects and other problems in the integrated supplier management process.

INTEGRATED TEAMING
A Project Management Process Area at Maturity Level 3

Purpose

The purpose of Integrated Teaming (IT) is to form and sustain an integrated team for the development of work products.

Introductory Notes

Integrated team members:

- Provide the needed skills and expertise to accomplish the team's tasks
- Provide the advocacy and representation necessary to address all essential phases of the product's life cycle
- Collaborate internally and externally with other teams and relevant stakeholders as appropriate
- Share a common understanding of the team's tasks and objectives
- Conduct themselves in accordance with established operating principles and ground rules

An integrated team (also known as an "Integrated Product Team" or IPT) is composed of relevant stakeholders who generate and implement decisions for the work product being developed. The members of the integrated team are collectively responsible for delivering the work product. (See the definition of "integrated team" in the glossary.) The integrated team receives its assignment from its sponsor. The sponsor of an integrated team is a person or a group (e.g., project manager or even another integrated team) who can assign work tasks and provide resources.

The following characteristics distinguish an integrated team in an Integrated Product and Process Development (IPPD) environment from other forms of specialty work or task groups:

- Team members include empowered representatives from both technical and business functional organizations involved with the product. Within defined boundaries, these representatives have decision-making authority and the responsibility to act for their respective organizations.

- Team members may include customers, suppliers, and other stakeholders outside of the organization as appropriate to the product being developed.
- An integrated team consists of people skilled in the functions that need to be performed to develop required work products. Some of them may represent a functional organization. These people have a dual responsibility to focus on the product while maintaining their connections with the functional organization that can assist the development with additional expertise and advice.
- An integrated team focuses on the product life cycle to the extent required by the project. Team members share and integrate considerations, expectations, and requirements of the product life-cycle phases.
- An integrated team understands its role in the structure of teams for the overall project.

Clearly defined and commonly understood objectives, tasks, responsibilities, authority, and context (of vertical and horizontal interfaces) provide a strong basis for implementing integrated teams.

Related Process Areas

Refer to the Project Planning process area for more information about planning for project execution within an IPPD environment where integrated teaming is involved.

Refer to the Organizational Environment for Integration process area for more information about establishing and maintaining an integrated work environment and creating organizational process assets for IPPD, including an organization's shared vision.

Refer to the Integrated Project Management process area for more information about coordinating and collaborating with relevant stakeholders, establishing the team structure, and considering IPPD organizational process assets.

Specific Practices by Goal

SG 1   ESTABLISH TEAM COMPOSITION

A team composition that provides the knowledge and skills required to deliver the team's product is established and maintained.

One of the main attributes of an integrated team is to be self-managed and empowered. Team membership is intended to be composed of people who can plan, execute, and implement decisions for all phases of the life cycle of the work product being acquired or developed. Team member selection and skill mix should be based on the assigned work product and the objectives

Practice-to-Goal Relationship Table

Continuous Representation	*Staged Representation*
SG 1 Establish Team Composition	SG 1 Establish Team Composition
SP 1.1-1 Identify Team Tasks	SP 1.1-1 Identify Team Tasks
SP 1.2-1 Identify Needed Knowledge and Skills	SP 1.2-1 Identify Needed Knowledge and Skills
SP 1.3-1 Assign Appropriate Team Members	SP 1.3-1 Assign Appropriate Team Members
SG 2 Govern Team Operation	SG 2 Govern Team Operation
SP 2.1-1 Establish a Shared Vision	SP 2.1-1 Establish a Shared Vision
SP 2.2-1 Establish a Team Charter	SP 2.2-1 Establish a Team Charter
SP 2.3-1 Define Roles and Responsibilities	SP 2.3-1 Define Roles and Responsibilities
SP 2.4-1 Establish Operating Procedures	SP 2.4-1 Establish Operating Procedures
SP 2.5-1 Collaborate among Interfacing Teams	SP 2.5-1 Collaborate among Interfacing Teams
GG 1 Achieve Specific Goals	
GP 1.1 Perform Base Practices	
GG 2 Institutionalize a Managed Process	GG 3 Institutionalize a Defined Process
GP 2.1 Establish an Organizational Policy	GP 2.1 Establish an Organizational Policy
GP 2.2 Plan the Process	GP 2.2 Plan the Process
GP 2.3 Provide Resources	GP 2.3 Provide Resources
GP 2.4 Assign Responsibility	GP 2.4 Assign Responsibility
GP 2.5 Train People	GP 2.5 Train People
GP 2.6 Manage Configurations	GP 2.6 Manage Configurations
GP 2.7 Identify and Involve Relevant Stakeholders	GP 2.7 Identify and Involve Relevant Stakeholders
GP 2.8 Monitor and Control the Process	GP 2.8 Monitor and Control the Process
GP 2.9 Objectively Evaluate Adherence	GP 2.9 Objectively Evaluate Adherence
GP 2.10 Review Status with Higher Level Management	GP 2.10 Review Status with Higher Level Management
GG 3 Institutionalize a Defined Process	
GP 3.1 Establish a Defined Process	GP 3.1 Establish a Defined Process
GP 3.2 Collect Improvement Information	GP 3.2 Collect Improvement Information
GG 4 Institutionalize a Quantitatively Managed Process	
GP 4.1 Establish Quantitative Objectives for the Process	
GP 4.2 Stabilize Subprocess Performance	
GG 5 Institutionalize an Optimizing Process	
GP 5.1 Ensure Continuous Process Improvement	
GP 5.2 Correct Root Causes of Problems	

IT

that are important to the different phases of that product's life cycle. Integrated teams should be cross-functional and involve relevant stakeholders.

SP 1.1-1 IDENTIFY TEAM TASKS

Identify and define the team's specific internal tasks to generate the team's expected output.

The sponsor of an integrated team typically provides the assigned product requirements, the initial technical and business interfaces, and the high-level task(s) each team will be responsible for satisfying. Integrated team tasks are based on these product requirements and interfaces. An integrated team understands its relationship to both the project and the organization, and structures its tasks accordingly to develop the work products.

Typical Work Products

1. Descriptions of internal work tasks
2. List of results the team is expected to achieve for all work tasks

Subpractices

1. Define team tasks required to deliver the assigned work products.
2. Decide which tasks need team or individual member input.

    Not all work efforts require the entire team; however, review and judgment are team responsibilities.

SP 1.2-1 IDENTIFY NEEDED KNOWLEDGE AND SKILLS

Identify the knowledge, skills, and functional expertise needed to perform team tasks.

Refer to the Plan for Needed Knowledge and Skills specific practice in the Project Planning process area. Staffing a team is similar to staffing a project, just at a lower level.

The functional knowledge and related job skills within the integrated team are directly related to specific team tasks and responsibilities. A fully effective integrated team is able to perform its tasks and is composed of the necessary technical and business specialties and expertise. An integrated team advocates appropriate coverage for all phases of the work product life cycle. A profile of essential skill mixes that are required at all team functions describes the core team, which can be supplemented with additional skill sets as needed for the extended team.

Typical Work Products

1. List of disciplines or functions required to perform the tasks
2. List of the knowledge, key skills, and critical expertise

3. Initial profiles of team skills and knowledge for the core team and the extended team

Subpractices

1. Identify the business functions and processes in which the integrated team must maintain competence to perform its objectives.
2. Identify the core competencies on which to base the integrated team's activities to sustain or achieve desired capability.
3. Establish knowledge and skill profiles underlying each core and extended team competency.
4. Define staffing and competency requirements.

SP 1.3-1 ASSIGN APPROPRIATE TEAM MEMBERS

Assign the appropriate personnel to be team members based on required knowledge and skills.

Team members are selected and positioned to perform team tasks based on their ability to satisfy required knowledge, skills, and functional expertise, and complement those of other team members. Team membership may not stay the same throughout the integrated team's period of performance. Selecting and assigning appropriate new members to the team to perform team tasks is an important element in maintaining proper team composition and output as members leave, team expectations change, or the team has evolved to the point where a different mix of personnel is necessary.

Examples of relevant criteria for evaluating potential team members include:
- Knowledge and skills related to tasks and responsibilities associated with the team's assigned work products
- Interpersonal skills and ability to work in a team environment
- Ability to complement the mix of knowledge and skills in the team
- Potential to fulfill a significant responsibility on the team
- Ability to acquire additional knowledge, skills, or expertise related to the team's tasks
- Existing workload and time available to fulfill responsibilities to the team
- Educational and cultural background
- Personal (self) motivation
- Ability to represent a functional area appropriately

Individual team members are empowered, within defined limits, by their respective functional managers to make decisions. Team members can be selected from both within or outside of the organization and can include suppliers, customers, and end users. Their roles and responsibilities in team operation need to be clearly defined.

Typical Work Products

1. Set of selection criteria
2. Revised skills matrix and knowledge profiles
3. List of team members
4. List of the level of effort and resources, including access to staff, to perform each team function

Subpractices

1. Establish relevant criteria for evaluating team members against established knowledge and skills profiles.
2. Utilize the criteria to qualify appropriate candidates against the knowledge and skills profiles.
3. Identify and orient team members to best contribute to the team's capability.
4. Assess and determine the integrated team's capability to meet its objectives based on initial staffing and positioning.

    It may be required to supplement the team's internal capability with external sources to maximize the team's ability to perform its function.

SG 2   GOVERN TEAM OPERATION

Operation of the integrated team is governed according to established principles.

An integrated team operates in a disciplined way that brings about effectiveness and productivity in meeting its objectives. Established operating principles help both the team leader and team members to manage group dynamics and to ensure successful interplay among the multiple functions within the team.

SP 2.1-1   ESTABLISH A SHARED VISION

Establish and maintain a shared vision for the integrated team that is aligned with any overarching or higher level vision.

Refer to the Provide IPPD Infrastructure specific goal in the Organizational Environment for Integration process area for more information about the organization's shared vision.
Refer to the Use the Project's Shared Vision for IPPD specific goal in the Integrated Project Management process area for more information about the project's shared vision.

The purpose of a shared vision is to provide a statement of an envisioned future and establish a common understanding of the aspirations and governing ideals of the team in the context of that desired end state. The shared vision anchors the team's governing ideas and principles and captures the objectives to be achieved. The shared vision guides the activities of the team and helps drive the team to achieve its mission and objectives. A shared vision facilitates working together and helps the team to attain unity of purpose among its members.

No team operates in isolation. A shared vision for the integrated team is critical to ensure that the team's charter, direction, and activities achieve a fit with any larger project objectives or other interfacing teams. A team's sponsor(s) or leader may establish the vision for the organization or project of which the integrated team is a part. An integrated team's shared vision must be aligned with and support the achievement of the project's and organization's higher level objectives as well as its own. When one team falls short of or strays from its objectives and vision, it is likely to have a significant impact on the overall success of the project.

Shared vision context has both an external and internal aspect. The external aspect entails the objectives and interfaces of the team's sponsor and overall organization, while the internal aspect is about aligning the group member's personal interests and vision with the team's mission and purpose. The shared vision must ensure a commitment of the integrated team members to both their team and to other interfacing teams and project responsibilities.

Aligning personal perceptions of the people within the team is an important part of understanding and accepting the shared vision. As such, a shared vision is usually not the product of one person's effort; however, the team's sponsor(s) or leader may begin the discussion of the vision for a team. It is important that all integrated team members understand and commit to a shared vision. The team should openly discuss and be given the opportunity to provide feedback on the vision and address inconsistencies and make revisions as appropriate. This openness creates a vision that belongs to everyone, provides an end-state view of the implementation of the team's responsibilities, is the basis for the team's charter, and is applied to all work. Benefits of a shared vision are that people understand and can adopt its principles to guide their own, as well as the whole team's, actions and decisions.

Typical Work Products

1. Boundary conditions and interfaces within which the team must operate
2. Documented shared vision
3. Presentation materials of the shared-vision statement suitable for team members and various audiences that need to be informed

Subpractices

1. Convey the shared vision context to team members to align personal aspirations and objectives with the team's expectations and envisioned future outcome.
2. Conduct meetings or workshops to discuss the shared vision.

3. Articulate the shared vision in terms of both core ideology and the desired future end state that each member can commit to.

4. Reinforce the relevance of the shared vision in performing individual and team activities and tasks.

5. Check the effectiveness of the shared vision and that individual and team activities or tasks are aligned with the shared vision.

6. Periodically reexamine clarity and applicability of the shared vision and revise or realign as necessary to better meet the current state of the team or project.

SP 2.2-1   ESTABLISH A TEAM CHARTER

Establish and maintain a team charter based on the integrated team's shared vision and overall team objectives.

The team charter is the contract among the team members and between the team and its sponsor for the expected work effort and level of performance. Charters solidify the rights, guarantees, privileges, and permissions for organizing and performing the team's objectives and tasks. Development of the team charter is a negotiated activity between the sponsor of the team and the integrated team. When approved by both the team and the sponsor, the team charter constitutes a recognized agreement with management authority.

The complexity of the team charter can vary depending on the scope of effort and the team objectives. Team objectives may be directly related to the assigned product requirements from the sponsor, specific project requirements, or identified internal team tasks. The charter typically identifies team responsibilities and authority and the measures by which the team's progress will be evaluated.

It is important that integrated teams exercise a level of authority in managing their activities and in making decisions in pursuit of their objectives. Team members need to assess whether the amount of power and control over decisions and actions has been properly delegated from upper management. The team decides whether the decision-making authority is appropriate to meet expectations and to accomplish the tasks accepted by the team. The team negotiates any disagreements with the organizations or entities that assigned them.

Typical Work Products

1. Team charter
2. Procedures for setting the expectations for the work to be done and for measuring team performance
3. List of critical success factors
4. List of specific strategies the team expects to employ

Subpractices

1. Define and list the team objectives.
2. Identify specific strategies for achieving the team objectives.
3. Establish the team's level of empowerment and independence.

   Empowerment is not likely to be unlimited. Every team must operate within some constraints, and these limits on authority must be identified and defined up front.

   Refer to the Manage People for Integration specific goal in the Organizational Environment for Integration process area for more information about the organization's guidelines for the degree of empowerment for people and integrated teams.

4. Identify how team and individual performance and accomplishments are measured.

   Refer to the Organizational Environment for Integration process area for more information about recognizing team as well as individual accomplishments.

5. Identify critical success factors.

SP 2.3-1 DEFINE ROLES AND RESPONSIBILITIES

Clearly define and maintain each team member's roles and responsibilities.

Defined roles and responsibilities provide a clear understanding of the team members' contributions, level of involvement, interfaces (with team members and other teams or groups), and the degree of influence or control each member has on the success and functioning of the team. Allocation of roles and responsibilities should be based on each member's abilities, skills, and other commitments. Roles and responsibilities include the following:

- Establish and maintain interfaces among integrated team members
- Determine how assignments are accepted
- Determine how resources and input are accessed
- Determine how work gets done
- Determine who checks and reviews work
- Determine how work is approved
- Determine how work is delivered and communicated
- Maintain interfaces with their functional area

Typical Work Products

1. Descriptions of roles and responsibilities
2. Assignment statements
3. Responsibility matrix

Subpractices

1. Map the roles, responsibilities, and expertise of the team members to the team tasks and expected deliverables.

   Ensure that assignments are made to integrate complementary knowledge and skills.

2. Define the working relationship and reporting structure for team members.

   Team members may have the responsibility to report to both the team leader and a functional organization and management chain.

SP 2.4-1 ESTABLISH OPERATING PROCEDURES

Establish and maintain integrated team operating procedures.

Operating procedures and ground rules serve to define and control how the team will interact and work together and to promote effective integration of efforts, high performance, and productivity for accomplishing objectives. Members especially need to understand the intended standards for work and to participate according to those precepts.

Typical Work Products

1. Operating procedures and ground rules
2. Procedures for work expectations and performance measures

Subpractices

1. Define the expectations and rules that will guide how the team works collectively and what the team members will use to moderate participation and interpersonal interaction.

2. Define the degree of collective decision making and the level of consensus needed for team decisions.

   Refer to the Organizational Environment for Integration process area for more information about establishing a process for setting the context for decision making.

3. Define how conflicts and differences of opinion within the team are addressed and resolved.

   Refer to the Organizational Environment for Integration process area for more information about establishing a process for resolving conflicts and differences of opinion.

SP 2.5-1 COLLABORATE AMONG INTERFACING TEAMS

Establish and maintain collaboration among interfacing teams.

The success of a team-based project will be a function of how effectively and successfully the integrated teams collaborate with each other while achieving their own and the project's objectives.

Refer to the Integrated Project Management for IPPD process area for more information about operating in an integrated environment, and about coordinating and collaborating with relevant stakeholders.

Typical Work Products

1. Work product and process deployment charts
2. Input to the integrated master plan and integrated schedules
3. Team work plans
4. Commitment lists

Subpractices

1. Collaboratively establish and maintain the work product ownership boundaries among interfacing teams within the project or organization.
2. Collaboratively establish and maintain interfaces and processes among interfacing teams for the exchange of inputs, outputs, or work products.

   Refer to the Integrated Project Management process area for more information about coordinating and collaborating with relevant stakeholders.

3. Collaboratively develop, communicate, and distribute among interfacing teams the commitment lists and work plans that are related to the work product or team interfaces.

Generic Practices by Goal

GG 1 ACHIEVE SPECIFIC GOALS

The process supports and enables achievement of the specific goals of the process area by transforming identifiable input work products to produce identifiable output work products.

GP 1.1 PERFORM BASE PRACTICES

Perform the base practices of the integrated teaming process to develop work products and provide services to achieve the specific goals of the process area.

GG 2 INSTITUTIONALIZE A MANAGED PROCESS

The process is institutionalized as a managed process.

GG 3 INSTITUTIONALIZE A DEFINED PROCESS

The process is institutionalized as a defined process.

> AUTHORS' NOTE: This generic goal's appearance here reflects its location in the staged representation.

CONTINUOUS ONLY

STAGED ONLY

Commitment to Perform

GP 2.1   ESTABLISH AN ORGANIZATIONAL POLICY

Establish and maintain an organizational policy for planning and performing the integrated teaming process.

Elaboration

This policy establishes organizational expectations for establishing and maintaining team composition and governing team operation.

Ability to Perform

GP 2.2   PLAN THE PROCESS

Establish and maintain the plan for performing the integrated teaming process.

Elaboration

Typically, this plan for performing the integrated teaming process is a part of the project plan as described in the Project Planning process area.

GP 2.3   PROVIDE RESOURCES

Provide adequate resources for performing the integrated teaming process, developing the work products, and providing the services of the process.

Elaboration

Examples of special equipment and facilities include:
- Team war rooms (for regular strategy development and communication meetings)

Examples of other resources provided include the following tools:
- Interactive electronic communication and data presentation tools (groupware)
- Team-building tools

GP 2.4   ASSIGN RESPONSIBILITY

Assign responsibility and authority for performing the process, developing the work products, and providing the services of the integrated teaming process.

GP 2.5   TRAIN PEOPLE

Train the people performing or supporting the integrated teaming process as needed.

Elaboration

> Examples of training topics include the following:
> - Use of integrated work environments
> - Interpersonal skills
> - Communication skills
> - Team building
> - Collaborative problem solving and decision making

Directing Implementation

GP 2.6   *MANAGE CONFIGURATIONS*

Place designated work products of the integrated teaming process under appropriate levels of configuration management.

Elaboration

> Examples of work products placed under configuration management include the following:
> - List of team members
> - List of the level of effort and resources, including access to staff to perform each team function
> - Work task formal commitment lists
> - Team shared vision statement
> - Team charter

GP 2.7   *IDENTIFY AND INVOLVE RELEVANT STAKEHOLDERS*

Identify and involve the relevant stakeholders of the integrated teaming process as planned.

Elaboration

> Examples of activities for stakeholder involvement include the following:
> - Establishing and maintaining the team's shared vision
> - Establishing and maintaining the team's charter
> - Establishing and maintaining the team's operating procedures
> - Collaborating with interfacing teams

GP 2.8   *MONITOR AND CONTROL THE PROCESS*

Monitor and control the integrated teaming process against the plan for performing the process and take appropriate corrective action.

Elaboration

> Examples of measures used in monitoring and controlling include the following:
> - Performance according to plans, commitments, and procedures for the integrated team, and deviations from expectations
> - Ability to achieve team objectives

Verifying Implementation

GP 2.9 OBJECTIVELY EVALUATE ADHERENCE

Objectively evaluate adherence of the integrated teaming process against its process description, standards, and procedures, and address noncompliance.

Elaboration

> Examples of activities reviewed include the following:
> - Defined roles and responsibilities
> - Communication activities within and among integrated teams

> Examples of work products reviewed include the following:
> - Descriptions of roles and responsibilities
> - Descriptions of product ownership boundaries and team interfaces

GP 2.10 REVIEW STATUS WITH HIGHER LEVEL MANAGEMENT

Review the activities, status, and results of the integrated teaming process with higher level management and resolve issues.

GG 3 INSTITUTIONALIZE A DEFINED PROCESS

The process is institutionalized as a defined process.

> AUTHORS' NOTE: This generic goal's appearance here reflects its location in the continuous representation.

C ONLY

Ability to Perform

GP 3.1 ESTABLISH A DEFINED PROCESS

Establish and maintain the description of a defined integrated teaming process.

Directing Implementation

GP 3.2   COLLECT IMPROVEMENT INFORMATION

Collect work products, measures, measurement results, and improvement information derived from planning and performing the integrated teaming process to support the future use and improvement of the organization's processes and process assets.

GG 4   INSTITUTIONALIZE A QUANTITATIVELY MANAGED PROCESS

The process is institutionalized as a quantitatively managed process.

GP 4.1   ESTABLISH QUANTITATIVE OBJECTIVES FOR THE PROCESS

Establish and maintain quantitative objectives for the integrated teaming process that address quality and process performance based on customer needs and business objectives.

GP 4.2   STABILIZE SUBPROCESS PERFORMANCE

Stabilize the performance of one or more subprocesses to determine the ability of the integrated teaming process to achieve the established quantitative quality and process-performance objectives.

GG 5   INSTITUTIONALIZE AN OPTIMIZING PROCESS

The process is institutionalized as an optimizing process.

GP 5.1   ENSURE CONTINUOUS PROCESS IMPROVEMENT

Ensure continuous improvement of the integrated teaming process in fulfilling the relevant business objectives of the organization.

GP 5.2   CORRECT ROOT CAUSES OF PROBLEMS

Identify and correct the root causes of defects and other problems in the integrated teaming process.

CONTINUOUS ONLY

MEASUREMENT AND ANALYSIS
A Support Process Area at Maturity Level 2

Purpose

The purpose of Measurement and Analysis (MA) is to develop and sustain a measurement capability that is used to support management information needs.

Introductory Notes

The Measurement and Analysis process area involves the following:

- Specifying the objectives of measurement and analysis such that they are aligned with identified information needs and objectives
- Specifying the measures, data collection and storage mechanisms, analysis techniques, and reporting and feedback mechanisms
- Implementing the collection, storage, analysis, and reporting of the data
- Providing objective results that can be used in making informed decisions, and taking appropriate corrective actions

The integration of measurement and analysis activities into the processes of the project supports the following:

- Objective planning and estimating
- Tracking actual performance against established plans and objectives
- Identifying and resolving process-related issues
- Providing a basis for incorporating measurement into additional processes in the future

The staff required to implement a measurement capability may or may not be employed in a separate organization-wide program. Measurement capability may be integrated into individual projects or other organizational functions (e.g., Quality Assurance).

The initial focus for measurement activities is at the project level. However, a measurement capability may prove useful for addressing organization- and/or enterprise-wide information needs.

Projects may choose to store project-specific data and results in a project-specific repository. When data are shared more widely across projects, the data may reside in the organization's measurement repository.

> **FOR SUPPLIER SOURCING**
> Measurement and analysis of the product components provided by suppliers is essential for effective management of the quality and costs of the project. It may be possible, with careful management of supplier agreements, to provide insight into the data that support supplier-performance analysis.

Related Process Areas

Refer to the Project Planning process area for more information about estimating project attributes and other planning information needs.

Refer to the Project Monitoring and Control process area for more information about monitoring project performance information needs.

Refer to the Configuration Management process area for more information about managing measurement work products.

Refer to the Requirements Development process area for more information about meeting customer requirements and related information needs.

Refer to the Requirements Management process area for more information about maintaining requirements traceability and related information needs.

Refer to the Organizational Process Definition process area for more information about establishing the organization's measurement repository.

Refer to the Quantitative Project Management process area for more information about understanding variation and the appropriate use of statistical analysis techniques.

Specific Practices by Goal

SG 1   *ALIGN MEASUREMENT AND ANALYSIS ACTIVITIES*

Measurement objectives and activities are aligned with identified information needs and objectives.

The specific practices covered under this specific goal may be addressed concurrently or in any order:

• When establishing measurement objectives, experts often think ahead about necessary criteria for specifying measures and analysis procedures. They also

Practice-to-Goal Relationship Table

Continuous Representation	*Staged Representation*
SG 1 Align Measurement and Analysis Activities	SG 1 Align Measurement and Analysis Activities
SP 1.1-1 Establish Measurement Objectives	SP 1.1-1 Establish Measurement Objectives
SP 1.2-1 Specify Measures	SP 1.2-1 Specify Measures
SP 1.3-1 Specify Data Collection and Storage Procedures	SP 1.3-1 Specify Data Collection and Storage Procedures
SP 1.4-1 Specify Analysis Procedures	SP 1.4-1 Specify Analysis Procedures
SG 2 Provide Measurement Results	SG 2 Provide Measurement Results
SP 2.1-1 Collect Measurement Data	SP 2.1-1 Collect Measurement Data
SP 2.2-1 Analyze Measurement Data	SP 2.2-1 Analyze Measurement Data
SP 2.3-1 Store Data and Results	SP 2.3-1 Store Data and Results
SP 2.4-1 Communicate Results	SP 2.4-1 Communicate Results
GG 1 Achieve Specific Goals	
GP 1.1 Perform Base Practices	
GG 2 Institutionalize a Managed Process	GG 2 Institutionalize a Managed Process
GP 2.1 Establish an Organizational Policy	GP 2.1 Establish an Organizational Policy
GP 2.2 Plan the Process	GP 2.2 Plan the Process
GP 2.3 Provide Resources	GP 2.3 Provide Resources
GP 2.4 Assign Responsibility	GP 2.4 Assign Responsibility
GP 2.5 Train People	GP 2.5 Train People
GP 2.6 Manage Configurations	GP 2.6 Manage Configurations
GP 2.7 Identify and Involve Relevant Stakeholders	GP 2.7 Identify and Involve Relevant Stakeholders
GP 2.8 Monitor and Control the Process	GP 2.8 Monitor and Control the Process
GP 2.9 Objectively Evaluate Adherence	GP 2.9 Objectively Evaluate Adherence
GP 2.10 Review Status with Higher Level Management	GP 2.10 Review Status with Higher Level Management
GG 3 Institutionalize a Defined Process	GG 3 Institutionalize a Defined Process
GP 3.1 Establish a Defined Process	GP 3.1 Establish a Defined Process
GP 3.2 Collect Improvement Information	GP 3.2 Collect Improvement Information
GG 4 Institutionalize a Quantitatively Managed Process	
GP 4.1 Establish Quantitative Objectives for the Process	
GP 4.2 Stabilize Subprocess Performance	
GG 5 Institutionalize an Optimizing Process	
GP 5.1 Ensure Continuous Process Improvement	
GP 5.2 Correct Root Causes of Problems	

MA

C/ML 3–5

think concurrently about the constraints imposed by data collection and storage procedures.

- It often is important to specify the essential analyses that will be conducted before attending to details of measurement specification, data collection, or storage.

SP 1.1-1   ESTABLISH MEASUREMENT OBJECTIVES

Establish and maintain measurement objectives that are derived from identified information needs and objectives.

Measurement objectives document the purposes for which measurement and analysis are done, and specify the kinds of actions that may be taken based on the results of data analyses.

The sources for measurement objectives may be management, technical, project, product, or process implementation needs.

The measurement objectives may be constrained by existing processes, available resources, or other measurement considerations. Judgments may need to be made about whether the value of the results will be commensurate with the resources devoted to doing the work.

Modifications to identified information needs and objectives may, in turn, be indicated as a consequence of the process and results of measurement and analysis.

Sources of information needs and objectives may include the following:

- Project plans
- Monitoring of project performance
- Interviews with managers and others who have information needs
- Established management objectives
- Strategic plans
- Business plans
- Formal requirements or contractual obligations
- Recurring or other troublesome management or technical problems
- Experiences of other projects or organizational entities
- External industry benchmarks
- Process-improvement plans

Refer to the Project Planning process area for more information about estimating project attributes and other planning information needs.

Refer to the Project Monitoring and Control process area for more information about project performance information needs.

Refer to the Requirements Development process area for more information about meeting customer requirements and related information needs.

Refer to the Requirements Management process area for more information about maintaining requirements traceability and related information needs.

Typical Work Products

1. Measurement objectives

Subpractices

1. Document information needs and objectives.

   Information needs and objectives are documented to allow traceability to subsequent measurement and analysis activities.

2. Prioritize information needs and objectives.

   It may be neither possible nor desirable to subject all initially identified information needs to measurement and analysis. Priorities may also need to be set within the limits of available resources.

3. Document, review, and update measurement objectives.

   It is important to carefully consider the purposes and intended uses of measurement and analysis.

   The measurement objectives are documented, reviewed by management and other relevant stakeholders, and updated as necessary. Doing so enables traceability to subsequent measurement and analysis activities, and helps ensure that the analyses will properly address identified information needs and objectives.

   It is important that users of measurement and analysis results be involved in setting measurement objectives and deciding on plans of action. It may also be appropriate to involve those who provide the measurement data.

4. Provide feedback for refining and clarifying information needs and objectives as necessary.

   Identified information needs and objectives may need to be refined and clarified as a result of setting measurement objectives. Initial descriptions of information needs may be unclear or ambiguous. Conflicts may arise between existing needs and objectives. Precise targets on an already existing measure may be unrealistic.

5. Maintain traceability of the measurement objectives to the identified information needs and objectives.

   There must always be a good answer to the question, "Why are we measuring this?"

   Of course, the measurement objectives may also change to reflect evolving information needs and objectives.

SP 1.2-1 *SPECIFY MEASURES*

Specify measures to address the measurement objectives.

Measurement objectives are refined into precise, quantifiable measures.

Measures may be either "base" or "derived." Data for base measures are obtained by direct measurement. Data for derived measures come from other data, typically by combining two or more base measures.

Examples of commonly used base measures include the following:

- Estimates and actual measures of work product size (e.g., number of pages)
- Estimates and actual measures of effort and cost (e.g., number of person hours)
- Quality measures (e.g., number of defects, number of defects by severity)

Examples of commonly used derived measures include the following:

- Earned Value
- Schedule Performance Index
- Defect density
- Peer review coverage
- Test or verification coverage
- Reliability measures (e.g., mean time to failure)
- Quality measures (e.g., number of defects by severity/total number of defects)

Derived measures typically are expressed as ratios, composite indices, or other aggregate summary measures. They are often more quantitatively reliable and meaningfully interpretable than the base measures used to generate them.

Typical Work Products

1. Specifications of base and derived measures

Subpractices

1. Identify candidate measures based on documented measurement objectives.

   The measurement objectives are refined into specific measures. The identified candidate measures are categorized and specified by name and unit of measure.

2. Identify existing measures that already address the measurement objectives.

   Specifications for measures may already exist, perhaps established for other purposes earlier or elsewhere in the organization.

3. Specify operational definitions for the measures.

   Operational definitions are stated in precise and unambiguous terms. They address two important criteria as follows:

   - *Communication:* What has been measured, how was it measured, what are the units of measure, and what has been included or excluded?
   - *Repeatability:* Can the measurement be repeated, given the same definition, to get the same results?

4. Prioritize, review, and update measures.

> Proposed specifications of the measures are reviewed for their appropriateness with potential end users and other relevant stakeholders. Priorities are set or changed, and specifications of the measures are updated as necessary.

SP 1.3-1 SPECIFY DATA COLLECTION AND STORAGE PROCEDURES

Specify how measurement data will be obtained and stored.

Explicit specification of collection methods helps ensure that the right data are collected properly. It may also aid in further clarifying information needs and measurement objectives.

Proper attention to storage and retrieval procedures helps ensure that data are available and accessible for future use.

Typical Work Products

1. Data collection and storage procedures
2. Data collection tools

Subpractices

1. Identify existing sources of data that are generated from current work products, processes, or transactions.

> Existing sources of data may already have been identified when specifying the measures. Appropriate collection mechanisms may exist whether or not pertinent data have already been collected.

2. Identify measures for which data are needed, but are not currently available.
3. Specify how to collect and store the data for each required measure.

> Explicit specifications are made of how, where, and when the data will be collected. Procedures for collecting valid data are specified. The data are stored in an accessible manner for analysis, and it is determined whether they will be saved for possible reanalysis or documentation purposes.
>
> Questions to be considered typically include the following:
>
> - Have the frequency of collection and the points in the process where measurements will be made been determined?
> - Has the time line that is required to move measurement results from the points of collection to repositories, other databases, or end users been established?
> - Who is responsible for obtaining the data?
> - Who is responsible for data storage, retrieval, and security?
> - Have necessary supporting tools been developed or acquired?

4. Create data collection mechanisms and process guidance.

> Data collection and storage mechanisms are well integrated with other normal work processes. Data collection mechanisms may include manual or

automated forms and templates. Clear, concise guidance on correct procedures is available to those responsible for doing the work. Training is provided as necessary to clarify the processes necessary for collection of complete and accurate data and to minimize the burden on those who must provide and record the data.

5. Support automatic collection of the data where appropriate and feasible.

   Automated support can aid in collecting more complete and accurate data.

   > Examples of such automated support include the following:
   > - Timestamped activity logs
   > - Static or dynamic analyses of artifacts

   However, some data cannot be collected without human intervention (e.g., customer satisfaction or other human judgments), and setting up the necessary infrastructure for other automation may be costly.

6. Prioritize, review, and update data collection and storage procedures.

   Proposed procedures are reviewed for their appropriateness and feasibility with those who are responsible for providing, collecting, and storing the data. They also may have useful insights about how to improve existing processes, or be able to suggest other useful measures or analyses.

7. Update measures and measurement objectives as necessary.

   Priorities may need to be reset based on the following:
   - The importance of the measures
   - The amount of effort required to obtain the data

   Considerations include whether new forms, tools, or training would be required to obtain the data.

SP 1.4-1 SPECIFY ANALYSIS PROCEDURES

Specify how measurement data will be analyzed and reported.

Specifying the analysis procedures in advance ensures that appropriate analyses will be conducted and reported to address the documented measurement objectives (and thereby the information needs and objectives on which they are based). This approach also provides a check that the necessary data will in fact be collected.

Typical Work Products

1. Analysis specification and procedures
2. Data analysis tools

Subpractices

1. Specify and prioritize the analyses that will be conducted and the reports that will be prepared.

Early attention should be paid to the analyses that will be conducted and to the manner in which the results will be reported. These should meet the following criteria:

- The analyses explicitly address the documented measurement objectives
- Presentation of the results is clearly understandable by the audiences to whom the results are addressed

Priorities may have to be set within available resources.

2. Select appropriate data analysis methods and tools.

   Refer to the Select Measures and Analytic Techniques and Apply Statistical Methods to Understand Variation specific practices of the Quantitative Project Management process area for more information about the appropriate use of statistical analysis techniques and understanding variation, respectively.

   Issues to be considered typically include the following:

   - Choice of visual display and other presentation techniques (e.g., pie charts, bar charts, histograms, radar charts, line graphs, scatter plots, or tables)
   - Choice of appropriate descriptive statistics (e.g., arithmetic mean, median, or mode)
   - Decisions about statistical sampling criteria when it is impossible or unnecessary to examine every data element
   - Decisions about how to handle analysis in the presence of missing data elements
   - Selection of appropriate analysis tools

   Descriptive statistics are typically used in data analysis to do the following:

   - Examine distributions on the specified measures (e.g., central tendency, extent of variation, data points exhibiting unusual variation)
   - Examine the interrelationships among the specified measures (e.g., comparisons of defects by phase of the product's life cycle or by product component)
   - Display changes over time

3. Specify administrative procedures for analyzing the data and communicating the results.

   Issues to be considered typically include the following:

   - Identifying the persons and groups responsible for analyzing the data and presenting the results
   - Determining the time line to analyze the data and present the results
   - Determining the venues for communicating the results (e.g., progress reports, transmittal memos, written reports, or staff meetings)

4. Review and update the proposed content and format of the specified analyses and reports.

   All of the proposed content and format are subject to review and revision, including analytic methods and tools, administrative procedures, and priorities. The relevant stakeholders consulted should include intended end users, sponsors, data analysts, and data providers.

5. Update measures and measurement objectives as necessary.

Just as measurement needs drive data analysis, clarification of analysis criteria can affect measurement. Specifications for some measures may be refined further based on the specifications established for data analysis procedures. Other measures may prove to be unnecessary, or a need for additional measures may be recognized.

The exercise of specifying how measures will be analyzed and reported may also suggest the need for refining the measurement objectives themselves.

6. Specify criteria for evaluating the utility of the analysis results, and of the conduct of the measurement and analysis activities.

Criteria for evaluating the utility of the analysis might address the extent to which the following apply:

- The results are (1) provided on a timely basis, (2) understandable, and (3) used for decision making.
- The work does not cost more to perform than is justified by the benefits that it provides.

Criteria for evaluating the conduct of the measurement and analysis might include the extent to which the following apply:

- The amount of missing data or the number of flagged inconsistencies is beyond specified thresholds.
- There is selection bias in sampling (e.g., only satisfied end users are surveyed to evaluate end-user satisfaction, or only unsuccessful projects are evaluated to determine overall productivity).
- The measurement data are repeatable (e.g., statistically reliable).
- Statistical assumptions have been satisfied (e.g., about the distribution of data or about appropriate measurement scales).

SG 2 PROVIDE MEASUREMENT RESULTS

Measurement results that address identified information needs and objectives are provided.

The primary reason for doing measurement and analysis is to address identified information needs and objectives. Measurement results based on objective evidence can help to monitor performance, fulfill contractual obligations, make informed management and technical decisions, and enable corrective actions to be taken.

SP 2.1-1 COLLECT MEASUREMENT DATA

Obtain specified measurement data.

The data necessary for analysis are obtained and checked for completeness and integrity.

Typical Work Products

1. Base and derived measurement data sets
2. Results of data integrity tests

Subpractices

1. Obtain the data for base measures.

   Data are collected as necessary for previously used as well as for newly speci-fied base measures. Existing data are gathered from project records or from elsewhere in the organization.

   Note that data that were collected earlier may no longer be available for reuse in existing databases, paper records, or formal repositories.

2. Generate the data for derived measures.

   Values are newly calculated for all derived measures.

3. Perform data integrity checks as close to the source of the data as possible.

   All measurements are subject to error in specifying or recording data. It is always better to identify such errors and to identify sources of missing data early in the measurement and analysis cycle.

   Checks can include scans for missing data, out-of-bounds data values, and unusual patterns and correlation across measures. It is particularly important to do the following:

   - Test and correct for inconsistency of classifications made by human judg-ment (i.e., to determine how frequently people make differing classification decisions based on the same information, otherwise known as "inter-coder reliability").
   - Empirically examine the relationships among the measures that are used to calculate additional derived measures. Doing so can ensure that important distinctions are not overlooked and that the derived measures convey their intended meanings (otherwise known as "criterion validity").

SP 2.2-1 ANALYZE MEASUREMENT DATA

Analyze and interpret measurement data.

The measurement data are analyzed as planned, additional analyses are con-ducted as necessary, results are reviewed with relevant stakeholders, and nec-essary revisions for future analyses are noted.

Typical Work Products

1. Analysis results and draft reports

Subpractices

1. Conduct initial analyses, interpret the results, and draw preliminary conclusions.

    The results of data analyses are rarely self-evident. Criteria for interpreting the results and drawing conclusions should be stated explicitly.

2. Conduct additional measurement and analysis as necessary, and prepare results for presentation.

    The results of planned analyses may suggest (or require) additional, unanticipated analyses. In addition, they may identify needs to refine existing measures, to calculate additional derived measures, or even to collect data for additional primitive measures to properly complete the planned analysis. Similarly, preparing the initial results for presentation may identify the need for additional, unanticipated analyses.

3. Review the initial results with relevant stakeholders.

    It may be appropriate to review initial interpretations of the results and the way in which they are presented before disseminating and communicating them more widely.

    Reviewing the initial results before their release may prevent needless misunderstandings and lead to improvements in the data analysis and presentation.

    Relevant stakeholders with whom reviews may be conducted include intended end users and sponsors, as well as data analysts and data providers.

4. Refine criteria for future analyses.

    Valuable lessons that can improve future efforts are often learned from conducting data analyses and preparing results. Similarly, ways to improve measurement specifications and data collection procedures may become apparent, as may ideas for refining identified information needs and objectives.

SP 2.3-1 STORE DATA AND RESULTS

Manage and store measurement data, measurement specifications, and analysis results.

Storing measurement-related information enables the timely and cost-effective future use of historical data and results. The information also is needed to provide sufficient context for interpretation of the data, measurement criteria, and analysis results.

Information stored typically includes the following:

- Measurement plans
- Specifications of measures
- Sets of data that have been collected
- Analysis reports and presentations

The stored information contains or references the information needed to understand and interpret the measures and to assess them for reasonableness and applicability (e.g., measurement specifications used on different projects when comparing across projects).

Data sets for derived measures typically can be recalculated and need not be stored. However, it may be appropriate to store summaries based on derived measures (e.g., charts, tables of results, or report prose).

Interim analysis results need not be stored separately if they can be efficiently reconstructed.

Projects may choose to store project-specific data and results in a project-specific repository. When data are shared more widely across projects, the data may reside in the organization's measurement repository.

Refer to the Establish the Organization's Measurement Repository specific practice of the Organizational Process Definition process area for more information about establishing the organization's measurement repository.

Refer to the Configuration Management process area for information about managing measurement work products.

Typical Work Products

1. Stored data inventory

Subpractices

1. Review the data to ensure their completeness, integrity, accuracy, and currency.
2. Make the stored contents available for use only by appropriate groups and personnel.
3. Prevent the stored information from being used inappropriately.

> Examples of ways to prevent inappropriate use of the data and related information include controlling access to data and educating people on the appropriate use of data.

> Examples of inappropriate use include the following:
> - Disclosure of information that was provided in confidence
> - Faulty interpretations based on incomplete, out-of-context, or otherwise misleading information
> - Measures used to improperly evaluate the performance of people or to rank projects
> - Impugning the integrity of specific individuals

SP 2.4-1 COMMUNICATE RESULTS

Report results of measurement and analysis activities to all relevant stakeholders.

The results of the measurement and analysis process are communicated to relevant stakeholders in a timely and usable fashion to support decision making and assist in taking corrective action.

Relevant stakeholders include intended users, sponsors, data analysts, and data providers.

Typical Work Products

1. Delivered reports and related analysis results
2. Contextual information or guidance to aid in the interpretation of analysis results

Subpractices

1. Keep relevant stakeholders apprised of measurement results on a timely basis.

   Measurement results are communicated in time to be used for their intended purposes. Reports are unlikely to be used if they are distributed with little effort to follow up with those who need to know the results.

   To the extent possible and as part of the normal way they do business, users of measurement results are kept personally involved in setting objectives and deciding on plans of action for measurement and analysis. The users are regularly kept apprised of progress and interim results.

   Refer to the Project Monitoring and Control process area for more information about the use of measurement results.

2. Assist relevant stakeholders in understanding the results.

   Results are reported in a clear and concise manner appropriate to the methodological sophistication of the relevant stakeholders. They are understandable, easily interpretable, and clearly tied to identified information needs and objectives.

   The data are often not self-evident to practitioners who are not measurement experts. Measurement choices should be explicitly clear about the following:

   - How and why the base and derived measures were specified
   - How the data were obtained
   - How to interpret the results based on the data analysis methods that were used
   - How the results address information needs

Examples of actions to assist in understanding of results include the following:
- Discussing the results with the relevant stakeholders
- Providing a transmittal memo that provides background and explanation
- Briefing users on the results
- Providing training on the appropriate use and understanding of measurement results

Generic Practices by Goal

GG 1 ACHIEVE SPECIFIC GOALS

The process supports and enables achievement of the specific goals of the process area by transforming identifiable input work products to produce identifiable output work products.

GP 1.1 PERFORM BASE PRACTICES

Perform the base practices of the measurement and analysis process to develop work products and provide services to achieve the specific goals of the process area.

GG 2 INSTITUTIONALIZE A MANAGED PROCESS

The process is institutionalized as a managed process.

Commitment to Perform

GP 2.1 ESTABLISH AN ORGANIZATIONAL POLICY

Establish and maintain an organizational policy for planning and performing the measurement and analysis process.

Elaboration

This policy establishes organizational expectations for aligning measurement objectives and activities with identified information needs and objectives and for providing measurement results.

Ability to Perform

GP 2.2 PLAN THE PROCESS

Establish and maintain the plan for performing the measurement and analysis process.

MA

CONTINUOUS ONLY

Elaboration

Typically, this plan for performing the measurement and analysis process is included in (or referenced by) the project plan, which is described in the Project Planning process area.

GP 2.3 *PROVIDE RESOURCES*

Provide adequate resources for performing the measurement and analysis process, developing the work products, and providing the services of the process.

Elaboration

Measurement personnel may be employed full time or part time. A measurement group may or may not exist to support measurement activities across multiple projects.

Examples of other resources provided include the following tools:
- Statistical packages
- Packages that support data collection over networks

GP 2.4 *ASSIGN RESPONSIBILITY*

Assign responsibility and authority for performing the process, developing the work products, and providing the services of the measurement and analysis process.

GP 2.5 *TRAIN PEOPLE*

Train the people performing or supporting the measurement and analysis process as needed.

Elaboration

Examples of training topics include the following:
- Statistical techniques
- Data collection, analysis, and reporting processes
- Development of goal-related measurements (e.g., Goal Question Metric)

Directing Implementation

GP 2.6 *MANAGE CONFIGURATIONS*

Place designated work products of the measurement and analysis process under appropriate levels of configuration management.

Elaboration

> Examples of work products placed under configuration management include the following:
> - Specifications of base and derived measures
> - Data collection and storage procedures
> - Base and derived measurement data sets
> - Analysis results and draft reports
> - Data analysis tools

MA

GP 2.7   IDENTIFY AND INVOLVE RELEVANT STAKEHOLDERS

Identify and involve the relevant stakeholders of the measurement and analysis process as planned.

Elaboration

> Examples of activities for stakeholder involvement include the following:
> - Establishing measurement objectives and procedures
> - Assessing measurement data
> - Providing meaningful feedback to those responsible for providing the raw data on which the analysis and results depend

GP 2.8   MONITOR AND CONTROL THE PROCESS

Monitor and control the measurement and analysis process against the plan for performing the process and take appropriate corrective action.

Elaboration

> Examples of measures used in monitoring and controlling include the following:
> - Percentage of projects using progress and performance measures
> - Percentage of measurement objectives addressed

Verifying Implementation

GP 2.9   OBJECTIVELY EVALUATE ADHERENCE

Objectively evaluate adherence of the measurement and analysis process against its process description, standards, and procedures, and address noncompliance.

Elaboration

> Examples of activities reviewed include the following:
> - Aligning measurement and analysis activities
> - Providing measurement results

> Examples of work products reviewed include the following:
> - Specifications of base and derived measures
> - Data collection and storage procedures
> - Analysis results and draft reports

GP 2.10 REVIEW STATUS WITH HIGHER LEVEL MANAGEMENT

Review the activities, status, and results of the measurement and analysis process with higher level management and resolve issues.

AUTHORS' NOTE: GG3 and its practices do not apply for a
maturity level 2 rating, but do apply for a
maturity level 3 rating and above.

S ONLY

GG 3 INSTITUTIONALIZE A DEFINED PROCESS

The process is institutionalized as a defined process.

Ability to Perform

GP 3.1 ESTABLISH A DEFINED PROCESS

Establish and maintain the description of a defined measurement and analysis process.

Directing Implementation

GP 3.2 COLLECT IMPROVEMENT INFORMATION

Collect work products, measures, measurement results, and improvement information derived from planning and performing the measurement and analysis process to support the future use and improvement of the organization's processes and process assets.

GG 4 INSTITUTIONALIZE A QUANTITATIVELY MANAGED PROCESS

The process is institutionalized as a quantitatively managed process.

GP 4.1 ESTABLISH QUANTITATIVE OBJECTIVES FOR THE PROCESS

Establish and maintain quantitative objectives for the measurement and analysis process that address quality and process performance based on customer needs and business objectives.

CONTINUOUS/MATURITY LEVELS 3–5

CONTINUOUS ONLY

GP 4.2 STABILIZE SUBPROCESS PERFORMANCE

Stabilize the performance of one or more subprocesses to determine the ability of the measurement and analysis process to achieve the established quantitative quality and process-performance objectives.

GG 5 INSTITUTIONALIZE AN OPTIMIZING PROCESS

The process is institutionalized as an optimizing process.

GP 5.1 ENSURE CONTINUOUS PROCESS IMPROVEMENT

Ensure continuous improvement of the measurement and analysis process in fulfilling the relevant business objectives of the organization.

GP 5.2 CORRECT ROOT CAUSES OF PROBLEMS

Identify and correct the root causes of defects and other problems in the measurement and analysis process.

MA

CONTINUOUS ONLY

ORGANIZATIONAL ENVIRONMENT FOR INTEGRATION
A Support Process Area at Maturity Level 3

Purpose

The purpose of Organizational Environment for Integration (OEI) is to provide an Integrated Product and Process Development (IPPD) infrastructure and manage people for integration.

Introductory Notes

Successful integration of business and technical elements in projects is dependent on substantive and proactive organizational processes and guidelines. The organization is an integrated system capable of providing and sustaining the people, products, and processes necessary for the effective and efficient execution of its projects. The organization must raise performance expectations from all projects while providing mechanisms that stimulate both team and individual excellence.

Important characteristics of effective environments for integration include people trained to exploit the collaborative environment; a workplace that provides resources to maximize the productivity of people and facilitate integrated teams; and organization's set of standard processes and organizational process assets that culturally enable an IPPD environment that promotes and rewards team as well as individual excellence.

Related Process Areas

Refer to the Integrated Project Management process area for more information about managing relevant stakeholder involvement, resolving coordination issues, establishing the shared vision of a project, and organizing integrated teams.

Refer to the Organizational Process Definition process area for more information about establishing the organization's set of standard processes and process asset library.

Refer to the Organizational Training process area for more information about identifying training needs and providing the necessary training.

Specific Practices by Goal

SG 1 *PROVIDE IPPD INFRASTRUCTURE*

An infrastructure that maximizes the productivity of people and affects the collaboration necessary for integration is provided.

An organizational infrastructure that supports and promotes IPPD concepts is critical if IPPD is to be successfully sustained over the long term. An IPPD infrastructure includes the following:

- An organization's shared vision that promotes IPPD concepts such as concurrent development and integrated teaming
- A work environment that enables efficient and effective collaboration and integration
- People trained to collaborate, integrate, and lead others as necessary

SP 1.1-1 *ESTABLISH THE ORGANIZATION'S SHARED VISION*

Establish and maintain a shared vision for the organization.

Establishing and maintaining the organization's shared vision involves creating, communicating, using, and periodically evaluating and revising the shared vision. An organization's shared vision captures the organization's guiding principles including mission, objectives, expected behavior, and values. The shared visions of a project's integrated teams should be consistent with the project's shared vision, which in turn should be consistent with the organization's shared vision. (See the definition of "shared vision" in the glossary.)

Creating a shared vision involves establishing and actively maintaining agreement and commitment about what is to be done and how it will be accomplished, both procedurally and behaviorally. A shared vision is a result of an ongoing dialogue among all the people who will make it real. It continues to evolve as more ideas are shared.

The organization's shared vision facilitates people working together, helps those people to attain unity of purpose, and creates a common understanding of the end state that the organization is aiming to achieve. The organization's shared vision must speak to every element of the organization. Effectively impacting the lowest levels of the organization necessitates impacting the highest levels as well. The organization's leaders need to be role models for the actions of the organization. Their commitment to IPPD is critical to its success in the organization. They must clearly communicate their expectations for the organization's projects and integrated teams and what the projects and integrated teams can expect from management.

Practice-to-Goal Relationship Table

Continuous Representation	*Staged Representation*
SG 1 Provide IPPD Infrastructure	SG 1 Provide IPPD Infrastructure
SP 1.1-1 Establish the Organization's Shared Vision	SP 1.1-1 Establish the Organization's Shared Vision
SP 1.2-1 Establish an Integrated Work Environment	SP 1.2-1 Establish an Integrated Work Environment
SP 1.3-1 Identify IPPD-Unique Skill Requirements	SP 1.3-1 Identify IPPD-Unique Skill Requirements
SG 2 Manage People for Integration	SG 2 Manage People for Integration
SP 2.1-1 Establish Leadership Mechanisms	SP 2.1-1 Establish Leadership Mechanisms
SP 2.2-1 Establish Incentives for Integration	SP 2.2-1 Establish Incentives for Integration
SP 2.3-1 Establish Mechanisms to Balance Team and Home Organization Responsibilities	SP 2.3-1 Establish Mechanisms to Balance Team and Home Organization Responsibilities
GG 1 Achieve Specific Goals	
GP 1.1 Perform Base Practices	
GG 2 Institutionalize a Managed Process	GG 3 Institutionalize a Defined Process
GP 2.1 Establish an Organizational Policy	GP 2.1 Establish an Organizational Policy
GP 2.2 Plan the Process	GP 2.2 Plan the Process
GP 2.3 Provide Resources	GP 2.3 Provide Resources
GP 2.4 Assign Responsibility	GP 2.4 Assign Responsibility
GP 2.5 Train People	GP 2.5 Train People
GP 2.6 Manage Configurations	GP 2.6 Manage Configurations
GP 2.7 Identify and Involve Relevant Stakeholders	GP 2.7 Identify and Involve Relevant Stakeholders
GP 2.8 Monitor and Control the Process	GP 2.8 Monitor and Control the Process
GP 2.9 Objectively Evaluate Adherence	GP 2.9 Objectively Evaluate Adherence
GP 2.10 Review Status with Higher Level Management	GP 2.10 Review Status with Higher Level Management
GG 3 Institutionalize a Defined Process	
GP 3.1 Establish a Defined Process	GP 3.1 Establish a Defined Process
GP 3.2 Collect Improvement Information	GP 3.2 Collect Improvement Information
GG 4 Institutionalize a Quantitatively Managed Process	
GP 4.1 Establish Quantitative Objectives for the Process	
GP 4.2 Stabilize Subprocess Performance	
GG 5 Institutionalize an Optimizing Process	
GP 5.1 Ensure Continuous Process Improvement	
GP 5.2 Correct Root Causes of Problems	

OEI

The organization's shared vision needs to be grounded in reality. Organizations may be tempted to include in their shared vision broad statements about integrated teaming and employee empowerment. It is more important, however, to use the shared vision to set reasonable expectations on the rate of change in an organization. Unrealistic proclamations can transform the shared vision into a source of frustration and cause the organization to retreat from it after initial pilot demonstrations.

The organization's shared vision should be articulated in sufficient detail to provide criteria against which the shared visions of the projects and integrated teams can be aligned. For example, the organization's shared vision should address the use of integrated teams for projects, the focus on the customer, and the concurrent development of both product-related life-cycle processes and the product. These concepts, in turn, should be reflected in the shared visions of the projects and integrated teams. Guidelines for how projects and integrated teams should develop their shared visions should be made part of the organization's process asset library.

Maintenance of the organization's shared vision involves evaluating its use and currency. Results of evaluations may indicate the need to update the organization's shared vision or to establish and maintain organizational practices and structures that implement the shared vision.

Typical Work Products

1. Organization's shared vision
2. Evaluations of the organization's shared vision
3. Guidelines for shared vision building within projects and integrated teams

Subpractices

1. Identify expectations, constraints, interfaces, and boundary conditions applicable to the organization's shared vision.
2. Create a shared vision for the organization.

   The shared vision can include what the people in the organization can expect from the organization (e.g., some organizations have developed an "employees' bill of rights").
3. Communicate the shared vision both externally and internally.
4. Ensure that organizational practices and structures are aligned with the shared vision.

5. Periodically review the shared vision and update it as necessary.

Reexamine the shared vision to determine weaknesses and misunderstood parts. Revise the shared vision to improve its clarity and applicability to the current state of the organization. Periodically reinforce the clarity and reality of the shared vision.

6. Provide guidelines for shared vision building for use by projects and integrated teams.

These guidelines should establish the context for the shared visions of the projects and integrated teams.

Shared visions of the projects should be focused on product and contribute to achievement of the organization's shared vision. Shared visions of the projects could relate the minimum competencies, or demonstrated capabilities, for people assigned to integrated teams, such as individual leadership capabilities. Proposed products, activities, partnerships, organizational and project structures, and shared visions of the projects are tested against the organization's shared vision.

For the integrated teams, nurturing integration necessitates special attention to the objectives, values, and behaviors that are needed to affect integrated teamwork. Aspects, such as team operations, team behaviors, team responsibilities, and collaboration with interfacing teams, can be addressed.

SP 1.2-1 ESTABLISH AN INTEGRATED WORK ENVIRONMENT

Establish and maintain an integrated work environment that supports IPPD by enabling collaboration and concurrent development.

An integrated work environment includes the physical infrastructure (e.g., facilities, tools, equipment, and support needed to effectively use them) that people need to perform their jobs effectively. Properly functioning environments help people communicate clearly and efficiently about the product, processes, people needs, and organization. An integrated work environment helps integrate the business and technical functions and the interfaces among teams, projects, and organizations.

The integrated work environment must accommodate both collocated and distributed integrated teams as required. Two-way communications media should be easily accessible by all relevant stakeholders.

Encouraging open dialogue by providing communication mechanisms enables everyone to effectively engage in and contribute to information sharing.

Appropriate mechanisms might include meeting rooms, email, fax, FTP or Web sites, video teleconferencing capabilities, and others depending on the organization's culture and its project and integrated team preferences for efficient and effective information sharing. The types of information needed, which agents (projects, integrated teams, or individuals), and how many of them produce, own, and need that information should be considered in deciding the mechanisms to be used.

Integrated communication tool sets reduce time spent converting information from one medium or platform to another, and correcting transcriptions or misunderstandings when people do the conversions. Requirements for product and process information usability throughout the life of the product are important characteristics to consider in the selection of information-exchange tools. In an IPPD environment, it is particularly important that the tools for designing and developing the product-related life-cycle processes are integrated with the tools for designing and developing the product and product components.

Integrated work environments are developed with the same, or greater, rigor as that used to develop a specific product or service. Integrated work environments are capital assets that are often expensive, have unique implementations, are irreversible (their implementation can destroy or make unusable the assets being replaced), and whose modification disrupts ongoing activities. The rigor appropriate to the development should be matched to the magnitude of the needs to be resolved and the deployment risks.

Typical Work Products

1. Requirements for the integrated work environment
2. Design of the integrated work environment
3. Integrated work environment

Subpractices

1. Determine requirements for the integrated work environment.

   Requirements for the integrated work environment are typically based on the following:

   - The organization's set of standard processes
   - The objectives of the organization articulated in the organization's shared vision
   - The needs associated with developing, maintaining, and delivering the products and services of the organization

2. Regularly evaluate the effectiveness of the existing environment and forecast the need for additional, upgraded, or new tools or integrated work environment components.

3. Maintain awareness of current and emerging technologies, tools, and resources that are related to the integrated work environment.

> Maintaining awareness may be accomplished through industry journals, professional societies, conferences, trade shows, or benchmarking.

Examples of technologies, tools, and resources include the following:
- Computing resources and software productivity tools
- Communications systems, tools, and resources
- Communication tools (e.g., email, telephone, databases, archives)
- Manufacturing and production facilities
- Engineering or simulation tools
- Proprietary engineering tools
- Prototyping or production equipment
- Work space
- Office equipment and supplies
- Raw or stock input materials
- Transportation resources
- "Hotlines" and "help desks"
- Information brokerage services
- Support staff and/or services
- Information-technology capabilities
- Process enactment and management tools

4. Plan, design, and implement an integrated work environment.

> The critical aspects of the work environment are, like any other system, requirements driven. Work environment functionality (stimulated by customer needs and requirements) is explored with the same rigor as any other system development. Are the performance improvements (e.g., timely interoperable communications, safety, security, maintainability) worth the costs (e.g., capital outlays, training, support structure, disassembly and disposal of existing environments, performance and maintenance of the environment) and risks (e.g., workflow and project disruptions)?
>
> Requirements are developed for the duration of the work environment and address, as appropriate, the three different cases for work environment improvements: developing a new environment, migrating an existing environment to new capabilities, and maintaining awareness of new and evolving technologies to exploit improvement opportunities. As required, the integrated work environment or some of its components can be developed in house or acquired from external sources.

5. Provide ongoing maintenance and operational support for the integrated work environment.

> Maintenance and support of the integrated work environment can be accomplished either with capabilities found inside the organization or hired from outside the organization.

> Examples of maintenance and support methods include the following:
> - Hiring people to perform the maintenance and support
> - Training people to perform the maintenance and support
> - Contracting the maintenance and support
> - Developing expert users for selected automation tools

6. Monitor and evaluate the adequacy of the integrated work environment to satisfy user needs.

   Refer to the Project Monitoring and Control process area for more information about practices for monitoring and controlling the work environment.

   The work environment should be monitored throughout its existence to ascertain if, and when, its performance degrades below that expected (or specified) as well as to identify opportunities for improvements. The key operating characteristics of the integrated work environment should be identified. The key operating characteristics are those performance, product, and process characteristics that can be measured and compared against expected capabilities of the integrated work environment. End users should be surveyed to determine the adequacy of the current environment and to identify potential improvements. Changes should be planned and implemented based on the analysis of usage and performance data and on identified real and potential problems.

7. Revise the integrated work environment as necessary, by adding, deleting, or replacing components.

SP 1.3-1 *IDENTIFY IPPD-UNIQUE SKILL REQUIREMENTS*

Identify the unique skills needed to support the IPPD environment.

Refer to the Organizational Training process area for more information about determining training needs and delivering the training.

IPPD is a sufficiently different view of product development that the organization's leadership and workforce will need to develop new skills. IPPD requires integrative leadership, and interpersonal skills beyond those typically found in traditional environments where people tend to work alone or primarily interact with others from their own, or similar, functions or disciplines. Specific skills emphasized in an IPPD environment include the following:

- The skills to integrate all appropriate business and technical functions and their processes
- The interpersonal skills to coordinate and collaborate with others
- The leadership skills to act, and successfully influence others to act, to achieve the shared vision

Training to support these new skills must be established and maintained to sustain the ongoing adoption of IPPD in the organization.

Each integrated team member needs to understand what is vital to other team members in terms of product characteristics and the descriptions, expectations, and interfaces of the processes associated with the other functions represented on the team. This understanding can often be augmented through cross training of individuals across their function or discipline boundaries.

Collaboration among integrated team members is essential to create a team product rather than a collection of independent products. Enhanced interpersonal skills can help bridge the differences among disparate functions and disciplines as well as the differences in cultures, values, and backgrounds.

Leadership demands also increase under IPPD. Leadership challenges include: ensuring that all team members mutually understand their roles and responsibilities; employing people in their intended roles; and effectively accessing the depth and wealth of specific expertise resident in the organization and integrating it into the overall integrated team effort.

Typical Work Products

1. IPPD strategic training needs
2. IPPD tactical training needs

Subpractices

1. Provide requirements for IPPD skills for inclusion in the organization's strategic training needs.
2. Provide requirements for IPPD skills for inclusion in the organization's tactical training plan.

SG 2 MANAGE PEOPLE FOR INTEGRATION

People are managed to nurture the integrative and collaborative behaviors of an IPPD environment.

In an IPPD environment, special attention needs to be paid to aspects of organizational leadership and management. Nurturing integration necessitates focus on the objectives, values, and behaviors that are needed to affect integrated teamwork. The organization establishes the IPPD guidelines and processes that become part of the organization's set of standard processes and the project's defined process. The organization's standard processes enable, promote, and reinforce the integrative behaviors expected from projects, integrated teams, and people. For all IPPD processes and guidelines, people are recognized not as the tools or means to the end, but as part of a mutually beneficial collaboration to achieve the objectives.

In stimulating the integration needed, team-related incentives may be appropriate for people who work together. However, the value of individual excellence should not be overlooked. A balanced approach that addresses both individual performance as well as team performance would help maintain high standards of both team and individual achievement. Expectations from projects, integrated teams, and people are typically communicated in the form of policies, operating procedures, guidelines, and other organizational process assets.

SP 2.1-1 ESTABLISH LEADERSHIP MECHANISMS

Establish and maintain leadership mechanisms to enable timely collaboration.

Implementing IPPD introduces challenges to leadership because of the cultural changes required when people and integrated teams are empowered and decisions are driven to the lowest level appropriate. Effective and efficient communication mechanisms are critical to timely and sound decision making in the integrated work environment. Once an integrated work environment is established and training is provided, mechanisms to handle empowerment, decision making, and issue resolution also need to be provided to affect the timely collaboration of relevant stakeholders required for IPPD.

In an IPPD environment, it is particularly important that clear channels of responsibility and authority be established. Within the projects and the organization, issues can arise when individuals or integrated teams assume too much or too little authority and when the level at which decisions are made, or who owns what decisions, is unclear. Organizational guidelines that scope the degree of empowerment for integrated teams serve an issue-prevention role. Best practices promote documented and deployed organizational guidelines that can preclude issues arising from empowerment and authority misinterpretation.

Empowerment does not necessarily mean that every decision in an IPPD environment must occur at the lowest level, that it must be done collaboratively, or even that it must reflect consensus among all integrated team members or project participants. Decisions on the style and procedures for leadership and decision making for projects and among integrated teams need to be made in collaboration with the relevant stakeholders. In establishing the context for decision making, the various kinds of issues are described and agreements are reached on the decision type that will be used to resolve each kind of issue.

Some examples of decision types include the following:

- *Command.* The leader examines the issue and makes a decision alone.
- *Consultative.* The leader receives and examines inputs on the issue from relevant stakeholders and makes the decision.
- *Collaborative.* Issues are raised by any relevant stakeholders (including the leader), issues are discussed, and solutions are voted on. Rules are needed to determine whether this vote is binding on the leader.
- *Consensus.* Issues are raised by any relevant stakeholders, including the leader, and are discussed until all members of the integrated team can live with and support the decision.
- *Structured.* Major issues may be decided using formal evaluations. The steps in formal evaluations may be carried out in a collaborative way.

For many issues, a command decision may be adequate. For issues that require several different areas of expertise or that have far-reaching consequences, collaborative decisions may be more appropriate. Defining decision types and the authority of those entrusted to make decisions enables efficient operations.

Mechanisms that grow leadership talent enable lower organizational unit delegation, which, in turn, enables faster, better responses to changing customer needs, technology, and environmental conditions.

Leadership characteristics cannot be viewed as solely embodied in the manager/leader. When leadership characteristics are evident in more than the leader, individual group members lead decision making and activities that heavily involve their areas of expertise. This flexibility can result in improved group efficiency and effectiveness.

Even with well-intentioned empowerment, leadership, and decision making, issues will arise that cannot be resolved at the same level. An organizational process for issue resolution can form the basis for project- and integrated-team-specific procedures and help ensure that basic issue-resolution avenues are available to projects and integrated teams when unresolved issues must be escalated. An organizational process for issue resolution can serve both issue-resolution and issue-prevention roles.

Typical Work Products

1. Guidelines for determining the degree of empowerment of people and integrated teams
2. Guidelines for setting leadership and decision-making context
3. Organizational process documentation for issue resolution

Subpractices

1. Establish and maintain guidelines for the degree of empowerment provided to people and integrated teams.
2. Collaboratively determine rules for the use of different decision types in making various kinds of decisions.

   Refer to the Decision Analysis and Resolution process area for more information about approaches for evaluating and selecting among alternatives.
3. Define the process for using the decision-making rules.
4. Define a process for conflict resolution when an issue cannot be decided at the level at which it arose.

SP 2.2-1 ESTABLISH INCENTIVES FOR INTEGRATION

Establish and maintain incentives for adopting and demonstrating integrative and collaborative behaviors at all levels of the organization.

The recognition and reward systems in an organization are one of the motivators for behavior and value changes. To support IPPD, the recognition and reward systems (both positive rewards and negative consequences) need to recognize a shift in values from a single point of success or failure (e.g., providing a management incentive package to the product or program manager alone) to integrated team success or failure (e.g., providing layered incentives to integrated team members based on degree of involvement and contribution).

Individual excellence still should be recognized, but criteria should discern whether such excellence was achieved at the expense of the integrative behaviors expected or in support of them. For example, individuals (such as leaders) removing integration barriers or implementing collaboration capabilities may be just as important as an integrated team performing well. Care should be taken, however, not to single out individuals for recognition for a team's achievement.

Incentives should be consistent with the objectives of the organization and applied to achieve desired behavior at all levels of the organization. Criteria can establish guidelines for the reassignment of people who are unable to demonstrate desired behavior and the selection of people who can exhibit desired behavior for challenging or important jobs.

Compensation is not the only motivator, although giving an object of some value is an appropriate recognition. Reinforcement of positive behavior via thanks or praise is usually appropriate, especially soon after the observed performance of a task. Such immediate recognition reinforces the collaborative nature of working in an IPPD environment. If staff must wait for yearly performance appraisals, their motivation for working outside of their strict functional job description is lessened.

The yearly performance appraisals also need to be addressed. Review mechanisms should be structured so that both home organization supervisors and team leaders contribute to a person's performance review.

Typical Work Products

1. Policies and procedures for performance appraisal and recognition that reinforce collaboration
2. Integrated team and individual recognition and rewards

Subpractices

1. Structure the recognition and reward system to be consistent with the IPPD environment.

   The organization's recognition and reward system should recognize the value of individual and integrated team excellence and enable, promote, and reinforce integration.

2. Develop guidelines for team as well as individual recognition.
3. Define procedures for integrated review processes that involve both the integrated team leader and the functional manager.
4. Establish criteria for distinguishing behaviors that promote integrated team performance from those that establish barriers to team behaviors.

SP 2.3-1 ESTABLISH MECHANISMS TO BALANCE TEAM AND HOME ORGANIZATION RESPONSIBILITIES

Establish and maintain organizational guidelines to balance team and home organization responsibilities.

Here "home organization" refers to that part of the organization to which personnel are assigned when they are not in an integrated team. This home organization may be called the "functional organization," "home base," "home office," or "direct organization." Regardless of what it is called, it is often responsible for the career growth of the personnel assigned to it (e.g., performance appraisals and training to maintain functional and discipline expertise). In an IPPD environment, reporting procedures and rating systems should recognize that people's responsibility is focused on the integrated team, not on the traditional home organization. A balance must be struck, however, because the responsibility of integrated team members to their respective home organizations is still important, specifically for process implementation and improvement. Workloads should be balanced among projects and functions, while ensuring career growth and advancement. Mechanisms should be created that support the home organization responsibility but align the workforce to meet business objectives in a teaming environment.

Striking this balance is difficult for an organization but exceedingly important for the personnel and the success of IPPD implementation. The balance must be reflected in the personal or career development plans for each individual. The knowledge and skills needed for an individual to succeed in both their functional and integrated team role should be honed, taking into account current and future assignments.

Guidelines should also be in place for disbanding teams and maintaining home organizations. It has been observed that sometimes teams attempt to remain in place beyond their productive life in organizations that do not have a home organization for the team members to report back to after the team is dissolved.

Typical Work Products

1. Organizational guidelines for balancing team and home organization responsibilities
2. Performance review process that considers both functional supervisor and team leader input

Subpractices

1. Establish guidelines for home organization responsibilities in promoting integrated team behavior.
2. Establish guidelines for team management responsibilities to ensure integrated team members report appropriately to their home organization.
3. Establish a performance review process that considers input from home organization and integrated team leaders.

Generic Practices by Goal

GG 1 *ACHIEVE SPECIFIC GOALS*

The process supports and enables achievement of the specific goals of the process area by transforming identifiable input work products to produce identifiable output work products.

GP 1.1 *PERFORM BASE PRACTICES*

Perform the base practices of the organizational environment for integration process to develop work products and provide services to achieve the specific goals of the process area.

GG 2 *INSTITUTIONALIZE A MANAGED PROCESS*

The process is institutionalized as a managed process.

CONTINUOUS ONLY

GG 3 *INSTITUTIONALIZE A DEFINED PROCESS*

The process is institutionalized as a defined process.

AUTHORS' NOTE: This generic goal's appearance here reflects
its location in the staged representation.

Commitment to Perform

GP 2.1 *ESTABLISH AN ORGANIZATIONAL POLICY*

Establish and maintain an organizational policy for planning and performing the organizational environment for integration process.

Elaboration

This policy establishes organizational expectations for providing an IPPD infrastructure and managing people for integration.

Ability to Perform

GP 2.2 *PLAN THE PROCESS*

Establish and maintain the plan for performing the organizational environment for integration process.

Elaboration

This plan for performing the organizational environment for integration process may be included in or referenced by the organization's process improvement plan, which is described in the Organizational Process Focus process area, or it may be documented in a separate plan that describes only the plan for the organizational environment for integration process.

GP 2.3 *PROVIDE RESOURCES*

Provide adequate resources for performing the organizational environment for integration process, developing the work products, and providing the services of the process.

Elaboration

> Examples of special equipment and facilities include the following:
> - Manufacturing and production facilities
> - Prototyping or production equipment
> - Work space
> - Office equipment and supplies
> - Raw or stock input materials
> - Transportation resources
> - "Hotlines" and "help desks"
> - Information brokerage services
> - Support staff and/or services

> Examples of other resources provided include the following tools:
> - Communications systems, tools, and resources
> - Computing resources and software productivity tools
> - Engineering or simulation tools
> - Proprietary engineering tools
> - Information-technology capabilities

GP 2.4 ASSIGN RESPONSIBILITY

Assign responsibility and authority for performing the process, developing the work products, and providing the services of the organizational environment for integration process.

GP 2.5 TRAIN PEOPLE

Train the people performing or supporting the organizational environment for integration process as needed.

Elaboration

> Examples of training topics include the following:
> - Work environment development
> - Ergonomics
> - Leadership policies for IPPD
> - Managing people for integration and collaboration

Directing Implementation

GP 2.6 *Manage Configurations*

Place designated work products of the organizational environment for integration process under appropriate levels of configuration management.

Elaboration

> Examples of work products placed under configuration management include the following:
> - Organizational guidelines that determine the degree of empowerment of individuals and integrated teams
> - Organizational process documentation for issue resolution
> - Organization's shared vision

GP 2.7 *Identify and Involve Relevant Stakeholders*

Identify and involve the relevant stakeholders of the organizational environment for integration process as planned.

Elaboration

> Examples of activities for stakeholder involvement include the following:
> - Establishing and maintaining the organization's shared vision
> - Establishing and maintaining the integrated work environment
> - Establishing IPPD skill needs
> - Establishing and maintaining IPPD leadership mechanisms
> - Establishing and maintaining organizational policies for the management of people in an IPPD environment

GP 2.8 *Monitor and Control the Process*

Monitor and control the organizational environment for integration process against the plan for performing the process and take appropriate corrective action.

Elaboration

> Examples of measures used in monitoring and controlling include the following:
> - Parameters for key operating characteristics of the work environment

OEI

Verifying Implementation

GP 2.9 OBJECTIVELY EVALUATE ADHERENCE

Objectively evaluate adherence of the organizational environment for integration process against its process description, standards, and procedures, and address noncompliance.

Elaboration

> Examples of activities reviewed include the following:
> - Establishing the shared vision for the organization
> - Developing guidelines for the degree of empowerment provided to people and teams
> - Establishing and maintaining an issue-resolution process

> Examples of work products reviewed include the following:
> - Organization's shared vision
> - Organizational guidelines that determine the degree of empowerment of individuals and integrated teams
> - Organizational process documentation for issue resolution
> - Compensation policies and procedures

GP 2.10 REVIEW STATUS WITH HIGHER LEVEL MANAGEMENT

Review the activities, status, and results of the organizational environment for integration process with higher level management and resolve issues.

GG 3 INSTITUTIONALIZE A DEFINED PROCESS

The process is institutionalized as a defined process.

> AUTHORS' NOTE: This generic goal's appearance here reflects its location in the continuous representation.

C ONLY

Ability to Perform

GP 3.1 ESTABLISH A DEFINED PROCESS

Establish and maintain the description of a defined organizational environment for integration process.

Directing Implementation

GP 3.2 COLLECT IMPROVEMENT INFORMATION

Collect work products, measures, measurement results, and improvement information derived from planning and performing the organizational environment for integration process to support the future use and improvement of the organization's processes and process assets.

GG 4 INSTITUTIONALIZE A QUANTITATIVELY MANAGED PROCESS

The process is institutionalized as a quantitatively managed process.

GP 4.1 ESTABLISH QUANTITATIVE OBJECTIVES FOR THE PROCESS

Establish and maintain quantitative objectives for the organizational environment for integration process that address quality and process performance based on customer needs and business objectives.

GP 4.2 STABILIZE SUBPROCESS PERFORMANCE

Stabilize the performance of one or more subprocesses to determine the ability of the organizational environment for integration process to achieve the established quantitative quality and process-performance objectives.

GG 5 INSTITUTIONALIZE AN OPTIMIZING PROCESS

The process is institutionalized as an optimizing process.

GP 5.1 ENSURE CONTINUOUS PROCESS IMPROVEMENT

Ensure continuous improvement of the organizational environment for integration process in fulfilling the relevant business objectives of the organization.

GP 5.2 CORRECT ROOT CAUSES OF PROBLEMS

Identify and correct the root causes of defects and other problems in the organizational environment for integration process.

ORGANIZATIONAL INNOVATION AND DEPLOYMENT
A Process Management Process Area at Maturity Level 5

Purpose

The purpose of Organizational Innovation and Deployment (OID) is to select and deploy incremental and innovative improvements that measurably improve the organization's processes and technologies. The improvements support the organization's quality and process-performance objectives as derived from the organization's business objectives.

Introductory Notes

The Organizational Innovation and Deployment process area enables the selection and deployment of improvements that can enhance the organization's ability to meet its quality and process-performance objectives. (See the definition of "quality and process-performance objectives" in the glossary.) The term "improvement," as used in this process area, refers to all of the ideas (proven and unproven) that would change the organization's processes and technologies to better meet the organization's quality and process-performance objectives.

Quality and process-performance objectives that this process area might address include the following:

- Improved product quality (e.g., functionality, performance)
- Increased productivity
- Decreased cycle time
- Greater customer and end-user satisfaction
- Shorter development or production time to change functionality, add features, or adapt to new technologies

Achievement of these objectives depends on the successful establishment of an infrastructure that enables and encourages all people in the organization to propose potential improvements to the organization's processes and technologies. Achievement of these objectives also depends on being able to effectively evaluate and deploy proposed improvements to the organization's processes and technologies. All members of the organization can participate in the organization's process- and technology-improvement activities. Their proposals are systematically gathered and addressed.

Pilots are conducted to evaluate significant changes involving untried, high-risk, or innovative improvements before they are broadly deployed.

Process and technology improvements that will be deployed across the organization are selected from process- and technology-improvement proposals based on the following criteria:

- A quantitative understanding of the organization's current quality and process performance
- The organization's quality and process-performance objectives
- Estimates of the improvement in quality and process performance resulting from deploying the process and technology improvements
- Estimated costs of deploying process and technology improvements, and the resources and funding available for such deployment

The expected benefits added by the process and technology improvements are weighed against the cost and impact to the organization. Change and stability must be balanced carefully. Change that is too great or too rapid can overwhelm the organization, destroying its investment in organizational learning represented by organizational process assets. Rigid stability can result in stagnation, allowing the changing business environment to erode the organization's business position.

Improvements are deployed, as appropriate, to new and ongoing projects.

In this process area, the term "process and technology improvements" refers to incremental and innovative improvements to processes and also to process or product technologies.

The informative material in this process area is written with the assumption that the specific practices are applied to a quantitatively managed process. The specific practices of this process area may be applicable, but with reduced value, if the assumption is not met.

The specific practices in this process area complement and extend those found in the Organizational Process Focus process area. The focus of this process area is process improvement that is based on a quantitative knowledge of the organization's set of standard processes and technologies and their expected quality and performance in predictable situations. In the Organizational Process Focus process area, no assumptions are made about the quantitative basis of improvement.

Practice-to-Goal Relationship Table

Continuous Representation	**Staged Representation**

SG 1 Select Improvements

    SP 1.1-1 Collect and Analyze Improvement Proposals

    SP 1.2-1 Identify and Analyze Innovations

    SP 1.3-1 Pilot Improvements

    SP 1.4-1 Select Improvements for Deployment

SG 2 Deploy Improvements

    SP 2.1-1 Plan the Deployment

    SP 2.2-1 Manage the Deployment

    SP 2.3-1 Measure Improvement Effects

GG 1 Achieve Specific Goals

    GP 1.1 Perform Base Practices

GG 2 Institutionalize a Managed Process

    GP 2.1 Establish an Organizational Policy

    GP 2.2 Plan the Process

    GP 2.3 Provide Resources

    GP 2.4 Assign Responsibility

    GP 2.5 Train People

    GP 2.6 Manage Configurations

    GP 2.7 Identify and Involve Relevant Stakeholders

    GP 2.8 Monitor and Control the Process

    GP 2.9 Objectively Evaluate Adherence

    GP 2.10 Review Status with Higher Level Management

GG 3 Institutionalize a Defined Process

    GP 3.1 Establish a Defined Process

    GP 3.2 Collect Improvement Information

GG 4 Institutionalize a Quantitatively Managed Process

    GP 4.1 Establish Quantitative Objectives for the Process

    GP 4.2 Stabilize Subprocess Performance

GG 5 Institutionalize an Optimizing Process

    GP 5.1 Ensure Continuous Process Improvement

    GP 5.2 Correct Root Causes of Problems

Staged Representation

SG 1 Select Improvements

    SP 1.1-1 Collect and Analyze Improvement Proposals

    SP 1.2-1 Identify and Analyze Innovations

    SP 1.3-1 Pilot Improvements

    SP 1.4-1 Select Improvements for Deployment

SG 2 Deploy Improvements

    SP 2.1-1 Plan the Deployment

    SP 2.2-1 Manage the Deployment

    SP 2.3-1 Measure Improvement Effects

GG 3 Institutionalize a Defined Process

    GP 2.1 Establish an Organizational Policy

    GP 2.2 Plan the Process

    GP 2.3 Provide Resources

    GP 2.4 Assign Responsibility

    GP 2.5 Train People

    GP 2.6 Manage Configurations

    GP 2.7 Identify and Involve Relevant Stakeholders

    GP 2.8 Monitor and Control the Process

    GP 2.9 Objectively Evaluate Adherence

    GP 2.10 Review Status with Higher Level Management

    GP 3.1 Establish a Defined Process

    GP 3.2 Collect Improvement Information

Related Process Areas

Refer to the Organizational Process Definition process area for more information about incorporating the deployed process improvements into organizational process assets.

Refer to the Organizational Process Focus process area for more information about soliciting, collecting, and handling process improvement proposals and coordinating the deployment of process improvement into the project's defined processes.

Refer to the Organizational Training process area for more information about providing updated training to support deployment of process and technology improvements.

Refer to the Organizational Process Performance process area for more information about quality and process-performance objectives and process performance models. Quality and process-performance objectives are used to analyze and select process- and technology-improvement proposals for deployment. Process performance models are used to quantify the impact and benefits of innovations.

Refer to the Measurement and Analysis process area for more information about establishing objectives for measurement and analysis, specifying the measures and analyses to be performed, obtaining and analyzing measures, and reporting results.

Refer to the Integrated Project Management process area for more information about coordinating the deployment of process and technology improvements into the project's defined process.

Refer to the Decision Analysis and Resolution process area for more information about formal evaluations related to improvement proposals and innovations.

Specific Practices by Goal

SG 1 SELECT IMPROVEMENTS

Process and technology improvements that contribute to meeting quality and process-performance objectives are selected.

SP 1.1-1 COLLECT AND ANALYZE IMPROVEMENT PROPOSALS

Collect and analyze process- and technology-improvement proposals.

Each process- and technology-improvement proposal must be analyzed.

Simple process and technology improvements, with well-understood benefits and effects, will not usually undergo detailed evaluations.

Examples of simple process and technology improvements include the following:
- Add an item to a peer review checklist.
- Combine the technical review and management review for suppliers into a single technical/management review.

Typical Work Products

1. Analyzed process- and technology-improvement proposals

Subpractices

1. Collect process- and technology-improvement proposals.

   A process- and technology-improvement proposal documents proposed incremental and innovative improvements to specific processes and technologies. Managers and staff in the organization, as well as customers, end users, and suppliers can submit process- and technology-improvement proposals. Process and technology improvements may be implemented at the local level before being proposed for the organization.

   Examples of sources for process- and technology-improvement proposals include the following:

   - Findings and recommendations from process appraisals
   - The organization's quality and process-performance objectives
   - Analysis of data about customer and end-user problems as well as customer and end-user satisfaction
   - Analysis of data about project performance compared to quality and productivity objectives
   - Analysis of technical performance measures
   - Results of process and product benchmarking efforts
   - Analysis of data on defect causes
   - Measured effectiveness of process activities
   - Examples of process- and technology-improvement proposals that were successfully adopted elsewhere
   - Feedback on previously submitted process- and technology-improvement proposals
   - Spontaneous ideas from managers and staff

   Refer to the Organizational Process Focus process area for more information about process- and technology-improvement proposals.

2. Analyze the costs and benefits of process- and technology-improvement proposals as appropriate.

   Process- and technology-improvement proposals that have a large cost-to-benefit ratio are rejected.

   Criteria for evaluating costs and benefits include the following:

   - Contribution toward meeting the organization's quality and process-performance objectives
   - Effect on mitigating identified project and organizational risks
   - Ability to respond quickly to changes in project requirements, market situations, and the business environment
   - Effect on related processes and associated assets

- Cost of defining and collecting data that supports the measurement and analysis of the process- and technology-improvement proposal
- Expected life span of the proposal

Process- and technology-improvement proposals that would not improve the organization's processes are rejected.

Process performance models provide insight into the effect of process changes on process capability and performance.

Refer to the Organizational Process Performance process area for more information about process performance models.

3. Identify the process- and technology-improvement proposals that are innovative.

Innovative improvements are also identified and analyzed in the Identify and Analyze Innovations specific practice.

Whereas this specific practice analyzes proposals that have been passively collected, the purpose of the Identify and Analyze Innovations specific practice is to actively search for and locate innovative improvements. The search primarily involves looking outside the organization.

Innovative improvements are typically identified by reviewing process- and technology-improvement proposals or by actively investigating and monitoring innovations that are in use in other organizations or are documented in research literature. Innovation may be inspired by internal improvement objectives or by the external business environment.

Innovative improvements are typically major changes to the process that represent a break from the old way of doing things (e.g., changing the life-cycle model). Innovative improvements may also include changes in the products that support, enhance, or automate the process (e.g., using off-the-shelf products to support the process).

Examples of innovative improvements include the following:
- Advances in computer and related hardware products
- New support tools
- New techniques, methodologies, processes, or life-cycle models
- New interface standards
- New reusable components
- New management techniques
- New quality-improvement techniques
- New process-development and deployment-support tools

---

4. Identify potential barriers and risks to deploying each process- and technology-improvement proposal.

> Examples of barriers to deploying process and technology improvements include the following:
> - Turf guarding and parochial perspectives
> - Unclear or weak business rationale
> - Lack of short-term benefits and visible successes
> - Unclear picture of what is expected from everyone
> - Too many changes at the same time
> - Lack of involvement and support of relevant stakeholders

> Examples of risk factors that affect the deployment of process and technology improvements include the following:
> - Compatibility of the improvement with existing processes, values, and skills of potential end users
> - Complexity of the improvement
> - Difficulty implementing the improvement
> - Ability to demonstrate the value of the improvement before widespread deployment
> - Justification for large, up-front investments in areas such as tools and training
> - Inability to overcome "technology drag" where the current implementation is used successfully by a large and mature installed base of end users

5. Estimate the cost, effort, and schedule required for deploying each process- and technology-improvement proposal.

6. Select the process- and technology-improvement proposals to be piloted before broadscale deployment.

   Since innovations, by definition, usually represent a major change, most innovative improvements will be piloted.

7. Document the results of the evaluation of each process- and technology-improvement proposal.

8. Monitor the status of each process- and technology-improvement proposal.

SP 1.2-1 IDENTIFY AND ANALYZE INNOVATIONS

Identify and analyze innovative improvements that could increase the organization's quality and process performance.

The specific practice, Collect and Analyze Improvement Proposals, analyzes proposals that are passively collected. The purpose of this specific practice is to actively search for, locate, and analyze innovative improvements. This search primarily involves looking outside the organization.

Typical Work Products

1. Candidate innovative improvements
2. Analysis of proposed innovative improvements

Subpractices

1. Analyze the organization's set of standard processes to determine areas where innovative improvements would be most helpful.

   These analyses are performed to determine which subprocesses are critical to achieving the organization's quality and process-performance objectives and which ones are good candidates to be improved.

2. Investigate innovative improvements that may improve the organization's set of standard processes.

   Investigating innovative improvements involves the following:
   - Systematically maintaining awareness of leading relevant technical work and technology trends
   - Periodically searching for commercially available innovative improvements
   - Collecting proposals for innovative improvements from the projects and the organization
   - Systematically reviewing processes and technologies used externally and comparing them to those used within the organization
   - Identifying areas where innovative improvements have been used successfully, and reviewing data and documentation of experience using these improvements

3. Analyze potential innovative improvements to understand their effects on process elements and predict their influence on the process.

   Process performance models can provide a basis for analyzing possible effects of changes to process elements.

   Refer to the Organizational Process Performance process area for more information about process performance models.

4. Analyze the costs and benefits of potential innovative improvements.

   Innovative improvements that have a very large cost-to-benefit ratio are rejected.

5. Create process- and technology-improvement proposals for those innovative improvements that would result in improving the organization's processes or technologies.

6. Select the innovative improvements to be piloted before broadscale deployment.

   Since innovations, by definition, usually represent a major change, most innovative improvements will be piloted.

7. Document the results of the evaluations of innovative improvements.

SP 1.3-1 PILOT IMPROVEMENTS

Pilot process and technology improvements to select which ones to implement.

Pilots are performed to assess new and unproven major changes before they are broadly deployed, as appropriate.

The implementation of this specific practice may overlap with the implementation of the Implement the Action Proposals specific practice in the Causal Analysis and Resolution process area (e.g., when causal analysis and resolution is implemented organizationally or across multiple projects).

Typical Work Products

1. Pilot evaluation reports
2. Documented lessons learned from pilots

Subpractices

1. Plan the pilots.

    When planning pilots, it is critical to define criteria to be used for evaluating pilot results.

2. Review and get relevant stakeholder agreement on the plans for the pilots.
3. Consult with and assist the people performing the pilots.
4. Perform each pilot in an environment that is characteristic of the environment present in a broadscale deployment.
5. Track the pilots against their plans.
6. Review and document the results of pilots.

    Reviewing and documenting the results of pilots usually involves the following:

    - Deciding whether to terminate the pilot, replan and continue the pilot, or proceed with deploying the process and technology improvement
    - Updating the disposition of process- and technology-improvement proposals associated with the pilot
    - Identifying and documenting new process- and technology-improvement proposals as appropriate
    - Identifying and documenting lessons learned and problems encountered during the pilot

SP 1.4-1 SELECT IMPROVEMENTS FOR DEPLOYMENT

Select process- and technology-improvement proposals for deployment across the organization.

Selection of process- and technology-improvement proposals for deployment across the organization is based on quantifiable criteria derived from the organization's quality and process-performance objectives.

Typical Work Products

1. Process- and technology-improvement proposals selected for deployment

Subpractices

1. Prioritize the candidate process and technology improvements for deployment.

   Priority is based on an evaluation of the estimated cost-to-benefit ratio with regard to the quality and process-performance objectives.

   Refer to the Organizational Process Performance process area for more information about quality and process-performance objectives.

2. Select the process and technology improvements to be deployed.

   The selection of the process improvements is based on their priorities and the available resources.

3. Determine how each process and technology improvement will be deployed.

   > Examples of how the process and technology improvements may be deployed include incorporating these improvements into the following:
   > - Organizational process assets
   > - All or a subset of the organization's product families
   > - All or a subset of the organization's projects
   > - All or a subset of the organizational groups

4. Document the results of the selection process.

   The results of the selection process usually include the following:
   - The selection criteria
   - The disposition of each proposal
   - The rationale for the disposition of each proposal
   - The assets to be changed for each selected proposal

SG 2   DEPLOY IMPROVEMENTS

Measurable improvements to the organization's processes and technologies are continually and systematically deployed.

SP 2.1-1   PLAN THE DEPLOYMENT

Establish and maintain the plans for deploying the selected process and technology improvements.

The plans for deploying each process and technology improvement may be included in the organization's plan for organizational innovation and deployment or they may be documented separately.

This specific practice plans the deployment of individual process and technology improvements. The Plan the Process generic practice addresses comprehensive planning that covers the specific practices in this process area.

Typical Work Products

1. Deployment plan for selected process and technology improvements

Subpractices

1. Determine how each process and technology improvement must be adjusted for organization-wide deployment.

   Process and technology improvements proposed within a limited context (e.g., for a single project) might have to be modified to work across the organization.

2. Determine the changes necessary to deploy each process and technology improvement.

   > Examples of changes needed to deploy a process and technology improvement include the following:
   > - Process descriptions, standards, and procedures
   > - Development environments
   > - Education and training
   > - Skills
   > - Existing commitments
   > - Existing activities
   > - Continuing support to end users
   > - Organizational culture and characteristics

3. Identify strategies to address potential barriers to deploying each process and technology improvement.

4. Establish measures and objectives for determining the value of each process and technology improvement with respect to the organization's quality and process-performance objectives.

   > Examples of measures for determining the value of a process and technology improvement include the following:
   > - Return on investment
   > - Time to recover the cost of the process or technology improvement
   > - Measured improvement in the project's or organization's process performance
   > - Number and types of project and organizational risks mitigated by the process or technology improvement
   > - Ability to respond quickly to changes in project requirements, market situations, and the business environment

   Refer to the Measurement and Analysis process area for more information about establishing objectives for measurement and analysis, specifying the measures and analyses to be performed, obtaining and analyzing measures, and reporting results.

5. Document the plan for deploying each process and technology improvement.

6. Review and get agreement with relevant stakeholders on the plan for deploying each process and technology improvement.

7. Revise the plan for deploying each process and technology improvement as necessary.

SP 2.2-1 MANAGE THE DEPLOYMENT

Manage the deployment of the selected process and technology improvements.

The implementation of this specific practice may overlap with the implementation of the Implement the Action Proposals specific practice in the Causal Analysis and Resolution process area (e.g., when causal analysis and resolution is implemented organizationally or across multiple projects). The primary difference is that in the Causal Analysis and Resolution process area, planning is done to manage the removal of the root causes of defects or problems from the project's defined processes. In the Organizational Innovation and Deployment process area, planning is done to manage the deployment of improvements to the organization's processes and technologies that can be quantified against the organization's business objectives.

Typical Work Products

1. Updated training materials (to reflect deployed process and technology improvements)

2. Documented results of process- and technology-improvement deployment activities

3. Revised process- and technology-improvement measures, objectives, priorities, and deployment plans

Subpractices

1. Monitor the deployment of the process and technology improvements using the deployment plan.

2. Coordinate the deployment of process and technology improvements across the organization.

   Coordinating deployment includes the following activities:
   - Coordinating the activities of projects, support groups, and organizational groups for each process and technology improvement
   - Coordinating the activities for deploying related process and technology improvements

3. Quickly deploy process and technology improvements in a controlled and disciplined manner, as appropriate.

> Examples of methods for quickly deploying process and technology improvements include the following:
> - Using red-lines, process change notices, or other controlled process documentation as interim process descriptions
> - Deploying process and technology improvements incrementally, rather than as a single deployment
> - Providing comprehensive consulting to early adopters of the process and technology improvement in lieu of revised formal training

4. Incorporate the process and technology improvements into organizational process assets, as appropriate.

   Refer to the Organizational Process Definition process area for more information about organizational process assets.

5. Coordinate the deployment of the process and technology improvements into the projects' defined processes as appropriate.

   Refer to the Organizational Process Focus process area for more information about deploying organizational process assets.

6. Provide consulting, as appropriate, to support deployment of the process and technology improvements.

7. Provide updated training materials to reflect the improvements to the organizational process assets.

   Refer to the Organizational Training process area for more information about training materials.

8. Confirm that the deployment of all process and technology improvements is completed.

9. Determine whether the ability of the defined process to meet quality and process-performance objectives is adversely affected by the process and technology improvement, and take corrective action as necessary.

   Refer to the Quantitative Project Management process area for more information about quantitatively managing the project's defined process to achieve the project's established quality and process-performance objectives.

10. Document and review the results of process- and technology-improvement deployment.

    Documenting and reviewing the results includes the following:
    - Identifying and documenting lessons learned
    - Identifying and documenting new process- and technology-improvement proposals
    - Revising process- and technology-improvement measures, objectives, priorities, and deployment plans

SP 2.3-1 MEASURE IMPROVEMENT EFFECTS

Measure the effects of the deployed process and technology improvements.

Refer to the Measurement and Analysis process area for more information about establishing objectives for measurement and analysis, specifying the measures and analyses to be performed, obtaining and analyzing measures, and reporting results.

The implementation of this specific practice may overlap with the implementation of the Evaluate the Effect of Changes specific practice in the Causal Analysis and Resolution process area (e.g., when causal analysis and resolution is implemented organizationally or across multiple projects).

Typical Work Products

1. Documented measures of the effects resulting from the deployed process and technology improvements

Subpractices

1. Measure the actual cost, effort, and schedule for deploying each process and technology improvement.
2. Measure the value of each process and technology improvement.
3. Measure the progress toward achieving the organization's quality and process-performance objectives.
4. Analyze the progress toward achieving the organization's quality and process-performance objectives and take corrective action as needed.

   Refer to the Organizational Process Performance process area for more information about process performance analyses.

5. Store the measures in the organization's measurement repository.

Generic Practices by Goal

GG 1 ACHIEVE SPECIFIC GOALS

The process supports and enables achievement of the specific goals of the process area by transforming identifiable input work products to produce identifiable output work products.

GP 1.1 PERFORM BASE PRACTICES

Perform the base practices of the organizational innovation and deployment process to develop work products and provide services to achieve the specific goals of the process area.

CONTINUOUS ONLY

GG 2 *INSTITUTIONALIZE A MANAGED PROCESS*	C ONLY
The process is institutionalized as a managed process.	

GG 3 *INSTITUTIONALIZE A DEFINED PROCESS*	S ONLY
The process is institutionalized as a defined process.	
AUTHORS' NOTE: This generic goal's appearance here reflects its location in the staged representation.	

Commitment to Perform

GP 2.1   *ESTABLISH AN ORGANIZATIONAL POLICY*

Establish and maintain an organizational policy for planning and performing the organizational innovation and deployment process.

Elaboration

This policy establishes organizational expectations for identifying and deploying process and technology improvements that contribute to meeting quality and process-performance objectives.

Ability to Perform

GP 2.2   *PLAN THE PROCESS*

Establish and maintain the plan for performing the organizational innovation and deployment process.

Elaboration

This plan for performing the organizational innovation and deployment process differs from the deployment plans described in a specific practice in this process area. The plan called for in this generic practice would address the comprehensive planning for all of the specific practices in this process area, from collecting and analyzing improvement proposals all the way through to the measurement of improvement effects. In contrast, the deployment plans called for in the specific practice would address the planning needed for the deployment of individual process and technology improvements.

GP 2.3   *PROVIDE RESOURCES*

Provide adequate resources for performing the organizational innovation and deployment process, developing the work products, and providing the services of the process.

Elaboration

> Examples of resources provided include the following tools:
> - Simulation packages
> - Prototyping tools
> - Statistical packages
> - Dynamic systems modeling
> - Subscriptions to online technology databases
> - Process modeling tools

GP 2.4   ASSIGN RESPONSIBILITY

Assign responsibility and authority for performing the process, developing the work products, and providing the services of the organizational innovation and deployment process.

GP 2.5   TRAIN PEOPLE

Train the people performing or supporting the organizational innovation and deployment process as needed.

Elaboration

> Examples of training topics include the following:
> - Planning, designing, and conducting pilots
> - Cost/benefit analysis
> - Technology transition
> - Change management

Directing Implementation

GP 2.6   MANAGE CONFIGURATIONS

Place designated work products of the organizational innovation and deployment process under appropriate levels of configuration management.

Elaboration

> Examples of work products placed under configuration management include the following:
> - Documented lessons learned from pilots
> - Revised process- and technology-improvement measures, objectives, priorities, and deployment plans
> - Updated training material

GP 2.7 IDENTIFY AND INVOLVE RELEVANT STAKEHOLDERS

Identify and involve the relevant stakeholders of the organizational innovation and deployment process as planned.

Elaboration

Examples of activities for stakeholder involvement include:
- Reviewing process- and technology-improvement proposals that may have major impacts on process performance or on customer and end-user satisfaction
- Providing feedback to the organization on the status and results of the process- and technology-improvement deployment activities

The feedback typically involves:

- Informing the people who submit process- and technology-improvement proposals about the disposition of their proposals
- Regularly informing relevant stakeholders about the plans and status for selecting and deploying process and technology improvements
- Preparing and distributing a summary of process- and technology-improvement selection and deployment activities

GP 2.8 MONITOR AND CONTROL THE PROCESS

Monitor and control the organizational innovation and deployment process against the plan for performing the process and take appropriate corrective action.

Elaboration

Examples of measures used in monitoring and controlling include the following:
- Change in quality
- Change in process performance

Verifying Implementation

GP 2.9 OBJECTIVELY EVALUATE ADHERENCE

Objectively evaluate adherence of the organizational innovation and deployment process against its process description, standards, and procedures, and address noncompliance.

Elaboration

Examples of activities reviewed include the following:
- Selecting improvements
- Deploying improvements

> Examples of work products reviewed include the following:
> - Deployment plans
> - Revised process- and technology-improvement measures, objectives, priorities, and deployment plans
> - Updated training material

GP 2.10 REVIEW STATUS WITH HIGHER LEVEL MANAGEMENT

Review the activities, status, and results of the organizational innovation and deployment process with higher level management and resolve issues.

GG 3 INSTITUTIONALIZE A DEFINED PROCESS

The process is institutionalized as a defined process.

> AUTHORS' NOTE: This generic goal's appearance here reflects its location in the continuous representation.

C ONLY

Ability to Perform

GP 3.1 ESTABLISH A DEFINED PROCESS

Establish and maintain the description of a defined organizational innovation and deployment process.

Directing Implementation

GP 3.2 COLLECT IMPROVEMENT INFORMATION

Collect work products, measures, measurement results, and improvement information derived from planning and performing the organizational innovation and deployment process to support the future use and improvement of the organization's processes and process assets.

GG 4 INSTITUTIONALIZE A QUANTITATIVELY MANAGED PROCESS

The process is institutionalized as a quantitatively managed process.

GP 4.1 ESTABLISH QUANTITATIVE OBJECTIVES FOR THE PROCESS

Establish and maintain quantitative objectives for the organizational innovation and deployment process that address quality and process performance based on customer needs and business objectives.

CONTINUOUS ONLY

GP 4.2   STABILIZE SUBPROCESS PERFORMANCE

Stabilize the performance of one or more subprocesses to determine the ability of the organizational innovation and deployment process to achieve the established quantitative quality and process-performance objectives.

GG 5   INSTITUTIONALIZE AN OPTIMIZING PROCESS

The process is institutionalized as an optimizing process.

GP 5.1   ENSURE CONTINUOUS PROCESS IMPROVEMENT

Ensure continuous improvement of the organizational innovation and deployment process in fulfilling the relevant business objectives of the organization.

GP 5.2   CORRECT ROOT CAUSES OF PROBLEMS

Identify and correct the root causes of defects and other problems in the organizational innovation and deployment process.

ORGANIZATIONAL PROCESS DEFINITION

A Process Management Process Area at Maturity Level 3

Purpose

The purpose of Organizational Process Definition (OPD) is to establish and maintain a usable set of organizational process assets.

Introductory Notes

Organizational process assets enable consistent process performance across the organization and provide a basis for cumulative, long-term benefits to the organization. (See the definition of "organizational process assets" in the glossary.)

The organization's process asset library is a collection of items maintained by the organization for use by the people and projects of the organization. This collection of items includes descriptions of processes and process elements, descriptions of life-cycle models, process tailoring guidelines, process-related documentation, and data. The organization's process asset library supports organizational learning and process improvement by allowing the sharing of best practices and lessons learned across the organization.

The organization's set of standard processes is tailored by projects to create their defined processes. The other organizational process assets are used to support tailoring as well as the implementation of the defined processes.

A standard process is composed of other processes or process elements. A process element is the fundamental (e.g., atomic) unit of process definition and describes the activities and tasks to consistently perform work. Process architecture provides rules for connecting the process elements of a standard process. The organization's set of standard processes may include multiple process architectures.

(See the definitions of "standard process," "process architecture," and "process element" in the glossary.)

> The organizational process assets may be organized in many ways, depending on the implementation of the Organizational Process Definition process area. Examples include the following:
> - Descriptions of life-cycle models may be documented as part of the organization's set of standard processes, or they may be documented separately.
> - The organization's set of standard processes may be stored in the organization's process asset library, or they may be stored separately.
> - A single repository may contain both the measurements and the process-related documentation, or they may be stored separately.

Related Process Areas

Refer to the Organizational Process Focus process area for more information about organizational process-related matters.

Specific Practices by Goal

SG 1   ESTABLISH ORGANIZATIONAL PROCESS ASSETS

A set of organizational process assets is established and maintained.

> **FOR INTEGRATED PRODUCT AND PROCESS DEVELOPMENT**
> Integrated processes that emphasize parallel rather than serial development are a cornerstone of IPPD implementation. Product development processes and product-related life-cycle processes, such as the manufacturing process development and the support process development processes, are conducted concurrently. Such integrated processes should accommodate the information provided by stakeholders representing all phases of the product life cycle from both business and technical functions. Processes for effective teamwork are also needed.

SP 1.1-1   ESTABLISH STANDARD PROCESSES

Establish and maintain the organization's set of standard processes.

> **FOR INTEGRATED PRODUCT AND PROCESS DEVELOPMENT**
> In an IPPD environment, the organization's shared vision is included in the organizational process assets.

Standard processes may be defined at multiple levels in an enterprise and they may be related in a hierarchical manner. For example, an enterprise may have a set of standard processes that is tailored by individual organizations (e.g., a division or site) in the enterprise to establish their set of

Practice-to-Goal Relationship Table

Continuous Representation	*Staged Representation*
SG 1 Establish Organizational Process Assets	SG 1 Establish Organizational Process Assets
SP 1.1-1 Establish Standard Processes	SP 1.1-1 Establish Standard Processes
SP 1.2-1 Establish Life-Cycle Model Descriptions	SP 1.2-1 Establish Life-Cycle Model Descriptions
SP 1.3-1 Establish Tailoring Criteria and Guidelines	SP 1.3-1 Establish Tailoring Criteria and Guidelines
SP 1.4-1 Establish the Organization's Measurement Repository	SP 1.4-1 Establish the Organization's Measurement Repository
SP 1.5-1 Establish the Organization's Process Asset Library	SP 1.5-1 Establish the Organization's Process Asset Library
GG 1 Achieve Specific Goals	
GP 1.1 Perform Base Practices	
GG 2 Institutionalize a Managed Process	GG 3 Institutionalize a Defined Process
GP 2.1 Establish an Organizational Policy	GP 2.1 Establish an Organizational Policy
GP 2.2 Plan the Process	GP 2.2 Plan the Process
GP 2.3 Provide Resources	GP 2.3 Provide Resources
GP 2.4 Assign Responsibility	GP 2.4 Assign Responsibility
GP 2.5 Train People	GP 2.5 Train People
GP 2.6 Manage Configurations	GP 2.6 Manage Configurations
GP 2.7 Identify and Involve Relevant Stakeholders	GP 2.7 Identify and Involve Relevant Stakeholders
GP 2.8 Monitor and Control the Process	GP 2.8 Monitor and Control the Process
GP 2.9 Objectively Evaluate Adherence	GP 2.9 Objectively Evaluate Adherence
GP 2.10 Review Status with Higher Level Management	GP 2.10 Review Status with Higher Level Management
GG 3 Institutionalize a Defined Process	
GP 3.1 Establish a Defined Process	GP 3.1 Establish a Defined Process
GP 3.2 Collect Improvement Information	GP 3.2 Collect Improvement Information
GG 4 Institutionalize a Quantitatively Managed Process	
GP 4.1 Establish Quantitative Objectives for the Process	
GP 4.2 Stabilize Subprocess Performance	
GG 5 Institutionalize an Optimizing Process	
GP 5.1 Ensure Continuous Process Improvement	
GP 5.2 Correct Root Causes of Problems	

OPD

standard processes. The set of standard processes may also be tailored for each of the organization's business areas or product lines. Thus "the organization's set of standard processes" can refer to the standard processes established at the organization level and standard processes that may be established at lower levels, although some organizations may only have a single level of standard processes. (See the definitions of "standard process" and "organization's set of standard processes" in the glossary.)

Multiple standard processes may be needed to address the needs of different application domains, life-cycle models, methodologies, and tools. The organization's set of standard processes contains process elements (e.g., a work product size-estimating element) that may be interconnected according to one or more process architectures that describe the relationships among these process elements. Processes may be composed of other processes or process elements.

The organization's set of standard processes typically includes technical, management, administrative, support, and organizational processes.

The organization's set of standard processes should collectively cover all processes needed by the organization and projects, including those processes addressed by the process areas at Maturity Level 2.

Typical Work Products

1. Organization's set of standard processes

Subpractices

1. Decompose each standard process into constituent process elements to the detail needed to understand and describe the process.

   Each process element covers a bounded and closely related set of activities. The descriptions of the process elements may be templates to be filled in, fragments to be completed, abstractions to be refined, or complete descriptions to be tailored or used unmodified. These elements are described in sufficient detail such that the process, when fully defined, can be consistently performed by appropriately trained and skilled people.

   > Examples of process elements include the following:
   > - Template for generating work product size estimates
   > - Description of work product design methodology
   > - Tailorable peer review methodology
   > - Template for conduct of management reviews

2. Specify the critical attributes of each process element.

> **Examples of critical attributes include the following:**
> - Process roles
> - Applicable process and product standards
> - Applicable procedures, methods, tools, and resources
> - Process performance objectives
> - Entry criteria
> - Inputs
> - Product and process measures to be collected and used
> - Verification points (e.g., peer reviews)
> - Outputs
> - Interfaces
> - Exit criteria

3. Specify the relationships of the process elements.

> **Examples of relationships include the following:**
> - Ordering of the process elements
> - Interfaces among the process elements
> - Interfaces with external processes
> - Interdependencies among the process elements

The rules for describing the relationships among process elements are referred to as "process architecture." The process architecture covers the essential requirements and guidelines. The detailed specifications of these relationships are covered in the descriptions of the defined processes that are tailored from the organization's set of standard processes.

4. Ensure that the organization's set of standard processes adheres to applicable policies, process standards and models, and product standards.

Adherence to applicable process standards and models is typically demonstrated by developing a mapping from the organization's set of standard processes to the relevant process standards and models. In addition, this mapping will be a useful input to future appraisals.

5. Ensure that the organization's set of standard processes satisfies the process needs and objectives of the organization.

Refer to the Organizational Process Focus process area for more information about establishing and maintaining the organization's process needs and objectives.

6. Ensure that there is appropriate integration among the processes that are included in the organization's set of standard processes.

7. Document the organization's set of standard processes.

8. Conduct peer reviews on the organization's set of standard processes.

Refer to the Verification process area for more information about peer review.

9. Revise the organization's set of standard processes as necessary.

SP 1.2-1 *Establish Life-Cycle Model Descriptions*

Establish and maintain descriptions of the life-cycle models approved for use in the organization.

Life-cycle models may be developed for a variety of customers or in a variety of situations, since one life-cycle model may not be appropriate for all situations. The organization may identify more than one life-cycle model for use. Typically, the organization needs both product and project life-cycle models for the types of products that it produces and for defining the phases of the project.

Product life-cycle models partition the product life cycle into phases for which activities and requirements can be defined to promote a complete solution, from initiating development of the product to its ultimate disposal.

Typical Work Products

1. Descriptions of life-cycle models

Subpractices

1. Select life-cycle models based on the needs of projects and the organization.

   > For example, in the case of a development project, project life-cycle models include the following:
   > - Waterfall
   > - Spiral
   > - Evolutionary
   > - Incremental
   > - Iterative

   > Examples of project characteristics that could affect project life-cycle models include the following:
   > - Size of the project
   > - Experience and familiarity of project staff in implementing the process
   > - Constraints such as cycle time and acceptable defect levels

2. Document the descriptions of the life-cycle models.

   The life-cycle models may be documented as part of the organization's standard process descriptions or they may be documented separately.

3. Conduct peer reviews on the life-cycle models.

   Refer to the Verification process area for more information about conducting peer reviews.

4. Revise the descriptions of the life-cycle models as necessary.

SP 1.3-1 ESTABLISH TAILORING CRITERIA AND GUIDELINES

Establish and maintain the tailoring criteria and guidelines for the organization's set of standard processes.

> **FOR INTEGRATED PRODUCT AND PROCESS DEVELOPMENT**
> In creating the tailoring criteria and guidelines, include considerations for concurrent development and operating with integrated teams. For example, how one tailors the manufacturing process will be different depending on whether it is done serially after the product has been developed or in parallel with the development of the product, as in IPPD. Processes, such as resource allocation, will also be tailored differently if the project is operating with integrated teams.

The tailoring criteria and guidelines describe the following:

- How the organization's set of standard processes and organizational process assets are used to create the defined processes
- Mandatory requirements that must be satisfied by the defined processes (e.g., the subset of the organizational process assets that are essential for any defined process)
- Options that can be exercised and criteria for selecting among the options
- Procedures that must be followed in performing and documenting process tailoring

> Examples of reasons for tailoring include the following:
> - Adapting the process for a new product line or host environment
> - Customizing the process for a specific application or class of applications (e.g., initial development, maintenance, or creation of prototypes)
> - Elaborating the process description so that the resulting defined process can be performed

Flexibility in tailoring and defining processes is balanced with ensuring appropriate consistency in the processes across the organization. Flexibility is needed to address contextual variables such as the domain; nature of the customer; cost, schedule, and quality tradeoffs; technical difficulty of the work; and experience of the people implementing the process. Consistency across the organization is needed so that organizational standards, objectives, and strategies are appropriately addressed, and process data and lessons learned can be shared.

Tailoring criteria and guidelines may allow for using a standard process "as is," with no tailoring.

Typical Work Products

1. Tailoring guidelines for the organization's set of standard processes

Subpractices

1. Specify the selection criteria and procedures for tailoring the organization's set of standard processes.

> Examples of criteria and procedures include the following:
> - Criteria for selecting life-cycle models from those approved by the organization
> - Criteria for selecting process elements from the organization's set of standard processes
> - Procedures for tailoring the selected life-cycle models and process elements to accommodate specific process characteristics and needs

> Examples of tailoring actions include the following:
> - Modifying a life-cycle model
> - Combining elements of different life-cycle models
> - Modifying process elements
> - Replacing process elements
> - Reordering process elements

2. Specify the standards for documenting the defined processes.
3. Specify the procedures for submitting and obtaining approval of waivers from the requirements of the organization's set of standard processes.
4. Document the tailoring guidelines for the organization's set of standard processes.
5. Conduct peer reviews on the tailoring guidelines.

   Refer to the Verification process area for more information about conducting peer reviews.

6. Revise the tailoring guidelines as necessary.

SP 1.4-1 ESTABLISH THE ORGANIZATION'S MEASUREMENT REPOSITORY

Establish and maintain the organization's measurement repository.

Refer to the Use Organizational Process Assets for Planning Project Activities specific practice of the Integrated Project Management process area for more information about the use of the organization's measurement repository in planning project activities.

The repository contains both product and process measures that are related to the organization's set of standard processes. It also contains or refers to the information needed to understand and interpret the measures and assess them for reasonableness and applicability. For example, the definitions of the measures are used to compare similar measures from different processes.

Typical Work Products

1. Definition of the common set of product and process measures for the organization's set of standard processes
2. Design of the organization's measurement repository
3. Organization's measurement repository (that is, the repository structure and support environment)
4. Organization's measurement data

Subpractices

1. Determine the organization's needs for storing, retrieving, and analyzing measurements.
2. Define a common set of process and product measures for the organization's set of standard processes.

   The measures in the common set are selected based on the organization's set of standard processes. The common set of measures may vary for different standard processes.

   Operational definitions for the measures specify the procedures for collecting valid data and the point in the process where the data will be collected.

   Examples of classes of commonly used measures include the following:
   - Estimates of work product size (e.g., pages)
   - Estimates of effort and cost (e.g., person hours)
   - Actual measures of size, effort, and cost
   - Quality measures (e.g., number of defects found, severity of defects)
   - Peer review coverage
   - Test coverage
   - Reliability measures (e.g., mean time to failure)

   Refer to the Measurement and Analysis process area for more information about defining measures.

3. Design and implement the measurement repository.
4. Specify the procedures for storing, updating, and retrieving measures.
5. Conduct peer reviews on the definitions of the common set of measures and the procedures for storing and retrieving measures.

   Refer to the Verification process area for more information about conducting peer reviews.

6. Enter the specified measures into the repository.

   Refer to the Measurement and Analysis process area for more information about collecting and analyzing data.

7. Make the contents of the measurement repository available for use by the organization and projects as appropriate.

8. Revise the measurement repository, common set of measures, and procedures as the organization's needs change.

> Examples of when the common set of measures may need to be revised include the following:
> - New processes are added
> - Processes are revised and new product or process measures are needed
> - Finer granularity of data is required
> - Greater visibility into the process is required
> - Measures are retired

SP 1.5-1 *ESTABLISH THE ORGANIZATION'S PROCESS ASSET LIBRARY*

Establish and maintain the organization's process asset library.

> Examples of items to be stored in the organization's process asset library include the following:
> - Organizational policies
> - Defined process descriptions
> - Procedures (e.g., estimating procedure)
> - Development plans
> - Quality assurance plans
> - Training materials
> - Process aids (e.g., checklists)
> - Lessons-learned reports

Typical Work Products

1. Design of the organization's process asset library
2. Organization's process asset library
3. Selected items to be included in the organization's process asset library
4. Catalog of items in the organization's process asset library

Subpractices

1. Design and implement the organization's process asset library, including the library structure and support environment.
2. Specify the criteria for including items in the library.
   The items are selected based primarily on their relationship to the organization's set of standard processes.
3. Specify the procedures for storing and retrieving items.
4. Enter the selected items into the library and catalog them for easy reference and retrieval.
5. Make the items available for use by the projects.

6. Periodically review the use of each item and use the results to maintain the library contents.

7. Revise the organization's process asset library as necessary.

> Examples of when the library may need to be revised include the following:
> - New items are added
> - Items are retired
> - Current versions of items are changed

Generic Practices by Goal

GG 1 ACHIEVE SPECIFIC GOALS

The process supports and enables achievement of the specific goals of the process area by transforming identifiable input work products to produce identifiable output work products.

GP 1.1 PERFORM BASE PRACTICES

Perform the base practices of the organizational process definition process to develop work products and provide services to achieve the specific goals of the process area.

GG 2 INSTITUTIONALIZE A MANAGED PROCESS

The process is institutionalized as a managed process.

GG 3 INSTITUTIONALIZE A DEFINED PROCESS

The process is institutionalized as a defined process.

> AUTHORS' NOTE: This generic goal's appearance here reflects its location in the staged representation.

Commitment to Perform

GP 2.1 ESTABLISH AN ORGANIZATIONAL POLICY

Establish and maintain an organizational policy for planning and performing the organizational process definition process.

Elaboration

This policy establishes organizational expectations for establishing and maintaining a set of standard processes for use by the organization and making organizational process assets available across the organization.

Ability to Perform

GP 2.2 *PLAN THE PROCESS*

Establish and maintain the plan for performing the organizational process definition process.

Elaboration

Typically, this plan for performing the organizational process definition process is a part of the organization's process improvement plan.

GP 2.3 *PROVIDE RESOURCES*

Provide adequate resources for performing the organizational process definition process, developing the work products, and providing the services of the process.

Elaboration

A process group typically manages the organizational process definition activities. This group typically is staffed by a core of professionals whose primary responsibility is coordinating organizational process improvement. This group is supported by process owners and people with expertise in various disciplines such as the following:

- *Project management*
- *Appropriate engineering disciplines*
- *Configuration management*
- *Quality assurance*

Examples of other resources provided include the following tools:
- Database management systems
- Process modeling tools
- Web page builders and browsers

GP 2.4 *ASSIGN RESPONSIBILITY*

Assign responsibility and authority for performing the process, developing the work products, and providing the services of the organizational process definition process.

GP 2.5 *TRAIN PEOPLE*

Train the people performing or supporting the organizational process definition process as needed.

Elaboration

> Examples of training topics include the following:
> - CMMI and other process and process improvement reference models
> - Planning, managing, and monitoring processes
> - Process modeling and definition
> - Developing a tailorable standard process

Directing Implementation

GP 2.6 *MANAGE CONFIGURATIONS*

Place designated work products of the organizational process definition process under appropriate levels of configuration management.

Elaboration

> Examples of work products placed under configuration management include the following:
> - Organization's set of standard processes
> - Descriptions of the life-cycle models
> - Tailoring guidelines for the organization's set of standard processes
> - Definitions of the common set of product and process measures
> - Organization's measurement data

GP 2.7 *IDENTIFY AND INVOLVE RELEVANT STAKEHOLDERS*

Identify and involve the relevant stakeholders of the organizational process definition process as planned.

Elaboration

> Examples of activities for stakeholder involvement include the following:
> - Reviewing the organization's set of standard processes
> - Reviewing the organization's life-cycle models
> - Resolving issues on the tailoring guidelines
> - Assessing the definitions of the common set of process and product measures

GP 2.8 *MONITOR AND CONTROL THE PROCESS*

Monitor and control the organizational process definition process against the plan for performing the process and take appropriate corrective action.

Elaboration

> Examples of measures used in monitoring and controlling include the following:
> - Percentage of projects using the process architectures and process elements of the organization's set of standard processes
> - Defect density of each process element of the organization's set of standard processes

Verifying Implementation

GP 2.9   OBJECTIVELY EVALUATE ADHERENCE

Objectively evaluate adherence of the organizational process definition process against its process description, standards, and procedures, and address noncompliance.

Elaboration

> Examples of activities reviewed include the following:
> - Establishing organizational process assets

> Examples of work products reviewed include the following:
> - Organization's set of standard processes
> - Descriptions of the life-cycle models
> - Tailoring guidelines for the organization's set of standard processes
> - Organization's measurement data

GP 2.10   REVIEW STATUS WITH HIGHER LEVEL MANAGEMENT

Review the activities, status, and results of the organizational process definition process with higher level management and resolve issues.

GG 3   INSTITUTIONALIZE A DEFINED PROCESS

The process is institutionalized as a defined process.

> AUTHORS' NOTE: This generic goal's appearance here reflects its location in the continuous representation.

C ONLY

Ability to Perform

GP 3.1   ESTABLISH A DEFINED PROCESS

Establish and maintain the description of a defined organizational process definition process.

Directing Implementation

GP 3.2 COLLECT IMPROVEMENT INFORMATION

Collect work products, measures, measurement results, and improvement informa-tion derived from planning and performing the organizational process definition process to support the future use and improvement of the organization's processes and process assets.

GG 4 INSTITUTIONALIZE A **QUANTITATIVELY MANAGED PROCESS**

The process is institutionalized as a quantitatively managed process.

GP 4.1 ESTABLISH QUANTITATIVE OBJECTIVES FOR THE PROCESS

Establish and maintain quantitative objectives for the organizational process defini-tion process that address quality and process performance based on customer needs and business objectives.

GP 4.2 STABILIZE SUBPROCESS PERFORMANCE

Stabilize the performance of one or more subprocesses to determine the ability of the organizational process definition process to achieve the established quantita-tive quality and process-performance objectives.

GG 5 INSTITUTIONALIZE AN **OPTIMIZING PROCESS**

The process is institutionalized as an optimizing process.

GP 5.1 ENSURE CONTINUOUS PROCESS IMPROVEMENT

Ensure continuous improvement of the organizational process definition process in fulfilling the relevant business objectives of the organization.

GP 5.2 CORRECT ROOT CAUSES OF PROBLEMS

Identify and correct the root causes of defects and other problems in the organiza-tional process definition process.

ORGANIZATIONAL PROCESS FOCUS
A Process Management Process Area at Maturity Level 3

Purpose

The purpose of Organizational Process Focus (OPF) is to plan and implement organizational process improvement based on a thorough understanding of the current strengths and weaknesses of the organization's processes and process assets.

Introductory Notes

The organization's processes include the organization's set of standard processes and the defined processes that are tailored from them. The organizational process assets are used to establish, maintain, implement, and improve the defined processes. (See the definition of "organizational process assets" in the glossary.)

Candidate improvements to the organizational process assets are obtained from various sources, including measurement of the processes, lessons learned in implementing the processes, results of process appraisals, results of product evaluation activities, results of benchmarking against other organizations' processes, and recommendations from other improvement initiatives in the organization.

Process improvement occurs within the context of the organization's needs and is used to address the organization's objectives. The organization encourages participation in process improvement activities by those who will perform the process. The responsibility for facilitating and managing the organization's process improvement activities, including coordinating the participation of others, is typically assigned to a process group. The organization provides the long-term commitment and resources required to sponsor this group.

Careful planning is required to ensure that process improvement efforts across the organization are adequately managed and implemented. The organization's planning for process improvement results in a process improvement plan. The organization's process improvement plan will address appraisal planning, process action planning, pilot planning, and deployment planning. Appraisal plans describe the appraisal time line and schedule, the scope of the appraisal, the resources required to perform the appraisal, the reference model against which the appraisal will be performed, and the logistics for the appraisal. Process action plans usually result from appraisals and document how specific improvements targeting the weaknesses uncovered by an appraisal will be implemented. In cases in which it is determined that the improvement described in the process action plan should be tested on a small group before deploying it across the organization, a pilot plan is generated. Finally, when the improvement is to be deployed, a deployment plan is used. This plan describes when and how the improvement will be deployed across the organization.

Related Process Areas

Refer to the Organizational Process Definition process area for more information about the organizational process assets.

Specific Practices by Goal

SG 1 DETERMINE PROCESS-IMPROVEMENT OPPORTUNITIES

Strengths, weaknesses, and improvement opportunities for the organization's processes are identified periodically and as needed.

Strengths, weaknesses, and improvement opportunities may be determined relative to a process standard or model such as a CMMI model or International Organization for Standardization (ISO) standard. The process improvements should be selected specifically to address the organization's needs.

SP 1.1-1 ESTABLISH ORGANIZATIONAL PROCESS NEEDS

Establish and maintain the description of the process needs and objectives for the organization.

> **FOR INTEGRATED PRODUCT AND PROCESS DEVELOPMENT**
> Integrated processes that emphasize parallel rather than serial development are a cornerstone of IPPD implementation. Product development processes and product-related life-cycle processes, such as the manufacturing process development and the support process development processes, are conducted concurrently. Such integrated processes need to accommodate the information provided by stakeholders representing all phases of the product life cycle from both business and technical functions. Processes for effective teamwork will also be needed.

Practice-to-Goal Relationship Table

Continuous Representation	*Staged Representation*
SG 1 Determine Process Improvement Opportunities	**SG 1** Determine Process Improvement Opportunities
SP 1.1-1 Establish Organizational Process Needs	SP 1.1-1 Establish Organizational Process Needs
SP 1.2-1 Appraise the Organization's Processes	SP 1.2-1 Appraise the Organization's Processes
SP 1.3-1 Identify the Organization's Process Improvements	SP 1.3-1 Identify the Organization's Process Improvements
SG 2 Plan and Implement Process Improvement Activities	**SG 2** Plan and Implement Process Improvement Activities
SP 2.1-1 Establish Process Action Plans	SP 2.1-1 Establish Process Action Plans
SP 2.2-1 Implement Process Action Plans	SP 2.2-1 Implement Process Action Plans
SP 2.3-1 Deploy Organizational Process Assets	SP 2.3-1 Deploy Organizational Process Assets
SP 2.4-1 Incorporate Process-Related Experiences into the Organizational Process Assets	SP 2.4-1 Incorporate Process-Related Experiences into the Organizational Process Assets
GG 1 Achieve Specific Goals	
GP 1.1 Perform Base Practices	
GG 2 Institutionalize a Managed Process	**GG 3** Institutionalize a Defined Process
GP 2.1 Establish an Organizational Policy	GP 2.1 Establish an Organizational Policy
GP 2.2 Plan the Process	GP 2.2 Plan the Process
GP 2.3 Provide Resources	GP 2.3 Provide Resources
GP 2.4 Assign Responsibility	GP 2.4 Assign Responsibility
GP 2.5 Train People	GP 2.5 Train People
GP 2.6 Manage Configurations	GP 2.6 Manage Configurations
GP 2.7 Identify and Involve Relevant Stakeholders	GP 2.7 Identify and Involve Relevant Stakeholders
GP 2.8 Monitor and Control the Process	GP 2.8 Monitor and Control the Process
GP 2.9 Objectively Evaluate Adherence	GP 2.9 Objectively Evaluate Adherence
GP 2.10 Review Status with Higher Level Management	GP 2.10 Review Status with Higher Level Management
GG 3 Institutionalize a Defined Process	
GP 3.1 Establish a Defined Process	GP 3.1 Establish a Defined Process
GP 3.2 Collect Improvement Information	GP 3.2 Collect Improvement Information
GG 4 Institutionalize a Quantitatively Managed Process	
GP 4.1 Establish Quantitative Objectives for the Process	
GP 4.2 Stabilize Subprocess Performance	
GG 5 Institutionalize an Optimizing Process	
GP 5.1 Ensure Continuous Process Improvement	
GP 5.2 Correct Root Causes of Problems	

FOR INTEGRATED PRODUCT AND PROCESS DEVELOPMENT

Examples of processes for effective teamwork include the following:

- Communications
- Collaborative decision making
- Issue resolution
- Team building

The organization's processes operate in a business context that must be understood. The organization's business objectives, needs, and constraints determine the needs and objectives for the organization's processes. Typically, the issues related to financial, technological, quality, human resource, and marketing are important process considerations.

The organization's process needs and objectives cover aspects that include the following:

- Characteristics of the processes
- Process-performance objectives, such as time-to-market and product quality
- Process effectiveness

Typical Work Products

1. Organization's process needs and objectives

Subpractices

1. Identify the policies, standards, and business objectives that are applicable to the organization's processes.
2. Examine relevant process standards and models for best practices.
3. Determine the organization's process-performance objectives.

   Process-performance objectives may be expressed in quantitative or qualitative terms.

   Examples of process-performance objectives include the following:
   - Cycle time
   - Defect removal rates
   - Productivity

4. Define the essential characteristics of the organization's processes.

   The essential characteristics of the organization's processes are determined based on the following:
   - Processes currently being used in the organization
   - Process and product standards imposed by the organization
   - Process and product standards commonly imposed by customers of the organization

> Examples of process characteristics include the following:
> - Level of detail used to describe the processes
> - Process notation used
> - Granularity of the processes

5. Document the organization's process needs and objectives.
6. Revise the organization's process needs and objectives as needed.

SP 1.2-1 APPRAISE THE ORGANIZATION'S PROCESSES

Appraise the processes of the organization periodically and as needed to maintain an understanding of their strengths and weaknesses.

Process appraisals may be performed for the following reasons:

- To identify processes that should be improved
- To confirm progress and make the benefits of process improvement visible
- To satisfy the needs of a customer-supplier relationship
- To motivate and facilitate buy-in

The buy-in gained during a process appraisal can be eroded significantly if it is not followed by an appraisal-based action plan.

Typical Work Products

1. Plans for the organization's process appraisals
2. Appraisal findings that address strengths and weaknesses of the organization's processes
3. Improvement recommendations for the organization's processes

Subpractices

1. Obtain sponsorship of the process appraisal from senior management.

   Senior management sponsorship includes the commitment to have the organization's managers and staff participate in the process appraisal and to provide the resources and funding to analyze and communicate the findings of the appraisal.

2. Define the scope of the process appraisal.

   Process appraisals may be performed on the entire organization or may be performed on a smaller part of an organization such as a single project or business area.

   The scope of the process appraisal addresses the following:
   - Definition of the organization (e.g., sites or business areas) that will be covered by the appraisal

- Identification of the project and support functions that will represent the organization in the appraisal
- Processes that will be appraised

3. Determine the method and criteria for process appraisal.

   Process appraisals can occur in many forms. Process appraisals should address the needs and objectives of the organization, which may change over time. For example, the appraisal may be based on a process model, such as a CMMI model, or on a national or international standard, such as ISO 9001. The appraisals may also be based on a benchmark comparison with other organizations. The appraisal method may assume a variety of characteristics in terms of time and effort expended, makeup of the appraisal team, and the method and depth of investigation.

4. Plan, schedule, and prepare for the process appraisal.

5. Conduct the process appraisal.

6. Document and deliver the appraisal's activities and findings.

SP 1.3-1   IDENTIFY THE ORGANIZATION'S PROCESS IMPROVEMENTS

Identify improvements to the organization's processes and process assets.

Typical Work Products

1. Analysis of candidate process improvements
2. Identification of improvements for the organization's processes

Subpractices

1. Determine candidate process improvements.

   Candidate process improvements are typically determined by doing the following:
   - Measure the processes and analyze the measurement results
   - Review the processes for effectiveness and suitability
   - Review the lessons learned from tailoring the organization's set of standard processes
   - Review the lessons learned from implementing the processes
   - Review process improvement proposals submitted by the organization's managers and staff, and other relevant stakeholders
   - Solicit inputs on process improvements from senior management and leaders in the organization
   - Examine the results of process appraisals and other process-related reviews
   - Review results of other organization improvement initiatives

2. Prioritize the candidate process improvements.

   Criteria for prioritization are as follows:
   - Consider the estimated cost and effort to implement the process improvements

- Appraise the expected improvement against the organization's improvement objectives and priorities
- Determine the potential barriers to the process improvements and develop strategies for overcoming these barriers

---

Examples of techniques to help determine and prioritize the possible improvements to be implemented include the following:

- A gap analysis that compares current conditions in the organization with optimal conditions
- Force-field analysis of potential improvements to identify potential barriers and strategies for overcoming those barriers
- Cause-and-effect analyses to provide information on the potential effects of different improvements that can then be compared

---

3. Identify and document the process improvements that will be implemented.
4. Revise the list of planned process improvements to keep it current.

SG 2 PLAN AND IMPLEMENT PROCESS IMPROVEMENT ACTIVITIES

Improvements are planned and implemented, organizational process assets are deployed, and process-related experiences are incorporated into the organizational process assets.

Successful implementation of improvements requires participation in the process definition and improvement activities by process owners, those performing the process, and support organizations.

SP 2.1-1 ESTABLISH PROCESS ACTION PLANS

Establish and maintain process action plans to address improvements to the organization's processes and process assets.

Establishing and maintaining process action plans typically involves the following roles:

- Management steering committees to set strategies and oversee process improvement activities
- Process group staff to facilitate and manage the process improvement activities
- Process action teams to define and implement the improvement
- Process owners to manage the deployment
- Practitioners to perform the process

This involvement helps to obtain buy-in on the process improvements and increases the likelihood of effective deployment.

Process action plans are detailed implementation plans. These plans differ from the organization's process improvement plan in that they are plans targeting specific improvements that have been defined to address weaknesses usually uncovered by appraisals.

Typical Work Products

1. Organization's approved process action plans

Subpractices

1. Identify strategies, approaches, and actions to address the identified process improvements.

   New, unproven, and major changes are piloted before they are incorporated into normal use.

2. Establish process action teams to implement the actions.

   The teams and people performing the process improvement actions are called "process action teams." Process action teams typically include process owners and those who perform the process.

3. Document process action plans.

   Process action plans typically cover the following:
   • Process improvement infrastructure
   • Process-improvement objectives
   • Process improvements that will be addressed
   • Procedures for planning and tracking process actions
   • Strategies for piloting and implementing the process actions
   • Responsibility and authority for implementing the process actions
   • Resources, schedules, and assignments for implementing the process actions
   • Methods for determining the effectiveness of the process actions
   • Risks associated with process action plans

4. Review and negotiate process action plans with relevant stakeholders.

5. Review process action plans as necessary.

SP 2.2-1 *IMPLEMENT PROCESS ACTION PLANS*

Implement process action plans across the organization.

Typical Work Products

1. Commitments among the various process action teams
2. Status and results of implementing process action plans
3. Plans for pilots

Subpractices

1. Make process action plans readily available to relevant stakeholders.
2. Negotiate and document commitments among the process action teams and revise their process action plans as necessary.
3. Track progress and commitments against process action plans.
4. Conduct joint reviews with the process action teams and relevant stakeholders to monitor the progress and results of the process actions.
5. Plan pilots needed to test selected process improvements.
6. Review the activities and work products of process action teams.
7. Identify, document, and track to closure issues in implementing process action plans.
8. Ensure that the results of implementing process action plans satisfy the organization's process-improvement objectives.

SP 2.3-1 DEPLOY ORGANIZATIONAL PROCESS ASSETS

Deploy organizational process assets across the organization.

Deployment of organizational process assets or of changes to organizational process assets should be performed in an orderly manner. Some organizational process assets or changes to organizational process assets may not be appropriate for implementation in some parts of the organization (because of customer requirements or the current life-cycle phase being implemented, for example). It is therefore important that those that are or will be executing the process, as well as other organization functions (such as training and quality assurance) be involved in the deployment as necessary.

Refer to the Organizational Process Definition process area for more information about how the deployment of organizational process assets is supported and enabled by the organization's process asset library.

Typical Work Products

1. Plans for deploying the organizational process assets and changes to organizational process assets
2. Training materials for deploying the organizational process assets and changes to organizational process assets
3. Documentation of changes to the organizational process assets
4. Support materials for deploying the organizational process assets and changes to organizational process assets

Subpractices

1. Deploy organizational process assets and associated methods and tools.

    Typical activities performed as a part of this deployment include the following:
    - Planning the deployment
    - Identifying the organizational process assets that should be adopted by those who will be performing the process
    - Ensuring that training is available for the organizational process assets that are being deployed
    - Identifying the support resources (e.g., tools) needed to transition the deployed organizational process assets
    - Determining the schedule for deploying the organizational process assets

    Refer to the Organizational Training process area for more information about coordination of training.

2. Deploy the changes that were made to the organizational process assets.

    Typical activities performed as a part of this deployment include the following:
    - Planning the deployment
    - Determining which changes are appropriate for those that are or will be performing the process
    - Determining the time frame for deploying the changes
    - Arranging for the associated support needed to successfully transition the changes

3. Document the changes to the organizational process assets.

    The documentation of changes is used to understand the relationship of the changes to resulting changes in process performance and results.

4. Provide guidance and consultation on the use of the organizational process assets.

SP 2.4-1 INCORPORATE PROCESS-RELATED EXPERIENCES INTO THE ORGANIZATIONAL PROCESS ASSETS

Incorporate process-related work products, measures, and improvement information derived from planning and performing the process into the organizational process assets.

Typical Work Products

1. Process improvement proposals
2. Process lessons learned
3. Measurements on the organizational process assets
4. Improvement recommendations for the organizational process assets
5. Records of the organization's process improvement activities
6. Information on the organizational process assets and improvements to them

Subpractices

1. Conduct periodic reviews of the effectiveness and suitability of the organization's set of standard processes and related organizational process assets relative to the organization's business objectives.
2. Obtain feedback about the use of the organizational process assets.
3. Derive lessons learned from defining, piloting, implementing, and deploying the organizational process assets.
4. Make lessons learned available to the people in the organization as appropriate.

    Actions may have to be taken to ensure that lessons learned are used appropriately.

    > Examples of inappropriate use of lessons learned include the following:
    > - Evaluating the performance of people
    > - Judging process performance or results

    > Examples of ways to prevent inappropriate use of lessons learned include the following:
    > - Controlling access to the lessons learned
    > - Educating people about the appropriate use of lessons learned

5. Analyze the organization's common set of measures.

    Refer to the Measurement and Analysis process area for more information about analyzing measures.

    Refer to the Organizational Process Definition process area for more information about establishing an organizational measurement repository, including common measures.

6. Appraise the processes, methods, and tools in use in the organization and develop recommendations for improving the organizational process assets.

    This appraisal typically includes the following:
    - Determining which of the processes, methods, and tools are of potential use to other parts of the organization
    - Appraising the quality and effectiveness of the organizational process assets
    - Identifying candidate improvements to the organizational process assets
    - Determining compliance with the organization's set of standard processes and tailoring guidelines

7. Make the best use of the organization's processes, methods, and tools available to the people in the organization as appropriate.
8. Manage process improvement proposals.

    The activities for managing process improvement proposals typically include the following:
    - Soliciting process improvement proposals
    - Collecting process improvement proposals
    - Reviewing the process improvement proposals

- Selecting the process improvement proposals that will be implemented
- Tracking the implementation of the process improvement proposals

Process improvement proposals are documented as process change requests or problem reports, as appropriate.

   Some process improvement proposals may be incorporated into the organization's process action plans.

9. Establish and maintain records of the organization's process improvement activities.

Generic Practices by Goal

GG 1   ACHIEVE SPECIFIC GOALS

The process supports and enables achievement of the specific goals of the process area by transforming identifiable input work products to produce identifiable output work products.

GP 1.1   PERFORM BASE PRACTICES

Perform the base practices of the organizational process focus process to develop work products and provide services to achieve the specific goals of the process area.

GG 2   INSTITUTIONALIZE A MANAGED PROCESS

The process is institutionalized as a managed process.

GG 3   INSTITUTIONALIZE A DEFINED PROCESS

The process is institutionalized as a defined process.

   AUTHORS' NOTE: This generic goal's appearance here reflects its location in the staged representation.

CONTINUOUS ONLY

S ONLY

Commitment to Perform

GP 2.1   ESTABLISH AN ORGANIZATIONAL POLICY

Establish and maintain an organizational policy for planning and performing the organizational process focus process.

Elaboration

This policy establishes organizational expectations for determining process improvement opportunities for the processes being used and for planning and implementing process improvement activities across the organization.

Ability to Perform

GP 2.2   PLAN THE PROCESS

Establish and maintain the plan for performing the organizational process focus process.

Elaboration

The plan for performing the organizational process focus process, which is often called "the process improvement plan," differs from the process action plans described in specific practices in this process area. The plan called for in this generic practice addresses the comprehensive planning for all of the specific practices in this process area, from the establishment of organizational process needs all the way through to the incorporation of process-related experiences into the organizational process assets.

GP 2.3   PROVIDE RESOURCES

Provide adequate resources for performing the organizational process focus process, developing the work products, and providing the services of the process.

Elaboration

Examples of resources provided include the following tools:
- Database management systems
- Process improvement tools
- Web page builders and browsers
- Groupware
- Quality-improvement tools (e.g., cause-and-effect diagrams, affinity diagrams, Pareto charts)

GP 2.4   ASSIGN RESPONSIBILITY

Assign responsibility and authority for performing the process, developing the work products, and providing the services of the organizational process focus process.

Elaboration

Two groups are typically established and assigned responsibility for process improvement: (1) a management steering committee for process improvement to provide senior management sponsorship, and (2) a process group to facilitate and manage the process improvement activities.

GP 2.5   TRAIN PEOPLE

Train the people performing or supporting the organizational process focus process as needed.

Elaboration

> Examples of training topics include the following:
> - CMMI and other process and process improvement reference models
> - Planning and managing process improvement
> - Tools, methods, and analysis techniques
> - Process modeling
> - Facilitation techniques
> - Change management

Directing Implementation

GP 2.6 MANAGE CONFIGURATIONS

Place designated work products of the organizational process focus process under appropriate levels of configuration management.

Elaboration

> Examples of work products placed under configuration management include the following:
> - Process improvement proposals
> - Organization's approved process action plans
> - Training materials for deploying organizational process assets
> - Plans for the organization's process appraisals

GP 2.7 IDENTIFY AND INVOLVE RELEVANT STAKEHOLDERS

Identify and involve the relevant stakeholders of the organizational process focus process as planned.

Elaboration

> Examples of activities for stakeholder involvement include the following:
> - Coordinating and collaborating on process improvement activities with process owners, those who are or will be performing the process, and support organizations (e.g., training staff and quality assurance representatives)
> - Establishing the organizational process needs and objectives
> - Appraising the organization's processes
> - Implementing process action plans
> - Coordinating and collaborating on the execution of pilots to test selected improvements
> - Deploying organizational process assets and changes to organizational process assets
> - Communicating the plans, status, activities, and results related to the implementation of process improvement activities

GP 2.8 MONITOR AND CONTROL THE PROCESS

Monitor and control the organizational process focus process against the plan for performing the process and take appropriate corrective action.

Elaboration

Examples of measures used in monitoring and controlling include the following:
- Number of process improvement proposals submitted, accepted, or implemented
- CMMI maturity level or capability level

Verifying Implementation

GP 2.9 OBJECTIVELY EVALUATE ADHERENCE

Objectively evaluate adherence of the organizational process focus process against its process description, standards, and procedures, and address noncompliance.

Elaboration

Examples of activities reviewed include the following:
- Determining process improvement opportunities
- Planning and coordinating process improvement activities

Examples of work products reviewed include the following:
- Process improvement plans
- Process action plans
- Plans for the organization's process appraisals

GP 2.10 REVIEW STATUS WITH HIGHER LEVEL MANAGEMENT

Review the activities, status, and results of the organizational process focus process with higher level management and resolve issues.

Elaboration

These reviews are typically in the form of a briefing presented to the management steering committee by the process group and the process action teams.

Examples of presentation topics include the following:
- Status of improvements being developed by process action teams
- Results of pilots
- Results of deployments
- Schedule status for achieving significant milestones (e.g., readiness for an appraisal, or progress toward achieving a targeted organizational maturity level or capability level profile)

GG 3   *INSTITUTIONALIZE A DEFINED PROCESS*

The process is institutionalized as a defined process.

> AUTHORS' NOTE: This generic goal's appearance here reflects
> its location in the continuous representation.

Ability to Perform

GP 3.1   *ESTABLISH A DEFINED PROCESS*

Establish and maintain the description of a defined organizational process focus process.

Directing Implementation

GP 3.2   *COLLECT IMPROVEMENT INFORMATION*

Collect work products, measures, measurement results, and improvement information derived from planning and performing the organizational process focus process to support the future use and improvement of the organization's processes and process assets.

GG 4   *INSTITUTIONALIZE A QUANTITATIVELY MANAGED PROCESS*

The process is institutionalized as a quantitatively managed process.

GP 4.1   *ESTABLISH QUANTITATIVE OBJECTIVES FOR THE PROCESS*

Establish and maintain quantitative objectives for the organizational process focus process that address quality and process performance based on customer needs and business objectives.

GP 4.2   *STABILIZE SUBPROCESS PERFORMANCE*

Stabilize the performance of one or more subprocesses to determine the ability of the organizational process focus process to achieve the established quantitative quality and process-performance objectives.

GG 5   *INSTITUTIONALIZE AN OPTIMIZING PROCESS*

The process is institutionalized as an optimizing process.

GP 5.1   *ENSURE CONTINUOUS PROCESS IMPROVEMENT*

Ensure continuous improvement of the organizational process focus process in fulfilling the relevant business objectives of the organization.

GP 5.2   *CORRECT ROOT CAUSES OF PROBLEMS*

Identify and correct the root causes of defects and other problems in the organizational process focus process.

CONTINUOUS ONLY

ORGANIZATIONAL PROCESS PERFORMANCE
A Process Management Process Area at Maturity Level 4

Purpose

The purpose of Organizational Process Performance (OPP) is to establish and maintain a quantitative understanding of the performance of the organization's set of standard processes in support of quality and process-performance objectives, and to provide the process performance data, baselines, and models to quantitatively manage the organization's projects.

Introductory Notes

Process performance is a measure of the actual results achieved by following a process. Process performance is characterized by both process measures (e.g., effort, cycle time, and defect removal effectiveness) and product measures (e.g., reliability and defect density).

The common measures for the organization are composed of process and product measures that can be used to summarize the actual performance of processes in individual projects in the organization. The organizational data for these measures are analyzed to establish a distribution and range of results, which characterize the expected performance of the process when used on any individual project in the organization.

In this process area, the phrase "quality and process-performance objectives" covers objectives and requirements for product quality, service quality, and process performance. As indicated above, the term "process performance" includes product quality; however, to emphasize the importance of product quality, the phrase "quality and process-performance objectives" is used rather than just "process-performance objectives."

The expected process performance can be used in establishing the project's quality and process-performance objectives and can be used as a baseline against which actual project performance can be compared. This information is used to quantitatively manage the project. Each quantitatively managed project, in turn, provides actual performance results that become a part of the baseline data for the organizational process assets.

The associated process performance models are used to represent past and current process performance and to predict future results of the process. For example, the latent defects in the delivered product can be predicted using measurements of defects identified during product-verification activities.

When the organization has measures, data, and analytical techniques for critical process and product characteristics, it is able to do the following:

- Determine whether processes are behaving consistently or have stable trends (i.e., are predictable)
- Identify processes where the performance is within natural bounds that are consistent across process implementation teams
- Establish criteria for identifying whether a process or process element should be statistically managed, and determine pertinent measures and analytical techniques to be used in such management
- Identify processes that show unusual (e.g., sporadic or unpredictable) behavior
- Identify any aspects of the processes that can be improved in the organization's set of standard processes
- Identify the implementation of a process which performs best

Related Process Areas

Refer to the Quantitative Project Management process area for more information about the use of process performance baselines and models.

Refer to the Measurement and Analysis process area for more information about specifying measures and collecting and analyzing data.

Specific Practices by Goal

SG 1   ESTABLISH PERFORMANCE BASELINES AND MODELS

Baselines and models that characterize the expected process performance of the organization's set of standard processes are established and maintained.

Prior to establishing process performance baselines and models, it is necessary to determine which processes are suitable to be measured (the Select Processes specific practice), which measures are useful for determining process performance (the Establish Process Performance Measures specific practice), and the quality and process-performance objectives for those processes (the Establish Quality and Process-Performance Objectives specific practice). These specific practices are often interrelated and may need to be performed concurrently to select the appropriate processes, measures,

Practice-to-Goal Relationship Table

Continuous Representation	*Staged Representation*
SG 1 Establish Performance Baselines and Models	**SG 1** Establish Performance Baselines and Models
SP 1.1-1 Select Processes	SP 1.1-1 Select Processes
SP 1.2-1 Establish Process Performance Measures	SP 1.2-1 Establish Process Performance Measures
SP 1.3-1 Establish Quality and Process-Performance Objectives	SP 1.3-1 Establish Quality and Process-Performance Objectives
SP 1.4-1 Establish Process Performance Baselines	SP 1.4-1 Establish Process Performance Baselines
SP 1.5-1 Establish Process Performance Models	SP 1.5-1 Establish Process Performance Models
GG 1 Achieve Specific Goals	
GP 1.1 Perform Base Practices	
GG 2 Institutionalize a Managed Process	**GG 3** Institutionalize a Defined Process
GP 2.1 Establish an Organizational Policy	GP 2.1 Establish an Organizational Policy
GP 2.2 Plan the Process	GP 2.2 Plan the Process
GP 2.3 Provide Resources	GP 2.3 Provide Resources
GP 2.4 Assign Responsibility	GP 2.4 Assign Responsibility
GP 2.5 Train People	GP 2.5 Train People
GP 2.6 Manage Configurations	GP 2.6 Manage Configurations
GP 2.7 Identify and Involve Relevant Stakeholders	GP 2.7 Identify and Involve Relevant Stakeholders
GP 2.8 Monitor and Control the Process	GP 2.8 Monitor and Control the Process
GP 2.9 Objectively Evaluate Adherence	GP 2.9 Objectively Evaluate Adherence
GP 2.10 Review Status with Higher Level Management	GP 2.10 Review Status with Higher Level Management
GG 3 Institutionalize a Defined Process	
GP 3.1 Establish a Defined Process	GP 3.1 Establish a Defined Process
GP 3.2 Collect Improvement Information	GP 3.2 Collect Improvement Information
GG 4 Institutionalize a Quantitatively Managed Process	
GP 4.1 Establish Quantitative Objectives for the Process	
GP 4.2 Stabilize Subprocess Performance	
GG 5 Institutionalize an Optimizing Process	
GP 5.1 Ensure Continuous Process Improvement	
GP 5.2 Correct Root Causes of Problems	

OPP

and quality and process-performance objectives. Often, the selection of one process, measure, or objective will constrain the selection of the others. For example, if a certain process is selected, the measures and objectives for that process may be constrained by the process itself.

SP 1.1-1 SELECT PROCESSES

Select the processes or process elements in the organization's set of standard processes that are to be included in the organization's process performance analyses.

Refer to the Organizational Process Definition process area for more information about the structure of the organizational process assets.

The organization's set of standard processes consists of a set of standard processes that, in turn, are composed of process elements.

Typically, it will not be possible, useful, or economically justifiable to apply statistical management techniques to all processes or process elements of the organization's set of standard processes. Selection of the processes and/or process elements is based on the needs and objectives of both the organization and projects.

Typical Work Products

1. List of processes or process elements identified for process performance analyses

SP 1.2-1 ESTABLISH PROCESS PERFORMANCE MEASURES

Establish and maintain definitions of the measures that are to be included in the organization's process performance analyses.

Refer to the Measurement and Analysis process area for more information about selecting measures.

Typical Work Products

1. Definitions for the selected measures of process performance

Subpractices

1. Determine which of the organization's business objectives for quality and process performance need to be addressed by the measures.
2. Select measures that provide appropriate insight into the organization's quality and process performance.

    The Goal Question Metric paradigm is an approach that can be used to select measures that provide insight into the organization's business objectives.

Examples of criteria used to select measures include the following:
- Relationship of the measures to the organization's business objectives
- Coverage that the measures provide over the entire life of the product
- Visibility that the measures provide into the process performance
- Availability of the measures
- Extent to which the measures are objective
- Frequency at which the observations of the measure can be collected
- Extent to which the measures are controllable by changes to the process
- Extent to which the measures represent the users' view of effective process performance

3. Incorporate the selected measures into the organization's set of common measures.

> *Refer to the Organizational Process Definition process area for more information about establishing organizational process assets.*

4. Revise the set of measures as necessary.

SP 1.3-1 ESTABLISH QUALITY AND PROCESS-PERFORMANCE OBJECTIVES

Establish and maintain quantitative objectives for quality and process performance for the organization.

The organization's quality and process-performance objectives should have the following attributes:

- Based on the organization's business objectives
- Based on the past performance of projects
- Defined to gauge process performance in areas such as product quality, productivity, or cycle time
- Constrained by the inherent variability or natural bounds of the process

Typical Work Products

1. Organization's quality and process-performance objectives

Subpractices

1. Review the organization's business objectives related to quality and process performance.

Examples of business objectives include the following:
- Achieve a development cycle of a specified duration for a specified release of a product
- Decrease the cost of maintenance of the products by a specified percent

2. Define the organization's quantitative objectives for quality and process performance.

> Objectives may be established for both process measurements (e.g., effort, cycle time, and defect removal effectiveness) and product measurements (e.g., reliability and defect density).

Examples of quality and process-performance objectives include the following:
- Achieve a specified productivity
- Deliver work products with no more than a specified number of latent defects

---

3. Define the priorities of the organization's objectives for quality and process performance.
4. Review, negotiate, and obtain commitment for the organization's quality and process-performance objectives and their priorities from the relevant stakeholders.
5. Revise the organization's quantitative objectives for quality and process performance as necessary.

Examples of when the organization's quantitative objectives for quality and process performance may need to be revised include the following:
- When the organization's business objectives change
- When the organization's processes change
- When actual quality and process performance differs significantly from the objectives

---

SP 1.4-1 ESTABLISH PROCESS PERFORMANCE BASELINES

Establish and maintain the organization's process performance baselines.

The organization's process performance baselines are a measurement of performance for the organization's set of standard processes at various levels of detail, as appropriate. The processes include the following:

- Individual process elements (e.g., test-case inspection element)
- Sequence of connected processes
- Processes that cover the entire life of the project
- Processes for developing individual work products

There may be several process performance baselines to characterize performance for subgroups of the organization.

> Examples of criteria used to categorize subgroups include the following:
> - Product line
> - Application domain
> - Complexity
> - Team size
> - Work product size
> - Process elements from the organization's set of standard processes

Allowable tailoring of the organization's set of standard processes may significantly affect the comparability of the data for inclusion in process performance baselines. The effects of tailoring should be considered in establishing baselines.

Refer to the Quantitative Project Management process area for more information about the use of process performance baselines.

Typical Work Products

1. Baseline data on the organization's process performance

Subpractices

1. Collect measurements from the organization's projects.

   The process in use when the measurement was taken is recorded to enable appropriate use at a later date.

   Refer to the Measurement and Analysis process area for information about collecting and analyzing data.

2. Establish and maintain the organization's process performance baselines from the collected measurements and analyses.

   Refer to the Measurement and Analysis process area for information about establishing objectives for measurement and analysis, specifying the measures and analyses to be performed, obtaining and analyzing measures, and reporting results.

   Process performance baselines are derived by analyzing the collected measures to establish a distribution and range of results that characterize the expected performance for selected processes when used on any individual project in the organization.

   The measurements from stable processes from projects should be used; other data may not be reliable.

3. Review and get agreement with relevant stakeholders about the organization's process performance baselines.

4. Make the organization's process performance information available across the organization in the organization's measurement repository.

   The organization's process performance baselines are used by the projects to estimate the natural bounds for process performance.

Refer to the Organizational Process Definition process area for more information about establishing the organization's measurement repository.

5. Compare the organization's process performance baselines to the associated objectives.

6. Revise the organization's process performance baselines as necessary.

> Examples of when the organization's process performance baselines may need to be revised include the following:
> - When the processes change
> - When the organization's results change
> - When the organization's needs change

SP 1.5-1 ESTABLISH PROCESS PERFORMANCE MODELS

Establish and maintain the process performance models for the organization's set of standard processes.

Process performance models are used to estimate or predict the value of a process performance measure from the values of other process and product measurements. These process performance models typically use process and product measurements collected throughout the life of the project to estimate progress toward achieving objectives that cannot be measured until later in the project's life.

The process performance models are used as follows:

- The organization uses them for estimating, analyzing, and predicting the process performance associated with the processes in the organization's set of standard processes.
- The organization uses them to assess the (potential) return on investment for process improvement activities.
- Projects use them for estimating, analyzing, and predicting the process performance for their defined processes.
- Projects use them for selecting processes for use.

These measures and models are defined to provide insight into and to provide the ability to predict critical process and product characteristics that are relevant to business value.

Examples of areas of concern to projects in which models may be useful include the following:
- Schedule and cost
- Reliability
- Defect identification and removal rates
- Defect removal effectiveness
- Latent defect estimation
- Project progress
- Combinations of these areas

Examples of process performance models include the following:
- System dynamics models
- Reliability growth models
- Complexity models

Refer to the Quantitative Project Management process area for more information about the use of process performance models.

Typical Work Products

1. Process performance models

Subpractices

1. Establish the process performance models based on the organization's set of standard processes and the organization's process performance baselines.
2. Calibrate the process performance models based on the organization's past results and current needs.
3. Review the process performance models and get agreement with relevant stakeholders.
4. Support the projects' use of the process performance models.
5. Revise the process performance models as necessary.

Examples of when the process performance models may need to be revised include the following:
- When the processes change
- When the organization's results change
- When the organization's needs change

Generic Practices by Goal

GG 1 ACHIEVE SPECIFIC GOALS

The process supports and enables achievement of the specific goals of the process area by transforming identifiable input work products to produce identifiable output work products.

GP 1.1 PERFORM BASE PRACTICES

Perform the base practices of the organizational process performance process to develop work products and provide services to achieve the specific goals of the process area.

GG 2 INSTITUTIONALIZE A MANAGED PROCESS

The process is institutionalized as a managed process.

GG 3 INSTITUTIONALIZE A DEFINED PROCESS

The process is institutionalized as a defined process.

> AUTHORS' NOTE: This generic goal's appearance here reflects its location in the staged representation.

Commitment to Perform

GP 2.1 ESTABLISH AN ORGANIZATIONAL POLICY

Establish and maintain an organizational policy for planning and performing the organizational process performance process.

Elaboration
This policy establishes organizational expectations for establishing and maintaining process performance baselines for the organization's set of standard processes.

Ability to Perform

GP 2.2 PLAN THE PROCESS

Establish and maintain the plan for performing the organizational process performance process.

Elaboration
This plan for performing the organizational process performance process may be included in or referenced by the organization's process improvement plan, which is described in the Organizational Process Focus process area, or it may be

documented in a separate plan that describes only the plan for the organizational process performance process.

GP 2.3   PROVIDE RESOURCES

Provide adequate resources for performing the organizational process performance process, developing the work products, and providing the services of the process.

Elaboration

Special expertise in statistics and statistical process control may be needed to establish the process performance baselines for the organization's set of standard processes.

> Examples of other resources provided include the following tools:
> - Database management systems
> - System dynamics model
> - Process modeling tools
> - Statistical analysis packages
> - Problem-tracking packages

GP 2.4   ASSIGN RESPONSIBILITY

Assign responsibility and authority for performing the process, developing the work products, and providing the services of the organizational process performance process.

GP 2.5   TRAIN PEOPLE

Train the people performing or supporting the organizational process performance process as needed.

Elaboration

> Examples of training topics include the following:
> - Process and process-improvement modeling
> - Quantitative and statistical methods (e.g., estimating models, Pareto analysis, and control charts)

Directing Implementation

GP 2.6   MANAGE CONFIGURATIONS

Place designated work products of the organizational process performance process under appropriate levels of configuration management.

OPP

Elaboration

> Examples of work products placed under configuration management include the following:
> - Organization's quality and process-performance objectives
> - Definitions of the selected measures of process performance
> - Baseline data on the organization's process performance

GP 2.7 *IDENTIFY AND INVOLVE RELEVANT STAKEHOLDERS*

Identify and involve the relevant stakeholders of the organizational process perform-ance process as planned.

Elaboration

> Examples of activities for stakeholder involvement include the following:
> - Establishing the organization's quality and process-performance objectives and their priorities
> - Reviewing and resolving issues on the organization's process performance baselines
> - Reviewing and resolving issues on the organization's process performance models

GP 2.8 *MONITOR AND CONTROL THE PROCESS*

Monitor and control the organizational process performance process against the plan for performing the process and take appropriate corrective action.

Elaboration

> Examples of measures used in monitoring and controlling include the following:
> - Trends in the organization's process performance with respect to changes in work products and task attributes (e.g., size growth, effort, schedule, and quality)

Verifying Implementation

GP 2.9 *OBJECTIVELY EVALUATE ADHERENCE*

Objectively evaluate adherence of the organizational process performance process against its process description, standards, and procedures, and address noncompliance.

Elaboration

> Examples of activities reviewed include the following:
> - Establishing process performance baselines and models

Examples of work products reviewed include the following:
- Process performance plans
- Organization's quality and process-performance objectives
- Definitions of the selected measures of process performance

GP 2.10 REVIEW STATUS WITH HIGHER LEVEL MANAGEMENT

Review the activities, status, and results of the organizational process performance process with higher level management and resolve issues.

GG 3 INSTITUTIONALIZE A DEFINED PROCESS

The process is institutionalized as a defined process.

AUTHORS' NOTE: This generic goal's appearance here reflects its location in the continuous representation.

Ability to Perform

GP 3.1 ESTABLISH A DEFINED PROCESS

Establish and maintain the description of a defined organizational process performance process.

Directing Implementation

GP 3.2 COLLECT IMPROVEMENT INFORMATION

Collect work products, measures, measurement results, and improvement information derived from planning and performing the organizational process performance process to support the future use and improvement of the organization's processes and process assets.

GG 4 INSTITUTIONALIZE A QUANTITATIVELY MANAGED PROCESS

The process is institutionalized as a quantitatively managed process.

GP 4.1 ESTABLISH QUANTITATIVE OBJECTIVES FOR THE PROCESS

Establish and maintain quantitative objectives for the organizational process performance process that address quality and process performance based on customer needs and business objectives.

GP 4.2 STABILIZE SUBPROCESS PERFORMANCE

Stabilize the performance of one or more subprocesses to determine the ability of the organizational process performance process to achieve the established quantitative quality and process-performance objectives.

GG 5 INSTITUTIONALIZE AN OPTIMIZING PROCESS

The process is institutionalized as an optimizing process.

GP 5.1 ENSURE CONTINUOUS PROCESS IMPROVEMENT

Ensure continuous improvement of the organizational process performance process in fulfilling the relevant business objectives of the organization.

GP 5.2 CORRECT ROOT CAUSES OF PROBLEMS

Identify and correct the root causes of defects and other problems in the organizational process performance process.

CONTINUOUS ONLY

ORGANIZATIONAL TRAINING
A Process Management Process Area at Maturity Level 3

Purpose

The purpose of Organizational Training (OT) is to develop the skills and knowledge of people so they can perform their roles effectively and efficiently.

Introductory Notes

Organizational Training includes training to support the organization's strategic business objectives and to meet the tactical training needs that are common across projects and support groups. Specific training needs identified by individual projects and support groups are handled at the project and support group level and are outside the scope of Organizational Training. Project and support groups are responsible for identifying and addressing their specific training needs.

Refer to the Project Planning process area for more information about the specific training needs identified by projects.

An organizational training program involves the following:

- Identifying the training needed by the organization
- Obtaining and providing training to address those needs
- Establishing and maintaining training capability
- Establishing and maintaining training records
- Assessing training effectiveness

Effective training requires assessment of needs, planning, instructional design, and appropriate training media (e.g., workbooks, computer software), as well as a repository of training process data. As an organizational process, the main components of training include a managed training development program, documented plans, personnel with appropriate mastery of specific disciplines and other areas of knowledge, and mechanisms for measuring the effectiveness of the training program.

The identification of process training needs is primarily based on the skills that are required to perform the organization's set of standard processes. *Refer to the Organizational Process Definition process area for more information about the organization's set of standard processes.*

Certain skills may be effectively and efficiently imparted through vehicles other than in-class training experiences (e.g., informal mentoring). Other skills require more formalized training vehicles, such as in a classroom, by Web-based training, through guided self-study, or via a formalized on-the-job training program. The formal or informal training vehicles employed for each situation should be based on an assessment of the need for training and the performance gap to be addressed. The term "training" used throughout this process area is used broadly to include all of these learning options.

Success in training can be measured in terms of the availability of opportunities to acquire the skills and knowledge needed to perform new and ongoing enterprise activities.

Skills and knowledge may be technical, organizational, or contextual. Technical skills pertain to the ability to use the equipment, tools, materials, data, and processes required by a project or a process. Organizational skills pertain to behavior within and according to the employee's organization structure, role and responsibilities, and general operating principles and methods. Contextual skills are the self-management, communication, and interpersonal abilities needed to successfully perform in the organizational and social context of the project and support groups.

The phrase "project and support groups" is used frequently in the text of the process area description to indicate an organization-level perspective.

Related Process Areas

Refer to the Organizational Process Definition process area for more information about the organization's process assets.

Refer to the Project Planning process area for more information about the specific training needs identified by projects.

Refer to the Decision Analysis and Resolution process area for how to apply decision-making criteria when determining training approaches.

Specific Practices by Goal

SG 1   ESTABLISH AN ORGANIZATIONAL TRAINING CAPABILITY

A training capability that supports the organization's management and technical roles is established and maintained.

Practice-to-Goal Relationship Table

Continuous Representation	*Staged Representation*
SG 1 Establish an Organizational Training Capability	SG 1 Establish an Organizational Training Capability
SP 1.1-1 Establish the Strategic Training Needs	SP 1.1-1 Establish the Strategic Training Needs
SP 1.2-1 Determine Which Training Needs Are the Responsibility of the Organization	SP 1.2-1 Determine Which Training Needs Are the Responsibility of the Organization
SP 1.3-1 Establish an Organizational Training Tactical Plan	SP 1.3-1 Establish an Organizational Training Tactical Plan
SP 1.4-1 Establish Training Capability	SP 1.4-1 Establish Training Capability
SG 2 Provide Necessary Training	SG 2 Provide Necessary Training
SP 2.1-1 Deliver Training	SP 2.1-1 Deliver Training
SP 2.2-1 Establish Training Records	SP 2.2-1 Establish Training Records
SP 2.3-1 Assess Training Effectiveness	SP 2.3-1 Assess Training Effectiveness
GG 1 Achieve Specific Goals	
GP 1.1 Perform Base Practices	
GG 2 Institutionalize a Managed Process	GG 3 Institutionalize a Defined Process
GP 2.1 Establish an Organizational Policy	GP 2.1 Establish an Organizational Policy
GP 2.2 Plan the Process	GP 2.2 Plan the Process
GP 2.3 Provide Resources	GP 2.3 Provide Resources
GP 2.4 Assign Responsibility	GP 2.4 Assign Responsibility
GP 2.5 Train People	GP 2.5 Train People
GP 2.6 Manage Configurations	GP 2.6 Manage Configurations
GP 2.7 Identify and Involve Relevant Stakeholders	GP 2.7 Identify and Involve Relevant Stakeholders
GP 2.8 Monitor and Control the Process	GP 2.8 Monitor and Control the Process
GP 2.9 Objectively Evaluate Adherence	GP 2.9 Objectively Evaluate Adherence
GP 2.10 Review Status with Higher Level Management	GP 2.10 Review Status with Higher Level Management
GG 3 Institutionalize a Defined Process	
GP 3.1 Establish a Defined Process	GP 3.1 Establish a Defined Process
GP 3.2 Collect Improvement Information	GP 3.2 Collect Improvement Information
GG 4 Institutionalize a Quantitatively Managed Process	
GP 4.1 Establish Quantitative Objectives for the Process	
GP 4.2 Stabilize Subprocess Performance	
GG 5 Institutionalize an Optimizing Process	
GP 5.1 Ensure Continuous Process Improvement	
GP 5.2 Correct Root Causes of Problems	

The organization identifies the training required to develop the skills and the knowledge necessary to perform enterprise activities. Once the needs are identified, a training program addressing those needs is developed.

> **FOR INTEGRATED PRODUCT AND PROCESS DEVELOPMENT**
> Cross-functional training, leadership training, interpersonal skills training, and training in the skills needed to integrate appropriate business and technical functions is needed by integrated team members. The potentially wider range of requirements and participant backgrounds may require relevant stakeholders who were not involved in requirements development to take cross training in the disciplines involved in product design in order to commit to requirements with a full understanding of the range of requirements and their interrelationships.

SP 1.1-1   *ESTABLISH THE STRATEGIC TRAINING NEEDS*

Establish and maintain the strategic training needs of the organization.

> Examples of sources of strategic training needs include the following:
> • Organization's standard processes
> • Organization's strategic business plan
> • Organization's process improvement plan
> • Enterprise-level initiatives
> • Skill appraisals
> • Risk analyses

Typical Work Products

1. Training needs
2. Assessment analysis

Subpractices

1. Analyze the organization's strategic business objectives and process improvement plan to identify potential future training needs.
2. Document the strategic training needs of the organization.

> Examples of categories of training needs include (but are not limited to) the following:
> • Process analysis and documentation
> • Engineering (e.g., requirements analysis, design, testing, configuration management, and quality assurance)
> • Selection and management of suppliers
> • Management (e.g., estimating, tracking, and risk management)

3. Determine the roles and skills needed to perform the organization's set of standard processes.
4. Document the training needed to perform the roles in the organization's set of standard processes.
5. Revise the organization's strategic needs and required training as necessary.

SP 1.2-1 DETERMINE WHICH TRAINING NEEDS ARE THE RESPONSIBILITY OF THE ORGANIZATION

Determine which training needs are the responsibility of the organization and which will be left to the individual project or support group.

Refer to the Project Planning process area for more information about project- and support-group-specific plans for training.

In addition to strategic training needs, organizational training addresses training requirements that are common across projects and support groups. Projects and support groups have the primary responsibility for identifying and addressing their specific training needs. The organization's training staff is only responsible for addressing common cross-project and support group training needs. In some cases, however, the organization's training staff may address additional training needs of projects and support groups, as negotiated with them, within the context of the training resources available and the organization's training priorities.

Typical Work Products

1. Common project and support group training needs
2. Training commitments

Subpractices

1. Analyze the training needs identified by the various projects and support groups.

    Analysis of project and support group needs is intended to identify common training needs that can be most efficiently addressed organization-wide. These needs-analysis activities are used to anticipate future training needs that are first visible at the project and support group level.

2. Negotiate with the various projects and support groups on how their specific training needs will be satisfied.

    The support provided by the organization's training staff depends on the training resources available and the organization's training priorities.

> Examples of training appropriately performed by the project or support group include the following:
> - Training in the application domain of the project
> - Training in the unique tools and methods used by the project or support group

3. Document the commitments for providing training support to the projects and support groups.

SP 1.3-1 ESTABLISH AN ORGANIZATIONAL TRAINING TACTICAL PLAN

Establish and maintain an organizational training tactical plan.

The organizational training tactical plan is the plan to deliver the training that is the responsibility of the organization. This plan is adjusted periodically in response to changes (e.g., in needs or resources) and to evaluations of effectiveness.

Typical Work Products

1. Organizational training tactical plan

Subpractices

1. Establish plan content.

    Organizational training tactical plans typically contain the following:
    - Training needs
    - Training topics
    - Schedules based on training activities and their dependencies
    - Methods used for training
    - Requirements and quality standards for training materials
    - Training tasks, roles, and responsibilities
    - Required resources including tools, facilities, environments, staffing, and skills and knowledge

2. Establish commitments to the plan.

    Documented commitments by those responsible for implementing and supporting the plan are essential for the plan to be effective.

3. Revise plan and commitments as necessary.

SP 1.4-1 ESTABLISH TRAINING CAPABILITY

Establish and maintain training capability to address organizational training needs.

Refer to the Decision Analysis and Resolution process area for how to apply decision-making criteria when selecting training approaches and developing training materials.

Typical Work Products

1. Training materials and supporting artifacts

Subpractices

1. Select the appropriate approaches to satisfy specific organizational training needs.

Many factors may affect the selection of training approaches, including audience-specific knowledge, costs and schedule, work environment, and so on. Selection of an approach requires consideration of the means to provide skills and knowledge in the most effective way possible given the constraints.

Examples of training approaches include the following:
- Classroom training
- Computer-aided instruction
- Guided self-study
- Formal apprenticeship and mentoring programs
- Facilitated videos
- Chalk talks
- Brown-bag lunch seminars
- Structured on-the-job training

---

2. Determine whether to develop training materials internally or acquire them externally.

   Determine the costs and benefits of internal training development or of obtaining training externally.

Example criteria that can be used to determine the most effective mode of knowledge or skill acquisition include the following:
- Performance objectives
- Time available to prepare for project execution
- Business objectives
- Availability of in-house expertise
- Availability of training from external sources

Examples of external sources of training include the following:
- Customer-provided training
- Commercially available training courses
- Academic programs
- Professional conferences
- Seminars

---

3. Develop or obtain training materials.

   Training may be provided by the project, by support groups, by the organization, or by an external organization. The organization's training staff coordinates the acquisition and delivery of training regardless of its source.

Examples of training materials include the following:
- Courses
- Computer-aided instruction
- Videos

4. Develop or obtain qualified instructors.

To ensure that internally provided training instructors have the necessary knowledge and training skills, criteria can be defined to identify, develop, and qualify them. In the case of externally provided training, the organization's training staff can investigate how the training provider determines which instructors will deliver the training. This can also be a factor in selecting or continuing to use a specific training provider.

5. Describe the training in the organization's training curriculum.

> Examples of the information provided in the training descriptions for each course include the following:
> - Topics covered in the training
> - Intended audience
> - Prerequisites and preparation for participating
> - Training objectives
> - Length of the training
> - Lesson plans
> - Completion criteria for the course
> - Criteria for granting training waivers

6. Revise the training materials and supporting artifacts as necessary.

> Examples of situations in which the training materials and supporting artifacts may need to be revised include the following:
> - Training needs change (e.g., when new technology associated with the training topic is available)
> - An evaluation of the training identifies the need for change (e.g., evaluations of training effectiveness surveys, training program performance assessments, or instructor evaluation forms)

SG 2   PROVIDE NECESSARY TRAINING

Training necessary for individuals to perform their roles effectively is provided.

In selecting people to be trained, the following should be taken into consideration:

- Background of the target population of training participants
- Prerequisite background to receive training
- Skills and abilities needed by people to perform their roles
- Need for cross-discipline technical management training for all disciplines, including project management
- Need for managers to have training in appropriate organizational processes

- Need for training in the basic principles of discipline-specific engineering to support personnel in quality management, configuration management, and other related support functions
- Need to provide competency development for critical functional areas

SP 2.1-1 DELIVER TRAINING

Deliver the training following the organizational training tactical plan.

Typical Work Products

1. Delivered training course

Subpractices

1. Select the people who will receive the training.

   Training is intended to impart knowledge and skills to people performing various roles within the organization. Some people already possess the knowledge and skills required to perform well in their designated roles. Training can be waived for these people, but care should be taken that training waivers are not abused.

2. Schedule the training, including any resources, as necessary (e.g., facilities and instructors).

   Training should be planned and scheduled. Training is provided that has a direct bearing on the expectations of work performance. Therefore, optimal training occurs in a timely manner with regard to imminent job-performance expectations. These expectations often include the following:
   - Training in the use of specialized tools
   - Training in procedures that are new to the individual who will perform them

3. Conduct the training.

   Experienced instructors should perform training. When possible, training is conducted in settings that closely resemble actual performance conditions and includes activities to simulate actual work situations. This approach includes integration of tools, methods, and procedures for competency development. Training is tied to work responsibilities so that on-the-job activities or other outside experiences will reinforce the training within a reasonable time after the training.

4. Track the delivery of training against the plan.

SP 2.2-1 ESTABLISH TRAINING RECORDS

Establish and maintain records of the organizational training.

Refer to the Project Monitoring and Control process area for information about how project or support group training records are maintained.

The scope of this practice is for the training performed at the organizational level. Establishment and maintenance of training records for project- or support-group-sponsored training is the responsibility of each individual project or support group.

Typical Work Products

1. Training records
2. Training updates to the organizational repository

Subpractices

1. Keep records of all students who successfully complete each training course or other approved training activity as well as those who are unsuccessful.
2. Keep records of all staff who have been waived from specific training.

   The rationale for granting a waiver should be documented, and both the manager responsible and the manager of the excepted individual should approve the waiver for organizational training.
3. Keep records of all students who successfully complete their designated required training.
4. Make training records available to the appropriate people for consideration in assignments.

   Training records may be part of a skills matrix developed by the training organization to provide a summary of the experience and education of people, as well as training sponsored by the organization.

SP 2.3-1 ASSESS TRAINING EFFECTIVENESS

Assess the effectiveness of the organization's training program.

A process should exist to determine the effectiveness of training (i.e., how well the training is meeting the organization's needs).

> Examples of methods used to assess training effectiveness include the following:
> - Testing in the training context
> - Post-training surveys of training participants
> - Surveys of managers' satisfaction with post-training effects
> - Assessment mechanisms embedded in courseware

Measures may be taken to assess the added value of the training against both the project's and organization's objectives. Particular attention should be paid to the need for various training methods, such as training teams as integral work units. When used, performance objectives should be shared with course participants, and should be unambiguous, observable, and verifiable. The results of the training-effectiveness assessment should be used to revise training materials as described in the Establish Training Capability specific practice.

Typical Work Products

1. Training-effectiveness surveys
2. Training program performance assessments
3. Instructor evaluation forms
4. Training examinations

Subpractices

1. Assess in-progress or completed projects to determine whether staff knowledge is adequate for performing project tasks.
2. Provide a mechanism for assessing the effectiveness of each training course with respect to established organizational, project, or individual learning (or performance) objectives.
3. Obtain student evaluations of how well training activities met their needs.

Generic Practices by Goal

GG 1 ACHIEVE SPECIFIC GOALS

The process supports and enables achievement of the specific goals of the process area by transforming identifiable input work products to produce identifiable output work products.

GP 1.1 PERFORM BASE PRACTICES

Perform the base practices of the organizational training process to develop work products and provide services to achieve the specific goals of the process area.

GG 2 INSTITUTIONALIZE A MANAGED PROCESS

The process is institutionalized as a managed process.

GG 3 INSTITUTIONALIZE A DEFINED PROCESS

The process is institutionalized as a defined process.

AUTHORS' NOTE: This generic goal's appearance here reflects its location in the staged representation.

CONTINUOUS ONLY

STAGED ONLY

OT

Commitment to Perform

GP 2.1 ESTABLISH AN ORGANIZATIONAL POLICY

Establish and maintain an organizational policy for planning and performing the organizational training process.

Elaboration
This policy establishes organizational expectations for identifying the strategic training needs of the organization, and providing that training.

Ability to Perform

GP 2.2 PLAN THE PROCESS

Establish and maintain the plan for performing the organizational training process.

Elaboration
This plan for performing the organizational training process differs from the tactical plan for organizational training described in a specific practice in this process area. The plan called for in this generic practice would address the comprehensive planning for all of the specific practices in this process area, from the establishment of strategic training needs all the way through to the assessment of the effectiveness of the organizational training effort. In contrast, the organizational training tactical plan called for in the specific practice would address the periodic planning for the delivery of individual training offerings.

GP 2.3 PROVIDE RESOURCES

Provide adequate resources for performing the organizational training process, developing the work products, and providing the services of the process.

Elaboration

Examples of people (full or part time, internal or external), and skills needed include the following:
- Subject-matter experts
- Curriculum designers
- Instructional designers
- Instructors
- Training administrators

Special facilities may be required for training. When necessary, the facilities required for the activities in the Organizational Training process area are developed or purchased.

> Examples of other resources provided include the following tools:
> - Instruments for analyzing training needs
> - Workstations to be used for training
> - Instructional design tools
> - Packages for developing presentation materials

GP 2.4 ASSIGN RESPONSIBILITY

Assign responsibility and authority for performing the process, developing the work products, and providing the services of the organizational training process.

GP 2.5 TRAIN PEOPLE

Train the people performing or supporting the organizational training process as needed.

Elaboration

> Examples of training topics include the following:
> - Knowledge and skills needs analysis
> - Instructional design
> - Instructional techniques (e.g., train the trainer)
> - Refresher training on subject matter

Directing Implementation

GP 2.6 MANAGE CONFIGURATIONS

Place designated work products of the organizational training process under appropriate levels of configuration management.

Elaboration

> Examples of work products placed under configuration management include the following:
> - Organizational training tactical plan
> - Training records
> - Training materials and supporting artifacts
> - Instructor evaluation forms

GP 2.7 IDENTIFY AND INVOLVE RELEVANT STAKEHOLDERS

Identify and involve the relevant stakeholders of the organizational training process as planned.

Elaboration

> Examples of activities for stakeholder involvement include the following:
> - Establishing a collaborative environment for discussion of training needs and training effectiveness to ensure that the organization's training needs are met
> - Identifying training needs
> - Reviewing the organizational training tactical plan
> - Assessing training effectiveness

GP 2.8   MONITOR AND CONTROL THE PROCESS

Monitor and control the organizational training process against the plan for performing the process and take appropriate corrective action.

Elaboration

> Examples of measures used in monitoring and controlling include the following:
> - Number of training courses delivered (e.g., planned versus actual)
> - Post-training evaluation ratings
> - Training program quality survey ratings

Verifying Implementation

GP 2.9   OBJECTIVELY EVALUATE ADHERENCE

Objectively evaluate adherence of the organizational training process against its process description, standards, and procedures, and address noncompliance.

Elaboration

> Examples of activities reviewed include the following:
> - Identifying training needs and making training available
> - Providing necessary training

> Examples of work products reviewed include the following:
> - Organizational training tactical plan
> - Training materials and supporting artifacts
> - Instructor evaluation forms

GP 2.10 REVIEW STATUS WITH HIGHER LEVEL MANAGEMENT

Review the activities, status, and results of the organizational training process with higher level management and resolve issues.

GG 3 INSTITUTIONALIZE A DEFINED PROCESS

The process is institutionalized as a defined process.

> AUTHORS' NOTE: This generic goal's appearance here reflects
> its location in the continuous representation.

C ONLY

Ability to Perform

GP 3.1 ESTABLISH A DEFINED PROCESS

Establish and maintain the description of a defined organizational training process.

Directing Implementation

GP 3.2 COLLECT IMPROVEMENT INFORMATION

Collect work products, measures, measurement results, and improvement information derived from planning and performing the organizational training process to support the future use and improvement of the organization's processes and process assets.

GG 4 INSTITUTIONALIZE A QUANTITATIVELY MANAGED PROCESS

The process is institutionalized as a quantitatively managed process.

GP 4.1 ESTABLISH QUANTITATIVE OBJECTIVES FOR THE PROCESS

Establish and maintain quantitative objectives for the organizational training process that address quality and process performance based on customer needs and business objectives.

GP 4.2 STABILIZE SUBPROCESS PERFORMANCE

Stabilize the performance of one or more subprocesses to determine the ability of the organizational training process to achieve the established quantitative quality and process-performance objectives.

CONTINUOUS ONLY

GG 5   *Institutionalize an Optimizing Process*

The process is institutionalized as an optimizing process.

GP 5.1   *Ensure Continuous Process Improvement*

Ensure continuous improvement of the organizational training process in fulfilling the relevant business objectives of the organization.

GP 5.2   *Correct Root Causes of Problems*

Identify and correct the root causes of defects and other problems in the organizational training process.

Continuous Only

PRODUCT INTEGRATION
An Engineering Process Area at Maturity Level 3

Purpose

The purpose of Product Integration (PI) is to assemble the product from the product components, ensure that the product, as integrated, functions properly, and deliver the product.

Introductory Notes

This process area addresses the integration of product components into more complex product components or into complete products. The term "integration" is used in this sense throughout this process area and is not to be confused with integration of people or activities that may be described elsewhere in the model.

The scope of this process area is to achieve complete product integration through progressive assembly of product components, in one stage or in incremental stages, according to a defined integration sequence and procedures.

A critical aspect of product integration is the management of internal and external interfaces of the products and product components to ensure compatibility among the interfaces. Attention should be paid to interface management throughout the project.

Product integration is more than just a one-time assembly of the product components at the conclusion of design and fabrication. Product integration can be conducted incrementally, using an iterative process of assembling product components, evaluating them, and then assembling more product components. This process may begin with analysis and simulations (e.g., threads, rapid prototypes, virtual prototypes, and physical prototypes) and steadily progress through increasingly more realistic incremental functionality until the final product is achieved. In each successive build, prototypes (virtual, rapid, or physical) are constructed, evaluated, improved, and reconstructed based on knowledge gained in the evaluation process. The degree of virtual versus physical prototyping required depends on the functionality of the design tools, the complexity of the product, and its associated risk. There is a high probability that the product, integrated in this manner, will pass product verification and validation. For some products, the last integration phase will occur when the product is deployed at its intended operational site.

Related Process Areas

Refer to the Requirements Development process area for more information about identifying interface requirements.

Refer to the Technical Solution process area for more information about defining the interfaces and the integration environment (when the integration environment needs to be developed).

Refer to the Verification process area for more information about verifying the interfaces, the integration environment, and the progressively assembled product components.

Refer to the Validation process area for more information about performing validation of the product components and the integrated product.

Refer to the Risk Management process area for more information about identifying risks and the use of prototypes in risk mitigation for both interface compatibility and product-component integration.

Refer to the Decision Analysis and Resolution process area for more information about using a formal evaluation process for selecting the appropriate integration sequence and procedures and for deciding whether the integration environment should be acquired or developed.

Refer to the Configuration Management process area for more information about managing changes to interface definitions and about the distribution of information.

Refer to the Supplier Agreement Management process area for more information about acquiring product components or parts of the integration environment.

Specific Practices by Goal

SG 1   PREPARE FOR PRODUCT INTEGRATION

Preparation for product integration is conducted.

Preparing for integration of product components involves establishing and maintaining an integration sequence, the environment for performing the integration, and integration procedures. The specific practices of the Prepare for Product Integration specific goal build on each other in the following way. The first specific practice determines the sequence for product and product-component integration. The second determines the environment that will be used to carry out the product and product-component integration. The third develops procedures and criteria for product and product-

Practice-to-Goal Relationship Table

Continuous Representation	Staged Representation

Continuous Representation

SG 1 Prepare for Product Integration
    SP 1.1-1 Determine Integration Sequence
    SP 1.2-2 Establish the Product
              Integration Environment
    SP 1.3-3 Establish Product Integration
              Procedures and Criteria

SG 2 Ensure Interface Compatibility
    SP 2.1-1 Review Interface Descriptions
              for Completeness
    SP 2.2-1 Manage Interfaces

SG 3 Assemble Product Components and
    Deliver the Product
    SP 3.1-1 Confirm Readiness of Product
              Components for Integration
    SP 3.2-1 Assemble Product Components
    SP 3.3-1 Evaluate Assembled Product
              Components
    SP 3.4-1 Package and Deliver the
              Product or Product Component

GG 1 Achieve Specific Goals
    P 1.1 Perform Base Practices

GG 2 Institutionalize a Managed Process
    GP 2.1 Establish an Organizational Policy
    GP 2.2 Plan the Process
    GP 2.3 Provide Resources
    GP 2.4 Assign Responsibility
    GP 2.5 Train People
    GP 2.6 Manage Configurations
    GP 2.7 Identify and Involve Relevant
            Stakeholders
    GP 2.8 Monitor and Control the Process
    GP 2.9 Objectively Evaluate Adherence
   GP 2.10 Review Status with Higher Level
            Management

GG 3 Institutionalize a Defined Process
    GP 3.1 Establish a Defined Process
    GP 3.2 Collect Improvement Information

GG 4 Institutionalize a Quantitatively
    Managed Process
    GP 4.1 Establish Quantitative Objectives
            for the Process
    GP 4.2 Stabilize Subprocess Performance

GG 5 Institutionalize an Optimizing Process
    GP 5.1 Ensure Continuous Process
            Improvement
    GP 5.2 Correct Root Causes of Problems

Staged Representation

SG 1 Prepare for Product Integration
    SP 1.1-1 Determine Integration Sequence
    SP 1.2-2 Establish the Product
              Integration Environment
    SP 1.3-3 Establish Product Integration
              Procedures and Criteria

SG 2 Ensure Interface Compatibility
    SP 2.1-1 Review Interface Descriptions
              for Completeness
    SP 2.2-1 Manage Interfaces

SG 3 Assemble Product Components and
    Deliver the Product
    SP 3.1-1 Confirm Readiness of Product
              Components for Integration
    SP 3.2-1 Assemble Product Components
    SP 3.3-1 Evaluate Assembled Product
              Components
    SP 3.4-1 Package and Deliver the
              Product or Product Component

GG 3 Institutionalize a Defined Process
    GP 2.1 Establish an Organizational Policy
    GP 2.2 Plan the Process
    GP 2.3 Provide Resources
    GP 2.4 Assign Responsibility
    GP 2.5 Train People
    GP 2.6 Manage Configurations
    GP 2.7 Identify and Involve Relevant
            Stakeholders
    GP 2.8 Monitor and Control the Process
    GP 2.9 Objectively Evaluate Adherence
   GP 2.10 Review Status with Higher Level
            Management

    GP 3.1 Establish a Defined Process
    GP 3.2 Collect Improvement
            Information

PI

component integration. Preparation for integration starts early in the project and the integration sequence is developed concurrently with the practices in the Technical Solution process area.

SP 1.1-1 DETERMINE INTEGRATION SEQUENCE

Determine the product-component integration sequence.

The product components that are integrated may include those that are a part of the product to be delivered along with test equipment, test software, or other integration items such as fixtures. Once you have analyzed alternative test and assembly integration sequences, select the best integration sequence.

The product integration sequence can provide for incremental assembly and evaluation of product components that provide a problem-free foundation for incorporation of other product components as they become available, or for prototypes of high-risk product components.

The integration sequence should be harmonized with the selection of solutions and the design of product and product components in the Technical Solution process area.

Refer to the Decision Analysis and Resolution process area for more information about using a formal evaluation process to select the appropriate product integration sequence.

Refer to the Risk Management process area for more information about identifying and handling risks associated with the integration sequence.

Refer to the Supplier Agreement Management process area for more information about transitioning acquired product components and the need for handling those product components in the product integration sequence.

Typical Work Products

1. Product integration sequence
2. Rationale for selecting or rejecting integration sequences

Subpractices

1. Identify the product components to be integrated.
2. Identify the product integration verifications to be performed using the definition of the interfaces between the product components.
3. Identify alternative product-component integration sequences.

    This can include defining the specific tools and test equipment to support the product integration.
4. Select the best integration sequence.

5. Periodically review the product integration sequence and revise as needed.

  Assess the product integration sequence to ensure that variations in production and delivery schedules have not had an adverse impact on the sequence or compromised the factors on which earlier decisions were made.

6. Record the rationale for decisions made and deferred.

SP 1.2-2 ESTABLISH THE PRODUCT INTEGRATION ENVIRONMENT

Establish and maintain the environment needed to support the integration of the product components.

Refer to the Technical Solution process area for more information about make-or-buy decisions.

The environment for product integration can either be acquired or developed. To establish an environment, requirements for the purchase or development of equipment, software, or other resources will need to be developed. These requirements are gathered when implementing the processes associated with the Requirements Development process area. The product integration environment may include the reuse of existing organizational resources. The decision to acquire or develop the product integration environment is addressed in the processes associated with the Technical Solution process area.

  The environment required at each step of the product integration process may include test equipment, simulators (taking the place of nonavailable product components), pieces of real equipment, and recording devices.

Typical Work Products

1. Verified environment for product integration
2. Support documentation for the product integration environment

Subpractices

1. Identify the requirements for the product integration environment.
2. Identify verification criteria and procedures for the product integration environment.
3. Decide whether to make or buy the needed product integration environment.

  Refer to the Supplier Agreement Management process area for more information about acquiring parts of the integration environment.

4. Develop an integration environment if a suitable environment cannot be acquired.

  For unprecedented, complex projects, the product integration environment can be a major development. As such, it would involve project planning, requirements development, technical solutions, verification, validation, and risk management.

5. Maintain the product integration environment throughout the project.
6. Dispose of those portions of the environment that are no longer useful.

SP 1.3-3   ESTABLISH PRODUCT INTEGRATION PROCEDURES AND CRITERIA

Establish and maintain procedures and criteria for integration of the product components.

Procedures for the integration of the product components can include such things as the number of incremental iterations to be performed and details of the expected tests and other evaluations to be carried out at each stage.

Criteria can indicate the readiness of a product component for integration or its acceptability.

Procedures and criteria for product integration address the following:

- Level of testing for build components
- Verification of interfaces
- Thresholds of performance deviation
- Derived requirements for the assembly and its external interfaces
- Allowable substitutions of components
- Testing environment parameters
- Limits on cost of testing
- Quality/cost tradeoffs for integration operations
- Probability of proper functioning
- Delivery rate and its variation
- Lead time from order to delivery
- Personnel availability
- Availability of the integration facility/line/environment

Criteria can be defined for how the product components are to be verified and the functions they are expected to have. Criteria can be defined for how the assembled product components and final integrated product are to be validated and delivered.

Criteria may also constrain the degree of simulation permitted for a product component to pass a test, or may constrain the environment to be used for the integration test.

FOR SUPPLIER SOURCING

Pertinent parts of the schedule and criteria for assembly should be shared with suppliers of work products to reduce the occurrence of delays and component failure.

Typical Work Products

1. Product integration procedures
2. Product integration criteria

Subpractices

1. Establish and maintain product integration procedures for the product components.
2. Establish and maintain criteria for product-component integration and evaluation.
3. Establish and maintain criteria for validation and delivery of the integrated product.

SG 2 ENSURE INTERFACE COMPATIBILITY

The product-component interfaces, both internal and external, are compatible.

Many product integration problems arise from unknown or uncontrolled aspects of both internal and external interfaces. Effective management of product-component interface requirements, specifications, and designs helps ensure that implemented interfaces will be complete and compatible.

SP 2.1-1 REVIEW INTERFACE DESCRIPTIONS FOR COMPLETENESS

Review interface descriptions for coverage and completeness.

The interfaces should include, in addition to product-component interfaces, all the interfaces with the product integration environment.

Typical Work Products

1. Categories of interfaces
2. List of interfaces per category
3. Mapping of the interfaces to the product components and the product integration environment

Subpractices

1. Review interface data for completeness and ensure complete coverage of all interfaces.

Consider all the product components and prepare a relationship table. Interfaces are usually classified in three main classes: environmental, physical, and functional. Typical categories for these classes include the following: mechanical, fluid, sound, electrical, climatic, electromagnetic, thermal, message, and the human-machine or human interface.

FOR SOFTWARE ENGINEERING

In the message category for software, interfaces include the following:

- Origination
- Destination
- Stimulus
- Protocols and data characteristics

FOR SYSTEMS ENGINEERING

For mechanical and electronic components, the interface data should include the following:

- Mechanical interfaces (e.g., weight and size, center of gravity, clearance of parts in operation, space required for maintenance, fixed links, mobile links, shocks and vibrations received from the bearing structure)
- Noise interfaces (e.g., noise transmitted by the structure, noise transmitted in the air, acoustics)
- Climatic interfaces (e.g., temperature, humidity, pressure, salinity)
- Thermal interfaces (e.g., heat dissipation, transmission of heat to the bearing structure, air conditioning characteristics)
- Fluid interfaces (e.g., fresh water inlet/outlet, seawater inlet/outlet for a naval/coastal product, air conditioning, compressed air, nitrogen, fuel, lubricating oil, exhaust gas outlet)
- Electrical interfaces (e.g., power supply consumption by network with transients and peak values; nonsensitive control signal for power supply and communications; sensitive signal [e.g., analog links]; disturbing signal [e.g., microwave]; grounding signal to comply with the TEMPEST standard)
- Electromagnetic interfaces (e.g., magnetic field, radio and radar links, optical band link wave guides, coaxial and optical fibers)
- Human-machine interface (e.g., audio or voice synthesis, audio or voice recognition, display [analog dial, television screen, or liquid-crystal display, indicators' light-emitting diodes], manual controls [pedal, joystick, ball, keys, push buttons, touchscreen])

2. Ensure that product components and interfaces are marked to ensure easy and correct connection to the joining product component.

3. Periodically review the adequacy of interface descriptions.

 Once established, the interface descriptions must be periodically reviewed to ensure there is no deviation between the existing descriptions and the products being developed, processed, produced, or bought.

> **FOR SUPPLIER SOURCING**
> The interface descriptions for product components should be reviewed with relevant suppliers to avoid misinterpretations, reduce delays, and prevent the development of interfaces that do not work properly.

SP 2.2-1 MANAGE INTERFACES

Manage internal and external interface definitions, designs, and changes for products and product components.

Interface requirements drive the development of the interfaces necessary to integrate product components. Managing product and product-component interfaces starts very early in the development of the product. The definitions and designs for interfaces affect not only the product components and external systems, but can also affect the verification and validation environments.

Refer to the Requirements Development process area for more information about requirements for interfaces.

Refer to the Technical Solution process area for more information about design of interfaces between product components.

Refer to the Requirements Management process area for more information about managing the changes to the interface requirements.

Refer to the Configuration Management process area for more information about distributing changes to the interface descriptions (specifications) so that everyone can know the current state of the interfaces.

Management of the interfaces includes maintenance of the consistency of the interfaces throughout the life of the product, and resolution of conflict, noncompliance, and change issues.

The interfaces should include, in addition to product-component interfaces, all the interfaces with the environment as well as other environments for verification, validation, operations, and support.

The interface changes are documented, maintained, and readily accessible.

Typical Work Products

1. Table of relationships among the product components and the external environment (e.g., main power supply, fastening product, computer bus system)

2. Table of relationships among the different product components
3. List of agreed-to interfaces defined for each pair of product components, when applicable
4. Reports from the interface control working group meetings
5. Action items for updating interfaces
6. Application program interface (API)
7. Updated interface description or agreement

Subpractices

1. Ensure the compatibility of the interfaces throughout the life of the product.
2. Resolve conflict, noncompliance, and change issues.
3. Maintain a repository for interface data accessible to project participants.

   A common accessible repository for interface data provides a mechanism to ensure that everyone knows where the current interface data resides and can access it for use.

SG 3   *ASSEMBLE PRODUCT COMPONENTS AND DELIVER THE PRODUCT*

Verified product components are assembled and the integrated, verified, and validated product is delivered.

Integration of product components proceeds according to the product integration sequence and available procedures. Before integration, each product component should be confirmed to be compliant with its interface requirements. Product components are assembled into larger, more complex product components. These assembled product components are checked for correct interoperation. This process continues until product integration is complete. If, during this process, problems are identified, the problem should be documented and a corrective action process initiated.

Ensure that the assembly of the product components into larger and more complex product components is conducted according to the product integration sequence and available procedures. The timely receipt of needed product components and the involvement of the right people contribute to the successful integration of the product components that compose the product.

SP 3.1-1   *CONFIRM READINESS OF PRODUCT COMPONENTS FOR INTEGRATION*

Confirm, prior to assembly, that each product component required to assemble the product has been properly identified, functions according to its description, and that the product-component interfaces comply with the interface descriptions.

Refer to the Verification process area for more information about verifying product components.

Refer to the Technical Solution process area for more information about unit test of product components.

The purpose of this specific practice is to ensure that the properly identified product component that meets its description can actually be assembled according to the product integration sequence and available procedures. The product components are checked for quantity, obvious damage, and consistency between the product component and interface descriptions.

PI

Those conducting product integration are ultimately responsible for checking to make sure everything is proper with the product components before assembly.

Typical Work Products

1. Acceptance documents for the received product components
2. Delivery receipts
3. Checked packing lists
4. Exception reports
5. Waivers

Subpractices

1. Track the status of all product components as soon as they become available for integration.
2. Ensure that product components are delivered to the product integration environment in accordance with the product integration sequence and available procedures.
3. Confirm the receipt of each properly identified product component.
4. Ensure that each received product component meets its description.
5. Check the configuration status against the expected configuration.
6. Perform a pre-check (e.g., by a visual inspection and using basic measures) of all the physical interfaces before connecting product components together.

SP 3.2-1   ASSEMBLE PRODUCT COMPONENTS

Assemble product components according to the product integration sequence and available procedures.

Refer to the Verification process area for more information about verifying assembled product components.
Refer to the Validation process area for more information about validating assembled product components.

For users of the continuous representation, this is a capability level 1 specific practice. Product integration processes at capability level 1 or 2 may not include procedures and criteria that are created in the Establish Product Integration Procedures and Criteria specific practice at capability level 3. When there are no procedures or criteria established, use the sequence established by the Determine Integration Sequence specific practice to accomplish capability level 1 performance.

CONTINUOUS ONLY

The assembly activities of this specific practice and the evaluation activities of the next specific practice are conducted iteratively, from the initial product components, through the interim assemblies of product components, to the product as a whole.

FOR SUPPLIER SOURCING
The project should exercise reasonable oversight of these assembly processes. The supplier agreements should specify appropriate oversight for critical components.

Typical Work Products

1. Assembled product or product components

Subpractices

1. Ensure the readiness of the product integration environment.
2. Ensure that the assembly sequence is properly performed.
   Record all appropriate information (e.g., configuration status, serial numbers of the product components, types, and calibration date of the meters).
3. Revise the product integration sequence and available procedures as appropriate.

SP 3.3-1 *EVALUATE ASSEMBLED PRODUCT COMPONENTS*

Evaluate assembled product components for interface compatibility.

This evaluation involves examining and testing assembled product components for performance, suitability, or readiness using the available procedures and environment. It is performed as appropriate for different stages of assembly of product components as identified in the product integration sequence and available procedures. The product integration sequence and available procedures may define a more refined integration and evaluation sequence than might be envisioned just by examining the product architecture. For example, if an assembly of product components is composed of four less complex product components, the integration sequence will not necessarily call for the simultaneous integration and evaluation of the four units as one. Rather, the four less complex units may be integrated progressively, one at a time, with an evaluation after each assembly operation prior to realizing the more complex product component that matched the specification in the product architecture. Alternatively, the product integration sequence and available procedures could have determined that only a final evaluation was the best one to perform.

Typical Work Products

1. Exception reports
2. Interface evaluation reports
3. Product integration summary reports

Subpractices

1. Conduct the evaluation of assembled product components following the product integration sequence and available procedures.
2. Record the evaluation results.

> Example results include the following:
> - Any adaptation required to the integration procedure
> - Any change to the product configuration (spare parts, new release)
> - Evaluation procedure deviations

SP 3.4-1 PACKAGE AND DELIVER THE PRODUCT OR PRODUCT COMPONENT

Package the assembled product or product component and deliver it to the appropriate customer.

Refer to the Verification process area for more information about verifying the product or an assembly of product components before packaging.

Refer to the Validation process area for more information about validating the product or an assembly of product components before packaging.

The packaging requirements for some products can be addressed in their specifications and verification criteria. This is especially important when items are stored and transported by the customer. In such cases, there may be a spectrum of environmental and stress conditions specified for the package. In other circumstances, factors such as the following may become important:

- Economy and ease of transportation (e.g., containerization)
- Accountability (e.g., shrinkwrapping)
- Ease and safety of unpacking (e.g., sharp edges, strength of binding methods, childproofing, environmental friendliness of packing material, weight)

The adjustment required to fit product components together in the factory could be different from the one required to fit product components together when installed on the operational site. In that case, the product's logbook for the customer should be used to record such specific parameters.

Typical Work Products

1. Packaged product or product components
2. Delivery documentation

Subpractices

1. Review the requirements, design, product, verification results, and documentation to ensure that issues affecting the packaging and delivery of the product are identified and resolved.
2. Use effective methods to package and deliver the assembled product.

> **FOR SOFTWARE ENGINEERING**
> Examples of software packaging and delivery methods include the following:
> - Magnetic tape
> - Diskettes
> - Hardcopy documents
> - Compact disks
> - Other electronic distribution such as the Internet

3. Satisfy the applicable requirements and standards for packaging and delivering the product.

> **FOR SOFTWARE ENGINEERING**
> Examples of requirements and standards for packaging and delivering software include the following:
> - Type of storage and delivery media
> - Custodians of the master and backup copies
> - Required documentation
> - Copyrights
> - License provisions
> - Security of the software

> **FOR SYSTEMS ENGINEERING**
> Examples of requirements and standards include those for safety, the environment, security, and transportability.

4. Prepare the operational site for installation of the product.

   Preparing the operational site may be the responsibility of the customer or end users.

5. Deliver the product and related documentation and confirm receipt.

6. Install the product at the operational site and confirm correct operation.

   Installing the product may be the responsibility of the customer or the end users. In some circumstances, very little may need to be done to confirm correct operation. In other circumstances, final verification of the integrated product occurs at the operational site.

Generic Practices by Goal

GG 1 ACHIEVE SPECIFIC GOALS

The process supports and enables achievement of the specific goals of the process area by transforming identifiable input work products to produce identifiable output work products.

GP 1.1 PERFORM BASE PRACTICES

Perform the base practices of the product integration process to develop work products and provide services to achieve the specific goals of the process area.

GG 2 INSTITUTIONALIZE A MANAGED PROCESS

The process is institutionalized as a managed process.

GG 3 INSTITUTIONALIZE A DEFINED PROCESS

The process is institutionalized as a defined process.

> AUTHORS' NOTE: This generic goal's appearance here reflects its location in the staged representation.

CONTINUOUS ONLY

STAGED ONLY

Commitment to Perform

GP 2.1 ESTABLISH AN ORGANIZATIONAL POLICY

Establish and maintain an organizational policy for planning and performing the product integration process.

Elaboration

This policy establishes organizational expectations for developing product integration sequences, procedures, and an environment; ensuring interface compatibility among product components; assembling the product components; and delivering the product and product components.

Ability to Perform

GP 2.2 *PLAN THE PROCESS*

Establish and maintain the plan for performing the product integration process.

Elaboration

This plan for performing the product integration process addresses the comprehensive planning for all of the specific practices in this process area, from the preparation for product integration all the way through to the delivery of the final product.

GP 2.3 *PROVIDE RESOURCES*

Provide adequate resources for performing the product integration process, developing the work products, and providing the services of the process.

Elaboration

Product-component interface coordination may be accomplished with an Interface Control Working Group consisting of people who represent external and internal interfaces. Such groups can be used to elicit needs for interface requirements development.

Special facilities may be required for assembling and delivering the product. When necessary, the facilities required for the activities in the Product Integration process area are developed or purchased.

Examples of other resources provided include the following tools:
- Prototyping tools
- Analysis tools
- Simulation tools
- Interface management tools
- Assembly tools (e.g., compilers, make files, joining tools, jigs and fixtures)

GP 2.4 *ASSIGN RESPONSIBILITY*

Assign responsibility and authority for performing the process, developing the work products, and providing the services of the product integration process.

GP 2.5 *TRAIN PEOPLE*

Train the people performing or supporting the product integration process as needed.

Elaboration

> Examples of training topics include the following:
> - Application domain
> - Product integration procedures and criteria
> - Organization's facilities for integration and assembly
> - Assembly methods
> - Packaging standards

Directing Implementation

GP 2.6   MANAGE CONFIGURATIONS

Place designated work products of the product integration process under appropriate levels of configuration management.

Elaboration

> Examples of work products placed under configuration management include the following:
> - Acceptance documents for the received product components
> - Evaluated assembled product and product components
> - Product integration sequence
> - Product integration procedures and criteria
> - Updated interface description or agreement

GP 2.7   IDENTIFY AND INVOLVE RELEVANT STAKEHOLDERS

Identify and involve the relevant stakeholders of the product integration process as planned.

Elaboration

Select relevant stakeholders from customers, end users, developers, producers, testers, suppliers, marketers, maintainers, disposal personnel, and others who may be affected by, or may affect, the product as well as the process.

> Examples of activities for stakeholder involvement include the following:
> - Reviewing interface descriptions for completeness
> - Establishing the product integration sequence
> - Establishing the product integration procedures and criteria
> - Assembling and delivering the product and product components
> - Communicating the results after evaluation
> - Communicating new, effective product integration processes to give affected people the opportunity to improve their performance

GP 2.8 *Monitor and Control the Process*

Monitor and control the product integration process against the plan for performing the process and take appropriate corrective action.

Elaboration

Examples of measures used in monitoring and controlling include the following:
- Product-component integration profile (e.g., product-component assemblies planned and performed, and number of exceptions found)
- Integration evaluation problem report trends (e.g., number written and number closed)
- Integration evaluation problem report aging (i.e., how long each problem report has been open)

Verifying Implementation

GP 2.9 *Objectively Evaluate Adherence*

Objectively evaluate adherence of the product integration process against its process description, standards, and procedures, and address noncompliance.

Elaboration

Examples of activities reviewed include the following:
- Establishing and maintaining a product integration sequence
- Ensuring interface compatibility
- Assembling product components and delivering the product

Examples of work products reviewed include the following:
- Product integration sequence
- Product integration procedures and criteria
- Acceptance documents for the received product components
- Assembled product and product components

GP 2.10 *Review Status with Higher Level Management*

Review the activities, status, and results of the product integration process with higher level management and resolve issues.

GG 3 *Institutionalize a Defined Process*

The process is institutionalized as a defined process.

AUTHORS' NOTE: This generic goal's appearance here reflects its location in the continuous representation.

C ONLY

Ability to Perform

GP 3.1   ESTABLISH A DEFINED PROCESS

Establish and maintain the description of a defined product integration process.

Directing Implementation

GP 3.2   COLLECT IMPROVEMENT INFORMATION

Collect work products, measures, measurement results, and improvement information derived from planning and performing the product integration process to support the future use and improvement of the organization's processes and process assets.

GG 4   INSTITUTIONALIZE A QUANTITATIVELY MANAGED PROCESS

The process is institutionalized as a quantitatively managed process.

GP 4.1   ESTABLISH QUANTITATIVE OBJECTIVES FOR THE PROCESS

Establish and maintain quantitative objectives for the product integration process that address quality and process performance based on customer needs and business objectives.

GP 4.2   STABILIZE SUBPROCESS PERFORMANCE

Stabilize the performance of one or more subprocesses to determine the ability of the product integration process to achieve the established quantitative quality and process-performance objectives.

GG 5   INSTITUTIONALIZE AN OPTIMIZING PROCESS

The process is institutionalized as an optimizing process.

GP 5.1   ENSURE CONTINUOUS PROCESS IMPROVEMENT

Ensure continuous improvement of the product integration process in fulfilling the relevant business objectives of the organization.

GP 5.2   CORRECT ROOT CAUSES OF PROBLEMS

Identify and correct the root causes of defects and other problems in the product integration process.

CONTINUOUS ONLY

PROJECT MONITORING AND CONTROL
A Project Management Process Area at Maturity Level 2

Purpose

The purpose of Project Monitoring and Control (PMC) is to provide an understanding of the project's progress so that appropriate corrective actions can be taken when the project's performance deviates significantly from the plan.

Introductory Notes

A project's documented plan is the basis for monitoring activities, communicating status, and taking corrective action. Progress is primarily determined by comparing actual work product and task attributes, effort, cost, and schedule to the plan at prescribed milestones or control levels within the project schedule or work breakdown structure (WBS). Appropriate visibility enables timely corrective action to be taken when performance deviates significantly from the plan. A deviation is significant if, when left unresolved, it precludes the project from meeting its objectives.

The term "project plan" is used throughout these practices to refer to the overall plan for controlling the project.

When actual status deviates significantly from the expected values, corrective actions are taken as appropriate. These actions may require replanning, which may include revising the original plan, establishing new agreements, or including additional mitigation activities within the current plan.

Related Process Areas

Refer to the Project Planning process area for more information about the project plan, including how it specifies the appropriate level of project monitoring, the measures used to monitor progress, and known risks.

Refer to the Measurement and Analysis process area for information about the process of measuring, analyzing, and recording information.

Specific Practices by Goal

SG 1   *Monitor Project Against Plan*

Actual performance and progress of the project are monitored against the project plan.

SP 1.1-1   *Monitor Project Planning Parameters*

Monitor the actual values of the project planning parameters against the project plan.

Project planning parameters constitute typical indicators of project progress and performance and include attributes of work products and tasks, cost, effort, and schedule. Attributes of the work products and tasks include such items as size, complexity, weight, form, fit, or function.

Monitoring typically involves measuring the actual values of project planning parameters, comparing actual values to the estimates in the plan, and identifying significant deviations. Recording actual values of the project planning parameters includes recording associated contextual information to help understand the measures. An analysis of the impact that significant deviations have on determining what corrective actions to take is handled in the second specific goal and its specific practices in this process area.

Typical Work Products

1. Records of project performance
2. Records of significant deviations

Subpractices

1. Monitor progress against the schedule.

   Progress monitoring typically includes the following:

   - Periodically measuring the actual completion of activities and milestones
   - Comparing actual completion of activities and milestones against the schedule documented in the project plan
   - Identifying significant deviations from the schedule estimates in the project plan

2. Monitor the project's cost and expended effort.

   Effort and cost monitoring typically includes the following:

   - Periodically measuring the actual effort and cost expended and staff assigned
   - Comparing actual effort, costs, staffing, and training to the estimates and budgets documented in the project plan
   - Identifying significant deviations from the budgets in the project plan

Practice-to-Goal Relationship Table

Continuous Representation	*Staged Representation*

SG 1 Monitor Project Against Plan

SP 1.1-1 Monitor Project Planning Parameters

SP 1.2-1 Monitor Commitments

SP 1.3-1 Monitor Project Risks

SP 1.4-1 Monitor Data Management

SP 1.5-1 Monitor Stakeholder Involvement

SP 1.6-1 Conduct Progress Reviews

SP 1.7-1 Conduct Milestone Reviews

SG 2 Manage Corrective Action to Closure

SP 2.1-1 Analyze Issues

SP 2.2-1 Take Corrective Action

SP 2.3-1 Manage Corrective Action

GG 1 Achieve Specific Goals

GP 1.1 Perform Base Practices

GG 2 Institutionalize a Managed Process

GP 2.1 Establish an Organizational Policy

GP 2.2 Plan the Process

GP 2.3 Provide Resources

GP 2.4 Assign Responsibility

GP 2.5 Train People

GP 2.6 Manage Configurations

GP 2.7 Identify and Involve Relevant Stakeholders

P 2.8 Monitor and Control the Process

GP 2.9 Objectively Evaluate Adherence

GP 2.10 Review Status with Higher Level Management

GG 3 Institutionalize a Defined Process

GP 3.1 Establish a Defined Process

GP 3.2 Collect Improvement Information

GG 4 Institutionalize a Quantitatively Managed Process

GP 4.1 Establish Quantitative Objectives for the Process

GP 4.2 Stabilize Subprocess Performance

GG 5 Institutionalize an Optimizing Process

GP 5.1 Ensure Continuous Process Improvement

GP 5.2 Correct Root Causes of Problems

SG 1 Monitor Project Against Plan

SP 1.1-1 Monitor Project Planning Parameters

SP 1.2-1 Monitor Commitments

SP 1.3-1 Monitor Project Risks

SP 1.4-1 Monitor Data Management

SP 1.5-1 Monitor Stakeholder Involvement

SP 1.6-1 Conduct Progress Reviews

SP 1.7-1 Conduct Milestone Reviews

SG 2 Manage Corrective Action to Closure

SP 2.1-1 Analyze Issues

SP 2.2-1 Take Corrective Action

SP 2.3-1 Manage Corrective Action

GG 2 Institutionalize a Managed Process

GP 2.1 Establish an Organizational Policy

GP 2.2 Plan the Process

GP 2.3 Provide Resources

GP 2.4 Assign Responsibility

GP 2.5 Train People

GP 2.6 Manage Configurations

GP 2.7 Identify and Involve Relevant Stakeholders

GP 2.8 Monitor and Control the Process

GP 2.9 Objectively Evaluate Adherence

GP 2.10 Review Status with Higher Level Management

GG 3 Institutionalize a Defined Process

GP 3.1 Establish a Defined Process

GP 3.2 Collect Improvement Information

C/ML 3–5

3. Monitor the attributes of the work products and tasks.

   Refer to the Project Planning process area for information about the attributes of work products and tasks.

   Monitoring the attributes of the work products and tasks typically includes the following:
   - Periodically measuring the actual attributes of the work products and tasks, such as size or complexity (and the changes to the attributes)
   - Comparing the actual attributes of the work products and tasks (and the changes to the attributes) to the estimates documented in the project plan
   - Identifying significant deviations from the estimates in the project plan

4. Monitor resources provided and used.

   Refer to the Project Planning process area for information about planned resources.

Examples of resources include:
- Physical facilities
- Computers, peripherals, and software used in design, manufacturing, testing, and operation
- Networks
- Security environment
- Project staff
- Processes

FOR SOFTWARE ENGINEERING

Examples of software engineering resources include the following:
- Host computers and peripherals
- Networks
- Software test computers and peripherals
- Target computer environment software
- Software engineering environment (e.g., software tools)

5. Monitor the knowledge and skills of project personnel.

   Refer to the Project Planning process area for information about planning for knowledge and skills needed to perform the project.

   Monitoring the knowledge and skills of the project personnel typically includes the following:
   - Periodically measuring the acquisition of knowledge and skills by project personnel
   - Comparing actual training obtained to that documented in the project plan
   - Identifying significant deviations from estimates in the project plan

6. Document the significant deviations in the project planning parameters.

SP 1.2-1   MONITOR COMMITMENTS

Monitor commitments against those identified in the project plan.

Typical Work Products

1. Records of commitment reviews

Subpractices

1. Regularly review commitments (both external and internal).
2. Identify commitments that have not been satisfied or that are at significant risk of not being satisfied.
3. Document the results of the commitment reviews.

SP 1.3-1 MONITOR PROJECT RISKS

Monitor risks against those identified in the project plan.

Refer to the Project Planning process area for more information about identifying project risks.

Refer to the Risk Management process area for more information about risk management activities.

Typical Work Products

1. Records of project risk monitoring

Subpractices

1. Periodically review the documentation of the risks in the context of the project's current status and circumstances.
2. Revise the documentation of the risks, as additional information becomes available, to incorporate changes.
3. Communicate risk status to relevant stakeholders.

> Examples of risk status include the following:
> - A change in the probability that the risk occurs
> - A change in risk priority

SP 1.4-1 MONITOR DATA MANAGEMENT

Monitor the management of project data against the project plan.

Refer to the Plan for Data Management specific practice in the Project Planning process area for more information about identifying the types of data that should be managed and how to plan for their management.

Once the plans for the management of project data are made, the management of that data must be monitored to ensure that those plans are accomplished.

Typical Work Products

1. Records of data management

Subpractices

1. Periodically review data management activities against their description in the project plan.
2. Identify and document significant issues and their impacts.
3. Document the results of data management activity reviews.

SP 1.5-1 MONITOR STAKEHOLDER INVOLVEMENT

Monitor stakeholder involvement against the project plan.

Refer to the Plan Stakeholder Involvement specific practice in the Project Planning process area for more information about identifying relevant stakeholders and planning the appropriate involvement with them.

Once the stakeholders are identified and the extent of their involvement within the project is specified in project planning, that involvement must be monitored to ensure that the appropriate interactions are occurring.

Typical Work Products

1. Records of stakeholder involvement

Subpractices

1. Periodically review the status of stakeholder involvement.
2. Identify and document significant issues and their impacts.
3. Document the results of the stakeholder involvement status reviews.

SP 1.6-1 CONDUCT PROGRESS REVIEWS

Periodically review the project's progress, performance, and issues.

Progress reviews are reviews on the project to keep stakeholders informed. These project reviews can be informal reviews and may not be specified explicitly in the project plans.

Examples of these reviews include the following:
- Reviews with staff
- Reviews with project engineers and support
- Reviews with management

FOR SUPPLIER SOURCING

Examples of these reviews also include the following:

• Reviews with key suppliers

Typical Work Products

1. Documented project review results

Subpractices

1. Regularly communicate status on assigned activities and work products to relevant stakeholders.

   Managers, staff members, customers, end users, suppliers, and other relevant stakeholders within the organization are included in the reviews as appropriate.

2. Review the results of collecting and analyzing measures for controlling the project.

   Refer to the Measurement and Analysis process area for more information about the process for measuring and analyzing project performance data.

3. Identify and document significant issues and deviations from the plan.

4. Document change requests and problems identified in any of the work products and processes.

   Refer to the Configuration Management process area for more information about how changes are managed.

5. Document the results of the reviews.

6. Track change requests and problem reports to closure.

SP 1.7-1   *CONDUCT MILESTONE REVIEWS*

Review the accomplishments and results of the project at selected project milestones.

Refer to the Project Planning process area for more information about milestone planning.

Milestone reviews are planned during project planning and are typically formal reviews.

Typical Work Products

1. Documented milestone review results

Subpractices

1. Conduct reviews at meaningful points in the project's schedule, such as the completion of selected stages, with relevant stakeholders.

   Managers, staff members, customers, end users, suppliers, and other relevant stakeholders within the organization are included in the milestone reviews as appropriate.

2. Review the commitments, plan, status, and risks of the project.

3. Identify and document significant issues and their impacts.

4. Document the results of the review, action items, and decisions.

5. Track action items to closure.

SG 2 *MANAGE CORRECTIVE ACTION TO CLOSURE*

Corrective actions are managed to closure when the project's performance or results deviate significantly from the plan.

SP 2.1-1 *ANALYZE ISSUES*

Collect and analyze the issues and determine the corrective actions necessary to address the issues.

Typical Work Products

1. List of issues needing corrective actions

Subpractices

1. Gather issues for analysis.

Issues are collected from reviews and the execution of other processes.

> Examples of issues to be gathered include:
> - Issues discovered through performing verification and validation activities
> - Significant deviations in the project planning parameters from the estimates in the project plan
> - Commitments (either internal or external) that have not been satisfied
> - Significant changes in risk status
> - Data access, collection, privacy, or security issues
> - Stakeholder representation or involvement issues

2. Analyze issues to determine need for corrective action.

Refer to the Project Planning process area for information about corrective action criteria.

Corrective action is required when the issue, if left unresolved, may prevent the project from meeting its objectives.

SP 2.2-1 *TAKE CORRECTIVE ACTION*

Take corrective action on identified issues.

Typical Work Products

1. Corrective action plan

Subpractices

1. Determine and document the appropriate actions needed to address the identified issues.

   Refer to the Project Planning process area for more information about the project plan when replanning is needed.

Examples of potential actions include the following:
• Modifying the statement of work
• Modifying requirements
• Revising estimates and plans
• Renegotiating commitments
• Adding resources
• Changing processes
• Revising project risks

2. Review and get agreement with relevant stakeholders on the actions to be taken.

3. Negotiate changes to internal and external commitments.

SP 2.3-1 MANAGE CORRECTIVE ACTION

Manage corrective actions to closure.

Typical Work Products

1. Corrective action results

Subpractices

1. Monitor corrective actions for completion.
2. Analyze results of corrective actions to determine the effectiveness of the corrective actions.
3. Determine and document appropriate actions to correct deviations from planned results for corrective actions.

   Lessons learned as a result of taking corrective action can be inputs to planning and risk management processes.

Generic Practices by Goal

GG 1 ACHIEVE SPECIFIC GOALS

The process supports and enables achievement of the specific goals of the process area by transforming identifiable input work products to produce identifiable output work products.

> **GP 1.1**   PERFORM BASE PRACTICES
>
> *Perform the base practices of the project monitoring and control process to develop work products and provide services to achieve the specific goals of the process area.*

GG 2   INSTITUTIONALIZE A MANAGED PROCESS

The process is institutionalized as a managed process.

Commitment to Perform

GP 2.1   ESTABLISH AN ORGANIZATIONAL POLICY

Establish and maintain an organizational policy for planning and performing the project monitoring and control process.

Elaboration

This policy establishes organizational expectations for monitoring performance against the project plan and managing corrective action to closure when actual performance or results deviate significantly from the plan.

Ability to Perform

GP 2.2   PLAN THE PROCESS

Establish and maintain the plan for performing the project monitoring and control process.

Elaboration

This plan for performing the project monitoring and control process is typically a part of the project plan, as described in the Project Planning process area.

GP 2.3   PROVIDE RESOURCES

Provide adequate resources for performing the project monitoring and control process, developing the work products, and providing the services of the process.

Elaboration

Examples of resources provided include the following tools:
- Cost tracking systems
- Effort reporting systems
- Action-item-tracking systems
- Project-management and scheduling programs

GP 2.4 ASSIGN RESPONSIBILITY

Assign responsibility and authority for performing the process, developing the work products, and providing the services of the project monitoring and control process.

GP 2.5 TRAIN PEOPLE

Train the people performing or supporting the project monitoring and control process as needed.

Elaboration

Examples of training topics include the following:
- Monitoring and control of projects
- Risk management
- Data management

Directing Implementation

GP 2.6 MANAGE CONFIGURATIONS

Place designated work products of the project monitoring and control process under appropriate levels of configuration management.

GP 2.7 IDENTIFY AND INVOLVE RELEVANT STAKEHOLDERS

Identify and involve the relevant stakeholders of the project monitoring and control process as planned.

Elaboration

This generic practice is different from monitoring stakeholder interaction for the project, which is covered by a specific practice in this process area.

Examples of activities for stakeholder involvement include the following:
- Assessing the project against the plan
- Reviewing commitments and resolving issues
- Reviewing project risks
- Reviewing data management activities
- Reviewing project progress
- Managing corrective actions to closure

GP 2.8 MONITOR AND CONTROL THE PROCESS

Monitor and control the project monitoring and control process against the plan for performing the process and take appropriate corrective action.

Elaboration

Examples of measures used in monitoring and controlling include the following:
- Number of open and closed corrective actions
- Project milestone dates (e.g., planned versus actual and slipped milestones)
- Number and types of reviews performed
- Review schedule (planned versus actual and slipped target dates)

Verifying Implementation

GP 2.9 OBJECTIVELY EVALUATE ADHERENCE

Objectively evaluate adherence of the project monitoring and control process against its process description, standards, and procedures, and address noncompliance.

Elaboration

Examples of activities reviewed include the following:
- Monitoring project performance against the project plan
- Managing corrective actions to closure

Examples of work products reviewed include the following:
- Records of project performance
- Project review results

GP 2.10 REVIEW STATUS WITH HIGHER LEVEL MANAGEMENT

Review the activities, status, and results of the project monitoring and control process with higher level management and resolve issues.

AUTHORS' NOTE: GG3 and its practices do not apply for a maturity level 2 rating, but do apply for a maturity level 3 rating and above.

S ONLY

GG 3 INSTITUTIONALIZE A DEFINED PROCESS

The process is institutionalized as a defined process.

Ability to Perform

GP 3.1 ESTABLISH A DEFINED PROCESS

Establish and maintain the description of a defined project monitoring and control process.

C/ML 3–5

Directing Implementation

GP 3.2   COLLECT IMPROVEMENT INFORMATION

Collect work products, measures, measurement results, and improvement information derived from planning and performing the project monitoring and control process to support the future use and improvement of the organization's processes and process assets.

GG 4   INSTITUTIONALIZE A QUANTITATIVELY MANAGED PROCESS

The process is institutionalized as a quantitatively managed process.

GP 4.1   ESTABLISH QUANTITATIVE OBJECTIVES FOR THE PROCESS

Establish and maintain quantitative objectives for the project monitoring and control process that address quality and process performance based on customer needs and business objectives.

GP 4.2   STABILIZE SUBPROCESS PERFORMANCE

Stabilize the performance of one or more subprocesses to determine the ability of the project monitoring and control process to achieve the established quantitative quality and process-performance objectives.

GG 5   INSTITUTIONALIZE AN OPTIMIZING PROCESS

The process is institutionalized as an optimizing process.

GP 5.1   ENSURE CONTINUOUS PROCESS IMPROVEMENT

Ensure continuous improvement of the project monitoring and control process in fulfilling the relevant business objectives of the organization.

GP 5.2   CORRECT ROOT CAUSES OF PROBLEMS

Identify and correct the root causes of defects and other problems in the project monitoring and control process.

PROJECT PLANNING
A Project Management Process Area at Maturity Level 2

Purpose

The purpose of Project Planning (PP) is to establish and maintain plans that define project activities.

Introductory Notes

The Project Planning process area involves the following:

- Developing the project plan
- Interacting with stakeholders appropriately
- Getting commitment to the plan
- Maintaining the plan

Planning begins with requirements that define the product and project.

Planning includes estimating the attributes of the work products and tasks, determining the resources needed, negotiating commitments, producing a schedule, and identifying and analyzing project risks. Iterating through these activities may be necessary to establish the project plan. The project plan provides the basis for performing and controlling the project's activities that address the commitments with the project's customer.

The project plan will usually need to be revised as the project progresses to address changes in requirements and commitments, inaccurate estimates, corrective actions, and process changes. Specific practices describing both planning and replanning are contained in this process area.

The term "project plan" is used throughout the generic and specific practices in this process area to refer to the overall plan for controlling the project.

Related Process Areas

Refer to the Requirements Development process area for more information about developing requirements that define the product and product components. Product and product-

component requirements and changes to those requirements serve as a basis for planning and replanning.

Refer to the Requirements Management process area for more information about managing requirements needed for planning and replanning.

Refer to the Risk Management process area for more information about identifying and managing risks.

Refer to the Technical Solution process area for more information about transforming requirements into product and product-component solutions.

Specific Practices by Goal

SG 1   ESTABLISH ESTIMATES

Estimates of project planning parameters are established and maintained.

Project planning parameters include all information needed by the project to perform the necessary planning, organizing, staffing, directing, coordinating, reporting, and budgeting.

Estimates of planning parameters should have a sound basis to instill confidence that any plans based on these estimates are capable of supporting project objectives.

Factors that are typically considered when estimating these parameters include the following:

- Project requirements, including the product requirements, the requirements imposed by the organization, the requirements imposed by the customer, and other requirements that impact the project
- Scope of the project
- Identified tasks and work products
- Technical approach
- Selected project life-cycle model (e.g., waterfall, incremental, or spiral)
- Attributes of the work products and tasks (e.g., size or complexity)
- Schedule
- Models or historical data for converting the attributes of the work products and tasks into labor hours and cost
- Methodology (e.g., models, data, algorithms) used to determine needed material, skills, labor hours, and cost

Documentation of the estimating rationale and supporting data is needed for stakeholders' review and commitment to the plan and for maintenance of the plan as the project progresses.

Practice-to-Goal Relationship Table

Continuous Representation	*Staged Representation*

SG 1 Establish Estimates
  SP 1.1-1 Estimate the Scope of the Project
  SP 1.2-1 Establish Estimates of Work Product and Task Attributes
  SP 1.3-1 Define Project Life Cycle
  SP 1.4-1 Determine Estimates of Effort and Cost

SG 2 Develop a Project Plan
  SP 2.1-1 Establish the Budget and Schedule
  SP 2.2-1 Identify Project Risks
  SP 2.3-1 Plan for Data Management
  SP 2.4-1 Plan for Project Resources
  SP 2.5-1 Plan for Needed Knowledge and Skills
  SP 2.6-1 Plan Stakeholder Involvement
  SP 2.7-1 Establish the Project Plan

SG 3 Obtain Commitment to the Plan
  SP 3.1-1 Review Plans that Affect the Project
  SP 3.2-1 Reconcile Work and Resource Levels
  SP 3.3-1 Obtain Plan Commitment

GG 1 Achieve Specific Goals
  GP 1.1 Perform Base Practices

GG 2 Institutionalize a Managed Process
  GP 2.1 Establish an Organizational Policy
  GP 2.2 Plan the Process
  GP 2.3 Provide Resources
  GP 2.4 Assign Responsibility
  GP 2.5 Train People
  GP 2.6 Manage Configurations
  GP 2.7 Identify and Involve Relevant Stakeholders
  GP 2.8 Monitor and Control the Process
  GP 2.9 Objectively Evaluate Adherence
  GP 2.10 Review Status with Higher Level Management

GG 3 Institutionalize a Defined Process
  GP 3.1 Establish a Defined Process
  GP 3.2 Collect Improvement Information

GG 4 Institutionalize a Quantitatively Managed Process
  GP 4.1 Establish Quantitative Objectives for the Process
  GP 4.2 Stabilize Subprocess Performance

GG 5 Institutionalize an Optimizing Process
  GP 5.1 Ensure Continuous Process Improvement
  GP 5.2 Correct Root Causes of Problems

SG 1 Establish Estimates
  SP 1.1-1 Estimate the Scope of the Project
  SP 1.2-1 Establish Estimates of Work Product and Task Attributes
  SP 1.3-1 Define Project Life Cycle
  SP 1.4-1 Determine Estimates of Effort and Cost

SG 2 Develop a Project Plan
  SP 2.1-1 Establish the Budget and Schedule
  SP 2.2-1 Identify Project Risks
  SP 2.3-1 Plan for Data Management
  SP 2.4-1 Plan for Project Resources
  SP 2.5-1 Plan for Needed Knowledge and Skills
  SP 2.6-1 Plan Stakeholder Involvement
  SP 2.7-1 Establish the Project Plan

SG 3 Obtain Commitment to the Plan
  SP 3.1-1 Review Plans that Affect the Project
  SP 3.2-1 Reconcile Work and Resource Levels
  SP 3.3-1 Obtain Plan Commitment

GG 2 Institutionalize a Managed Process
  GP 2.1 Establish an Organizational Policy
  GP 2.2 Plan the Process
  GP 2.3 Provide Resources
  GP 2.4 Assign Responsibility
  GP 2.5 Train People
  GP 2.6 Manage Configurations
  GP 2.7 Identify and Involve Relevant Stakeholders
  GP 2.8 Monitor and Control the Process
  GP 2.9 Objectively Evaluate Adherence
  GP 2.10 Review Status with Higher Level Management

GG 3 Institutionalize a Defined Process
  GP 3.1 Establish a Defined Process
  GP 3.2 Collect Improvement Information

PP

C/ML 3–5

Establish a top-level work breakdown structure (WBS) to estimate the scope of the project.

The WBS evolves with the project. Initially a top-level WBS can serve to structure the initial estimating. The development of a WBS divides the overall project into an interconnected set of manageable components. Typically, the WBS is a product oriented structure that provides a scheme for identifying and organizing the logical units of work to be managed, which are called "work packages." The WBS provides a reference and organizational mechanism for assigning effort, schedule, and responsibility and is used as the underlying framework to plan, organize, and control the work done on the project.

Typical Work Products

1. Task descriptions
2. Work package descriptions
3. WBS

Subpractices

1. Develop a WBS based on the product architecture.

   The WBS provides a scheme for organizing the project's work around the products that the work supports. The WBS should permit the identification of the following items:

   - Identified risks and their mitigation tasks
   - Tasks for deliverables and supporting activities
   - Tasks for skill and knowledge acquisition
   - Tasks for development of needed support plans, such as configuration management, quality assurance, and verification plans
   - Tasks for integration and management of nondevelopmental items

2. Identify the work packages in sufficient detail to specify estimates of project tasks, responsibilities, and schedule.

   The top-level WBS is intended to help in gauging the project work effort in terms of tasks and organizational roles and responsibilities. The amount of detail in the WBS at this more detailed level helps in developing realistic schedules, thereby minimizing the need for management reserve.

3. Identify work products (or components of work products) that will be externally acquired.

   Refer to the Supplier Agreement Management process area for more information about acquiring work products from sources external to the project.

4. Identify work products that will be reused.

SP 1.2-1 *ESTABLISH ESTIMATES OF WORK PRODUCT AND TASK ATTRIBUTES*

Establish and maintain estimates of the attributes of the work products and tasks.

Size is the primary input to many models used to estimate effort, cost, and schedule. The models can also be based on inputs such as connectivity, complexity, and structure.

Examples of types of work products for which size estimates are made include the following:
- Deliverable and nondeliverable work products
- Documents
- Operational and support software

Examples of size measures include the following:
- Number of functions
- Function points
- Source lines of code
- Number of classes and objects
- Number of requirements
- Number of interfaces
- Number of pages
- Number of inputs and outputs
- Number of technical risk items
- Volume of data

The estimates should be consistent with project requirements to determine the project's effort, cost, and schedule. A relative level of difficulty or complexity should be assigned for each size attribute.

Typical Work Products

1. Technical approach
2. Size and complexity of tasks and work products
3. Estimating models
4. Attribute estimates

Subpractices

1. Determine the technical approach for the project.

   The technical approach defines a top-level strategy for development of the products. It includes decisions on architectural features, such as distributed or client/server; state-of-the-art or established technologies to be applied, such as robotics, composite materials, or artificial intelligence; and breadth of the functionality expected in the final products, such as safety, security, and ergonomics.

2. Use appropriate methods to determine the attributes of the work products and tasks that will be used to estimate the resource requirements.

Methods for determining size and complexity should be based on validated models or historical data.

The methods for determining attributes evolve as our understanding of the relationship of product characteristics to attributes increases.

Examples of current methods include the following:
- Number of logic gates for integrated circuit design
- Lines of code or function points for software
- Number/complexity of requirements for systems engineering
- Number of square feet for standard-specified residential homes

---

3. Estimate the attributes of the work products and tasks.
4. Estimate, as appropriate, the labor, machinery, materials, and methods that will be required by the project.

SP 1.3-1   DEFINE PROJECT LIFE CYCLE

Define the project life-cycle phases on which to scope the planning effort.

The determination of a project's life-cycle phases provides for planned periods of evaluation and decision making. These are normally defined to support logical decision points at which significant commitments are made concerning resources and technical approach. Such points provide planned events at which project course corrections and determinations of future scope and cost can be made.

> **FOR SOFTWARE ENGINEERING**
> The determination of project phases for software typically includes selection and refinement of a software development model to address interdependencies and appropriate sequencing of software project activities.

> **FOR SYSTEMS ENGINEERING**
> Identify the major product phase (e.g., concept exploration or development) for the current state of the product, expected future phases, and the relationships and effects among phases. Adjust planning parameters to account for relationships and effects among phases.

The project life cycle consists of phases that need to be defined depending on the scope of requirements, the estimates for project resources, and the nature of the project. Larger projects may contain multiple phases, such as concept exploration, development, production, operations, and disposal.

Within these phases, subphases may be needed. A development phase may include subphases such as requirements analysis, design, fabrication, integration, and verification. Depending on the strategy for development, there may be intermediate phases for the creation of prototypes, increments of capability, or spiral model cycles.

Understanding the project life cycle is crucial in determining the scope of the planning effort and the timing of the initial planning, as well as the timing and criteria (critical milestones) for replanning.

Typical Work Products

1. Project life-cycle phases

SP 1.4-1   DETERMINE ESTIMATES OF EFFORT AND COST

Estimate the project effort and cost for the work products and tasks based on estimation rationale.

Estimates of effort and cost are generally based on the results of analysis using models or historical data applied to size, activities, and other planning parameters. Confidence in these estimates is based on the rationale for the selected model and the nature of the data. There may be occasions when the available historical data does not apply, such as where efforts are unprecedented or where the type of task does not fit available models. An effort is unprecedented (to some degree) if a similar product or component has never been built. An effort may also be unprecedented if the development group has never built such a product or component.

Unprecedented efforts are more risky, require more research to develop reasonable bases of estimate, and require more management reserve. The uniqueness of the project must be documented when using these models to ensure a common understanding of any assumptions made in the initial planning stages.

Typical Work Products

1. Estimation rationale
2. Project effort estimates
3. Project cost estimates

Subpractices

1. Collect the models or historical data that will be used to transform the attributes of the work products and tasks into estimates of the labor hours and cost.

FOR SOFTWARE ENGINEERING

Within the software engineering area, many parametric models have been developed to aid in estimating cost and schedule. The use of these models as the sole source of estimation is not recommended because these models are based on historical project data that may or may not be pertinent to your project. Multiple models and/or methods can be used to ensure a high level of confidence in the estimate.

Historical data include the cost, effort, and schedule data from previously executed projects, plus appropriate scaling data to account for differing sizes and complexity.

2. Include supporting infrastructure needs when estimating effort and cost.

    The support infrastructure includes items needed from a development and sustainment perspective for the product.

FOR SOFTWARE ENGINEERING

Consider critical computer resources in the host environment, in the test environment, in the target environment, or in any combination of these. Computer resource estimation typically includes the following:

- Identifying the critical computer resources for the software project
- Basing estimates of critical computer resources on allocated requirements

FOR SOFTWARE ENGINEERING

Examples of critical computer resources include the following:

- Memory, disk, and network capacity
- Processor power
- Communications channel capacity
- Workstation power
- Peripheral capacity

FOR SOFTWARE ENGINEERING

Examples of software engineering facilities include the following:

- Host computers, peripherals, and networks
- Software test computers and peripherals
- Target computer environment software
- Software engineering environment (i.e., software tools)

3. Estimate effort and cost using models and/or historical data.

    Effort and cost inputs used for estimating typically include the following:

    - Judgmental estimates provided by an expert or group of experts (e.g., Delphi Method)
    - Risks, including the extent to which the effort is unprecedented

- Critical competencies and roles needed to perform the work
- Product and product-component requirements
- Technical approach
- WBS
- Size estimates of work products and anticipated changes
- Cost of externally acquired work products
- Selected project life-cycle model and processes
- Life-cycle cost estimates
- Capability of tools provided in engineering environment
- Skill levels of managers and staff needed to perform the work
- Knowledge, skill, and training needs
- Facilities needed (e.g., office and meeting space and workstations)
- Engineering facilities needed
- Capability of manufacturing process(es)
- Travel
- Level of security required for tasks, work products, hardware, software, personnel, and work environment
- Service level agreements for call centers and warranty work
- Direct labor and overhead

SG 2   DEVELOP A PROJECT PLAN

A project plan is established and maintained as the basis for managing the project.

A project plan is a formal, approved document used to manage and control the execution of the project. It is based on the project requirements and the established estimates.

The project plan should consider all phases of the project life cycle. Project planning should ensure that all plans affecting the project are consistent with the overall project plan.

SP 2.1-1   ESTABLISH THE BUDGET AND SCHEDULE

Establish and maintain the project's budget and schedule.

The project's budget and schedule are based on the developed estimates and ensure that budget allocation, task complexity, and task dependencies are appropriately addressed.

Event-driven, resource-limited schedules have proven to be effective in dealing with project risk. Identifying accomplishments to be demonstrated before initiation of the event provides some flexibility in the timing of the event, a common understanding of what is expected, a better vision of the state of the project, and a more accurate status of the project's tasks.

Typical Work Products

1. Project schedules
2. Schedule dependencies
3. Project budget

Subpractices

1. Identify major milestones.

   Milestones are often imposed to ensure completion of certain deliverables by the milestone. Milestones can be event based or calendar based. If calendar based, once milestone dates have been agreed on, it is often very difficult to change them.

2. Identify schedule assumptions.

   When schedules are initially developed, it is common to make assumptions about the duration of certain activities. These assumptions are frequently made on items for which little if any estimation data is available. Identifying these assumptions provides insight into the level of confidence (uncertainties) in the overall schedule.

3. Identify constraints.

   Factors that limit the flexibility of management options need to be identified as early as possible. The examination of the attributes of the work products and tasks often will bring these issues to the surface. Such attributes can include task duration, resources, inputs, and outputs.

4. Identify task dependencies.

   Typically, the tasks for a project can be accomplished in some ordered sequence that will minimize the duration of the project. This involves the identification of predecessor and successor tasks to determine the optimal ordering.

   > Examples of tools that can help determine an optimal ordering of task activities include the following:
   > - Critical Path Method (CPM)
   > - Program Evaluation and Review Technique (PERT)
   > - Resource-limited scheduling

5. Define the budget and schedule.

   Establishing and maintaining the project's budget and schedule typically includes the following:
   - Defining the committed or expected availability of resources and facilities
   - Determining time phasing of activities
   - Determining a breakout of subordinate schedules
   - Defining the dependencies between the activities (predecessor or successor relationships)

- Defining the schedule activities and milestones to support accuracy in progress measurement
- Identifying milestones for delivery of products to the customer
- Defining activities of appropriate duration
- Defining milestones of appropriate time separation
- Defining a management reserve based on the confidence level in meeting the schedule and budget
- Using appropriate historical data to verify the schedule
- Defining incremental funding requirements
- Documenting project assumptions and rationale

6. Establish corrective action criteria.

   Criteria are established for determining what constitutes a significant deviation from the project plan. A basis for gauging issues and problems is necessary to determine when a corrective action should be taken. The corrective actions may require replanning, which may include revising the original plan, establishing new agreements, or including mitigation activities within the current plan.

SP 2.2-1 IDENTIFY PROJECT RISKS

Identify and analyze project risks.

Refer to the Risk Management process area for more information about risk management activities.

Refer to the Monitor Project Risks specific practice in the Project Monitoring and Control process area for more information about risk monitoring activities.

Risks are identified or discovered and analyzed to support project planning. This specific practice should be extended to all the plans that affect the project to ensure that the appropriate interfacing is taking place between all relevant stakeholders on identified risks. Project planning risk identification and analysis typically include the following:

- Identifying risks
- Analyzing the risks to determine the impact, probability of occurrence, and time frame in which problems are likely to occur
- Prioritizing risks

Typical Work Products

1. Identified risks
2. Risk impacts and probability of occurrence
3. Risk priorities

Subpractices

1. Identify risks.

    The identification of risks involves the identification of potential issues, hazards, threats, vulnerabilities, and so on that could negatively affect work efforts and plans. Risks must be identified and described in an understandable way before they can be analyzed. When identifying risks, it is good to use a standard method for defining risks. Risk identification and analysis tools can be used to help identify possible problems.

    > Examples of risk identification and analysis tools include the following:
    > - Risk taxonomies
    > - Risk assessments
    > - Checklists
    > - Structured interviews
    > - Brainstorming
    > - Performance models
    > - Cost models
    > - Network analysis
    > - Quality factor analysis

2. Document the risks.
3. Review and obtain agreement with relevant stakeholders on the completeness and correctness of the documented risks.
4. Revise the risks as appropriate.

    > Examples of when identified risks may need to be revised include the following:
    > - When new risk is identified
    > - When risks become problems
    > - When risks are retired
    > - When project circumstances change significantly

SP 2.3-1 PLAN FOR DATA MANAGEMENT

Plan for the management of project data.

> **FOR INTEGRATED PRODUCT AND PROCESS DEVELOPMENT**
> When integrated teams are formed, project data includes data developed and used solely within a particular team as well as data applicable across integrated team boundaries if there are multiple integrated teams.

Data are the various forms of documentation required to support a program in all of its areas (e.g., administration, engineering, configuration management, financial, logistics, quality, safety, manufacturing, and procurement). The data can take any form (e.g., reports, manuals, notebooks, charts, drawings, specifications, files, or correspondence). The data may exist in any medium (e.g., printed or drawn on various materials, photographs, electronic, or multimedia). Data may be deliverable (e.g., items identified by a program's contract data requirements) or data may be nondeliverable (e.g., informal data, trade studies and analyses, internal meeting minutes, internal design review documentation, lessons learned, and action items). Distribution can take many forms, including electronic transmission.

The data requirements for the project should be established for both the data items to be created and their content and form, based on a common or standard set of data requirements. Uniform content and format requirements for data items facilitate understanding of data content and help with consistent management of the data resources.

The reason for collecting each document should be clear. This task includes the analysis and verification of project deliverables and nondeliverables, contract and noncontract data requirements, and customer-supplied data. Often, data is collected with no clear understanding of how it will be used. Data is costly and should be collected only when needed.

Typical Work Products

1. Data management plan
2. Master list of managed data
3. Data content and format description
4. Data requirements lists for acquirers and for suppliers
5. Privacy requirements
6. Security requirements
7. Security procedures
8. Mechanism for data retrieval, reproduction, and distribution
9. Schedule for collection of project data
10. Listing of project data to be collected

Subpractices

1. Establish requirements and procedures to ensure privacy and security of the data.

   Not everyone will have the need or clearance necessary to access the project data. Procedures must be established to identify who has access to what data as well as when they have access to the data.

2. Establish a mechanism to archive data and to access archived data.

   Accessed information should be in an understandable form (e.g., electronic or computer output from a database) or represented as originally generated.

3. Determine the project data to be identified, collected, and distributed.

SP 2.4-1   *PLAN FOR PROJECT RESOURCES*

Plan for necessary resources to perform the project.

> **FOR INTEGRATED PRODUCT AND PROCESS DEVELOPMENT**
> When integrated teams are formed, planning for project resources has to consider staffing of the integrated teams.

Defining project resources (labor, machinery/equipment, materials, and methods) and quantities needed to perform project activities builds on the initial estimates and provides additional information that can be applied to expand the WBS used to manage the project.

The top-level WBS developed earlier as an estimation mechanism is typically expanded by decomposing these top levels into work packages that represent singular work units that can be separately assigned, performed, and tracked. This subdivision is done to distribute management responsibility and provide better management control. Each work package or work product in the WBS should be assigned a unique identifier (e.g., number) to permit tracking. A WBS can be based on requirements, activities, work products, or a combination of these items. A dictionary that describes the work for each work package in the WBS should accompany the work breakdown structure.

Typical Work Products

1. WBS work packages
2. WBS task dictionary
3. Staffing requirements based on project size and scope
4. Critical facilities/equipment list
5. Process/workflow definitions and diagrams
6. Program administration requirements list

Subpractices

1. Determine process requirements.

   The processes used to manage a project must be identified, defined, and co-ordinated with all the relevant stakeholders to ensure efficient operations during project execution.

2. Determine staffing requirements.

   The staffing of a project depends on the decomposition of the project requirements into tasks, roles, and responsibilities for accomplishing the project requirements as laid out within the work packages of the WBS.

   Staffing requirements must consider the knowledge and skills required for each of the identified positions, as defined in the Plan for Needed Knowledge and Skills specific practice.

3. Determine facilities, equipment, and component requirements.

> Most projects are unique in some sense and require some set of unique assets to accomplish the objectives of the project. The determination and acquisition of these assets in a timely manner are crucial to project success.
>
> Lead-time items need to be identified early to determine how they will be addressed. Even when the required assets are not unique, compiling a list of all of the facilities, equipment, and parts (e.g., number of computers for the personnel working on the project, software applications, and office space) provides insight into aspects of the scope of an effort that are often overlooked.

SP 2.5-1 *PLAN FOR NEEDED KNOWLEDGE AND SKILLS*

Plan for knowledge and skills needed to perform the project.

Refer to the Organizational Training process area for more information about knowledge and skills information to be incorporated into the project plan.

Knowledge delivery to projects involves both training of project personnel and acquisition of knowledge from outside sources.

> Staffing requirements are dependent on the knowledge and skills available to support the execution of the project.

Typical Work Products

1. Inventory of skill needs
2. Staffing and new hire plans
3. Databases (e.g., skills and training)

Subpractices

1. Identify the knowledge and skills needed to perform the project.
2. Assess the knowledge and skills available.
3. Select mechanisms for providing needed knowledge and skills.

> | Example mechanisms include the following: |
> | :--- |
> | • In-house training (both organizational and project) |
> | • External training |
> | • Staffing and new hires |
> | • External skill acquisition |

> The choice of in-house training or external outsourcing for the needed knowledge and skills is determined by the availability of training expertise, the project's schedule, and the business objectives.

4. Incorporate selected mechanisms into the project plan.

SP 2.6-1 PLAN STAKEHOLDER INVOLVEMENT

Plan the involvement of identified stakeholders.

> **FOR INTEGRATED PRODUCT AND PROCESS DEVELOPMENT**
> When integrated teams are formed, stakeholder involvement needs to be planned down to the integrated team level.

Stakeholders are identified from all phases of the project life cycle by identifying the type of people and functions needing representation in the project and describing their relevance and the degree of interaction for specific project activities. A two-dimensional matrix with stakeholders along one axis and project activities along the other axis is a convenient format for accomplishing this identification. Relevance of the stakeholder to the activity in a particular project phase and the amount of interaction expected would be shown at the intersection of the project phase activity axis and the stakeholder axis.

For the inputs of stakeholders to be useful, careful selection of relevant stakeholders is necessary. For each major activity, identify the stakeholders who are affected by the activity and those who have expertise that is needed to conduct the activity. This list of relevant stakeholders will probably change as the project moves through the phases of the project life cycle. It is important, however, to ensure that relevant stakeholders in the latter phases of the life cycle have early input to requirements and design decisions that affect them.

> Examples of the type of material that should be included in a plan for stakeholder interaction include the following:
> - List of all relevant stakeholders
> - Rationale for stakeholder involvement
> - Roles and responsibilities of the relevant stakeholders with respect to the project, by project life-cycle phase
> - Relationships between stakeholders
> - Relative importance of the stakeholder to success of the project, by project life-cycle phase
> - Resources (e.g., training, materials, time, funding) needed to ensure stakeholder interaction
> - Schedule for phasing of stakeholder interaction

Conduct of this specific practice relies on shared or exchanged information with the previous Plan for Needed Knowledge and Skills specific practice.

Typical Work Products

1. Stakeholder involvement plan

SP 2.7-1 Establish the Project Plan

Establish and maintain the overall project plan content.

FOR SYSTEMS ENGINEERING

Systems engineering planning details the work activities and work products of the integrated technical effort across the project.

FOR SYSTEMS ENGINEERING

Examples of plans that have been used in the U.S. Department of Defense community include the following:

- *Integrated Master Plan*—an event-driven plan that documents significant accomplishments with pass/fail criteria for both business and technical elements of the project and that ties each accomplishment to a key program event.
- *Integrated Master Schedule*—an integrated and networked multi-layered schedule of program tasks required to complete the work effort documented in a related Integrated Master Plan.
- *Systems Engineering Management Plan*—a plan that details the integrated technical effort across the project.
- *Systems Engineering Master Schedule*—an event-based schedule that contains a compilation of key technical accomplishments, each with measurable criteria, requiring successful completion to pass identified events.
- *Systems Engineering Detailed Schedule*—a detailed, time-dependent, task-oriented schedule that associates specific dates and milestones with the Systems Engineering Master Schedule.

FOR SOFTWARE ENGINEERING

For software, the planning document is often referred to as one of the following:

- Software development plan
- Software project plan
- Software plan

A documented plan that addresses all relevant planning items is necessary to achieve the mutual understanding, commitment, and performance of individuals, groups, and organizations that must execute or support the plans. The plan generated for the project defines all aspects of the effort, tying together in a logical manner: project life-cycle considerations; technical and management tasks; budgets and schedules; milestones; data management, risk identification, resource and skill requirements; and stakeholder identification and interaction. Infrastructure descriptions include responsibility and authority relationships for project staff, management, and support organizations.

Typical Work Products

1. Overall project plan

SG 3 OBTAIN COMMITMENT TO THE PLAN

Commitments to the project plan are established and maintained.

To be effective, plans require commitment by those responsible for implementing and supporting the plan.

SP 3.1-1 REVIEW PLANS THAT AFFECT THE PROJECT

Review all plans that affect the project to understand project commitments.

> **FOR INTEGRATED PRODUCT AND PROCESS DEVELOPMENT**
> When integrated teams are formed, their integrated work plans are among the plans to review.

Plans developed within other process areas will typically contain information similar to that called for in the overall project plan. These plans may provide additional detailed guidance and should be compatible with and support the overall project plan to indicate who has the authority, responsibility, accountability, and control. All plans that affect the project should be reviewed to ensure a common understanding of the scope, objectives, roles, and relationships that are required for the project to be successful. Many of these plans are described by the Plan the Process generic practice in each of the process areas.

Typical Work Products

1. Record of the reviews of plans that affect the project

SP 3.2-1 RECONCILE WORK AND RESOURCE LEVELS

Reconcile the project plan to reflect available and estimated resources.

> **FOR INTEGRATED PRODUCT AND PROCESS DEVELOPMENT**
> When integrated teams are formed, special attention needs to be paid to resource commitments in circumstances of distributed integrated teams and when people are on multiple integrated teams in one or many projects.

To obtain commitment from relevant stakeholders, it is important to reconcile any differences between the estimates and the available resources. Reconciliation is typically accomplished by lowering or deferring technical performance requirements, negotiating more resources, finding ways to increase productivity, outsourcing, adjusting the staff skill mix, or revising all plans that affect the project or schedules.

Typical Work Products

1. Revised methods and corresponding estimating parameters (e.g., better tools, use of off-the-shelf components)
2. Renegotiated budgets
3. Revised schedules
4. Revised requirements list
5. Renegotiated stakeholder agreements

SP 3.3-1 OBTAIN PLAN COMMITMENT

Obtain commitment from relevant stakeholders responsible for performing and supporting plan execution.

> **FOR INTEGRATED PRODUCT AND PROCESS DEVELOPMENT**
> When integrated teams are formed, the integrated team plans will need buy-in from the team members, the interfacing teams, the project, and the process owners of the standard processes that team has selected for tailored application.

Obtaining commitment involves interaction among all relevant stakeholders both internal and external to the project. The individual or group making a commitment should have confidence that the work can be performed within cost, schedule, and performance constraints. Often, a provisional commitment is adequate to allow the effort to begin and to permit research to be performed to increase confidence to the appropriate level needed to obtain a full commitment.

Typical Work Products

1. Documented requests for commitments
2. Documented commitments

Subpractices

1. Identify needed support and negotiate commitments with relevant stakeholders.

    The WBS can be used as a checklist for ensuring that commitments are obtained for all tasks.

    The plan for stakeholder interaction should identify all parties from whom commitment should be obtained.

2. Document all organizational commitments, both full and provisional, ensuring appropriate level of signatories.

   Commitments must be documented to ensure a consistent mutual understanding as well as for tracking and maintenance. Provisional commitments should be accompanied by a description of the risks associated with the relationship.

3. Review internal commitments with senior management as appropriate.

4. Review external commitments with senior management as appropriate.

   Management may have the necessary insight and authority to reduce risks associated with external commitments.

5. Identify commitments on interfaces between elements in the project, and with other projects and organizational units so that they can be monitored.

   Well-defined interface specifications form the basis for commitments.

Generic Practices by Goal

GG 1 ACHIEVE SPECIFIC GOALS

The process supports and enables achievement of the specific goals of the process area by transforming identifiable input work products to produce identifiable output work products.

GP 1.1 PERFORM BASE PRACTICES

Perform the base practices of the project planning process to develop work products and provide services to achieve the specific goals of the process area.

CONTINUOUS ONLY

GG 2 INSTITUTIONALIZE A MANAGED PROCESS

The process is institutionalized as a managed process.

Commitment to Perform

GP 2.1 ESTABLISH AN ORGANIZATIONAL POLICY

Establish and maintain an organizational policy for planning and performing the project planning process.

Elaboration

This policy establishes organizational expectations for estimating the planning parameters, making internal and external commitments, and developing the plan for managing the project.

Ability to Perform

GP 2.2 PLAN THE PROCESS

Establish and maintain the plan for performing the project planning process.

Elaboration

This plan for performing the project planning process differs from the project plan described in specific practices in this process area. The plan called for in this generic practice would address the comprehensive planning for all of the specific practices in this process area, from estimating the scope of the project all the way to obtaining commitment for the project plan. In other words, this generic practice calls for one to "plan the plan." In contrast, the project plan called for in the specific practices would address planning for the project effort itself in a comprehensive manner.

GP 2.3 PROVIDE RESOURCES

Provide adequate resources for performing the project planning process, developing the work products, and providing the services of the process.

Elaboration

Special expertise, equipment, and facilities in project planning may be required. Special expertise in project planning may include the following:

- *Experienced estimators*
- *Schedulers*
- *Technical experts in applicable areas (e.g., product domain and technology)*

Examples of other resources provided include the following tools:
- Spreadsheet programs
- Estimating models
- Project planning and scheduling packages

GP 2.4 ASSIGN RESPONSIBILITY

Assign responsibility and authority for performing the process, developing the work products, and providing the services of the project planning process.

GP 2.5 TRAIN PEOPLE

Train the people performing or supporting the project planning process as needed.

Elaboration

> Examples of training topics include the following:
> - Estimating
> - Budgeting
> - Negotiating
> - Risk identification and analysis
> - Data management
> - Planning
> - Scheduling

Directing Implementation

GP 2.6   MANAGE CONFIGURATIONS

Place designated work products of the project planning process under appropriate levels of configuration management.

Elaboration

> Examples of work products placed under configuration management include the following:
> - Work breakdown structure
> - Project plan
> - Data management plan
> - Stakeholder involvement plan

GP 2.7   IDENTIFY AND INVOLVE RELEVANT STAKEHOLDERS

Identify and involve the relevant stakeholders of the project planning process as planned.

Elaboration

This generic practice is different from developing the plan for stakeholder involvement for the project itself, which is covered in a specific practice of this process area.

Select relevant stakeholders from senior managers, project managers, project functional managers (e.g., systems engineering, software engineering, other disciplines), software engineers, systems engineers, manufacturing engineers, logisticians, suppliers, customers, and others who may be affected by, or may affect, the project.

> Examples of activities for stakeholder involvement include the following:
> - Establishing estimates
> - Reviewing and resolving issues on the completeness and correctness of the project risks
> - Reviewing data management plans
> - Establishing project plans
> - Reviewing project plans and resolving issues on work and resource issues

GP 2.8 *MONITOR AND CONTROL THE PROCESS*

Monitor and control the project planning process against the plan for performing the process and take appropriate corrective action.

Elaboration

> Examples of measures used in monitoring and controlling include the following:
> - Number of revisions to the plan
> - Cost, schedule, and effort variance per plan revision

Verifying Implementation

GP 2.9 *OBJECTIVELY EVALUATE ADHERENCE*

Objectively evaluate adherence of the project planning process against its process description, standards, and procedures, and address noncompliance.

Elaboration

> Examples of activities reviewed include the following:
> - Establishing estimates
> - Developing a project plan
> - Obtaining commitments to the project plan

> Examples of work products reviewed include the following:
> - WBS
> - Project plan
> - Data management plan
> - Stakeholder involvement plan

GP 2.10 *REVIEW STATUS WITH HIGHER LEVEL MANAGEMENT*

Review the activities, status, and results of the project planning process with higher level management and resolve issues.

AUTHORS' NOTE: GG3 and its practices do not apply for
a maturity level 2 rating, but do apply for
a maturity level 3 rating and above.

GG 3   INSTITUTIONALIZE A DEFINED PROCESS

The process is institutionalized as a defined process.

Ability to Perform

GP 3.1   ESTABLISH A DEFINED PROCESS

Establish and maintain the description of a defined project planning process.

Directing Implementation

GP 3.2   COLLECT IMPROVEMENT INFORMATION

Collect work products, measures, measurement results, and improvement informa-
tion derived from planning and performing the project planning process to support
the future use and improvement of the organization's processes and process assets.

GG 4   INSTITUTIONALIZE A QUANTITATIVELY MANAGED PROCESS

The process is institutionalized as a quantitatively managed process.

GP 4.1   ESTABLISH QUANTITATIVE OBJECTIVES FOR THE PROCESS

Establish and maintain quantitative objectives for the project planning process that ad-
dress quality and process performance based on customer needs and business objectives.

GP 4.2   STABILIZE SUBPROCESS PERFORMANCE

Stabilize the performance of one or more subprocesses to determine the ability of
the project planning process to achieve the established quantitative quality and
process-performance objectives.

GG 5   INSTITUTIONALIZE AN OPTIMIZING PROCESS

The process is institutionalized as an optimizing process.

GP 5.1   ENSURE CONTINUOUS PROCESS IMPROVEMENT

Ensure continuous improvement of the project planning process in fulfilling the rele-
vant business objectives of the organization.

GP 5.2   CORRECT ROOT CAUSES OF PROBLEMS

Identify and correct the root causes of defects and other problems in the project
planning process.

PROCESS AND PRODUCT QUALITY ASSURANCE
A Support Process Area at Maturity Level 2

Purpose

The purpose of Process and Product Quality Assurance (PPQA) is to provide staff and management with objective insight into processes and associated work products.

Introductory Notes

The Process and Product Quality Assurance process area involves the following:

- Objectively evaluating performed processes, work products, and services against the applicable process descriptions, standards, and procedures
- Identifying and documenting noncompliance issues
- Providing feedback to project staff and managers on the results of quality assurance activities
- Ensuring that noncompliance issues are addressed

The Process and Product Quality Assurance process area supports the delivery of high-quality products and services by providing the project staff and managers at all levels with appropriate visibility into, and feedback on, processes and associated work products throughout the life of the project.

The practices in the Process and Product Quality Assurance process area ensure that planned processes are implemented, while the practices in the Verification process area ensure that the specified requirements are satisfied. These two process areas may on occasion address the same work product but from different perspectives. Projects should take care to minimize duplication of effort.

Objectivity in process and product quality assurance evaluations is critical to the success of the project. (See the definition of "objectively evaluate" in the glossary.) Objectivity is achieved by both independence and the use of criteria. Traditionally, a quality assurance group that is independent of the project provides this objectivity. It may be appropriate in some organizations, however, to implement the process and product quality assurance role without that kind of independence. For example, in an organization with an open, quality-oriented culture, the process and product quality assurance role may be performed, partially or completely, by peers; and the quality assurance function may be embedded in the process.

If quality assurance is embedded in the process, several issues must be addressed to ensure objectivity. Everyone performing quality assurance activities should be trained in quality assurance. Those performing quality assurance activities for a work product should be separate from those directly involved in developing or maintaining the work product. An independent reporting channel to the appropriate level of organizational management must be available so that noncompliance issues can be escalated as necessary.

Quality assurance should begin in the early phases of a project to establish plans, processes, standards, and procedures that will add value to the project and satisfy the requirements of the project and the organizational policies. Those performing quality assurance participate in establishing the plans, processes, standards, and procedures to ensure that they fit the project's needs and that they will be useable for performing quality assurance evaluations. In addition, the specific processes and associated work products that will be evaluated during the project are designated. This designation may be based on sampling or on objective criteria that are consistent with organizational policies and project requirements and needs.

When noncompliance issues are identified, they are first addressed within the project and resolved there if possible. Any noncompliance issues that cannot be resolved within the project are escalated to an appropriate level of management for resolution.

This process area primarily applies to evaluations of products and services, but it also applies to evaluations of nonproject activities and work products such as training activities. For these activities and work products, the term "project" should be appropriately interpreted.

Related Process Areas

Refer to the Project Planning process area for more information about identifying processes and associated work products that will be objectively evaluated.

Refer to the Verification process area for more information about satisfying specified requirements.

Practice-to-Goal Relationship Table

Continuous Representation	Staged Representation
SG 1 Objectively Evaluate Processes and Work Products	**SG 1** Objectively Evaluate Processes and Work Products
SP 1.1-1 Objectively Evaluate Processes	SP 1.1-1 Objectively Evaluate Processes
SP 1.2-1 Objectively Evaluate Work Products and Services	SP 1.2-1 Objectively Evaluate Work Products and Services
SG 2 Provide Objective Insight	**SG 2** Provide Objective Insight
SP 2.1-1 Communicate and Ensure Resolution of Noncompliance Issues	SP 2.1-1 Communicate and Ensure Resolution of Noncompliance Issues
SP 2.2-1 Establish Records	SP 2.2-1 Establish Records
GG 1 Achieve Specific Goals	
GP 1.1 Perform Base Practices	
GG 2 Institutionalize a Managed Process	**GG 2** Institutionalize a Managed Process
GP 2.1 Establish an Organizational Policy	GP 2.1 Establish an Organizational Policy
GP 2.2 Plan the Process	GP 2.2 Plan the Process
GP 2.3 Provide Resources	GP 2.3 Provide Resources
GP 2.4 Assign Responsibility	GP 2.4 Assign Responsibility
GP 2.5 Train People	GP 2.5 Train People
GP 2.6 Manage Configurations	GP 2.6 Manage Configurations
GP 2.7 Identify and Involve Relevant Stakeholders	GP 2.7 Identify and Involve Relevant Stakeholders
GP 2.8 Monitor and Control the Process	GP 2.8 Monitor and Control the Process
GP 2.9 Objectively Evaluate Adherence	GP 2.9 Objectively Evaluate Adherence
GP 2.10 Review Status with Higher Level Management	GP 2.10 Review Status with Higher Level Management
GG 3 Institutionalize a Defined Process	**GG 3** Institutionalize a Defined Process
GP 3.1 Establish a Defined Process	GP 3.1 Establish a Defined Process
GP 3.2 Collect Improvement Information	GP 3.2 Collect Improvement Information
GG 4 Institutionalize a Quantitatively Managed Process	
GP 4.1 Establish Quantitative Objectives for the Process	
GP 4.2 Stabilize Subprocess Performance	
GG 5 Institutionalize an Optimizing Process	
GP 5.1 Ensure Continuous Process Improvement	
GP 5.2 Correct Root Causes of Problems	

PPQA

C/ML 3-5

Specific Practices by Goal

SG 1 OBJECTIVELY EVALUATE PROCESSES AND WORK PRODUCTS

Adherence of the performed process and associated work products and services to applicable process descriptions, standards, and procedures is objectively evaluated.

SP 1.1-1 OBJECTIVELY EVALUATE PROCESSES

Objectively evaluate the designated performed processes against the applicable process descriptions, standards, and procedures.

Objectivity in quality assurance evaluations is critical to the success of the project. A description of the quality assurance reporting chain and how it ensures objectivity should be defined.

Typical Work Products

1. Evaluation reports
2. Noncompliance reports
3. Corrective actions

Subpractices

1. Promote an environment (created as part of project management) that encourages employee participation in identifying and reporting quality issues.
2. Establish and maintain clearly stated criteria for the evaluations.

    The intent of this subpractice is to provide criteria, based on business needs, such as the following:

    - What will be evaluated
    - When or how often a process will be evaluated
    - How the evaluation will be conducted
    - Who must be involved in the evaluation

3. Use the stated criteria to evaluate performed processes for adherence to process descriptions, standards, and procedures.
4. Identify each noncompliance found during the evaluation.
5. Identify lessons learned that could improve processes for future products and services.

SP 1.2-1 OBJECTIVELY EVALUATE WORK PRODUCTS AND SERVICES

Objectively evaluate the designated work products and services against the applicable process descriptions, standards, and procedures.

Typical Work Products

1. Evaluation reports
2. Noncompliance reports
3. Corrective actions

Subpractices

1. Select work products to be evaluated, based on documented sampling criteria if sampling is used.
2. Establish and maintain clearly stated criteria for the evaluation of work products.

   The intent of this subpractice is to provide criteria, based on business needs, such as the following:

   - What will be evaluated during the evaluation of a work product
   - When or how often a work product will be evaluated
   - How the evaluation will be conducted
   - Who must be involved in the evaluation

3. Use the stated criteria during the evaluations of work products.
4. Evaluate work products before they are delivered to the customer.
5. Evaluate work products at selected milestones in their development.
6. Perform in-progress or incremental evaluations of work products and services against process descriptions, standards, and procedures.
7. Identify each case of noncompliance found during the evaluations.
8. Identify lessons learned that could improve processes for future products and services.

SG 2   PROVIDE OBJECTIVE INSIGHT

Noncompliance issues are objectively tracked and communicated, and resolution is ensured.

SP 2.1-1   COMMUNICATE AND ENSURE RESOLUTION OF NONCOMPLIANCE ISSUES

Communicate quality issues and ensure resolution of noncompliance issues with the staff and managers.

Noncompliance issues are problems identified in evaluations that reflect a lack of adherence to applicable standards, process descriptions, or procedures. The status of noncompliance issues provides an indication of quality trends. Quality issues include noncompliance issues and results of trend analysis.

When local resolution of noncompliance issues cannot be obtained, use established escalation mechanisms to ensure that the appropriate level of management can resolve the issue. Track noncompliance issues to resolution.

Typical Work Products

1. Corrective action reports
2. Evaluation reports
3. Quality trends

Subpractices

1. Resolve each noncompliance with the appropriate members of the staff where possible.
2. Document noncompliance issues when they cannot be resolved within the project.

> Examples of ways to resolve noncompliance within the project include the following:
> - Fixing the noncompliance
> - Changing the process descriptions, standards, or procedures that were violated
> - Obtaining a waiver to cover the noncompliance issue

3. Escalate noncompliance issues that cannot be resolved within the project to the appropriate level of management designated to receive and act on noncompliance issues.
4. Analyze the noncompliance issues to see if there are any quality trends that can be identified and addressed.
5. Ensure that relevant stakeholders are aware of the results of evaluations and the quality trends in a timely manner.
6. Periodically review open noncompliance issues and trends with the manager designated to receive and act on noncompliance issues.
7. Track noncompliance issues to resolution.

SP 2.2-1 ESTABLISH RECORDS

Establish and maintain records of the quality assurance activities.

Typical Work Products

1. Evaluation logs
2. Quality assurance reports
3. Status reports of corrective actions
4. Reports of quality trends

Subpractices

1. Record process and product quality assurance activities in sufficient detail such that status and results are known.
2. Revise the status and history of the quality assurance activities as necessary.

Generic Practices by Goal

GG 1 ACHIEVE SPECIFIC GOALS

The process supports and enables achievement of the specific goals of the process area by transforming identifiable input work products to produce identifiable output work products.

GP 1.1 PERFORM BASE PRACTICES

Perform the base practices of the process and product quality assurance process to develop work products and provide services to achieve the specific goals of the process area.

GG 2 INSTITUTIONALIZE A MANAGED PROCESS

The process is institutionalized as a managed process.

Commitment to Perform

GP 2.1 ESTABLISH AN ORGANIZATIONAL POLICY

Establish and maintain an organizational policy for planning and performing the process and product quality assurance process.

Elaboration

This policy establishes organizational expectations for objectively evaluating whether processes and associated work products adhere to the applicable process descriptions, standards, and procedures, and ensuring that noncompliance is addressed.

This policy also establishes organizational expectations for process and product quality assurance being in place for all projects. Process and product quality assurance must possess sufficient independence from project management to provide objectivity in identifying and reporting noncompliance issues.

Ability to Perform

GP 2.2 PLAN THE PROCESS

Establish and maintain the plan for performing the process and product quality assurance process.

PPQA

CONTINUOUS ONLY

Elaboration

This plan for performing the process and product quality assurance process may be included in (or referenced by) the project plan, which is described in the Project Planning process area.

GP 2.3 PROVIDE RESOURCES

Provide adequate resources for performing the process and product quality assurance process, developing the work products, and providing the services of the process.

Elaboration

Examples of resources provided include the following tools:
- Evaluation tools
- Noncompliance tracking tool

GP 2.4 ASSIGN RESPONSIBILITY

Assign responsibility and authority for performing the process, developing the work products, and providing the services of the process and product quality assurance process.

Elaboration

To guard against subjectivity or bias, ensure that those people assigned responsibility and authority for process and product quality assurance can perform their evaluations with sufficient independence and objectivity.

GP 2.5 TRAIN PEOPLE

Train the people performing or supporting the process and product quality assurance process as needed.

Elaboration

Examples of training topics include the following:
- Application domain
- Customer relations
- Process descriptions, standards, procedures, and methods for the project
- Quality assurance objectives, process descriptions, standards, procedures, methods, and tools

Directing Implementation

GP 2.6 MANAGE CONFIGURATIONS

Place designated work products of the process and product quality assurance process under appropriate levels of configuration management.

Elaboration

Examples of work products placed under configuration management include the following:
- Noncompliance reports
- Evaluation logs and reports

GP 2.7 IDENTIFY AND INVOLVE RELEVANT STAKEHOLDERS

Identify and involve the relevant stakeholders of the process and product quality assurance process as planned.

Elaboration

Examples of activities for stakeholder involvement include the following:
- Establishing criteria for the objective evaluations of processes and work products
- Evaluating processes and work products
- Resolving noncompliance issues
- Tracking noncompliance issues to closure

GP 2.8 MONITOR AND CONTROL THE PROCESS

Monitor and control the process and product quality assurance process against the plan for performing the process and take appropriate corrective action.

Elaboration

Examples of measures used in monitoring and controlling include the following:
- Variance of objective process evaluations planned and performed
- Variance of objective work product evaluations planned and performed

Verifying Implementation

GP 2.9 OBJECTIVELY EVALUATE ADHERENCE

Objectively evaluate adherence of the process and product quality assurance process against its process description, standards, and procedures, and address noncompliance.

Elaboration

Examples of activities reviewed include the following:
- Objectively evaluating processes and work products
- Tracking and communicating noncompliance issues

Examples of work products reviewed include the following:
- Noncompliance reports
- Evaluation logs and reports

GP 2.10 REVIEW STATUS WITH HIGHER LEVEL MANAGEMENT

Review the activities, status, and results of the process and product quality assurance process with higher level management and resolve issues.

AUTHORS' NOTE: GG3 and its practices do not apply for a maturity level 2 rating, but do apply for a maturity level 3 rating and above.

S ONLY

GG 3 INSTITUTIONALIZE A DEFINED PROCESS

The process is institutionalized as a defined process.

Ability to Perform
GP 3.1 ESTABLISH A DEFINED PROCESS

Establish and maintain the description of a defined process and product quality assurance process.

Directing Implementation
GP 3.2 COLLECT IMPROVEMENT INFORMATION

Collect work products, measures, measurement results, and improvement information derived from planning and performing the process and product quality assurance process to support the future use and improvement of the organization's processes and process assets.

CONTINUOUS/MATURITY LEVELS 3–5

GG 4 INSTITUTIONALIZE A QUANTITATIVELY MANAGED PROCESS

The process is institutionalized as a quantitatively managed process.

GP 4.1 ESTABLISH QUANTITATIVE OBJECTIVES FOR THE PROCESS

Establish and maintain quantitative objectives for the process and product quality assurance process that address quality and process performance based on customer needs and business objectives.

CONTINUOUS ONLY

GP 4.2 STABILIZE SUBPROCESS PERFORMANCE

Stabilize the performance of one or more subprocesses to determine the ability of the process and product quality assurance process to achieve the established quantitative quality and process-performance objectives.

GG 5 INSTITUTIONALIZE AN OPTIMIZING PROCESS

The process is institutionalized as an optimizing process.

GP 5.1 ENSURE CONTINUOUS PROCESS IMPROVEMENT

Ensure continuous improvement of the process and product quality assurance process in fulfilling the relevant business objectives of the organization.

GP 5.2 CORRECT ROOT CAUSES OF PROBLEMS

Identify and correct the root causes of defects and other problems in the process and product quality assurance process.

PPQA

CONTINUOUS ONLY

QUANTITATIVE PROJECT MANAGEMENT
A Project Management Process Area at Maturity Level 4

Purpose

The purpose of the Quantitative Project Management (QPM) process area is to quantitatively manage the project's defined process to achieve the project's established quality and process-performance objectives.

Introductory Notes

The Quantitative Project Management process area involves the following:

- Establishing and maintaining the project's quality and process-performance objectives
- Identifying suitable subprocesses that compose the project's defined process based on historical stability and capability data found in process performance baselines or models
- Selecting the subprocesses of the project's defined process to be statistically managed
- Monitoring the project to determine whether the project's objectives for quality and process performance are being satisfied, and identifying appropriate corrective action
- Selecting the measures and analytic techniques to be used in statistically managing the selected subprocesses
- Establishing and maintaining an understanding of the variation of the selected subprocesses using the selected measures and analytic techniques
- Monitoring the performance of the selected subprocesses to determine whether they are capable of satisfying their quality and process-performance objectives, and identifying corrective action
- Recording statistical and quality management data in the organization's measurement repository

The quality and process-performance objectives, measures, and baselines identified here are developed as described in the Organizational Process Performance process area. Subsequently, the results of performing the processes associated with the Quantitative Project Management process area (e.g., measurement definitions and measurement data) become part of the organizational process assets referred to in the Organizational Process Performance process area.

To effectively address the specific practices in this process area, the organization should have already established a set of standard processes and related organizational process assets, such as the organization's measurement repository and the organization's process asset library for use by each project in establishing its defined process. The project's defined process is a set of subprocesses that form an integrated and coherent life cycle for the project. It is established, in part, through selecting and tailoring processes from the organization's set of standard processes. (See the definition of "defined process" in the glossary.)

> **FOR SUPPLIER SOURCING**
>
> The quality and timeliness of the products delivered by a supplier can have a significant impact on the performance of the project's processes. To meet the objectives of the project requires careful handling of the supplier agreements to ensure that the measurements and progress of the supplier's efforts are made available to the project. The practices of the Supplier Agreement Management and Integrated Supplier Management process areas should be coordinated with this process area. Establishment of effective relationships with suppliers is necessary for the successful implementation of this process area's specific practices.

Process performance is a measure of the actual process results achieved. Process performance is characterized by both process measures (e.g., effort, cycle time, and defect removal efficiency) and product measures (e.g., reliability, defect density, and response time).

Subprocesses are defined components of a larger defined process. For example, a typical organization's development process may be defined in terms of subprocesses such as requirements development, design, build, test, and peer review. The subprocesses themselves may be further decomposed as necessary into other subprocesses and process elements.

One essential element of quantitative management is having confidence in estimates (i.e., being able to predict the extent to which the project can fulfill its quality and process-performance objectives). The subprocesses that will be statistically managed are chosen based on identified needs for predictable performance. (See the definitions of "statistically managed process," "quality and process-performance objective," and "quantitatively managed process" in the glossary.)

Another essential element of quantitative management is understanding the nature and extent of the variation experienced in process performance,

Practice-to-Goal Relationship Table

Continuous Representation	*Staged Representation*
SG 1 Quantitatively Manage the Project	SG 1 Quantitatively Manage the Project
SP 1.1-1 Establish the Project's Objectives	SP 1.1-1 Establish the Project's Objectives
SP 1.2-1 Compose the Defined Process	SP 1.2-1 Compose the Defined Process
SP 1.3-1 Select the Subprocesses that Will Be Statistically Managed	SP 1.3-1 Select the Subprocesses that Will Be Statistically Managed
SP 1.4-1 Manage Project Performance	SP 1.4-1 Manage Project Performance
SG 2 Statistically Manage Subprocess Performance	SG 2 Statistically Manage Subprocess Performance
SP 2.1-1 Select Measures and Analytic Techniques	SP 2.1-1 Select Measures and Analytic Techniques
SP 2.2-1 Apply Statistical Methods to Understand Variation	SP 2.2-1 Apply Statistical Methods to Understand Variation
SP 2.3-1 Monitor Performance of the Selected Subprocesses	SP 2.3-1 Monitor Performance of the Selected Subprocesses
SP 2.4-1 Record Statistical Management Data	SP 2.4-1 Record Statistical Management Data
GG 1 Achieve Specific Goals	
GP 1.1 Perform Base Practices	
GG 2 Institutionalize a Managed Process	GG 3 Institutionalize a Defined Process
GP 2.1 Establish an Organizational Policy	GP 2.1 Establish an Organizational Policy
GP 2.2 Plan the Process	GP 2.2 Plan the Process
GP 2.3 Provide Resources	GP 2.3 Provide Resources
GP 2.4 Assign Responsibility	GP 2.4 Assign Responsibility
GP 2.5 Train People	GP 2.5 Train People
GP 2.6 Manage Configurations	GP 2.6 Manage Configurations
GP 2.7 Identify and Involve Relevant Stakeholders	GP 2.7 Identify and Involve Relevant Stakeholders
GP 2.8 Monitor and Control the Process	GP 2.8 Monitor and Control the Process
GP 2.9 Objectively Evaluate Adherence	GP 2.9 Objectively Evaluate Adherence
GP 2.10 Review Status with Higher Level Management	GP 2.10 Review Status with Higher Level Management
GG 3 Institutionalize a Defined Process	
GP 3.1 Establish a Defined Process	GP 3.1 Establish a Defined Process
GP 3.2 Collect Improvement Information	GP 3.2 Collect Improvement Information
GG 4 Institutionalize a Quantitatively Managed Process	
GP 4.1 Establish Quantitative Objectives for the Process	
GP 4.2 Stabilize Subprocess Performance	
GG 5 Institutionalize an Optimizing Process	
GP 5.1 Ensure Continuous Process Improvement	
GP 5.2 Correct Root Causes of Problems	

and recognizing when the project's actual performance may not be adequate to achieve the project's quality and process-performance objectives.

Statistical management involves statistical thinking and the correct use of a variety of statistical techniques, such as run charts, control charts, confidence intervals, prediction intervals, and tests of hypotheses. Quantitative management uses data from statistical management to help the project predict whether it will be able to achieve its quality and process-performance objectives and identify what corrective action should be taken.

This process area applies to managing a project, but the concepts found here also apply to managing other groups and functions. Applying these concepts to managing other groups and functions may not necessarily contribute to achieving the organization's business objectives, but may help these groups and functions control their own processes.

Examples of other groups and functions include the following:
- Quality assurance
- Process definition and improvement
- Effort reporting
- Customer complaint handling
- Problem tracking and reporting

Related Process Areas

Refer to the Project Monitoring and Control process area for more information about monitoring and controlling the project and taking corrective action.

Refer to the Measurement and Analysis process area for more information about establishing measurable objectives, specifying the measures and analyses to be performed, obtaining and analyzing measures, and providing results.

Refer to the Organizational Process Performance process area for more information about the organization's quality and process-performance objectives, process performance analyses, process performance baselines, and process performance models.

Refer to the Organizational Process Definition process area for more information about the organizational process assets, including the organization's measurement repository.

Refer to the Integrated Project Management process area for more information about establishing and maintaining the project's defined process.

Refer to the Causal Analysis and Resolution process area for more information about how to identify the causes of defects and other problems, and taking action to prevent them from occurring in the future.

Refer to the Organizational Innovation and Deployment process area for more information about selecting and deploying improvements that support the organization's quality and process-performance objectives.

Specific Practices by Goal

SG 1 *QUANTITATIVELY MANAGE THE PROJECT*

The project is quantitatively managed using quality and process-performance objectives.

SP 1.1-1 *ESTABLISH THE PROJECT'S OBJECTIVES*

Establish and maintain the project's quality and process-performance objectives.

When establishing the project's quality and process-performance objectives, it is often useful to think ahead about which processes from the organization's set of standard processes will be included in the project's defined process, and what the historical data indicates regarding their process performance. These considerations will help in establishing realistic objectives for the project. Later, as the project's actual performance becomes known and more predictable, the objectives may need to be revised.

Typical Work Products

1. The project's quality and process-performance objectives

Subpractices

1. Review the organization's objectives for quality and process performance.

    The intent of this review is to ensure that the project understands the broader business context in which the project will need to operate. The project's objectives for quality and process performance are developed in the context of these overarching organizational objectives.

    Refer to the Organizational Process Performance process area for more information about the organization's quality and process-performance objectives.

2. Identify the quality and process performance needs and priorities of the customer, end users, and other relevant stakeholders.

    > Examples of quality and process performance attributes for which needs and priorities might be identified include the following:
    > - Functionality
    > - Reliability
    > - Maintainability
    > - Usability
    > - Duration
    > - Predictability
    > - Timeliness
    > - Accuracy

3. Identify how process performance is to be measured.

   Consider whether the measures established by the organization are adequate for assessing progress in fulfilling customer, end-user, and other stakeholder needs and priorities. It may be necessary to supplement these with additional measures.

   Refer to the Measurement and Analysis process area for more information about defining measures.

4. Define and document measurable quality and process-performance objectives for the project.

   Defining and documenting objectives for the project involve the following:

   • Incorporating the organization's quality and process-performance objectives
   • Writing objectives that reflect the quality and process performance needs and priorities of the customer, end users, and other stakeholders, and the way these objectives should be measured

   ---

   Examples of quality attributes for which objectives might be written include the following:
   • Mean time between failures
   • Critical resource utilization
   • Number and severity of defects in the released product
   • Number and severity of customer complaints concerning the provided service

   ---

   Examples of process performance attributes for which objectives might be written include the following:
   • Percentage of defects removed by product verification activities (perhaps by type of verification, such as peer reviews and testing)
   • Defect escape rates
   • Number and density of defects (by severity) found during the first year following product delivery (or start of service)
   • Cycle time
   • Percentage of rework time

   ---

5. Derive interim objectives for each life-cycle phase, as appropriate, to monitor progress toward achieving the project's objectives.

   An example of a method to predict future results of a process is the use of process performance models to predict the latent defects in the delivered product using interim measures of defects identified during product verification activities (e.g., peer reviews and testing).

   ---

6. Resolve conflicts among the project's quality and process-performance objectives (e.g., if one objective cannot be achieved without compromising another objective).

Resolving conflicts involves the following:
- Setting relative priorities for the objectives
- Considering alternative objectives in light of long-term business strategies as well as short-term needs
- Involving the customer, end users, senior management, project management, and other relevant stakeholders in the tradeoff decisions
- Revising the objectives as necessary to reflect the results of the conflict resolution

7. Establish traceability to the project's quality and process-performance objectives from their sources.

> Examples of sources for objectives include the following:
> - Requirements
> - Organization's quality and process-performance objectives
> - Customer's quality and process-performance objectives
> - Business objectives
> - Discussions with customers and potential customers
> - Market surveys

> An example of a method to identify and trace these needs and priorities is Quality Function Deployment (QFD).

8. Define and negotiate quality and process-performance objectives for suppliers.

   Refer to the Supplier Agreement Management process area for more information about establishing and maintaining agreements with suppliers.

9. Revise the project's quality and process-performance objectives as necessary.

SP 1.2-1   COMPOSE THE DEFINED PROCESS

Select the subprocesses that compose the project's defined process based on historical stability and capability data.

Refer to the Integrated Project Management process area for more information about establishing and maintaining the project's defined process.

Refer to the Organizational Process Definition process area for more information about the organization's process asset library, which might include a process element of known and needed capability.

Refer to the Organizational Process Performance process area for more information about the organization's process performance baselines and process performance models.

Subprocesses are identified from the process elements in the organization's set of standard processes and the process artifacts in the organization's process asset library.

Typical Work Products

1. Criteria used in identifying which subprocesses are valid candidates for inclusion in the project's defined process
2. Candidate subprocesses for inclusion in the project's defined process
3. Subprocesses to be included in the project's defined process
4. Identified risks when selected subprocesses lack a process performance history

Subpractices

1. Establish the criteria to use in identifying which subprocesses are valid candidates for use.

   Identification may be based on the following:
   - Quality and process-performance objectives
   - Existence of process performance data
   - Product line standards
   - Project life-cycle models
   - Customer requirements
   - Laws and regulations

2. Determine whether the subprocesses that are to be statistically managed, and that were obtained from the organizational process assets, are suitable for statistical management.

   A subprocess may be more suitable for statistical management if it has a history of the following:
   - Stable performance in previous comparable instances
   - Process performance data that satisfies the project's quality and process-performance objectives

   Historical data are primarily obtained from the organization's process performance baselines. However, these data may not be available for all subprocesses.

3. Analyze the interaction of subprocesses to understand the relationships among the subprocesses and the measured attributes of the subprocesses.

   > Examples of analysis techniques include system dynamics models and simulations.

4. Identify the risk when no subprocess is available that is known to be capable of satisfying the quality and process-performance objectives (i.e., no capable subprocess is available or the capability of the subprocess is not known).

   Even when a subprocess has not been selected to be statistically managed, historical data and process performance models may indicate that the subprocess is not capable of satisfying the quality and process-performance objectives.

   Refer to the Risk Management process area for more information about risk identification and analysis.

SP 1.3-1   SELECT THE SUBPROCESSES THAT WILL BE STATISTICALLY MANAGED

Select the subprocesses of the project's defined process that will be statistically managed.

Selecting the subprocesses to be statistically managed is often a concurrent and iterative process of identifying applicable project and organization quality and process-performance objectives, selecting the subprocesses, and identifying the process and product attributes to measure and control. Often the selection of a process, quality and process-performance objective, or measurable attribute will constrain the selection of the other two. For example, if a particular process is selected, the measurable attributes and quality and process-performance objectives may be constrained by that process.

Typical Work Products

1. Quality and process-performance objectives that will be addressed by statistical management
2. Criteria used in selecting which subprocesses will be statistically managed
3. Subprocesses that will be statistically managed
4. Identified process and product attributes of the selected subprocesses that should be measured and controlled

Subpractices

1. Identify which of the quality and process-performance objectives of the project will be statistically managed.
2. Identify the criteria to be used in selecting the subprocesses that are the main contributors to achieving the identified quality and process-performance objectives and for which predictable performance is important.

> Examples of sources for criteria used in selecting subprocesses include the following:
> - Customer requirements related to quality and process performance
> - Quality and process-performance objectives established by the customer
> - Quality and process-performance objectives established by the organization
> - Organization's performance baselines and models
> - Stable performance of the subprocess on other projects
> - Laws and regulations

3. Select the subprocesses that will be statistically managed using the selection criteria.

   It may not be possible to statistically manage some subprocesses (e.g., where new subprocesses and technologies are being piloted). In other cases, it may not be economically justifiable to apply statistical techniques to certain subprocesses.

4. Identify the product and process attributes of the selected subprocesses that will be measured and controlled.

> Examples of product and process attributes include the following:
> - Defect density
> - Cycle time
> - Test coverage

SP 1.4-1   MANAGE PROJECT PERFORMANCE

Monitor the project to determine whether the project's objectives for quality and process performance will be satisfied, and identify corrective action as appropriate.

Refer to the Measurement and Analysis process area for more information about analyzing and using measures.

A prerequisite for such a comparison is that the selected subprocesses of the project's defined process are being statistically managed and their process capability is understood.

Typical Work Products

1. Estimates (predictions) of the achievement of the project's quality and process-performance objectives
2. Documentation of the risks in achieving the project's quality and process-performance objectives
3. Documentation of actions needed to address the deficiencies in achieving the project's objectives

Subpractices

1. Periodically review the performance of each subprocess and the capability of each subprocess selected to be statistically managed to appraise progress toward achieving the project's quality and process-performance objectives.

   The process capability of each selected subprocess is determined with respect to that subprocess' established quality and process-performance objectives. These objectives are derived from the project's quality and process-performance objectives, which are for the project as a whole.

2. Periodically review the actual results achieved against established interim objectives for each phase of the project life cycle to appraise progress toward achieving the project's quality and process-performance objectives.

3. Track suppliers' results for achieving their quality and process-performance objectives.

4. Use process performance models calibrated with obtained measures of critical attributes to estimate progress toward achieving the project's quality and process-performance objectives.

Process performance models are used to estimate progress toward achieving objectives that cannot be measured until a future phase in the project life cycle. An example is the use of process performance models to predict the latent defects in the delivered product using interim measures of defects identified during peer reviews.

Refer to the Organizational Process Performance process area for more information about process performance models.

The calibration is based on the results obtained from performing the previous subpractices.

5. Identify and manage the risks associated with achieving the project's quality and process-performance objectives.

Refer to the Risk Management process area for more information about identifying and managing risks.

Example sources of the risks include the following:

- Inadequate stability and capability data in the organization's measurement repository
- Subprocesses having inadequate performance or capability
- Suppliers not achieving their quality and process-performance objectives
- Lack of visibility into supplier capability
- Inaccuracies in the organization's process performance models for predicting future performance
- Deficiencies in predicted process performance (estimated progress)
- Other identified risks associated with identified deficiencies

---

6. Determine and document actions needed to address the deficiencies in achieving the project's quality and process-performance objectives.

The intent of these actions is to plan and deploy the right set of activities, resources, and schedule to place the project back on track as much as possible to meet its objectives.

Examples of actions that can be taken to address deficiencies in achieving the project's objectives include the following:

- Changing quality or process-performance objectives so that they are within the expected range of the project's defined process
- Improving the implementation of the project's defined process so as to reduce its normal variability (reducing variability may bring the project's performance within the objectives without having to move the mean)
- Adopting new subprocesses and technologies that have the potential for satisfying the objectives and managing the associated risks
- Identifying the risk and risk mitigation strategies for the deficiencies
- Terminating the project

Refer to the Project Monitoring and Control process area for more information about taking corrective action.

QPM

SG 2 STATISTICALLY MANAGE SUBPROCESS PERFORMANCE

The performance of selected subprocesses within the project's defined process is statistically managed.

This specific goal describes an activity critical to achieving the Quantitatively Manage the Project specific goal of this process area. The specific practices under this specific goal describe how to statistically manage the subprocesses whose selection was described in the specific practices under the first specific goal. When the selected subprocesses are statistically managed, their capability to achieve their objectives can be determined. By these means, it will be possible to predict whether the project will be able to achieve its objectives, which is key to quantitatively managing the project.

SP 2.1-1 SELECT MEASURES AND ANALYTIC TECHNIQUES

Select the measures and analytic techniques to be used in statistically managing the selected subprocesses.

Refer to the Measurement and Analysis process area for more information about establishing measurable objectives; on defining, collecting, and analyzing measures; and on revising measures and statistical analysis techniques.

Typical Work Products

1. Definitions of the measures and analytic techniques to be used in (or proposed for) statistically managing the subprocesses
2. Operational definitions of the measures, their collection points in the subprocesses, and how the integrity of the measures will be determined
3. Traceability of measures back to the project's quality and process-performance objectives
4. Instrumented organizational support environment to support automatic data collection

Subpractices

1. Identify common measures from the organizational process assets that support statistical management.

   Refer to the Organizational Process Definition process area for more information about common measures.

   Product lines or other stratification criteria may categorize common measures.

2. Identify additional measures that may be needed for this instance to cover critical product and process attributes of the selected subprocesses.

In some cases, measures may be research oriented. Such measures should be explicitly identified.

3. Identify the measures that are appropriate for statistical management.

Critical criteria for selecting statistical management measures include the following:

- Controllable (e.g., can a measure's values be changed by changing how the subprocess is implemented?)
- Adequate performance indicator (e.g., is the measure a good indicator of how well the subprocess is performing relative to the objectives of interest?)

> Examples of subprocess measures include the following:
> - Requirements volatility
> - Ratios of estimated to measured values of the planning parameters (e.g., size, cost, and schedule)
> - Coverage and efficiency of peer reviews
> - Test coverage and efficiency
> - Effectiveness of training (e.g., percent of planned training completed and test scores)
> - Reliability
> - Percentage of the total defects inserted or found in the different phases of the project life cycle
> - Percentage of the total effort expended in the different phases of the project life cycle

4. Specify the operational definitions of the measures, their collection points in the subprocesses, and how the integrity of the measures will be determined.

Operational definitions are stated in precise and unambiguous terms. They address two important criteria as follows:

- *Communication:* What has been measured, how it was measured, what the units of measure are, and what has been included or excluded
- *Repeatability:* Whether the measurement can be repeated, given the same definition, to get the same results

5. Analyze the relationship of the identified measures to the organization's and project's objectives, and derive objectives that state specific target measures or ranges to be met for each measured attribute of each selected subprocess.

6. Instrument the organizational support environment to support collection, derivation, and analysis of statistical measures.

The instrumentation is based on the following:

- Description of the organization's set of standard processes
- Description of the project's defined process
- Capabilities of the organizational support environment

7. Identify the appropriate statistical analysis techniques that are expected to be useful in statistically managing the selected subprocesses.

> The concept of "one size does not fit all" applies to statistical analysis techniques. What makes a particular technique appropriate is not just the type of measures, but more important, how the measures will be used and whether the situation warrants applying that technique. The appropriateness of the selection may need to be investigated from time to time.

> Examples of statistical analysis techniques are given in the next specific practice.

8. Revise the measures and statistical analysis techniques as necessary.

SP 2.2-1   *APPLY STATISTICAL METHODS TO UNDERSTAND VARIATION*

Establish and maintain an understanding of the variation of the selected subprocesses using the selected measures and analytic techniques.

Refer to the Measurement and Analysis process area for more information about collecting, analyzing, and using measurement results.

Understanding variation is achieved, in part, by collecting and analyzing process and product measures so that special causes of variation can be identified and addressed to achieve predictable performance.

A special cause of process variation is characterized by an unexpected change in process performance. Special causes are also known as "assignable causes" because they can be identified, analyzed, and addressed to prevent recurrence.

The identification of special causes of variation is based on departures from the system of common causes of variation. These departures can be identified by the presence of extreme values, or other identifiable patterns in the data collected from the subprocess or associated work products. Knowledge of variation and insight about potential sources of anomalous patterns are typically needed to detect special causes of variation.

Sources of anomalous patterns of variation may include the following:
- Lack of process compliance
- Undistinguished influences of multiple underlying subprocesses on the data
- Ordering or timing of activities within the subprocess
- Uncontrolled inputs to the subprocess
- Environmental changes during subprocess execution
- Schedule pressure
- Inappropriate sampling or grouping of data

Typical Work Products

1. Collected measures
2. Natural bounds of process performance for each measured attribute of each selected subprocess
3. Process performance compared to the natural bounds of process performance for each measured attribute of each selected subprocess

Subpractices

1. Establish trial natural bounds for subprocesses having suitable historical performance data.

   Refer to the Organizational Process Performance process area for more information about organizational process performance baselines.

   Natural bounds of an attribute are the range within which variation normally occurs. All processes will show some variation in process and product measures each time they are executed. The issue is whether this variation is due to common causes of variation in the normal performance of the process or to some special cause that can and should be identified and removed.

   When a subprocess is initially executed, suitable data for establishing trial natural bounds are sometimes available from prior instances of the subprocess or comparable subprocesses, process performance baselines, or process performance models. These data are typically contained in the organization's measurement repository. As the subprocess is executed, data specific to that instance are collected and used to update and replace the trial natural bounds. However, if the subprocess in question has been materially tailored, or if the conditions are materially different from those in previous instantiations, the data in the repository may not be relevant and should not be used.

   In some cases, there may be no historical comparable data (e.g., when introducing a new subprocess, when entering a new application domain, or when significant changes have been made to the subprocess). In such cases, trial natural bounds will have to be made from early process data of this subprocess. These trial natural bounds must then be refined and updated as subprocess execution continues.

   > Examples of criteria for determining whether data are comparable include the following:
   > - Product lines
   > - Application domain
   > - Work product and task attributes (e.g., size of product)
   > - Size of project

2. Collect data, as defined by the selected measures, on the subprocesses as they execute.

3. Calculate the natural bounds of process performance for each measured attribute.

> Examples of where the natural bounds are calculated include the following:
> - Control charts
> - Confidence intervals (for parameters of distributions)
> - Prediction intervals (for future outcomes)

4. Identify special causes of variation.

> An example of a criterion for detecting a special cause of process variation in a control chart is a data point that falls outside of the 3-sigma control limits.

The criteria for detecting special causes of variation are based on statistical theory and experience and depend on economic justification. As criteria are added, special causes are more likely to be identified if present, but the likelihood of false alarms also increases.

5. Analyze the special cause of process variation to determine the reasons the anomaly occurred.

> Examples of techniques for analyzing the reasons for special causes of variation include the following:
> - Cause-and-effect (fishbone) diagrams
> - Designed experiments
> - Control charts (applied to subprocess inputs or to lower level subprocesses)
> - Subgrouping (analyzing the same data segregated into smaller groups based on an understanding of how the subprocess was implemented facilitates isolation of special causes)

Some anomalies may simply be extremes of the underlying distribution rather than problems. The people implementing a subprocess are usually the ones best able to analyze and understand special causes of variation.

6. Determine what corrective action should be taken when special causes of variation are identified.

Removing a special cause of process variation does not change the underlying subprocess. It addresses an error in the way the subprocess is being executed.

Refer to the Project Monitoring and Control process area for more information about taking corrective action.

7. Recalculate the natural bounds for each measured attribute of the selected subprocesses as necessary.

Recalculating the (statistically estimated) natural bounds is based on measured values that signify that the subprocess has changed, not on expectations or arbitrary decisions.

> Examples of when the natural bounds may need to be recalculated include the following:
> - There are incremental improvements to the subprocess
> - New tools are deployed for the subprocess
> - A new subprocess is deployed
> - The collected measures suggest that the subprocess mean has permanently shifted or the subprocess variation has permanently changed

SP 2.3-1   Monitor Performance of the Selected Subprocesses

Monitor the performance of the selected subprocesses to determine their capability to satisfy their quality and process-performance objectives, and identify corrective action as necessary.

The intent of this specific practice is to do the following:

- Determine statistically the process behavior expected from the subprocess
- Appraise the probability that the process will meet its quality and process-performance objectives
- Identify the corrective action to be taken, based on a statistical analysis of the process performance data

Corrective action may include renegotiating the affected project objectives, identifying and implementing alternative subprocesses, or identifying and measuring lower level subprocesses to achieve greater detail in the performance data. Any or all of these actions are intended to help the project use a more capable process. (See the definition of "capable process" in the glossary.)

A prerequisite for comparing the capability of a selected subprocess against its quality and process-performance objectives is that the performance of the subprocess is stable and predictable with respect to its measured attributes.

Process capability is analyzed for those subprocesses and those measured attributes for which (derived) objectives have been established. Not all subprocesses or measured attributes that are statistically managed are analyzed regarding process capability.

The historical data may be inadequate for initially determining whether the subprocess is capable. It also is possible that the estimated natural bounds for subprocess performance may shift away from the quality and process-performance objectives. In either case, statistical control implies monitoring capability as well as stability.

Typical Work Products

1. Natural bounds of process performance for each selected subprocess compared to its established (derived) objectives
2. For each subprocess, its process capability
3. For each subprocess, the actions needed to address deficiencies in its process capability

Subpractices

1. Compare the quality and process-performance objectives to the natural bounds of the measured attribute.

    This comparison provides an appraisal of the process capability for each measured attribute of a subprocess. These comparisons can be displayed graphically, in ways that relate the estimated natural bounds to the objectives or as process capability indices, which summarize the relationship of the objectives to the natural bounds.

2. Monitor changes in quality and process-performance objectives and selected subprocess' process capability.
3. Identify and document subprocess capability deficiencies.
4. Determine and document actions needed to address subprocess capability deficiencies.

> Examples of actions that can be taken when a selected subprocess's performance does not satisfy its objectives include the following:
> - Changing quality and process-performance objectives so that they are within the subprocess' process capability
> - Improving the implementation of the existing subprocess so as to reduce its normal variability (reducing variability may bring the natural bounds within the objectives without having to move the mean)
> - Adopting new process elements and subprocesses and technologies that have the potential for satisfying the objectives and managing the associated risks
> - Identifying risks and risk mitigation strategies for each subprocess's process capability deficiency

Refer to the Project Monitoring and Control process area for more information about taking corrective action.

SP 2.4-1 RECORD STATISTICAL MANAGEMENT DATA

Record statistical and quality management data in the organization's measurement repository.

Refer to the Measurement and Analysis process area for more information about managing and storing data, measurement definitions, and results.

Refer to the Organizational Process Definition process area for more information about the organization's measurement repository.

Typical Work Products

1. Statistical and quality management data recorded in the organization's measurement repository

Generic Practices by Goal

GG 1 ACHIEVE SPECIFIC GOALS

The process supports and enables achievement of the specific goals of the process area by transforming identifiable input work products to produce identifiable output work products.

GP 1.1 PERFORM BASE PRACTICES

Perform the base practices of the quantitative project management process to develop work products and provide services to achieve the specific goals of the process area.

GG 2 INSTITUTIONALIZE A MANAGED PROCESS

The process is institutionalized as a managed process.

GG 3 INSTITUTIONALIZE A DEFINED PROCESS

The process is institutionalized as a defined process.

> AUTHORS' NOTE: This generic goal's appearance here reflects its location in the staged representation.

Commitment to Perform

GP 2.1 ESTABLISH AN ORGANIZATIONAL POLICY

Establish and maintain an organizational policy for planning and performing the quantitative project management process.

Elaboration

This policy establishes organizational expectations for quantitatively managing the project using quality and process-performance objectives, and statistically managing selected subprocesses within the project's defined process.

Ability to Perform

GP 2.2 PLAN THE PROCESS

Establish and maintain the plan for performing the quantitative project management process.

Elaboration

Typically, this plan for performing the quantitative project management process is included in (or referenced by) the project plan, which is described in the Project Planning process area.

GP 2.3 PROVIDE RESOURCES

Provide adequate resources for performing the quantitative project management process, developing the work products, and providing the services of the process.

Elaboration

Special expertise in statistics and statistical process control may be needed to define the techniques for statistical management of selected subprocesses, but staff will use the tools and techniques to perform the statistical management. Special expertise in statistics may also be needed for analyzing and interpreting the measures resulting from statistical management.

Examples of other resources provided include the following tools:
- System dynamics models
- Automated test-coverage analyzers
- Statistical process and quality control packages
- Statistical analysis packages

GP 2.4 ASSIGN RESPONSIBILITY

Assign responsibility and authority for performing the process, developing the work products, and providing the services of the quantitative project management process.

GP 2.5 TRAIN PEOPLE

Train the people performing or supporting the quantitative project management process as needed.

Elaboration

Examples of training topics include the following:
- Process modeling and analysis
- Process measurement data selection, definition, and collection

Directing Implementation

GP 2.6 MANAGE CONFIGURATIONS

Place designated work products of the quantitative project management process under appropriate levels of configuration management.

Elaboration

Examples of work products placed under configuration management include the following:

- Subprocesses to be included in the project's defined process
- Operational definitions of the measures, their collection points in the subprocesses, and how the integrity of the measures will be determined
- Collected measures

GP 2.7 IDENTIFY AND INVOLVE RELEVANT STAKEHOLDERS

Identify and involve the relevant stakeholders of the quantitative project management process as planned.

Elaboration

Examples of activities for stakeholder involvement include the following:

- Establishing project objectives
- Resolving issues among the project's quality and process-performance objectives
- Appraising performance of the selected subprocesses
- Identifying and managing the risks in achieving the project's quality and process-performance objectives
- Identifying what corrective action should be taken

GP 2.8 MONITOR AND CONTROL THE PROCESS

Monitor and control the quantitative project management process against the plan for performing the process and take appropriate corrective action.

Elaboration

Examples of measures used in monitoring and controlling include the following:

- Profile of subprocesses under statistical management (e.g., number planned to be under statistical management, number currently being statistically managed, and number that are statistically stable)
- Number of special causes of variation identified

Verifying Implementation

GP 2.9 OBJECTIVELY EVALUATE ADHERENCE

Objectively evaluate adherence of the quantitative project management process against its process description, standards, and procedures, and address noncompliance.

Elaboration

Examples of activities reviewed include the following:
- Quantitatively managing the project using quality and process-performance objectives
- Statistically managing selected subprocesses within the project's defined process

Examples of work products reviewed include the following:
- Subprocesses to be included in the project's defined process
- Operational definitions of the measures
- Collected measures

GP 2.10 REVIEW STATUS WITH HIGHER LEVEL MANAGEMENT

Review the activities, status, and results of the quantitative project management process with higher level management and resolve issues.

GG 3 INSTITUTIONALIZE A DEFINED PROCESS

The process is institutionalized as a defined process.

> AUTHORS' NOTE: This generic goal's appearance here reflects its location in the continuous representation.

C ONLY

Ability to Perform

GP 3.1 ESTABLISH A DEFINED PROCESS

Establish and maintain the description of a defined quantitative project management process.

Directing Implementation

GP 3.2 COLLECT IMPROVEMENT INFORMATION

Collect work products, measures, measurement results, and improvement information derived from planning and performing the quantitative project management process to support the future use and improvement of the organization's processes and process assets.

GG 4   *INSTITUTIONALIZE A QUANTITATIVELY MANAGED PROCESS*

The process is institutionalized as a quantitatively managed process.

GP 4.1   *ESTABLISH QUANTITATIVE OBJECTIVES FOR THE PROCESS*

Establish and maintain quantitative objectives for the quantitative project management process that address quality and process performance based on customer needs and business objectives.

GP 4.2   *STABILIZE SUBPROCESS PERFORMANCE*

Stabilize the performance of one or more subprocesses to determine the ability of the quantitative project management process to achieve the established quantitative quality and process-performance objectives.

GG 5   *INSTITUTIONALIZE AN OPTIMIZING PROCESS*

The process is institutionalized as an optimizing process.

GP 5.1   *ENSURE CONTINUOUS PROCESS IMPROVEMENT*

Ensure continuous improvement of the quantitative project management process in fulfilling the relevant business objectives of the organization.

GP 5.2   *CORRECT ROOT CAUSES OF PROBLEMS*

Identify and correct the root causes of defects and other problems in the quantitative project management process.

REQUIREMENTS DEVELOPMENT
An Engineering Process Area at Maturity Level 3

Purpose

The purpose of Requirements Development (RD) is to produce and analyze customer, product, and product-component requirements.

Introductory Notes

This process area describes three types of requirements: customer requirements, product requirements, and product-component requirements. Taken together, these requirements address the needs of relevant stakeholders, including those pertinent to various product life-cycle phases (e.g., acceptance testing criteria) and product attributes (e.g., safety, reliability, maintainability). Requirements also address constraints caused by the selection of design solutions (e.g., integration of commercial off-the-shelf products).

Requirements are the basis for design. The development of requirements includes the following activities:

- Elicitation, analysis, validation, and communication of customer needs, expectations, and constraints to obtain customer requirements that constitute an understanding of what will satisfy stakeholders
- Collection and coordination of stakeholder needs
- Development of the life-cycle requirements of the product
- Establishment of the customer requirements
- Establishment of initial product and product-component requirements consistent with customer requirements

This process area addresses all customer requirements rather than only product-level requirements because the customer may also provide specific design requirements.

Customer requirements are further refined into product and product-component requirements. In addition to customer requirements, product and product-component requirements are derived from the selected design solutions.

Requirements are identified and refined throughout the phases of the product life cycle. Design decisions, subsequent corrective actions, and feedback during each phase of the product's life cycle are analyzed for impact on derived and allocated requirements.

The Requirements Development process area includes three specific goals. The Develop Customer Requirements specific goal addresses defining a set of customer requirements to use in the development of product requirements. The Develop Product Requirements specific goal addresses defining a set of product or product-component requirements to use in the design of products and product components. The Analyze and Validate Requirements specific goal addresses the necessary analysis of customer, product, and product-component requirements to define, derive, and understand the requirements. The specific practices of the third specific goal are intended to assist the specific practices in the first two specific goals. The processes associated with the Requirements Development process area and those associated with the Technical Solution process area may interact recursively with one another.

Analyses are used to understand, define, and select the requirements at all levels from competing alternatives. These analyses include the following:

- Analysis of needs and requirements for each product life-cycle phase, including needs of relevant stakeholders, the operational environment, and factors that reflect overall customer and end-user expectations and satisfaction, such as safety, security, and affordability
- Development of an operational concept
- Definition of the required functionality

The definition of functionality, also referred to as "functional analysis," is not the same as structured analysis in software development and does not presume a functionally oriented software design. In object-oriented software design, it relates to defining the services. The definition of functions, their logical groupings, and their association with requirements is referred to as a "functional architecture."

Analyses occur recursively at successively more detailed layers of a product's architecture until sufficient detail is available to enable detailed design, acquisition, and testing of the product to proceed. As a result of the analysis of requirements and the operational concept (including functionality, support, maintenance, and disposal), the manufacturing or production concept produces more derived requirements, including consideration of the following:

- Constraints of various types
- Technological limitations
- Cost and cost drivers

Practice-to-Goal Relationship Table

Continuous Representation	**Staged Representation**
SG 1 Develop Customer Requirements	SG 1 Develop Customer Requirements
SP 1.1-1 Collect Stakeholder Needs	SP 1.1-2 Elicit Needs
SP 1.1-2 Elicit Needs	SP 1.2-1 Develop the Customer Requirements
SP 1.2-1 Develop the Customer Requirements	
SG 2 Develop Product Requirements	SG 2 Develop Product Requirements
SP 2.1-1 Establish Product and Product-Component Requirements	SP 2.1-1 Establish Product and Product-Component Requirements
SP 2.2-1 Allocate Product-Component Requirements	SP 2.2-1 Allocate Product-Component Requirements
SP 2.3-1 Identify Interface Requirements	SP 2.3-1 Identify Interface Requirements
SG 3 Analyze and Validate Requirements	SG 3 Analyze and Validate Requirements
SP 3.1-1 Establish Operational Concepts and Scenarios	SP 3.1-1 Establish Operational Concepts and Scenarios
SP 3.2-1 Establish a Definition of Required Functionality	SP 3.2-1 Establish a Definition of Required Functionality
SP 3.3-1 Analyze Requirements	SP 3.3-1 Analyze Requirements
SP 3.4-3 Analyze Requirements to Achieve Balance	SP 3.4-3 Analyze Requirements to Achieve Balance
SP 3.5-1 Validate Requirements	SP 3.5-2 Validate Requirements with Comprehensive Methods
SP 3.5-2 Validate Requirements with Comprehensive Methods	
GG 1 Achieve Specific Goals	
GP 1.1 Perform Base Practices	
GG 2 Institutionalize a Managed Process	GG 3 Institutionalize a Defined Process
GP 2.1 Establish an Organizational Policy	GP 2.1 Establish an Organizational Policy
GP 2.2 Plan the Process	GP 2.2 Plan the Process
GP 2.3 Provide Resources	GP 2.3 Provide Resources
GP 2.4 Assign Responsibility	GP 2.4 Assign Responsibility
GP 2.5 Train People	GP 2.5 Train People
GP 2.6 Manage Configurations	GP 2.6 Manage Configurations
GP 2.7 Identify and Involve Relevant Stakeholders	GP 2.7 Identify and Involve Relevant Stakeholders
GP 2.8 Monitor and Control the Process	GP 2.8 Monitor and Control the Process
GP 2.9 Objectively Evaluate Adherence	GP 2.9 Objectively Evaluate Adherence
GP 2.10 Review Status with Higher Level Management	GP 2.10 Review Status with Higher Level Management
GG 3 Institutionalize a Defined Process	
GP 3.1 Establish a Defined Process	GP 3.1 Establish a Defined Process
GP 3.2 Collect Improvement Information	GP 3.2 Collect Improvement Information
GG 4 Institutionalize a Quantitatively Managed Process	
GP 4.1 Establish Quantitative Objectives for the Process	
GP 4.2 Stabilize Subprocess Performance	
GG 5 Institutionalize an Optimizing Process	
GP 5.1 Ensure Continuous Process Improvement	
GP 5.2 Correct Root Causes of Problems	

RD

- Time constraints and schedule drivers
- Risks
- Consideration of issues implied but not explicitly stated by the customer or end user
- Factors introduced by the developer's unique business considerations, regulations, and laws

A hierarchy of logical entities (functions and subfunctions, object classes and subclasses) is established through iteration with the evolving operational concept. Requirements are refined, derived, and allocated to these logical entities. Requirements and logical entities are allocated to products, product components, people, associated processes, or services.

Involvement of relevant stakeholders in both requirements development and analysis gives them visibility into the evolution of requirements. This activity continually assures them that the requirements are being properly defined.

Related Process Areas

Refer to the Requirements Management process area for more information about managing customer and product requirements, obtaining agreement with the requirements provider, obtaining commitments with those implementing the requirements, and maintaining traceability.

Refer to the Technical Solution process area for more information about how the outputs of the requirements development processes are used, and the development of alternative solutions and designs used in refining and deriving requirements.

Refer to the Product Integration process area for more information about interface requirements and interface management.

Refer to the Verification process area for more information about verifying that the resulting product meets the requirements.

Refer to the Validation process area for more information about how the product built will be validated against the customer needs.

Refer to the Risk Management process area for more information about identifying and managing risks that are related to requirements.

Refer to the Configuration Management process area for information about ensuring that key work products are controlled and managed.

Specific Practices by Goal

SG 1 DEVELOP CUSTOMER REQUIREMENTS

Stakeholder needs, expectations, constraints, and interfaces are collected and translated into customer requirements.

The needs of stakeholders (e.g., customers, end users, suppliers, builders, and testers) are the basis for determining customer requirements. The stakeholder needs, expectations, constraints, interfaces, operational concepts, and product concepts are analyzed, harmonized, refined, and elaborated for translation into a set of customer requirements.

Frequently, stakeholder needs, expectations, constraints, and interfaces are poorly identified or conflicting. Since stakeholder needs, expectations, constraints, and limitations should be clearly identified and understood, an iterative process is used throughout the life of the project to accomplish this objective. To facilitate the required interaction, a surrogate for the end user or customer is frequently involved to represent their needs and help resolve conflicts. The customer relations or marketing part of the organization as well as members of the development team from disciplines such as human engineering or support can be used as surrogates. Environmental, legal, and other constraints should be considered when creating and resolving the set of customer requirements.

The following specific practice is subsumed in the staged representation by SP 1.1-2, Elicit Needs.

SP 1.1-1 *COLLECT STAKEHOLDER NEEDS*

Identify and collect stakeholder needs, expectations, constraints, and interfaces for all phases of the product life cycle.

This practice addresses the receipt of requirements that a customer provides to define what is needed or desired. These requirements may or may not be stated in technical terms. They should address the various product life-cycle activities and their impact on the product.

SP 1.1-2 *ELICIT NEEDS*

Elicit stakeholder needs, expectations, constraints, and interfaces for all phases of the product life cycle.

Eliciting goes beyond collecting requirements by proactively identifying additional requirements not explicitly provided by customers. Additional requirements should address the various product life-cycle activities and their impact on the product.

Examples of techniques to elicit needs include the following:
- Technology demonstrations
- Interface control working groups
- Technical control working groups
- Interim project reviews
- Questionnaires, interviews, and operational scenarios obtained from end users
- Operational walkthroughs and end-user task analysis
- Prototypes and models
- Brainstorming
- Quality Function Deployment
- Market surveys
- Beta testing
- Extraction from sources such as documents, standards, or specifications
- Observation of existing products, environments, and workflow patterns
- Use cases
- Business case analysis
- Reverse engineering (for legacy products)

Subpractices

1. Engage relevant stakeholders using methods for eliciting needs, expectations, constraints, and external interfaces.

SP 1.2-1   *DEVELOP THE CUSTOMER REQUIREMENTS*

Transform stakeholder needs, expectations, constraints, and interfaces into customer requirements.

> **FOR INTEGRATED PRODUCT AND PROCESS DEVELOPMENT**
> Relevant stakeholders representing all phases of the product's life cycle should include business as well as technical functions. In this way, concepts for all product-related life-cycle processes are considered concurrently with the concepts for the products. Customer requirements result from informed decisions on the business as well as technical effects of their requirements.

The various inputs from the customer must be consolidated, missing information must be obtained, and conflicts must be resolved in documenting the recognized set of customer requirements. The customer requirements may include needs, expectations, and constraints with regard to verification and validation.

Typical Work Products

1. Customer requirements
2. Customer constraints on the conduct of verification
3. Customer constraints on the conduct of validation

Subpractices

1. Translate the stakeholder needs, expectations, constraints, and interfaces into documented customer requirements.
2. Define constraints for verification and validation.

SG 2 DEVELOP PRODUCT REQUIREMENTS

Customer requirements are refined and elaborated to develop product and product-component requirements.

Customer requirements are analyzed in conjunction with the development of the operational concept to derive more detailed and precise sets of requirements called "product and product-component requirements." Product and product-component requirements address the needs associated with each product life-cycle phase. Derived requirements arise from constraints, consideration of issues implied but not explicitly stated in the customer requirements baseline, and factors introduced by the selected architecture, the design, and the developer's unique business considerations. The requirements are reexamined with each successive, lower level set of requirements and functional architecture, and the preferred product concept is refined.

The requirements are allocated to product functions and product components including objects, people, and processes. The traceability of requirements to functions, objects, tests, issues, or other entities is documented. The allocated requirements and functions are the basis for the synthesis of the technical solution. As internal components are developed, additional interfaces are defined and interface requirements are established.

Refer to the Maintain Bidirectional Traceability of Requirements specific practice of the Requirements Management process area for more information about maintaining bidirectional traceability.

SP 2.1-1 ESTABLISH PRODUCT AND PRODUCT-COMPONENT REQUIREMENTS

Establish and maintain product and product-component requirements, which are based on the customer requirements.

The customer requirements may be expressed in the customer's terms and may be nontechnical descriptions. The product requirements are the expression of these requirements in technical terms that can be used for design decisions. An example of this translation is found in the first House of Quality Functional Deployment, which maps customer desires into technical parameters. For instance, "solid sounding door" might be mapped to size, weight, fit, dampening, and resonant frequencies.

Product and product-component requirements address the satisfaction of customer, business, and project objectives and associated attributes, such as effectiveness and affordability.

Design constraints include specifications on product components that are derived from design decisions rather than higher level requirements.

> **FOR SOFTWARE ENGINEERING**
> For example, application components that must interface with an off-the-shelf database component must comply with interface requirements imposed by the selected database. Such product-component requirements are generally not traceable to higher level requirements.

Derived requirements also address the cost and performance of other life-cycle phases (e.g., production, operations, and disposal) to the extent compatible with business objectives.

The modification of requirements due to approved requirement changes is covered by the "maintain" function of this specific practice; whereas, the administration of requirement changes is covered by the Requirements Management process area.

Refer to the Requirements Management process area for more information about managing changes to requirements.

Typical Work Products

1. Derived requirements
2. Product requirements
3. Product-component requirements

Subpractices

1. Develop requirements in technical terms necessary for product and product-component design.

   Develop architecture requirements addressing critical product qualities and performance necessary for product architecture design.

2. Derive requirements that result from design decisions.

   Refer to the Technical Solution process area for more information about developing the solutions that generate additional derived requirements.

   Selection of a technology brings with it additional requirements. For instance, use of electronics requires additional technology-specific requirements such as electromagnetic interference limits.

3. Establish and maintain relationships between requirements for consideration during change management and requirements allocation.

   Refer to the Requirements Management process area for more information about maintaining requirements traceability.

   Relationships between requirements can aid in evaluating the impact of changes.

SP 2.2-1 ALLOCATE PRODUCT-COMPONENT REQUIREMENTS

Allocate the requirements for each product component.

Refer to the Technical Solution process area for more information about allocation of requirements to products and product components. This specific practice provides information for defining the allocation of requirements but must interact with the specific practices in the Technical Solution process area to establish solutions to which the requirements are allocated.

The requirements for product components of the defined solution include allocation of product performance; design constraints; and fit, form, and function to meet requirements and facilitate production. In cases where a higher level requirement specifies performance that will be the responsibility of two or more product components, the performance must be partitioned for unique allocation to each product component as a derived requirement.

Typical Work Products

1. Requirement allocation sheets
2. Provisional requirement allocations
3. Design constraints
4. Derived requirements
5. Relationships among derived requirements

Subpractices

1. Allocate requirements to functions.
2. Allocate requirements to product components.

3. Allocate design constraints to product components.

4. Document relationships among allocated requirements.

> Relationships include dependencies in which a change in one requirement may affect other requirements.

SP 2.3-1 *IDENTIFY INTERFACE REQUIREMENTS*

Identify interface requirements.

Interfaces between functions (or between objects) are identified. Functional interfaces may drive the development of alternative solutions described in the Technical Solution process area.

Refer to the Product Integration process area for more information about the management of interfaces and the integration of products and product components.

Interface requirements between products or product components identified in the product architecture are defined. They are controlled as part of product and product-component integration and are an integral part of the architecture definition.

Typical Work Products

1. Interface requirements

Subpractices

1. Identify interfaces both external to the product and internal to the product (i.e., between functional partitions or objects).

   As the design progresses, the product architecture will be altered by technical solution processes, creating new interfaces between product components and components external to the product.

   Interfaces with product-related life-cycle processes should also be identified.

> Examples of these interfaces include interfaces with test equipment, transportation systems, support systems, and manufacturing facilities.

2. Develop the requirements for the identified interfaces.

   Refer to the Technical Solution process area for more information about generating new interfaces during the design process.

   Requirements for interfaces are defined in terms of origination, destination, stimulus, data characteristics for software, and electrical and mechanical characteristics for hardware.

SG 3 ANALYZE AND VALIDATE REQUIREMENTS

The requirements are analyzed and validated, and a definition of required functionality is developed.

The specific practices of the Analyze and Validate Requirements specific goal support the development of the requirements in both the Develop Customer Requirements specific goal and the Develop Product Requirements specific goal. The specific practices associated with this specific goal cover analyzing and validating the requirements with respect to the user's intended environment.

Analyses are performed to determine what impact the intended operational environment will have on the ability to satisfy the stakeholders' needs, expectations, constraints, and interfaces. Considerations, such as feasibility, mission needs, cost constraints, potential market size, and acquisition strategy, must all be taken into account, depending on the product context. A definition of required functionality is also established. All specified usage modes for the product are considered, and a timeline analysis is generated for time-critical sequencing of functions.

The objectives of the analyses are to determine candidate requirements for product concepts that will satisfy stakeholder needs, expectations, and constraints; and then to translate these concepts into requirements. In parallel with this activity, the parameters that will be used to evaluate the effectiveness of the product are determined based on customer input and the preliminary product concept.

Requirements are validated to increase the probability that the resulting product will perform as intended in the use environment.

SP 3.1-1 ESTABLISH OPERATIONAL CONCEPTS AND SCENARIOS

Establish and maintain operational concepts and associated scenarios.

Refer to the Technical Solution process area for more information about detailed development of operational concepts that are dependent on the selected designs.

A scenario is a sequence of events that might occur in the use of the product, which is used to make explicit some of the needs of the stakeholders. In contrast, an operational concept for a product usually depends on both the design solution and the scenario. For example, the operational concept for a satellite-based communications product is quite different from one based on landlines. Since the alternative solutions have not usually been defined when preparing the initial operational concepts, conceptual solutions are developed for use when analyzing the requirements. The operational concepts are refined as solution decisions are made and lower level detailed requirements are developed.

Just as a design decision for a product may become a requirement for product components, the operational concept may become the scenarios (requirements) for product components.

The scenarios may include operational sequences, provided those sequences are an expression of customer requirements rather than operational concepts.

Typical Work Products

1. Operational concept
2. Product installation, operational, maintenance, and support concepts
3. Disposal concepts
4. Use cases
5. Timeline scenarios
6. New requirements

Subpractices

1. Develop operational concepts and scenarios that include functionality, performance, maintenance, support, and disposal as appropriate.

   Identify and develop scenarios, consistent with the level of detail in the stakeholder needs, expectations, and constraints in which the proposed product is expected to operate.

2. Define the environment the product will operate in, including boundaries and constraints.

3. Review operational concepts and scenarios to refine and discover requirements.

   Operational concept and scenario development is an iterative process. The reviews should be held periodically to ensure that they agree with the requirements. The review may be in the form of a walkthrough.

4. Develop a detailed operational concept, as products and product components are selected, that defines the interaction of the product, the end user, and the environment, and that satisfies the operational, maintenance, support, and disposal needs.

SP 3.2-1   *ESTABLISH A DEFINITION OF REQUIRED FUNCTIONALITY*

Establish and maintain a definition of required functionality.

The definition of functionality, also referred to as "functional analysis," is the description of what the product is intended to do. The definition of functionality can include actions, sequence, inputs, outputs, or other information that communicates the manner in which the product will be used.

Functional analysis is not the same as structured analysis in software development and does not presume a functionally oriented software design. In object-oriented software design, it relates to defining the services. The definition of functions, their logical groupings, and their association with requirements is referred to as a functional architecture. (See the definition of "functional architecture" in the glossary.)

Typical Work Products

1. Functional architecture
2. Activity diagrams and use cases
3. Object-oriented analysis with services identified

Subpractices

1. Analyze and quantify functionality required by end users.
2. Analyze requirements to identify logical or functional partitions (e.g., subfunctions).
3. Partition requirements into groups, based on established criteria (e.g., similar functionality, performance, or coupling), to facilitate and focus the requirements analysis.
4. Consider the sequencing of time-critical functions both initially and subsequently during product-component development.
5. Allocate customer requirements to functional partitions, objects, people, or support elements to support the synthesis of solutions.
6. Allocate functional and performance requirements to functions and subfunctions.

SP 3.3-1 ANALYZE REQUIREMENTS

Analyze requirements to ensure that they are necessary and sufficient.

In light of the operational concept and scenarios, the requirements for one level of the product hierarchy are analyzed to determine whether they are necessary and sufficient to meet the objectives of higher levels of the product hierarchy. The analyzed requirements then provide the basis for more detailed and precise requirements for lower levels of the product hierarchy.

As requirements are defined, their relationship to higher level requirements and the higher level defined functionality must be understood. One of the other actions is the determination of which key requirements will be used to track technical progress. For instance, the weight of a product or size of a software product may be monitored through development based on its risk.

Typical Work Products

1. Requirements defects reports
2. Proposed requirements changes to resolve defects
3. Key requirements
4. Technical performance measures

Subpractices

1. Analyze stakeholder needs, expectations, constraints, and external interfaces to remove conflicts and to organize into related subjects.
2. Analyze requirements to determine whether they satisfy the objectives of higher level requirements.
3. Analyze requirements to ensure that they are complete, feasible, realizable, and verifiable.

   While design determines the feasibility of a particular solution, this subpractice addresses knowing which requirements affect feasibility.
4. Identify key requirements that have a strong influence on cost, schedule, functionality, risk, or performance.
5. Identify technical performance measures that will be tracked during the development effort.

   Refer to the Measurement and Analysis process area for more information about the use of measurements.
6. Analyze operational concepts and scenarios to refine the customer needs, constraints, and interfaces and to discover new requirements.

   This analysis may result in more detailed operational concepts and scenarios as well as supporting the derivation of new requirements.

SP 3.4-3 ANALYZE REQUIREMENTS TO ACHIEVE BALANCE

Analyze requirements to balance stakeholder needs and constraints.

Stakeholder needs and constraints can address cost, schedule, performance, functionality, reusable components, maintainability, or risk.

Typical Work Products

1. Assessment of risks related to requirements

Subpractices

1. Use proven models, simulations, and prototyping to analyze the balance of stakeholder needs and constraints.

   Results of the analyses can be used to reduce the cost of the product and the risk in developing the product.

2. Perform a risk assessment on the requirements and functional architecture.

   Refer to the Risk Management process area for information about performing a risk assessment on customer and product requirements and the functional architecture.

3. Examine product life-cycle concepts for impacts of requirements on risks.

The following specific practice is subsumed in the staged representation by SP 3.5-2, Validate Requirements with Comprehensive Methods.

SP 3.5-1 *VALIDATE REQUIREMENTS*

Validate requirements to ensure the resulting product will perform appropriately in its intended-use environment.

Typical Work Products

1. Results of requirements validation

Subpractices

1. Analyze the requirements to determine the risk that the resulting product will not perform appropriately in its intended-use environment.

SP 3.5-2 *VALIDATE REQUIREMENTS WITH COMPREHENSIVE METHODS*

Validate requirements to ensure the resulting product will perform as intended in the user's environment using multiple techniques as appropriate.

Requirements validation is performed early in the development effort to gain confidence that the requirements are capable of guiding a development that results in successful final validation. This activity should be integrated with risk management activities. Mature organizations will typically perform requirements validation in a more sophisticated way and will broaden the basis of the validation to include other stakeholder needs and expectations. These organizations will typically perform analyses, simulations, or prototypes to ensure that requirements will satisfy stakeholder needs and expectations.

Typical Work Products

1. Record of analysis methods and results

Subpractices

1. Analyze the requirements to determine the risk that the resulting product will not perform appropriately in its intended-use environment.
2. Explore the adequacy and completeness of requirements by developing product representations (e.g., prototypes, simulations, models, scenarios, and storyboards) and by obtaining feedback about them from relevant stakeholders.
3. Assess the design as it matures in the context of the requirements validation environment to identify validation issues and expose unstated needs and customer requirements.

Generic Practices by Goal

GG 1 *ACHIEVE SPECIFIC GOALS*

The process supports and enables achievement of the specific goals of the process area by transforming identifiable input work products to produce identifiable output work products.

GP 1.1 *PERFORM BASE PRACTICES*

Perform the base practices of the requirements development process to develop work products and provide services to achieve the specific goals of the process area.

GG 2 *INSTITUTIONALIZE A MANAGED PROCESS*

The process is institutionalized as a managed process.

GG 3 *INSTITUTIONALIZE A DEFINED PROCESS*

The process is institutionalized as a defined process.

> AUTHORS' NOTE: This generic goal's appearance here reflects its location in the staged representation.

CONTINUOUS ONLY

STAGED ONLY

Commitment to Perform

GP 2.1 *ESTABLISH AN ORGANIZATIONAL POLICY*

Establish and maintain an organizational policy for planning and performing the requirements development process.

Elaboration

This policy establishes organizational expectations for collecting stakeholder needs, formulating product and product-component requirements, and analyzing and validating those requirements.

Ability to Perform

GP 2.2 PLAN THE PROCESS

Establish and maintain the plan for performing the requirements development process.

Elaboration

Typically, this plan for performing the requirements development process is a part of the project plan as described in the Project Planning process area.

GP 2.3 PROVIDE RESOURCES

Provide adequate resources for performing the requirements development process, developing the work products, and providing the services of the process.

Elaboration

Special expertise in the application domain, methods for eliciting stakeholder needs, and methods and tools for specifying and analyzing customer, product, and product-component requirements may be required.

> Examples of other resources provided include the following tools:
> - Requirements specification tools
> - Simulators and modeling tools
> - Prototyping tools
> - Scenario definition and management tools
> - Requirements tracking tools

GP 2.4 ASSIGN RESPONSIBILITY

Assign responsibility and authority for performing the process, developing the work products, and providing the services of the requirements development process.

GP 2.5 TRAIN PEOPLE

Train the people performing or supporting the requirements development process as needed.

Elaboration

> Examples of training topics include the following:
> - Application domain
> - Requirements definition and analysis
> - Requirements elicitation
> - Requirements specification and modeling
> - Requirements tracking

Directing Implementation

GP 2.6 MANAGE CONFIGURATIONS

Place designated work products of the requirements development process under appropriate levels of configuration management.

Elaboration

> Examples of work products placed under configuration management include the following:
> - Customer requirements
> - Functional architecture
> - Product and product-component requirements
> - Interface requirements

GP 2.7 IDENTIFY AND INVOLVE RELEVANT STAKEHOLDERS

Identify and involve the relevant stakeholders of the requirements development process as planned.

Elaboration

Select relevant stakeholders from customers, end users, developers, producers, testers, suppliers, marketers, maintainers, disposal personnel, and others who may be affected by, or may affect, the product as well as the process.

> Examples of activities for stakeholder involvement include the following:
> - Reviewing the adequacy of requirements in meeting needs, expectations, constraints, and interfaces
> - Establishing operational concepts and scenarios
> - Assessing the adequacy of requirements
> - Establishing product and product-component requirements
> - Assessing product cost, schedule, and risk

GP 2.8 MONITOR AND CONTROL THE PROCESS

Monitor and control the requirements development process against the plan for performing the process and take appropriate corrective action.

Elaboration

> Examples of measures used in monitoring and controlling include the following:
> - Cost, schedule, and effort expended for rework
> - Defect density of requirements specifications

Verifying Implementation

GP 2.9 OBJECTIVELY EVALUATE ADHERENCE

Objectively evaluate adherence of the requirements development process against its process description, standards, and procedures, and address noncompliance.

Elaboration

> Examples of activities reviewed include the following:
> - Collecting stakeholder needs
> - Formulating product and product-component requirements
> - Analyzing and validating product and product-component requirements

> Examples of work products reviewed include the following:
> - Product requirements
> - Product-component requirements
> - Interface requirements
> - Functional architecture

GP 2.10 REVIEW STATUS WITH HIGHER LEVEL MANAGEMENT

Review the activities, status, and results of the requirements development process with higher level management and resolve issues.

GG 3 INSTITUTIONALIZE A DEFINED PROCESS

The process is institutionalized as a defined process.

> AUTHORS' NOTE: This generic goal's appearance here reflects its location in the continuous representation.

C ONLY

Ability to Perform

> *GP 3.1* ESTABLISH A DEFINED PROCESS
>
> *Establish and maintain the description of a defined requirements development process.*

Directing Implementation

> *GP 3.2* COLLECT IMPROVEMENT INFORMATION
>
> *Collect work products, measures, measurement results, and improvement information derived from planning and performing the requirements development process to support the future use and improvement of the organization's processes and process assets.*

GG 4 INSTITUTIONALIZE A QUANTITATIVELY MANAGED PROCESS

The process is institutionalized as a quantitatively managed process.

> *GP 4.1* ESTABLISH QUANTITATIVE OBJECTIVES FOR THE PROCESS
>
> *Establish and maintain quantitative objectives for the requirements development process that address quality and process performance based on customer needs and business objectives.*

> *GP 4.2* STABILIZE SUBPROCESS PERFORMANCE
>
> *Stabilize the performance of one or more subprocesses to determine the ability of the requirements development process to achieve the established quantitative quality and process-performance objectives.*

GG 5 INSTITUTIONALIZE AN OPTIMIZING PROCESS

The process is institutionalized as an optimizing process.

> *GP 5.1* ENSURE CONTINUOUS PROCESS IMPROVEMENT
>
> *Ensure continuous improvement of the requirements development process in fulfilling the relevant business objectives of the organization.*

> *GP 5.2* CORRECT ROOT CAUSES OF PROBLEMS
>
> *Identify and correct the root causes of defects and other problems in the requirements development process.*

CONTINUOUS ONLY

REQUIREMENTS MANAGEMENT
An Engineering Process Area at Maturity Level 2

Purpose

The purpose of Requirements Management (REQM) is to manage the requirements of the project's products and product components and to identify inconsistencies between those requirements and the project's plans and work products.

Introductory Notes

Requirements management processes manage all requirements received or generated by the project, including both technical and nontechnical requirements as well as those requirements levied on the project by the organization. In particular, if the Requirements Development process area is implemented, its processes will generate product and product-component requirements that will also be managed by the requirements management processes. When the Requirements Management, Requirements Development, and Technical Solution process areas are all implemented, their associated processes may be closely tied and be performed concurrently.

The project takes appropriate steps to ensure that the agreed-on set of requirements is managed to support the planning and execution needs of the project. When a project receives requirements from an approved requirements provider, the requirements are reviewed with the requirements provider to resolve issues and prevent misunderstanding before the requirements are incorporated into the project's plans. Once the requirements provider and the requirements receiver reach an agreement, commitment to the requirements is obtained from the project participants. The project manages changes to the requirements as they evolve and identifies any inconsistencies that occur among the plans, work products, and requirements.

Part of the management of requirements is to document requirements changes and rationale and to maintain bidirectional traceability between source requirements and all product and product-component requirements.

Related Process Areas

Refer to the Requirements Development process area for more information about transforming stakeholder needs into product requirements and deciding how to allocate or distribute requirements among the product components.

Refer to the Technical Solution process area for more information about transforming requirements into technical solutions.

Refer to the Project Planning process area for more information about how project plans reflect requirements and need to be revised as requirements change.

Refer to the Configuration Management process area for more information about baselines and controlling changes to configuration documentation for requirements.

Refer to the Project Monitoring and Control process area for more information about tracking and controlling the activities and work products that are based on the requirements and taking appropriate corrective action.

Refer to the Risk Management process area for more information about identifying and handling risks associated with requirements.

Specific Practices by Goal

SG 1   MANAGE REQUIREMENTS

Requirements are managed and inconsistencies with project plans and work products are identified.

The project maintains a current and approved set of requirements over the life of the project by doing the following:

- Managing all changes to the requirements
- Maintaining the relationships among the requirements, the project plans, and the work products
- Identifying inconsistencies among the requirements, the project plans, and the work products
- Taking corrective action

Refer to the Technical Solution process area for more information about determining the feasibility of the requirements.

Refer to the Requirements Development process area for more information about ensuring that the requirements reflect the needs and expectations of the customer.

Refer to the Project Monitoring and Control process area for more information about taking corrective action.

Practice-to-Goal Relationship Table

Continuous Representation	*Staged Representation*
SG 1 Manage Requirements	SG 1 Manage Requirements
SP 1.1-1 Obtain an Understanding of Requirements	SP 1.1-1 Obtain an Understanding of Requirements
SP 1.2-2 Obtain Commitment to Requirements	SP 1.2-2 Obtain Commitment to Requirements
SP 1.3-1 Manage Requirements Changes	SP 1.3-1 Manage Requirements Changes
SP 1.4-2 Maintain Bidirectional Traceability of Requirements	SP 1.4-2 Maintain Bidirectional Traceability of Requirements
SP 1.5-1 Identify Inconsistencies between Project Work and Requirements	SP 1.5-1 Identify Inconsistencies between Project Work and Requirements

REQM

Continuous Representation	Staged Representation
GG 1 Achieve Specific Goals	
GP 1.1 Perform Base Practices	
GG 2 Institutionalize a Managed Process	GG 2 Institutionalize a Managed Process
GP 2.1 Establish an Organizational Policy	GP 2.1 Establish an Organizational Policy
GP 2.2 Plan the Process	GP 2.2 Plan the Process
GP 2.3 Provide Resources	GP 2.3 Provide Resources
GP 2.4 Assign Responsibility	GP 2.4 Assign Responsibility
GP 2.5 Train People	GP 2.5 Train People
GP 2.6 Manage Configurations	GP 2.6 Manage Configurations
GP 2.7 Identify and Involve Relevant Stakeholders	GP 2.7 Identify and Involve Relevant Stakeholders
GP 2.8 Monitor and Control the Process	GP 2.8 Monitor and Control the Process
GP 2.9 Objectively Evaluate Adherence	GP 2.9 Objectively Evaluate Adherence
GP 2.10 Review Status with Higher Level Management	GP 2.10 Review Status with Higher Level Management
GG 3 Institutionalize a Defined Process	GG 3 Institutionalize a Defined Process
GP 3.1 Establish a Defined Process	GP 3.1 Establish a Defined Process
GP 3.2 Collect Improvement Information	GP 3.2 Collect Improvement Information
GG 4 Institutionalize a Quantitatively Managed Process	
GP 4.1 Establish Quantitative Objectives for the Process	
GP 4.2 Stabilize Subprocess Performance	
GG 5 Institutionalize an Optimizing Process	
GP 5.1 Ensure Continuous Process Improvement	
GP 5.2 Correct Root Causes of Problems	

C/ML 3–5

> **FOR SOFTWARE ENGINEERING**
>
> The requirements may be a subset of the overall product requirements, or they may constitute the entire product requirements.

> **FOR SYSTEMS ENGINEERING**
>
> Each level of product-component design (e.g., segment, subsystem) receives the requirements from the higher level.

SP 1.1-1   OBTAIN AN UNDERSTANDING OF REQUIREMENTS

Develop an understanding with the requirements providers on the meaning of the requirements.

As the project matures and requirements are derived, all activities or disciplines will receive requirements. To avoid requirements creep, criteria are established to designate appropriate channels, or official sources, from which to receive requirements. The receiving activities conduct analyses of the requirements with the requirements provider to ensure that a compatible, shared understanding is reached on the meaning of the requirements. The result of this analysis and dialog is an agreed-to set of requirements.

Typical Work Products

1. Lists of criteria for distinguishing appropriate requirements providers
2. Criteria for evaluation and acceptance of requirements
3. Results of analyses against criteria
4. An agreed-to set of requirements

Subpractices

1. Establish criteria for distinguishing appropriate requirements providers.
2. Establish objective criteria for the acceptance of requirements.

   Lack of acceptance criteria often results in inadequate verification, costly rework, or customer rejection.

> Examples of acceptance criteria include the following:
> - Clearly and properly stated
> - Complete
> - Consistent with each other
> - Uniquely identified
> - Appropriate to implement
> - Verifiable (testable)
> - Traceable

3. Analyze requirements to ensure that the established criteria are met.

4. Reach an understanding of the requirements with the requirements provider so that the project participants can commit to them.

SP 1.2-2　OBTAIN COMMITMENT TO REQUIREMENTS

Obtain commitment to the requirements from the project participants.

Refer to the Project Monitoring and Control process area for more information about monitoring the commitments made.

> **FOR INTEGRATED PRODUCT AND PROCESS DEVELOPMENT**
> When integrated teams are formed, the project participants are the integrated teams and their members. Commitment to the requirement for interacting with other integrated teams is as important for each integrated team as its commitments to product and other project requirements.

Whereas the previous specific practice dealt with reaching an understanding with the requirements providers, this specific practice deals with agreements and commitments among those who have to carry out the activities necessary to implement the requirements. Requirements evolve throughout the project, especially as described by the specific practices of the Requirements Development process area and the Technical Solution process area. As the requirements evolve, this specific practice ensures that project participants commit to the current, approved requirements and the resulting changes in project plans, activities, and work products.

Typical Work Products

1. Requirements impact assessments
2. Documented commitments to requirements and requirements changes

Subpractices

1. Assess the impact of requirements on existing commitments.

    The impact on the project participants should be evaluated when the requirements change or at the start of a new requirement.

2. Negotiate and record commitments.

    Changes to existing commitments should be negotiated before project participants commit to the requirement or requirement change.

SP 1.3-1 MANAGE REQUIREMENTS CHANGES

Manage changes to the requirements as they evolve during the project.

Refer to the Configuration Management process area for more information about maintaining and controlling the requirements baseline and on making the requirements and change data available to the project.

During the project, requirements change for a variety of reasons. As needs change and as work proceeds, additional requirements are derived and changes may have to be made to the existing requirements. It is essential to manage these additions and changes efficiently and effectively. To effectively analyze the impact of the changes, it is necessary that the source of each requirement is known and the rationale for any change is documented. The project manager may, however, want to track appropriate measures of requirements volatility to judge whether new or revised controls are necessary.

Typical Work Products

1. Requirements status
2. Requirements database
3. Requirements decision database

Subpractices

1. Capture all requirements and requirements changes that are given to or generated by the project.
2. Maintain the requirements change history with the rationale for the changes.
   Maintaining the change history helps track requirements volatility.
3. Evaluate the impact of requirement changes from the standpoint of relevant stakeholders.
4. Make the requirements and change data available to the project.

SP 1.4-2 MAINTAIN BIDIRECTIONAL TRACEABILITY OF REQUIREMENTS

Maintain bidirectional traceability among the requirements and the project plans and work products.

The intent of this specific practice is to maintain the bidirectional traceability of requirements for each level of product decomposition. When the requirements are managed well, traceability can be established from the source requirement to its lower level requirements and from the lower level requirements back to their source. Such bidirectional traceability helps determine that all source requirements have been completely addressed and that all lower level requirements can be traced to a valid source. Requirements traceability can also cover the relationships to other entities such as intermediate and final work products, changes in design documentation, test plans, and work tasks. The traceability should cover both the horizontal and vertical relationships, such as across interfaces. Traceability is particularly needed in conducting the impact assessment of requirements changes on the project plans, activities, and work products.

Typical Work Products

1. Requirements traceability matrix
2. Requirements tracking system

Subpractices

1. Maintain requirements traceability to ensure that the source of lower level (derived) requirements is documented.
2. Maintain requirements traceability from a requirement to its derived requirements and allocation to functions, objects, people, processes, and work products.
3. Maintain horizontal traceability from function to function and across interfaces.
4. Generate the requirements traceability matrix.

SP 1.5-1 IDENTIFY INCONSISTENCIES BETWEEN PROJECT WORK AND REQUIREMENTS

Identify inconsistencies between the project plans and work products and the requirements.

Refer to the Project Monitoring and Control process area for more information about monitoring and controlling the project plans and work products for consistency with requirements and taking corrective actions when necessary.

This specific practice finds the inconsistencies between the requirements and the project plans and work products and initiates the corrective action to fix them.

Typical Work Products

1. Documentation of inconsistencies including sources, conditions, and rationale
2. Corrective actions

Subpractices

1. Review the project's plans, activities, and work products for consistency with the requirements and the changes made to them.
2. Identify the source of the inconsistency and the rationale.

3. Identify changes that need to be made to the plans and work products resulting from changes to the requirements baseline.

4. Initiate corrective actions.

Generic Practices by Goal

GG 1 *ACHIEVE SPECIFIC GOALS*

The process supports and enables achievement of the specific goals of the process area by transforming identifiable input work products to produce identifiable output work products.

GP 1.1 *PERFORM BASE PRACTICES*

Perform the base practices of the requirements management process to develop work products and provide services to achieve the specific goals of the process area.

CONTINUOUS ONLY

GG 2 *INSTITUTIONALIZE A MANAGED PROCESS*

The process is institutionalized as a managed process.

Commitment to Perform

GP 2.1 *ESTABLISH AN ORGANIZATIONAL POLICY*

Establish and maintain an organizational policy for planning and performing the requirements management process.

Elaboration
This policy establishes organizational expectations for managing requirements and identifying inconsistencies between the requirements and the project plans and work products.

Ability to Perform

GP 2.2 *PLAN THE PROCESS*

Establish and maintain the plan for performing the requirements management process.

Elaboration
Typically, this plan for performing the requirements management process is a part of the project plan as described in the Project Planning process area.

GP 2.3 PROVIDE RESOURCES

Provide adequate resources for performing the requirements management process, developing the work products, and providing the services of the process.

Elaboration

> Examples of resources provided include the following tools:
> * Requirements tracking tools
> * Traceability tools

GP 2.4 ASSIGN RESPONSIBILITY

Assign responsibility and authority for performing the process, developing the work products, and providing the services of the requirements management process.

GP 2.5 TRAIN PEOPLE

Train the people performing or supporting the requirements management process as needed.

Elaboration

> Examples of training topics include the following:
> * Application domain
> * Requirements definition, analysis, review, and management
> * Requirements management tools
> * Configuration management
> * Negotiation and conflict resolution

Directing Implementation

GP 2.6 MANAGE CONFIGURATIONS

Place designated work products of the requirements management process under appropriate levels of configuration management.

Elaboration

> Examples of work products placed under configuration management include the following:
> * Requirements
> * Requirements traceability matrix

GP 2.7 *IDENTIFY AND INVOLVE RELEVANT STAKEHOLDERS*

Identify and involve the relevant stakeholders of the requirements management process as planned.

Elaboration

Select relevant stakeholders from customers, end users, developers, producers, testers, suppliers, marketers, maintainers, disposal personnel, and others who may be affected by, or may affect, the product as well as the process.

Examples of activities for stakeholder involvement include:
- Resolving issues on the understanding of the requirements
- Assessing the impact of requirements changes
- Communicating the bidirectional traceability
- Identifying inconsistencies among project plans, work products, and requirements

---

GP 2.8 *MONITOR AND CONTROL THE PROCESS*

Monitor and control the requirements management process against the plan for performing the process and take appropriate corrective action.

Elaboration

Examples of measures used in monitoring and controlling include the following:
- Requirements volatility (percentage of requirements changed)

Verifying Implementation

GP 2.9 *OBJECTIVELY EVALUATE ADHERENCE*

Objectively evaluate adherence of the requirements management process against its process description, standards, and procedures, and address noncompliance.

Elaboration

Examples of activities reviewed include the following:
- Managing requirements
- Identifying inconsistencies among project plans, work products, and requirements

---

Examples of work products reviewed include the following:
- Requirements
- Requirements traceability matrix

GP 2.10 REVIEW STATUS WITH HIGHER LEVEL MANAGEMENT

Review the activities, status, and results of the requirements management process with higher level management and resolve issues.

Elaboration

Proposed changes to commitments to be made external to the organization are reviewed with higher level management to ensure that all commitments can be accomplished.

AUTHORS' NOTE: GG3 and its practices do not apply for a maturity level 2 rating, but do apply for a maturity level 3 rating and above.

S ONLY

GG 3 INSTITUTIONALIZE A DEFINED PROCESS

The process is institutionalized as a defined process.

Ability to Perform

GP 3.1 ESTABLISH A DEFINED PROCESS

Establish and maintain the description of a defined requirements management process.

Directing Implementation

GP 3.2 COLLECT IMPROVEMENT INFORMATION

Collect work products, measures, measurement results, and improvement information derived from planning and performing the requirements management process to support the future use and improvement of the organization's processes and process assets.

CONTINUOUS/MATURITY LEVELS 3–5

GG 4 INSTITUTIONALIZE A QUANTITATIVELY MANAGED PROCESS

The process is institutionalized as a quantitatively managed process.

GP 4.1 ESTABLISH QUANTITATIVE OBJECTIVES FOR THE PROCESS

Establish and maintain quantitative objectives for the requirements management process that address quality and process performance based on customer needs and business objectives.

GP 4.2 STABILIZE SUBPROCESS PERFORMANCE

Stabilize the performance of one or more subprocesses to determine the ability of the requirements management process to achieve the established quantitative quality and process-performance objectives.

CONTINUOUS ONLY

GG 5   INSTITUTIONALIZE AN OPTIMIZING PROCESS

The process is institutionalized as an optimizing process.

GP 5.1   ENSURE CONTINUOUS PROCESS IMPROVEMENT

Ensure continuous improvement of the requirements management process in fulfilling the relevant business objectives of the organization.

GP 5.2   CORRECT ROOT CAUSES OF PROBLEMS

Identify and correct the root causes of defects and other problems in the requirements management process.

CONTINUOUS ONLY

RISK MANAGEMENT
A Project Management Process Area at Maturity Level 3

Purpose

The purpose of Risk Management (RSKM) is to identify potential problems before they occur so that risk-handling activities can be planned and invoked as needed across the life of the product or project to mitigate adverse impacts on achieving objectives.

Introductory Notes

Risk management is a continuous, forward-looking process that is an important part of the business and technical management processes. Risk management should address issues that could endanger achievement of critical objectives. A continuous risk management approach is applied to effectively anticipate and mitigate the risks that may have a critical impact on the project.

Effective risk management includes early and aggressive risk identification through the collaboration and involvement of relevant stakeholders, as described in the stakeholder involvement plan addressed in the Project Planning process area. Strong leadership across all relevant stakeholders is needed to establish an environment for the free and open disclosure and discussion of risk.

While technical issues are a primary concern both early on and throughout all project phases, risk management must consider both internal and external sources for cost, schedule, and technical risk. Early and aggressive detection of risk is important because it is typically easier, less costly, and less disruptive to make changes and correct work efforts during the earlier, rather than the later, phases of the project.

Risk management can be divided into three parts: defining a risk management strategy; identifying and analyzing risks; and handling identified risks, including the implementation of risk mitigation plans when needed.

As represented in the Project Planning and Project Monitoring and Control process areas, organizations may initially focus simply on risk identification for awareness, and react to the realization of these risks as they occur.

The Risk Management process area describes an evolution of these specific practices to systematically plan, anticipate, and mitigate risks to proactively minimize their impact on the project.

Although the primary emphasis of the Risk Management process area is on the project, the concepts can also be applied to manage organizational risks.

Related Process Areas

Refer to the Project Planning process area for more information about identification of project risks and planning for involvement of relevant stakeholders.

Refer to the Project Monitoring and Control process area for more information about monitoring project risks.

Refer to the Decision Analysis and Resolution process area for more information about using a formal evaluation process to evaluate alternatives for selection and mitigation of identified risks.

Specific Practices by Goal

SG 1   PREPARE FOR RISK MANAGEMENT

Preparation for risk management is conducted.

Preparation is conducted by establishing and maintaining a strategy for identifying, analyzing, and mitigating risks. This is typically documented in a risk management plan. The risk management strategy addresses the specific actions and management approach used to apply and control the risk management program. This includes identifying the sources of risk; the scheme used to categorize risks; and the parameters used to evaluate, bound, and control risks for effective handling.

SP 1.1-1   DETERMINE RISK SOURCES AND CATEGORIES

Determine risk sources and categories.

Identification of risk sources provides a basis for systematically examining changing situations over time to uncover circumstances that impact the ability of the project to meet its objectives. Risk sources are both internal and external to the project. As the project progresses, additional sources of risk may be identified. Establishing categories for risks provides a mechanism for collecting and organizing risks as well as ensuring appropriate scrutiny and management attention for those risks that can have more serious consequences on meeting project objectives.

Practice-to-Goal Relationship Table

Continuous Representation	*Staged Representation*
SG 1 Prepare for Risk Management	SG 1 Prepare for Risk Management
SP 1.1-1 Determine Risk Sources and Categories	SP 1.1-1 Determine Risk Sources and Categories
SP 1.2-1 Define Risk Parameters	SP 1.2-1 Define Risk Parameters
SP 1.3-1 Establish a Risk Management Strategy	SP 1.3-1 Establish a Risk Management Strategy
SG 2 Identify and Analyze Risks	SG 2 Identify and Analyze Risks
SP 2.1-1 Identify Risks	SP 2.1-1 Identify Risks
SP 2.2-1 Evaluate, Categorize, and Prioritize Risks	SP 2.2-1 Evaluate, Categorize, and Prioritize Risks
SG 3 Mitigate Risks	SG 3 Mitigate Risks
SP 3.1-1 Develop Risk Mitigation Plans	SP 3.1-1 Develop Risk Mitigation Plans
SP 3.2-1 Implement Risk Mitigation Plans	SP 3.2-1 Implement Risk Mitigation Plans
GG 1 Achieve Specific Goals	
GP 1.1 Perform Base Practices	
GG 2 Institutionalize a Managed Process	GG 3 Institutionalize a Defined Process
GP 2.1 Establish an Organizational Policy	GP 2.1 Establish an Organizational Policy
GP 2.2 Plan the Process	GP 2.2 Plan the Process
GP 2.3 Provide Resources	GP 2.3 Provide Resources
GP 2.4 Assign Responsibility	GP 2.4 Assign Responsibility
GP 2.5 Train People	GP 2.5 Train People
GP 2.6 Manage Configurations	GP 2.6 Manage Configurations
GP 2.7 Identify and Involve Relevant Stakeholders	GP 2.7 Identify and Involve Relevant Stakeholders
GP 2.8 Monitor and Control the Process	GP 2.8 Monitor and Control the Process
GP 2.9 Objectively Evaluate Adherence	GP 2.9 Objectively Evaluate Adherence
GP 2.10 Review Status with Higher Level Management	GP 2.10 Review Status with Higher Level Management
GG 3 Institutionalize a Defined Process	
GP 3.1 Establish a Defined Process	GP 3.1 Establish a Defined Process
GP 3.2 Collect Improvement Information	GP 3.2 Collect Improvement Information
GG 4 Institutionalize a Quantitatively Managed Process	
GP 4.1 Establish Quantitative Objectives for the Process	
GP 4.2 Stabilize Subprocess Performance	
GG 5 Institutionalize an Optimizing Process	
GP 5.1 Ensure Continuous Process Improvement	
GP 5.2 Correct Root Causes of Problems	

Typical Work Products

1. Risk source lists (external and internal)
2. Risk categories list

Subpractices

1. Determine risk sources.

   Risk sources are the fundamental drivers that cause risks within a project or organization. There are many sources of risks, both internal and external, to a project. Risk sources identify common areas where risks may originate. Typical internal and external risk sources include the following:

   • Uncertain requirements
   • Unprecedented efforts—estimates unavailable
   • Infeasible design
   • Unavailable technology
   • Unrealistic schedule estimates or allocation
   • Inadequate staffing and skills
   • Cost or funding issues
   • Uncertain or inadequate subcontractor capability
   • Uncertain or inadequate vendor capability

   Many of these sources of risk are often accepted without adequate planning. Early identification of both internal and external sources of risk can lead to early identification of risks. Risk mitigation plans can then be implemented early in the project to preclude occurrence of the risks or reduce the consequences of their occurrence.

2. Determine risk categories.

   Risk categories reflect the "bins" for collecting and organizing risks. A reason for identifying risk categories is to help in the future consolidation of the activities in the risk mitigation plans.

   > The following factors may be considered when determining risk categories:
   > • The phases of the project's life-cycle model (e.g., requirements, design, manufacturing, test and evaluation, delivery, disposal)
   > • The types of processes used
   > • The types of products used
   > • Program management risks (e.g., contract risks, budget/cost risks, schedule risks, resources risks, performance risks, supportability risks)

   A risk taxonomy can be used to provide a framework for determining risk sources and categories.

SP 1.2-1 *DEFINE RISK PARAMETERS*

Define the parameters used to analyze and categorize risks, and the parameters used to control the risk management effort.

Parameters for evaluating, categorizing, and prioritizing risks include the following:

- Risk likelihood (i.e., probability of risk occurrence)
- Risk consequence (i.e., impact and severity of risk occurrence)
- Thresholds to trigger management activities

Risk parameters are used to provide common and consistent criteria for comparing the various risks to be managed. Without these parameters, it would be very difficult to gauge the severity of the unwanted change caused by the risk and to prioritize the necessary actions required for risk mitigation planning.

Typical Work Products

1. Risk evaluation, categorization, and prioritization criteria
2. Risk management requirements (e.g., control and approval levels, reassessment intervals)

Subpractices

1. Define consistent criteria for evaluating and quantifying risk likelihood and severity levels.

   Consistently used criteria (e.g., the bounds on the likelihood and severity levels) allow the impacts of different risks to be commonly understood, to receive the appropriate level of scrutiny, and to obtain the management attention warranted. In managing dissimilar risks (e.g., personnel safety versus environmental pollution), it is important to ensure consistency in end result (e.g., a high risk of environmental pollution is as important as a high risk to personnel safety).

2. Define thresholds for each risk category.

   For each risk category, thresholds can be established to determine acceptability or unacceptability of risks, prioritization of risks, or triggers for management action.

   Examples of thresholds include the following:
   - Project-wide thresholds could be established to involve senior management when product costs exceed 10 percent of the target cost or when Cost Performance Indexes (CPIs) fall below 0.95.
   - Schedule thresholds could be established to involve senior management when Schedule Performance Indexes (SPIs) fall below 0.95.
   - Performance thresholds could be set to involve senior management when specified key design items (e.g., processor utilization) exceed 125 percent of the intended design.

These may be refined later, for each identified risk, to establish points at which more aggressive risk monitoring is employed or to signal the implementation of risk mitigation plans.

3. Define bounds on the extent to which thresholds are applied against or within a category.

There are few limits to which risks can be assessed in either a quantitative or qualitative fashion. Definition of bounds (or boundary conditions) can be used to help scope the extent of the risk management effort and avoid excessive resource expenditures. Bounds may include exclusion of a risk source from a category. These bounds can also exclude any condition that occurs less than a given frequency.

SP 1.3-1 ESTABLISH A RISK MANAGEMENT STRATEGY

Establish and maintain the strategy to be used for risk management.

A comprehensive risk management strategy addresses items such as the following:

- The scope of the risk management effort
- Methods and tools to be used for risk identification, risk analysis, risk mitigation, risk monitoring, and communication
- Project-specific sources of risks
- How these risks are to be organized, categorized, compared, and consolidated
- Parameters, including likelihood, consequence, and thresholds, for taking action on identified risks
- Risk mitigation techniques to be used, such as prototyping, simulation, alternative designs, or evolutionary development
- Definition of risk measures to monitor the status of the risks
- Time intervals for risk monitoring or reassessment

The risk management strategy should be guided by a common vision of success that describes the desired future project outcomes in terms of the product that is delivered, its cost, and its fitness for the task. The risk management strategy is often documented in an organizational or a project risk management plan. The risk management strategy is reviewed with relevant stakeholders to promote commitment and understanding.

Typical Work Products

1. Project risk management strategy

SG 2 *IDENTIFY AND ANALYZE RISKS*

Risks are identified and analyzed to determine their relative importance.

The degree of risk impacts the resources assigned to handle an identified risk and the determination of when appropriate management attention is required.

Analyzing risks entails identifying risks from the internal and external sources identified and then evaluating each identified risk to determine its likelihood and consequences. Categorization of the risk, based on an evaluation against the established risk categories and criteria developed for the risk management strategy, provides the information needed for risk handling. Related risks may be grouped for efficient handling and effective use of risk management resources.

SP 2.1-1 *IDENTIFY RISKS*

Identify and document the risks.

> **FOR INTEGRATED PRODUCT AND PROCESS DEVELOPMENT**
> The particular risks associated with conducting the project using integrated teams should be considered, such as risks associated with loss of inter-team or intra-team coordination.

The identification of potential issues, hazards, threats, and vulnerabilities that could negatively affect work efforts or plans is the basis for sound and successful risk management. Risks must be identified and described in an understandable way before they can be analyzed and managed properly. Risks are documented in a concise statement that includes the context, conditions, and consequences of risk occurrence.

Risk identification should be an organized, thorough approach to seek out probable or realistic risks in achieving objectives. To be effective, risk identification should not be an attempt to address every possible event regardless of how highly improbable it may be. Use of the categories and parameters developed in the risk management strategy, along with the identified sources of risk, can provide the discipline and streamlining appropriate to risk identification. The identified risks form a baseline to initiate risk management activities. The list of risks should be reviewed periodically to reexamine possible sources of risk and changing conditions to uncover sources and risks previously overlooked or nonexistent when the risk management strategy was last updated.

Risk identification activities focus on the identification of risks, not placement of blame. The results of risk identification activities are not used by management to evaluate the performance of individuals.

There are many methods for identifying risks. Typical identification methods include the following:

- Examine each element of the project work breakdown structure to uncover risks.
- Conduct a risk assessment using a risk taxonomy.
- Interview subject matter experts.
- Review risk management efforts from similar products.
- Examine lessons-learned documents or databases.
- Examine design specifications and agreement requirements.

Typical Work Products

1. List of identified risks, including the context, conditions, and consequences of risk occurrence

Subpractices

1. Identify the risks associated with cost, schedule, and performance in all appropriate product life-cycle phases.

    Cost, schedule, and performance risks should be examined during all phases of the product life cycle to the extent that they impact project objectives. There may be potential risks discovered that are outside the scope of the project's objectives but vital to customer interests. For example, the risks in development costs, product acquisition costs, cost of spare (or replacement) products, and product disposition (or disposal) costs have design implications. The customer may not have provided requirements for the cost of supporting the fielded product. The customer should be informed of such risks, but actively managing those risks may not be necessary. The mechanisms for making such decisions should be examined at project and organization levels and put in place if deemed appropriate, especially for risks that impact the ability to verify and validate the product.

    In addition to the cost risks identified above, other cost risks may include those associated with funding levels, funding estimates, and distributed budgets.

    Schedule risks may include risks associated with planned activities, key events, and milestones.

    Performance risks may include risks associated with the following:
    - Requirements
    - Analysis and design
    - Application of new technology
    - Physical size
    - Shape
    - Weight
    - Manufacturing and fabrication

- Functional performance and operation
- Verification
- Validation
- Performance maintenance attributes

Performance maintenance attributes are those characteristics that enable an in-use product to provide originally required performance, such as maintaining safety and security performance.

There are other risks that do not fall into cost, schedule, or performance categories.

Examples of these other risks include the following:
- Risks associated with strikes
- Diminishing sources of supply
- Technology cycle time
- Competition

---

2. Review environmental elements that may impact the project.

Risks to a project that frequently are missed include those supposedly outside the scope of the project (i.e., the project does not control whether they occur but can mitigate their impact), such as weather, natural disasters, political changes, and telecommunications failures.

3. Review all elements of the work breakdown structure as part of identifying risks to help ensure that all aspects of the work effort have been considered.

4. Review all elements of the project plan as part of identifying risks to help ensure that all aspects of the project have been considered.

Refer to the Project Planning process area for more information about identifying project risks.

5. Document the context, conditions, and potential consequences of the risk.

Risks statements are typically documented in a standard format that contains the risk context, conditions, and consequences of occurrence. The risk context provides additional information such that the intent of the risk can be easily understood. In documenting the context of the risk, consider the relative time frame of the risk, the circumstances or conditions surrounding the risk that has brought about the concern, and any doubt or uncertainty.

6. Identify the relevant stakeholders associated with each risk.

SP 2.2-1 EVALUATE, CATEGORIZE, AND PRIORITIZE RISKS

Evaluate and categorize each identified risk using the defined risk categories and parameters, and determine its relative priority.

The evaluation of risks is needed to assign relative importance to each identified risk, and is used in determining when appropriate management attention is required. Often it is useful to aggregate risks based on their interrelationships, and develop options at an aggregate level. When an aggregate risk is formed by a roll up of lower level risks, care must be taken to ensure that important lower level risks are not ignored.

Collectively, the activities of risk evaluation, categorization, and prioritization are sometimes called "risk assessment" or "risk analysis."

Typical Work Products

1. List of risks, with a priority assigned to each risk

Subpractices

1. Evaluate the identified risks using the defined risk parameters.

   Each risk is evaluated and assigned values in accordance with the defined risk parameters, which may include likelihood, consequence (severity, or impact), and thresholds. The assigned risk parameter values can be integrated to produce additional measures, such as risk exposure, which can be used to prioritize risks for handling.

   Often, a scale with three to five values is used to evaluate both likelihood and consequence. Likelihood, for example, can be categorized as remote, unlikely, likely, highly likely, or a near certainty.

   > **Examples for consequences include the following:**
   > - Low
   > - Medium
   > - High
   > - Negligible
   > - Marginal
   > - Significant
   > - Critical
   > - Catastrophic

   Probability values are frequently used to quantify likelihood. Consequences are generally related to cost, schedule, environmental impact, or human measures (e.g., labor hours lost, severity of injury).

   This evaluation is often a difficult and time-consuming task. Specific expertise or group techniques may be needed to assess the risks and gain confidence in the prioritization. In addition, priorities may require reevaluation as time progresses.

2. Categorize and group risks according to the defined risk categories.

   Risks are categorized into the defined risk categories, providing a means to look at risks according to their source, taxonomy, or project component. Related or equivalent risks may be grouped for efficient handling. The cause-and-effect relationships between related risks are documented.

3. Prioritize risks for mitigation.

A relative priority is determined for each risk based on the assigned risk parameters. Clear criteria should be used to determine the risk priority. The intent of prioritization is to determine the most effective areas to which resources for mitigation of risks can be applied with the greatest positive impact to the project.

SG 3 MITIGATE RISKS

Risks are handled and mitigated, where appropriate, to reduce adverse impacts on achieving objectives.

The steps in handling risks include developing risk-handling options, monitoring risks, and performing risk-handling activities when defined thresholds are exceeded. Risk mitigation plans are developed and implemented for selected risks to proactively reduce the potential impact of risk occurrence. This can also include contingency plans to deal with the impact of selected risks that may occur despite attempts to mitigate them. The risk parameters used to trigger risk-handling activities are defined by the risk management strategy.

SP 3.1-1 DEVELOP RISK MITIGATION PLANS

Develop a risk mitigation plan for the most important risks to the project, as defined by the risk management strategy.

A critical component of a risk mitigation plan is to develop alternative courses of action, workarounds, and fallback positions, with a recommended course of action for each critical risk. The risk mitigation plan for a given risk includes techniques and methods used to avoid, reduce, and control the probability of occurrence of the risk, the extent of damage incurred should the risk occur (sometimes called a "contingency plan"), or both. Risks are monitored and when they exceed the established thresholds, the risk mitigation plans are deployed to return the impacted effort to an acceptable risk level. If the risk cannot be mitigated, a contingency plan can be invoked. Both risk mitigation and contingency plans are often generated only for selected risks where the consequences of the risks are determined to be high or unacceptable; other risks may be accepted and simply monitored.

Options for handling risks typically include alternatives such as the following:

- *Risk avoidance:* Changing or lowering requirements while still meeting the user's needs

- *Risk control:* Taking active steps to minimize risks
- *Risk transfer:* Reallocating design requirements to lower the risks
- *Risk monitoring:* Watching and periodically reevaluating the risk for changes to the assigned risk parameters
- *Risk acceptance:* Acknowledgment of risk but not taking any action

Often, especially for high risks, more than one approach to handling a risk should be generated.

In many cases, risks will be accepted or watched. Risk acceptance is usually done when the risk is judged too low for formal mitigation, or when there appears to be no viable way to reduce the risk. If a risk is accepted, the rationale for this decision should be documented. Risks are watched when there is an objectively defined, verifiable, and documented threshold of performance, time, or risk exposure (the combination of likelihood and consequence) that will trigger risk mitigation planning or invoke a contingency plan if it is needed.

Adequate consideration should be given early to technology demonstrations, models, simulations, and prototypes as part of risk mitigation planning.

Typical Work Products

1. Documented handling options for each identified risk
2. Risk mitigation plans
3. Contingency plans
4. List of those responsible for tracking and addressing each risk

Subpractices

1. Determine the levels and thresholds that define when a risk becomes unacceptable and triggers the execution of a risk mitigation plan or a contingency plan.

    Risk level (derived using a risk model) is a measure combining the uncertainty of reaching an objective with the consequences of failing to reach the objective.

    Risk levels and thresholds that bound planned or acceptable performance must be clearly understood and defined to provide a means with which risk can be understood. Proper categorization of risk is essential for ensuring appropriate priority based on severity and the associated management response. There may be multiple thresholds employed to initiate varying levels of management response. Typically, thresholds for the execution of risk mitigation plans are set to engage before the execution of contingency plans.

2. Identify the person or group responsible for addressing each risk.

3. Determine the cost-to-benefit ratio of implementing the risk mitigation plan for each risk.

   Risk mitigation activities should be examined for the benefits they provide versus the resources they will expend. Just like any other design activity, alternative plans may need to be developed and the costs and benefits of each alternative assessed. The most appropriate plan is then selected for implementation. At times the risk may be significant and the benefits small, but the risk must be mitigated to reduce the probability of incurring unacceptable consequences.

4. Develop an overall risk mitigation plan for the project to orchestrate the implementation of the individual risk mitigation and contingency plans.

   The complete set of risk mitigation plans may not be affordable. A tradeoff analysis should be performed to prioritize the risk mitigation plans for implementation.

5. Develop contingency plans for selected critical risks in the event their impacts are realized.

   Risk mitigation plans are developed and implemented as needed to proactively reduce risks before they become problems. Despite best efforts, some risks may be unavoidable and will become problems that impact the project. Contingency plans can be developed for critical risks to describe the actions a project may take to deal with the occurrence of this impact. The intent is to define a proactive plan for handling the risk, either to reduce the risk (mitigation) or respond to the risk (contingency), but in either event to manage the risk.

   Some risk management literature may consider contingency plans a synonym or subset of risk mitigation plans. These plans also may be addressed together as risk-handling or risk action plans.

SP 3.2-1 IMPLEMENT RISK MITIGATION PLANS

Monitor the status of each risk periodically and implement the risk mitigation plan as appropriate.

To effectively control and manage risks during the work effort, follow a proactive program to regularly monitor risks and the status and results of risk-handling actions. The risk management strategy defines the intervals at which the risk status should be revisited. This activity may result in the discovery of new risks or new risk-handling options that can require replanning and reassessment. In either event, the acceptability thresholds associated with the risk should be compared against the status to determine the need for implementing a risk mitigation plan.

Typical Work Products

1. Updated lists of risk status
2. Updated assessments of risk likelihood, consequence, and thresholds
3. Updated lists of risk-handling options
4. Updated list of actions taken to handle risks
5. Risk mitigation plans

Subpractices

1. Monitor risk status.

    After a risk mitigation plan is initiated, the risk is still monitored. Thresholds are assessed to check for the potential execution of a contingency plan.

    A periodic mechanism for monitoring should be employed.

2. Provide a method for tracking open risk-handling action items to closure.

    Refer to the Project Monitoring and Control process area for more information about tracking action items.

3. Invoke selected risk-handling options when monitored risks exceed the defined thresholds.

    Quite often, risk handling is only performed for those risks judged to be "high" and "medium." The risk-handling strategy for a given risk may include techniques and methods to avoid, reduce, and control the likelihood of the risk or the extent of damage incurred should the risk (anticipated event or situation) occur or both. In this context, risk handling includes both risk mitigation plans and contingency plans.

    Risk-handling techniques are developed to avoid, reduce, and control adverse impact to project objectives and to bring about acceptable outcomes in light of probable impacts. Actions generated to handle a risk require proper resource loading and scheduling within plans and baseline schedules. This replanning effort needs to closely consider the effects on adjacent or dependent work initiatives or activities.

    Refer to the Project Monitoring and Control process area for more information about revising the project plan.

4. Establish a schedule or period of performance for each risk-handling activity that includes the start date and anticipated completion date.

5. Provide continued commitment of resources for each plan to allow successful execution of the risk-handling activities.

6. Collect performance measures on the risk-handling activities.

Generic Practices by Goal

GG 1 *ACHIEVE SPECIFIC GOALS*

The process supports and enables achievement of the specific goals of the process area by transforming identifiable input work products to produce identifiable output work products.

GP 1.1 *PERFORM BASE PRACTICES*

Perform the base practices of the risk management process to develop work products and provide services to achieve the specific goals of the process area.

GG 2 *INSTITUTIONALIZE A MANAGED PROCESS*

The process is institutionalized as a managed process.

GG 3 *INSTITUTIONALIZE A DEFINED PROCESS*

The process is institutionalized as a defined process.

> AUTHORS' NOTE: This generic goal's appearance here reflects
> its location in the staged representation.

(side tab: RSKM)

(side tab: CONTINUOUS ONLY)

(side tab: STAGED ONLY)

Commitment to Perform

GP 2.1 *ESTABLISH AN ORGANIZATIONAL POLICY*

Establish and maintain an organizational policy for planning and performing the risk management process.

Elaboration

This policy establishes organizational expectations for defining a risk management strategy and identifying, analyzing, and mitigating risks.

Ability to Perform

GP 2.2 *PLAN THE PROCESS*

Establish and maintain the plan for performing the risk management process.

Elaboration

Typically, this plan for performing the risk management process is included in (or referenced by) the project plan, which is described in the Project Planning process *area. The plan for performing the risk management process differs from the risk mitigation plans described in the specific practices in this process area. The plan called for in this generic practice would address the comprehensive planning for all of the specific practices in this process area, from determining risk sources and categories all the way through to the implementation of risk mitigation plans. In contrast, the risk mitigation plans called for in another specific practice would address more focused items such as the levels that trigger risk-handling activities.*

GP 2.3   PROVIDE RESOURCES

Provide adequate resources for performing the risk management process, developing the work products, and providing the services of the process.

Elaboration

Examples of resources provided include the following tools:
- Risk management databases
- Risk mitigation tools
- Prototyping tools
- Modeling and simulation

GP 2.4   ASSIGN RESPONSIBILITY

Assign responsibility and authority for performing the process, developing the work products, and providing the services of the risk management process.

GP 2.5   TRAIN PEOPLE

Train the people performing or supporting the risk management process as needed.

Elaboration

Examples of training topics include the following:
- Risk management concepts and activities (e.g., risk identification, evaluation, monitoring, mitigation)
- Measure selection for risk mitigation

Directing Implementation

GP 2.6   MANAGE CONFIGURATIONS

Place designated work products of the risk management process under appropriate levels of configuration management.

Elaboration

> Examples of work products placed under configuration management include the following:
> - Risk management strategy
> - Identified risk items
> - Risk mitigation plans

GP 2.7 *IDENTIFY AND INVOLVE RELEVANT STAKEHOLDERS*

Identify and involve the relevant stakeholders of the risk management process as planned.

Elaboration

> Examples of activities for stakeholder involvement include the following:
> - Establishing a collaborative environment for free and open discussion of risk
> - Reviewing the risk management strategy and risk mitigation plans
> - Participating in risk identification, analysis, and mitigation activities
> - Communicating and reporting risk management status

GP 2.8 *MONITOR AND CONTROL THE PROCESS*

Monitor and control the risk management process against the plan for performing the process and take appropriate corrective action.

Elaboration

> Examples of measures used in monitoring and controlling include the following:
> - Number of risks identified, managed, tracked, and controlled
> - Risk exposure and changes to the risk exposure for each assessed risk, and as a summary percentage of management reserve
> - Change activity for the risk mitigation plans (e.g., processes, schedule, funding)
> - Occurrence of unanticipated risks
> - Risk categorization volatility
> - Comparison of estimated versus actual risk mitigation effort and impact

Verifying Implementation

GP 2.9   OBJECTIVELY EVALUATE ADHERENCE

Objectively evaluate adherence of the risk management process against its process description, standards, and procedures, and address noncompliance.

Elaboration

Examples of activities reviewed include the following:
- Establishing and maintaining a risk management strategy
- Identifying and analyzing risks
- Mitigating risks

Examples of work products reviewed include the following:
- Risk management strategy
- Risk mitigation plans

GP 2.10   REVIEW STATUS WITH HIGHER LEVEL MANAGEMENT

Review the activities, status, and results of the risk management process with higher level management and resolve issues.

Elaboration

Reviews of the project risk status are held on a periodic and event-driven basis, with appropriate levels of management, to provide visibility into the potential for project risk exposure and appropriate corrective action.

Typically, these reviews include a summary of the most critical risks, key risk parameters (such as likelihood and consequence of the risks), and the status of risk mitigation efforts.

GG 3   INSTITUTIONALIZE A DEFINED PROCESS

The process is institutionalized as a defined process.

AUTHORS' NOTE: This generic goal's appearance here reflects its location in the continuous representation.

C ONLY

Ability to Perform

GP 3.1   ESTABLISH A DEFINED PROCESS

Establish and maintain the description of a defined risk management process.

Directing Implementation

GP 3.2 COLLECT IMPROVEMENT INFORMATION

Collect work products, measures, measurement results, and improvement information derived from planning and performing the risk management process to support the future use and improvement of the organization's processes and process assets.

GG 4 INSTITUTIONALIZE A QUANTITATIVELY MANAGED PROCESS

The process is institutionalized as a quantitatively managed process.

GP 4.1 ESTABLISH QUANTITATIVE OBJECTIVES FOR THE PROCESS

Establish and maintain quantitative objectives for the risk management process that address quality and process performance based on customer needs and business objectives.

GP 4.2 STABILIZE SUBPROCESS PERFORMANCE

Stabilize the performance of one or more subprocesses to determine the ability of the risk management process to achieve the established quantitative quality and process-performance objectives.

GG 5 INSTITUTIONALIZE AN OPTIMIZING PROCESS

The process is institutionalized as an optimizing process.

GP 5.1 ENSURE CONTINUOUS PROCESS IMPROVEMENT

Ensure continuous improvement of the risk management process in fulfilling the relevant business objectives of the organization.

GP 5.2 CORRECT ROOT CAUSES OF PROBLEMS

Identify and correct the root causes of defects and other problems in the risk management process.

CONTINUOUS ONLY

SUPPLIER AGREEMENT MANAGEMENT
A Project Management Process Area at Maturity Level 2

Purpose

The purpose of Supplier Agreement Management (SAM) is to manage the acquisition of products from suppliers for which there exists a formal agreement.

Introductory Notes

The Supplier Agreement Management process area involves the following:

- Determining the type of acquisition that will be used for the products to be acquired
- Selecting suppliers
- Establishing and maintaining agreements with suppliers
- Executing the supplier agreement
- Accepting delivery of acquired products
- Transitioning acquired products to the project

This process area primarily applies to the acquisition of products and product components that are delivered to the project's customer. To minimize risks to the project, this process area can also be applied to the acquisition of significant products and product components not delivered to the project's customer (for example, development tools and test environments).

This process area does not directly address arrangements in which the supplier is integrated into the project team (for example, integrated product teams). Typically, these situations are handled by other processes or functions, possibly external to the project, though some of the specific practices of this process area may be useful in managing the formal agreement with such a supplier.

Suppliers may take many forms depending on business needs, including in-house vendors (i.e., vendors that are in the same organization but are external to the project), fabrication capabilities and laboratories, and commercial vendors. (See the definition of "supplier" in the glossary.)

A formal agreement is any legal agreement between the organization (representing the project) and the supplier. This agreement may be a contract, a license, or a memorandum of agreement. The acquired product is delivered to the project from the supplier and becomes part of the products delivered to the customer. (See the definition of "product" in the glossary.)

Refer to the Integrated Supplier Management process area for more information about analyzing sources of products and monitoring selected supplier processes and work products.

Related Process Areas

Refer to the Project Monitoring and Control process area for more information about monitoring projects and taking corrective action.

Refer to the Requirements Development process area for more information about defining requirements.

Refer to the Requirements Management process area for more information about managing requirements, including the traceability of requirements for products acquired from suppliers.

Refer to the Technical Solution process area for more information about determining the products and product components that may be acquired from suppliers.

Specific Practices by Goal

SG 1   ESTABLISH SUPPLIER AGREEMENTS

Agreements with the suppliers are established and maintained.

SP 1.1-1   DETERMINE ACQUISITION TYPE

Determine the type of acquisition for each product or product component to be acquired.

Refer to the Technical Solution process area for more information about identifying the products and product components to be acquired.

There are many different types of acquisition that can be used to acquire products and product components that will be used by the project.

Practice-to-Goal Relationship Table

Continuous Representation	*Staged Representation*
SG 1 Establish Supplier Agreements	SG 1 Establish Supplier Agreements
SP 1.1-1 Determine Acquisition Type	SP 1.1-1 Determine Acquisition Type
SP 1.2-1 Select Suppliers	SP 1.2-1 Select Suppliers
SP 1.3-1 Establish Supplier Agreements	SP 1.3-1 Establish Supplier Agreements
SG 2 Satisfy Supplier Agreements	SG 2 Satisfy Supplier Agreements
SP 2.1-1 Review COTS Products	SP 2.1-1 Review COTS Products
SP 2.2-1 Execute the Supplier Agreement	SP 2.2-1 Execute the Supplier Agreement
SP 2.3-1 Accept the Acquired Product	SP 2.3-1 Accept the Acquired Product
SP 2.4-1 Transition Products	SP 2.4-1 Transition Products
GG 1 Achieve Specific Goals	
GP 1.1 Perform Base Practices	
GG 2 Institutionalize a Managed Process	GG 2 Institutionalize a Managed Process
GP 2.1 Establish an Organizational Policy	GP 2.1 Establish an Organizational Policy
GP 2.2 Plan the Process	GP 2.2 Plan the Process
GP 2.3 Provide Resources	GP 2.3 Provide Resources
GP 2.4 Assign Responsibility	GP 2.4 Assign Responsibility
GP 2.5 Train People	GP 2.5 Train People
GP 2.6 Manage Configurations	GP 2.6 Manage Configurations
GP 2.7 Identify and Involve Relevant Stakeholders	GP 2.7 Identify and Involve Relevant Stakeholders
GP 2.8 Monitor and Control the Process	GP 2.8 Monitor and Control the Process
GP 2.9 Objectively Evaluate Adherence	GP 2.9 Objectively Evaluate Adherence
GP 2.10 Review Status with Higher Level Management	GP 2.10 Review Status with Higher Level Management
GG 3 Institutionalize a Defined Process	GG 3 Institutionalize a Defined Process
GP 3.1 Establish a Defined Process	GP 3.1 Establish a Defined Process
GP 3.2 Collect Improvement Information	GP 3.2 Collect Improvement Information
GG 4 Institutionalize a Quantitatively Managed Process	
GP 4.1 Establish Quantitative Objectives for the Process	
GP 4.2 Stabilize Subprocess Performance	
GG 5 Institutionalize an Optimizing Process	
GP 5.1 Ensure Continuous Process Improvement	
GP 5.2 Correct Root Causes of Problems	

SAM

C/ML 3–5

Examples of types of acquisition include the following:
- Purchasing commercial off-the-shelf (COTS) products
- Obtaining products through a contractual agreement
- Obtaining products from an in-house vendor
- Obtaining products from the customer
- Combining some of the above (e.g., contracting for a modification to a COTS product or having another part of the business enterprise codevelop products with an external supplier)

Typical Work Products

1. List of the acquisition types that will be used for all products and product components to be acquired

SP 1.2-1   SELECT SUPPLIERS

Select suppliers based on an evaluation of their ability to meet the specified requirements and established criteria.

Refer to the Decision Analysis and Resolution process area for more information about formal evaluation approaches that can be used to select suppliers.

Refer to the Requirements Management process area for more information about specified requirements.

Refer to the Integrated Supplier Management process area for more information about analyzing sources of products.

Criteria should be established to address factors that are important to the project.

Examples of factors include the following:
- Geographical location of the supplier
- Supplier's performance records on similar work
- Engineering capabilities
- Staff and facilities available to perform the work
- Prior experience in similar applications

Typical Work Products

1. List of candidate suppliers
2. Preferred supplier list
3. Rationale for selection of suppliers
4. Advantages and disadvantages of candidate suppliers
5. Evaluation criteria
6. Solicitation materials and requirements

Subpractices

1. Establish and document criteria for evaluating potential suppliers.
2. Identify potential suppliers and distribute solicitation material and requirements to them.
3. Evaluate proposals according to evaluation criteria.
4. Evaluate risks associated with each proposed supplier.

    Refer to the Risk Management process area for more information about evaluating project risks.

5. Evaluate proposed suppliers' ability to perform the work.

    Examples of methods to evaluate the proposed supplier's ability to perform the work include the following:
    - Evaluation of prior experience in similar applications
    - Evaluation of prior performance on similar work
    - Evaluation of management capabilities
    - Capability evaluations
    - Evaluation of staff available to perform the work
    - Evaluation of available facilities and resources
    - Evaluation of the project's ability to work with the proposed supplier

6. Select the supplier.

SP 1.3-1 ESTABLISH SUPPLIER AGREEMENTS

Establish and maintain formal agreements with the supplier.

> **FOR INTEGRATED PRODUCT AND PROCESS DEVELOPMENT**
> When integrated teams are formed, team membership should be negotiated with suppliers and incorporated into the agreement. The agreement should identify any integrated decision making, reporting requirements (business and technical), and trade studies requiring supplier involvement. The supplier efforts should be orchestrated to support the IPPD efforts undertaken by the acquirer.

A formal agreement is any legal agreement between the organization (representing the project) and the supplier. This agreement may be a contract, a license, or a memorandum of agreement.

Typical Work Products

1. Statements of work
2. Contracts
3. Memoranda of agreement
4. Licensing agreement

Subpractices

1. Revise the requirements to be fulfilled by the supplier to reflect negotiations with the supplier when necessary.

   Refer to the Requirements Development process area for more information about revising requirements.

   Refer to the Requirements Management process area for more information about managing changes to requirements.

2. Document what the project will provide to the supplier.

   Include the following:
   - Project-furnished facilities
   - Documentation
   - Services

3. Document the supplier agreement.

   The supplier agreement should include a statement of work, a specification, terms and conditions, a list of deliverables, a schedule, a budget, and a defined acceptance process.

   This subpractice typically includes the following:
   - Establishing the statement of work, specification, terms and conditions, list of deliverables, schedule, budget, and acceptance process
   - Identifying who from the project and supplier are responsible and authorized to make changes to the supplier agreement
   - Identifying how requirements changes and changes to the supplier agreement are to be determined, communicated, and addressed
   - Identifying standards and procedures that will be followed
   - Identifying critical dependencies between the project and the supplier
   - Identifying the type and depth of project oversight of the supplier, procedures, and evaluation criteria to be used in monitoring supplier performance
   - Identifying the types of reviews that will be conducted with the supplier
   - Identifying the supplier's responsibilities for ongoing maintenance and support of the acquired products
   - Identifying warranty, ownership, and usage rights for the acquired products
   - Identifying acceptance criteria

   Refer to the Integrated Supplier Management process area for more information about monitoring selected supplier processes and work products.

4. Ensure that all parties to the agreement understand and agree to all requirements before implementing the agreement.

5. Revise the supplier agreement as necessary.

6. Revise the project's plans and commitments as necessary to reflect the supplier agreement.

   Refer to the Project Monitoring and Control process area for more information about revising the project plan.

SG 2   SATISFY SUPPLIER AGREEMENTS

Agreements with the suppliers are satisfied by both the project and the supplier.

Refer to the Monitor Selected Supplier Processes specific practice in the Integrated Supplier Management process area. Monitoring a supplier's work products and processes helps the project achieve the Satisfy Supplier Agreements goal in this process area.

SP 2.1-1   REVIEW COTS PRODUCTS

Review candidate COTS products to ensure that they satisfy the specified requirements that are covered under a supplier agreement.

In the event that COTS products are desired, care in evaluating and selecting these products and the vendor may be critical to the project.

> **FOR SUPPLIER SOURCING**
> Integral to the selection decision are proprietary issues and the availability of the products.

Typical Work Products

1. Trade studies
2. Price lists
3. Evaluation criteria
4. Supplier performance reports
5. Reviews of COTS products

Subpractices

1. Develop criteria for evaluating COTS products.
2. Evaluate candidate COTS products against the associated requirements and criteria.

   Refer to the Requirements Development process area for more information about the requirements that will be used to evaluate candidate products.

   These requirements address the following:
   - Functionality, performance, quality, and reliability
   - Terms and conditions of warranties for the products
   - Risk
   - Suppliers' responsibilities for ongoing maintenance and support of the products

3. Evaluate the impact of candidate COTS products on the project's plans and commitments.

Evaluate according to the following:
- Cost of the COTS products
- Cost and effort to incorporate the COTS products into the project
- Security requirements
- Benefits and impacts that may result from future product releases

Future product releases may provide additional features that support planned or anticipated enhancements for the project, but may also result in the supplier withdrawing support of the version for the product that is acquired by the project.

4. Assess the suppliers' performance and ability to deliver.

Refer to the Integrated Supplier Management process area for more information about analyzing sources of products and monitoring selected supplier processes.

5. Identify risks associated with the selected COTS product and the supplier agreement.

Refer to the Project Planning process area for more information about identifying project risks.

Refer to the Risk Management process area for more information about identifying project risks.

6. Select the COTS product to be acquired.

In some cases, selection of COTS products may require a supplier agreement in addition to the agreements in the product's license.

Examples of agreements with COTS suppliers include the following:
- Discounts for large quantity purchases
- Coverage of relevant stakeholders under the licensing agreement, including project suppliers, team members, and the project's customer
- Plans for future enhancements
- On-site support, such as responses to queries and problem reports
- Additional capabilities that are not in the product
- Maintenance support, including support after the product is withdrawn from general availability

---

7. Plan for the maintenance of the COTS product.

SP 2.2-1 *EXECUTE THE SUPPLIER AGREEMENT*

Perform activities with the supplier as specified in the supplier agreement.

Refer to the Project Monitoring and Control process area for more information about monitoring projects and taking corrective action.

Typical Work Products

1. Supplier progress reports and performance measures
2. Supplier review materials and reports
3. Action items tracked to closure
4. Documentation of product and document deliveries

Subpractices

1. Monitor supplier progress and performance (schedule, effort, cost, and technical performance) as defined in the supplier agreement.
2. Monitor selected supplier processes and take corrective action when necessary.

> Examples of processes to be monitored are quality assurance and configuration management.

> *Refer to the Integrated Supplier Management process area for more information about monitoring selected supplier processes.*

3. Conduct reviews with the supplier as specified in the supplier agreement.

   Refer to the Project Monitoring and Control process area for more information about conducting reviews.

   Reviews cover both formal and informal reviews and include the following steps:

   - Preparing for the review
   - Ensuring that relevant stakeholders participate
   - Conducting the review
   - Identifying, documenting, and tracking all action items to closure
   - Preparing and distributing to the relevant stakeholders a summary report of the review

4. Conduct technical reviews with the supplier as defined in the supplier agreement.

   Technical reviews typically include the following:

   - Providing the supplier with visibility into the needs and desires of the project's customers and end users, as appropriate
   - Reviewing the supplier's technical activities and verifying that the supplier's interpretation and implementation of the requirements are consistent with the project's interpretation
   - Ensuring that technical commitments are being met and that technical issues are communicated and resolved in a timely manner
   - Obtaining technical information about the supplier's products
   - Providing appropriate technical information and support to the supplier

5. Conduct management reviews with the supplier as defined in the supplier agreement.

    Management reviews typically include the following:
    - Reviewing critical dependencies
    - Reviewing project risks involving the supplier
    - Reviewing schedule and budget

    Technical and management reviews may be coordinated and held jointly.

6. Use the results of reviews to improve the supplier's performance and to establish and nurture long-term relationships with preferred suppliers.

7. Monitor risks involving the supplier and take corrective action as necessary.

    Refer to the Project Monitoring and Control process area for more information about monitoring project risks.

8. Revise the supplier agreement and project plans and schedules as necessary.

SP 2.3-1 ACCEPT THE ACQUIRED PRODUCT

Ensure that the supplier agreement is satisfied before accepting the acquired product.

Acceptance reviews and tests and configuration audits should be completed before accepting the product as defined in the supplier agreement.

Typical Work Products

1. Acceptance test procedures
2. Acceptance test results
3. Discrepancy reports or corrective action plans

Subpractices

1. Define the acceptance procedures.
2. Review and obtain agreement with relevant stakeholders on the acceptance procedures before the acceptance review or test.
3. Verify that the acquired products satisfy their requirements.

    Refer to the Verification process area for more information about verifying products.

4. Confirm that the nontechnical commitments associated with the acquired work product are satisfied.

    This may include confirming that the appropriate license, warranty, ownership, usage, and support or maintenance agreements are in place and that all supporting materials are received.

5. Document the results of the acceptance review or test.
6. Establish and obtain supplier agreement on an action plan for any acquired work products that do not pass their acceptance review or test.

7. Identify, document, and track action items to closure.

> *Refer to the Project Monitoring and Control process area for more information about tracking action items.*

SP 2.4-1   TRANSITION PRODUCTS

Transition the acquired products from the supplier to the project.

Before the acquired product is transferred to the project for integration, appropriate planning and evaluation should occur to ensure a smooth transition.

Refer to the Product Integration process area for more information about integrating the acquired products.

Typical Work Products

1. Transition plans
2. Training reports
3. Support and maintenance reports

Subpractices

1. Ensure that there are appropriate facilities to receive, store, use, and maintain the acquired products.
2. Ensure that appropriate training is provided for those involved in receiving, storing, using, and maintaining the acquired products.
3. Ensure that storing, distributing, and using the acquired products are performed according to the terms and conditions specified in the supplier agreement or license.

Generic Practices by Goal

GG 1   ACHIEVE SPECIFIC GOALS

The process supports and enables achievement of the specific goals of the process area by transforming identifiable input work products to produce identifiable output work products.

GP 1.1   PERFORM BASE PRACTICES

Perform the base practices of the supplier agreement management process to develop work products and provide services to achieve the specific goals of the process area.

GG 2   INSTITUTIONALIZE A MANAGED PROCESS

The process is institutionalized as a managed process.

Commitment to Perform

GP 2.1   ESTABLISH AN ORGANIZATIONAL POLICY

Establish and maintain an organizational policy for planning and performing the supplier agreement management process.

Elaboration

This policy establishes organizational expectations for establishing, maintaining, and satisfying supplier agreements.

Ability to Perform

GP 2.2   PLAN THE PROCESS

Establish and maintain the plan for performing the supplier agreement management process.

Elaboration

Typically, portions of this plan for performing the supplier agreement management process are a part of the project plan as described in the Project Planning process area. Often, however, some portions of the plan reside outside of the project with an independent group, such as contract management.

GP 2.3   PROVIDE RESOURCES

Provide adequate resources for performing the supplier agreement management process, developing the work products, and providing the services of the process.

Elaboration

Examples of resources provided include the following tools:
- Preferred supplier lists
- Requirements tracking programs
- Project-management and scheduling programs

GP 2.4   ASSIGN RESPONSIBILITY

Assign responsibility and authority for performing the process, developing the work products, and providing the services of the supplier agreement management process.

GP 2.5   TRAIN PEOPLE

Train the people performing or supporting the supplier agreement management process as needed.

Elaboration

Examples of training topics include the following:

- Regulations and business practices related to negotiating and working with suppliers
- Acquisition planning and preparation
- COTS products acquisition
- Supplier evaluation and selection
- Negotiation and conflict resolution
- Supplier management
- Testing and transitioning of acquired products
- Receiving, storing, using, and maintaining acquired products

Directing Implementation

GP 2.6 MANAGE CONFIGURATIONS

Place designated work products of the supplier agreement management process under appropriate levels of configuration management.

Elaboration

Examples of work products placed under configuration management include the following:

- Statements of work
- Supplier agreements
- Memoranda of agreement
- Subcontracts
- Preferred supplier lists

GP 2.7 IDENTIFY AND INVOLVE RELEVANT STAKEHOLDERS

Identify and involve the relevant stakeholders of the supplier agreement management process as planned.

Elaboration

Examples of activities for stakeholder involvement include the following:

- Establishing criteria for evaluation of potential suppliers
- Reviewing potential suppliers
- Establishing supplier agreements
- Resolving issues with suppliers
- Reviewing supplier performance

GP 2.8 *Monitor and Control the Process*

Monitor and control the supplier agreement management process against the plan for performing the process and take appropriate corrective action.

Elaboration

Examples of measures used in monitoring and controlling include the following:
- Number of changes made to the requirements for the supplier
- Cost and schedule variance per supplier agreement

Verifying Implementation

GP 2.9 *Objectively Evaluate Adherence*

Objectively evaluate adherence of the supplier agreement management process against its process description, standards, and procedures, and address noncompliance.

Elaboration

Examples of activities reviewed include the following:
- Establishing and maintaining supplier agreements
- Satisfying supplier agreements

Examples of work products reviewed include the following:
- Plan for Supplier Agreement Management
- Supplier agreements

GP 2.10 *Review Status with Higher Level Management*

Review the activities, status, and results of the supplier agreement management process with higher level management and resolve issues.

> AUTHORS' NOTE: GG3 and its practices do not apply for a maturity level 2 rating, but do apply for a maturity level 3 rating and above.

S ONLY

GG 3 *Institutionalize a Defined Process*

The process is institutionalized as a defined process.

C/ML 3–5

Ability to Perform

GP 3.1 *Establish a Defined Process*

Establish and maintain the description of a defined supplier agreement management process.

Directing Implementation

GP 3.2 COLLECT IMPROVEMENT INFORMATION

Collect work products, measures, measurement results, and improvement information derived from planning and performing the supplier agreement management process to support the future use and improvement of the organization's processes and process assets.

GG 4 INSTITUTIONALIZE A QUANTITATIVELY MANAGED PROCESS

The process is institutionalized as a quantitatively managed process.

GP 4.1 ESTABLISH QUANTITATIVE OBJECTIVES FOR THE PROCESS

Establish and maintain quantitative objectives for the supplier agreement management process that address quality and process performance based on customer needs and business objectives.

GP 4.2 STABILIZE SUBPROCESS PERFORMANCE

Stabilize the performance of one or more subprocesses to determine the ability of the supplier agreement management process to achieve the established quantitative quality and process-performance objectives.

GG 5 INSTITUTIONALIZE AN OPTIMIZING PROCESS

The process is institutionalized as an optimizing process.

GP 5.1 ENSURE CONTINUOUS PROCESS IMPROVEMENT

Ensure continuous improvement of the supplier agreement management process in fulfilling the relevant business objectives of the organization.

GP 5.2 CORRECT ROOT CAUSES OF PROBLEMS

Identify and correct the root causes of defects and other problems in the supplier agreement management process.

TECHNICAL SOLUTION
An Engineering Process Area at Maturity Level 3

Purpose

The purpose of Technical Solution (TS) is to design, develop, and implement solutions to requirements. Solutions, designs, and implementations encompass products, product components, and product-related life-cycle processes either singly or in combination as appropriate.

Introductory Notes

The Technical Solution process area is applicable at any level of the product architecture and to every product, product component, product-related life-cycle process, and service. The process area focuses on the following:

- Evaluating and selecting solutions (sometimes referred to as "design approaches," "design concepts," or "preliminary designs") that potentially satisfy an appropriate set of allocated requirements
- Developing detailed designs for the selected solutions (detailed in the context of containing all the information needed to manufacture, code, or otherwise implement the design as a product or product component)
- Implementing the designs as a product or product component

Typically, these activities interactively support each other. Some level of design, at times fairly detailed, may be needed to select solutions. Product-component prototypes may be used as a means of gaining sufficient knowledge to develop a technical data package or a complete set of requirements.

Technical Solution specific practices apply not only to the product and product components but also to services and product-related life-cycle processes. The product-related life-cycle processes are developed in concert with the product or product component. Such development may include selecting and adapting existing processes (including standard processes) for use as well as developing new processes.

Processes associated with the Technical Solution process area receive the product and product-component requirements from the requirements management processes. The requirements management processes place the requirements, which originate in requirements development processes, under appropriate configuration management and maintain their traceability to previous requirements.

For a maintenance or sustainment organization, the requirements in need of maintenance actions or redesign may be driven by user needs or latent defects in the product components. New requirements may arise from changes in the operating environment. Such requirements can be uncovered during verification of the product(s) where actual performance can be compared against the specified performance and unacceptable degradation can be identified. Processes associated with the Technical Solution process area should be used to perform the maintenance or sustainment design efforts.

Related Process Areas

Refer to the Requirements Development process area for more information about requirements allocations, establishing an operational concept, and interface requirements definition.

Refer to the Verification process area for more information about conducting peer reviews and verifying that the product and product components meet requirements.

Refer to the Decision Analysis and Resolution process area for more information about formal evaluation.

Refer to the Requirements Management process area for more information about managing requirements. The specific practices in the Requirements Management process area are performed interactively with those in the Technical Solution process area.

Refer to the Organizational Innovation and Deployment process area for more information about improving the organization's technology.

Specific Practices by Goal

SG 1   SELECT PRODUCT-COMPONENT SOLUTIONS

Product or product-component solutions are selected from alternative solutions.

Alternative solutions and their relative merits are considered in advance of selecting a solution. Key requirements, design issues, and constraints are established for use in alternative solution analysis. Architectural features that provide a foundation for product improvement and evolution are considered. Use of commercial off-the-shelf (COTS) product components are considered relative to cost, schedule, performance, and risk. COTS alternatives may be used with or without modification. Sometimes such items may

Practice-to-Goal Relationship Table

Continuous Representation	*Staged Representation*
SG 1 Select Product-Component Solutions	SG 1 Select Product-Component Solutions
SP 1.1-1 Develop Alternative Solutions and Selection Criteria	
SP 1.1-2 Develop Detailed Alternative Solutions and Selection Criteria	SP 1.1-2 Develop Detailed Alternative Solutions and Selection Criteria
SP 1.2-2 Evolve Operational Concepts and Scenarios	SP 1.2-2 Evolve Operational Concepts and Scenarios
SP 1.3-1 Select Product-Component Solutions	SP 1.3-1 Select Product-Component Solutions
SG 2 Develop the Design	SG 2 Develop the Design
SP 2.1-1 Design the Product or Product Component	SP 2.1-1 Design the Product or Product Component
SP 2.2-3 Establish a Technical Data Package	SP 2.2-3 Establish a Technical Data Package
SP 2.3-1 Establish Interface Descriptions	
SP 2.3-3 Design Interfaces Using Criteria	SP 2.3-3 Design Interfaces Using Criteria
SP 2.4-3 Perform Make, Buy, or Reuse Analyses	SP 2.4-3 Perform Make, Buy, or Reuse Analyses
SG 3 Implement the Product Design	SG 3 Implement the Product Design
SP 3.1-1 Implement the Design	SP 3.1-1 Implement the Design
SP 3.2-1 Develop Product Support Documentation	SP 3.2-1 Develop Product Support Documentation
GG 1 Achieve Specific Goals	
GP 1.1 Perform Base Practices	
GG 2 Institutionalize a Managed Process	GG 3 Institutionalize a Defined Process
GP 2.1 Establish an Organizational Policy	GP 2.1 Establish an Organizational Policy
GP 2.2 Plan the Process	GP 2.2 Plan the Process
GP 2.3 Provide Resources	GP 2.3 Provide Resources
GP 2.4 Assign Responsibility	GP 2.4 Assign Responsibility
GP 2.5 Train People	GP 2.5 Train People
GP 2.6 Manage Configurations	GP 2.6 Manage Configurations
GP 2.7 Identify and Involve Relevant Stakeholders	GP 2.7 Identify and Involve Relevant Stakeholders
GP 2.8 Monitor and Control the Process	GP 2.8 Monitor and Control the Process
GP 2.9 Objectively Evaluate Adherence	GP 2.9 Objectively Evaluate Adherence
GP 2.10 Review Status with Higher Level Management	GP 2.10 Review Status with Higher Level Management
GG 3 Institutionalize a Defined Process	
GP 3.1 Establish a Defined Process	GP 3.1 Establish a Defined Process
GP 3.2 Collect Improvement Information	GP 3.2 Collect Improvement Information
GG 4 Institutionalize a Quantitatively Managed Process	
GP 4.1 Establish Quantitative Objectives for the Process	
GP 4.2 Stabilize Subprocess Performance	
GG 5 Institutionalize an Optimizing Process	
GP 5.1 Ensure Continuous Process Improvement	
GP 5.2 Correct Root Causes of Problems	

TS

require modifications to aspects such as interfaces or a customization of some of the features to better achieve product requirements.

One indicator of a good design process is that the design was chosen after comparing and evaluating it against alternative solutions. Decisions on architecture, custom development versus off the shelf, and product-component modularization are typical of the design choices that are addressed.

Sometimes the search for solutions examines alternative instances of the same requirements with no allocations needed for lower level product components. Such is the case at the bottom of the product architecture. There are also cases where one or more of the solutions are fixed (e.g., a specific solution is directed or available product components, such as COTS, are investigated for use).

In the general case, solutions are defined as a set. That is, when defining the next layer of product components, the solution for each of the product components in the set is established. The alternative solutions are not only different ways of addressing the same requirements, but they also reflect a different allocation of requirements among the product components comprising the solution set. The objective is to optimize the set as a whole and not the individual pieces. There will be significant interaction with processes associated with the Requirements Development process area to support the provisional allocations to product components until a solution set is selected and final allocations established.

Product-related life-cycle processes are among the product-component solutions that are selected from alternative solutions. Examples of these product-related life-cycle processes are the manufacturing and the support processes.

The following specific practice is subsumed in the staged representation by SP 1.1-2, Develop Detailed Alternative Solutions and Selection Criteria.

SP 1.1-1   *DEVELOP ALTERNATIVE SOLUTIONS AND SELECTION CRITERIA*

Develop alternative solutions and selection criteria.

Refer to the Allocate Product-Component Requirements specific practice in the Requirements Development process area for more information about obtaining provisional allocations of requirements to solution alternatives for the product components.

Refer to the Decision Analysis and Resolution process area for more information about establishing selection criteria and identifying alternatives.

Refer to the Requirements Management process area for more information about managing the provisional and established allocated requirements.

Alternatives are based on potential product architectures and span a design space of feasible solutions. The Design Product or Product Component specific practice of the Develop the Design specific goal contains more information about developing potential product architectures to incorporate into alternative solutions for the product.

As selections are made, the design space can be constricted and other alternatives examined until the most promising (i.e., optimal) solutions that meet requirements and criteria are identified. The selection criteria identify the key factors that provide a basis for the selection of the solution. These criteria should provide clear discrimination and an indication of success in arriving at a balanced solution across the life of the product. They typically include measures of cost, schedule, performance, and risk.

The alternative solutions evaluated frequently encompass alternative requirement allocations to different product components. These alternatives also can be structured to evaluate the use of COTS solutions in the product architecture. Processes associated with the Requirements Development process area would then be employed to provide a more complete and robust provisional allocation of requirements to the alternative solutions.

Selection of the best solution establishes the requirements provisionally allocated to that solution as the set of allocated requirements. The circumstances in which it would not be useful to examine alternative solutions are infrequent in new developments. However, developments of precedented product components are candidates for not examining, or only minimally examining, alternative solutions.

Typical Work Products

1. Alternative solutions
2. Selection criteria

Subpractices

1. Establish and maintain a process or processes for identifying solution alternatives, selection criteria, and design issues.

   Selection criteria are influenced by a wide variety of factors driven by the requirements imposed on the project as well as the product life cycle. For example, criteria related to mitigating cost and schedule risks may influence a greater preference for COTS solutions provided such selections do not result in unacceptable risks for the remaining product components to be developed. When using existing items, such as COTS, either with or without modification, criteria dealing with diminishing sources of supply or technological obsolescence should be examined, as well as criteria for capturing the benefits of standardization, maintaining relationships with suppliers, and so forth. The criteria used in selections should provide a balanced approach to costs, benefits, and risks.

2. Identify alternative groupings of requirements that characterize sets of solution alternatives that span the feasible design space.

   Effective employment of COTS alternatives can provide special challenges. Knowledgeable designers familiar with candidate COTS alternatives may explore architectural opportunities to exploit potential COTS payoffs.

3. Identify design issues for each solution alternative in each set of alternatives.

4. Characterize design issues and take appropriate action.

   Appropriate action could be to characterize the issues as a risk for risk management, adjust the solution alternative to preclude the issues, or reject the solution alternative and replace it with a different alternative.

5. Obtain a complete requirements allocation for each alternative.

6. Document the rationale for each alternative set of solutions.

CONTINUOUS ONLY

SP 1.1-2   *DEVELOP DETAILED ALTERNATIVE SOLUTIONS AND SELECTION CRITERIA*

Develop detailed alternative solutions and selection criteria.

Refer to the Decision Analysis and Resolution process area for more information about establishing criteria used in making decisions.

> **FOR INTEGRATED PRODUCT AND PROCESS DEVELOPMENT**
> The activity of selecting alternative solutions and issues to be subject to decision analyses and trade studies is accomplished by the involvement of relevant stakeholders. These stakeholders represent both business and technical functions and the concurrent development of the product and the product-related life-cycle processes (e.g., manufacturing, support, training, verification, and disposal). In this way, important issues surface earlier in product development than with traditional serial development and can be addressed before they become costly mistakes.

Detailed alternative solutions are an essential concept of the Technical Solution process area. They provide more accurate and comprehensive information about the solution than nondetailed alternatives. For example, characterization of performance based on design content rather than on simple estimating enables effective assessment and understanding of environment and operating concept impacts. Alternative solutions need to be identified and analyzed to enable the selection of a balanced solution across the life of the product in terms of cost, schedule, and technical performance. These solutions are based on proposed product architectures that address critical product qualities. Specific practices associated with the Develop the Design specific goal provide more information on developing potential product architectures that can be incorporated into alternative solutions for the product.

Alternative solutions span the acceptable range of cost, schedule, and performance. The product-component requirements are received and used along with design issues, constraints, and criteria to develop the alternative solutions. Selection criteria would typically address costs (e.g., time, people, money), benefits (e.g., performance, capability, effectiveness), and risks (e.g., technical, cost, schedule). Considerations for detailed alternative solutions and selection criteria include the following:

- Cost (development, procurement, support, product life cycle)
- Technical performance
- Complexity of the product component and product-related life-cycle processes
- Robustness to product operating and use conditions, operating modes, environments, and variations in product-related life-cycle processes
- Product expansion and growth
- Technology limitations
- Sensitivity to construction methods and materials
- Risk
- Evolution of requirements and technology
- Disposal
- Capabilities and limitations of end users and operators

The considerations listed here are a basic set; organizations should develop screening criteria to narrow down the list of alternatives that are consistent with their business objectives. Product life-cycle cost, while being a desirable parameter to minimize, may be outside the control of development organizations. A customer may not be willing to pay for features that cost more in the short term but ultimately decrease cost over the life of the product. In such cases, customers should at least be advised of any potential for reducing life-cycle costs. The criteria used in selections of final solutions should provide a balanced approach to costs, benefits, and risks.

Typical Work Products

1. Alternative solution screening criteria
2. Evaluations of new technologies

3. Alternative solutions

4. Selection criteria for final selection

Subpractices

1. Identify screening criteria to select a set of alternative solutions for consideration.

2. Identify technologies currently in use and new product technologies for competitive advantage.

   Refer to the Organizational Innovation and Deployment process area for more information about improving the organization's technology.

   The project should identify technologies applied to current products and processes and monitor the progress of currently used technologies throughout the life of the project. The project should identify, select, evaluate, and invest in new technologies to achieve competitive advantage. Alternative solutions could include newly developed technologies, but could also include applying mature technologies in different applications or to maintain current methods.

3. Generate alternative solutions.

4. Obtain a complete requirements allocation for each alternative.

5. Develop the criteria for selecting the best alternative solution.

   Criteria should be included that address design issues for the life of the product, such as provisions for more easily inserting new technologies or the ability to better exploit commercial products. Examples include criteria related to open design or open architecture concepts for the alternatives being evaluated.

6. Develop timeline scenarios for product operation and user interaction for each alternative solution.

SP 1.2-2 EVOLVE OPERATIONAL CONCEPTS AND SCENARIOS

Evolve the operational concept, scenarios, and environments to describe the conditions, operating modes, and operating states specific to each product component.

Refer to the Establish Operational Concepts and Scenarios specific practice of the Requirements Development process area for information on product-level influences and implications of product-component operations.

> **FOR SYSTEMS ENGINEERING**
> Integrate the operational concepts and scenarios produced by various individuals or groups for each level of physical product decomposition.

Operational concepts and scenarios are evolved to facilitate the selection of product-component solutions that, when implemented, will satisfy the intended use of the product. Operational concepts and scenarios document the interaction of the product components with the environment, users, and other product components, regardless of engineering discipline. They should be documented for operations, product deployment, delivery, support (including maintenance and sustainment), training, and disposal and for all modes and states.

The environments (e.g., operating, support, training) also need to be evolved. The environment of any given product component will be influenced by other product components as well as the external environment.

Typical Work Products

1. Product-component operational concepts, scenarios, and environments for all product-related life-cycle processes (e.g., operations, support, training, manufacturing, deployment, fielding, delivery, and disposal)
2. Timeline analyses of product-component interactions
3. Use cases

Subpractices

1. Evolve the operational concepts and scenarios to a degree of detail appropriate for the product component.
2. Evolve the operational environments for the product components.

    The environments may include thermal, stress, and electromagnetic and other elements that need to be documented.

SP 1.3-1 SELECT PRODUCT-COMPONENT SOLUTIONS

Select the product-component solutions that best satisfy the criteria established.

Refer to the Allocate Product-Component Requirements and Identify Interface Requirements specific practices of the Requirements Development process area for information on establishing the allocated requirements for product components and interface requirements among product components.

Refer to the Decision Analysis and Resolution process area for more information about formal evaluations.

Selecting product components that best satisfy the criteria establishes the requirement allocations to product components. Lower level requirements are generated from the selected alternative and used to develop the product-component design. Interface requirements among product components are described, primarily functionally. Physical interface descriptions are included in the documentation for interfaces to items and activities external to the product.

The description of the solutions and the rationale for selection are documented. The documentation evolves throughout development as solutions and detailed designs are developed and those designs are implemented. Maintaining a record of rationale is critical to downstream decision making. Such records keep downstream stakeholders from redoing work and provide insights to apply technology as it becomes available in applicable circumstances.

Typical Work Products

1. Product-component selection decisions and rationale
2. Documented relationships between requirements and product components
3. Documented solutions, evaluations, and rationale

Subpractices

1. Evaluate each alternative solution/set of solutions against the selection criteria established in the context of the operating concepts, operating modes, and operating states.
2. Based on the evaluation of alternatives, assess the adequacy of the selection criteria and update these criteria as necessary.
3. Identify and resolve issues with the alternative solutions and requirements.
4. Select the best set of alternative solutions that satisfy the established selection criteria.
5. Establish the requirements associated with the selected set of alternatives as the set of allocated requirements to those product components.
6. Identify the product-component solutions that will be reused or acquired.

    Refer to the Supplier Agreement Management process area for more information about acquiring products and product components.

7. Establish and maintain the documentation of the solutions, evaluations, and rationale.

SG 2 DEVELOP THE DESIGN

Product or product-component designs are developed.

Product or product-component designs must provide the appropriate content not only for implementation, but also for other phases of the product life cycle such as modification, reprocurement, maintenance, sustainment, and installation. The design documentation provides a reference to support mutual understanding of the design by relevant stakeholders and supports future changes to the design both during development and in subsequent phases of the product life cycle. A complete design description is documented in a technical data package that includes a full range of features and parameters including form, fit, function, interface, manufacturing process characteristics, and other parameters. Established organizational or project design standards (e.g., checklists, templates, object frameworks) form the basis for achieving a high degree of definition and completeness in design documentation.

FOR INTEGRATED PRODUCT AND PROCESS DEVELOPMENT

The integrated teams develop the designs of the appropriate product-related life-cycle processes concurrently with the design of the product. These processes may be selected without modification from the organization's set of standard processes, if appropriate.

SP 2.1-1 DESIGN THE PRODUCT OR PRODUCT COMPONENT

Develop a design for the product or product component.

Product design consists of two broad phases that may overlap in execution: preliminary and detailed design. Preliminary design establishes product capabilities and the product architecture, including product partitions, product-component identifications, system states and modes, major inter-component interfaces, and external product interfaces. Detailed design fully defines the structure and capabilities of the product components.

Refer to the Requirements Development process area for more information about developing architecture requirements.

Architecture definition is driven from a set of architectural requirements developed during the requirements development processes. These requirements express the qualities and performance points that are critical to the success of the product. The architecture defines structural elements and coordination mechanisms that either directly satisfy requirements or support the achievement of the requirements as the details of the product design are established. Architectures may include standards and design rules governing development of product components and their interfaces as well as guidance to aid product developers. Specific practices in the Select Product-Component Solutions specific goal contain more information about using product architectures as a basis for alternative solutions.

Architects postulate and develop a model of the product, making judgments about allocation of requirements to product components including hardware and software. Multiple architectures, supporting alternative solutions, may be developed and analyzed to determine the advantages and disadvantages in the context of the architectural requirements.

Operational concepts and scenarios are used to generate use cases and quality scenarios that are used to refine the architecture. They are also used as a means to evaluate the suitability of the architecture for its intended purpose during architecture evaluations, which are conducted periodically throughout product design. The Evolve Operational Concepts and Scenarios specific practice gives more information about elaborating operational concepts and scenarios used in architecture evaluation.

Refer to the Establish Operational Concepts and Scenarios specific practice of the Requirements Development process area for information about developing operational concepts and scenarios used in architecture evaluation.

FOR SOFTWARE ENGINEERING

In addition to tasks just identified, software architecture definition may include:

- Establishing the structural relations of partitions and rules regarding interfaces between elements within partitions, and between partitions
- Identifying major internal interfaces and all external interfaces of software
- Identifying software product components
- Defining software coordination mechanisms
- Establishing infrastructure capabilities and services
- Developing product-component templates or classes and frameworks
- Establishing design rules and authority for making decisions
- Defining a process/thread model
- Defining physical deployment of software to hardware
- Identifying major reuse approaches and sources

During detailed design, the product architecture details are finalized, product components are completely defined, and interfaces are fully characterized. Product-component designs may be optimized for certain qualities or performance characteristics. Designers may evaluate the use of legacy or COTS products for the product components. As the design matures, the requirements assigned to lower level product components are tracked to ensure that those requirements are satisfied.

Refer to the Requirements Management process area for more information about tracking requirements for product components.

FOR SOFTWARE ENGINEERING

Detailed design is focused on software product-component development. The internal structure of product components is defined, data schema are generated, algorithms are developed, and heuristics are established to provide product-component capabilities that satisfy allocated requirements.

Typical Work Products

1. Product architecture
2. Product-component designs

Subpractices

1. Establish and maintain criteria against which the design can be evaluated.

   > Examples of attributes, in addition to expected performance, for which design criteria can be established, include the following:
   > - Modular
   > - Clear
   > - Simple
   > - Maintainable
   > - Verifiable
   > - Portable
   > - Reliable
   > - Accurate
   > - Secure
   > - Scalable
   > - Usable

2. Identify, develop, or acquire the design methods appropriate for the product.

   Effective design methods can embody a wide range of activities, tools, and descriptive techniques. Whether a given method is effective or not depends on the situation. Two companies may have very effective design methods for products in which they specialize, but these methods may not be effective in cooperative ventures. Highly sophisticated methods are not necessarily effective in the hands of designers who have not been trained in the use of the methods.

   Whether a method is effective also depends on how much assistance it provides the designer, and the cost effectiveness of that assistance. For example, a multiyear prototyping effort may not be appropriate for a simple product component but might be the right thing to do for an unprecedented, expensive, and complex product development. Rapid prototyping techniques, however, can be highly effective for many product components. Methods that use tools to ensure that a design will encompass all the necessary attributes needed to implement the product-component design can be very effective. For example, a design tool that "knows" the capabilities of the manufacturing processes can allow the variability of the manufacturing process to be accounted for in the design tolerances.

> Examples of techniques and methods that facilitate effective design include the following:
> - Prototypes
> - Structural models
> - Object-oriented design
> - Essential systems analysis
> - Entity relationship models
> - Design reuse
> - Design patterns

3. Ensure that the design adheres to applicable design standards and criteria.

> Examples of design standards include the following (some or all of these standards may be design criteria, particularly in circumstances where the standards have not been established):
> - Operator interface standards
> - Safety standards
> - Production constraints
> - Design tolerances
> - Parts standards (e.g., production scrap and waste)

4. Ensure that the design adheres to allocated requirements.

    Identified COTS product components must be taken into account. For example, putting existing product components into the product architecture might modify the requirements and the requirements allocation.

5. Document the design.

SP 2.2-3 ESTABLISH A TECHNICAL DATA PACKAGE

Establish and maintain a technical data package.

A technical data package provides the developer with a comprehensive description of the product or product component as it is developed. Such a package also provides procurement flexibility in a variety of circumstances such as performance-based contracting or build to print.

The design is recorded in a technical data package that is created during preliminary design to document the architecture definition. This technical data package is maintained throughout the life of the product to record essential details of the product design. The technical data package provides the description of a product or product component (including product-related life-cycle processes if not handled as separate product components) that supports an acquisition strategy, or the implementation, production, engineering, and logistics support phases of the product life cycle. The description includes the definition of the required design configuration and procedures to ensure adequacy of product or product-component performance. It includes all applicable technical data such as drawings, associated lists, specifications, design descriptions, design databases, standards, performance requirements, quality assurance provisions, and packaging details. The technical data package includes a description of the selected alternative solution that was chosen for implementation.

A technical data package should include the following if such information is appropriate for the type of product and product component (for example, material and manufacturing requirements may not be useful for product components associated with software services or processes):

- Product architecture description
- Allocated requirements
- Product-component descriptions
- Product-related life-cycle process descriptions, if not described as separate product components
- Key product characteristics
- Required physical characteristics and constraints
- Interface requirements
- Materials requirements (bills of material and material characteristics)
- Fabrication and manufacturing requirements (for both the original equipment manufacturer and field support)
- The verification criteria used to ensure that requirements have been achieved
- Conditions of use (environments) and operating/usage scenarios, modes and states for operations, support, training, manufacturing, disposal, and verifications throughout the life of the product
- Rationale for decisions and characteristics (requirements, requirement allocations, and design choices)

Because design descriptions can involve a very large amount of data and can be crucial to successful product-component development, it is advisable to establish criteria for organizing the data and for selecting the data content. It is particularly useful to use the product architecture as a means of organizing this data and abstracting views that are clear and relevant to an issue or feature of interest. These views include the following:

- Customers
- Requirements
- The environment
- Functional
- Logical

- Security
- Data
- States/modes
- Construction
- Management

These views are documented in the technical data package.

Typical Work Products

1. Technical data package

Subpractices

1. Determine the number of levels of design and the appropriate level of documentation for each design level.

   Determining the number of levels of product components (e.g., subsystem, hardware configuration item, circuit board, computer software configuration item [CSCI], computer software product component, computer software unit) that require documentation and requirements traceability is important to manage documentation costs and to support integration and verification plans.

2. Base detailed design descriptions on the allocated product-component requirements, architecture, and higher level designs.

3. Document the design in the technical data package.

4. Document the rationale for key (i.e., significant effect on cost, schedule, or technical performance) decisions made or defined.

5. Revise the technical data package as necessary.

The following specific practice is subsumed in the staged representation by SP 2.3-3, Design Interfaces Using Criteria.

SP 2.3-1 ESTABLISH INTERFACE DESCRIPTIONS

Establish and maintain the solution for product-component interfaces.

The product-component interface description covers interfaces between the following:

- Product components and product components
- Lower level product components and higher level product components
- Product components and product-related life-cycle processes
- Product components and external items

CONTINUOUS ONLY

Typical Work Products

1. Interface design
2. Interface design documents

Subpractices

1. Identify and document interfaces associated with other product components.
2. Identify interfaces associated with external items.
3. Identify interfaces between product components and the product-related life-cycle processes.

   For example, such interfaces could include those between a product component to be fabricated and the jigs and fixtures used to enable that fabrication during the manufacturing process.

4. Ensure that the solution includes the interface requirements developed in the requirements development processes.

   Refer to the Identify Interface Requirements specific practice in the Requirements Development process area for more information about identifying product and product-component interface requirements.

SP 2.3-3   DESIGN INTERFACES USING CRITERIA

Design comprehensive product-component interfaces in terms of established and maintained criteria.

Interface designs include the following:

- Origination
- Destination
- Stimulus and data characteristics for software
- Electrical, mechanical, and functional characteristics for hardware

The criteria for interfaces frequently reflect a comprehensive list of critical parameters that must be defined, or at least investigated, to ascertain their applicability. These parameters are often peculiar to a given type of product (e.g., software, mechanical, electrical) and are often associated with safety, security, durability, and mission-critical characteristics.

Typical Work Products

1. Interface design specifications
2. Interface control documents

3. Interface specification criteria

4. Rationale for selected interface design

Subpractices

1. Define interface criteria.

These criteria can be a part of the organizational process assets.

Refer to the Organizational Process Definition process area for more information about establishing and maintaining organizational process assets.

2. Apply the criteria to the interface design alternatives.

Refer to the Decision Analysis and Resolution process area for more information about identifying criteria and selecting alternatives based on those criteria.

3. Document the selected interface designs and the rationale for the selection.

SP 2.4-3 *PERFORM MAKE, BUY, OR REUSE ANALYSES*

Evaluate whether the product components should be developed, purchased, or re-used based on established criteria.

The determination of what products or product components will be acquired is frequently referred to as a "make-or-buy analysis." It is based on an analysis of the needs of the project. This make-or-buy analysis begins early in the project during the first iteration of design; continues during the design process; and is completed with the decision to develop, acquire, or reuse the product.

Refer to the Requirements Development process area for more information about determining the product and product-component requirements.

Refer to the Requirements Management process area for more information about managing requirements.

Factors affecting the make-or-buy decision include the following:

- Functions the products or services will provide and how these functions will fit into the project
- Available project resources and skills
- Costs of acquiring versus developing internally
- Critical delivery and integration dates
- Strategic business alliances, including high-level business requirements
- Market research of available products, including COTS products
- Functionality and quality of available products
- Skills and capabilities of potential suppliers

- Impact on core competencies
- Licenses, warranties, responsibilities, and limitations associated with products being acquired
- Product availability
- Proprietary issues
- Risk reduction

Many of these factors are addressed by the project.

The make-or-buy decision can be conducted using a formal evaluation approach.

Refer to the Decision Analysis and Resolution process area for more information about defining criteria and alternatives and performing formal evaluations.

As technology evolves, so does the rationale for choosing to develop or purchase a product component. While complex development efforts may favor purchasing an off-the-shelf product component, advances in productivity and tools may provide an opposing rationale. Off-the-shelf products may have incomplete or inaccurate documentation and may or may not be supported in the future.

Once the decision is made to purchase an off-the-shelf product component, the requirements are used to establish a supplier agreement. There are times when "off the shelf" refers to an existing item that may not be readily available in the marketplace. For example, some types of aircraft and engines are not truly "off the shelf" but can be readily procured. In some cases the use of such nondeveloped items is because the specifics of the performance and other product characteristics expected need to be within the limits specified. In these cases, the requirements and acceptance criteria may need to be included in the supplier agreement and managed. In other cases, the off-the-shelf product is literally off the shelf (word processing software, for example) and there is no agreement with the supplier that needs to be managed.

Refer to the Supplier Agreement Management process area for more information about how to address the acquisition of the product components that will be purchased.

Typical Work Products

1. Criteria for design and product-component reuse
2. Make-or-buy analyses
3. Guidelines for choosing COTS product components

Subpractices

1. Develop criteria for the reuse of product-component designs.

2. Analyze designs to determine if product components should be developed, reused, or purchased.

3. When purchased or nondevelopmental (COTS, government off the shelf, and reuse) items are selected, plan for their maintenance.

> **FOR SOFTWARE ENGINEERING**
> Consider how the compatibility of future releases of an operating system and a database manager will be handled.

SG 3   *IMPLEMENT THE PRODUCT DESIGN*

Product components, and associated support documentation, are implemented from their designs.

Product components are implemented from the designs established by the specific practices in the Develop the Design specific goal. The implementation usually includes unit testing of the product components before sending them to product integration and development of end-user documentation.

SP 3.1-1   *IMPLEMENT THE DESIGN*

Implement the designs of the product components.

> **FOR SOFTWARE ENGINEERING**
> Software code is a typical software product component.

Once the design has been completed, it is implemented as a product component. The characteristics of that implementation depend on the type of product component.

Design implementation at the top level of the product hierarchy involves the specification of each of the product components at the next level of the product hierarchy. This activity includes the allocation, refinement, and verification of each product component. It also involves the coordination between the various product-component development efforts.

Refer to the Requirements Development process area for more information about the allocation and refinement of requirements.

Refer to the Product Integration process area for more information about the management of interfaces and the integration of products and product components.

Example characteristics of this implementation are as follows:
- Software is coded.
- Data is documented.
- Services are documented.
- Electrical and mechanical parts are fabricated.
- Product-unique manufacturing processes are put into operation.
- Processes are documented.
- Facilities are constructed.
- Materials are produced (e.g., a product-unique material could be a petroleum, oil, or lubricant, or a new alloy).

Typical Work Products

1. Implemented design

Subpractices

1. Use effective methods to implement the product components.

FOR SOFTWARE ENGINEERING
Examples of software coding methods include the following:
- Structured programming
- Object-oriented programming
- Automatic code generation
- Software code reuse
- Use of applicable design patterns

FOR SYSTEMS ENGINEERING
Examples of appropriate fabrication methods include the following:
- Casting
- Molding
- Forming
- Joining
- Machining
- Tooling
- Welding
- Extruding

2. Adhere to applicable standards and criteria.

FOR SOFTWARE ENGINEERING

Examples of software coding standards include the following:

- Language standards
- Naming conventions for variables
- Acceptable language structures
- Structure and hierarchy of software product components
- Format of code and comments

FOR SOFTWARE ENGINEERING

Examples of software coding criteria include the following:

- Modularity
- Clarity
- Simplicity
- Structured (e.g., no GOTOs, one entrance, and one exit)
- Maintainability

FOR SYSTEMS ENGINEERING

Examples of standards include the following:

- Standard parts lists
- Standard drawing requirements
- Standards for manufactured parts

FOR SYSTEMS ENGINEERING

Examples of criteria include the following:

- Maintainability
- Reliability
- Safety

3. Conduct peer reviews of the selected product components.

   Refer to the Verification process area for more information about conducting peer reviews.

4. Perform unit testing of the product component as appropriate.

   Note that unit testing is not limited to software. Unit testing involves the testing of individual hardware or software units or groups of related items prior to integration of those items.

   Refer to the Verification process area for more information about verification methods and procedures and about verifying work products against their specified requirements.

FOR SOFTWARE ENGINEERING

Examples of unit testing methods include the following:

- Statement coverage testing
- Branch coverage testing
- Predicate coverage testing
- Path coverage testing
- Boundary value testing
- Special value testing

5. Revise the product component as necessary.

> An example of when the product component may need to be revised is when problems surface during implementation that could not be foreseen during design.

SP 3.2-1   DEVELOP PRODUCT SUPPORT DOCUMENTATION

Develop and maintain the end-use documentation.

This specific practice develops and maintains the documentation that will be used to install, operate, and maintain the product.

Typical Work Products

1. End-user training materials
2. User's manual
3. Operator's manual
4. Maintenance manual
5. Online help

Subpractices

1. Review the requirements, design, product, and test results to ensure that issues affecting the installation, operation, and maintenance documentation are identified and resolved.
2. Use effective methods to develop the installation, operation, and maintenance documentation.
3. Adhere to the applicable documentation standards.

> Examples of documentation standards include the following:
> - Compatibility with designated word processors
> - Acceptable fonts
> - Numbering of pages, sections, and paragraphs
> - Consistency with a designated style manual
> - Use of abbreviations
> - Security classification markings
> - Internationalization requirements

4. Develop preliminary versions of the installation, operation, and maintenance documentation in early phases of the project life cycle for review by the relevant stakeholders.

5. Conduct peer reviews of the installation, operation, and maintenance documentation.

    Refer to the Verification process area for more information about conducting peer reviews.

6. Revise the installation, operation, and maintenance documentation as necessary.

> Examples of when documentation may need to be revised include when the following events occur:
> - Requirements change
> - Design changes are made
> - Product changes are made
> - Documentation errors are identified
> - Workaround fixes are identified

Generic Practices by Goal

GG 1 ACHIEVE SPECIFIC GOALS

The process supports and enables achievement of the specific goals of the process area by transforming identifiable input work products to produce identifiable output work products.

GP 1.1 PERFORM BASE PRACTICES

Perform the base practices of the technical solution process to develop work products and provide services to achieve the specific goals of the process area.

GG 2 INSTITUTIONALIZE A MANAGED PROCESS

The process is institutionalized as a managed process.

CONTINUOUS ONLY

GG 3 *INSTITUTIONALIZE A DEFINED PROCESS*

The process is institutionalized as a defined process.

AUTHORS' NOTE: This generic goal's appearance here reflects
its location in the staged representation.

Commitment to Perform

GP 2.1 *ESTABLISH AN ORGANIZATIONAL POLICY*

Establish and maintain an organizational policy for planning and performing the technical solution process.

Elaboration

This policy establishes organizational expectations for addressing the iterative cycle in which product-component solutions are selected, product and product-component designs are developed, and the product-component designs are implemented.

Ability to Perform

GP 2.2 *PLAN THE PROCESS*

Establish and maintain the plan for performing the technical solution process.

Elaboration

Typically, this plan for performing the technical solution process is a part of the project plan as described in the Project Planning process area.

GP 2.3 *PROVIDE RESOURCES*

Provide adequate resources for performing the technical solution process, developing the work products, and providing the services of the process.

Elaboration

Special facilities may be required for developing, designing, and implementing solutions to requirements. When necessary, the facilities required for the activities in the Technical Solution process area are developed or purchased.

Examples of other resources provided include the following tools:
- Design specification tools
- Simulators and modeling tools
- Prototyping tools
- Scenario definition and management tools
- Requirements tracking tools
- Interactive documentation tools

GP 2.4 ASSIGN RESPONSIBILITY

Assign responsibility and authority for performing the process, developing the work products, and providing the services of the technical solution process.

GP 2.5 TRAIN PEOPLE

Train the people performing or supporting the technical solution process as needed.

Elaboration

> Examples of training topics include the following:
> - Application domain of the product and product components
> - Design methods
> - Interface design
> - Unit testing techniques
> - Standards (e.g., product, safety, human factors, environmental)

Directing Implementation

GP 2.6 MANAGE CONFIGURATIONS

Place designated work products of the technical solution process under appropriate levels of configuration management.

Elaboration

> Examples of work products placed under configuration management include the following:
> - Product, product component, process, service, and interface designs
> - Technical data packages
> - Interface design documents
> - Criteria for design and product-component reuse
> - Implemented designs (e.g., software code, fabricated product components)
> - User, installation, operation, and maintenance documentation

GP 2.7 IDENTIFY AND INVOLVE RELEVANT STAKEHOLDERS

Identify and involve the relevant stakeholders of the technical solution process as planned.

Elaboration

Select relevant stakeholders from customers, end users, developers, producers, testers, suppliers, marketers, maintainers, disposal personnel, and others who may be affected by, or may affect, the product as well as the process.

Examples of activities for stakeholder involvement include the following:
- Developing alternative solutions and selection criteria
- Evolving operational concept and scenarios
- Obtaining approval on external interface specifications and design descriptions
- Developing the technical data package
- Assessing the make, buy, or reuse alternatives for product components
- Implementing the design

GP 2.8 Monitor and Control the Process

Monitor and control the technical solution process against the plan for performing the process and take appropriate corrective action.

Elaboration

Examples of measures used in monitoring and controlling include the following:
- Cost, schedule, and effort expended for rework
- Percentage of requirements addressed in the product or product-component design
- Size and complexity of the product, product components, interfaces, and documentation
- Defect density of technical solutions work products

Verifying Implementation

GP 2.9 Objectively Evaluate Adherence

Objectively evaluate adherence of the technical solution process against its process description, standards, and procedures, and address noncompliance.

Elaboration

Examples of activities reviewed include the following:
- Selecting product-component solutions
- Developing product and product-component designs
- Implementing product-component designs

Examples of work products reviewed include the following:
- Technical data packages
- Product, product-component, and interface designs
- Implemented designs (e.g., software code, fabricated product components)
- User, installation, operation, and maintenance documentation

GP 2.10 Review Status with Higher Level Management

Review the activities, status, and results of the technical solution process with higher level management and resolve issues.

GG 3 INSTITUTIONALIZE A DEFINED PROCESS

The process is institutionalized as a defined process.

AUTHORS' NOTE: This generic goal's appearance here reflects its location in the continuous representation.

C ONLY

Ability to Perform

GP 3.1 ESTABLISH A DEFINED PROCESS

Establish and maintain the description of a defined technical solution process.

Directing Implementation

GP 3.2 COLLECT IMPROVEMENT INFORMATION

Collect work products, measures, measurement results, and improvement information derived from planning and performing the technical solution process to support the future use and improvement of the organization's processes and process assets.

GG 4 INSTITUTIONALIZE A QUANTITATIVELY MANAGED PROCESS

The process is institutionalized as a quantitatively managed process.

GP 4.1 ESTABLISH QUANTITATIVE OBJECTIVES FOR THE PROCESS

Establish and maintain quantitative objectives for the technical solution process that address quality and process performance based on customer needs and business objectives.

GP 4.2 STABILIZE SUBPROCESS PERFORMANCE

Stabilize the performance of one or more subprocesses to determine the ability of the technical solution process to achieve the established quantitative quality and process-performance objectives.

GG 5 INSTITUTIONALIZE AN OPTIMIZING PROCESS

The process is institutionalized as an optimizing process.

CONTINUOUS ONLY

GP 5.1 ENSURE CONTINUOUS PROCESS IMPROVEMENT

Ensure continuous improvement of the technical solution process in fulfilling the relevant business objectives of the organization.

GP 5.2 CORRECT ROOT CAUSES OF PROBLEMS

Identify and correct the root causes of defects and other problems in the technical solution process.

VALIDATION
An Engineering Process Area at Maturity Level 3

Purpose

The purpose of Validation (VAL) is to demonstrate that a product or product component fulfills its intended use when placed in its intended environment.

Introductory Notes

Validation activities can be applied to all aspects of the product in any of its intended environments, such as operation, training, manufacturing, maintenance, and support services. The methods employed to accomplish validation can be applied to work products as well as to the product and product components. The work products (e.g., requirements, designs, prototypes) should be selected on the basis of which are the best predictors of how well the product and product component will satisfy user needs.

The validation environment should represent the intended environment for the product and product components as well as represent the intended environment suitable for validation activities with work products.

Validation demonstrates that the product, as provided, will fulfill its intended use; whereas, verification addresses whether the work product properly reflects the specified requirements. In other words, verification ensures that "you built it right"; whereas, validation ensures that "you built the right thing." Validation activities use approaches similar to verification (e.g., test, analysis, inspection, demonstration, or simulation). Often, the end users are involved in the validation activities. Both validation and verification activities often run concurrently and may use portions of the same environment.

Refer to the Verification process area for more information about verification activities.

Whenever possible, validation should be accomplished using the product or product component operating in its intended environment. The entire environment can be used or only part of it. However, validation issues can be discovered early in the life of the project using work products.

When validation issues are identified, they are referred to the processes associated with the Requirements Development, Technical Solution, or Project Monitoring and Control process areas for resolution.

The specific practices of this process area build on each other in the following way:

- The Select Products for Validation specific practice enables the identification of the product or product component to be validated and the methods to be used to perform the validation.
- The Establish the Validation Environment specific practice enables the determination of the environment that will be used to carry out the validation.
- The Establish Validation Procedures and Criteria specific practice enables the development of validation procedures and criteria that are aligned with the characteristics of selected products, customer constraints on validation, methods, and the validation environment.
- The Perform Validation specific practice enables the performance of validation according to the methods, procedures, and criteria.

Related Process Areas

Refer to the Requirements Development process area for more information about requirements validation.

Refer to the Technical Solution process area for more information about transforming requirements into product specifications and for corrective action when validation issues are identified that affect the product or product-component design.

Refer to the Verification process area for more information about verifying that the product or product component meets its requirements.

Specific Practices by Goal

SG 1 PREPARE FOR VALIDATION

Preparation for validation is conducted.

Preparation activities include selecting products and product components for validation and establishing and maintaining the validation environment, procedures, and criteria. The items selected for validation may include only the product or it may include appropriate levels of the product components that are used to build the product. Any product or product component may be subject to validation, including replacement, maintenance, and training products, to name a few.

The environment required to validate the product or product component is prepared. The environment may be purchased or may be specified, designed, and built. The environments used for product integration and verification may be considered in collaboration with the validation environment to reduce cost and improve efficiency or productivity.

Practice-to-Goal Relationship Table

Continuous Representation	*Staged Representation*
SG 1 Prepare for Validation	SG 1 Prepare for Validation
SP 1.1-1 Select Products for Validation	SP 1.1-1 Select Products for Validation
SP 1.2-2 Establish the Validation Environment	SP 1.2-2 Establish the Validation Environment
SP 1.3-3 Establish Validation Procedures and Criteria	SP 1.3-3 Establish Validation Procedures and Criteria
SG 2 Validate Product or Product Components	SG 2 Validate Product or Product Components
SP 2.1-1 Perform Validation	SP 2.1-1 Perform Validation
SP 2.2-1 Analyze Validation Results	SP 2.2-1 Analyze Validation Results
GG 1 Achieve Specific Goals	
GP 1.1 Perform Base Practices	
GG 2 Institutionalize a Managed Process	GG 3 Institutionalize a Defined Process
GP 2.1 Establish an Organizational Policy	GP 2.1 Establish an Organizational Policy
GP 2.2 Plan the Process	GP 2.2 Plan the Process
GP 2.3 Provide Resources	GP 2.3 Provide Resources
GP 2.4 Assign Responsibility	GP 2.4 Assign Responsibility
GP 2.5 Train People	GP 2.5 Train People
GP 2.6 Manage Configurations	GP 2.6 Manage Configurations
GP 2.7 Identify and Involve Relevant Stakeholders	GP 2.7 Identify and Involve Relevant Stakeholders
GP 2.8 Monitor and Control the Process	GP 2.8 Monitor and Control the Process
GP 2.9 Objectively Evaluate Adherence	GP 2.9 Objectively Evaluate Adherence
GP 2.10 Review Status with Higher Level Management	GP 2.10 Review Status with Higher Level Management
GG 3 Institutionalize a Defined Process	
GP 3.1 Establish a Defined Process	GP 3.1 Establish a Defined Process
GP 3.2 Collect Improvement Information	GP 3.2 Collect Improvement Information
GG 4 Institutionalize a Quantitatively Managed Process	
GP 4.1 Establish Quantitative Objectives for the Process	
GP 4.2 Stabilize Subprocess Performance	
GG 5 Institutionalize an Optimizing Process	
GP 5.1 Ensure Continuous Process Improvement	
GP 5.2 Correct Root Causes of Problems	

VAL

SP 1.1-1 *Select Products for Validation*

Select products and product components to be validated and the validation methods that will be used for each.

Products and product components are selected for validation on the basis of their relationship to user needs. For each product component, the scope of the validation (e.g., operational behavior, maintenance, training, and user interface) should be determined.

The requirements and constraints for performing validation are collected. Then, validation methods are selected based on their ability to demonstrate that user needs are satisfied. The validation methods not only define the technical approach to product validation, but also drive the needs for the facilities, equipment, and environments. This may result in the generation of lower level product-component requirements that are handled by the requirements development processes. Derived requirements, such as interface requirements to test sets and test equipment, can be generated. These requirements are also passed to the requirements development processes to ensure that the product or product components can be validated in an environment that supports the methods.

Validation methods should be selected early in the life of the project so that they are clearly understood and agreed to by the relevant stakeholders.

The validation methods address the development, maintenance, support, and training for the product or product component as appropriate.

Typical Work Products

1. Lists of products and product components selected for validation
2. Validation methods for each product or product component
3. Requirements for performing validation for each product or product component
4. Validation constraints for each product or product component

Subpractices

1. Identify the key principles, features, and phases for product or product-component validation throughout the life of the project.
2. Determine which categories of user needs (operational, maintenance, training, or support) are to be validated.

   The product or product component must be maintainable and supportable in its intended operational environment. This specific practice also addresses the actual maintenance, training, and support services that may be delivered along with the product.

An example of evaluation of maintenance concepts in the operational environment is a demonstration that maintenance tools are operating with the actual product.

3. Select the product and product components to be validated.
4. Select the evaluation methods for product or product-component validation.
5. Review the validation selection, constraints, and methods with relevant stakeholders.

SP 1.2-2 ESTABLISH THE VALIDATION ENVIRONMENT

Establish and maintain the environment needed to support validation.

The requirements for the validation environment are driven by the product or product components selected, by the type of the work products (e.g., design, prototype, final version), and by the methods of validation. These may yield requirements for the purchase or development of equipment, software, or other resources. These requirements are provided to the requirements development processes for development. The validation environment may include the reuse of existing resources. In this case, arrangements for the use of these resources must be made. Examples of the type of elements in a validation environment include the following:

- Test tools interfaced with the product being validated (e.g., scope, electronic devices, probes)
- Temporary embedded test software
- Recording tools for dump or further analysis and replay
- Simulated subsystems or components (by software, electronics, or mechanics)
- Simulated interfaced systems (e.g., a dummy warship for testing a naval radar)
- Real interfaced systems (e.g., aircraft for testing a radar with trajectory tracking facilities)
- Facilities and customer-supplied products
- The skilled people to operate or use all the preceding elements
- Dedicated computing or network test environment (e.g., pseudo-operational telecommunications-network testbed or facility with actual trunks, switches, and systems established for realistic integration and validation trials)

Early selection of the products or product components to be validated, the work products to be used in the validation, and the validation methods is needed to ensure that the validation environment will be available when necessary.

The validation environment should be carefully controlled to provide for replication, analysis of results, and revalidation of problem areas.

Typical Work Products

1. Validation environment

Subpractices

1. Identify validation environment requirements.
2. Identify customer-supplied products.
3. Identify reuse items.
4. Identify test equipment and tools.
5. Identify validation resources that are available for reuse and modification.
6. Plan the availability of resources in detail.

SP 1.3-3   *ESTABLISH VALIDATION PROCEDURES AND CRITERIA*

Establish and maintain procedures and criteria for validation.

Validation procedures and criteria are defined to ensure that the product or product component will fulfill its intended use when placed in its intended environment. Acceptance test cases and procedures may meet the need for validation procedures.

The validation procedures and criteria include test and evaluation of maintenance, training, and support services.

Examples of sources for validation criteria include the following:
- Product and product-component requirements
- Standards
- Customer acceptance criteria
- Environmental performance
- Thresholds of performance deviation

Typical Work Products

1. Validation procedures
2. Validation criteria
3. Test and evaluation procedures for maintenance, training, and support

Subpractices

1. Review the product requirements to ensure that issues affecting validation of the product or product component are identified and resolved.
2. Document the environment, operational scenario, procedures, inputs, outputs, and criteria for the validation of the selected product or product component.

3. Assess the design as it matures in the context of the validation environment to identify validation issues.

SG 2 VALIDATE PRODUCT OR PRODUCT COMPONENTS

The product or product components are validated to ensure that they are suitable for use in their intended operating environment.

The validation methods, procedures, and criteria are used to validate the selected products and product components and any associated maintenance, training, and support services using the appropriate validation environment.

SP 2.1-1 PERFORM VALIDATION

Perform validation on the selected products and product components.

To be acceptable to users, a product or product component must perform as expected in its intended operational environment.

Validation activities are performed and the resulting data are collected according to the established methods, procedures, and criteria.

The as-run validation procedures should be documented and the deviations occurring during the execution should be noted, as appropriate.

For users of the continuous representation, this is a capability level 1 specific practice. Validation processes at capability level 1 or 2 may not include procedures and criteria, which are created in the Establish Validation Procedures and Criteria specific practice at capability level 3. When there are no procedures or criteria established, use the methods established by the Select Products for Validation specific practice to accomplish capability level 1 performance.

Typical Work Products

1. Validation reports
2. Validation results
3. Validation cross-reference matrix
4. As-run procedures log
5. Operational demonstrations

SP 2.2-1 ANALYZE VALIDATION RESULTS

Analyze the results of the validation activities and identify issues.

The data resulting from validation tests, inspections, demonstrations, or evaluations are analyzed against the defined validation criteria. Analysis reports indicate whether the needs were met; in the case of deficiencies, these reports document the degree of success or failure and categorize probable cause of failure. The collected test, inspection, or review results are compared with established evaluation criteria to determine whether to proceed or to address requirements or design issues in the requirements development or technical solution processes.

Analysis reports or as-run validation documentation may also indicate that bad test results are due to a validation procedure problem or a validation environment problem.

Typical Work Products

1. Validation deficiency reports
2. Validation issues
3. Procedure change request

Subpractices

1. Compare actual results to expected results.
2. Based on the established validation criteria, identify products and product components that do not perform suitably in their intended operating environments, or identify problems with the methods, criteria, and/or environment.
3. Analyze the validation data for defects.
4. Record the results of the analysis and identify issues.
5. Use validation results to compare actual measurements and performance to intended use or operational need.

Generic Practices by Goal

GG 1 *ACHIEVE SPECIFIC GOALS*

The process supports and enables achievement of the specific goals of the process area by transforming identifiable input work products to produce identifiable output work products.

GP 1.1 *PERFORM BASE PRACTICES*

Perform the base practices of the validation process to develop work products and provide services to achieve the specific goals of the process area.

GG 2 *INSTITUTIONALIZE A MANAGED PROCESS*

The process is institutionalized as a managed process.

CONTINUOUS ONLY

GG 3 **INSTITUTIONALIZE A DEFINED PROCESS**

The process is institutionalized as a defined process.

AUTHORS' NOTE: This generic goal's appearance here reflects
its location in the staged representation.

Commitment to Perform

GP 2.1 ESTABLISH AN ORGANIZATIONAL POLICY

Establish and maintain an organizational policy for planning and performing the validation process.

Elaboration

This policy establishes organizational expectations for selecting products and product components for validation; for selecting validation methods; and for establishing and maintaining validation procedures, criteria, and environments that ensure the products and product components satisfy user needs in their intended operating environment.

Ability to Perform

GP 2.2 PLAN THE PROCESS

Establish and maintain the plan for performing the validation process.

Elaboration

Typically, this plan for performing the validation process is included in (or referenced by) the project plan, which is described in the Project Planning process area.

GP 2.3 PROVIDE RESOURCES

Provide adequate resources for performing the validation process, developing the work products, and providing the services of the process.

Elaboration

Special facilities may be required for validating the product or product components. When necessary, the facilities required for validation are developed or purchased.

Examples of other resources provided include the following tools:
- Test-management tools
- Test-case generators
- Test-coverage analyzers
- Simulators
- Load, stress, and performance tools

GP 2.4   *ASSIGN RESPONSIBILITY*

Assign responsibility and authority for performing the process, developing the work products, and providing the services of the validation process.

GP 2.5   *TRAIN PEOPLE*

Train the people performing or supporting the validation process as needed.

Elaboration

Examples of training topics include the following:
- Application domain
- Validation principles, standards, and methods
- Intended-use environment

Directing Implementation

GP 2.6   *MANAGE CONFIGURATIONS*

Place designated work products of the validation process under appropriate levels of configuration management.

Elaboration

Examples of work products placed under configuration management include the following:
- Lists of products and product components selected for validation
- Validation methods, procedures, and criteria
- Validation reports

GP 2.7   *IDENTIFY AND INVOLVE RELEVANT STAKEHOLDERS*

Identify and involve the relevant stakeholders of the validation process as planned.

Elaboration

Select relevant stakeholders from customers, end users, developers, producers, testers, suppliers, marketers, maintainers, disposal personnel, and others who may be affected by, or may affect, the product as well as the process.

Examples of activities for stakeholder involvement include the following:
- Selecting the products and product components to be validated
- Establishing the validation methods, procedures, and criteria
- Reviewing results of product and product-component validation and resolving issues
- Resolving issues with the customers or end users

Issues with the customers or end users are resolved particularly when there are significant deviations from their baseline needs for the following:

- Waivers on the contract or agreement (what, when, and for which products, services, or manufactured products)
- Additional in-depth studies, trials, tests, or evaluations
- Possible changes in the contracts or agreements

GP 2.8   MONITOR AND CONTROL THE PROCESS

Monitor and control the validation process against the plan for performing the process and take appropriate corrective action.

Elaboration

> Examples of measures used in monitoring and controlling include the following:
> - Number of validation activities completed (planned versus actual)
> - Validation problem report trends (e.g., number written and number closed)
> - Validation problem report aging (i.e., how long each problem report has been open)

Verifying Implementation

GP 2.9   OBJECTIVELY EVALUATE ADHERENCE

Objectively evaluate adherence of the validation process against its process description, standards, and procedures, and address noncompliance.

Elaboration

> Examples of activities reviewed include the following:
> - Selecting the products and product components to be validated
> - Establishing and maintaining validation methods, procedures, and criteria
> - Validating products or product components

> Examples of work products reviewed include the following:
> - Validation methods, procedures, and criteria

GP 2.10   REVIEW STATUS WITH HIGHER LEVEL MANAGEMENT

Review the activities, status, and results of the validation process with higher level management and resolve issues.

GG 3   *INSTITUTIONALIZE A **DEFINED PROCESS***

The process is institutionalized as a defined process.

> AUTHORS' NOTE: This generic goal's appearance here reflects
> its location in the continuous representation.

C ONLY

Ability to Perform

GP 3.1   *ESTABLISH A **DEFINED PROCESS***

Establish and maintain the description of a defined validation process.

Directing Implementation

GP 3.2   *COLLECT **IMPROVEMENT INFORMATION***

*Collect work products, measures, measurement results, and improvement informa-
tion derived from planning and performing the validation process to support the
future use and improvement of the organization's processes and process assets.*

GG 4   *INSTITUTIONALIZE A **QUANTITATIVELY MANAGED PROCESS***

The process is institutionalized as a quantitatively managed process.

GP 4.1   *ESTABLISH **QUANTITATIVE OBJECTIVES FOR THE PROCESS***

*Establish and maintain quantitative objectives for the validation process that address
quality and process performance based on customer needs and business objectives.*

GP 4.2   *STABILIZE **SUBPROCESS PERFORMANCE***

*Stabilize the performance of one or more subprocesses to determine the ability of
the validation process to achieve the established quantitative quality and process-
performance objectives.*

GG 5   *INSTITUTIONALIZE AN **OPTIMIZING PROCESS***

The process is institutionalized as an optimizing process.

GP 5.1   *ENSURE **CONTINUOUS PROCESS IMPROVEMENT***

*Ensure continuous improvement of the validation process in fulfilling the relevant
business objectives of the organization.*

GP 5.2   *CORRECT **ROOT CAUSES OF PROBLEMS***

*Identify and correct the root causes of defects and other problems in the validation
process.*

CONTINUOUS ONLY

VERIFICATION
An Engineering Process Area at Maturity Level 3

Purpose

The purpose of Verification (VER) is to ensure that selected work products meet their specified requirements.

Introductory Notes

The Verification process area involves the following: verification preparation, verification performance, and identification of corrective action.

Verification includes verification of the product and intermediate work products against all selected requirements, including customer, product, and product-component requirements.

Verification is inherently an incremental process because it occurs throughout the development of the product and work products, beginning with verification of the requirements, progressing through the verification of the evolving work products, and culminating in the verification of the completed product.

The specific practices of this process area build on each other in the following way:

- The Select Work Products for Verification specific practice enables the identification of the work products to be verified, the methods to be used to perform the verification, and the requirements to be satisfied by each selected work product.
- The Establish the Verification Environment specific practice enables the determination of the environment that will be used to carry out the verification.
- The Establish Verification Procedures and Criteria specific practice then enables the development of verification procedures and criteria that are aligned with the selected work products, requirements, methods, and characteristics of the verification environment.
- The Perform Verification specific practice conducts the verification according to the available methods, procedures, and criteria.

Verification of work products substantially increases the likelihood that the product will meet the customer, product, and product-component requirements.

The Verification and Validation process areas are similar, but they address different issues. Validation demonstrates that the product, as provided (or as it will be provided), will fulfill its intended use, whereas verification addresses whether the work product properly reflects the specified requirements. In other words, verification ensures that "you built it right"; whereas, validation ensures that "you built the right thing."

Peer reviews are an important part of verification and are a proven mechanism for effective defect removal. An important corollary is to develop a better understanding of the work products and the processes that produced them so that defects can be prevented and process improvement opportunities can be identified.

Peer reviews involve a methodical examination of work products by the producers' peers to identify defects and other changes that are needed.

Examples of peer review methods include the following:
- Inspections
- Structured walkthroughs

Related Process Areas

Refer to the Validation process area for more information about confirming that a product or product component fulfills its intended use when placed in its intended environment.

Refer to the Requirements Development process area for more information about the generation and development of customer, product, and product-component requirements.

Refer to the Requirements Management process area for more information about managing requirements.

Specific Practices by Goal

SG 1   PREPARE FOR VERIFICATION

Preparation for verification is conducted.

Up-front preparation is necessary to ensure that verification provisions are embedded in product and product-component requirements, designs, developmental plans, and schedules. Verification includes selection, inspection, testing, analysis, and demonstration of work products.

Methods of verification include, but are not limited to, inspections, peer reviews, audits, walkthroughs, analyses, simulations, testing, and demonstrations.

Preparation also entails the definition of support tools, test equipment and software, simulations, prototypes, and facilities.

Practice-to-Goal Relationship Table

Continuous Representation	**Staged Representation**

SG 1 Prepare for Verification
    SP 1.1-1 Select Work Products for Verification
    SP 1.2-2 Establish the Verification Environment
    SP 1.3-3 Establish Verification Procedures and Criteria

SG 2 Perform Peer Reviews
    SP 2.1-1 Prepare for Peer Reviews
    SP 2.2-1 Conduct Peer Reviews
    SP 2.3-2 Analyze Peer Review Data

SG 3 Verify Selected Work Products
    SP 3.1-1 Perform Verification
    SP 3.2-2 Analyze Verification Results and Identify Corrective Action

GG 1 Achieve Specific Goals
    GP 1.1 Perform Base Practices

GG 2 Institutionalize a Managed Process
    GP 2.1 Establish an Organizational Policy
    GP 2.2 Plan the Process
    GP 2.3 Provide Resources
    GP 2.4 Assign Responsibility
    GP 2.5 Train People
    GP 2.6 Manage Configurations
    GP 2.7 Identify and Involve Relevant Stakeholders
    GP 2.8 Monitor and Control the Process
    GP 2.9 Objectively Evaluate Adherence
    GP 2.10 Review Status with Higher Level Management

GG 3 Institutionalize a Defined Process
    GP 3.1 Establish a Defined Process
    GP 3.2 Collect Improvement Information

GG 4 Institutionalize a Quantitatively Managed Process
    GP 4.1 Establish Quantitative Objectives for the Process
    GP 4.2 Stabilize Subprocess Performance

GG 5 Institutionalize an Optimizing Process
    GP 5.1 Ensure Continuous Process Improvement
    GP 5.2 Correct Root Causes of Problems

Staged Representation

SG 1 Prepare for Verification
    SP 1.1-1 Select Work Products for Verification
    SP 1.2-2 Establish the Verification Environment
    SP 1.3-3 Establish Verification Procedures and Criteria

SG 2 Perform Peer Reviews
    SP 2.1-1 Prepare for Peer Reviews
    SP 2.2-1 Conduct Peer Reviews
    SP 2.3-2 Analyze Peer Review Data

SG 3 Verify Selected Work Products
    SP 3.1-1 Perform Verification
    SP 3.2-2 Analyze Verification Results and Identify Corrective Action

GG 3 Institutionalize a Defined Process
    GP 2.1 Establish an Organizational Policy
    GP 2.2 Plan the Process
    GP 2.3 Provide Resources
    GP 2.4 Assign Responsibility
    GP 2.5 Train People
    GP 2.6 Manage Configurations
    GP 2.7 Identify and Involve Relevant Stakeholders
    GP 2.8 Monitor and Control the Process
    GP 2.9 Objectively Evaluate Adherence
    GP 2.10 Review Status with Higher Level Management

    GP 3.1 Establish a Defined Process
    GP 3.2 Collect Improvement Information

SP 1.1-1 *Select Work Products for Verification*

Select the work products to be verified and the verification methods that will be used for each.

Work products are selected based on their contribution to meeting project objectives and requirements, and to addressing project risks.

The work products to be verified may include those associated with maintenance, training, and support services. The work product requirements for verification are included with the verification methods. The verification methods address the technical approach to work product verification and the specific approaches that will be used to verify that specific work products meet their requirements.

> **For Software Engineering**
> Examples of verification methods include the following:
> - Path coverage testing
> - Load, stress, and performance testing
> - Decision-table-based testing
> - Functional decomposition-based testing
> - Test-case reuse
> - Acceptance tests

> **For Supplier Sourcing**
> Products supplied from outside of the project should be considered for verification.

Selection of the verification methods typically begins with involvement in the definition of product and product-component requirements to ensure that these requirements are verifiable. Reverification should be addressed by the verification methods to ensure that rework performed on work products does not cause unintended defects.

> **For Integrated Product and Process Development**
> The verification methods should be developed concurrently and iteratively with the product and product-component designs.

> **For Supplier Sourcing**
> Verification methods should be coordinated with suppliers to ensure applicability of the project's methods to the supplier's environment.

Typical Work Products

1. Lists of work products selected for verification
2. Verification methods for each selected work product

Subpractices

1. Identify work products for verification.
2. Identify the requirements to be satisfied by each selected work product.

   Refer to the Maintain Bidirectional Traceability of Requirements specific practice in the Requirements Management process area to help identify the requirements for each work product.

3. Identify the verification methods that are available for use.
4. Define the verification methods to be used for each selected work product.
5. Submit for integration with the project plan the identification of work products to be verified, the requirements to be satisfied, and the methods to be used.

   Refer to the Project Planning process area for information about coordinating with project planning.

SP 1.2-2 ESTABLISH THE VERIFICATION ENVIRONMENT

Establish and maintain the environment needed to support verification.

An environment must be established to enable verification to take place. The verification environment can be acquired, developed, reused, modified, or a combination of these, depending on the needs of the project.

The type of environment required will depend on the work products selected for verification and the verification methods used. A peer review may require little more than a package of materials, reviewers, and a room. A product test may require simulators, emulators, scenario generators, data reduction tools, environmental controls, and interfaces with other systems.

Typical Work Products

1. Verification environment

Subpractices

1. Identify verification environment requirements.
2. Identify verification resources that are available for reuse and modification.
3. Identify verification equipment and tools.
4. Acquire verification support equipment and an environment, such as test equipment and software.

SP 1.3-3 *ESTABLISH VERIFICATION PROCEDURES AND CRITERIA*

Establish and maintain verification procedures and criteria for the selected work products.

> **FOR INTEGRATED PRODUCT AND PROCESS DEVELOPMENT**
> The verification procedures and criteria should be developed concurrently and iteratively with the product and product-component designs.

Verification criteria are defined to ensure that the work products meet their requirements.

> Examples of sources for verification criteria include the following:
> - Product and product-component requirements
> - Standards
> - Organizational policies
> - Test type
> - Test parameters
> - Parameters for tradeoff between quality and cost of testing
> - Type of work products

> **FOR SUPPLIER SOURCING**
> The verification criteria affecting a supplier should be shared with the supplier to reduce the probability that a work product will fail its verification.

Typical Work Products

1. Verification procedures
2. Verification criteria

Subpractices

1. Generate the set of comprehensive, integrated verification procedures for work products and any commercial off-the-shelf products, as necessary.
2. Develop and refine the verification criteria when necessary.
3. Identify the expected results, any tolerances allowed in observation, and other criteria for satisfying the requirements.
4. Identify any equipment and environmental components needed to support verification.

SG 2 *PERFORM PEER REVIEWS*

Peer reviews are performed on selected work products.

Peer reviews involve a methodical examination of work products by the producers' peers to identify defects for removal and to recommend other changes that are needed.

The peer review is an important and effective engineering method implemented via inspections, structured walkthroughs, or a number of other collegial review methods.

Peer reviews are primarily applied to work products developed by the projects, but they can also be applied to other work products such as documentation and training work products that are typically developed by support groups.

SP 2.1-1   PREPARE FOR PEER REVIEWS

Prepare for peer reviews of selected work products.

Preparation activities for peer reviews typically include identifying the staff who will be invited to participate in the peer review of each work product; identifying the key reviewers who must participate in the peer review; preparing and updating any materials that will be used during the peer reviews, such as checklists and review criteria, and scheduling peer reviews.

Typical Work Products

1. Peer review schedule
2. Peer review checklist
3. Entry and exit criteria for work products
4. Criteria for requiring another peer review
5. Peer review training material
6. Selected work products to be reviewed

Subpractices

1. Determine what type of peer review will be conducted.

   > Examples of types of peer reviews include the following:
   > - Inspections
   > - Structured walkthroughs
   > - Active reviews

2. Define requirements for collecting data during the peer review.
   > *Refer to the Measurement and Analysis process area for information about identifying and collecting data.*

3. Establish and maintain entry and exit criteria for the peer review.
4. Establish and maintain criteria for requiring another peer review.

5. Establish and maintain checklists to ensure that the work products are reviewed consistently.

> Examples of items addressed by the checklists include the following:
> - Rules of construction
> - Design guidelines
> - Completeness
> - Correctness
> - Maintainability
> - Common defect types

The checklists are modified as necessary to address the specific type of work product and peer review. The peers of the checklist developers and potential users review the checklists.

6. Develop a detailed peer review schedule, including the dates for peer review training and for when materials for peer reviews will be available.

7. Ensure that the work product satisfies the peer review entry criteria prior to distribution.

8. Distribute the work product to be reviewed and its related information to the participants early enough to enable participants to adequately prepare for the peer review.

9. Assign roles for the peer review as appropriate.

> Examples of roles include the following:
> - Leader
> - Reader
> - Recorder
> - Author

10. Prepare for the peer review by reviewing the work product prior to conducting the peer review.

SP 2.2-1 CONDUCT PEER REVIEWS

Conduct peer reviews on selected work products and identify issues resulting from the peer review.

One of the purposes of conducting a peer review is to find and remove defects early. Peer reviews are performed incrementally as work products are being developed. These reviews are structured and are not management reviews.

Peer reviews may be performed on key work products of specification, design, test, and implementation activities and specific planning work products.

The focus of the peer review should be on the work product in review, not on the person who produced it.

When issues arise during the peer review, they should be communicated to the primary developer of the work product for correction.

Refer to the Project Monitoring and Control process area for information about tracking issues that arise during a peer review.

Peer reviews should address the following guidelines: there must be sufficient preparation, the conduct must be managed and controlled, consistent and sufficient data must be recorded (an example is conducting a formal inspection), and action items must be recorded.

Typical Work Products

1. Peer review results
2. Peer review issues
3. Peer review data

Subpractices

1. Perform the assigned roles in the peer review.
2. Identify and document defects and other issues in the work product.
3. Record the results of the peer review, including the action items.
4. Collect peer review data.

   Refer to the Measurement and Analysis process area for more information about data collection.

5. Identify action items and communicate the issues to relevant stakeholders.
6. Conduct an additional peer review if the defined criteria indicate the need.
7. Ensure that the exit criteria for the peer review are satisfied.

SP 2.3-2 ANALYZE PEER REVIEW DATA

Analyze data about preparation, conduct, and results of the peer reviews.

Refer to the Measurement and Analysis process area for more information about obtaining and analyzing data.

Typical Work Products

1. Peer review data
2. Peer review action items

Subpractices

1. Record data related to the preparation, conduct, and results of the peer reviews.

   Typical data are product name, product size, composition of the peer review team, type of peer review, preparation time per reviewer, length of the review meeting, number of defects found, type and origin of defect, and so on.

Additional information on the work product being peer reviewed may be collected, such as size, development stage, operating modes examined, and requirements being evaluated.

2. Store the data for future reference and analysis.

3. Protect the data to ensure that peer review data are not used inappropriately.

> Examples of inappropriate use of peer review data include using data to evaluate the performance of people and using data for attribution.

4. Analyze the peer review data.

SG 3 VERIFY SELECTED WORK PRODUCTS

Selected work products are verified against their specified requirements.

SP 3.1-1 PERFORM VERIFICATION

Perform verification on the selected work products.

Verifying products and work products incrementally promotes early detection of problems and can result in the early removal of defects. The results of verification save considerable cost of fault isolation and rework associated with troubleshooting problems.

> For users of the continuous representation, this is a capability level 1 specific practice. Verification processes at capability level 1 or 2 may not include procedures and criteria that are created in the Establish Verification Procedures and Criteria specific practice at capability level 3. When there are no procedures or criteria established, use the methods established by the Select Work Products for Verification specific practice to accomplish capability level 1 performance. *CONTINUOUS ONLY*

Typical Work Products

1. Verification results
2. Verification reports
3. Demonstrations
4. As-run procedures log

Subpractices

1. Perform verification of selected work products against their requirements.
2. Record the results of verification activities.
3. Identify action items resulting from verification of work products.
4. Document the "as-run" verification method and the deviations from the available methods and procedures discovered during its performance.

SP 3.2-2 ANALYZE VERIFICATION RESULTS AND IDENTIFY CORRECTIVE ACTION

Analyze the results of all verification activities and identify corrective action.

Actual results must be compared to established verification criteria to determine acceptability.

The results of the analysis are recorded as evidence that verification was conducted.

For each work product, all available verification results are incrementally analyzed and corrective actions are initiated to ensure that the requirements have been met. Since a peer review is one of several verification methods, peer review data should be included in this analysis activity to ensure that the verification results are analyzed sufficiently. Analysis reports or "as-run" method documentation may also indicate that bad verification results are due to method problems, criteria problems, or a verification environment problem.

Refer to the corrective action practices of Project Monitoring and Control process area for more information about implementing corrective action.

Typical Work Products

1. Analysis report (e.g., statistics on performances, causal analysis of nonconformances, comparison of the behavior between the real product and models, and trends)
2. Trouble reports
3. Change requests for the verification methods, criteria, and environment
4. Corrective actions to verification methods, criteria, and environment

Subpractices

1. Compare actual results to expected results.
2. Based on the established verification criteria, identify products that have not met their requirements or identify problems with the methods, procedures, criteria, and verification environment.
3. Analyze the verification data on defects.
4. Record all results of the analysis in a report.
5. Use verification results to compare actual measurements and performance to technical performance parameters.
6. Provide information on how defects can be resolved (including verification methods, criteria, and verification environment) and formalize it in a plan.

FOR SUPPLIER SOURCING
Distribute pertinent verification results to the supplier of the work product.

Generic Practices by Goal

GG 1   *ACHIEVE SPECIFIC GOALS*

The process supports and enables achievement of the specific goals of the process area by transforming identifiable input work products to produce identifiable output work products.

GP 1.1   *PERFORM BASE PRACTICES*

Perform the base practices of the verification process to develop work products and provide services to achieve the specific goals of the process area.

GG 2   *INSTITUTIONALIZE A MANAGED PROCESS*

The process is institutionalized as a managed process.

GG 3   *INSTITUTIONALIZE A DEFINED PROCESS*

The process is institutionalized as a defined process.

AUTHORS' NOTE: This generic goal's appearance here reflects its location in the staged representation.

Commitment to Perform

GP 2.1   *ESTABLISH AN ORGANIZATIONAL POLICY*

Establish and maintain an organizational policy for planning and performing the verification process.

Elaboration
This policy establishes organizational expectations for establishing and maintaining verification methods, procedures, criteria, verification environment, performing peer reviews, and verifying selected work products.

Ability to Perform

GP 2.2   *PLAN THE PROCESS*

Establish and maintain the plan for performing the verification process.

Elaboration
Typically, this plan for performing the verification process is included in (or referenced by) the project plan, which is described in the Project Planning process area.

GP 2.3 PROVIDE RESOURCES

Provide adequate resources for performing the verification process, developing the work products, and providing the services of the process.

Elaboration

Special facilities may be required for verifying selected work products. When necessary, the facilities required for the activities in the Verification process area are developed or purchased.

Certain verification methods may require special tools, equipment, facilities, and training (e.g., peer reviews may require meeting rooms and trained moderators; certain verification tests may require special test equipment and people skilled in the use of the equipment).

> Examples of other resources provided include the following tools:
> - Test management tools
> - Test-case generators
> - Test-coverage analyzers
> - Simulators

GP 2.4 ASSIGN RESPONSIBILITY

Assign responsibility and authority for performing the process, developing the work products, and providing the services of the verification process.

GP 2.5 TRAIN PEOPLE

Train the people performing or supporting the verification process as needed.

Elaboration

> Examples of training topics include the following:
> - Application domain
> - Verification principles, standards, and methods (e.g., analysis, demonstration, inspection, test)
> - Verification tools and facilities
> - Peer review preparation and procedures
> - Meeting facilitation

Directing Implementation

GP 2.6 MANAGE CONFIGURATIONS

Place designated work products of the verification process under appropriate levels of configuration management.

Elaboration

Examples of work products placed under configuration management include the following:
- Verification procedures and criteria
- Peer review training material
- Peer review data
- Verification reports

GP 2.7 IDENTIFY AND INVOLVE RELEVANT STAKEHOLDERS

Identify and involve the relevant stakeholders of the verification process as planned.

Elaboration

Select relevant stakeholders from customers, end users, developers, producers, testers, suppliers, marketers, maintainers, disposal personnel, and others who may be affected by, or may affect, the product as well as the process.

Examples of activities for stakeholder involvement include the following:
- Selecting work products and methods for verification
- Establishing verification procedures and criteria
- Conducting peer reviews
- Assessing verification results and identifying corrective action

GP 2.8 MONITOR AND CONTROL THE PROCESS

Monitor and control the verification process against the plan for performing the process and take appropriate corrective action.

Elaboration

Examples of measures used in monitoring and controlling include the following:
- Verification profile (e.g., the number of verifications planned and performed, and the defects found; perhaps categorized by verification method or type)
- Number of defects detected by defect category
- Verification problem report trends (e.g., number written and number closed)
- Verification problem report status (i.e., how long each problem report has been open)

Verifying Implementation

GP 2.9 OBJECTIVELY EVALUATE ADHERENCE

Objectively evaluate adherence of the verification process against its process description, standards, and procedures, and address noncompliance.

Elaboration

Examples of activities reviewed include the following:
- Selecting work products for verification
- Establishing and maintaining verification procedures and criteria
- Performing peer reviews
- Verifying selected work products

Examples of work products reviewed include the following:
- Verification procedures and criteria
- Peer review checklists
- Verification reports

GP 2.10 REVIEW STATUS WITH HIGHER LEVEL MANAGEMENT

Review the activities, status, and results of the verification process with higher level management and resolve issues.

GG 3 INSTITUTIONALIZE A DEFINED PROCESS

The process is institutionalized as a defined process.

AUTHORS' NOTE: This generic goal's appearance here reflects its location in the continuous representation.

Ability to Perform

GP 3.1 ESTABLISH A DEFINED PROCESS

Establish and maintain the description of a defined verification process.

Directing Implementation

GP 3.2 COLLECT IMPROVEMENT INFORMATION

Collect work products, measures, measurement results, and improvement information derived from planning and performing the verification process to support the future use and improvement of the organization's processes and process assets.

GG 4 INSTITUTIONALIZE A QUANTITATIVELY MANAGED PROCESS

The process is institutionalized as a quantitatively managed process.

GP 4.1 ESTABLISH QUANTITATIVE OBJECTIVES FOR THE PROCESS

Establish and maintain quantitative objectives for the verification process that address quality and process performance based on customer needs and business objectives.

GP 4.2 STABILIZE SUBPROCESS PERFORMANCE

Stabilize the performance of one or more subprocesses to determine the ability of the verification process to achieve the established quantitative quality and process-performance objectives.

GG 5 INSTITUTIONALIZE AN OPTIMIZING PROCESS

The process is institutionalized as an optimizing process.

GP 5.1 ENSURE CONTINUOUS PROCESS IMPROVEMENT

Ensure continuous improvement of the verification process in fulfilling the relevant business objectives of the organization.

GP 5.2 CORRECT ROOT CAUSES OF PROBLEMS

Identify and correct the root causes of defects and other problems in the verification process.

CONTINUOUS ONLY

PART THREE

The Appendices and Glossary

APPENDIX A

REFERENCES

Publicly Available Sources

Ahern 01   Ahern, Dennis; Clouse, Aaron; and Turner, Richard. *CMMI Distilled: A Practical Introduction to Integrated Process Improvement*. Boston: Addison-Wesley, 2001.

Bate 95   Bate, Roger; et al. *Systems Engineering Capability Maturity Model, Version 1.1 (CMU/SEI-95-MM-003)*. Pittsburgh, PA: Software Engineering Institute, Carnegie Mellon University, November 1995.

Crosby 79   Crosby, P. B. *Quality Is Free*. New York: McGraw-Hill, 1979.

Curtis 01   Curtis, Bill; Hefley, William E.; and Miller, Sally. *The People Capability Maturity Model*. Boston: Addison-Wesley, 2001.

Deming 86   Deming, W. Edwards. *Out of the Crisis*. Cambridge, MA: MIT Center for Advanced Engineering, 1986.

DoD 91   Department of Defense. *DoD Directive 5000.1: Defense Acquisition*. Washington, DC, 1991.

DoD 96a   Department of Defense. *DoD Regulation 5000.2: Mandatory Procedures for Major Defense Acquisition Programs and Major Automated Information Systems*. Washington, DC, 1996.

DoD 96b   Department of Defense. *DoD Guide to Integrated Product and Process Development (Version 1.0)*. Washington, DC: Office of the Under Secretary of Defense (Acquisition and Technology), February 5, 1996.
<http://www.acq.osd.mil/te/ survey/table_of_contents.html>

Dunaway 96   Dunaway, D.; and Masters, S. *CMM-Based Appraisal for Internal Process Improvement (CBA IPI): Method Description (CMU/SEI-96-TR-007)*. Pittsburgh, PA: Software Engineering Institute, Carnegie Mellon University, April 1996.
<http://www.sei.cmu.edu/publications/documents/96.reports/96.tr.007.html>

Dymond 95   Dymond, Kenneth M. *A Guide to the CMM: Understanding the Capability Maturity Model for Software*. Annapolis, MD: Process Inc., 1995.

EIA 94   Electronic Industries Alliance. *EIA Interim Standard: Systems Engineering (EIA/IS-632)*. Washington, DC, 1994.

EIA 95   Electronic Industries Alliance. *EIA Interim Standard: National Consensus Standard for Configuration Management (EIA/IS-649)*. Washington, DC, 1995.

EIA 98   Electronic Industries Alliance. *Systems Engineering Capability Model (EIA/IS-731)*. Washington, DC, 1998.
<http://geia.org/sstc/G47/731dwnld.htm>

FAA 97   Federal Aviation Administration. *Integrated Capability Maturity Model, Version 1.0 (FAA-iCMM)*, November 1997.
<http://www.faa.gov/aio/ProcessEngr/iCMM/index.htm>

Hefner 01   Hefner, Rick. CMMI Risk Management Requirements. Presentation at SEPG Conference, 2001.

Herbsleb 97   Herbsleb, James; Zubrow, David; Goldenson, Dennis; Hayes, Will; and Paulk, Mark. "Software Quality and the Capability Maturity Model." *Communications of the ACM* 40, 6 (June 1997): 30–40.

Humphrey 89   Humphrey, Watts S. *Managing the Software Process*. Reading, MA: Addison-Wesley, 1989.

IEEE 90   Institute of Electrical and Electronics Engineers. *IEEE Standard Computer Dictionary: A Compilation of IEEE Standard Computer Glossaries*. New York: IEEE, 1990.

INCOSE 96   International Council on Systems Engineering. *Systems Engineering Capability Assessment Model, Version 1.50*. Seattle, June 1996.

ISO 87   International Organization for Standardization. *ISO 9000: International Standard*. New York, 1987.
<http://www.iso.ch/>

ISO 95   International Organization for Standardization and International Electrotechnical Commission. *ISO/IEC TR 12207 Information Technology—Software Life Cycle Processes, 1995*.
<http://www.iso.ch/>

ISO 98   International Organization for Standardization and International Electrotechnical Commission. *ISO/IEC TR 15504 Information Technology—Software Process Assessment, 1998*.
<http://www.iso.ch/>

ISO 00   International Organization for Standardization. *ISO 9001, Quality Management Systems—Requirements, 2000*.
<http://www.iso.ch/>

ISO 02   International Organization for Standardization and International Electrotechnical Commission. *ISO/IEC 15939 Software Engineering—Software Measurement Process, 2002*.
<http://www.iso.ch/>

Juran 88   Juran, J. M. *Juran on Planning for Quality.* New York: Macmillan, 1988.

Masters 95   Masters, S.; and Bothwell, C. *CMM Appraisal Framework (CMU/ SEI-95-TR-001).* Pittsburgh, PA: Software Engineering Institute, Carnegie Mellon University, February 1995.
<http://www.sei.cmu.edu/publications/documents/95.reports/95-tr-001/95-tr-001-abstract.html>

McGarry 00   McGarry, John; Card, David; Jones, Cheryl; Layman, Beth; Clark, Elizabeth; Dean, Joseph; and Hall, Fred. *Practical Software Measurement: Objective Information for Decision Makers.* Boston: Addison-Wesley, 2002.

SEI 95   Software Engineering Institute. *The Capability Maturity Model: Guidelines for Improving the Software Process.* Reading, MA: Addison-Wesley, 1995.

SEI 97a   *Integrated Product Development Capability Maturity Model, Draft Version 0.98.* Pittsburgh, PA: Enterprise Process Improvement Collaboration and Software Engineering Institute, Carnegie Mellon University, July 1997.
<ftp://ftp.sei.cmu.edu/pub/CMMI/ipd-cmm-draft/>

SEI 97b   Software Engineering Institute. *Software CMM, Version 2.0 (Draft C),* October 22, 1997.
<http://www.sei.cmu.edu/activities/cmm/draft-c/c.html>

SEI 99   Software Engineering Institute. *CMMI A-Specification, Version 1.4,* April 1999.
<http://www.sei.cmu.edu/cmmi/org-docs/aspec1.4.html>

SEI 01a   CMMI Product Development Team. *ARC v1.1, Appraisal Requirements for CMMI, Version 1.1 (CMU/SEI-2001-TR-034, ESC-TR-2001-034).* Pittsburgh, PA: Software Engineering Institute, Carnegie Mellon University, December 2001.
<http://www.sei.cmu.edu/publications/documents/01.reports/01tr034.html>

SEI 01b   CMMI Product Development Team. *SCAMPI v1.1, Standard CMMI Appraisal Method for Process Improvement, Version 1.1: Method Definition Document (CMU/SEI-2001-HB-001).* Pittsburgh, PA: Software Engineering Institute, Carnegie Mellon University, December 2001.
<http://www.sei.cmu.edu/publications/documents/01.reports/01hb001.html>

SEI 01c   Paulk, Mark; and Chrissis, Mary Beth. *The 2001 High Maturity Workshop (CMU/SEI-2001-SR-014).* Pittsburgh, PA: Software Engineering Institute, Carnegie Mellon University, January 2002.
<http://www.sei.cmu.edu/publications/documents/01.reports/01sr014.html>

SEI 02a   CMMI Product Development Team. *CMMI for Systems Engineering/Software Engineering, Version 1.1 Staged Representation (CMU/SEI-2002-TR-002, ESC-TR-2002-002).* Pittsburgh, PA: Software Engineering Institute, Carnegie Mellon University, January 2002.
<http://www.sei.cmu.edu/publications/documents/02.reports/02tr002.html>

SEI 02b CMMI Product Development Team. *CMMI for Systems Engineering/ Software Engineering, Version 1.1 Continuous Representation (CMU/SEI-2002-TR-001, ESC-TR-2002-001)*. Pittsburgh, PA: Software Engineering Institute, Carnegie Mellon University, January 2002.
<http://www.sei.cmu.edu/publications/documents/02.reports/02tr001.html>

SEI 02c CMMI Product Development Team. *CMMI for Systems Engineering/ Software Engineering/Integrated Product and Process Development, Version 1.1 Staged Representation (CMU/SEI-2002-TR-004, ESC-TR-2002-004)*. Pittsburgh, PA: Software Engineering Institute, Carnegie Mellon University, January 2002.
<http://www.sei.cmu.edu/publications/documents/02.reports/02tr004.html>

SEI 02d CMMI Product Development Team. *CMMI for Systems Engineering/ Software Engineering/Integrated Product and Process Development, Version 1.1 Continuous Representation (CMU/SEI-2002-TR-003, ESC-TR-2002-003)*. Pittsburgh, PA: Software Engineering Institute, Carnegie Mellon University, January 2002.
<http://www.sei.cmu.edu/publications/documents/02.reports/02tr003.html>

SEI 02e CMMI Product Development Team. *CMMI for Systems Engineering/ Software Engineering/Integrated Product and Process Development/Supplier Sourcing, Version 1.1 Staged Representation (CMU/SEI-2002-TR-012, ESC-TR-2002-012)*. Pittsburgh, PA: Software Engineering Institute, Carnegie Mellon University, March 2002.
<http://www.sei.cmu.edu/publications/documents/02.reports/02tr012.html>

SEI 02f CMMI Product Development Team. *CMMI for Systems Engineering/ Software Engineering/Integrated Product and Process Development/Supplier Sourcing, Version 1.1 Continuous Representation (CMU/SEI-2002-TR-011, ESC-TR-2002-011)*. Pittsburgh, PA: Software Engineering Institute, Carnegie Mellon University, March 2002.
<http://www.sei.cmu.edu/publications/documents/02.reports/02tr011.html>

SEI 02g Software Engineering Institute. *The Measurement and Analysis Process Area in CMMI, 2002*.
<http://www.sei.cmu.edu/cmmi/publications/meas-anal-cmmi.html>

SEI 02h Software Engineering Institute. *Software Acquisition Capability Maturity Model (SA-CMM) Version 1.03 (CMU/SEI-2002-TR-010, ESC-TR-2002-010)*. Pittsburgh, PA: Software Engineering Institute, Carnegie Mellon University, March 2002.
<http://www.sei.cmu.edu/publications/documents/02.reports/02tr010.html>

Shewhart 31 Shewhart, Walter A. *Economic Control of Quality of Manufactured Product*. New York: Van Nostrand, 1931.

SPMN 97 Software Program Managers Network. *Program Managers Guide to Software Acquisition Best Practices, Version 2.31, 1998*.
<http://www.spmn.com/products_guidebooks.html>

Regularly Updated Sources

DoD 1   Department of Defense. Defense Acquisition Deskbook, Version 3.2.
<http://web2.deskbook.osd.mil/default.asp>

Paulk 1   Paulk, Mark. Software Capability Maturity Model (SW-CMM®) Case Study Bibliography.
<http://www.sei.cmu.edu/activities/cmm/docs/roi.html>

SEI 1   Software Engineering Institute. Transitioning Your Organization from Software CMM Version 1.1 to CMMI-SW Version 1.0.
<http://www.sei.cmu.edu/cmmi/publications/white-paper.html>

SEI 2   Software Engineering Institute. The IDEAL Model.
<http://www.sei.cmu.edu/ideal/ideal.html>

SEI 3   Software Engineering Institute. Advice for Change Agents.
<http://www.sei.cmu.edu/asta/advice.html>

SEI 4   Software Engineering Institute. CMMI Frequently Asked Questions (FAQ).
<http://www.sei.cmu.edu/cmmi/adoption/cmmi-faq.html>

STSC 1   Software Technology Support Center. Mapping of the Capability Maturity Model.
<http://www.stsc.hill.af.mil/consulting/cmmi/cmmiseswippdv11.pdf>

APPENDIX B

ACRONYMS

ARC Appraisal requirements for CMMI
CAF CMM Appraisal Framework
CAR Causal Analysis and Resolution (process area)
CAU Cockpit Avionics Upgrade
CBA IPI CMM-Based Appraisal for Internal Process Improvement
CBT computer-based training
CCB configuration control board
CM Configuration Management (process area)
CMM Capability Maturity Model
CMMI Capability Maturity Model Integration
CMMI-SE/SW Capability Maturity Model Integration for Systems Engineering and Software Engineering
CMMI-SE/SW/IPPD Capability Maturity Model Integration for Systems Engineering, Software Engineering, and Integrated Product and Process Development
CMMI-SE/SW/IPPD/SS Capability Maturity Model Integration for Systems Engineering, Software Engineering, Integrated Product and Process Development, and Supplier Sourcing
COTS commercial off the shelf
CPM critical path method
DAR Decision Analysis and Resolution (process area)
DoD Department of Defense
EIA Electronic Industries Alliance
EIA/IS Electronic Industries Alliance Interim Standard
FAA Federal Aviation Administration
FAA-iCMM Federal Aviation Administration Integrated Capability Maturity Model
GG generic goal
GP generic practice
IDEAL Initiating, Diagnosing, Establishing, Acting, Learning
IEEE Institute of Electrical and Electronics Engineers
INCOSE International Council on Systems Engineering

IPD-CMM Integrated Product Development Capability Maturity Model

IPM Integrated Project Management (process area)

IPPD Integrated Product and Process Development

IPT Integrated Product Team

ISM Integrated Supplier Management (process area)

ISO International Organization for Standardization

ISO/IEC International Organization for Standardization and International Electrotechnical Commission

IT Integrated Teaming (process area)

KSLOC thousand source lines of code

MA Measurement and Analysis (process area)

MOA memorandum of agreement

NASA National Aeronautics and Space Administration

NDI nondevelopmental item

NDIA National Defense Industrial Association

OEI Organizational Environment for Integration (process area)

OID Organizational Innovation and Deployment (process area)

OPD Organizational Process Definition (process area)

OPF Organizational Process Focus (process area)

OPP Organizational Process Performance (process area)

OT Organizational Training (process area)

OUSD/AT&L Office of the Under Secretary of Defense, Acquisition, Technology, and Logistics

P-CMM People Capability Maturity Model

PA process area

PAIS Process Appraisal Information System

PASS Primary Avionics Software System

PERT Program Evaluation and Review Technique

PI Product Integration (process area)

PMC Project Monitoring and Control (process area)

PP Project Planning (process area)

PPQA Process and Product Quality Assurance (process area)

QFD Quality Function Deployment

QPM Quantitative Project Management (process area)

RD Requirements Development (process area)

REQM Requirements Management (process area)

RSKM Risk Management (process area)

SA-CMM Software Acquisition Capability Maturity Model

SAM Supplier Agreement Management (process area)

SCAMPI Standard CMMI Appraisal Method for Process Improvement

SDMP software development management plan

SE systems engineering

SE-CMM   Systems Engineering Capability Maturity Model
SEC   Software Executive Council
SECAM   Systems Engineering Capability Assessment Model
SECM   Systems Engineering Capability Model
SEI   Software Engineering Institute
SE/SW   systems engineering and software engineering
SEPG   software engineering process group
SG   specific goal
SP   specific practice
SPMN   Software Program Managers Network
SS   supplier sourcing
STSC   Software Technology Support Center
SW   software engineering
SW-CMM   Capability Maturity Model for Software
TS   Technical Solution (process area)
URL   Uniform Resource Locator
USA   United Space Alliance
VAL   Validation (process area)
VER   Verification (process area)
WBS   work breakdown structure

APPENDIX C

CMMI PROJECT PARTICIPANTS

Many talented people were part of the product team for the CMMI Product Suite. Five primary groups involved in this development have been the Product Team, Sponsors, Steering Group, Configuration Control Board, and Stakeholders/Reviewers. Both present and emeritus members of these groups are listed here.

Product Team

The Product Team wrote, reviewed, revised, discussed, and agreed on the structure and technical content of the CMMI Product Suite, including the framework, models, training, and appraisal materials. Development activities were based on an A-Specification provided by the Steering Group, the three source models, and comments from Stakeholders and Steering Group members.

AT&T Labs
    Midha, Anil
Automatic Data Processing,
Inc.
    Eagan, Robert
BAE Systems
    Cole, David
    Gunning, Kelly
Boeing
    Beshore, David
    Brayer, Gil
    Schoening, Bill
Comarco Systems, Inc.
    Brown, Linda

Computer Sciences Corporation
    Irion-Talbot, Wendy
    Keeler, Kristi
Defense Logistics Agency
    Roberts, John
    Zentner, David T.
EER Systems
    Cepeda, Sandra
IBM
    McNeill, Bob
    Akiyama, Yoshihiro
Institute for Defense Analyses
    Kind, Peter
    Richter, Karen

Integrated System Diagnostics, Inc.
  Morin, Joseph F.
Jacobs Sverdrup Advanced Systems
Group
  Dutton, Jeffrey L.
KPMG Consulting
  Pomietto, Robert J.
Lockheed Martin
  Angstadt, Kim
  Blasewitz, Bob
  Busby, Mary
  Kellogg, David
  Weiser, Bob
  Wells, Curt
MitoKen Solutions
  Iyer, Seshadri
Ericsson
  Pesant, Jérôme
Federal Aviation Administration
  Turner, Richard
General Dynamics
  Consiglio, John
Harris Corporation
  Draper, Geoff
Hewlett-Packard Company
  Schurkus, Fred
Honeywell Corporation
  Graffius, Joe
Motorola
  Glick, Bud
National Reconnaissance Office
  Benhoff, Melanie
National Security Agency
  Kormos, Christina
Northrop Grumman Corporation
  Ahern, Dennis
  Hollenbach, Craig
  Steiner, Cliff

Pacific Bell
  Granger-Parker, Carol
  Stratton, Duane
Q-Labs. Inc.
  Hefley, Bill
  Menezes, Winifred
Raytheon
  Berauer, Ben
  Clouse, Aaron
  Moon, Jane
  Norton, John
  Wolf, Gary
Rockwell Collins
  Denny, Barbara
Science Applications International
Corporation
  Blazer, Dan
  Herndon, Mary Anne
  Rose, Kevin
  West, Laura
Siemens
  Hertneck, Christian
Software Engineering Institute
  Baker, Michele
  Barbour, Rick
  Bate, Roger
  Batman, Joe
  Bennett, Dan
  Biesecker, Carol
  Brownsword, Lisa
  Capell, Peter
  Carter, Lynn
  Cavanaugh, Mark
  Chrissis, Mary Beth
  Cooper, Jack
  Curtis, Pamela
  Dunaway, Donna
  Dymond, Ken
  Dzmura, Lucas

Fantazier, Bob
Ferguson, Jack
Fisher, Matt
Gallagher, Brian
Garcia, SuZ
Gibson, Diane
Goldenson, Dennis
Graffius, Joe
Gross, Jon
Guerin, Joan
Hayes, Will
Johnson, Martha
Jones, Larry
Kasse, Tim
Kitson, Dave
Kitson, Jeanie
Konrad, Mike
Martinez-Eskenasy, Antonio
Masters, Steve
McFeeley, Bob
McSteen, Bill
Miluk, Gene
Minnich, Ilene
Mogilensky, Judah
Peters, Wendy
Phillips, David M. (Mike)
Ryan, Charlie
Shrum, Sandy
Siviy, Jeannine
Straitiff, Betsy
Svolou, Agapi
Tady, Carolyn
Tyson, Barbara
Waclo, John
Weber, Charles
Wemyss, Gian
White, David
Williams, Ray
Zubrow, Dave

Software Productivity Consortium
   Armstrong, Jim
TeraQuest, Inc.
   Curtis, Bill
TRW
   Hefner, Rick
   Shuster, David
   Ulrich, Ron
THALES
   Bonnet, Thierry
   Cattan, Denise
   Des Rochettes, Gilles
   Hozhabrafkan, Fariba
US Air Force
   Allgood, Bruce
   Baxter, Brent
   Bernard, Tom
   Craig, Rushby
   Duquette, Joe
   Jarzombek, Joe
   Kordik, John
   Lanier, Kelly
   Price, John
   Richins, Kevin
   Swarz, Robert
US Army
   Ferraro, Alison
   Gordon, Chuck
   Gregg, Mary E.
   Riviere, Paul
   Sherer, S. Wayne
US Navy
   Gramoy, Beth
   Jacobson, Sherwin
   Taylor, Guy D

Sponsors

The CMMI project is sponsored by both government and industry. Government sponsorship is provided by the US Department of Defense (DoD), specifically the Office of the Under Secretary of Defense, Acquisition, Technology, and Logistics (OUSD/AT&L). Industry sponsorship is provided by the Systems Engineering Committee of the National Defense Industrial Association (NDIA).

National Defense Industrial Association
    Rassa, Bob, NDIA Systems Engineering Committee
Office of the Secretary of Defense
    Etter, Dolores, OUSD (S&T)*
    Garber, V., OUSD (AT&L)
    Shaffer, Mark, OUSD (AT&L)*
    Spruill, Nancy, OUSD (AT&L)
    Wilson, John, OUSD (AT&L)*

Steering Group

The Steering Group has guided and approved the plans of the Product Team, provided consultation on significant CMMI project issues, and ensured involvement from a variety of interested communities.

Federal Aviation Administration
    Ibrahim, Linda
General Dynamics
    Lentz, Robert
Lockheed Martin
    Weszka, Joan
Motorola
    Brown, Leroy
Northrop Grumman Corporation
    Wilson, Hal
Office of the Secretary of Defense
    Aggers, Richard[†]
    Desiderio, George
    Ferguson, Jack[†]
    Jarzombek, Joe

    Parry, Tom[†]
    Sylvester, Richard
    Zsak, Mike[†]
Raytheon
    Rassa, Bob
Software Engineering Institute
    Chittister, Clyde
    Peterson, Bill
    Phillips, David M. (Mike)[†]
Steering Group Support Staff
    Farinello, Joe, USAF, Meeting Facilitator
    Kayuha, Bob, Dayton Aerospace, Recording Secretary

*Emeritus sponsors
[†]Emeritus members

US Air Force
  Babel, Phil†
  Dulai, Ajmel†
  Nicol, Mike
US Army
  Castellano, David R.
  Devine, Michael P.*

US Navy
  McConnell, David*
  Zettervall, Brenda

Configuration Control Board

The Configuration Control Board is the official mechanism for controlling changes to the CMMI models. This group is responsible for product integrity over the life of the Product Suite by reviewing all changes to the baselines and approving only changes that meet the criteria for an upcoming release.

Boeing
  Schoening, Bill
Computer Sciences Corporation
  Croll, Paul
Institute for Defense Analyses
  Richter, Karen
Lockheed Martin
  Schwomeyer, Warren
  Wood, William A. (Bill)
Motorola
  Jacobsen, Nils
Raytheon
  Rassa, Bob
  Wolf, Gary
Reuters
  Gristock, Stephen
Software Engineering Institute
  Bate, Roger
  Chrissis, Mary Beth

  Gross, Jon
  Konrad, Mike
  Peterson, Bill
  Phillips, David M. (Mike)
  Shrum, Sandy
TRW
  Hefner, Rick
US Air Force
  Sapp, Millee
  Totty, Lonnie*
US Army
  Sherer, S. Wayne
US Navy
  Dudash, Edward

---

*Emeritus members

Stakeholders/Reviewers

The Stakeholder/Reviewer group of organizations provided valuable insight into the early effort toward combining the source models. Their review of multiple versions of the CMMI products gave the Product Team valuable perspectives.

AAI Corporation
Abelia Corporation
Aerospace Corporation
aimware, Inc.
Alcatel Space
Alcyonix, Inc.
Alexanna—LLC.
ARINC
Asea Brown Boveri
Automatic Data Processing, Inc.
AverStar Corporation
Bloodworth Integrated Technology, Inc.
Boeing
Burdeshaw Associates, LTD.
Celotex Corporation
Center for Naval Analysis
Change Bridge, Inc.
Chase Manhattan Bank
Citicorp
Computer Sciences Corporation
CS Draper Labs
Defense Contract Management Command
DELTA—Danish Electronic, Light & Acoustic
Eastman Kodak Company
EDS, Inc.
EntekIRD International
Ericsson AB
ETSS, Inc.
European Software Institute
Federal Aviation Administration
Fraunhofer Center/University of Maryland

GDE Systems, Inc.
GE Fanuc Automation NA, Inc.
General Dynamics
GenRad
GRC International, Inc.
Harris Corporation
Hughes Space and Communications
IBM
IEEE Computer Society
Institute for Software Process Improvement
Interim Technology Consulting
Jacobs Sverdrup Advanced Systems Group
Japan Ministry of Economy, Trade, and Industry
KAMO Consultancy
Kasse Initiatives, LLC.
KPMG Consulting
Lockheed Martin
Logistics Management Institute
Lucent Technologies
Mars Electronics International
Mitron Corporation
Motorola
M/S Inter Solutions P., Ltd.
Multi-Dimensional Maturity
NASA
Nokia Research Center
Nomura Research Institute, Ltd.
Northern Utah Process Improvement Technology
Northrop Grumman Corporation
Northwestern Mutual Life Insurance

Portland State University
Process Enhancement Partners, Inc.
Process Focus Software
Process Plus, Inc.
Process Transition Int'l, Inc.
Q-Labs, Inc.
Qwest Communications
Raytheon
Rockwell Collins, Inc.
Science Applications International
  Corporation
SECAT LLC
Smiths Industries
Software Engineering Institute
Software Productivity Consortium
Software Quality Institute
  (Brisbane, Australia)

Software Research Associates, Inc.
Software Systems Quality Consulting
Sterling Software
St. Paul Fire & Marine Insurance
  Company
THALES
Theta Information Systems
TRW
United Defense, L.P.
University of Maryland
US Air Force
US Army
US Navy
Washington Department of
  Information Services
Waynesburg College
Xerox Corporation

GLOSSARY

The CMMI glossary defines the basic terms used in the CMMI models. Glossary entries are typically multiple-word terms consisting of a noun and one or more restrictive modifiers. (There are some exceptions to this rule that account for one-word terms in the glossary.)

When selecting definitions for terms in the CMMI glossary, we used definitions from recognized sources as much possible. Definitions were selected first from existing sources that have a widespread readership. The order of precedence we used when selecting definitions was as follows:

1. *Webster's* OnLine dictionary (*www.m-w.com*)
2. ISO/IEC 9000
3. ISO/IEC 12207
4. ISO/IEC 15504
5. ISO/IEC 15288
6. CMMI Source Models
   - EIA/IS 731 (SECM)
   - SW-CMM v2, draft C
   - IPD-CMM v0.98
7. CMMI A-Spec
8. IEEE
9. SW-CMM v1.1
10. EIA 632
11. SA-CMM
12. FAA-iCMM
13. P-CMM

We developed the glossary recognizing the importance of using terminology that all model users can understand. We also recognized that words and terms can have different meanings in different contexts and environments. The glossary in CMMI models is designed to document the meanings of words and terms that should have the widest use and understanding by users of CMMI products.

ability to perform   A common feature of CMMI model process areas with a staged representation that groups the generic practices related to ensuring that the project and/or organization has the resources it needs.

acceptance criteria   The criteria that a product or product component must satisfy to be accepted by a user, customer, or other authorized entity.

acceptance testing   Formal testing conducted to enable a user, customer, or other authorized entity to determine whether to accept a product or product component. (See also "unit testing.")

achievement profile   In the continuous representation, a list of process areas and their corresponding capability levels that represent the organization's progress for each process area while advancing through the capability levels. (See also "capability level profile," "target profile," and "target staging.")

acquisition   The process of obtaining, through contract, any discrete action or proposed action by the acquisition entity that would commit to invest (appropriated funds) for obtaining products and services.

acquisition strategy   The specific approach to acquiring products and services that is based on considerations of supply sources, acquisition methods, requirements specification types, contract or agreement types, and the related acquisition risk.

adequate   This word is used so that you can interpret goals and practices in light of your organization's business objectives. When using any CMMI model, you must interpret the practices so that they work for your organization. This term is used in goals and practices where certain activities may not be done all of the time. (See also "appropriate" and "as needed.")

advanced practices   In the continuous representation, all the specific practices with a capability level of 2 or higher.

agreement/contract requirements   All technical and nontechnical requirements related to an acquisition.

allocated requirement   Requirement that levies all or part of the performance and functionality of a higher level requirement on a lower level architectural element or design component.

alternative practice   A practice that is a substitute for one or more generic or specific practices contained in CMMI models that achieves an equivalent effect toward satisfying the generic or specific goal associated with model practices. Alternative practices are not necessarily one-for-one replacements for the generic or specific practices.

appraisal   In the CMMI Product Suite, an examination of one or more processes by a trained team of professionals using an appraisal reference model as the basis for determining strengths and weaknesses. (See also "assessment" and "capability evaluation.")

appraisal findings   The conclusions of an appraisal that identify the most important issues, problems, or opportunities within the appraisal scope. Findings include, at a minimum, strengths and weaknesses based on valid observations.

appraisal participants   Members of the organizational unit who participate in providing information during the appraisal.

appraisal rating As used in CMMI appraisal materials, the value assigned by an appraisal team to (1) a CMMI goal or process area, (2) the capability level of a process area, or (3) the maturity level of an organizational unit. The rating is determined by enacting the defined rating process for the appraisal method being employed.

appraisal reference model As used in CMMI appraisal materials, the CMMI model to which an appraisal team correlates implemented process activities.

appraisal scope The definition of the boundaries of the appraisal encompassing the organizational limits and the CMMI model limits.

appraisal tailoring Selection of options within the appraisal method for use in a specific instance.

The intent of appraisal tailoring is to assist an organization in aligning application of the method with its business objectives.

appraisal team leader A person who leads the activities of an appraisal and has satisfied the qualification criteria for experience, knowledge, and skills defined by the appraisal method.

appropriate This word is used so that you can interpret goals and practices in light of your organization's business objectives. When using any CMMI model, you must interpret the practices so that they work for your organization. This term is used in goals and practices where certain activities may not be done all of the time. (See also "adequate" and "as needed.")

as needed This phrase is used so that you can interpret goals and practices in light of your organization's business objectives. When using any CMMI model, you must interpret the practices so that they work for your organization. This term is used in goals and practices where certain activities may not be done all the time. (See also "adequate" and "appropriate.")

assessment In the CMMI Product Suite, an appraisal that an organization does internally for the purposes of process improvement. The word *assessment* is also used in the CMMI Product Suite in an everyday English sense (e.g., risk assessment). (See also "appraisal" and "capability evaluation.")

assignable cause of process variation In CMMI, the term *special cause of process variation* is used in place of *assignable cause of process variation* to ensure consistency. The two terms are defined identically. (See "special cause of process variation.")

audit In CMMI process improvement work, an independent examination of a work product or set of work products to determine whether requirements are being met.

base measure A distinct property or characteristic of an entity and the method for quantifying it. (See also "derived measures.")

base practices In the continuous representation, all the specific practices with a capability level of 1.

baseline A set of specifications or work products that has been formally reviewed and agreed on, which thereafter serves as the basis for further development, and which can be changed only through change control procedures (See also "configuration baseline" and "product baseline.")

business objectives (See "organization's business objectives.")

capability evaluation An appraisal by a trained team of professionals used as a discriminator to select suppliers, for contract monitoring, or for incentives. Evaluations are used to help decision makers make better acquisition decisions, improve subcontractor performance, and provide insight to a purchasing organization. (See also "appraisal" and "assessment.")

capability level Achievement of process improvement within an individual process area. A capability level is defined by the appropriate specific and generic practices for a process area. (See also "generic goal," "generic practice," "maturity level," and "process area.")

capability level profile In the continuous representation, a list of process areas and their corresponding capability levels. (See also "achievement profile," "target profile," and "target staging.")

The profile may be an achievement profile when it represents the organization's progress for each process area while advancing through the capability levels. Or, the profile may be a target profile when it represents an objective for process improvement.

capability maturity model A model that contains the essential elements of effective processes for one or more disciplines and describes an evolutionary improvement path from ad hoc, immature processes to disciplined, mature processes with improved quality and effectiveness.

capable process A process that can satisfy its specified product quality, service quality, and process-performance objectives. (See also "stable process," "standard process," and "statistically managed process.")

causal analysis The analysis of defects to determine their cause.

change management Judicious use of means to effect a change, or proposed change, on a product or service. (See also "configuration management.")

CMMI Framework The basic structure that organizes CMMI components, including common elements of the current CMMI models as well as rules and methods for generating models, their appraisal methods (including associated artifacts), and their training materials. The framework enables new disciplines to be added to CMMI so that the new disciplines will integrate with the existing ones. (See also "CMMI model" and "CMMI Product Suite.")

CMMI model One from the entire collection of possible models that can be generated from the CMMI Framework. Since the CMMI Framework can generate different models based on the needs of the organization using it, there are multiple CMMI models. (See also "CMMI Framework" and "CMMI Product Suite.")

CMMI model component Any of the main architectural elements that compose a CMMI model. Some of the main elements of a CMMI model include specific practices, generic practices, specific goals, generic goals, process areas, capability levels, and maturity levels.

CMMI model tailoring The use of a subset of a CMMI model for the purpose of making it suitable for a specific application. The intent of model tailoring is to assist an organization in aligning application of a model with its business objectives.

CMMI Product Suite The complete set of products developed around the CMMI concept. These products include the framework itself, models, appraisal methods, appraisal materials, and various types of training. (See also "CMMI Framework" and "CMMI model.")

commitment to perform A common feature of CMMI model process areas with a staged representation that groups the generic practices related to creating policies and securing sponsorship.

common cause of process variation The variation of a process that exists because of normal and expected interactions among the components of a process. (See also "special cause of process variation.")

concept of operations (See "operational concept.")

configuration audit An audit conducted to verify that a configuration item conforms to a specified standard or requirement. (See also "audit" and "configuration item.")

configuration baseline The configuration information formally designated at a specific time during a product's or product component's life. Configuration baselines, plus approved changes from those baselines, constitute the current configuration information. (See also "product life cycle.")

configuration control An element of configuration management consisting of the evaluation, coordination, approval or disapproval, and implementation of changes to configuration items after formal establishment of their configuration identification. (See also "configuration identification," "configuration item," and "configuration management.")

configuration control board A group of people responsible for evaluating and approving or disapproving proposed changes to configuration items, and for ensuring implementation of approved changes. (See also "configuration item.")
 Configuration control boards are also known as change control boards.

configuration identification An element of configuration management consisting of selecting the configuration items for a product, assigning unique identifiers to them, and recording their functional and physical characteristics in technical documentation. (See also "configuration item," "configuration management," and "product.")

configuration item An aggregation of work products that is designated for configuration management and treated as a single entity in the configuration management process. (See also "configuration management.")

configuration management A discipline applying technical and administrative direction and surveillance to (1) identify and document the functional and physical characteristics of a configuration item, (2) control changes to those characteristics, (3) record and report change processing and implementation status, and (4) verify compliance with specified requirements [IEEE Std 610. 1990]. (See also "configuration audit," "configuration control," "configuration identification," and "configuration status accounting.")

configuration status accounting An element of configuration management consisting of the recording and reporting of information needed to manage a configuration effectively. This information includes a listing of the approved configuration identification, the status of proposed changes to the configuration, and the implementation status of approved changes. (See also "configuration identification" and "configuration management.")

continuous representation A capability maturity model structure wherein capability levels provide a recommended order for approaching process improvement within each specified process area. (See also "capability level," "process area," and "staged representation.")

contractor (See "supplier.")

corrective action Acts or deeds used to remedy a situation, remove an error, or adjust a condition.

COTS Items that can be purchased from a commercial vendor. (COTS stands for "commercial off the shelf.")

customer The party (individual, project, or organization) responsible for accepting the product or for authorizing payment. The customer is external to the project (except possibly when Integrated Product Teams are used, as in IPPD), but not necessarily external to the organization. The customer may be a higher level project. Customers are a subset of stakeholders. (See also "stakeholder.")

data management Principles, processes, and systems for the sharing and management of data.

defect density Number of defects per unit of product size (e.g., problem reports per thousand lines of code).

defined process A managed process that is tailored from the organization's set of standard processes according to the organization's tailoring guidelines; has a maintained process description; and contributes work products, measures, and other process improvement information to the organizational process assets. (See also "managed process.")

derived measures Data resulting from the mathematical function of two or more base measures. (See also "base measure.")

derived requirements Requirements that are not explicitly stated in the customer requirements, but are inferred (1) from contextual requirements (e.g., applicable standards, laws, policies, common practices, and management decisions), or (2) from requirements needed to specify a product component. Derived requirements can also arise during analysis and design of components of the product or system. (See also "product requirements.")

design review A formal, documented, comprehensive, and systematic examination of a design to evaluate the design requirements and the capability of the design to meet these requirements, and to identify problems and propose solutions.

development In the CMMI Product Suite, not only development activities but also maintenance activities may be included. Projects that benefit from the best practices of CMMI can focus on development, maintenance, or both.

developmental plan   A plan for guiding, implementing, and controlling the design and development of one or more products. (See also "product life cycle" and "project plan.")

directing implementation   A common feature of CMMI model process areas with a staged representation that groups the generic practices related to managing the performance of the process, managing the integrity of its work products, and involving relevant stakeholders.

discipline   In the CMMI Product Suite, the bodies of knowledge available to you when selecting a CMMI model (e.g., systems engineering). The CMMI Product Team envisions that other bodies of knowledge will be integrated into the CMMI Framework in the future.

discipline amplification   Discipline amplifications are informative model components that contain information relevant to a particular discipline. For example, to find a discipline amplification for software engineering, you would look in the model for items labeled "For Software Engineering." The same is true for other disciplines.

document   A collection of data, regardless of the medium on which it is recorded, that generally has permanence and can be read by humans or machines. So, documents include both paper and electronic documents.

enterprise   The full composition of companies. Companies may consist of many organizations in many locations with different customers. (See also "organization.")

entry criteria   States of being that must be present before an effort can begin successfully.

equivalent staging   A target staging, created using the continuous representation, that is defined so that the results of using the target staging can be compared to the maturity levels of the staged representation. (See also "capability level profile," "maturity level," "target profile," and "target staging.")

Such staging permits benchmarking of progress among organizations, enterprises, and projects, regardless of the CMMI representation used. The organization may implement components of CMMI models beyond those reported as part of equivalent staging. Equivalent staging is only a measure to relate how the organization is compared to other organizations in terms of maturity levels.

establish and maintain   In the CMMI Product Suite, you will encounter goals and practices that include the phrase "establish and maintain." This phrase connotes a meaning beyond the component terms; it includes documentation and usage. For example, "Establish and maintain an organizational policy for planning and performing the organizational process focus process" means that not only must a policy be formulated, but it also must be documented and it must be used throughout the organization.

evidence   (See "objective evidence.")

executive   (See "senior manager.")

exit criteria States of being that must be present before an effort can end successfully.

expected CMMI components CMMI components that explain what may be done to satisfy a required CMMI component. Model users can implement the expected components explicitly or implement equivalent alternative practices to these components. Specific and generic practices are expected model components.

finding (See "appraisal findings.")

formal evaluation process A structured approach to evaluating alternative solutions against established criteria to determine a recommended solution to address an issue.

framework (See "CMMI Framework.")

functional analysis Examination of a defined function to identify all the subfunctions necessary to the accomplishment of that function; identification of functional relationships and interfaces (internal and external) and capturing these in a functional architecture; and flow down of upper level performance requirements and assignment of these requirements to lower level subfunctions. (See also "functional architecture.")

functional architecture The hierarchical arrangement of functions, their internal and external (external to the aggregation itself) functional interfaces and external physical interfaces, their respective functional and performance requirements, and their design constraints.

generic goal A required model component that describes the characteristics that must be present to satisfy the institutionalization of the processes that implement a process area. (See also "institutionalization.")

generic practice An expected model component that is considered important in achieving the associated generic goal. The generic practices associated with a generic goal describe the activities that are expected to result in achievement of the generic goal and contribute to the institutionalization of the processes associated with a process area.

generic practice elaboration An informative model component that appears after a generic practice to provide guidance on how the generic practices should be applied to the process area.

goal A required CMMI component that can be either a generic goal or a specific goal. When you see the word *goal* in a CMMI model, it always refers to a model component (e.g., generic goal and specific goal). (See also "generic goal," "objective," and "specific goal.")

incomplete process A process that is not performed or is performed only partially (also known as capability level 0). One or more of the specific goals of the process area are not satisfied.

informative CMMI components CMMI components that help model users understand the required and expected components of a model. These components can contain examples, detailed explanations, or other helpful information. Subpractices, notes, references, goal titles, practice titles, sources, typical work products, discipline amplifications, and generic practice elaborations are informative model components.

institutionalization The ingrained way of doing business that an organization follows routinely as part of its corporate culture.

integrated product and process development A systematic approach to product development that achieves a timely collaboration of relevant stakeholders throughout the product life cycle to better satisfy customer needs.

integrated team A group of people with complementary skills and expertise who are committed to delivering specified work products in timely collaboration. Integrated team members provide skills and advocacy appropriate to all phases of the work products' life and are collectively responsible for delivering the work products as specified. An integrated team should include empowered representatives from organizations, disciplines, and functions that have a stake in the success of the work products.

interface control In configuration management, the process of (1) identifying all functional and physical characteristics relevant to the interfacing of two or more configuration items provided by one or more organizations, and (2) ensuring that the proposed changes to these characteristics are evaluated and approved prior to implementation [IEEE 828-1983]. (See also "configuration item" and "configuration management.")

lead appraiser As used in the CMMI Product Suite, a person who has achieved recognition from an authorizing body to perform as an appraisal team leader for a particular appraisal method.

life-cycle model A partitioning of the life of a product or project into phases.

managed process A performed process that is planned and executed in accordance with policy; employs skilled people having adequate resources to produce controlled outputs; involves relevant stakeholders; is monitored, controlled, and reviewed; and is evaluated for adherence to its process description. (See also "performed process.")

manager In the CMMI Product Suite, a person who provides technical and administrative direction and control to those performing tasks or activities within the manager's area of responsibility. The traditional functions of a manager include planning, organizing, directing, and controlling work within an area of responsibility.

maturity level Degree of process improvement across a predefined set of process areas in which all goals in the set are attained. (See also "capability level" and "process area.")

memorandum of agreement Binding documents of understanding or agreements between two or more parties. Also known as a "memorandum of understanding."

natural bounds The inherent process reflected by measures of process performance, sometimes referred to as "voice of the process." Techniques such as control charts, confidence intervals, and prediction intervals are used to determine whether the variation is due to common causes (i.e., the process is predictable or "stable") or is due to some special cause that can and should be identified and removed.

nondevelopmental item (NDI)   An item of supply that was developed previous to its current use in an acquisition or development process. Such an item may require minor modifications to meet the requirements of its current intended use.

nontechnical requirements   Contractual provisions, commitments, conditions, and terms that affect how products or services are to be acquired. Examples include products to be delivered, data rights for delivered commercial off-the-shelf (COTS) non-developmental items (NDIs), delivery dates, and milestones with exit criteria. Other nontechnical requirements include training requirements, site requirements, and deployment schedules.

objective   When used as a noun in the CMMI Product Suite, the term *objective* replaces the word *goal* as used in its common everyday sense, since the word *goal* is reserved for use when referring to the CMMI model components called specific goals and generic goals. (See also "goal.")

objective evidence   As used in CMMI appraisal materials, qualitative or quantitative information, records, or statements of fact pertaining to the characteristics of an item or service or to the existence and implementation of a process element, which are based on observation, measurement, or test and which are verifiable.

objectively evaluate   To review activities and work products against criteria that minimize subjectivity and bias by the reviewer. An example of an objective evaluation is an audit against requirements, standards, or procedures by an independent quality assurance function. (See also "audit.")

observation   As used in CMMI appraisal materials, a written record that represents the appraisal team members' understanding of information either seen or heard during the appraisal data collection activities. The written record may take the form of a statement or may take alternative forms as long as the information content is preserved.

operational concept   A general description of the way in which an entity is used or operates. (Also known as "concept of operations.")

operational scenario   A description of an imagined sequence of events that includes the interaction of the product with its environment and users, as well as interaction among its product components. Operational scenarios are used to evaluate the requirements and design of the system and to verify and validate the system.

optimizing process   A quantitatively managed process that is improved based on an understanding of the common causes of variation inherent in the process. The focus of an optimizing process is on continually improving the range of process performance through both incremental and innovative improvements. (See also "common cause of process variation," "defined process," and "quantitatively managed process.")

organization   An administrative structure in which people collectively manage one or more projects as a whole, and whose projects share a senior manager and operate under the same policies. However, the word *organization* as used throughout CMMI models can also apply to one person who performs a function in a small organization that might be performed by a group of people in a large organization. (See also "enterprise" and "organizational unit.")

organizational maturity The extent to which an organization has explicitly and consistently deployed processes that are documented, managed, measured, controlled, and continually improved. Organizational maturity may be measured via appraisals.

organizational policy A guiding principle typically established by senior management that is adopted by an organization to influence and determine decisions.

organizational process assets Artifacts that relate to describing, implementing, and improving processes (e.g., policies, measurements, process descriptions, and process implementation support tools). The term *process assets* is used to indicate that these artifacts are developed or acquired to meet the business objectives of the organization, and they represent investments by the organization that are expected to provide current and future business value. (See also "process asset library.")

organizational unit The part of an organization that is the subject of an appraisal; also known as the organizational scope of the appraisal.

An organizational unit deploys one or more processes that have a coherent process context and operates within a coherent set of business objectives. An organizational unit is typically part of a larger organization, although in a small organization, the organizational unit may be the whole organization.

organization's business objectives Senior management developed strategies designed to ensure an organization's continued existence and enhance its profitability, market share, and other factors influencing the organization's success. (See also "quality and process-performance objectives" and "quantitative objective.")

Such objectives may include reducing the number of change requests during a system's integration phase, reducing development cycle time, increasing the number of errors found in a product's first or second phase of development, and reducing the number of customer-reported defects, when applied to systems engineering activities.

organization's measurement repository A repository used to collect and make available measurement data on processes and work products, particularly as they relate to the organization's set of standard processes. This repository contains or references actual measurement data and related information needed to understand and analyze the measurement data.

organization's process asset library A library of information used to store and make available process assets that are useful to those who are defining, implementing, and managing processes in the organization. This library contains process assets that include process-related documentation such as policies, defined processes, checklists, lessons-learned documents, templates, standards, procedures, plans, and training materials.

organization's set of standard processes   A collection of definitions of the processes that guide activities in an organization. These process descriptions cover the fundamental process elements (and their relationships to each other, such as ordering and interfaces) that must be incorporated into the defined processes that are implemented in projects across the organization. A standard process enables consistent development and maintenance activities across the organization and is essential for long-term stability and improvement. (See also "defined process" and "process element.")

outsourcing   (See "acquisition.")

peer review   The review of work products performed by peers during development of the work products to identify defects for removal. The term *peer review* is used in the CMMI Product Suite instead of the term *work product inspection.* Essentially, these terms mean the same thing. (See also "work product.")

performance parameters   The measures of effectiveness and other key measures used to guide and control progressive development.

performed process   A process that accomplishes the needed work to produce work products. The specific goals of the process area are satisfied.

planned process   A process that is documented both by a description and a plan. The description and plan should be coordinated, and the plan should include standards, requirements, objectives, resources, assignments, and so on.

policy   (See "organizational policy.")

process   In the CMMI Product Suite, activities that can be recognized as implementations of practices in a CMMI model. These activities can be mapped to one or more practices in CMMI process areas to allow a model to be useful for process improvement and process appraisal. (See also "process area.")

There is a special use of the phrase *the process* in the statements and descriptions of the generic goals and generic practices. "The process," as used in chapter 3 and in Part Two (in the section of each process area that contains the generic components), is the process or processes that implement the process area.

process action plan   A plan, usually resulting from appraisals, that documents how specific improvements targeting the weaknesses uncovered by an appraisal will be implemented.

process action team   A team that has the responsibility to develop and implement process improvement activities for an organization as documented in a process action plan.

process and technology improvements   Incremental and innovative improvements to processes and also to process or product technologies.

process architecture   The ordering, interfaces, interdependencies, and other relationships among the process elements in a standard process. Process architecture also describes the interfaces, interdependencies, and other relationships between process elements and external processes (e.g., contract management).

process area   A cluster of related practices in an area that, when implemented collectively, satisfy a set of goals considered important for making significant improvement in that area. All CMMI process areas are common to both continuous and staged representations.

process asset Anything that the organization considers useful in attaining the goals of a process area. (See also "organizational process assets.")

process asset library A collection of process asset holdings that can be used by an organization or project. (See also "organization's process asset library.")

process attribute A measurable characteristic of process capability applicable to any process.

process capability The range of expected results that can be achieved by following a process [EIA/IS 731, v1.0].

process context The set of factors, documented in the appraisal input, that influences the judgment and comparability of appraisal ratings.

These include, but are not limited to, the size of the organizational unit to be appraised; the demographics of the organizational unit; the application domain of the products or services; the size, criticality, and complexity of the products or services; and the quality characteristics of the products or services.

process definition The act of defining and describing a process. The result of process definition is a process description. (See also "process description.")

process description A documented expression of a set of activities performed to achieve a given purpose that provides an operational definition of the major components of a process. The documentation specifies, in a complete, precise, and verifiable manner, the requirements, design, behavior, or other characteristics of a process. It also may include procedures for determining whether these provisions have been satisfied. Process descriptions can be found at the activity, project, or organizational level.

process element The fundamental unit of a process. A process can be defined in terms of subprocesses or process elements. A subprocess can be further decomposed; a process element cannot.

Each process element covers a closely related set of activities (e.g., estimating element, peer review element). Process elements can be portrayed using templates to be completed, abstractions to be refined, or descriptions to be modified or used. A process element can be an activity or task.

process group A collection of specialists who facilitate the definition, maintenance, and improvement of the process(es) used by the organization.

process improvement A program of activities designed to improve the performance and maturity of the organization's processes, and the results of such a program.

process-improvement objectives A set of target characteristics established to guide the effort to improve an existing process in a specific, measurable way either in terms of resultant product characteristics (e.g., quality, performance, conformance to standards) or in the way in which the process is executed (e.g., elimination of redundant process steps, combination of process steps, improvement of cycle time). (See also "organization's business objectives" and "quantitative objective.")

process improvement plan   A plan for achieving organizational process-improvement objectives based on a thorough understanding of the current strengths and weaknesses of the organization's processes and process assets.

process measurement   The set of definitions, methods, and activities used to take measurements of a process and its resulting products for the purpose of characterizing and understanding the process.

process owner   The person (or team) responsible for defining and maintaining a process. At the organizational level, the process owner is the person (or team) responsible for the description of a standard process; at the project level, the process owner is the person (or team) responsible for the description of the defined process. A process may therefore have multiple owners at different levels of responsibility. (See also "defined process" and "standard process.")

process performance   A measure of actual results achieved by following a process. It is characterized by both process measures (e.g., effort, cycle time, and defect removal efficiency) and product measures (e.g., reliability, defect density, and response time).

process performance baseline   A documented characterization of the actual results achieved by following a process, which is used as a benchmark for comparing actual process performance against expected process performance. (See also "process performance.")

process performance model   A description of the relationships among attributes of a process and its work products that are developed from historical process performance data and calibrated using collected process and product measures from the project and that are used to predict results to be achieved by following a process.

process tailoring   Making, altering, or adapting a process description for a particular end. For example, a project tailors its defined process from the organization's set of standard processes to meet the objectives, constraints, and environment of the project. (See also "defined process," "organization's set of standard processes," and "process description.")

product   In the CMMI Product Suite, any tangible output or service that is a result of a process and that is intended for delivery to a customer or end user. A product is a work product that is delivered to the customer. (See also "customer" and "work product.")

product baseline   In configuration management, the initial approved technical data package (including, for software, the source code listing) defining a configuration item during the production, operation, maintenance, and logistic support of its life cycle. (See also "configuration item" and "configuration management.")

product component   In the CMMI Product Suite, lower level components of the product. Product components are integrated to "build" the product. There may be multiple levels of product components. A product component is any work product that must be engineered (requirements defined and designs developed and implemented) to achieve the intended use of the product throughout its life and that is delivered to the customer. (See also "product" and "work product.")

product-component requirements   A complete specification of a product component, including fit, form, function, performance, and any other requirement.

product life cycle   The period of time, consisting of phases, that begins when a product is conceived and ends when the product is no longer available for use. Since an organization may be producing multiple products for multiple customers, one description of a product life cycle may not be adequate. Therefore, the organization may define a set of approved product life-cycle models. These models are typically found in published literature and are likely to be tailored for use in an organization.

A product life cycle could consist of the following phases: (1) concept/vision, (2) feasibility, (3) design/development, (4) production, and (5) phase out.

product line   A group of products sharing a common, managed set of features that satisfy specific needs of a selected market or mission.

product-related life-cycle processes   Processes associated with a product throughout one or more phases of its life (e.g., from conception through disposal), such as the manufacturing and support processes.

product requirements   A refinement of the customer requirements into the developers' language, making implicit requirements into explicit derived requirements. (See also "derived requirements" and "product-component requirements.")

The developer uses the product requirements to guide the design and building of the product.

product suite   (See "CMMI Product Suite.")

profile   (See "achievement profile" and "target profile.")

program   (1) A project. (2) A collection of related projects and the infrastructure that supports them, including objectives, methods, activities, plans, and success measures. (See also "project.")

project   In the CMMI Product Suite, a managed set of interrelated resources that delivers one or more products to a customer or end user. A project has a definite beginning and end and typically operates according to a plan. Such a plan is frequently documented and specifies the product to be delivered or implemented, the resources and funds to be used, the work to be done, and a schedule for doing the work. A project can be composed of projects.

project manager   In the CMMI Product Suite, the person responsible for planning, directing, controlling, structuring, and motivating the project. The project manager is responsible for satisfying the customer.

project plan   A plan that provides the basis for performing and controlling the project's activities, which addresses the commitments to the project's customer.

Project planning includes estimating the attributes of the work products and tasks, determining the resources needed, negotiating commitments, producing a schedule, and identifying and analyzing project risks. Iterating through these activities may be necessary to establish the project plan.

project progress and performance What a project achieves with respect to implementing project plans, including effort, cost, schedule, and technical performance.

project's defined process The integrated and defined process that is tailored from the organization's set of standard processes. (See also "defined process.")

prototype A preliminary type, form, or instance of a product or product component that serves as a model for later stages or for the final, complete version of the product. This model (e.g., physical, electronic, digital, analytical) can be used for the following (and other) purposes:

- assessing the feasibility of a new or unfamiliar technology
- assessing or mitigating technical risk
- validating requirements
- demonstrating critical features
- qualifying a product
- qualifying a process
- characterizing performance or product features
- elucidating physical principles

quality The ability of a set of inherent characteristics of a product, product component, or process to fulfill requirements of customers.

quality and process-performance objectives Objectives and requirements for product quality, service quality, and process performance. Process-performance objectives include product quality; however, to emphasize the importance of product quality in the CMMI Product Suite, the phrase *quality and process-performance objectives* is used rather than just *process-performance objectives*.

quality assurance A planned and systematic means for assuring management that the defined standards, practices, procedures, and methods of the process are applied.

quality control The operational techniques and activities that are used to fulfill requirements for quality [ISO 8402-1994]. (See also "quality assurance.")

quantitative objective Desired target value expressed as quantitative measures. (See also "process-improvement objectives" and "quality and process-performance objectives.")

quantitatively managed process A defined process that is controlled using statistical and other quantitative techniques. The product quality, service quality, and process performance attributes are measurable and controlled throughout the project. (See also "defined process," "optimizing process," and "statistically managed process.")

rating (See "appraisal rating.")

reference An informative model component that points to additional or more detailed information in related process areas.

reference model A model that is used as a benchmark for measuring some attribute.

relevant stakeholder A stakeholder that is identified for involvement in specified activities and is included in a plan. (See also "stakeholder.")

representation The organization, use, and presentation of a CMM's components. Overall, two types of approaches to presenting best practices are evident: the staged representation and the continuous representation.

required CMMI components CMMI components that are essential to achieving process improvement in a given process area. These components are used in appraisals to determine process capability. Specific goals and generic goals are required model components.

requirement (1) A condition or capability needed by a user to solve a problem or achieve an objective. (2) A condition or capability that must be met or possessed by a product or product component to satisfy a contract, standard, specification, or other formally imposed documents. (3) A documented representation of a condition or capability as in (1) or (2) [IEEE 610.12-1990].

requirements analysis The determination of product-specific performance and functional characteristics based on analyses of customer needs, expectations, and constraints; operational concept; projected utilization environments for people, products, and processes; and measures of effectiveness.

requirements elicitation Using systematic techniques, such as prototypes and structured surveys, to proactively identify and document customer and end-user needs.

requirements management The management of all requirements received by or generated by the project, including both technical and nontechnical requirements as well as those requirements levied on the project by the organization.

requirements traceability The evidence of an association between a requirement and its source requirement, its implementation, and its verification.

return on investment The ratio of revenue from output (product) to production costs, which determines whether an organization benefits from performing an action to produce something.

risk analysis The evaluation, classification, and prioritization of risks.

risk identification An organized, thorough approach to seek out probable or realistic risks in achieving objectives.

risk management An organized, analytic process to identify what might cause harm or loss (identify risks); to assess and quantify the identified risks; and to develop and, if needed, implement an appropriate approach to prevent or handle causes of risk that could result in significant harm or loss.

risk management strategy An organized, technical approach to identify what might cause harm or loss (identify risks); to assess and quantify the identified risks; and to develop and, if needed, implement an appropriate approach to prevent or handle causes of risk that could result in significant harm or loss. Typically, risk management is performed for project, organization, or product developing organizational units.

root cause A source of a defect such that if it is removed, the defect is decreased or removed.

senior manager   In the CMMI Product Suite, a management role at a high enough level in an organization that the primary focus of the person filling the role is the long-term vitality of the organization rather than short-term project and contractual concerns and pressures. A senior manager has authority to direct the allocation or reallocation of resources in support of organizational process improvement effectiveness.

   A senior manager can be any manager who satisfies this description, including the head of the organization. Synonyms for "senior manager" include "executive" and "top-level manager." However, to ensure consistency and usability, these synonyms are not used in CMMI models.

shared vision   In the CMMI Product Suite, a common understanding of guiding principles including mission, objectives, expected behavior, values, and final outcomes, which are developed and used by a group such as an organization, project, or team. Creating a shared vision requires that all people in the group have an opportunity to speak and be heard about what really matters to them.

software engineering   (1) The application of a systematic, disciplined, quantifiable approach to the development, operation, and maintenance of software. (2) The study of approaches as in (1).

solicitation   The process of preparing a package to be used in selecting a supplier (contractor). (See also "solicitation package.")

solicitation package   A formal document delineating technical and nontechnical requirements that is used to request offers on invitations for bid (bids) and requests for proposal (proposals), or to request statements of capabilities and price quotations (quotes). It is otherwise used as a basis for selecting a supply source or sources to provide products or services.

special cause of process variation   A cause of a defect that is specific to some transient circumstance and not an inherent part of a process. (See also "common cause of process variation.")

specific goal   A required model component that describes the unique characteristics that must be present to satisfy the process area. (See also "capability level," "generic goal," "organization's business objectives," and "process area.")

specific practice   An expected model component that is considered important in achieving the associated specific goal. The specific practices describe the activities expected to result in achievement of the specific goals of a process area. (See also "process area" and "specific goal.")

   In the continuous representation, every specific practice is associated with a capability level. The staged representation does not recognize capability levels, so all specific practices are treated equally.

stable process   The state in which all special causes of process variation have been removed and prevented from recurring so that only the common causes of process variation of the process remain. (See also "capable process," "common cause of variation," "special cause of process variation," "standard process," and "statistically managed process.")

staged representation A model structure wherein attaining the goals of a set of process areas establishes a maturity level; each level builds a foundation for subsequent levels. (See also "maturity level" and "process area.")

stakeholder In the CMMI Product Suite, a group or individual that is affected by or is in some way accountable for the outcome of an undertaking. Stakeholders may include project members, suppliers, customers, end users, and others. (See also "customer" and "relevant stakeholder.")

standard When you see the word *standard* used as a noun in a CMMI model, it refers to the formal mandatory requirements developed and used to prescribe consistent approaches to development (e.g., ISO/IEC standards, IEEE standards, organizational standards). Instead of using *standard* in its common everyday sense, we chose another term that means the same thing (e.g., *typical, traditional, usual,* or *customary*).

standard process An operational definition of the basic process that guides the establishment of a common process in an organization [ISO/IEC 15504-9].

A standard process describes the fundamental process elements that are expected to be incorporated into any defined process. It also describes the relationships (e.g., ordering and interfaces) among these process elements. (See also "defined process.")

statement of work A description of contracted work required to complete a project.

statistical predictability The performance of a quantitative process that is controlled using statistical and other quantitative techniques.

statistical process control Statistically based analysis of a process and measurements of process performance, which will identify common and special causes of variation in the process performance, and maintain process performance within limits. (See also "common cause of process variation," "special cause of process variation," and "statistically managed process.")

statistical techniques An analytic technique that employs statistical methods (e.g., statistical process control, confidence intervals, and prediction intervals).

statistically managed process A process that is managed by a statistically based technique in which processes are analyzed, special causes of process variation are identified, and performance is contained within well-defined limits. (See also "capable process," "special cause of process variation," "stable process," "standard process," and "statistical process control.")

strength As used in CMMI appraisal materials, an exemplary or noteworthy implementation of a CMMI model practice.

subpractice An informative model component that provides guidance for interpreting and implementing specific or generic practices. Subpractices may be worded as if prescriptive, but are actually meant only to provide ideas that may be useful for process improvement.

subprocess A process that is part of a larger process. (See also "process description.")

supplier (1) An entity delivering products or performing services being acquired. (2) An individual, partnership, company, corporation, association, or other service having an agreement (contract) with an acquirer for the design, development, manufacture, maintenance, modification, or supply of items under the terms of an agreement (contract).

sustainment The processes used to ensure that a product can be utilized operationally by its end users or customers. Sustainment ensures that maintenance is done such that the product is in an operable condition whether or not the product is in use by customers or end users.

systems engineering The interdisciplinary approach governing the total technical and managerial effort required to transform a set of customer needs, expectations, and constraints into a product solution and to support that solution throughout the product's life.

This includes the definition of technical performance measures, the integration of engineering specialties toward the establishment of a product architecture, and the definition of supporting life-cycle processes that balance cost, performance, and schedule objectives.

tailoring Tailoring a process makes, alters, or adapts the process description for a particular end. For example, a project establishes its defined process by tailoring from the organization's set of standard processes to meet the objectives, constraints, and environment of the project.

tailoring guidelines Organizational guidelines that enable projects, groups, and organizational functions to appropriately adapt standard processes for their use. The organization's set of standard processes is described at a general level that may not be directly usable to perform a process.

Tailoring guidelines aid those who establish the defined processes for projects. Tailoring guidelines cover (1) selecting a standard process, (2) selecting an approved life-cycle model, and (3) tailoring the selected standard process and life-cycle model to fit project needs. Tailoring guidelines describe what can and cannot be modified and identify process components that are candidates for modification.

target profile In the continuous representation, a list of process areas and their corresponding capability levels that represent an objective for process improvement. (See also "achievement profile" and "capability level profile.")

target staging In the continuous representation, a sequence of target profiles that describes the path of process improvement to be followed by the organization. (See also "achievement profile," "capability level profile," and "target profile.")

technical data package A collection of items that can include the following if such information is appropriate to the type of product and product component (e.g., material and manufacturing requirements may not be useful for product components associated with software services or processes):

- product architecture description
- allocated requirements

- product-component descriptions
- product-related life-cycle process descriptions if not described as separate product components
- key product characteristics
- required physical characteristics and constraints
- interface requirements
- materials requirements (bills of material and material characteristics)
- fabrication and manufacturing requirements (for both the original equipment manufacturer and field support)
- verification criteria used to ensure requirements have been achieved
- conditions of use (environments) and operating/usage scenarios, modes and states for operations, support, training, manufacturing, disposal, and verifications throughout the life of the product
- rationale for decisions and characteristics (e.g., requirements, requirement allocations, design choices)

technical requirements Properties (attributes) of products or services to be acquired or developed.

test procedure Detailed instructions for the setup, execution, and evaluation of results for a given test.

traceability (See "requirements traceability.")

trade study An evaluation of alternatives, based on criteria and systematic analysis, to select the best alternative for attaining determined objectives.

training Formal and informal learning options, which may include in-class training, informal mentoring, Web-based training, guided self-study, and formalized on-the-job training programs. The learning options selected for each situation are based on an assessment of the need for training and the performance gap to be addressed.

typical work product An informative model component that provides sample outputs from a specific practice. These examples are called *typical work products* because there are often other work products that are just as effective, but are not listed.

unit testing Testing of individual hardware or software units or groups of related units. (See also "acceptance testing.")

validation Confirmation that the product, as provided (or as it will be provided), will fulfill its intended use. In other words, validation ensures that "you built the right thing." (See also "verification.")

verification Confirmation that work products properly reflect the requirements specified for them. In other words, verification ensures that "you built it right." (See also "validation.")

verifying implementation A common feature of CMMI model process areas with a staged representation that groups the generic practices related to review by higher level management, and objective evaluation of conformance to process descriptions, procedures, and standards.

version control The establishment and maintenance of baselines and the identification of changes to baselines that make it possible to return to the previous baseline.

weakness As used in CMMI appraisal materials, the ineffective, or lack of, implementation of one or more CMMI model practices.

work breakdown structure (WBS) An arrangement of work elements and their relationship to each other and to the end product.

work product In the CMMI Product Suite, any artifact produced by a process. These artifacts can include files, documents, parts of the product, services, processes, specifications, and invoices. Examples of processes to be considered as work products include a manufacturing process, a training process, and a disposal process for the product. A key distinction between a work product and a product component is that a work product need not be engineered or be part of the end product. (See also "product" and "product component.")

In CMMI models, you will see the phrase *work products and services*. Even though the definition of *work product* includes services, this phrase is used to emphasize the inclusion of services in the discussion.

work product and task attributes Characteristics of products, services, and project tasks used to help in estimating project work. These characteristics include items such as size, complexity, weight, form, fit, and function. They are typically used as one input to deriving other project and resource estimates (e.g., effort, cost, and schedule).

INDEX

Note: Italicized page locators refer to figures and/or tables.

The SEI Series in Software Engineering

ISBN 0-201-73500-8

ISBN 0-321-11886-3

ISBN 0-201-73723-X

ISBN 0-201-54664-7

ISBN 0-321-15496-7

ISBN 0-201-70372-6

ISBN 0-201-70482-X

ISBN 0-201-70332-7

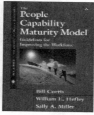

ISBN 0-201-60445-0

ISBN 0-201-60444-2

ISBN 0-201-25592-8

ISBN 0-201-54597-7

ISBN 0-201-54809-7

ISBN 0-201-18095-2

ISBN 0-201-54610-8

ISBN 0-201-47719-X

ISBN 0-201-77639-1

ISBN 0-201-61626-2

ISBN 0-201-70454-4

ISBN 0-201-73409-5

ISBN 0-201-85480-5

ISBN 0-321-11884-7

ISBN 0-201-70064-6

ISBN 0-201-17782-X

ISBN 0-201-52577-1

Please see our Web site at http://www.awprofessional.com for more information on these titles.

Process Areas as Presented in the Staged Representation

Maturity Level 2

REQM Requirements Management

PP   Project Planning

PMC   Project Monitoring and Control

SAM   Supplier Agreement Management

MA   Measurement and Analysis

PPQA Process and Product Quality Assurance

CM   Configuration Management

Maturity Level 3

RD   Requirements Development

TS   Technical Solution

PI   Product Integration

VER   Verification

VAL   Validation

OPF   Organizational Process Focus

OPD   Organizational Process Definition

OT   Organizational Training

IPM   Integrated Project Management

RSKM Risk Management

IT   Integrated Teaming

ISM   Integrated Supplier Management

DAR   Decision Analysis and Resolution

OEI   Organizational Environment for Integration

Maturity Level 4

OPP   Organizational Process Performance

QPM   Quantitative Project Management

Maturity Level 5

OID   Organizational Innovation and Deployment

CAR   Causal Analysis and Resolution